REPORTING FOR THE MEDIA

EIGHTH EDITION

REPORTING FOR THE MEDIA

FRED FEDLER

JOHN R. BENDER

LUCINDA DAVENPORT

MICHAEL W. DRAGER

New York Oxford

OXFORD UNIVERSITY PRESS

2005

Oxford University Press

Oxford New York
Auckland Bangkok Buenos Aires Cape Town Chennai
Dar es Salaam Delhi Hong Kong Istanbul Karachi Kolkata
Kuala Lumpur Madrid Melbourne Mexico City Mumbai Nairobi
São Paulo Shanghai Taipei Tokyo Toronto

Published by Oxford University Press, Inc.
198 Madison Avenue, New York, New York 10016
www.oup.com

Library of Congress Cataloging-in-Publication Data
Reporting for the media / Fred Fedler . . . [et al.].—8th ed.
p. cm.
Includes bibliographical references and index.
ISBN-13 978-0-19-516999-7
ISBN 0-19-516999-9 (alk. paper)
1. Reporters and reporting—Problems, exercises, etc. I. Fedler, Fred.

PN4781.F4 2004
070.4′3—dc22 2004041579

Printing number: 9 8 7 6 5 4 3

Printed in the United States of America
on acid-free paper

CONTENTS

Preface xi

CHAPTER 1 The Basics: Format, Copy Editing and AP Style 1

Producing Copy 2
News Story Format 2
Copy-editing Symbols 4
The Associated Press Stylebook and Briefing on Media Law 8
Accuracy of Names and Facts 9
The Writing Coach—The Lucky 13 Ways to Become a Good Writer 10
Checklist for Copy Preparation 11
Suggested Readings 11
Useful Web Sites 11
Exercises 12

CHAPTER 2 Grammar and Spelling 29

The Parts of Speech 29
Basic Sentence Structure 36
Active and Passive Voice 38
Agreement 38
Ambiguous Pronouns 40
Plurals and Possessives 40
"That" and "Which" 41
"Who" and "Whom" 42
Misplaced Modifiers 42
Dangling Modifiers 43
Personification 43
Parallel Form 44
"Because" and "Due To" 44
Spelling 44
Grammar Checklist 45
The Writing Coach—Acronyms Lift Your Writing
Suggested Readings 47
Useful Web Sites 48
Exercises 49

CHAPTER 3 Newswriting Style 59

Prewriting 59
Simplify Words, Sentences and Paragraphs 62
Remain Objective 66
Checklist for Newswriting Style 71
The Writing Coach–Find the Clear Path to Writing Glory 72
Suggested Readings 74
Exercises 76

CHAPTER 4 The Language of News 90

The Effectiveness of Words 90
Be Precise 91
Use Strong Verbs 93
Avoiding Problems in Your Writing 94
Words to Avoid 94
Other Problems to Avoid 99
Checklist for the Language of News 103
The Writing Coach—Become a Power Lifter When Picking Verbs 103
Suggested Readings 104
Exercises 105

CHAPTER 5 Selecting and Reporting the News 122

The Characteristics of News 123
Two Views of 9/11 126
Types of News 131
Public/Civic Journalism 133
Applying the Principles of News Selection 135
The Concept of Objectivity 135
Details Newspapers Are Reluctant to Publish 136
The Importance of Accuracy 138
Suggested Readings 141
Exercises 143

CHAPTER 6 Basic News Leads 146

The Summary News Lead 146
Sentence Structure in Leads 148
Guidelines for Writing Effective Leads 149
Avoiding Some Common Errors 154
Apply the Guidelines to Other Kinds of Leads 157
Checklist for Writing Leads 158
The Writing Coach—Oh Where, Oh Where Does the Time Element Go? 159
Suggested Readings 160
Exercises 161

CHAPTER 7 Alternative Leads 181

Criticisms 182
"Buried" or "Delayed" Leads 183
Multiparagraph Leads 184
Using Quotations 184
Using Questions 185
Suspenseful Leads 186

Descriptive Leads 186
Shockers—Leads With a Twist 187
Ironic Leads 187
Direct-Address Leads 187
Words Used in Unusual Ways 188
Other Unusual Leads 188
The Writing Coach—Too Many Words Can Muddle Writing 189
Exercises 192

CHAPTER 8 The Body of a News Story 200

The Inverted-Pyramid Style 200
The Hourglass Style 206
The Focus Style 208
The Narrative Style 211
Using Transitions 215
Explain the Unfamiliar 217
The Importance of Examples 219
The Use of Description 219
The Use of Humor 221
The Need to Be Fair 221
The Final Step: Edit Your Story 222
Checklist for Writing News Stories 222
The Writing Coach—How to Find the Endings to Stories 223
Suggested Readings 223
Exercises 224

CHAPTER 9 Quotations and Attribution 239

Quotations 239
Blending Quotations and Narrative 243
Attribution 246
Guidelines for Capitalizing and Punctuating Quotations 253
Checklists for Quotations and Attribution 255
A Memo From the Editor—Descriptive Writing: Turning a Good Story Into a Great Story 256
Suggested Readings 258
Useful Web Sites 259
Exercises 260

CHAPTER 10 Interviews 269

Why Am I Interviewing? 269
Whom Should I Interview? 270
When Should I Conduct My Interviews? 272
Where Should I Conduct the Interview? 273
What Questions Should I Ask? 274
How Should I Conduct Interviews? 275
Writing the Interview Story 277
The Writing Coach—Figure It: Poetry Can Be in Newspaper Stories 278
Suggested Readings 279
Useful Web Sites 279
Exercises 280

CHAPTER 11 Writing Obituaries 292

Types of Death Reports 293
Jim Nicholson: No. 1 in Obituaries 297
Obituary Writing Considerations 301
Checklists for Reporting and Writing Obituaries 302
Suggested Readings 302
Useful Web Sites 302
Exercises 303

CHAPTER 12 Speeches and Meetings 312

Advance Stories 312
Covering the Speech or Meeting 313
Follow Stories 314
Internet Brings Pornography to Children, Researcher Says 317
Remember Your Readers 320
Adding Color 321
Checklists for Reporting Speeches and Meetings 322
The Writing Coach—Go Beyond the Stick 323
Suggested Readings 323
Useful Web Sites 323
Exercises 324

CHAPTER 13 Specialized Types of Stories 343

Brights 343
Follow-ups 345
Roundups 347
Sidebars 347
Checklists for Writing Specialized Stories 348
A Memo From the Editor—History, Traditions and Culture: Old Glory and Noodle 349
Suggested Readings 351
Useful Web Sites 351
Exercises 352

CHAPTER 14 Feature Stories 368

Selecting a Topic and Gathering Information 368
Types of Feature Stories 370
Types of Feature Leads 380
The Body of a Feature Story 381
The Ending of a Feature Story 382
What does It Take to Be a Top-Notch Writer? 383
Suggested Readings 384
Useful Web Sites 384
Exercises 385

CHAPTER 15 Public Affairs Reporting 393

Crime and Accidents 394
Covering the Search for a Serial Killer 395
Local Government 403
Courts 410
Checklists for Public Affairs Reporting 416

A Note About This Chapter's Exercises **417**
The Writing Coach—The "Knows" Have It for Police and Court Reporters **417**
Suggested Readings **418**
Useful Web Sites **418**
Exercises **419**

CHAPTER 16 Understanding and Using the Internet 446

A Brief History **446**
Journalists and the Internet **447**
E-Mail **447**
Internet Addresses, Web Sites or URLs (Universal Resource Locators) **448**
Search Engines and Subject Directories **451**
Mailing Lists and Newsgroups **453**
Ethical Considerations **456**
Suggested Readings **457**
Useful Web Sites **457**
Exercises **458**

CHAPTER 17 Advanced Reporting 467

Using Statistics **468**
Conducting Informal Polls **469**
Using Computers to Get Answers **471**
Converging Media **472**
Checklist for Using Statistics **473**
Checklist for Conducting Informal Polls **473**
A Memo From the Editor—Good Writing's Great, but It's Not Enough **473**
Suggested Readings **475**
Exercises **476**

CHAPTER 18 Writing for Broadcast 498

Writing for Your Listener **498**
Writing for Your Announcer **501**
Leads for Broadcast Stories **502**
The Body of a Broadcast News Story **504**
Updating Broadcast News Stories **505**
Guidelines for Copy Preparation **505**
Editing Copy **507**
Putting Together a Newscast **508**
Sources for Broadcast News **509**
The Newsroom Environment **510**
Checklists for Broadcast News Writing **511**
Suggested Readings **511**
Useful Web Sites **511**
Exercises **512**

CHAPTER 19 The News Media and PR Practitioners 524

What Is Public Relations? **524**
Becoming a Public Relations Practitioner **526**
Working with News Media **526**
Elements of a News Release **527**
Types of News Releases **530**

The Journalist's Perspective: Working with Press Releases 533
The No. 1 Problem: Lack of Newsworthiness 534
The No. 2 Problem: Lack of Objectivity 536
Other Problems with News Releases 538
Some Final Guidelines 540
Checklist for PR Practitioners 540
Checklist for Handling News Releases 541
Guest Column—Transparency Is Paramount 541
Suggested Readings 543
Exercises 544

CHAPTER 20 Communications Law 561

Libel 561
12 Steps for Avoiding Libel Suits 572
Privacy 572
Newsgathering 578
Bar-Press Guidelines 583
Checklists 584
Suggested Readings 586
Useful Web Sites 586
Exercises 587

CHAPTER 21 Ethics 593

Media Credibility 594
Ethical Decision-Making 594
Ethics Issues 596
Codes of Ethics 610
Checklist for Improving Media Credibility 610
A Memo From the Editor—Some Thoughts on Plagiarism 611
Suggested Readings 613
Useful Web Sites 614
Exercises 615

CHAPTER 22 Careers 622

A Journalist's Attributes 623
Be the Applicant Who Gets Hired 624
The Industry Needs More Women and Minorities 628
Freelance Writing 629
Checklist for Finding the Right Journalism Job 629
Suggested Readings 630
Useful Web Sites 630

Appendix A City Directory 631
Appendix B The Associated Press Stylebook 646
Appendix C Rules for Forming Possessives 655
Appendix D Answer Keys 657
Appendix E Common Writing Errors 665
Credit Lines 669
Index 671

PREFACE

Is journalism a social science or a humanity? Do journalists have more in common with sociologists, political scientists and economists or with poets, philosophers and artists? These questions may seem esoteric, but the answers describe what journalists do and suggest how they should be trained.

The subject matter of most news stories falls squarely within the domain of the social sciences: crime, the economy, government policies, international relations. Reporters must be familiar with those fields. Some reporters have studied law, economics or diplomacy. Yet the practice of journalism has more to do with the humanities than with the social sciences. Like novelists and playwrights, reporters are storytellers. Like poets and artists, they seek compelling, emotionally powerful images. So what does it take to be a reporter?

Good reporters need two characteristics:

1. They must be engaged in the world around them.
2. They must be articulate.

Being engaged in the world means reporters have a high degree of curiosity about their beats and life in general, and they feel empathy for the people who are the subjects of their stories.

Curiosity helps reporters generate story ideas and develop the stories assigned to them. Good stories emerge when reporters ask why things work as they do, what's wrong, what's right and who makes a difference. The more sophisticated the questions reporters ask, the more sophisticated—and interesting—the stories they tell. Curiosity leads reporters to ask about things others may not have considered newsworthy or interesting. The incurious reporter might have a parent who is facing a debilitating disease and see it only as a personal problem. The curious reporter in the same situation recognizes that many people are living with the same problem and looking for support, information and encouragement. From that recognition emerges a great story idea. The incurious reporter may watch the city council award contract after contract to the same company and not wonder why that happens. The curious reporter will ask why the contractor is so successful, whether that success carries over to competition for private sector projects and what connections to the city council the contractor might have. From those questions emerges a prize-winning investigative project.

Reporters must be constantly curious, asking about the details of their beats. How do police work? What do they do at a crime scene? How do they handle interrogations? Reporters should ask such questions with no expectation the answers will lead to stories. No reporter can predict what tidbit of information may help unravel a great story. But even if the information yields no story, it might be a fact or insight that helps the reporter understand and explain events to readers and viewers.

Being engaged also means having empathy for the sources and subjects of news stories. People in the news often confront highly emotional situations. The sources and subjects may be victims of crime or the relatives of a victim; they may be people who have lost loved ones in a plane crash; they may be athletes who have just suffered a defeat; or they may be community residents worried about how a proposed development might affect their lives and their property. A story about a knife attack by a male employee on a female supervisor is not just an antiseptic crime story or an exercise in deductive logic. It is a story about anger, frustration, betrayal, terror and humiliation. A reporter who cannot empathize with the people involved cannot truly understand their experiences or tell their stories.

The ability to empathize does not require reporters to abandon objectivity and impartiality. Empathy differs from sympathy. Sympathy requires one to have the same feelings as another or to achieve a mutual understanding with another. Empathy means projecting one's personality into that of another so as to understand the other person better. Reporters who have empathy for others can understand them without embracing or approving their emotions. Empathy not only is consistent with objectivity, but it also is probably indispensable for producing a truly objective and thorough story. If reporters cannot understand the emotional states of the people they write about or assess the emotional changes events inflict on sources, they will fail to report the full story.

Curiosity and empathy enable reporters to get the who, what, when, where, why and how of a story. Putting those elements into a coherent, interesting and readable story requires that reporters be articulate.

Being articulate combines at least two skills. One is the ability to use words effectively, to select the appropriate words and use them correctly, and to arrange them in sentences that are grammatical and properly punctuated. The other skill is the ability to organize the elements of the story—the facts, the quotations and the anecdotes—in a manner that is captivating, informative and dramatic.

Reporters who understand grammar and diction can construct sentences that are clear and precise. The skillful writer knows that the following sentences mean very different things:

> She only kissed him on the lips.
>
> She kissed him only on the lips.

The skillful writer would also know that one of these sentences accuses the subject of a crime:

> Wanda sent her husband Bob to the store.
>
> Wanda sent her husband, Bob, to the store.

The first sentence uses "Bob" as an essential modifier of "husband," meaning that Wanda has more than one husband and the one she sent to the store is Bob. The sentence implies Wanda has committed the crime of bigamy. The second sentence, because it uses commas before and after "Bob," makes it clear that Wanda has only one husband, and his name is Bob.

The ability to construct clear, correct sentences is fundamental. But a news story may contain nothing but clear, correct sentences and still be impossible to read because the writer has failed to organize the material. Readers crave organization; if they don't find it, they may stop reading. A story that jumps from one topic to another and back to the first without any sense of direction will confuse readers and drive them elsewhere for information. Reporters need to know how to organize information in a way that makes its significance and drama clear. Usually for news stories, this means placing the newest, most newsworthy information early in the story. But sometimes, writers want to hold some particularly dramatic or poignant fact for the end of the story.

All of the skills one needs to become a great reporter—curiosity, empathy, a knowledge of grammar and the ability to organize stories—are skills a person can learn. Some people may learn them more easily than others, or some may develop one set of skills more than the others. But anybody who can handle college-level course work can cultivate the skills a professional reporter needs. This eighth edition of "Reporting for the Media" offers many features—some new to this edition—to help students master the skills of news reporting.

Features of Interest

As with the previous editions of this textbook, the eighth edition contains several changes. But it also adheres to the approach and practice Fred Fedler developed when he created this textbook 30 years ago. The co-authors who have taken over much of the responsibility for this book hope longtime users will be comfortable with it and new users will find it attractive.

Although the eighth edition contains hundreds of changes, some major ones are worth noting:

- Electronic supplements to the textbook in the form of Web sites accessible through Oxford University Press contain additional exercises. Some of these exercises are old ones that have been deleted from this or previous editions of the book. Others are new ones we were unable to fit into the book. Material that might update or elaborate on points discussed in the text will be added to the electronic supplements in coming years.
- The chapter on grammar has been expanded to include a discussion of the parts of speech. This discussion should lay the foundation for the points of grammar discussed throughout the book.
- New and updated examples and illustrations have been added throughout the book. Many of these examples deal with news events that have occurred since the publication of the seventh edition, such as the terrorist attacks of Sept. 11 and the war in Iraq.
- New exercises have been added to almost every chapter in the book. Like the old exercises, they are devised to help reporting and newswriting students learn the basics of how to structure news stories, and they challenge students to find and correct many of the errors of grammar and spelling that commonly appear in news stories.
- Almost every chapter includes a list of Web sites students can use for finding additional information and instruction. The list of Web sites can be found at the end of the chapters following the bibliography of print sources.
- Joe Hight, managing editor of The Daily Oklahoman, has updated some of the columns he contributed to the last edition of the book.
- Tommy Miller, the former managing editor of the Houston Chronicle and now a professor at California State University, Fresno, has contributed four columns, which appear at the end of various chapters.
- Two journalists who had front-row seats to the Sept. 11 terrorist attacks, Erin Schulte of The Wall Street Journal and Jeff Zeleny of the Chicago Tribune, have contributed columns describing their experiences. Those columns are included in Chapter 5.
- Chapter 19 on public relations includes a column by Robert S. Saline, a public relations professional, and Chapter 14 includes a column by Bryan Denham, an assistant professor at Clemson University, on writing good feature stories.
- New photographs and illustrations have been added, some to chapters that had no illustrations in the past.

Other Features of Interest to Faculty Members

Answer Keys

Some students want more practice after they read the chapters and work on their exercises. They can complete the extra exercises marked "Answer Key Provided," then correct their own work. The answers to those exercises appear in Appendix D.

Appendices

"Reporting for the Media" provides five appendices: (A) a city directory, (B) a summary of The Associated Press Stylebook and Briefing on Media Law, (C) rules for forming possessives, (D) answer keys for some exercises and (E) a discussion of common writing problems.

Checklists and Other End-of-Chapter Materials

A variety of supplemental teaching materials appears at the end of each chapter. The materials include expanded checklists that review and reinforce the chapter's primary instructions. Other materials vary from chapter to chapter but typically include (1) lists of readings, (2) helpful Web sites, (3) discussion questions, (4) suggested projects and (5) sidebars or columns.

Flexibility

"Reporting for the Media" is flexible. Teachers can assign the chapters in almost any order. Moreover, the book provides enough exercises that faculty members can assign their favorites, then assign extra exercises for students who need more help. Some teachers use the book for two semesters: for basic and advanced reporting classes. There are enough exercises for both terms.

The book can be used in general media writing classes and those specific to newswriting and reporting. Still, faculty members who prefer the book's traditional emphasis on the print media can assign the chapters on public relations and writing for the broadcast media as optional readings.

Hundreds of Examples

"Reporting for the Media" contains hundreds of examples, some written by students and some by professionals. While introducing a new topic or discussing an error, this book typically shows students examples. For errors, the book also shows students how to avoid or correct them.

Some examples have been written by prize-winning professionals, and students can use their stories as models. For instance, examples from The Associated Press, The New York Times, The Washington Post and several other U.S. newspapers, large and small, illustrate many of the concepts discussed in the text. And Jim Nicholson of the Philadelphia Daily News, considered by many journalists to be the nation's best obituary writer, is quoted extensively in Chapter 11 (Writing Obituaries).

Realistic and Often Genuine Exercises

This book contains a multitude of exercises, and teachers can select the ones most appropriate for their students. Many are real. Chapter 12 (Speeches and Meetings) includes President Bill Clinton's address at a memorial service for victims of the Oklahoma City bombing and President George W. Bush's speech announcing the end of major combat operations in Iraq. Chapter 15 includes an exercise based on 911 tapes involved in the investigation of serial killer Jeffrey L. Dahmer. Exercises in other chapters, although fictionalized, are drawn from real events.

To add to the realism, many of the exercises contain ethical problems: profanities, sexist comments, the names of rape victims, bloody details and other material that many editors would be reluctant to publish. Students completing those exercises will have to deal with the problems, and their decisions are likely to provoke class discussion.

Instructor's Manual

The authors provide a detailed Instructor's Manual: more than 120 pages of ideas, recommendations, answers and quizzes. The manual's introductory sections discuss accuracy, grades, suggested policies and assignments. Those sections are followed by sample course outlines and lists of the exercises that contain ethical dilemmas and sexist remarks. Other lists tell you which exercises mention your city, state or school and can be localized. Later sections provide answers for many of the exercises. The manual also has tests covering style, vocabulary, attribution and spelling, as well as true/false questions for most chapters. (If you would like your city or school mentioned in an exercise in the next edition, contact any of the authors.)

Practical Approach

Like previous editions, the eighth is concrete, not abstract or theoretical. Its tone is practical and realistic. Its language is readable: clear, concise, simple and direct. Because of the book's realism, students will encounter the types of problems and assignments they are likely to find when they graduate and take entry-level jobs with the media.

Pro Challenge

Several exercises in the chapters about leads and the body of news stories are subtitled "Pro Challenge." Professionals have completed the exercises so students assigned the same exercises can compare their work to that of the professionals. The professionals' examples are in the Instructor's Manual.

A Single Volume

By combining everything students need in a single volume, "Reporting for the Media" provides a convenient package at a reasonable price. Like earlier editions, the eighth edition includes both the instructions and examples that students need to learn to write more effectively. It also includes a multitude of exercises and a summary of The Associated Press Stylebook. Thus students do not have to buy separate workbooks and stylebooks along with the text.

A Note of Thanks

Journalists are wonderful people: enthusiastic, interesting and helpful. While working on this book, we wrote to dozens of them. Reporters, photographers and editors from Portland to Philadelphia, from Miami to New York, answered our letters and provided advice and samples of their work.

We would especially like to thank the many professionals who gave us permission to quote their work: Roy Peter Clark of the Poynter Institute for Media Studies; Don Fry of the Poynter Institute for Media Studies; Ken Fuson, a reporter for the Des Moines Register; Jack Hart, managing editor of The Oregonian in Portland; Matthew Hansen of the Lincoln (Neb.) Journal Star; Joe Hight, managing editor of The Oklahoman; Kelly Luvison, publisher of The Evening News of Hornell, N.Y.; Tommy Miller, former managing editor of the Houston Chronicle and now a professor of journalism at California State University at Fresno; Henry McNulty, a former associate editor of the Hartford (Conn.) Courant; John Mollwitz, formerly of the Milwaukee Journal-Sentinel, who has worked in almost every newspaper job from paper boy to copy editor to board of directors member; Melissa Moore, former police reporter for The Advocate of Baton Rouge, La., and now adviser to Reveille, the Louisiana State University student newspaper; Robert S. Saline, APR, a public relations professional; Jim Nicholson, an obituary writer for the Philadelphia Daily News; Erin Schulte, a reporter for The Wall Street Journal Online; and Jeff Zeleny, a reporter in the Chicago Tribune's Washington, D.C., bureau.

Some teaching colleagues also gave us permission to quote their work: Bryan Denham, an assistant professor at Clemson University; Eugene Goodwin, a retired journalist, professor and author of "Groping for Ethics in Journalism"; M. Timothy O'Keefe, a professor at the University of Central Florida and a freelance writer; and Jim Underwood, a professor at Ohio Wesleyan University.

Numerous organizations, publications and news services gave us permission to quote their stories or republish their photographs: Albany (N.Y.) Times Union, Ann Arbor (Mich.) News, Associated Press, Atlanta Journal-Constitution, Boston Globe, Boston Herald; Chambersburg (Pa.) Public Opinion; Cheboygan (Mich.) Daily Tribune, Chicago Tribune, Dallas Morning

News, Denver Post, Detroit Free Press, Detroit News, Great Falls (Mont.) Tribune, Harrisburg (Pa.) Patriot-News, Houston Chronicle, Knight Ridder, Lansing (Mich.) State Journal, the Lincoln (Neb.) Journal Star, Los Angeles Times, Miami Herald, New York Times, New York Daily News, New York Post, Newsweek, Orlando (Fla.) Sentinel, Philadelphia Inquirer, Pittsburgh Post-Gazette, San Francisco Chronicle, Sioux Falls (S.D.) Argus Leader, Sacramento (Calif.) Bee, St. Louis Post-Dispatch, Tampa (Fla.) Tribune, Time, U.S. News & World Report, USA Today, Wall Street Journal, Washington Post, and Westchester (N.Y.) Journal News.

These professionals, all former students, completed the exercises titled "Pro Challenge": Melanie M. Sidwell of the Marco Island Eagle/Naples (Fla.) Daily News; Dane and Veronica Stickney of the Grand Junction (Colo.) Free Press; and Gwen Tietgen of the Garden City (Kan.) Telegram.

We would also like to thank two other colleagues: Geri Alumit-Zeldes, Ph.D., instructor for the School of Journalism at Michigan State University; and Pat Mills of the department of journalism at Ball State University, for her help during a previous edition in revising and improving the chapter on feature stories.

For their insightful comments and useful suggestions during the development process, thanks go to Deborah Davis, an adjunct professor at Kent State University in Ohio; Richard D. Hendrickson, assistant professor in the department of communications at John Carroll University in University Heights, Ohio; and Jackie M. Young, a student at the University of Hawaii.

We would also like to thank the staff at Oxford University Press: Peter Labella, acquisitions editor; Sean Mahoney, associate editor; Shiwani Srivastava, editorial assistant; and Karen Shapiro, managing editor.

The Authors

John R. Bender is an associate professor in the news-editorial sequence of the College of Journalism and Mass Communications at the University of Nebraska-Lincoln. Bender worked for six years for the Pittsburg (Kan.) Morning Sun, starting as a reporter covering local government and politics. He became the paper's assignment editor, news editor and then managing editor. During his term as managing editor, the Morning Sun won awards for farm coverage, photography and editorial writing. Bender has taught at the college or university level for 20 years. He was a journalism instructor at Culver-Stockton College in Canton, Mo., for five years, and he joined the faculty of the University of Nebraska in 1990. His teaching and research areas include news reporting and writing, communications law, media history and controls of information. He is also executive director of the Nebraska High School Press Association. As an undergraduate, Bender majored in sociology at Westminster College in Fulton, Mo. He holds a master's degree in journalism from the University of Kansas and a doctorate in journalism from the University of Missouri at Columbia.

Lucinda Davenport is a professor in the School of Journalism at Michigan State University and is associate dean for the College of Communication Arts and Sciences. During her 16 years at MSU, Davenport has served as assistant director and acting director of the department and director of the journalism graduate program. She received a university teaching award from MSU, and has developed and taught more than 15 different courses. Davenport is on numerous committees concerning journalism education and advises many students and student organizations, including being president of the board of directors for MSU's independent student newspaper. Davenport also has earned national awards for her research, which focuses mainly on newspaper ethics, computer-assisted reporting and media history. Davenport has worked as a newspaper reporter, broadcast news director and reporter, public relations practitioner and online news editor. As an undergraduate at Baylor University, Davenport earned a double-major in journalism and radio/TV/film. She received a master's degree in journalism from the University of Iowa and a doctorate in mass media from Ohio University. Both her thesis and dissertation were firsts about online news and information.

Michael W. Drager is an assistant professor in the Department of Communication/Journalism at Shippensburg University of Pennsylvania. He graduated with a bachelor's degree in art from Millersville University in Pennsylvania. While working as a newspaper reporter,

Drager earned a master's degree in communication at Shippensburg University. Drager received his doctorate from Michigan State University. As a journalist, Drager has worked as a reporter, copy editor, editorial writer, columnist and photographer. He has also worked in public relations as a writer and publications designer. As an educator, Drager has 18 years of experience in both public and higher education. He has taught courses in news reporting, news editing and design, public relations writing, photojournalism, magazine design and media ethics. His research explores the relationship between mass media and public policy. In addition, he conducts workshops and seminars on the relationship between journalism and public institutions.

Fred Fedler received his bachelor's degree from the University of Wisconsin in Madison, then worked as a newspaper reporter in Dubuque and Davenport, Iowa, and as a copy editor in Sacramento, Calif. He received his master's degree from the University of Kentucky and doctorate from the University of Minnesota. Since 1971, Fedler has taught at the University of Central Florida in Orlando and for 16 years headed the School of Communication's Journalism Division. He regularly conducts research in the field of journalism but also continues to freelance for popular publications. Fedler's other books include "Introduction to the Mass Media," "Media Hoaxes" and "Lessons from the Past: Journalists' Lives and Work—1850–1950." In addition, Fedler has served on numerous committees concerned with journalism education.

Many students and teachers have written us over the years telling us what they like and dislike about this book and suggesting new features. We have adopted many of those ideas, and we would like to hear from you. If you have a comment or suggestion, please write any of us:

Fred Fedler
School of Communication
University of Central Florida
Orlando, Fla. 32816-1344
ffedler@pegasus.cc.ucf.edu

John R. Bender
College of Journalism and
Mass Communications
University of Nebraska-Lincoln
Lincoln, Neb. 68588-0474
jbender1@unl.edu

Lucinda Davenport
School of Journalism
Michigan State University
East Lansing, Mich. 48824-1212
ludavenp@msu.edu

Michael W. Drager
Department of Communication/Journalism
Shippensburg University of Pennsylvania
1871 Old Main Drive
Shippensburg, Pa. 17257
mwdrag@wharf.ship.edu

REPORTING FOR THE MEDIA

CHAPTER 1

THE BASICS: FORMAT, COPY EDITING AND AP STYLE

True ease in writing comes from art, not chance,
As those move easiest who have learned to dance.
(Alexander Pope, English poet)

Training to become a journalist can be one of the most challenging and rewarding adventures of your life. Learning how to write in journalistic style—researching events and issues, identifying leads, organizing thoughts and writing concisely—will be one of your most useful experiences because the ability to communicate will benefit you throughout life.

For centuries, journalists have inspired people. The town crier told people the news, which they discussed among themselves. Then they waited to hear from the town crier again for updates. The town criers now are print, broadcast or online journalists, telling people in the community the news and information they need to make productive decisions about their lives. Journalism requires honest hard work and dedication. To what profession did the world turn to find out news in the wake of the Sept. 11 terrorist attacks? Who told the stories that were unfolding in the midst of the war in Iraq? And, where do people go to learn the results of local elections or road closings?

Although the purpose of reporting the news has remained the same for decades, the methods of gathering, producing and presenting information have changed. Only 15 years ago most editors thought online databases were unimportant, and few knew what an online database was. Today, reporters must know how to gather information using the Internet, CD-ROMs, public records, databases, electronic archives and newspaper databases in addition to traditional reporting skills.

Only recently, the issue of media convergence (or multimedia reporting) has been considered and debated. Convergence generally means journalists are using their writing skills to report the news through more than one medium. For example, in Tampa, Fla., Media General Inc. houses its media properties—the Tampa Tribune, WFLA-TV and TBO.com—in the same building. The newspaper reporters often "go live" on the television newscast, online reporters might write a column for the newspaper and broadcast videographers carry digital still cameras for print and online reporting. Other news organizations have shared resources, created partnerships or offered crossover news. This blending of media has caused critics to raise concern about diluted news and the fewer number of voices in the community. But proponents say convergence enables media organizations to provide more depth to their reporting by bringing additional resources to each story.

Nonetheless, reporters still must know how to report and write well. Once journalists understand the fundamentals of traditional print reporting and writing, they can transfer those skills to the different media. Thus, this chapter focuses on basic newspaper copy-editing skills and Associated Press style.

PRODUCING COPY

More changes than ever are happening in newsrooms. Until about 20 years ago, reporters typed their stories on sheets of paper, then used a pencil to correct their errors before giving the paper to an editor. The editor would often make further changes on the paper before giving the reporter's story to a typesetter. Starting in the 1970s, media organizations experienced rapid technological change. Most journalists now type their stories on computers or word processors and correct their errors instantly. When the journalists finish their work, their stories are stored in a computer until an editor is ready to view them on another terminal. Finally, the edited stories are transmitted to another computer, which sets them in type. Everything is done electronically, and the system can save a single news organization millions of dollars a year by eliminating its need for typesetters, other skilled workers and equipment.

Reporting students must still learn the traditional format and copy-editing symbols. Reporters and editors handle printed copy from freelance writers, public relations agencies and a variety of other sources. Also, the traditional format and copy-editing symbols are helpful in college classes in which their stories are printed for instructors' comments and editing.

Although most assignments must be typed, students may notice an error in their work after their story is printed. In making corrections on paper, students are expected to use the proper format and copy-editing symbols. These are the same format, editing and style guidelines that journalists across the country use when editing on paper. Accordingly, we review these guidelines in this chapter.

NEWS STORY FORMAT

Reporters have developed a standard format for their stories, and each story they write follows the guidelines presented here. Although minor variations exist from one news organization to another, most publications are remarkably consistent in their adherence to these rules:

- Type or print each news story on one side only of separate $8\frac{1}{2}$-by-11-inch sheets of paper.
- Type your name as the journalist, the date the story is written and a slugline describing the story on the upper left-hand corner of the first page:

  Fred Fedler
  April 7, 2005
  Child Genius

Sluglines help editors identify and keep track of stories that are being prepared for publication. They also provide a quick summary of each story's topic. A story that reports an increase in the city's unemployment might be slugged "Unemployment Increases"; a story about a fund-raiser for homeless children might be slugged "Homeless Children Fund-raiser." Sluglines should not exceed three words and should be as specific as possible. Vague sluglines, such as "Unemployment" or "Fund-raiser," might be used on more than one story; and the stories, their headlines and their placement in the paper might then become mixed up with one another.

In devising a slugline, journalists avoid jokes, sarcasm, insensitivity and statements of opinion that would cause embarrassment if the slugline were accidentally published, as sometimes happens. A reporter in Texas was irritated when she was told to cover a story at the local high school. It was about a talk given by a 22-year-old high school dropout urging others to complete their schooling. The reporter thought the story was unimportant and uninteresting. Angrily, she slugged it "Wannabe Whines." She was almost fired when the slugline inadvertently appeared in print. Similarly, a writer in Michigan wrote a story about a man who had kept his dead mother in a lifelike position in the house for several years. Another employee thought the writer's slugline was the headline—and an accurate one. It was set in type, and the story the next morning bore the insensitive headline "Mommie's a Mummy."

- Begin each story about one-third of the way down the first page. In a news organization, the space at the top of the first page provides room for a byline, a headline and special instructions to production workers. In class, the space provides room for instructors to evaluate students' work.
- Leave a 1-inch margin on each side and at the bottom of every page. Standard margins help editors and production workers gauge the length of each story. Instructors use this space to write comments.
- Indent five spaces at the beginning of each paragraph. Type and double-space each story so that it is neat, uniform and easy to read. Editing should be placed clearly in the skipped spaces. The spacing should make editing easier to do and see. Do not leave any extra space between paragraphs.
- To save time, learn to type the first draft of every story. Deadlines are missed and effort is wasted if news stories are written in longhand first. Slow typists should practice until they can manage at least 30 words a minute.
- Traditionally, journalists never divided a word at the end of a line because typesetters might mistakenly assume that the hyphen was part of the word and set it in type. Today, computer software can automatically move an entire word to the next line rather than hyphenate it.
- Also traditionally, journalists never divided a paragraph between pages. A story would often go to the production department in pages. If a news reporter broke a paragraph between pages, then the production staff would have to delay moving the story through the production process. Keeping a paragraph together keeps its information together should following pages be misplaced. A student using a computer can insert a page break between paragraphs. Sometimes a page break is not necessary because production processes are electronic.
- If a story continues on a second page, type the word "more" centered at the bottom of the first page to indicate to the editor and production staff that the story does not end on the first page; more information is on an additional page.
- Begin the second page and all later pages about 1 inch from the top of the page. Type your last name, the page number of the story and the slugline in the upper left-hand corner:

  Fedler
  Child Genius
  Page 2

- At the end of the story, type an end mark to show that the story is complete. If no mark appears, then composers do not know if more information is coming and time is lost finding out. Telegraphers used to end their messages with the Roman numerals XXX to indicate the end of a message. Eventually, editors put it at the end of a story indicating its completion, and the Roman numerals ultimately migrated into the Arabic "30." Traditional end marks to Linotype operators were "-30-" or three pound signs ("###"). Printers preferred "#" because it avoided confusion between "30" and "—3—" or "3-em," a sign that called for the insertion of a dash to separate parts of a story. Since the early 1900s, reporters have typed or written "#."

Be aware that news organizations use different terms to mean the same thing. Instead of using the word "paragraph," some journalists call it a "graph" or "graf." Other journalists refer to a page of a story as an "add" or a "take." And still others use the word "copy" instead of "story" to refer to the written version of a news report. News organizations also vary on the use of datelines, which indicate the place where the event took place. Datelines are placed at the beginning of the story and normally include the name of the city, printed entirely in capital letters and followed by a comma, the abbreviation for the state in upper and lower case and a dash (for example: DANSVILLE, Mich. —). Names of major cities that have large populations and are synonymous with a state or nation (such as Denver, Pittsburgh, San Francisco, Toronto and Tokyo) are used alone. Most news organizations do not use datelines for stories that originate within their own communities. When they use the names of other cities within their own state, they omit the name of the state.

Datelines routinely used to include the date the story was written. Because communication was slower in the 19th century, the dates in datelines helped readers know how fresh the news was. Now, most stories are published the day they are written or the day after. A few news organizations, such as The New York Times, retain the dates in datelines.

News organizations also have different policies about when to use datelines. Some organizations tell their reporters to use datelines to indicate where the basic information in the story came from even if the writer of the story was in another city. Other news organizations say datelines should be used only when the principal reporter of the story is physically in the city named in the dateline.

COPY-EDITING SYMBOLS

Reporters should edit their stories and correct all their errors before giving the final version to an editor. If the editor finds a problem, the story is often returned to the reporter for revisions. Almost all journalists correct their work using a standard method. Correcting stories is called editing; symbols used to edit are called copy-editing symbols.

Most stories written for reporting classes will not have to be typed perfectly, but they should be neat and easy to read. To edit a story after typing it, use a pencil to insert the copy-editing symbols shown in the paragraphs below. Ink cannot be erased and the original markings may be confused with revised editing.

If several errors appear within one word, draw one line through the word and place the correct spelling above it. Make these copy-editing symbols and corrections plain and obvious. If several major errors appear in a paragraph or section of a story, retype that section. If corrections become too numerous and messy, retype the entire story so that it is easy to read. The following is an example of copy-editing for print publications. Copy-editing symbols for broadcast are discussed in Chapter 18.

Double-space your story. Indent every paragraph in a news story, and mark the beginning of each paragraph with the proper copy-editing symbol: ⌊____ If you want to mark a paragraph to be divided into two shorter paragraphs, you can use either the same copy-editing symbol or this one: ¶ .

If you indent a line and then decide that you do not want to start a new paragraph, link the lines together with a pencil, as shown here.

The same symbol is used to link the remaining parts of a sentence or paragraph after a major deletion ~~involving the elimination of a great many words and more than one line of type, or even a complete sentence or two,~~ as shown here.

Always use a pencil, not a pen, to correct any errors that appear in your stories. If you make a mistake in correcting your story with a pen, the correction will be difficult to change.

Write "OK" above facts or spellings that are so unusual that your editors are likely to question their accuracy, and circle the letters. (For example, you might need to check again the spelling of Suzanne Schlovitkowitz, when writing that she became a millionaire at the age of 13.) The notation "OK" indicates that the information is correct, regardless of how odd, unlikely or bizarre it may appear to be.

If you accidentally type an extra word or letter, cross out with one line the word or ~~or~~ letter, then draw an arc above it to link the remaining portions of the sentence. An arc drawn above a deletion indicates that the remaining segments of the sentence or paragraph should be moved closer together, but a space should be left between them. To eliminate a space within a word, draw an arc both above and below i t. To eliminate an unnecessary letter, draw an arc both above and below ixt, plus a *vertical* line through it. To delete a letter or punctuation at the end of a word, you can draw a symbol through it like this.

When two words or letters are inverted, use symbol this to indicate that they should be transposed. If you want to move an entire paragraph, retype that portion of the story. Particularly if the transposed paragraphs are on different pages, several errors are likely to occur if you fail to retype them.

draw three lines under a letter to indicate that it should be capitalized. If a letter is capitalized, but should not be, draw a *slanted* line Through it. If two words are incorrectly run together, draw a *straight*, vertical line between them to indicate that a spaceshould be added.

If you make a correction and then decide that the correction is unnecessary or mistaken, write the word "stet" (from the Latin word "stare," meaning "let it stand") alongside the correction to indicate that you want to retain the original version.

If you want to add or change a letter, word or phrase, write or type the change abve the lyne, then use a caret to indicate where it fits into the sentence. Many punctuation marks, including colons, semicolons, exclamation points and question marks, are added in the same manner (for example: When will he have dinner ready). Make certain that your caret is legible by inserting it in the space above or below the text line.

To add a comma, draw a comma in the proper place and put a caret *over* it (for example: The dog is big, black and furry.). If you add an apostrophe or quotation mark, place a caret *under* it (for example: He said, "Im going to the store"). To add a period, draw either a dot or a small "x" and circle it. A hyphen is indicated by the symbol =, and a dash by the symbol)—(.

Never type or write over a letter or word. Also, place all corrections above (never below) the typed line and error. Otherwise, an editor won't know if your correction goes with the line above or below it.

As you examine various newspapers, you will see that they never underline ~~because typesetters do not have a key to underline.~~ However, you can use the symbol shown here to indicate that a word needs to be set in italics, and you can use the symbol shown here to indicate that a word needs to be set in boldface. You can use this symbol to center a line on the page:

]By Gordon Elliott[

This symbol means flush left. This symbol means flush right.

Spell out most numbers below 10 and use numerals for the number 10 and most larger numbers. Consult The Associated Press Stylebook and Libel Manual for more exact guidelines. If you type a numeral, but want it spelled out, circle it (for example: She has 4 dogs.). If you spell out a number, but want to use the numeral, circle it (for example: She has twelve horses.). Similarly, circle words that are spelled out, but should be abbreviated (for example: He is from Madison, Wisconsin), and words that are abbreviated but should be spelled out (for example: Her dad is from Tex.). Do not use a circle to indicate that a letter should or should not be capitalized.

Below the last line of each news story, in the center of the page, place one of these "end marks":

-30-

-0-

###

Calvin and Hobbes **by Bill Watterson**

Reprinted with permission of Universal Press Syndicate.

Reporters usually do not write headlines for their stories, nor do they put their byline on the stories. Editors write the headlines after they determine the size of the headline and where to place the stories in their papers. Editors also control the use of bylines.

THE ASSOCIATED PRESS STYLEBOOK AND BRIEFING ON MEDIA LAW

Most news organizations have adopted The Associated Press Stylebook and Briefing on Media Law. The stylebook presents rules in alphabetical order for abbreviations, capitalization, punctuation, grammar, spelling and word usage. A summary of the stylebook appears in Appendix B of this book, and students should study it and learn all its rules. The complete stylebook is available at most campus and community bookstores.

The stylebook helps journalists avoid misspellings and errors in grammar and word usage. In addition, the stylebook saves journalists time, because it answers most of the questions they are likely to ask about the proper use of the language. Thus, journalists seldom must search through several reference books or interrupt more experienced colleagues with questions. Further, news organizations have found it less expensive and much easier to follow a nationally accepted stylebook.

Large news organizations employ dozens or hundreds of journalists. By specifying a single set of rules for everyone to follow, The Associated Press Stylebook also encourages consistency. Without a single set of rules, news organizations would publish more errors, which could be both costly and embarrassing. For example, four reporters within the same news organization might use a different style for the same phrase. One reporter might spell "percent" as one word (17 percent), another might use two words (17 per cent), a third might use the percentage sign (17%), and a fourth might spell out the number 17 (seventeen percent). The first version (17 percent) is correct. Reading newspapers is also easier if the style is consistent.

Over the years the stylebook has grown to include information necessary for journalists, such as guidelines for the Internet, sports and business, media law and photo captions. In addition to its other uses, the stylebook helps students prepare for their first jobs. If beginning journalists learn the book's basic rules while enrolled in college, they can easily begin writing for the media—and move from one employer to another. Because most news organizations have adopted The Associated Press Stylebook, reporters do not have to learn a new set of rules each time they move to another newsroom.

A few large newspapers, such as The New York Times and The Washington Post, have published stylebooks of their own. Other large news organizations publish brief supplements to The Associated Press Stylebook that specify the rules for handling unusual stylistic problems that arise in their communities. Similarly, some college newspapers publish supplements that specify a standardized set of rules for common usage on their campuses.

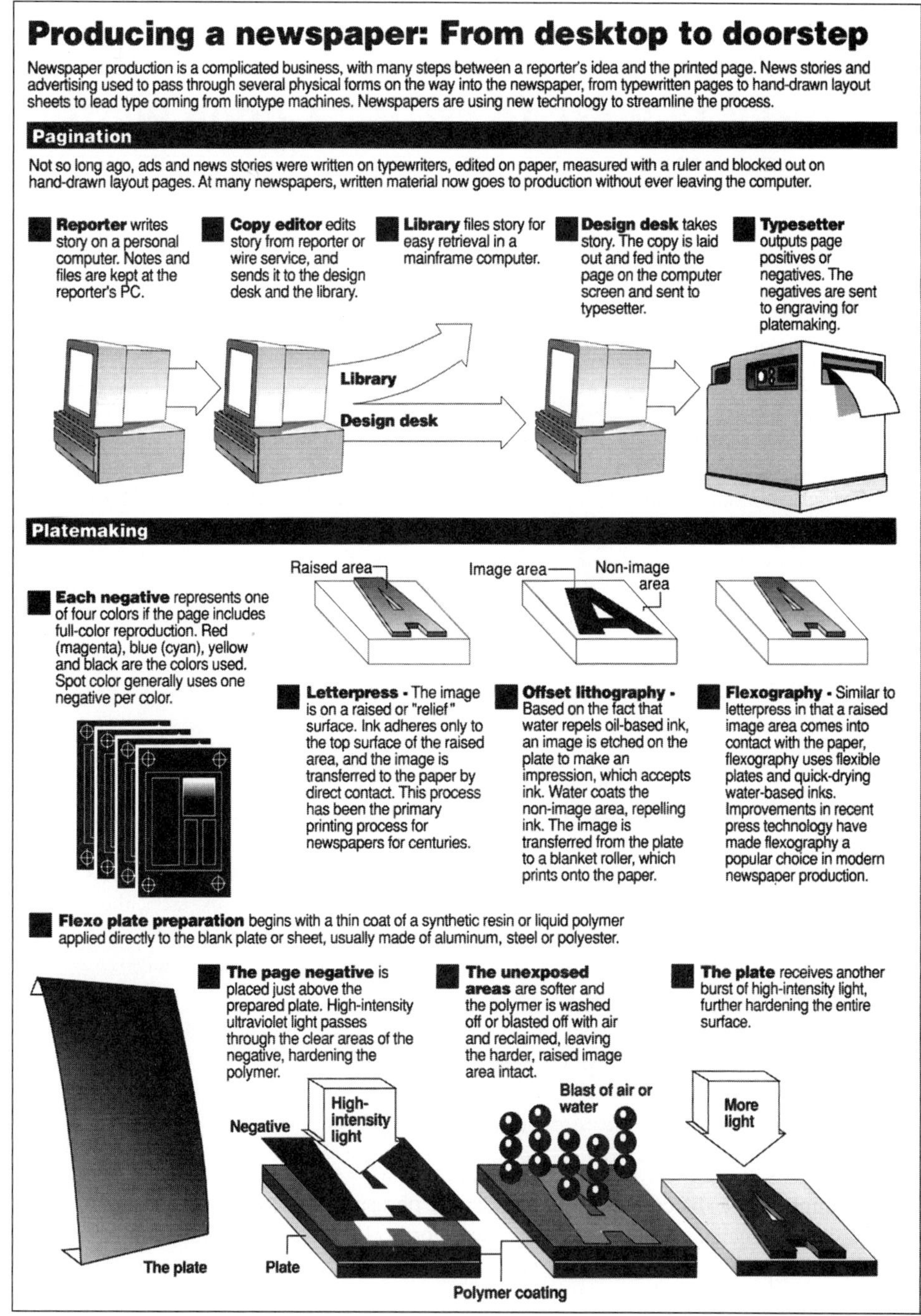

Knight-Ridder Tribune/CHUCK CARTER

ACCURACY OF NAMES AND FACTS

Editors and instructors do not tolerate sloppiness of any kind, and they are particularly critical of spelling errors, and incorrect names and facts, because there is rarely any excuse for them.

Be especially careful to check the spelling of people's names. Most misspellings are the result of carelessness, and they anger two sets of people—those who were intended to be named as well as those who are inadvertently named. Most editors require their reporters to consult a second source, usually a telephone book or a city directory, to verify the way names are spelled. Always confirm the spelling of a source's name and title before ending the interview.

THE WRITING COACH

THE LUCKY 13 WAYS TO BECOME A GOOD WRITER

By **Joe Hight**
Managing Editor of The Oklahoman

1. Realize you are human and will make mistakes. So that means that you need to self-edit, and double-check your facts, etc.
2. Always get the names right. Ever had your name misspelled?
3. Double-check your facts. Mistakes will be made, but careful writers and editors catch as many as possible.
4. Know grammar. Didn't listen to your English teacher? Well, there are lots of books to help you catch up.
5. Use simple words. Clarity in writing is vital, and the basic components of clear writing are simple: brevity and simplicity. Author Paula LaRocque writes that poor writers and editors claim this is oversimplification, dumbs down the product by writing "on a first-grade basis."
6. Use those simple words correctly. Understand the differences between words that look or sound similar, such as "peak," "peek" and "pique."
7. Shorten your sentences. Your stories should contain sentences with a variety of lengths, but most should be fewer than 30 words.
8. Listen. Ever know a person who didn't listen? Good interviewers ask well-prepared questions, then listen for answers.
9. Use great quotes! Don't use them for facts; use them for emphasis and flow.
10. Think, write and rewrite. First prepare for your story through research, then write it and then rewrite it. The rewrite may be most important.
11. Just write! After you've done your research, then write. Let your rewrite become your masterpiece.
12. Be original and relate to your reader. The best writers eliminate clichés, journalese and jargon and find ways to explain and use elements that readers will understand.
13. MOST IMPORTANT: Feature people, not things. People add life to stories. Help people relate to statistics, help them form opinions about issues.

For the exercises in this textbook, use the city directory that appears in Appendix A to verify the spelling of names, titles and addresses. Names in some exercises have deliberately been misspelled. Draw a box around the names to show that you have checked their spelling and that they are accurate (for example: Mayor Sabrina Datolli has resigned). To avoid inconsistent spellings, check and box a name every time it appears in a news story, not just the first time it is used.

Like other city directories, the directory in this book does not list people who live in other parts of the country. Thus, if a story mentions that someone lives in another city, assume that the person's name is spelled correctly. Because the name will not be listed in the city directory, it will be impossible to check.

Journalists understand the importance of double-checking the accuracy of every fact in every news story. Any factual error will damage a news organization's reputation and may seriously harm people mentioned in the stories. Because of the serious consequences of inaccuracies, an instructor is likely to lower grades significantly for a factual error. Students are also penalized for errors in diction, grammar and style. If an instructor accepts late assignments (most do not), grades on them may be lowered because of a missed deadline. All media organizations must meet rigid deadlines, and editors expect work to be turned in on time.

CHECKLIST FOR COPY PREPARATION

1. Devise a slugline that describes the story's content.
2. Start typing the story one-third of the way down the first page and 1 inch from the top of all following pages.
3. Double-space each story.
4. Indent each paragraph.
5. Use a pencil and the proper copy-editing symbols to correct errors.
6. Make certain that no words are divided and hyphenated at the end of a line and that no paragraphs are divided between pages.
7. Print separate stories on separate pages and do not use the back of pages.
8. If the story continues on a second page, type "more" at the bottom of the first page; type your name, page number and slugline at the top of the second page; and type an end mark at the end of the story.
9. If the story originated outside your community, add the proper dateline.
10. Use the city directory to verify the spelling of all names used in the story; check and draw a box around those names every time they are used.

SUGGESTED READINGS

Born, Roscoe C. *The Suspended Sentence: A Guide for Writers*. Ames, Iowa: Iowa State University Press, 1993.

Cappon, Rene J. *Associated Press Guide to Newswriting*. 3rd ed., New York: Arco Publishing, 2000.

Goldstein, Norm, ed. *The Associated Press Stylebook and Briefing on Media Law*. New York: The Associated Press, 2000.

Kessler, Lauren, and Duncan McDonald. *When Words Collide: A Media Writer's Guide to Grammar and Style*, 4th ed. Belmont, Calif.: Wadsworth, 1999.

USEFUL WEB SITES

American Copy Editors Society (ACES): www.copydesk.org
Words at Work (Ron Hartung and Gerald Grow): www.longleaf.net/newsroom101

Name ________________________ Class ____________________ Date ______

EXERCISE 1

FORMAT AND COPY-EDITING SYMBOLS

Using the proper copy-editing symbols, correct the errors in the following stories. Use the reference chart for copy-editing symbols on the inside of the front and back covers to help you.

Except for some obvious errors, the stories' style (the abbreviations, for example) is correct. There is one exception: You will have to form all the possessives. If you need help, see Appendix C, "Rules for Forming Possessives." Use Appendix A to check names and addresses.

1. BACKGROUND INVESTIGATIONS

for $150, threee retirde detective s will Help you investigate a potential date roommmate, em-ploeye or anyone else you are curous abou.t

one year ago, the detectivrs openedBackgroundds Unlimited and, for $150, will conduct a basic background investigation. The investigation includes on an examinatino of an Individu-als criminal record, driving record, employment history credit historyy and educational back-ground

"People have started coming to us, askingus to on check there spouses, tenants nannies -- anyone you nac can imagin," said Roger datolla, retired who after wworking 26 years for the city s police department,. HIS partners, Betsy Aaron and Myron Hansen, retired after 20years "We re friendds, and this seemed like a natural for us," Datolla said. "Were all familiar with the routnie, and its catching on faster than we expected. Of coarse, some people want us cond-cutt more detailed investigations, and we chagre more for that."

Lar ge corporations ask bBackgrounds Unlimited to investigate potential employes. "They want to find out about soneone before they hire the person, before its two late,"" Datolli continued "A charming personality isn't enough these days for someone loking for a good job. People in personnel offices realizze they can't rely on instinct, refences, or even diplomas or written employment histories. Its too easy to fake all that.plus, small businessses, especially, don"t have the contacts or know-how to conduct good background checks."

Aaronadded: “WE started fo off thinking almost all our worlk would be from businesses, mainly checking on ojb applicamnts, possibly employee thefts and that type of thing. Sudenly, we re getting other people, and that part of our business is mushrooming, almost half ofwhatdo we now. We ve had mothers comein,checking on guys their daughterss are dating, and couples checking onneighbors. We even had a colllege teacher ask u s to cheCk on a student he thought was dangereous.

2. JURY AWARD

A judge Monday ordered the cityy to pay $2.8 million too Caleb Draia, a thieve from Chicago shot in the back

A polic officer fired threee shotsat Dr aia, and one hit him, paralyzing him for live.

Draia admitted that he grabed a purse from 74 year old Celia Favata as she as was returning to hwrher car in parking lot at cColonial Mall. He pleaded guilty to a charge of robbary and was sentenced to five yearns in prison, a ternm he;s now serving.

Draias lawyer argued that the police were not justified in shooting, his client in the bcak as he fled. A judge agree, ruling that Draia was the victim of excessive, deadly policcpolice force.

Favata testified tht she was nearly chokked todeath. “I tried to holler for help, and he threatened to choke me to death if I didn’t shut up,” she said Her glassses were broken her dress torn, her nose bloodied and her left arm broken when Draia through her to tHE ground.

“Thiis wasn’t just a mugigng,” city atorney Allen Farci argud.”This was really a case of attempted murder.”

After Judge Marilyn PIcot annnounced her verdict, FAvata said: “Its not right. I never got 10 centts, and now this thug gets nearly $3 million. He deserved to be hurt,.”

Patrolmen George Oldaker was shoppiing at the hall heard Favatas cries, and asw her lying injued on the ground. “Officer Oldaker was justified in shooting Draia because he was preventing the flight of a violent felon,” the citey attorney argued. “Theirwas no other way to stop

Draia, to keep from him escaping. N o one know who he was, so if he got away, chances were he'd never be CAUGHT."

Farci said hewill apppeal the judges decison. "Its ludicrous," he siad said. "This verdict sends a message to people that you can be rewarded if anything happens to you, even iff you're hurt while connitting a very serious crime. HE could've killed thtat poorold woman.

3. PUBLIC ART

Spending money on art is a poor ppriority and sinful waist of the publics money, Mayor Sabrina datoli said during a press converence friday.

A new state la w requires public agencies to spend one-half of 1 percent of the cost of every mew new governmentt buildingon art for the building

"We re planing to buidl a new city hall, and thiSS law would force us to spend $460,000 on art," Datolli said. "Wee need that money to erect the cityhalll, not for atart no one in the city wants. Thats a lot of money, all the money we"d typicallly collect in property taxes in a year from 230 or more homes. That's not what citizens pay their taxes for,not what they want done with their hard-earned noney.."

Datolli said the state flaw forces the city to spend, on art, mony also needed for schools parsk roads and other essential services, including police and fire protection. "government should limit IT's spending to exxessential servizes, and letprivatte donors and buyers deal in art," Datoli.

Carmen Foucault, chaeir of the State art Federation, said the federation supported the laws pas sage and will oppose any effort to change it. "We'll due everything we can to fight it," Fou cault said. "Governmend ought to be supporting art and artists. Itsimportnat for us as a people as a culture, tohavesome public expresion of our artistic side, to expose more people to art and culture. ART iss an uplifting, civilizing force in our world, and we need nmore of it. BE sides, goverments have always subsidized art, and the amount involved here isn't all that significant,"

Name ______________________________ Class ______________________ Date ______

EXERCISE 2

FORMAT AND COPY-EDITING SYMBOLS

Using the proper copy-editing symbols, correct the errors in the following stories. Use the reference chart for copy-editing symbols on the inside of the front and back covers to help you.

Except for some obvious errors, the stories' style (the abbreviations, for example) is correct. There is one exception: You will have to form all the possessives. If you need help, see Appendix C, "Rules for Forming Possessives." Use Appendix A to check names and addresses.

1. ISLAND PRISONS

WASHINGTON, D.C. -- Membbers ofthe House Armed Ser vices COIommitteee today recommendde that the united Stats imprison dtrug addicts and dealers on two remote islands,.

THE U.S. Navey plans to abandon its bases on Midway and Wake Islands, and committee menmbers saidthe basis should be conv ertted to prsonsprisons to alleviate overcrowding at other federal failities

"Labor coxts in the region are loW, and the inmates could be required to do a lot more themselfs," sad Sen. arlen Hoyniak, D-Ill. ""Plus,this would be a real punishmnet and deterrent."

Wake is a three-square mileatoll located abotu 2,300 miles wetwest of Hawaii. Midway is 1 mile widee and 15 miles long, and locatd 1,150 miles northwest of Hawaii. I t was the sitte of decisive U.S. naval victory during World War II.

Since World II, the isljands have been U.S. possessions, and the military used has them for emergency airfields and com munications stations.

Hoyniak proposedtheidea, and the Armed Services Commiitee voted unanimously in favo r of it. The committee wants the secretary of defense to study idea the and report back to it

"Sending drug criminals to faraway islands makes more sense than building new prisons," HOyniak said. He axxedadded that the Pacific islands could be reservde for volunters. Asanincentive, he suggewsted that convicts who agreed to be imprisoned on the islands could have their sentences reduced by one-third:

"Theres not much change they're going to get anything but rehabilitated on too little islands like these, and theislands are isoladted enough to deter any thoughtt of escpe," hoyniak continued. "You can't go anywhere.The only thing prisoners can do there IS think about there mistakes and how they'ddd improve their lives"

Hoyniaksaid he thought of the idea after visit ing Midway and Wake during commmittee trips. Neither ilandisland has any native inhabitants, only military personnel.

HOwever, Nicole Ezzell, direcotr of Humanity Internatonal in new York, City considers the idea a giantt step backward. "This is astonishing," she said. "It takes penologyback two centur ies, to the days when the British shipped their hardened criminals off to Australia and the French se nt their convicts to Devil's Island off coast the of Sout america.

2. TRUANCY

judge JoAnne Kaeppler wednesday sentenced Rosalind McGowin to thrfee days in jail, and McGowins husban, Bill, will be gin a thrree-day sentence the moment she is released.Kaeppler found that the two failed to make their15-year-old daghter, Claire, atttend school. Claire a sophomore at kennedy High School, was absent 11 out of 20 days month last, and 10 out of 19 days thE previous month, acording to school records.

"We generally wiffwill not prosecute unless the shool system has exhausted every possibble way to convinceparents to get their kids in school," District Attorney Ramon Hernandez said; in an interview to day. "Generally, this is the last thing we want to DO."

Hernandez added, however, that his sttaff is also pursuing three other truancy cases. "We want people to take this seriously" he explained. "Childre are our fOuture Hopefully, the mc-Gowins and oterother parents like them will get the message."

State law requries childrem between

the ages of 6 and 16 to atend schol. Violationsofthe law are a second-degree misdemeanor, punishable by sentenbces of up 60 days in jail, six months probation and $500 fines.

The McGowinns pleaded guiltky to violating the law. In addition to sentencing htem to jail, KAEPPLER placed them on probatiom for six months and orderd them to perform 100 hours of community serve.

THeY promised Kaeppler that their daugher would return classes to to day,but school oficials could not immediately confirm that she aws present. The McGowinns initially told the judge that their daughter did not want to attend school and that there was nothing they could do to make her.

"Tryharder,"Kaeppler responded.

The school system normally refer five to 10 cascs a year to prosecuters, but the McGowins are the first sentenced parents to jail. "Our system hasn't been vrey aggressife in forcing the issue," Hernandez said. "In this case the parents had repeated warnings, and we decided it was time to begin cracking down on the problem, especially since kids who aren t in school get into all sorts of othertrouble.

Super intendent of Shools GARY Hebert said he wswas disappointed that the McGowins had to be prosecuted, but that parentts must make therechildren attend school.

3. POLICE STING

tHe policehavearrested 114 people who thought they inherited $14,000.

"Most evrey criminal i s greedy," PoliceChief Barry Kopp errud said, "and we appealed to their greed."

THe police created a fictitious law firm, then spent $1,100 for a fake

sign and for pprinting and postage send to letters to 441 peeple wanted on warrants issued in the past three year. Each leterletter was mailed to the persons last known a ddress and said the recipient had inherited $14,200 from a distaant relative. The letter set An appointment time for each person to come to the firm and pick up acheck.

Fourteen officers posing as lawyers and their asistants were assigned to donated space and workeed from there 8 a.m.to 9 p.m monday through Friday last week. Recipients who appeared to collect their money were led to a back room and quietly arrested.

Koperrud siad offficers are often unable to find people wanted on w arrants. "When we go to tyhere homes and try to pick these peopl up, we often mis s them, and that warnz them we're after them.They disappear, staying with friends or relatives or moving toother cities."

DetectiveManuel Cortez added: "Ths was a good tactic. I dont have any qualms about telling a little white lie to criminls trying to ezcape the law. Be sides, it saved a tonn of money. Normally, too make these arrests would take hundreds of hoUrs of our time, and some of these people would commit new crimes before we caught hemthem, if we caught them at all."

MOst of the people policc arrested weer wanted for probation violations drunken driving writing bad checks failure to pay child support and other nonviolent crimes. However, seven were wanted for burglary, thee for car theft, thre for robbery and one for aiding an escape

Name ____________________ Class ____________________ Date ______

EXERCISE 3

AP STYLE

Circle the correct AP style within the parentheses. Use the condensed Associated Press Stylebook in Appendix B for help with your answers. Use Appendix C for help with possessives.

1. Sooyoung ran a red light at the intersection of Brown and Grant (Streets / streets).
2. The (first lady / First Lady) will return to the (presidential / Presidential) suites at 3 p.m.
3. The ophthalmologist office is at (nine / 9) Westwind (Avenue / avenue / Ave. / ave.)
4. Emily is taking a course in the (Sociology / sociology) and (English / english) (Departments / departments).
5. Copy-editing symbols have not changed much since the (1920s / 1920's).
6. Only (three / 3) (% / per cent / percent) of the population in 2003 bought duct tape and plastic for their windows when (President / president) Bush put the country on high alert for terrorist attacks.
7. The (girl / woman) celebrated her 19th birthday yesterday.
8. Danny got his (first / 1st) story published in (Sports Illustrated / *Sports Illustrated* / "Sports Illustrated" / **Sports Illustrated**) (Magazine / magazine).
9. The horse knows (its / it's) way home.
10. (Mrs. Fred Greene / Josephine Greene) won the (womans / womens / woman's / women's) (golf / Golf) (Tournament / tournament).
11. The (winter's / Winter's) lowest temperature was (minus / -) (fourty / forty / 40) (degree's / degrees / °).
12. One of the (potato / potatoe) sacks weighted (4 / four) (lbs. / pounds) and the other weighed (11 / eleven) (oz. / ounces).
13. Harry (Potter, of Phoenix, / Potter of Phoenix) was at the wizard's convention.

14. (Codys / Cody's) birthday is in (Sept. / September).
15. The flag is (red, white, and blue / red; white; and blue / red, white and blue / red, white & blue).
16. The soldier came home from Iraq on a (Tuesday / Tues. / tuesday / tues.).
17. Jamie (drove / drived) (South / south) to (Texas / Tex.).
18. Many people in the (US / U.S. / United States / united states) are worried about the SARS (Virus / virus).
19. Shaun lives in (Central / central) (Penn. / PA. / Pennsylvania).
20. The textbook cost (forty dollars / 40 dollars / $40).

Name ______________________ Class ______________________ Date ______

EXERCISE 4

AP STYLE

Circle the correct AP style within the parentheses. Use the condensed Associated Press Stylebook in Appendix B for help with your answers. Use Appendix C for help with possessives. Answer key provided, see Appendix D.

1. The (priest / Priest) (said / celebrated) (Mass / mass) during their marriage ceremony.
2. Morgan's new book is (entitled / titled) ("Rachael's New Glasses" / Rachael's New Glasses).
3. His (dad / Dad) celebrates his birthday in (August / Aug.).
4. The jury found him (not guilty / innocent).
5. The miniature ponies were (reared / raised) in Elliott (county / County).
6. The mayor lives at (forty-nine / fourty-nine / 49) Morning Glory (Street, St.).
7. Seven of the (people / persons) in the room were reading newspapers.
8. (Jean and Diane's / Jean's and Diane's) room was in a mess.
9. Neither Jason nor his friends (was / were) going to the party.
10. The wine was bottled in (October 2002 / Oct. 2002 / October, 2002).
11. Most news organizations want a reporter with a (Bachelor's degree / Bachelor degree / bachelor degree / bachelor's degree) in journalism.
12. The (Police / police) clocked the (mayor / Mayor) going (thirty / 30) (m.p.h. / mph / miles per hour) over the speed limit.
13. The address is (twenty-one / 21) Merryweather (Road / Rd.)
14. The (atty. / attorney) and her (ass't. / assistant) went into the (government / govt.) (building / bldg.) to meet with their clients.
15. She will remember (September 11, 2001 / Sept. 11, 2001,) always.

16. Manuel (Middlebrooks, Jr. / Middlebrooks Jr.) works for the (Federal Bureau of Investigations / F.B.I / FBI).
17. (Pres. / President) Bush has a ranch in Crawford, (TX / Tex. / Texas).
18. The (capitol / Capitol / capital / Capital) of Idaho is (Lewiston / Boise).
19. The journalism class had (it's / its / they're / their) last meeting (Wed. / Wednesday).
20. (Her's / Hers) was the (number one / number 1 / No. 1 / Number One) book on the best sellers list.

Name ______________________ Class ______________________ Date ______

EXERCISE 5

AP STYLE AND COPY EDITING

Use the proper copy-editing symbols to correct the mechanical, spelling and stylistic errors in the following sentences. Refer to The Associated Press Stylebook in Appendix B, the common writing errors in Appendix E and the copy-editing symbols on the front and back covers of the textbook to help you.

Remember that none of the possessives have been formed for you. If you need help in forming the possessives, see the guidelines in Appendix C.

1. Next Summer, Maurice Reimer, an accountant with an office on Bender Ave., wants to buy a 4-door toyota avalon that costs about 29000 dollars.
2. Atty. Miguel Acevedo, who lives on Bell Ave. said his seven-yr.-old son received serious injuries when hit by the drunk driver in a ford van.
3. United States Senator Connie Mack, a republican from Florida, said the social security system is bankrupt and, in ten years, the Federal Government will slash its benefits.
4. Prof. Denise Bealle, a member of the History Dept., estimated that one third of her students will seek a Masters Degree within 5 years.
5. Fire totally destroyed the Dries Manufacturing Company at 3130 River Rd., and the damage is estimated at 4,000,000 to 5,000,000 dollars.
6. The boy, an 18 year old College Freshman, arrived in Green Bay Wisc. at 12 noon and will stay until February 14th.
7. 50 youths met in the YMCA at 3010 1st Avenue yesterday and agreed to return at 7:00PM October 4 to view the film titled Sports.
8. Irregardless of the investigations outcome, the thirty two White youths at Colonial high school want Mr. Tony Guarinno to continue as their Coach.

9. During the 1920s, the Federal Government allocated 820000 dollars for the project, and Mrs. Mildred Berg, who has a Ph.D. in Sociology, said 8% of the money was wasted.
10. On February 14 1996 the temperature fell to 0 in Athens Georgia and on February 15th it fell to -14.
11. Yesterday the United States President promised that the United States Congress would help the flood victims in Miss., Ala., Ga., and La.
12. He wants to duplicate copies of the e mail he received last Spring and to mail copies to 8 members of the Eastwind Homeowners Assn.
13. The jury reached their verdict at 12 midnight November 4th, finding Kevin Blohm, age 41, not guilty of the 3 charges.
14. Doctor Rachael Rosolowski, of Boston, said the X rays taken yesterday reveal that the Popes cancer is spreading.
15. Police said the ford mustang driven by Anne Capiello of 8210 University Boulevard was traveling sixty mph when it collided with a tree at the corner of Wilson and Hampshire Avenues.
16. The building on Grand Av. was totally demolished during the 1990s, and the state legislature yesterday voted 120-14 to spend 14,300,000 million dollars to rebuild it.
17. Four fifths of the hispanic medical students said they watched the television program entitled "ER" at 10:00PM last Thur. night.
18. 24 women, led by Prof. Maxine Cessarini, met at 9:00p.m. last night and concluded that their childrens 3rd grade teacher lacks a Bachelors Degree and lied at the P.T.A. meeting held last Aug. 29th.

19. Michael Beverly, age three, and his baby sitter, Trina Lasiter found 3000 dollars on Wilson Ave. yesterday, and his parents have hired Atty. Enrique Diaz to represent them.

20. The chemistry major ran South towards the Graumann Building and, afterwards, explained that she was late for a meeting with her adviser and, irregardless of the outcome, will transfer to another College.

Name ______________________ Class ______________________ Date ______

EXERCISE 6

AP STYLE AND COPY EDITING

Use the proper copy-editing symbols to correct the mechanical, spelling and stylistic errors in the following sentences. Refer to The Associated Press Stylebook in Appendix B, the common writing errors in Appendix E and the copy-editing symbols on the front and back covers of the textbook to help you.

Remember that none of the possessives have been formed for you. If you need help in forming the possessives, see the guidelines in Appendix C.

1. After earning her Masters Degree the Mayor of Boulder Colorado resigned and, on January 1st, established the Colorado Corporation at 8192 South Hawkins Dr.
2. On August 7th 2004 the First Lady, her aide, and 4 members of the United States Congress flew South to meet the governors of the ten States.
3. Ms. Delta Comanche, the Presidents Number 1 choice for the job of Secretary of State, estimated that 80% of the U.S. Senators favor the Summer program.
4. In January as the Priest celebrated a high mass at St. Margaret Mary Church on Park Ave., Ronal Sheppard, Junior, age 3, fell asleep.
5. The American Civil Liberties Union (A.C.L.U.) charged that during the Twentieth Century both the democratic and the republican parties repeatedly violated the United States Constitution.
6. The ford mustang driven by a white male in his 20s sped South on Pennsylvania Av., then turned left onto Franklin Dr. at speeds up to 80 m.p.h.
7. Chapter 20 in the book entitled Wasteful Solutions charges that in May, 2004 the congressional delegation wasted 2 to 2.3 million dollars sightseeing in Portland Oregon and Sacramento California.
8. James Eastland, III, a Lieutenant Colonel in the United States marines, received an M.A. in Business Administration and will speak at 2:00pm Sunday afternoon to the Small Business Owners Assn. at 626 North 3rd Street.

9. Reverend Audrey Van Pelt, of 420 North Wilkes Rd., arrived October 20th at 6:00 p.m. in a white Cadillac he bought last Summer.
10. The twelve youths from Syracuse New York said yesterday that their number one fear is the rising cost of College tuition.
11. The President of People's Gas Company said the new building at 1840 North Hampton Rd. will cost $12,400,000 dollars and be completed in 2 years.
12. Two teenagers saw the 8 year old boy in a car and said the driver was about 30, 6 ft. tall, and weighed 180 lbs.
13. The conference started at 12 noon yesterday and, ten minutes later, the groups President introduced the 3 Congressmen from N.Y.
14. Prof. Mayerline Valderama of Carbondale Illinois arrived for work on February 23 2004 when two college Freshmen, both majoring in Political science, stepped towards her and demanded her resignation.
15. The clubs Vice-President said his seven year old son found a wallet containing $1434, and that 7 persons have claimed it.
16. Afterwards, the Calif. Governor estimated that 1/4 the teenagers and 80% of their parents favor tougher standards, but implementing them would cost $1,000,000,000 a year.
17. The youth was born in Seminole county in January 1986 and is minoring in german. At 8:00pm Tuesday night, she attended a meeting of the German Friendship Assn. with 3 friends.
18. After leaving the white house, Pres. Ronald Reagan retired from the Federal Government and moved to southern California but continued to meet with republican leaders.

19. The F.B.I. found that, during the 1990s, congress spent $42,680,000 million remodeling the Senate Office Bldg., and that 3/4 of its employes thought $10 to $12 million was wasted.
20. Reaching for a tissue, Dist. Atty. Ramon Hernandez said as a child during the 1950s he paid $0.25 for a coke or for “Time Magazine” and watched as his citys Aldermen voted 7 to 5 to repeal a 12 midnight curfew on teenagers.

CHAPTER 2

GRAMMAR AND SPELLING

Never use a metaphor, simile or other figure of speech which you are not used to seeing in print; never use a long word where a short one will do; if it is possible to cut a word out, always cut it out; never use the passive voice when you can use the active; never use a foreign phrase, a scientific word or jargon if you can think of an everyday English equivalent; and break any of these rules sooner than say anything outright barbarous.

(George Orwell, author)

Good reporters have good news judgment and write well. Some students taking their first journalism class have wonderful news sense but do not know the basics of good grammar. They perform poorly in class because they cannot communicate news and ideas in ways others can easily understand.

To become effective writers, journalists must understand more than the basics of grammar and word usage. They have to become experts. Understanding the following areas of good grammar will help.

THE PARTS OF SPEECH

All words are classified as one of the parts of speech—nouns, verbs, prepositions, adjectives and so forth. Understanding grammar begins with an understanding of the parts of speech and how they are used.

Nouns

A noun is a name for any animate or inanimate thing: people, animals, places, qualities, acts or ideas.

Common nouns name any member of a class of things: "cow," "town," "soldier," "refrigerator," "computer," "honesty." Proper nouns are names for specific individuals, animals, places or brands: "Robert," "Bessie," "Gateway," "St. Louis." The first letter of a proper noun is always capitalized; the first letter of a common noun is capitalized only when it is the first word in a sentence.

Nouns are also concrete or abstract. Concrete nouns name tangible objects, such as "table," "book" or "tree." Abstract nouns name intangible things or ideas: "laziness," "creativity" or "beauty." Nouns may indicate various levels of abstraction, becoming more abstract as they become more general. "Animal" may refer to any of millions of kinds of organisms from bacteria to humans. "Mammal" is more specific, referring to thousands of species that share certain physiological characteristics. "Dog" is still more specific, identifying a particular species of mammal. And "Fido," a name for a specific dog, represents the most concrete level.

Newswriters try to use the most concrete and most specific nouns possible. Stories filled with such words are more easily understood and more interesting than stories filled with abstract nouns.

Verbs

Verbs are the most important part of speech. While nouns are static, verbs describe action; they tell what things and people do. Examples are "run," "steal," "hesitate" and "reflect." Not only do verbs show action, but they also change form to tell the reader who is doing the acting and when it was done. "Ran" is the past-tense form of "run," so the reader knows the action being described has been completed. All verb tenses use one of four principal forms: the present, the present participle, the past and the past participle. These are called the principal parts of a verb. Most verbs add "ed" to form the past and past participle and "ing" to form the present participle. These are regular verbs. Some verbs are irregular, and dictionary entries usually list the principal parts for irregular verbs. Here are the principal parts of a few common verbs:

	Present	**Present Participle**	**Past**	**Past Participle**
Sail	sail	sailing	sailed	sailed
Talk	talk	talking	talked	talked
Write	write	writing	wrote	written
Run	run	running	ran	ran

English has dozens of possible tenses, but six are used most often: simple present, simple past, simple future, present perfect, past perfect, and future perfect. Here's an example of what a verb looks like in all six tenses:

Simple present: I vote.	*Present perfect:* I have voted.
Simple past: I voted.	*Past perfect:* I had voted.
Simple future: I will vote.	*Future perfect:* I will have voted.

Verbs also give readers hints as to who is doing the action. For most verbs, the third person singular in the present tense has a distinct form, usually created by adding "s" to the end of the verb. "Runs," for example, tells the reader that the running is going on in the present, and that only one person is doing the running.

Because verbs pack so much information, good writers give extra attention to the selection of verbs. The best verbs convey strong actions that readers can easily visualize. Sentences with strong verbs and concrete nouns need little help from adjectives and adverbs.

Adjectives

Adjectives describe or limit nouns and pronouns. In many instances, the adjectives precede the nouns they modify: "the thick book," "the yellow flower," "the sleepy town." Other times, the adjective follows some form of the verb "to be": The town is sleepy.

Adjectives may have "more," "most," "less" or "least" before them or have "er" or "est" attached at the end to indicate degrees of comparison. English has three degrees of comparison: positive, comparative and superlative. The positive degree is the basic form of the adjective and merely states that a particular thing possesses a quality. The comparative degree is used when comparing two things in the degree to which they possess a quality. The superlative degree is used when three or more things are being compared. Here are some examples:

Positive Degree	**Comparative Degree**	**Superlative Degree**
the thick book	the thicker book	the thickest book
the beautiful flower	the more beautiful flower	the most beautiful flower
the popular candidate	the less popular candidate	the least popular candidate

Some adjectives take irregular forms when they are in the comparative or superlative degree. These are a few examples:

Positive Degree	**Comparative Degree**	**Superlative Degree**
good	better	best
bad	worse	worst
little	less	least

Almost any word can be used as an adjective to modify nouns or two or more words can be combined to create adjectival phrases, as in these examples:

Nouns modifying nouns: car insurance, school assignments, government official.

Present participles modifying nouns: soaring airplane, ironing board, winding road.

Past participles modifying nouns: hardened criminal, trusted friend, weakened opponent.

Adjectival phrases: wine-red sea, sky-blue shirt, full-time employee, man-eating shark.

Note that the words combined to form adjectival phrases are often hyphenated.

Articles

The indefinite articles are "a" and "an." The definite article is "the." The use of an indefinite article implies the writer is referring to any member of a class of people or things. The definite article implies the writer is referring to a specific member of a class.

Jane checked out a book from the library. (The book could be any in the library.)

Jane checked out the book from the library. (She checked out a book that had already been specified.)

"A" is used before nouns that begin with consonant sounds; "an" is used before nouns that begin with vowel sounds. In most cases, the choice is obvious, but some words that start with consonants sound as if they start with vowels. In "honor," for example, the "h" is silent, so it requires "an" instead of "a."

He received an honorary degree.

In other cases, words that start with vowels sound as if they start with consonants. "Europe" sounds as if it starts with a "y"; therefore, it use the indefinite article "a."

They plan a European vacation.

Reporters who misuse the definite article confuse readers by implying that an object being referred to is the only such object in existence. If a story reports three people were taken to "the hospital," yet the story's earlier paragraphs never mentioned any hospital, the use of "the" implies the area has only one hospital. Similarly, a story reporting someone ate lunch at "the McDonald's in New York," implies, wrongly, that there is only one McDonald's in the entire city.

Adverbs

Adverbs modify verbs, adjectives and other adverbs. Like adjectives, adverbs limit or qualify the words they modify. They may show manner, degree, direction, cause, affirmation, negation, frequency, time or place. Many, but not all, adverbs end in "ly."

The following sentences illustrate some of the uses of adverbs. The adverbs are italicized:

Rose *quickly* paid her bills.
U.S. forces are *fully* committed to the mission.
He recited the alphabet *backward.*
Gordon travels *weekly* to Los Angeles.
The couple walked *arm in arm* down the aisle.

Like adjectives, adverbs may show degrees of comparison. Most adverbs form the comparative and superlative degrees by combining with "more," "most," "less" or "least." Here are some examples:

Positive degree: The Salt Valley bus runs frequently.
Comparative degree: The Arapahoe bus runs more frequently than the Salt Valley bus.
Superlative degree: The 27th Street bus runs most frequently of all city buses.

Pronouns

Pronouns can take the place of proper or common nouns, allowing the writer to avoid needless and confusing repetition of a noun. The noun the pronoun replaces is called its antecedent. "Antecedent" means that which goes before, and usually the pronoun follows its antecedent, although that is not always true.

Bill overcame his fear and took the test.

In spite of his fear, Bill took the test.

In both of the sentences above, "Bill" is the antecedent for the pronoun "his," but in the second sentence, the pronoun precedes the antecedent. Whether the pronoun follows or precedes its antecedent, the writer must be sure the meaning is clear.

Some pronouns may have indefinite antecedents, or the antecedent may be so obvious it is unstated. The pronouns "I" and "you" obviously refer to the speaker and the listener; usually they have no antecedents. But in the sentence "It often rains in Seattle," "it" has no clear antecedent.

Grammarians recognize several kinds of pronouns: adjective, demonstrative, indefinite, interrogative, personal and relative.

Adjective

An adjective pronoun is one that modifies another noun or pronoun. Some common adjective pronouns are "all," "any," "each," "few," "little," "many," "much" and the possessive forms of personal pronouns. In some cases, the adjective pronoun may replace the noun it modifies.

Few soldiers survived the battle.

Few survived the battle.

In the second sentence, "soldiers" may be understood from the context in which the sentence appears.

Demonstrative

Demonstrative pronouns designate or point out the things referred to. English has two demonstrative pronouns and their plural forms.

Singular	**Plural**
this	these
that	those

"This" and "these" refer to things that are close in time and space; "that" and "those" refer to things that are more remote.

The fruit from this tree is sweeter than the fruit from that one.

These students have better test scores than those students.

Demonstrative pronouns may have specific nouns as their antecedents, or they may have entire phrases or clauses as antecedents. In the following sentence, the antecedent for "that" is the entire opening clause.

The bill may be amended before it is enacted, but that will be up to the committee.

Indefinite

Indefinite pronouns refer to objects or people generally or indeterminately. The pronoun may refer to any of a class of people. In the following sentence "each" is an indefinite pronoun:

Each of the workers received a pay voucher.

Some of the common indefinite pronouns are "all," "another," "any," "anybody," "anyone," "both," "each," "either," "every," "everybody," "everyone," "few," "many," "much," "neither," "nobody," "none," "one," "other," "several," "some," "somebody," "someone" and "such."

Some indefinite pronouns may be used as nouns, as adjectives or even as adverbs or conjunctions.

Interrogative

Pronouns used to ask questions—"who," "which" and "what"—are called interrogatives. "Who" and "which" are also used as relative pronouns. "Who" should be used to refer to people. "Which" and "what" may be used for inanimate things, abstractions and lower animals. The antecedents for interrogative pronouns often are in the answers to the questions:

Question: Who has the key?
Answer: Jane does.

"Jane" is the antecedent for "who" in the above example. But if the respondent doesn't know the answer, the interrogative pronoun effectively has no antecedent.

Question: Who has the key?
Answer: I don't know.

Personal

Personal pronouns are the most easily recognized pronouns. They take the place of names of people, although the third person neuter "it" can replace a noun for any living or inanimate object or abstraction.

The personal pronouns are the most fully inflected words in English. That means the pronouns change their form to show whether they are the subject of the sentence, a direct or an indirect object or a possessive. The forms used for subjects are called the nominative case. The forms used for objects are called the objective case, and those used for possessives are called the possessive case.

Person	Nominative Case	Objective Case	Possessive Case
1st person singular	I	me	my or mine
2nd person singular	you	you	your or yours
3rd person masculine	he	him	his
3rd person feminine	she	her	her or hers
3rd person neuter	it	it	its
1st person plural	we	us	our or ours
2nd person plural	you	you	your or yours
3rd person plural	they	them	their or theirs

Personal pronouns must agree with their antecedents in number and gender. A singular masculine antecedent requires a singular masculine pronoun; a plural antecedent requires a plural pronoun. But the case of the pronoun depends on its function in the clause in which it stands. In the examples below, the pronouns are italicized.

> The president says Congress will send *him* the legislation.
>
> Coach Jane Harris told *her* players *they* would make the playoffs this year.
>
> *I* told Sara this side of the fence is *my* property and that side is *hers*.

In the first example, "president" is the antecedent of "him," which is in the objective case because it functions as an indirect object in the clause in which it appears. In the second example, "Coach Jane Harris" is the antecedent for "her," which is a possessive used to describe "players." "Players" is the antecedent for "they," which functions as the subject of a clause. In the final example, "I" is the subject of the sentence and its antecedent is understood to be the speaker. The possessive "my" has "I" as its antecedent and modifies "property." "Hers" has "Sara" as its antecedent and is an independent possessive—that is, it stands alone because the word it modifies ("property") is understood from the context.

Reflexive forms of personal pronouns add "self" or "selves" at the end. Reflexive pronouns are used when the action of the verb affects the actor, as in the first sentence below, and to intensify or emphasize who is doing the acting, as in the second sentence.

> William cut *himself* while slicing the carrots.
>
> The plumber fixed the drain, but I replaced the faucet *myself*.

Relative

Relative pronouns serve a double function: They refer to a noun or another pronoun, and they connect or relate two parts of the sentence. The most common relative pronouns are "who" (and "whom"), "which," "what" and "that." The following sentence illustrates the dual role relative pronouns play.

> The governor has a plan *that* will hold down taxes.

The relative pronoun "that" stands in for the noun "plan." It also relates the first and second clauses of the sentence. The same idea could have been expressed as two separate sentences:

> The governor has a plan. The plan will hold down taxes.

Using the relative pronoun allows the writer to combine the two clauses and avoid the awkward repetition of "plan."

Prepositions

A preposition shows a relationship between a word that comes before it, called an antecedent, and a word that follows, called an object or a subsequent. The antecedent of a preposition can be any part of speech or a phrase; the object is usually a noun or pronoun. The following sentence contains two prepositional phrases. In the first, "order" is the antecedent of the preposition "from," and "headquarters" is the object. In the second, "will apply" is the antecedent of the preposition "to," and "everyone" is the object.

The new order from headquarters will apply to everyone.

Here are some of the more common prepositions:

at	from	spite
about	in	through
above	inside	throughout
after	into	till
along	of	under
below	on	until
beside	onto	up
between	opposite	upon
beyond	outside	with
by	over	within
down	since	without
for		

English also has some phrases that function as prepositions. Some of the common ones are "because of," "in spite of," "on account of," "out of," "owing to," "with respect to," "in addition to" and "together with."

The phrase a preposition introduces has the effect of describing or limiting the antecedent, as in these examples: a book about genetics, a brownie with ice cream, the beach beside the lake, the rocks on the mountainside.

The uses of prepositions are the most idiomatic in English. Writers cannot simply rely on dictionary definitions to know which preposition best fits a sentence. Instead, they must become familiar with the language through reading and listening. Nevertheless, the use of the wrong preposition can convey a false or misleading meaning. The following sentences are the same except for the preposition, but their meanings are very different:

I bought a book by Professor Smith.

I bought a book from Professor Smith.

The first sentence tells the reader who wrote the book but nothing about where the speaker bought it. The second tells the reader where the speaker bought the book, but not who wrote it.

Sometimes prepositions combine with verbs to create idiomatic phrases. The addition of the preposition can dramatically change the meaning of the verb. "To break" means something different from "to break into" or "to break down." The last of these three illustrates the idiomatic nature of prepositions. A person whose car has stopped running might say, "My car broke down." Logic does not compel this use of "down"; it's just the way people speak.

Conjunctions

Conjunctions are words or phrases that connect other words, phrases, clauses or sentences. Conjunctions are generally classified as coordinating and subordinating. Coordinating conjunctions connect elements of equal grammatical standing—words to words, phrases to phrases, clauses to clauses, sentences to sentences. Subordinating conjunctions connect dependent units to ones that are grammatically independent.

The most common coordinating conjunctions are "and," "or," "but," "nor," for," "yet" and "so." Each conjunction may show a slightly different relation: addition, contrast, separation, consequence. Writers can make transitions smooth and clear by selecting the conjunction that most accurately reflects their meaning.

Subordinating conjunctions are more numerous than coordinating conjunctions, but they, too, may show a variety of relationships: cause, comparison, concession, condition, manner, place, purpose or time. Here are some of the more common subordinating conjunctions:

After, although, because, before, hence, if, inasmuch, otherwise, provided, since, though, unless, until, when, whenever, while, whereas, wherefore.

Independent clauses joined by a coordinating conjunction should use a comma before the conjunction.

The message arrived, but she ignored it.

The afternoon was hot, so I went for a swim.

If the independent clauses have no coordinating conjunction linking them, use a semicolon.

The company issued its report Wednesday; the price of its stock fell 40 percent the next day.

Use a semicolon, too, if the independent clauses are linked by a conjunctive adverb. Some of the conjunctive adverbs are "however," "moreover," "nevertheless" and "therefore."

The governor agreed to the tax increase; however, she vetoed the plan for a new prison.

We were out of town last week; therefore, we missed the show.

Some conjunctions come in pairs. These are called correlative conjunctions. The main ones are:

both–and: Both the president and the vice president will attend the dinner.
either–or: Either the president or the vice president will attend the dinner.
neither–nor: Neither the president nor the vice president will attend the dinner.
whether–or: Whether the president or the vice president will attend the dinner is unclear.
not only–but also: Not only the president but also the Cabinet members will attend the dinner.
as–as: Workers hope their pay increase will be as large this year as it was last year.
if–then: If the company refuses to increase pay, then the workers will strike.
so–that: The workers were so angry at management that they rejected the contract.

Interjection

Interjections are words or short phrases that express strong, sudden emotions. Interjections bear no grammatical relation to the rest of the sentence and are considered independent or absolute constructions. Some common interjections are "aw," "bravo," "goodbye," "hey," "hush," "nonsense," "oh," "oh, dear," "ouch," "well," "whew" and "yea."

Interjections usually are punctuated with exclamation points, which may come either after the interjection itself or at the end of the sentence containing the interjection.

Nonsense! I never said such a thing.

Nonsense, I never said such a thing!

The placement of the exclamation point depends on whether the strong emotion attaches to the interjection alone or to the entire sentence.

BASIC SENTENCE STRUCTURE

Simple sentences usually include a subject, a verb and a direct object. The subject is the person or thing doing the action. The verb describes the action. And the direct object is the person or thing acted upon. Consider this sentence:

The batter hit the ball.

"Batter" is the actor (the subject of the sentence). "Hit" is the action (the verb), and "ball" is the thing acted upon (the object).

Sometimes sentences include indirect objects, which tell to whom or for whom an action was done. The test for an indirect object is to place "to" or "for" before the word. The following sentences have both direct and indirect objects.

Juan sent Maria a Valentine card.

Samantha bought her mother a new CD player.

Subject	**Verb**	**Indirect Object**	**Direct Object**
Juan	sent	Maria	a Valentine card
Samantha	bought	her mother	a new CD player

When a noun alone is used as an indirect object, it usually comes between the verb and the direct object, as in the examples above. But when the indirect object takes the form of a prepositional phrase, it usually follows the direct object.

Juan sent a Valentine card to Maria.

Samatha bought a new CD player for her mother.

Verbs that have direct objects are called transitive verbs, because they indicate that the action is transferred to a direct object. Some verbs are intransitive—their action is not transferred to another object. And many verbs can be used in both transitive and intransitive ways. The verb "lie" is intransitive. In the sentence "I will lie down," the action is done by the actor but is not transferred to anything else. In the sentence "She flies the flag," "flies" is used in a transitive sense; the action is transferred to the flag, which is the direct object. But in "The flag flies from the pole," "flies" is used in an intransitive way; the verb merely describes the flag's action.

A complete sentence needs at least a subject and a verb. And the subject may be implied or understood, as in a command such as "Go!" Sentences may need direct or indirect objects, depending on whether the verb is transitive.

Writers can embellish the simple sentence in a number of ways. One way is to combine two independent clauses—clauses that could stand alone as sentences—to make a compound sentence.

Ice skating is her favorite sport, but she enjoys roller skating, too.

She is an engineer, and he is a teacher.

Another way is to combine an independent clause with a dependent one to make a complex sentence. Dependent clauses are introduced by subordinating conjunctions, which make the clauses incapable of standing alone.

Subordinating conjunctions are words and phrases like "because," "as a result of," "after," "before," "whenever" and "as long as."

I eat dinner after my last class is over.

I visit my aunt whenever I go home for the holidays.

Writers also may use one or more dependent clauses together with two or more independent clauses to create compound-complex sentences.

I visit my aunt whenever I go home for the holidays, but I call her almost every week.

Sentences may also contain phrases, which are related groups of words that lack both a subject and a verb. Prepositional phrases and verbal phrases are common types. They may be incorporated in the body of the sentence, or they may introduce the main clause. The first of the following sentences ends with a prepositional phrase, and the second begins with a verbal phrase:

People spend more time outdoors in the springtime.

Tired from her bicycle ride, Suzanna took a nap.

Sentence parts can be combined and arranged in many ways. Varying sentence structure can keep one's writing from becoming too predictable and simplistic, but simple sentences that stick to subject-verb-object order are the clearest and most easily understood.

ACTIVE AND PASSIVE VOICE

Sentences that use the subject-verb-object order are active-voice sentences. A passive-voice sentence turns that order around. The direct object of the active-voice sentence becomes the subject of the passive-voice sentence; the subject becomes part of a prepositional phrase; and the verb is replaced with its past participle and some form of the verb "to be."

Notice that in the following examples, the passive-voice sentence is two words longer than the active-voice sentence, but it says the same thing. Those extra words are unnecessary stumbling blocks for readers.

ACTIVE VOICE: The batter hit the ball.
PASSIVE VOICE: The ball was hit by the batter.

Notice, too, that the actor or subject can disappear from a passive-voice sentence:

ACTIVE VOICE: The mayor gave Alex an award.
ACTIVE VOICE: The mayor gave an award to Alex.

PASSIVE VOICE: An award was given to Alex.

Some writers make the mistake of using the indirect object as the subject of the passive-voice sentence. This mistake is most common with verbs like "give" or "present." In the example above, for instance, some writers might try to make "Alex" the subject of the passive-voice sentence. Some grammarians call this a false passive and consider it an error.

FALSE PASSIVE: Alex was given an award.
TRUE PASSIVE: An award was given to Alex.

The false passive is an error because it suggests that "Alex" is what was given. But the award is what was given, and Alex was the recipient of the award.

Writers should avoid the passive voice not only because it is wordier than the active voice but also because it often camouflages responsibility. If a disaster strikes or a defective product harms someone, then government or business officials may admit "mistakes were made," but that passive construction reveals nothing about who made the mistakes or why. The passive voice is the ally of all who seek to evade responsibility; it is the enemy of all who seek clarity.

AGREEMENT

Nouns, pronouns and verbs are either singular or plural. Nouns and pronouns also indicate gender: masculine, feminine or neuter. A basic principle of grammar is that nouns and verbs should agree with each other, and so should nouns and pronouns. Singular subjects should have singular verbs; plural nouns should have plural pronouns. The principle is simple, but the opportunities for error are numerous.

Subjects and Verbs

If the subject of a sentence is singular, use a singular verb, and if the subject is plural, use a plural verb. Getting subjects and verbs to agree is easy when sentences are simple. But when prepositional phrases separate subjects and verbs or when the subject is a collective noun, agreement becomes trickier. In the first example below, the singular noun "team" is the subject, and the prepositional phrase "of researchers" describes the subject. The verb must agree with the singular "team," not the plural "researchers." In the example below, the subject is in italics and the verb is underlined:

A *team* of researchers <u>have gathered</u> the information.
REVISED: A *team* of researchers <u>has gathered</u> the information.

Three *teams* from the university <u>is gathering</u> the information.
REVISED: Three *teams* from the university <u>are gathering</u> the information.

Some nouns may appear to be plural because they end in "s," but they are considered singular in some senses. Some examples are "economics," "politics" and "physics."

Economics are a required course.
REVISED: Economics is a required course.

Nouns that refer to a group or a collection of individuals as one whole are called collective nouns. Words like "committee," "club," "jury," "regiment" and "team" are examples. Proper nouns that identify organizations also are collective nouns: "Congress" and "Microsoft," for instance. Usually collective nouns are considered singular and require singular verbs and pronouns:

The jury announce their verdict.

REVISED: The jury announces its verdict.

The American Society of Newspaper Editors have begun a program to help journalists with their writing.

REVISED: The American Society of Newspaper Editors has begun a program to help journalists with their writing.

Nouns and Pronouns

Not only must pronouns agree with verbs, but they must also have the same number and gender as their antecedents. A singular feminine noun requires a singular feminine pronoun, and a plural neuter noun requires a plural neuter pronoun. In the following examples, the pronouns are underlined and their antecedents are in italics.

Rachael took <u>her</u> work with <u>her</u> when <u>she</u> visited New York.

The carpenter replaced the *nails* in <u>their</u> container.

Collective nouns like "team," "jury," "group," "committee," "family" and "faculty" cause the most problems with noun-pronoun agreement. Not being sure whether a collective noun is singular or plural, beginning writers try to have it both ways. They use singular verbs with collective nouns, but then use plural pronouns to take their place:

General Motors is expanding <u>their</u> product line.
REVISED: *General Motors* is expanding <u>its</u> product line.

The *team* won <u>their</u> third victory in a row.
REVISED: The *team* won <u>its</u> third victory in a row.

However, if a collective noun is used in a plural sense, then a plural pronoun is needed:

The *committees* reviewed its goal of curbing children's access to Internet pornography.

REVISED: The *committees* reviewed their goal of curbing children's access to Internet pornography.

AMBIGUOUS PRONOUNS

Pronouns can lead to ambiguity. In the following example, readers do not know whose mother is being asked for permission:

Walter and Taylor went to his mother for permission to stay out late.

Too many pronouns within one sentence or paragraph can perplex readers:

The committee took its recommendation to the board. It discussed it before returning it to it for further consideration.

Limit the use of pronouns, and make sure each one has a clear antecedent. Revised, the sentence above might read, "The committee took its recommendation to the board, which revised and returned it to the committee for further consideration."

Reporters use words such as "this" or "those" with caution because their meanings often are unclear. Reporters are particularly careful to avoid starting a sentence or paragraph with "it," "this," "these," "those" or "that." When one of these words starts a sentence, readers may have trouble determining its antecedent. Reporters can avoid confusion by repeating a key word or rewriting a foggy sentence:

Commissioner Terry Benham, who represents Scott County on the Transit Authority, said the bus system has stopped losing money. He attributed this to the elimination of consistently unprofitable routes.

REVISED: Commissioner Terry Benham, who represents Scott County on the Transit Authority, said the bus system has stopped losing money because consistently unprofitable routes have been eliminated.

PLURALS AND POSSESSIVES

Nouns can be singular ("cat") or plural ("cats"). Generally, one makes a noun plural by adding an "s" at the end. For example, the plural of "student" is "students."

The plural of nouns ending in "s," "z," "x," "sh" and "ch" is often formed by adding an "es." For instance, "church" becomes "churches," "dish" becomes "dishes," "business" becomes "businesses," and "cake mix" becomes "cake mixes."

Other plural endings are irregular. A method left over from old English is to add "en," as in "child" to "children" and "woman" to "women." Some nouns ending in "f," such as "wolf," change to "ves" to become "wolves."

Possessives sometimes show ownership of one noun by another (Susan's glove). But they may indicate other kinds of relationships. Possessives may classify or describe nouns (states' rights) or describe purpose (a children's book). Possessives and plurals are easily confused because an "s" often is used to form both.

Singular and plural nouns not ending in "s" require adding an apostrophe and "s" ('s) to become a possessive:

Noun not ending in "s"	possessive	sentence
singular: dog	dog's	The dog's water dish was empty.
singular: Jean	Jean's	Jean's bracelet was missing.
plural: children	children's	The children's party was successful.
plural: geese	geese's	The geese's formation was in a "V."

Plural nouns ending in "s" need just an apostrophe (') to form a possessive:

Plural noun ending in "s"	possessive	sentence
monkeys	monkeys'	The monkeys' antics were hilarious.
churches	churches'	The churches' pastors meet weekly.

Singular common nouns that end in "s" need an apostrophe and an "s" ('s) to form the possessive. If the word immediately following the possessive starts with an "s," add only the apostrophe.

Singular common noun ending in "s"	possessive	sentence
witness	witness's	The witness's testimony failed to sway the jury.
hostess	hostess'	The hostess' seat was at the head of the table.

Singular proper names that end in "s" use only the apostrophe to form the possessive.

Singular proper name ending in "s"	possessive	sentence
Arkansas	Arkansas'	Arkansas' budget was approved.
Dickens	Dickens'	Dickens' novels are still in print.

Pronouns have distinct possessive forms and do not need an apostrophe or an "s" to show possession:

pronoun	possessive
her	her
him	his
they	their
it	its

Many students confuse "its" with "it's." The first is the possessive pronoun, which does not need an apostrophe. The second is the contraction for "it is," and the apostrophe substitutes for the "i" in "is." Similarly, the possessive pronouns "his" and "hers" do not need apostrophes. Students also confuse the plural possessive pronoun "their" with "there," which refers to a place, or "they're," which is the contraction for "they are."

More guidelines for forming possessives are in Appendix C.

"THAT" AND "WHICH"

"That" and "which" are little words, but they can make a big difference in the meaning of a sentence. The sentences below illustrate how changing "that" to "which" changes the meaning of the sentence:

> She told Shannon to take the lawn mower that is in the barn to Jaysen.
>
> She told Shannon to take the lawn mower, which is in the barn, to Jaysen.

In the first sentence, the use of "that" implies many lawn mowers exist on the property—in the yard, the garage and the barn—but Shannon should take the lawn mower from the barn. In the second sentence, the clause introduced by "which" is not essential. There is only one lawn mower on the property, so it is the only one Shannon can take to Jaysen. It is helpful to know where the lawn mower is, but the information in the clause is not necessary to understand the meaning of the sentence.

Here's a rule that can help decide between "that" and "which": If the sentence is read without the subordinate clause and the meaning does not change, then "which" should introduce the clause. Otherwise, use "that."

"WHO" AND "WHOM"

"That," "which," "who" and "whom" are relative pronouns. "That" and "which" introduce clauses referring to ideas, inanimate objects or animals without names. "Who" and "whom" begin clauses that refer to people and animals with names.

> It was Morgan that came by the house yesterday.
> REVISED: It was Morgan who came by the house yesterday.

> It was a stray cat who ate the bird.
> REVISED: It was a stray cat that ate the bird.

The distinction between "who" and "whom" causes problems for some writers. "Who" is the subject of a clause; "whom" is the object of a verb or a preposition. Whether a word is a subject or an object may not always be clear in relative clauses or questions, either of which may depart from normal word order.

Either "who" or "whom" may appear as the first word in a question, but which a writer uses depends on its grammatical relationship to the rest of the sentence. These two sentences illustrate the difference:

> Who gave you the scarf?

> Whom do you prefer as student body president?

In the first example, "who" is the subject of the clause, the initiator of the action "gave." In the second sentence, "whom" is the direct object of the verb "prefer." Here are two more examples:

> Who did you speak to?
> REVISED: To whom did you speak?

> The report names the man who the police suspect of the crime.
> REVISED: The report names the man whom the police suspect of the crime.

In the first example, the relative pronoun is the object of the preposition "to." In the second, it is the direct object; it refers to the person the police suspect. Both should be "whom."

One way to avoid or reduce confusion over "who" and "whom" is to replace them with a personal pronoun. Isolate the who or whom phrase. If "he" or "she" sounds right, then use "who." If "him" or "her" would be more natural, use "whom." Do that in the following sentence and it is easy to see that "whom" is wrong:

> The candidates argued about whom was responsible for the tax increase.

At first the relative pronoun "whom" appears to be the object of the preposition "about," but when it is replaced with a personal pronoun, it doesn't sound right. That's because the relative pronoun is the subject of the clause "was responsible for the tax increase." No one would say "her was responsible. . . ." But "she was responsible . . ." makes sense. The relative pronoun to use here is "who."

MISPLACED MODIFIERS

Modifiers are words or phrases that limit, restrict or qualify some other word or phrase. Modifiers should appear as close as possible to the word or phrase they modify. Misplaced modifiers can make sentences ambiguous, confusing or nonsensical:

> She retold the ordeal of being held hostage with tears running down her cheeks.
> REVISED: She retold, with tears running down her cheeks, the ordeal of being held hostage.
> OR: With tears running down her cheeks, she retold the ordeal of being held hostage.

The gunmen tied the victim and left him with his hands and feet taped and lying on the back seat.

REVISED: The gunmen tied the victim, taped his hands and feet and left him lying on the back seat.

He is making a list of the empty lots in the neighborhood so he can track down their owners and ask if he can plant them next summer.

REVISED: He wants to plant the empty lots in the neighborhood next summer and is making a list of them so he can find their owners.

In the first example, the phrase "with tears running down her cheeks" follows "hostage," and readers might think the phrase modifies "hostage"—that she was crying while she was a hostage. But the phrase really tells how the woman behaved as she talked about her ordeal. The word being modified is "retold." In the second example, the revision says the victim is left lying on the back seat, not just his hands and feet. The changes to the last example make it clear that it is the empty lots that will be planted, not their owners.

Sometimes the meaning of a sentence can change dramatically simply by moving a modifying word or phrase. Look at how the following sentences change in meaning by moving the word "only":

Only Jenkins' farm produces the best apples in the county.
Jenkins' only farm produces the best apples in the county.
Jenkins' farm only produces the best apples in the county.
Jenkins' farm produces only the best apples in the county.
Jenkins' farm produces the best apples only in the county.

Careful writers choose the word order that accurately conveys their meaning.

DANGLING MODIFIERS

Modifiers dangle when the word or phrase they are supposed to modify does not appear in the sentence. That may happen when a thoughtless or hurried writer starts a sentence intending to say an idea one way and then switches in midsentence to express it in another way:

Pleased with everyone's papers, the class received congratulations.

REVISED: Pleased with everyone's papers, the teacher congratulated the class.

Angered by the unannounced closure of the plant, security guards hurriedly cleared the area.

REVISED: Security guards hurriedly cleared the area of employees who were angered by the unannounced closure of the plant.

Readers understand introductory words and phrases to modify the subject of the sentence. If that is not the case, the modifiers are either misplaced or dangling.

PERSONIFICATION

Avoid treating inanimate objects or abstractions as if they were human. Objects such as buildings, cars, stores and trees cannot hear, think, feel or talk. Yet some writers treat them as people. The writers see—and repeat—the error so often they fail to recognize it and continue to personify such things as corporations, countries and machines.

Memorial Hospital treated her for shock and a broken arm.

She was driving west on Hullett Avenue when two cars in front of her slammed on their brakes.

Can a hospital treat patients, or is that the job of a hospital's staff? Can a car slam on its own brakes? Of course not! Such personifications are easy to correct:

> The store said it will not reopen.
> REVISED: The owner of the store said she will not reopen it.

> The intention of the road was to help farmers transport their crops to market.
> REVISED: Highway planners intended the road to help farmers transport their crops to market.

Personification also contributes to two other problems. First, audiences cannot determine a story's credibility if reporters fail to identify their sources. Readers can assess the credibility of a statement attributed to a mayor or governor, but not the credibility of a statement attributed to a city or state.

Second, personification allows people to escape responsibility for their actions. Officials cannot be held responsible for their actions if reporters attribute those actions to a business or government.

PARALLEL FORM

When writers link similar ideas, they do so with parallel structures. Grammatically parallel structures create harmony and balance in writing, and they help readers compare and contrast the ideas that are linked within the sentence.

The principle of parallelism requires that every item in a series takes the same grammatical form: all nouns, all verbs or all prepositional phrases. If the first verb in a series uses the past tense, every verb in the series must use the past tense. Or, if the first verb ends in "ing," all must end in "ing." If reporters fail to express like ideas in the same grammatical form, their sentences become convoluted and confusing:

> She enjoys writing, researching and reading her published work is great fun, too.
> PARALLEL FORM: She enjoys writing, researching and reading her published work.

> Police said the plastic handcuffs are less bulky, not as expensive and no key is needed to remove them from a suspect's wrists than metal handcuffs.
> PARALLEL FORM: Police said plastic handcuffs are less bulky, less expensive and less difficult to remove from a suspect's wrists than metal handcuffs.

> The Greenes have three children: 4-year-old Gordon, Andrea, who is 3, and little Fielding is not quite 25 months.
> PARALLEL FORM: The Greenes have three children: Gordon, 4; Andrea, 3; and Fielding, 2.

"BECAUSE" AND "DUE TO"

Students often misuse of "because" and "due to" when presenting a reason or a cause. "Because" modifies a verb. For instance, the sentence "She slipped because of the ice on the walkway" tells that a person slipped and explains why she slipped. "Due to" modifies a noun. And, it usually follows some form of the verb "to be." For instance, the sentence "The weird painting is due to his wife's eccentric taste in art" explains the painting.

SPELLING

Readers complain about inaccuracies in news stories, and what they are often referring to are spelling errors. Misspellings reflect laziness on the part of the writer, and they sometimes cause readers to doubt the facts in the story.

Correct spelling is as important for writers in broadcast journalism as it is for those in print journalism. News announcers often lack time to review the reporter's copy for misspelled words, and misspellings may cause them to make mistakes on air.

Common phrases such as "a lot" and "all right" are frequently misspelled. Five other words that students often misspell are: "medium," "datum," "graffito," "criterion" and "phenomenon." All five are singular forms. Students often incorrectly use the plural forms instead: "media," "data," "graffiti," "criteria" and "phenomena." Thus it would be correct to say, "The four criteria are adequate" or "The datum is lost," but not, "The media is inaccurate" or "The phenomenon are unusual." Commonly misspelled words make up some exercises at the end of this chapter.

Reporters are usually formal in their spelling. For example, they normally use "until" rather than "till" and "although" rather than "though." They also avoid slang.

A final point about spelling: Spell-check programs for computers help many writers. However, a computer program can look only at the spelling of a word and not how it is used. If a student were to write, "There cat's name is Savannah," the spell-checker would note that every word in the sentence is spelled correctly. However, "their" should replace "there." No one should depend solely on a spell-check program.

Confusing words, such as "accept/except" and "capital/capitol," are words that may look or sound alike but have different meanings. Test your vocabulary skills on confusing words with the exercises in Chapter 4.

GRAMMAR CHECKLIST

1. Use subject-verb-object order for sentences.
2. Use active-voice verbs, not passive ones.
3. Use singular verbs with singular subjects, and plural verbs with plural subjects.
4. Make sure that pronouns agree with their antecedents.
5. Spell plurals and possessives correctly.
6. Use "that," "which," "who" and "whom" correctly.
7. Place modifiers immediately before or after the noun they describe.
8. Avoid personification; do not suggest inanimate objects can talk, think or feel.
9. List items in a series in parallel form.
10. Use the articles, "a," "an" and "the" correctly.
11. Reread copy several times for spelling and other writing errors.
12. Do not depend on spell-check programs to find all misspelled words.

THE WRITING COACH

ACRONYMS LIFT YOUR WRITING

By **Joe Hight**
Managing Editor of The Oklahoman

Acronyms usually don't help your stories. Besides the obvious ones such as FBI or CIA, they're confusing to readers and can create a measles effect in your writing.

But one acronym will strengthen your writing every time. It's V.E.R.B.S.

And if you use V.E.R.B.S. you will become a better writer.

Here's the meaning of V.E.R.B.S.:

(*continued*)

V = VIGOR.

A major component of vigorous writing is verbs—stronger ones.

Strengthen your verbs by using ones that are specific, descriptive, show mood and are active: plunge, dive, decide, kick. Avoid the passive voice. Example: *Strong verbs are used by strong writers* is passive. The active sentence *Strong writers use strong verbs* cuts unnecessary words and is much stronger.

Likewise, trim weak linking verbs such as *is* (*there is,* for example), *has* and *make.* Verbal phrases that carry unnecessary prepositional phrases (*free up, check on, shut down*), abstract nouns or adjectives. Extending verbs with the suffix *"ize."* And tagging adverbs such as *very* to a verb when a stronger word would be better.

E = ENTHUSIASM.

The drive to want to learn more. The desire to get the interview that no one else can get. The attitude to check all names and facts one last time. The joy of seeing your byline on Page 1. Enthusiasm can drive an average writer to become a good writer and a good writer to become an outstanding writer.

William Faulkner should have been a loser. He did poorly in elementary school. Dropped out of high school. Dropped out after only three semesters in a University of Mississippi program for World War I veterans. Dropped out after a failed attempt to become a poet.

But the Mississippi native became one of the greatest writers in the 20th century because he wouldn't quit trying to write. He set short-term goals. Demanded a certain number of words from himself every day. Focused on what he wrote about and on minute details.

He was driven—enthusiastic. Enough that his writing eventually won two Pulitzer Prizes and the Nobel Prize in literature.

Remember, enthusiasm generates energy. Energy breeds experience. Experience creates expectations. And the only way to fulfill those expectations is through enthusiasm. A person with enthusiasm can influence one person, a few people or hundreds, thousands or millions now and in the future. Faulkner died in 1962, but his writing remains with us.

Likewise, your writing, your enthusiasm, will leave a lasting memory.

R = REWRITE, OR EDIT YOURSELF.

Rewrite your stories and reports as many times as possible. Ernest Hemingway was known for his rewrites, for saying that "Good writing is architecture, not interior decoration." Therefore, even on deadline, it's the rewrite that becomes the best story, not the first draft.

That involves editing yourself. Here are a few ways to self-edit (some you may know, but, hey, it won't hurt to review):

- Double-check, triple-check your facts and spelling of names. (And know the paper's style, too, because your editors will expect you to know it.)
- Trim your prepositions, adjectives and adverbs: The *captain of the police department* could easily be *police captain.* Adverbs usually add baggage to your sentences. And adjectives tend to tell readers what you think; you need to show them through details.
- Limit your clichés and trim or explain the jargon, the vocabulary of a certain profession, and cut the journalese, which is language used by journalists and not anyone else (He faced a firestorm of criticism).

- Get rid of quotations that don't add to your stories. Quotes filled with numbers, facts and jargon or repeat information already in the story should be paraphrased so you can save a few words for more details. Use quotes to emphasize, that are descriptive or provide flow to your story.
  In an Associated Press story about St. Louis Cardinal slugger Mark McGwire, the writer hit a home run of his own by including an excellent quote from McGwire on a recent slump: "I've been an ornament the last month."
- For editors, remember to double-check what you've just edited to ensure that you didn't edit a mistake into a reporter's story. Don't rush so much that you'll have regrets the next day.

B = BE SPECIFIC.

Find the details—the pertinent details—that will help the reader see, taste, smell or hear your story. When at the scene or interviewing, look for details that will help you show the scene to the reader. Instead of telling readers about a small group of protesters, tell them how many protesters are in the group, the group the protesters are with and what their signs say.

If you're interested in improving your V.E.R.B.S., you're interested in details, imagery and good writing.

S = SIMPLIFY TO SEEK CLARITY.

If you seek clarity, you want the reader to understand your writing.

It means simplicity. Remembering that the best sentences are subject, verb, object.

It means a focus—one idea per sentence. Eliminating the jargon, clichés and journalese that are misunderstood. Writing sentences of fewer than 30 words; most 23 to 25 words long. Placing fewer than three numbers or three prepositions in them.

It means trimming long, confusing words—terms that are not strong and not abstract. Avoiding misplaced modifiers or clauses. Avoiding sentences with long backed-in clauses that are unnecessary or delay the subject. Using good quotes instead of long, meaningless ones.

It means what I wrote earlier: using strong verbs and strong words: *He decided* instead of *He made the decision. She drove the car* instead of *The car was driven by her.* Unless, of course, you're using the passive voice to emphasize the sentence's object.

Use your experience in writing to become better understood—and that's what we should strive for in everything we write.

Strong writing means V.E.R.B.S.

VIGOR THROUGH VERBS, ENTHUSIASM, REWRITING, BEING SPECIFIC and SIMPLICITY TO SEEK CLARITY. Follow these traits and you're on your way to becoming a Hemingway or Faulkner.

SUGGESTED READINGS

Arnold, George T. *Media Writer's Handbook: A Guide to Common Writing and Editing Problems.* New York: McGraw-Hill, 1999.

Bremner, John B. *Words on Words: A Dictionary for Writers and Others Who Care About Words.* New York: Columbia University Press, 1980.

Bernstein, Theodore M. *The Careful Writer: A Modern Guide to English Usage.* New York: Atheneum, 1980.

Brooks, Brian S., and James L. Pinson. *Working With Words: A Handbook for Media Writer and Editors,* 4th ed. New York: Bedford/St. Martin's Press, 1999.

Kessler, Lauren, and Duncan McDonald. *When Words Collide: A Media Writer's Guide to Grammar and Style,* 5th ed. Belmont, Calif.: Wadsworth, 1999.
Strunk, William Jr., and E.B. White. *The Elements of Style,* 4th ed. Boston: Allyn and Bacon, 2000.

USEFUL WEB SITES

Guide to Grammar & Writing: http://webster.commnet.edu/grammar
The Grammar Lady: http://www.grammarlady.com
Webgrammar: http://www.webgrammar.com

Name ______________________ Class ______________________ Date ______

EXERCISE 1

RECOGNIZING AND CORRECTING NEWSWRITING ERRORS

Answer Key Provided: See Appendix D

SECTION I: AGREEMENT

Edit the following sentences, correcting agreement and other errors.

1. The committee submits their data this weekend and expects it to help their church.
2. She said the company failed to earn enough to repay their loans, and she does not expect them to reopen.
3. The jury reached their verdict at 1 a.m., concluding that the media was guilty of libeling the restaurant and their twenty-two employees.
4. The decision allowed the city council to postpone their vote for a week, and they suggested that the sites developer design a plan to save more of it's trees.
5. A representative for the organization said they help anyone that is on welfare obtain some job training and raise their self esteem.

SECTION II: PLURALS AND POSSESSIVES

Edit the following sentences, correcting for plurals, possessives and other errors.

1. The womens car was parked nearby, and sheriffs deputies asked to see the owners drivers license.
2. The juror said she opposes assisted suicide "because a doctors job is to save peoples lives, not end them."
3. Last years outstanding teacher insisted that peoples complaints about the schools problems are mistaken.

4. Manvel Jones parents said there younger childrens teacher earned her bachelors degree in philosophy and her masters degree in eductaion.
5. Everyones money was stolen, and the neighborhood associations president warned that the police are no longer able to guarantee peoples safety in the citys poorest neighborhoods.

SECTION III: PLACEMENT

Rewrite these sentences, keeping related words and ideas together. Correct all errors.

1. The board of trustees voted 8–1 to fire the college president for his sexual misconduct during an emergency meeting Thursday morning.
2. On their arrival, the hotel manager took the guests' bags to their rooms.
3. The union representative urged Americans to support better working conditions for the nations migrant workers at the Unitarian church Sunday.
4. Jogging around campus, a thorn bush ripped a hole in Zena's shirt.
5. A suspect in the burglary case was arrested after a high-speed chase involving two lawn mowers stolen from a hardware store.

SECTION IV: PERSONIFICATION

Rewrite the following sentences, eliminating personification and other errors.

1. Slamming on its brakes, the car turned to the left, narrowly missing the dog.
2. The city said it cannot help the three businesses who asked for better lighting.
3. After detecting the outbreak, the hospital admitted that 7 babies born this month were infected, including one that died.
4. The Fire Department treated the child for smoke inhalation, then transported her to Mercy Hospital, which treated her broken legs.
5. The corporation, which denied any responsibility for the deaths, will appear in court next month.

SECTION V: PARALLEL FORM

Rewrite these sentences in parallel form, and correct all errors.

1. He was charged with drunken driving and an expired drivers license.
2. Karen Kim was a full-time student, Air Force reservist, and she worked part-time for a veterinarian.
3. To join the club, one must be a sophomore, junior or senior; studying journalism; be in good academic standing; and have demonstrated professional journalistic ability.
4. The mayor warned that the neighborhoods high crime rate causes residents to flee, contributes to more unemployment for workers, and the city loses tax revenue, along with lowering everyones property values.
5. She said the other advantages of owning her own business include being independent, not having a boss, flexible hours and less stress.

SECTION VI: MULTIPLE ERRORS

Rewrite the following sentences, correcting all errors. Most sentences contain more than one error.

1. A sheriffs deputy saw the teenagers Chevrolet pull out of the alley, driving recklessly without its headlines on, and arrested it's driver.
2. The city also said that they cannot silence Sooyoung Li, the woman that fears pollution is likely to effect the neighborhoods 300 residents.
3. Seeking more money, publicity, and to help the poor, the churchs members said it wants the city to help it by providing food and offer housing for the homeless.
4. The Public Works Department said they could pave the developments road themselves for less than $1.2 million, the Roess Company submitted a bid of $2.74 million.
5. A jury awarded almost $10.5 million to the operators of an abortion clinic that charged that picketers tormented them and there clients. The clinics operators praised the jury's verdict, saying their courage and understanding set a needed precedent.

Name ______________________ Class ______________________ Date ______

EXERCISE 2

RECOGNIZING AND CORRECTING NEWS WRITING ERRORS

SECTION I: AGREEMENT

Edit the following sentences, correcting agreement and other errors.

1. Every one of the news stories were accurate in their description of the accused.
2. Are seven dollars enough to buy the book?
3. Spagetti and meatballs are my favoite dish.
4. The board voted to raise they're salaries 10 percent.
5. The cat and dog, whom ate off her plate, was punished severely.

SECTION II: PLURALS AND POSSESSIVES

Edit the following sentences correcting for plurals, possessives and other errors.

1. The women's liberation movement continue to help champion their cause for equality.
2. Experts fear the grey wolfs are a endangered species.
3. The fishes scales glowed in the dark from being exposed to pollution.
4. She acknowledged that the mistake was her's.
5. Their going to take they're trip to Jamaica this year.

SECTION III: PLACEMENT

Rewrite these sentences, keeping related words and ideas together. Correct all errors.

1. While baring it's teeth, the dogcatcher caught the racoon.
2. The teacher said that grading was tiring and exhausing for her students papers.
3. Too cold to move, her coat was inadequate for her outing.
4. The mother knew that going to war would be hard for her baby, who was a sergeant in the military.
5. The firefighter saved the child as she ran into the burning house.

SECTION IV: PERSONIFICATION

Rewrite the following sentences, eliminating personification and other errors.

1. The jets unloaded their bombs in the no-fly zone.
2. The funeral home said the former mayors burial was at 4 p.m.
3. What the newspaper says is all ways right.
4. The governors meeting voted to raise taxes.
5. Her watch said it was noon time.

SECTION V: PARALLEL FORM

Rewrite these sentences in parallel form, and correct all errors.

1. She goes to college majoring in journalism to write news.
2. The mayor promised improvements in employment, education and to fix up roads in the county.
3. Tracy went to the store for eggs and butter and also to buy milk.
4. Sept. 11, 2001, was sad, had offensiveness and many students believe it is upsetting to their classmates.
5. She asked the victim to describe the muggers's height, weight and if he knew what she wore.

SECTION VI: MULTIPLE ERRORS

Rewrite the following sentences, correcting all errors. Most sentences contain more than one error.

1. As it rolled along the floor, her foot was run over by the chair.
2. The electricians's union told their members to go on strike and to also demonstrate their disagreement.
3. Detailed and tricky, the class finished their exams.
4. The hockey team was given their five goals by their principal player, Annie Bearclaw.
5. None of the witnesses were available to the reporter that had a deadline.

6. The beautiful flower, black and blue, was stepped on by the gardeners dog.
7. The teacher that was interviewed by the reporter asked for her e-mail.
8. All the people in the neighborhood was given a good citizenship award by the mayor.
9. The woman could not be a juror due to she said the judge was an hypocrite with her rulings.
10. He likes to watch movies which make him cry and also gets him to feeling sentimental.

Name ______________________ Class ______________________ Date ______

EXERCISE 3

SPELLING

Cross off the word that is misspelled in each of the following pairs. Always use the spelling recommended by The Associated Press.

1. a lot/alot
2. acceptable/acceptible
3. accidently/accidentally
4. accommodate/accomodate
5. advertising/advertizing
6. adviser/advisor
7. afterward/afterwards
8. alright/all right
9. baptize/baptise
10. boy friend/ boyfriend
11. broccoli/brocolli
12. canceled/cancelled
13. catagorized/categorized
14. cemetery/cemetary
15. comming/coming
16. commited/committed
17. congradulations/ congratulations
18. conscious/concious
19. contraversial/ controversial
20. credability/credibility
21. critized/criticized
22. cryed/cried
23. defendant/defendent
24. desert/dessert (food)
25. despite/dispite
26. deterrant/deterrent
27. dilema/dilemma
28. disastrous/disasterous
29. dispise/despise
30. elite/elete
31. embarass/embarrass
32. emphasize/emphacize
33. employe/employee
34. endorsed/indorsed
35. exhorbitant/exorbitant
36. existance/existence
37. explaination/explanation
38. fascination/facination
39. favortism/favoritism
40. Febuary/February
41. fourty/forty
42. fulfil/fulfill
43. glamour/glamor
44. goverment/government
45. guerrilla/guerilla
46. harassment/harrassment
47. humorous/humerous
48. independant/independent
49. indispensable/ indispensible
50. infered/inferred
51. innuendo/inuendo
52. irrate/irate
53. irregardless/regardless
54. it's/its (possessive)
55. janiter/janitor
56. judgement/judgment
57. kindergarten/ kindergarden
58. license/liscense
59. lightning/lightening
60. likelyhood/likelihood
61. magazines/magasines

62. municipal/municiple
63. nickles/nickels
64. noticeable/noticable
65. occasionally/ocassionally
66. occured/occurred
67. oppertunity/opportunity
68. per cent/percent
69. permissable/permissible
70. personel/personnel
71. persue/pursue
72. picknicking/picnicking
73. plagiarism/plagarism
74. practice/practise
75. priviledge/privilege
76. protester/protestor
77. questionnaire/questionaire
78. receive/recieve
79. reckless/wreckless
80. re-elect/reelect
81. refering/referring
82. gardless/regardless
83. resturant/restaurant
84. roomate/roommate
85. saleries/salaries
86. sandwich/sandwhich
87. seige/siege
88. separate/seperate
89. sergeant/sargeant
90. sizable/sizeable
91. sophmore/sophomore
92. souvenir/sovenir
93. stab/stabb
94. strickly/strictly
95. suing/sueing
96. summarize/summerize
97. surgery/surgury
98. surprise/surprize
99. taxi/taxy
100. teen-ager/teenager
101. temperature/temperture
102. tendancy/tendency
103. their/thier
104. totaled/totalled
105. toward/towards
106. transfered/transferred
107. tries/trys
108. truely/truly
109. until/untill
110. useable/usable
111. vacinate/vaccinate
112. vacuum/vaccum
113. valedictorian/valdictorian
114. vetoes/vetos
115. victum/victim
116. villain/villan
117. Wednesday/Wedesday
118. wierd/weird
119. writing/writting
120. yield/yeild

Name ______________ Class ______________ Date ______

EXERCISE 4

SPELLING

Cross off the word that is misspelled in each of the following pairs. Always use the spelling recommended by The Associated Press.

1. abberation/aberration
2. abbreviate/abreviate
3. abdomen/abdoman
4. absence/absense
5. accessible/accessable
6. acknowlegement/ acknowledgment
7. acquaintance/acquantance
8. acter/actor
9. adherant/adherent
10. admissable/admissible
11. admited/admitted
12. affidavit/afidavit
13. allready/already
14. alotted/alloted
15. alphabet/alphebet
16. ambulance/ambulence
17. ammendment/ amendment
18. among/amoung
19. apologize/apologise
20. apparantly/apparently
21. arguement/argument
22. arithematic/arithmetic
23. assassinate/assasinate
24. athlete/athlite
25. auxiliary/auxillary
26. ax/axe
27. baby sit/baby-sit
28. bachelor's/ bachelors degree
29. backward/backwards
30. baloney/balogna
31. barbecue/barbeque
32. basically/basicly
33. becoming/becomming
34. believable/beleivable
35. beneficial/benificial
36. broadcast/broadcasted
37. bureacracy/bureaucracy
38. burglars/burglers
39. Caribbean/Carribean
40. catagorized/categorized
41. catalog/catalogue
42. catastrophe/catastraphe
43. champagne/champayne
44. changeable/changable
45. chauffeur/chaufeur
46. cigarettes/cigaretes
47. commited/committed
48. comparable/comperable
49. concensus/consensus
50. contemptible/ contemptable
51. definately/definitely
52. demagogue/demogog
53. dependent/dependant
54. desireable/desirable
55. destroyed/distroyed
56. deterant/deterrent
57. develop/develope
58. deviding/dividing
59. disasterous/disastrous
60. discrimination/ descrimination

61. drunkenness/drunkeness
62. exaggerate/exagerate
63. existence/existance
64. expelled/expeled
65. familiar/familar
66. fiery/fierey
67. forward/forwards
68. fourty/forty
69. goodby/goodbye
70. grammar/grammer
71. guarante/guarantee
72. hazzard/hazard
73. hemorrhage/hemorrage
74. heros/heroes
75. hitchiker/hitchhiker
76. imminent/imminant
77. imposter/impostor
78. innuendo/inuendo
79. involveing/involving
80. labelled/labeled
81. layed/laid
82. liaison/liason
83. likeable/likable
84. limousine/limousene
85. loneliness/lonelyness
86. maintnance/maintenance
87. mathematics/mathmatics
88. medias/media (plural)
89. millionaire/millionnaire
90. missile/missle
91. misspell/mispell
92. mortgage/morgage
93. mosquitos/mosquitoes
94. necesary/necessary
95. omitted/ommited
96. paniced/panicked
97. payed/paid
98. persistent/persistant
99. perspiration/persperation
100. potatoes/potatos
101. practise/practice
102. precede/preceed
103. preparing/prepairing
104. prevalent/prevalant
105. professor/proffessor
106. prominent/prominant
107. pryed/pried
108. realised/realized
109. receive/recieve
110. repetition/repitition
111. resturant/restaurant
112. saboteur/sabateur
113. sheriff/sherrif
114. singular/singuler
115. sophmore/sophomore
116. survivors/survivers
117. tenative/tentative
118. traveled/travelled
119. wintry/wintery
120. worrys/worries

CHAPTER 3

NEWSWRITING STYLE

I do not apologize for the effort of anybody in the news business to be entertaining, if the motive is to instruct and to teach and to elevate rather than to debase.

(Max Frankel, newspaper editor)

Newswriters have a challenging task. They must convey information, often complex information, to their readers and viewers. They have to tell a story by providing facts in a clear and concise manner using simple language. Simplicity of language is important because newswriters are trying to reach readers and viewers whose capabilities and interests vary greatly. Some may have a high school diploma, while others may have a doctoral degree. Some may be interested in world events, while others may be interested in the world of entertainment and celebrities. To communicate effectively to a mass audience, newswriters must learn to present information in a way that will allow almost everyone to read and understand it.

Newswriting style also demands that reporters present factual information succinctly and in an impartial or objective manner. Unlike some other forms of writing, newswriting often is constrained by the space and time available for each story. Yet even short stories must contain enough information that readers can understand what has happened. Also, one of the basic principles of journalism is the separation of fact and opinion. Reporters and editors strive to keep opinions out of news stories. Beginners may find newswriting style awkward at first; however, once it is mastered, students will find it can help them be more clear and concise in all writing.

The first step to a well-written story is planning and preparation. Before writers attempt to construct a news story—or any other piece of writing—they identify the main idea they want to convey to their readers and steps they must take to do so.

PREWRITING

Identifying the Central Point

Writing, whether about simple or complex topics, requires preparation and organization. The preparation begins even before the reporter starts gathering information, when the story is just an idea in the mind of the reporter, editor or producer. When reporters have gathered all the information they think they need for a story, they still face the task of organizing. The best way to do this, for long stories and short ones, is to write a central point and a brief outline.

A central point for a news story is a one- or two-sentence summary of what the story is about and why it is newsworthy. It is a statement of the topic—and more. Several stories may have the same topic, but the central point of each of those stories should be unique. If a jetliner crashed on landing at an airport, the next edition of the local paper probably would have several stories about the crash, each of which would have a unique central point. One story might have as its central point, "Wind and rain made airport runways treacherous, but other jetliners made successful landings." That story would report on weather conditions at the airport and whether air traffic controllers and other pilots considered them to be severe. The central point for another story might be "The heroism of passengers and flight attendants saved the lives of dozens of people." That story would report what happened in the passenger cabin after the crash and how those who survived made it to safety. And a third story's central point might be "Federal investigators have recovered the flight data recorders but will need days or weeks to figure out what caused the crash." That story would focus on what will likely happen in the investigation of the crash. Although each of these stories would be about the jetliner crash, each would have a distinct central point, and each would have only information relevant to that central point.

Good writers include a statement of the central point in each story. The central point may be in the first paragraph, called the "lead." Or it may be in a nut paragraph—called a "nut graf"—that follows a lead that tells an anecdote, describes a scene or uses some other storytelling device to entice the reader into the story. By including the central point, writers clearly tell readers what they will learn from reading the entire story.

News stories may have many possible central points. Which one reporters use may depend on their news judgment and their estimation of what the audiences for their publications or broadcasts want to know. If a flamboyant head of a major corporation resigns when the business is forced to pay millions of dollars in damages after losing a lawsuit, the story by a reporter for a local newspaper might focus on whether the company will have to eliminate jobs. A story in a financial newspaper might have as its central point the impact of the lawsuit on investors' confidence in the company. And a newspaper that covers legal affairs might emphasize the failure of the company's courtroom strategy. Although these publications and their reporters would select different central points for their stories, each choice would be appropriate for the publication's audience.

Story Outlines

Reporters usually have a good idea what the central point of their stories will be even as they begin gathering the information. Often, however, unexpected information may emerge that forces them to rethink the central point of the story. Therefore, reporters always review their notes and other materials they have gathered before they start writing. The review assures reporters they have identified the most newsworthy central point and have the information they need to develop it. It also helps them decide what the major sections of their stories will be. A reporter who has covered a city council's adoption of a new budget might write a central-point statement that says, "The city council eliminated several popular programs to avoid having to increase property taxes." The reporter then might decide that the story should have these major sections:

- What programs were cut.
- Why the city could not afford to keep them.
- Reaction to the cuts.

The central point and this brief outline of the major sections form the skeleton of the story. The reporter needs only to develop each section.

Once reporters have selected a central point and written a brief outline, they can go through their notes again to decide what information belongs where. Some reporters will number passages according to what section of the story they relate to. Others will use colored pens or markers to indicate where to put particular facts, quotes or anecdotes. They discard information that does not fit in any of the sections.

Reporters who fail to identify a central point for a story or who lose sight of that central point risk writing stories that are incoherent and incomplete. Here's a story by a student reporter that lacks a central focus:

> A loss of personal identity can mean a gain in unwanted headaches. When people lose their wallets, a sense of panic might come over them because they know they had tucked away a driver's license, a credit card and a student ID card, all of which might fall into the hands of an identity thief.
>
> The university issues student ID cards that have the students' Social Security numbers printed across the front. So some students may become concerned that they may lose their identity should their ID cards become lost or stolen.
>
> Marlene Ambroz, manager of the local Social Security Administration office, said there are people out there who feel the need to steal personal identities. She said chances of that happening are slim.
>
> "There is an element of risk. How much, I don't know," she said.
>
> Ambroz said the loss of an individual's identity would probably come once someone actively sought information about another person, such as birthdate or address.
>
> Fred Simmons, director of registration for the university, said people who lost their wallets would place themselves at risk for having credit cards stolen. But he said the risks created by having a thief learn one's Social Security number from a student ID were minor.
>
> Simmons said the student ID cards went through a computer system specifically designed to recognize Social Security numbers. He said it was of no great urgency to change the system, considering the expense of changing student ID numbers to something other than Social Security numbers. He said some institutions in the United States had decided to assign generic student numbers.
>
> "I can tell you that for those institutions that have switched, it was no simple and straightforward thing," Simmons said. "I know that at one major university it was more than a yearlong project. That's how long it took them to change all of their systems and reassign numbers and basically recard the whole campus."
>
> Ambroz agreed that if the university tried to design its own identification system, it would be cumbersome.

The story begins by suggesting that university students may be vulnerable to identity theft by having their student IDs, which bear Social Security numbers, stolen. However, the story does not explain what identity theft is or how someone whose Social Security number is stolen may be injured. Then the story jumps to why university officials are reluctant to change from Social Security numbers to a generic system of student ID numbers and the difficulties encountered by universities that have switched to generic numbers. Although all of these issues may be part of the same topic, they belong in separate stories with distinct central points. The writer of this story lost track of the story's central point and failed to find enough information to develop one central point thoroughly.

The process of identifying a central point and story outline has been described here in the context of routine news stories, which may have fewer than 1,000 words. This same process can help writers of much longer pieces, such as multipart newspaper series, magazine articles and books. Donald Barlett and James B. Steele, reporters who have produced a number of long investigative stories and books, say one of the keys to their success is organizing information. They spend months gathering documents and conducting interviews, all of which are filed by topic or name of individual, agency or corporation. Then they read the material several times because important issues and ideas often become clear only after time. Once they have an outline of the major sections of their piece, they start drafting the story section by section. Finally, they polish sections and spend most of their time working on leads and transitions between sections. Barlett and Steele's description of how they work confirms what most writers say: No one sits down and writes great stories. Writers must plan their work.

SIMPLIFY WORDS, SENTENCES AND PARAGRAPHS

George Orwell, in his classic commentary "Politics and the English Language," complained that too often writers replace simple verbs and appropriate nouns with complicated phrases. Such phrases tend to obscure facts and confuse the reader.

To simplify stories, avoid long, unfamiliar words. Whenever possible, substitute shorter and simpler words that convey the same meaning. Use "about" rather than "approximately," "build" rather than "construct," "call" rather than "summon" and "home" rather than "residence."

Also use short sentences and short paragraphs. Rewrite long or awkward sentences and divide them into shorter ones that are easier to read and understand. Research has consistently found a strong correlation between readability and sentence length: The longer a sentence is, the more difficult it is to understand. One survey found that 75 percent of readers were able to understand sentences containing an average of 20 words, but understanding dropped rapidly as the sentences became longer.

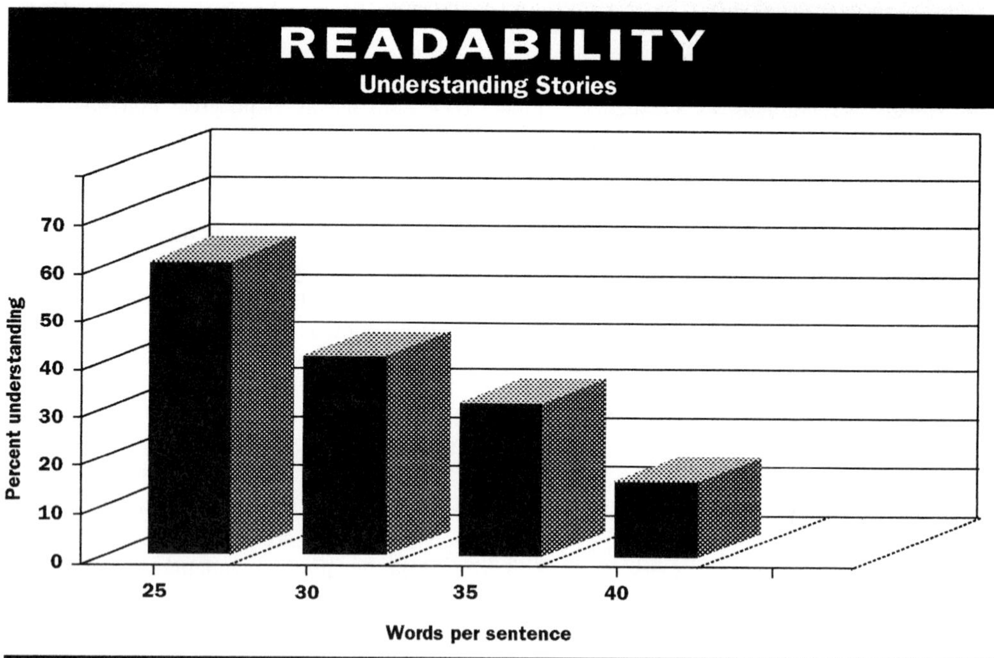

This does not mean all stories should have nothing but short sentences. Too many short sentences strung together will make the writing sound choppy. Long sentences, constructed and used with care, can be effective tools for the writer. Overuse of either long or very short sentences can make the writing awkward and difficult for the reader to comprehend.

Newswriters should write for the ear, listening to the natural rhythm, or flow, of the words and sentences they put on paper. They should test their stories by reading them aloud to themselves or to a friend. If the sentences sound awkward or inappropriate for a conversation with friends, the writer must rewrite them and be particularly careful to avoid complex phrases and long, awkward sentences.

The following three paragraphs written by Anne Hull of the St. Petersburg (Fla.) Times in a story about a teenager who pulled a gun on a female police officer illustrate the impact one can achieve by combining short and long sentences:

> The sound she heard from the gun would reverberate for months.
>
> Click.
>
> It was the same sound the key in the lock makes as the father comes home now to the empty apartment, greeted by the boy in the golden frame.

Notice the construction of those three paragraphs. One is the ultimate of brevity—only one word—while the other two sentences are 11 words and 29 words. The combination of the three sentences creates a vivid picture for the reader, as well as a rhythm that creates drama and touches the emotions.

Paula LaRocque, writing coach and author of books and columns on writing, notes that concise writing can be just as dramatic and have as much impact as long narrative passages. LaRocque says writers tend to overwrite when seeking drama or impact. Yet a few carefully selected words can better convey the story to readers.

Because of the strong correlation between readability and sentence length, publications quite obviously cater to their intended audiences. The sentences in comics contain an average of about eight words, while the sentences in publications for the general public average 15 to 20 words. Publications with sentences averaging 20 to 30 words are much more difficult to understand, and they appeal to more specialized and better-educated audiences. These publications include such magazines as The Atlantic Monthly, Harper's and scholarly, scientific or professional journals.

Many college students tend to write sentences that are much too long. Students are more likely to write sentences containing 40 or 50 words than sentences containing four or five. Yet short sentences are clearer and more forceful.

Edna Buchanan, who won a Pulitzer Prize when she was a police reporter for The Miami Herald, wrote in her best-selling book "The Corpse Had a Familiar Face":

> Dozens of fires erupted at intersections. Firefighters were forced back by gunfire. Businesses and stores burned unchecked. "It's absolutely unreal," said Miami Fire Inspector George Bilberry. "They're burning down the whole north end of town."
>
> Late Sunday, 15 major blazes still raged out of control. Snipers fired rifles at rescue helicopters. The looting and burning went on for three days. Public schools were closed, and an 8 p.m.-6 a.m. curfew was established.

Buchanan's sentences average only 8.1 words. Several of her sentences contain only five or six words. The longest contains 11. Yet the writing is graphic and dramatic, letting the reader feel the tension of the scene.

Compare Buchanan's writing style with the following sentence taken from William L. Shirer's book "Gandhi: A Memoir":

> Clever lawyer that he was, Jinnah took the independence that Gandhi had wrestled for India from the British by rousing the masses to non-violent struggle and used it to set up his own independent but shaky Moslem nation of Pakistan, destined, I believed then, to break up, as shortly happened when the eastern Bengali part, separated from the western part by a thousand miles of India's territory, broke away to form Bangladesh; destined eventually, I believed, to simply disappear.

Because of its length and complexity, this sentence is much more difficult to understand. It contains 80 words.

To make their newspapers more readable, many editors are demanding shorter stories and simpler writing, including shorter sentences and simpler words.

Some critics have charged that newspapers' emphasis on simplicity makes their stories dull, yet the opposite is true. When stories are well-written, simplicity makes them clearer and more interesting. Well-written stories contain no distracting clutter; instead, they emphasize the most important facts and report those facts in a clear, forceful manner.

There's another important reason for using short sentences and short paragraphs in news stories. Newspapers are printed in small type, with narrow columns, on cheap paper. Long paragraphs—producing large, gray blocks of type—discourage readers. So reporters divide stories into bite-sized chunks that are easy to read and understand. Also, from a newspaper design standpoint, the white space left at the ends of paragraphs helps brighten each page.

One way to keep sentences short, clear and conversational is to use the normal word order: subject, verb and direct object. Notice how much clearer and more concise the following sentence becomes when it uses this normal word order:

> Designing a new front page for the paper was undertaken by the publisher.
> REVISED: The publisher designed a new front page for the paper.

Also be certain the ideas in each sentence are related. If they are not, even short sentences can become confusing:

> Elected president of the student senate, he went to Parkdale Elementary School.
>
> Planning on being the first person in line for the concert, she bought her first car when she was 16.

Long introductory phrases and subordinate clauses make a sentence more difficult to understand. The phrases and clauses overload sentences, obscuring their main points:

> Fighting the wildfire from two fronts to keep the flames from engulfing the entire town, firefighters decided to let the house burn.
>
> REVISED: Firefighters decided to let the house burn. They had been fighting the wildfire on two fronts to keep the flames from engulfing the entire town.

Sometimes beginners pack too many ideas into a single sentence:

> The mayor said he was happy that the City Council had passed the resolution increasing the public library tax to provide more funds to expand the library's book collection, build a Web site and add a new wing to house government documents, but the amount of the increase was not enough to do everything that has to be done because repairs are needed to the roof of the public library building and facilities must be improved for the disabled.
>
> REVISED: The mayor said he was happy that the City Council passed the resolution increasing the public library tax. The amount of the increase, however, was not enough to do everything that has to be done. The tax increase will provide funds to expand the library's book collection, build a Web site and add a new wing to house government documents. Other needed improvements, according to the mayor, are repairs to the library's roof and better facilities for the disabled.

Paragraph length, as well as sentence length, varies from publication to publication. A paragraph should demonstrate relationships between ideas. It is a means of making complicated material clear. Like the words that form sentences, the sentences that form paragraphs should flow together, logically combining similar thoughts or ideas. Paragraphs should not combine unrelated ideas. But ideas that are related or belong together should not be artificially separated just to create shorter paragraphs. If you needlessly separate ideas, you risk producing choppy writing. According to Jack Hart, managing editor for staff training and development at The Oregonian in Portland, "A skilled writer who makes full use of various paragraph structures can create something that goes beyond making a single point of emphasis, grouping related material or connecting ideas in logical sequence."

Eliminate Unnecessary Words

Newswriters must learn to eliminate unnecessary words yet retain enough detail to make their stories informative.

QUIZ

Are you ready for a quiz? Do not rewrite the following redundant sentences; simply cross out the unnecessary words.

1. She was in a quick hurry and warned that, in the future, she will seek out textbooks that are sexist and demand that they be totally banned.
2. As it now stands, three separate members of the committee said they will try to prevent the city from closing down the park during the winter months.
3. His convertible was totally destroyed and, in order to obtain the money necessary to buy a new car, he now plans to ask a personal friend for a loan to help him along.
4. After police found the lifeless body, the medical doctor conducted an autopsy to determine the cause of death and concluded that the youth had been strangled to death.
5. In the past, he often met up with the students at the computer lab and, because of their future potential, invited them to attend the convention.
6. Based upon her previous experience as an architect, she warned the committee members that constructing the new hospital facility will be pretty expensive and suggested that they step in and seek more donors.
7. The two men were hunting in a wooded forest a total of 12 miles away from the nearest hospital in the region when both suffered severe bodily injuries.
8. Based upon several studies conducted in the past, he firmly believes that, when first started next year, the two programs should be very selective, similar in nature and conducted only in the morning hours.

Now count the number of words you eliminated—and your score. If you need help, the answers appear in Appendix D.

0-30: Amateur.	Were you really trying?
31-40: Copy kid.	Time to enroll in Newswriting 101.
41-50: Cub.	You've still got a lot to learn.
51-60: Pro.	You're getting there, but can do even better.
61+: Expert.	Time to ask your boss for a raise or your teacher for an "A."

Most news organizations can publish or air only a fraction of the information they receive each day. An editor for The New York Times once estimated The Times received 1.25 million to 1.5 million words every day but had enough space to publish only one-tenth of that material. By writing concisely, reporters present readers as much information as possible. Brevity also helps readers grasp the main idea of each story, because it eliminates unnecessary words. Writers who use two or more words when only one is necessary waste time and space. Some words are almost always unnecessary: "that," "then," "currently," "now" and "presently," for example. Because the verb tense and some nouns tell when an action occurred—in the past, present or future—it is redundant to add a second word reiterating the time, such as "*past* history," "is *now*" and "*future* plans."

Notice how easily several unnecessary words can be deleted from the following sentences without changing their meaning:

> She was able to begin college classes her senior year in high school
> REVISED: She began college classes her senior year in high school.

At the present time he is planning to leave for New York at 3 p.m. in the afternoon next Thursday.

REVISED: He plans to leave for New York at 3 p.m. next Thursday.

Be especially careful to avoid phrases and sentences that are redundant—that unnecessarily repeat the same idea. The following phrases contain only two or three words, yet at least one—the word in italics—is unnecessary:

bodily injuries	*lone* gunman
dropped *downward*	*new* innovation
end result	*now* serves
free *of charge*	*past* experiences
helped *along*	*physical* pain

Improving some redundant sentences requires more thought and effort:

Deaths are extremely rare, with only one fatality occurring in every 663,000 cases.

REVISED: One death occurs in every 663,000 cases.

Redundancy often arises because writers introduce a topic, then present some specific information about it. In most cases, only the more specific information is needed:

Trying to determine who was responsible for the burglary, police checked the door frame for fingerprints.

REVISED: Police checked the door frame for fingerprints.

Repetition is even more common in longer passages involving several sentences. Sentences appearing near the end of a paragraph should not repeat facts implied or mentioned earlier:

This is not the first elected office she has held in the city. She has been a city council member, a member of the library board and a tax collector.

REVISED: She has been a city council member, a member of the library board and a tax collector.

REMAIN OBJECTIVE

During the Revolutionary War, American newspapers were journals of opinion and frequently editorialized for or against the British. A colonial editor named Isaiah Thomas joined the militia that fired on British troops at Lexington, then reported the battle in his paper, the Massachusetts Spy. His May 3, 1775, story began:

AMERICANS! forever bear in mind the BATTLE OF LEXINGTON! where British troops, unmolested and unprovoked, wantonly and in a most inhuman manner, fired upon and killed a number of our countrymen, then robbed, ransacked, and burnt their houses! nor could the tears of defenseless women, some of whom were in the pains of childbirth, the cries of helpless babes, nor the prayers of old age, confined to beds of sickness, appease their thirst for blood!—or divert them from their DESIGN of MURDER and robbery!

Even today, some news organizations, such as Time magazine and Fox News, employ a similar—though less inflammatory—approach. In addition to reporting the news, Time and Fox interpret it, providing readers and viewers with their perspectives on events.

Today, most journalists strive to be as impartial or "objective" as possible. Reporters are neutral observers, not advocates or participants. They provide the facts and details of the stories they report, not their own interpretations or opinions of the facts and events. Journalists express their opinions only in editorials and commentaries, which usually appear in a section of the newspaper or a part of the news broadcast reserved for opinion. Sometimes, keeping fact and opinion separate is difficult.

Following the terrorist attacks of Sept. 11, reporters and anchors for some television networks started wearing American flag lapel pins, and most networks used flags or other red, white and blue motifs to signal stories about the war on terrorism. Some critics said these overt displays of patriotism were inconsistent with news organizations' obligation to separate news and opinion. Tasteful expressions of love of country, especially in a time of national crisis, do not necessarily conflict with the journalist's obligation to remain impartial, so long as they continue to examine government policies with diligence and skepticism.

More difficult problems with objectivity arose during the Second Gulf War when print and television reporters accompanied American soldiers, Marines and sailors into combat. The reporters who accompanied U.S. combat units spent weeks training, traveling and sharing hardships with the men and women they covered. Gordon Dillow, a columnist for the Orange County (Calif.) Register who covered a Marine company during the war, wrote in an article for the Columbia Journalism Review: "The biggest problem I faced as an embed with the marine grunts was that I found myself doing what journalists are warned from J-school not to do: I found myself falling in love with my subject. I fell in love with 'my' Marines."

The tendency for the reporter to identify with sources is natural, even in situations less extreme than combat, but good reporters strive to resist the temptation and to keep their stories free of opinion. When reporters inject their own opinions into a story, they risk offending readers and viewers who may not want reporters telling them how to think. Reporters assume audience members are intelligent and capable of reaching their own conclusions about issues in the news.

One way reporters keep their opinions out of stories is by avoiding loaded words, such as "demagogue," "extremist," "radical," "racist," "segregationist" and "zealot." Such words are often unnecessary and inaccurate. Many times, these loaded words state the obvious: that an argument was "heated," a rape "violent" or a death "unfortunate." Reporters can eliminate the opinions in some sentences simply by deleting a single adjective or adverb: "*alert* witness," "*famous* author," "*gala* reception," "*thoughtful* reply." Here are two more examples:

> The book costs just $49.95.
> REVISED: The book costs $49.95.
> They built a very expensive house.
> REVISED: They built a $1 million house.

Writers can avoid loaded words by reporting factual details as clearly and thoroughly as possible.

Entire sentences sometimes convey opinions, unsupported by facts. Good editors (and instructors) will eliminate those sentences. Often, deletion is the only way to correct the problem. Here are two examples:

> The candidate looks like a winner.
> Everyone is angry about the mayor's decision.

Newswriters can report the opinions expressed by other people—the sources for their stories—but must clearly attribute those opinions to the source. If reporters fail to provide the proper attribution, readers may think the reporters are expressing their own opinions or agreeing with the source:

> The family filed a lawsuit because the doctor failed to notice the injury.
> REVISED: The family's lawsuit charges the doctor failed to notice the injury.

A single word expressing an opinion can infuriate readers. When a college student was raped, a news story reported she suffered cuts on her arms and hands but "was not seriously injured." An irate reader asked, "Since when are rape and attempted sodomy, at knifepoint, not enough violence to constitute serious injury?"

Avoid Stereotypical "Isms"

Stereotyping occurs when a newswriter uses offensive, condescending or patronizing terms or phrases in describing other individuals, especially women, racial or religious minorities, the elderly or the disabled. Good newswriters are attuned to the "isms"—racism, sexism, ageism—that can appear in a story even unintentionally. They understand their audiences and the effect their words may have on some readers.

Racism

Journalists should avoid stereotypes of blacks, Asians, Hispanics, Native Americans and all other racial groups.

Reporters mention a person's race, religion or ethnic background only when the fact is clearly relevant to a story. Typically, employees at The New York Times are told: "The writer—or the characters quoted in the story—must demonstrate the relevance of ethnic background or religion. It isn't enough to assume that readers will find the fact interesting or evocative; experience shows that many will find it offensive and suspect us of relying on stereotypes."

Sometimes students and even professionals report that a "black" or "Hispanic" committed a crime, but usually the criminal's race is irrelevant to the story. Identifying a criminal by race, when that is the only characteristic known, is especially harmful because it casts suspicion upon every member of the race. Henry McNulty, a former associate editor of The Hartford (Conn.) Courant, explained his paper's policy on racial identification:

> A long-standing Courant policy states that race and sex alone do not constitute an adequate description. For instance, if the only thing a witness tells police is that a "white woman" or "black man" committed the crime, the Courant will not use any description. Only when such things as height, weight, hair length, scars, clothing and so forth are given will the newspaper print the information.

By that policy, the following description makes appropriate use of a person's race to describe a specific individual whom some readers might be able to identify:

> Witnesses said the bank robber was a white man, about 50 years old and 6 feet tall. He weighed about 250 pounds, was wearing a blue suit and escaped on a Honda motorcycle.

Other stories demean Native Americans by using descriptive words or phrases that cast them in a negative light. Avoid such obviously stereotypical words as "wampum," "warpath," "powwow," "tepee," "brave" and "squaw" and such offensive terms as "drunk," "irresponsible," "lazy" and "savage" in stories about Native Americans—or members of any ethnic group.

Sexism

In the past, news stories mentioning women often emphasized their roles as wives, mothers, cooks, seamstresses, housekeepers and sex objects. During the 1960s and 1970s, women began to complain that such stereotypes are false and demeaning because women are human beings, not primarily housewives and sex objects.

More women than ever are employed and hold high positions of responsibility in public and private organizations—including news organizations. Unfortunately, stereotypical statements continue to appear in news stories because reporters sometimes do not think about the consequences of what they write. It is offensive and demeaning to women when a newswriter uses words or phrases that suggest women are inferior to men. The offensive remark can be something as simple as describing a woman's physical appearance but not her male counterpart's physical appearance.

A headline announced, "Woman Exec Slain in Waldorf-Astoria." Critics said the slain person's sex was irrelevant to the story, and few journalists would have written, "Man Exec Slain." A headline in The Washington Post said, "School Job May Go to Woman Educator." Critics asked editors at The Post why they used the term "woman educator," because they would never use the term "man educator." Moreover, the headline's wording suggested it is unusual for a woman to achieve a position of importance.

A story in The New York Times reported a secretary "wore a full-length blue-tweed coat, leather boots and gold bangle bracelets." Critics said the secretary's clothing was neither unusual nor relevant to her involvement in the news, and the reporter would not have described the attire of a man in the same position.

A story published by a campus newspaper referred to women as "chicks." Several female students and faculty members were outraged. They complained the word implies women are cute, little, fluffy and helpless.

Some advertisements still contain sexual stereotypes. Radio advertisements have urged women to ask their husbands for money so they could shop at a certain clothing store. Another advertisement urged mothers (not fathers) to take their children to a certain amusement park.

Although reporters are expected to avoid demeaning comments and sexist stereotypes, they sometimes have difficulty breaking old ways of thinking, especially the stereotypes they developed in childhood.

As a first step, avoid occupational terms that exclude women: "fireman," "mailman," "policeman" and "workman," for example. Journalists substitute "firefighter," "mail carrier" or "postal worker," "police officer" and "worker." Similarly, use the words "reporter" and "journalist" instead of "newsman."

Although some groups favor their use, The Associated Press Stylebook recommends journalists avoid awkward or contrived words, such as "chairperson" and "spokesperson." Instead, the stylebook advises using "chairman" or "spokesman" when referring to a man or to the office in general, and using "chairwoman" or "spokeswoman" when referring to a woman. When appropriate, reporters can use a neutral word such as "leader" or "representative."

Also avoid using the words "female" and "woman" in places where you would not use the words "male" or "man" (for example: "woman doctor" or "female general"). Similarly, use unisex substitutes for words such as "authoress" (author), "actress" (actor), "aviatrix" (aviator) and "coed" (student).

Women object to being called "gals," "girls" or "ladies" and to being referred to by their first names. News stories do not call men "boys" and usually refer to them by their last names, rarely their first—except in stories in which multiple members of the same family are quoted as sources and first names are necessary to clarify who is being quoted.

Other unacceptable practices include:

- Suggesting homemaking is not work.
- Identifying a woman solely by her relationship with a man—for example, as a man's wife, daughter or secretary—unless the woman insists upon the use of her husband's name. One way to avoid this problem is to identify women by their own name, not their husband's:

  SEXIST: Mrs. Anthony Pedersen participated in the event.
  REVISED: Elizabeth Pedersen participated in the event.

- Describing a woman's hair, dress, voice or figure, when such characteristics are irrelevant to the story. To avoid problems, writers should ask themselves, "Under the same circumstances, would I describe a man's physical characteristics or marital status?"
- Mentioning a woman's marital status, especially if she is divorced, unless it is clearly relevant to your story. Even when a woman's marital status is relevant, it seldom belongs in the headline or the lead of the story.

Never assume everyone involved in a story is male, all people holding prestigious jobs are male or most women are full-time homemakers. Be especially careful to avoid using the pronouns "he," "his" and "him" while referring to a typical American or average person. Some readers will mistakenly assume you are referring exclusively to men.

Writers try to avoid, however, the cumbersome and repetitive "he/she" or "he and/or she." The effort to rid the language of male bias or female stereotyping should never become so strained that it distracts readers. Writers employ a couple of techniques to avoid those cumbersome terms:

1. Substitute an article for the male pronouns "he" and "his."

   A contractor must always consult his blueprints when building a house.
   REVISED: A contractor must always consult the blueprints when building a house.

2. Substitute plural nouns and pronouns for male nouns and pronouns.

   A soldier must train himself to be ready.
   REVISED: Soldiers must train themselves to be ready.

Ageism

Stereotypes of the elderly suggest older Americans are all lonely, inactive, unproductive, poor, passive, weak and sick. In fact, most are still active, and some continue to work into their late 70s. When asked to describe their health, a majority responded "good" to "excellent." Yet television programs often portray the elderly as eccentric, foolish, forgetful or feeble. Similarly, news stories express surprise when older people buy a sports car; fall in love; or remain alert, healthy, innovative and productive.

Avoid using terms such as "geezer" or "old fogey" when describing the elderly. Using the word "spry" when describing elderly people gives the impression that they are unusually active for their age. A person's age should not be a factor in a story about an accomplishment—getting elected to office, winning an award, being employed in an unusual occupation, for example—unless it is relevant to the story. The fact that a 70-year-old grandfather wins an election for state senator should not be treated any differently than if a 40-year-old father won the election. Neither should appear in the headline or the lead of the story.

Avoid Stereotyping Other Groups

Individuals with physical or mental disabilities often are stereotyped as helpless, deficient or unable to contribute to society. However, many physically and mentally disabled people lead active lives and contribute to society both professionally and personally. The terms "disabled" and "challenged" have replaced "handicapped." More acceptable is "person with a disability," "person who is blind" and so forth. Such phrasing emphasizes the individual before the condition.

Veterans' organizations have accused the media of portraying the men and women who served in Vietnam as violent and unstable. The media, critics explain, sometimes report that a person charged with a serious crime is "a Vietnam veteran," regardless of the fact's relevance.

Religious groups also accuse the media of bias in the portrayal of members of their faiths. Muslims around the world complain that Western media often portray Muslims as terrorists or inherently violent. Some Christian denominations are portrayed in the media as strange, different or extremist in their beliefs. Reporters must be careful when covering members of different faiths that they do not stereotype all members of a particular faith because of the actions of a branch of that faith.

DON'T WRITE LIKE THIS

Here are examples of bad writing that came from statements made on insurance forms. Car drivers attempted to summarize the details of their accidents in the fewest words possible.

- Coming home, I drove into the wrong house and collided with a tree I don't have.
- The other car collided with mine without warning of its intentions.

- I thought my window was down, but I found out it was up when I put my head through it.
- I collided with a stationary truck coming the other way.
- A truck backed through my windshield into my wife's face.
- The guy was all over the road. I had to swerve a number of times before I hit him.
- I pulled away from the side of the road, glanced at my mother-in-law and headed over the embankment.
- In my attempt to kill a fly, I drove into a telephone pole.
- I had been shopping for plants all day and was on my way home. As I reached an intersection, a hedge sprang up, obscuring my vision and I did not see the other car.
- I was on my way to the doctor with rear-end trouble when my universal joint gave way causing me to have engine trouble.
- I had been driving for 40 years when I fell asleep at the wheel and had an accident.
- My car was legally parked as it backed into another vehicle.
- The pedestrian had no idea which way to run, so I ran over him.
- A pedestrian hit me and went under my car.
- As I approached the intersection, a sign suddenly appeared in a place where no stop sign ever appeared before. I was unable to stop in time to avoid the accident.
- I was sure the old fellow would never make it to the other side of the road when I struck him.
- I saw a slow-moving, sad-faced old gentleman as he bounced off the roof of my car.
- I told police that I was not injured, but on removing my hat, I found that I had a fractured skull.
- An invisible car came out of nowhere, struck my car and vanished.
- The indirect cause of the accident was a little guy in a small car with a big mouth. I was thrown from my car as it left the road. I was later found in a ditch by some stray cows.
- The telephone pole was approaching. I was attempting to swerve out of its way when it struck the front end.
- To avoid hitting the bumper on the car in front, I hit a pedestrian.

CHECKLIST FOR NEWSWRITING STYLE

As you begin to write stories, check to make sure you follow these guidelines.

1. Identify the central point of the story.
2. Prepare a brief outline of the three or four major parts of the story.

3. Use short, familiar words.
4. Use short sentences and short paragraphs.
5. Eliminate unnecessary words.
6. Avoid overloading sentences with unrelated ideas.
7. Use relatively simple sentences that follow normal word order: subject-verb-direct object.
8. Avoid statements of opinion.
9. Avoid stereotyping people by race, gender, age, ethnic group or religion.

THE WRITING COACH

FIND THE CLEAR PATH TO WRITING GLORY

By **Joe Hight**
Managing Editor of The Oklahoman

Without clarity in every sentence of your story, you lose.

You lose what creativity you've used to write your story. You lose meaning because you can't be understood. You lose what time you took to write the story. You lose respect from peers. You lose readers because they don't have time to interpret the meaning of your words and sentences.

So for any story to succeed—for you to succeed—clarity becomes vital.

The (Portland) Oregonian has listed clarity as the No. 2 value (No. 1 is accuracy) of a good newspaper. Roy Peter Clark of the Poynter Institute for Media Studies writes, "The most valued quality of the language of journalism is clarity, and its most desired effect is to be understood." Paula LaRocque, writing coach and author, writes that clarity is crucial to good writing of any kind. And The Oklahoman demands that reporters must ensure that stories are accurate and clear to readers.

Writing coaches and experts have emphasized clarity for many years. Readability guides and computer programs have been developed to help writers check whether they have written understandable passages.

The guides and programs can be helpful, but they mean nothing if the writer doesn't seek clarity through simplicity, understanding, polishing and caring. Each element is related and plays a role in clear writing.

Here are summaries of each:

SIMPLICITY

Poor writers try to impress by being complex instead of simplifying their sentences and paragraphs. They fear that someone will ridicule them for being too simplistic.

But LaRocque writes, "Good, clear writing is neither dumb nor over simple. And unclear writing (unless also written by the unintelligent) is self-indulgent if not arrogant. The truth is that the best writers are and always have been the clearest writers—from Winston Churchill to Albert Einstein to Carl Sagan. They've learned that knowledge isn't worth much if we can't convey it to others."

Simplicity means:

- Using subject-verb-object whenever possible.
- Using active verbs.
- Reducing complicated words into single-syllable or simple terms.

- Using specific details instead of general terms. Concrete over abstract.
- Keeping sentences short but pacing them with a variety of lengths.
- Avoiding long backed-in clauses that only delay the subject.
- Avoiding too many statistics that tend to confuse. Or too many prepositions. LaRocque recommends no more than three statistics or prepositions per sentence.

UNDERSTANDING

A religious song titled "Prayer of St. Francis" has the following verse in it: "To be understood as to understand." The line should become a theme for anyone writing a newspaper story.

In their "Secrets of Great Writing," journalism professors Maureen A. Croteau and Wayne A. Worcester list understanding as one of their 20 tips: "You can't write what you don't understand. If you don't know what you're talking about, nobody else will either. You can parrot information, drop in some quotes and produce something that looks like a story. But if you don't understand what you're writing about, no one else will."

Understanding means:

- Translating jargon into terms that readers can understand. Avoid excessive use of bureaucratic terms or try to explain those that must be used. Avoid clichés that limit understanding. Avoid journalese—writing that speaks in terms that only a journalist can understand.
- Using quotations that are understandable to readers. How many times have you read a quote that's filled with so many parentheses, clichés or jargon that it's difficult to understand? Most are from reporters who fail to clarify or paraphrase quotes that are incomprehensible. Many longer quotes seem to come from tape recorders. But tape recorders aren't the problem. It's reporters who are so worried about transcribing that they forget to translate.
- Limiting the use of acronyms, except those that are commonly used. Mary Goddard, the late writing coach for The Oklahoman, gave this advice for anyone writing stories or headlines: "Would the first 10 people polled at a McDonald's know instantly what these letters stand for?"

POLISHING

Most writers should know William Strunk Jr.'s famous words: "Vigorous writing is concise. A sentence should contain no unnecessary words, a paragraph no unnecessary sentences, for the same reason that a drawing should have no unnecessary lines and a machine no unnecessary parts."

All of these quotes emphasize the need to draft, then polish.

Polishing means:

- Ensuring names are spelled correctly. The math is correct. The facts don't conflict. (Sure, good writers make mistakes, but they strive to prevent them.)
- Pruning words like the best hedge trimmer. Searching for dangling or misplaced modifiers. Rewriting to prevent double meanings. Carefully trimming away the excess until creating a precise work.

(continued)

- Eliminating the complex. Sarah Fritz of the Los Angeles Times calls it selection. She said good reporters, especially those who are investigative, are storytellers who select what is understandable and throw out material that is trivial or can't be understood.
- Finding better ways to self-edit. Reading sentences out loud. Talking with other reporters about complicated sentences. Working with editors to trim and edit, and editors working with reporters.

CARING

This is the most important element in seeking clear writing. Caring that you've done your best work and caring for the readers of that work.

Caring means:

- Using simplicity, understanding and polishing to create powerful writing.
- Seeking brevity so the readers get no more than what they need to read.
- Establishing a focus in the story. From the lead to the end, a focus on organizing your story to provide information that the reader should know.
- Providing meaning. Donald Murray, a writing expert and columnist who won the Pulitzer Prize for editorial writing in The Boston Herald, distinguishes between a reporter and a writer. He says in "Writer in the Newsroom" that writers and reporters both have goals of accuracy, simplicity and clarity. But the writer reveals meaning between pieces of information. The writer "collects accurate, specific, revealing pieces of information and constructs each draft by building firm, logical patterns of meaning. The writer is master of the craft of reporting—and the craft of writing."
- Hard work. "Writing is hard work," author William Zinsser writes. "A clear sentence is no accident. Very few sentences come out right the first time, or even the third time. Remember this in moments of despair. If you find that writing is hard, it's because it is hard. It's one of the hardest things people do."

Combined, these elements—simplicity, understanding, polishing and caring—produce clarity in your work. They also produce outstanding stories.

In your stories, they prevent you from losing.

SUGGESTED READINGS

Bazerman, Charles. *The Informed Writer*, 4th ed. Boston: Houghton Mifflin, 1992.

Clark, Roy Peter and Christopher Scanlon. *America's Best Newspaper Writing: A Collection of ASNE Prizewinners*. Boston: Bedford/St. Martin's, 2001.

Clark, Roy Peter. *The American Conversation and the Language of Journalism*. St. Petersburg, Fla.: Poynter Institute for Media Studies, 1994.

Flocke, Lynne, Dona Hayes and Anna L. Babic. *Journalism and the Aging Population*. Syracuse, N.Y.: Syracuse University Series in Gerontology Education, Center for Instructional Development, Syracuse University, 1990.

Franklin, Jon. *Writing for Story: Craft Secrets of Dramatic Nonfiction by a Two-Time Pulitzer Prize Winner*. New York: Plume/Penguin, 1986.

LaRocque, Paula. "It's Not Quantity But Quality That Defines Good Writing." *Quill*, December 1997, p. 19.

Murray, Donald M. *Write to Learn*, 4th ed. New York: Harcourt Brace Jovanovich, 1993.
Reporting on People with Disabilities. Washington, D.C.: Disabilities Committee of the American Society of Newspaper Editors, American Society of Newspaper Editors, 1990.
Rice, Scott. *Right Words, Right Places*. Belmont, Calif.: Wadsworth, 1993.
Roberts, Eugene L., Jr. "Writing for the Reader." *The Red Smith Lecture in Journalism. University of Notre Dame*, Department of American Studies, South Bend, Ind., May 1994.
Zinsser, William. *On Writing Well: An Informal Guide to Writing Nonfiction*, 4th ed. New York: Perennial Library, 1990.

CORRECTING WORDY PHRASES

It is easy to overwrite—use too many words when just one or two will do. Here are examples of wordy phrases and their more concise replacements.

WORDY PHRASE	REPLACEMENT
appoint to the post of	appoint
conduct an investigation into	investigate
rose to the defense of	defended
succeed in doing	do
came to a stop	stopped
devoured by flames	burned
shot to death	shot
have a need for	need
made contact with	met
promoted to the rank of	promoted

Name ______________________ Class ______________________ Date ______

EXERCISE 1

NEWSWRITING STYLE

DISCUSSION QUESTIONS

1. Imagine that you have just been named editor of your city's daily newspaper. Formulate a policy that specifies when your staff can report that a person is "adopted," "illegitimate," "receiving welfare," "gay" or an "ex-convict."

2. Imagine that your city's new mayor, elected today, had never met his father and did not even know his identity. He was raised by his mother, who never married. Would you report that fact while describing the new mayor? Why?

3. You are interviewing a source for a story, and the source uses an offensive stereotypical term about senior citizens. Would you print the word? Why?

4. Suppose a bank in your city today named a woman its president, and she was the first woman to head a bank in your city. Should your local daily publish a story about her promotion that emphasized she was the first woman to hold such a position? Why? Would you publish similar stories when the first women are named to head a local college, a local hospital and a local police department?

5. For one week, examine every story published on the front page of your local daily newspaper. Look for sentences or phrases that are not objective. Why is the sentence or phrase not objective? How would you rewrite it?

6. Think of your favorite television programs. How do the shows portray men? Women? Minorities? The elderly? Do the portrayals foster or break stereotypical images? Why?

7. For one week, examine every story published on the front page of your local daily newspaper. Circle words and phrases that you could replace with simpler ones. Do the simpler words and phrases change the meaning of the story? Why or why not?

Name ______________________ Class ______________________ Date ______

EXERCISE 2

NEWSWRITING STYLE

BEING CONCISE

SECTION I: USING SIMPLE WORDS

Substitute simpler and more common words for each of these words.

1. numerous
2. accomplish
3. ultimate
4. objective
5. imbibe
6. disclose
7. massive
8. utilize
9. expedite
10. apprehend
11. deceased
12. cognizant
13. lacerations
14. currently
15. attempt
16. inquire
17. consume
18. stated
19. obtain
20. commence

SECTION II: AVOIDING REDUNDANT PHRASES

Do not rewrite the following phrases; simply cross off the unnecessary words.

1. accidentally stumbled
2. eliminate altogther
3. qualified expert
4. face up to
5. seldom ever
6. armed gunman
7. bare essentials
8. totally destroyed
9. dangerous weapon
10. postponed until later
11. honest truth
12. future plans

13. awkward predicament
14. fully engulfed
15. dead body
16. cooperate together
17. free of charge
18. in order to
19. acute crisis
20. merge together

SECTION III: AVOIDING WORDY PHRASES

Use a single word to replace each of these phrases.

1. on account of
2. due to the fact that
3. at this point in time
4. in the not-too-distant future
5. take into consideration
6. united together in holy matrimony
7. give rise to
8. made the acquaintance of
9. consensus of opinion
10. despite the fact that
11. on the occasion of
12. arrived at a decision
13. made a motion
14. commented to the effect that
15. file a lawsuit against
16. was in possession of
17. caused injuries to
18. put emphasis on
19. draw to a close
20. gave their approval of

SECTION IV: ELIMINATING UNNECESSARY WORDS

Eliminate the unnecessary words from the following sentences. The sentences do not have to be rewritten; simply cross off the words that are not needed.

1. The T-shirts were free of charge to the first 50 customers.
2. The contractor did a totally complete job on the renovation.
3. The airline faced a crisis situation after the crash.
4. The mayor flatly rejected the ordinance.
5. Police said the armed gunman was caught near the bank.

SECTION V: REWRITING WORDY SENTENCES

Rewrite the following sentences, eliminating as many words as possible and correcting any other errors.

1. The accident victims were taken from the scene of the accident to the hospital in an ambulance.
2. The senator went on to say that the new legislation would leave the program in a state of paralysis.
3. The companys fines were in excess of $25,000.
4. The purpose of the new guidelines is to provide services to as many students as humanly possible.
5. The warden cited a lack of adequate and necessary funds as one of the many reasons prisoners were being released early.

SECTION VI: SIMPLIFYING OVERLOADED SENTENCES

Rewrite the following sentences, shortening and simplifying them and correcting any other errors.

1. Two university students, Jonathan Colson and Marie Parkinson, both seniors and both majoring in business in the Department of Economic Sciences, were driving south on Addison Drive during a thunderstorm when a tree, which was blown down by strong winds, fell across the road in front of them and Colson swerved to avoid the tree before hitting a utility pole with his car and causing more than 10,000 people to lose electricity to their homes.
2. Police officers chased the suspect, who had attempted to rob Robert Ames and his wife, Emily, who live at 1345 Grassland Avenue, of $3,500 in cash and jewelry that was in a small safe in their home, into the park where he tried to climb through the window of a childrens playhouse and got stuck in the window because his belt buckle caught on a protruding nail and officers had to cut the man's belt in order to get him out of the window and charge him with robbery, burglary and resisting arrest.

3. Mary Johnson, who is 51 and lives at 414 West Coast Boulevard and who is an emergency room nurse at Mercy Hospital and was on duty at 3 p.m. yesterday, was surprised when a woman who looked just like her was brought into the emergency room after a minor traffic accident at the intersection of Lakeview Drive and Darlington Avenue in which the woman's car was struck in the rear by a pickup truck while she was stopped at an intersection and Mary began asking the woman questions about her family and past history, discovering that the woman had been adopted, but had been told she had a twin sister who had been adopted by another family when the sisters were three years old, so Mary introduced herself to her long lost twin sister.
4. The mayor said she was more than willing to support the ordinance the city council was proposing to begin the building of a new facility to house elderly city residents who needed to have a place they could go when they could no longer live independently in their own homes, but the cost of such a facility had to fall within the current fiscal realities of the revenue stream city taxes could generate to support such a building program without raising taxes for city residents, which the mayor knows will upset city residents who will hold her responsible for any proposal the city counsel approves in the long run.

Name ______________________ Class ______________________ Date ______

EXERCISE 3

NEWSWRITING STYLE

-ISMS

SECTION I: AVOIDING SEXIST TITLES AND TERMS

Replace these words with ones that include both men and women.

1. fireman
2. workman
3. cameraman
4. councilman
5. salesman
6. chairman
7. policeman
8. mailman
9. assemblyman
10. statesman
11. repairman
12. doorman

SECTION II: AVOIDING EXCLUSIVELY MALE NOUNS AND PRONOUNS

Rewrite the following sentences, eliminating their use of male nouns and pronouns and correcting any other errors.

1. A policeman has to inspect his weapons before going on patrol.
2. Normally, a congressman represents his nation in the trade talks.
3. A paperboy has to get up early to deliver his papers.
4. If a patient is clearly dying of cancer, doctors may give him enough drugs to ease his pain, and perhaps even enough to hasten his death.
5. When a repairman finishes his job, he usually gives his customers a written guarantee that his work meets his industry's standards.

SECTION III: AVOIDING STEREOTYPES

Rewrite the following sentences, avoiding stereotypical language and comments and correcting any other errors.

1. Police said the Hispanic man is wanted in connection with the robbery of the black woman in her home.

2. John Peters, who was accompanied by his wife, Mrs. Paula Peters, an attractive woman dressed in a lavender blouse, tan skirt and black high heel shoes, attended the award ceremony as the first man to be president of the all-female University College.
3. As pressure from 20 men and 60 females protesting the club's policies increased, the spokesman for the club said it had reached a gentleman's agreement with the protesters.
4. Members of the American Indian Movement went on the warpath today when federal agents attempted to interrupt a powwow of tribal elders.
5. The town councilmen, with the exception of the lone female councilman, Margaret Walters, visited the hospital's new maternity ward, where male nurse James Lopez, a Mexican American, helped deliver the first baby.
6. Everyone was surprised and delighted that the old geezer Arnold Wilkinson, who amazingly is a spry 78 years young, was given the award for selling the most new homes in the month of January.

Name ____________________ Class ____________________ Date ________

EXERCISE 4

NEWSWRITING STYLE

TESTING ALL YOUR SKILLS

SECTION I: AVOIDING REDUNDANT PHRASES

The following phrases are redundant. They do not have to be rewritten; simply cross off the unnecessary words.

1. dangerous weapon
2. major breakthrough
3. refer back to
4. melted down
5. appeared on the scene
6. seal off
7. underlying purpose
8. narrow down
9. fully clothed
10. depreciate in value
11. enter into
12. young child
13. announce the names of
14. calm down
15. favored to win
16. radical transformation
17. died suddenly
18. perfectly clear
19. know about
20. conduct a poll

SECTION II: ELIMINATING UNNECESSARY WORDS

Eliminate the unnecessary words from the following sentences. The sentences do not have to be rewritten; simply cross off the words that are not needed.

1. The mayor arrived to speak at the press conference at 10 a.m. in the morning and told reporters she would vote for the newly created ordinance whether or not it was supported by city council.
2. Local residents applauded the major breakthrough in contract negotiations when teachers agreed to make out a list of the complaints against the school superintendent.

3. The newly renovated department store opened its doors to the public for the first time on Thursday and it was perfectly clear people were ready to personally experience one of the last remaining downtown department stores.
4. The chief of police responded by saying that he wanted all members of the police department to combine together their efforts to set a new record in raising charitable funds for the YMCA.
5. She asked the board for their mutual cooperation in developing the new innovation in programming so employees could merge together the company's high technology.

SECTION III: AVOIDING WORDY PHRASES

Substitute a single word for the wordy phrases in the following sentences.

1. The professor told his students he would be releasing their grades in the not-too-distant future.
2. The police department said it had arrested more than 40 motorists for exceeding the speed limit.
3. To be acquainted with the topic, the speaker said she had studied the basic fundamentals of the issue and as a consequence of that study she was ready to address the issue at this point in time.
4. The doctor said he resigned his position as head of the hospital after he found out that the board of directors was in possession of incriminating evidence.
5. All of a sudden, the police officer arrived at a decision to secure the site where the badly decomposed body was found.

SECTION IV: SIMPLIFYING SENTENCES

Rewrite the following sentences to make them more simple and clear and correct any other errors.

1. The attorney for the perpetrator said despite the fact that a dangerous weapon had been found at the scene of the crime it did not necessarily mean that the weapon happened to belong to his current client.

2. According to the currently held belief on the part of the design engineer, Jonathan Emory, who is 56 years old, the important essentials for completing the construction project on time will require an interim period between the design phase and the actual construction.
3. Doctors rushed the boy who had been injured in the collision between two cars at the intersection of Main and King streets into the emergency ward and later said the boy currently was in critically serious condition.
4. Police chased the suspects vehicle through town at a speed estimated to be in the vicinity of 80 miles per hour after it sped away from officers who had arrived at the scene of the accident.
5. While they had not come to a final conclusion in regard to the plans for the new educational program, the members of the school board said that tentatively a total of about more than 800 students would be served.

SECTION V: AVOIDING SEXUAL STEREOTYPES

Rewrite the following sentences, avoiding sexist language and comments.

1. Congressman Janice Byron, a petite 38-year-old mother of two children who has a sunny disposition, voted in favor of the education bill.
2. The girls were planning a trip to Florida even though their husbands wanted to go to the mountains.
3. Michelle Patterson recently was hired as a lineman for the electric company.
4. The senator and his wife, Mrs. James Rueben, an attractive woman who was wearing a pretty yellow flower-print dress, arrived at the airport at noon.
5. A Michigan man and his wife agreed to buy the antique car.

SECTION VI: REMAINING OBJECTIVE

The following sentences do not have to be rewritten; simply cross off the opinionated words and phrases.

1. It was miraculous that only three people were injured in the 20-vehicle chain-reaction collision on the fog-bound interstate.
2. Three soldiers training at a nearby army base died tragically in the helicopter accident despite heroic efforts to save them.
3. The city councilman claimed he was for the wonderful new recreation park, but voted against providing funding for it.
4. Tickets for a game at the new stadium will cost only $30 per person, which is really reasonable.
5. It was such a shame that the school board was unable to arrive at a decision to allow the surprisingly good student choral group to attend the music conference.

SECTION VII: TESTING ALL YOUR SKILLS

Rewrite the following sentences, correcting all their errors.

1. The board was comprised of seven highly educated and well-qualified persons, three men and four girls, two of whom are black and one of whom is Hispanic.
2. The program is free and open to the public, but the program director said it will cost a sum of $5000 to put the program on.
3. It was amazing that the spry 81-year-old man was gainfully employed as a maintenance worker.
4. The incumbent senator, a man with a questionable past, planned to introduce legislation in the not-too-distant future on the grounds that the poor needed jobs.
5. The students decision to protest the plan to implement the reconfiguration of the design for the new student education center angered the university president who was counting on the mutual cooperation of the students.

Name ______________________ Class ______________________ Date ________

EXERCISE 5

NEWSWRITING STYLE

REVIEW

SECTION I: REMAINING OBJECTIVE

Rewrite the following sentences, eliminating all their statements of opinion and other errors. Answer key provided: See Appendix D.

1. The famous speaker, who truly will delight her audience, will discuss the relationship of economics and poverty at tonights interesting presentation.
2. In a startling discovery, police claimed to have identified the despicable man who attacked the poor, defenseless 65-year-old woman.
3. The handsome man was presented with the prestigious award for his efforts on behalf of the agency.
4. Theater-goers are urged to buy their tickets, at a cost of only $20, early for the sensational community theater production of "Cats," which can look forward to a long run in the city.
5. Another important point was the boards decision to end the contract for water service with the company.

SECTION II: AVOIDING REDUNDANT PHRASES

The following phrases are redundant. They do not have to be rewritten; simply cross off the unnecessary words.

1. ultimate conclusion
2. personal experience
3. tracked down
4. tangled together
5. viable solution
6. root cause
7. hoist up
8. exactly identical
9. unpaid debt
10. green in color

SECTION III: AVOIDING WORDY PHRASES

Substitute a single word for each of the following phrases.

1. face up to
2. made good an escape
3. summoned to the scene
4. never at any time
5. exchanged wedding vows
6. a great deal of
7. be acquainted with
8. conducted an investigation of
9. postpone until later
10. favored to win

SECTION IV: AVOIDING UNNECESSARY WORDS

The following sentences do not have to be rewritten; simply cross off the unnecessary words.

1. Firefighters responding to the scene of the blaze found the warehouse fully engulfed in flames.
2. There is a possibility the board may postpone until later a decision on rezoning the city park.
3. The city council commented to the effect that no qualified experts were consulted in the report.
4. The woman set an all-time record in the marathon despite the fact that she was having muscle cramps the last two miles of the race.
5. The accident occurred when the driver of the pickup truck failed to yield the right of way.

SECTION V: TESTING ALL YOUR SKILLS

Rewrite the following sentences, correcting all their errors.

1. She sustained a broken leg and the loss of her sight in the accident.
2. The attorney was in possession of evidence that helped the jury to arrive at a decision.
3. It was the consensus of opinion of councilman Janet Rose and the others that the massively huge budget increase be eliminated altogether.

4. Police decided to release the Native American suspect from custody due to the fact that he was not identified as the armed gunman.
5. An attractive young brunette, Donna Moronesi, seems to be an unlikely candidate for the office, but she has surprisingly raised more than 1 million dollars before the campaign has even begun.
6. The informative information was presented at this point in time because all the members of the board were present and accounted for and would be able to vote on the proposal to increase contributions to the employees retirement accounts.
7. The purpose of the article is to examine the problems of migrant workers.
8. As a matter of fact, the mayor claimed she had already considered the attorneys proposal, but the terms of the agreement to settle with the bitter old man who filed a lawsuit against the city over the death of his dog which had been taken to the city pound was not in accordance with the best interests of the city and its local residents.
9. Mike Deacosta, his wife and their two children, Mark and Amy, were invited to meet the president.
10. Before a young child can begin school, they must be able to read and write their name.
11. The state representative gave a favorable recommendation to a proposal to purchase 150 acres of land near the capital to be combined together with the already existing 300 acres of the park to provide more recreation space.
12. The sheriff cited overcrowded conditions in the county jail as one of the reasons why he made an investigation of the possibility of getting a federal grant.

CHAPTER 4

THE LANGUAGE OF NEWS

The right to express yourself is not something that's inherently part of being a journalist; it's part of being a human being.

(Kanthan Pillay, South African newspaper editor)

"I'm nauseous," she said.

No, she wasn't. No matter how much her stomach churned or how strongly she felt the need to vomit, she was not nauseous. She was nauseated.

What's the difference? "Nauseous" is an adjective describing something that causes one to feel sick, such as an odor. "Nauseated" is a form of the verb that means to feel nausea. The words are used the same way as the words "poisonous" and "poisoned." One who has just ingested a lethal dose of arsenic would not exclaim, "Help! I'm poisonous!"

Learning what words mean and using them appropriately is one of the basic skills of a journalist. Good writers choose words that carry the intended meaning and assemble those words in sentences and paragraphs that paint an accurate and lively picture of the world in which they and their audiences live.

THE EFFECTIVENESS OF WORDS

Writers sometimes do not understand the words they use. Other times they fail to express their ideas clearly and precisely. In such cases, the sentences they write may state the obvious (or impossible), or they may carry unintended, often comical, meanings. Consider these examples:

> Gothic architecture is distinguished by flying buttocks.
>
> The horror gender is a complex field to study.
>
> Rural life is found mostly in the country.
>
> That summer I finally got my leg operated on, and what a relief! It had been hanging over my head for years.
>
> Theodore Roosevelt was saddened when his young wife died and went to a ranch in the Dakotas.

People expect more of journalists, who must master the English language. When news organizations hire a new reporter, they look for someone who understands and respects the language, knows spelling and grammar, possesses an extensive vocabulary and writes in a clear and interesting manner. Even careful writers make mistakes, sometimes hilarious ones. But if the errors become too numerous, they can damage a news organization's credibility and force it to print or broadcast costly and embarrassing corrections.

The men and women who devote their lives to journalism develop a respect for the language. They value prose that is clear, concise and accurate. They strive to select the exact word needed to convey an idea, use the word properly and place it in a sentence that is grammatically correct.

When a major event occurs, such as the Sept. 11 attack on the World Trade Center and the Pentagon or the war in Iraq, dozens and sometimes hundreds of journalists rush to the scene, gather information and then transmit it to the public. All journalists write about the same event, but some stories are much better than others. Why?

Some reporters are particularly adept at gathering the information needed to write exceptional stories. Other reporters produce exceptional stories because of their command of the English language. Their language is forceful, and their stories are written so clearly and simply that everyone can understand them. These reporters describe people, places and events involved in news stories and use quotations that enable those people to speak directly to the public.

Skilled reporters can transform even routine events into front-page stories. A reporter who is unimaginative about or indifferent to a topic may write a three-paragraph story that, because of its mediocre writing, will not be used. Another reporter, excited by the same topic, may go beyond the superficial—ask more questions, uncover unusual developments and inject color into the story. The second reporter may write a 20- or 30-inch story about the topic that, because of the reporter's command of language and excellent use of words, gets published at the top of Page 1.

BE PRECISE

To communicate effectively, reporters must be precise, particularly in their selection of words. Mark Twain wrote, "The difference between the right word and the almost right word is the difference between lightning and the lightning bug." The perfect choice makes a sentence forceful and interesting; imprecision creates confusion and misunderstanding.

Some words simply are inappropriate in news stories. Few editors or news directors permit the use of words such as "cop" or "kid" (unless the reporter is referring to a goat), or derogatory terms about a person's race or religion. News executives allow profanity only when it is essential to a story's meaning; even then, they refuse to publish the most offensive terms. They prefer the word "woman" to the archaic "lady." Many ban the use of contractions ("isn't," "can't," "don't") except in direct quotations. Professional journalists also object to using nouns as verbs. They would not write that someone "authored" a book, a city "headquartered" a company or an event "impacted" a community. Nor would they allow a reporter to write that food prices were "upped," plans "finalized" or children "parented."

Some errors occur because the reporter is unaware of a word's exact meaning. Few journalists would report that a car "collided" with a tree, a "funeral service" was held, a gunman "executed" his victim or a child "was drowned" in a lake. Why? Two objects collide only if both are moving; thus, a car can strike a tree but never "collide" with one. The term "funeral service" is redundant. "Executed" means put to death in accordance with a legally imposed sentence; therefore, only a state—never a murderer—can execute anyone. A report that a child "was drowned" would imply that someone held the child's head underwater until the victim died.

Such considerations are not trivial. Journalists who do not use words correctly can confuse or irritate their audience, undermining their credibility and causing their audience to question

THE FAR SIDE By GARY LARSON

"So, then . . . Would that be 'us the people' or 'we the people?'"

the accuracy of their stories. Thus, instructors will object when students use language that is sloppy and inaccurate.

Sloppy use of words can creep into anyone's writing. The word "epicenter," for example, means the point on the earth's surface directly above the source of an earthquake. "Epicenter" is often misused, however, as a synonym for "center." A story in The New York Times described the cult that has grown up around Harley-Davidson motorcycles and said: "This summer Milwaukee will be the cult's epicenter. More than 250,000 people and 10,000 Harleys are expected to converge for the centenary celebration. . . ." But the motorcyclists and their Harleys were going to gather in Milwaukee, not thousands of feet underneath the city. If all the writer means is that Milwaukee will be the center of activities for Harley riders, then "epi-" adds nothing to the sentence except confusion.

Another misused phrase is "beg the question." Begging the question is a logical fallacy in which a person constructs an argument using the conclusion he or she wishes to prove as a premise. Here's an example of an argument that begs the question: "Capitalist economies allow the greatest room for the exercise of individual initiative. Therefore, business owners in capitalist societies have the most opportunity to profit from their initiative." The premise and the conclusion in this example are saying the same thing. When the phrase "beg the question" appears in news stories, however, it usually is used as a synonym for "raise the question" or "ask the question," as in a passage from a Boston Herald sports story. The story said New England Patriots cornerback Tyrone Poole seemed dissatisfied even though he had signed a $6 million, four-year contract just months earlier: "Now Poole is hinting he wants out, which begs the question: What changed?"

When reporters fail to express their ideas clearly and precisely, audiences can derive meanings different from the one intended. The unintended meaning may be difficult for the writer to detect. Double meanings in the following headlines, all of which appeared in newspapers, illustrate the problem:

> Council Stands Against Drugs and Biting Dogs
> Breast implants prominent
> Juvenile Court to Try Shooting Defendant
> Japanese scientists grow frog eyes and ears
> Police Say Man Hid Crack in Buttocks
> Astronauts Practice Landing on Laptops
> Doughnut hole, nude dancing on council table

While readers often consider the double meanings humorous, few editors or news directors are amused when such errors appear. Yet even the best news organizations occasionally make mistakes. Here is an example from The New York Times:

> The State Health Department is surveying hospitals around the state to ascertain whether women patients are being given Pap tests to determine if they have uterine cancer as required by law.

Confusion sometimes arises because words look or sound alike. For example, a story reported, "About 40 years ago, she left her native Cypress for New York City and set up a bakery on Ninth Avenue near 40th Street." Few people are born in trees, and an editor wondered, "Could that have been 'Cyprus'?"

College students often confuse words such as "buses" and "busses," "naval" and "navel," and "reckless" and "wreckless." The word "busses" refers to kisses, not the vehicles people ride in. A "navel" is a belly button, and some motorists drive "wrecks," but are convicted of "reckless" driving.

USE STRONG VERBS

Verbs can transform a drab sentence into an interesting—or even horrifying—one. Notice the impact of "crashed," "collapsed," "rocked" and "spread" in the lead paragraph from an Associated Press story about the terrorist attacks on the World Trade Center and the Pentagon:

> NEW YORK (AP)—In a horrific sequence of destruction, terrorists crashed two planes into the World Trade Center, and the twin 110-story towers collapsed Tuesday morning. Explosions also rocked the Pentagon and spread fear across the nation.

Strong verbs like these help readers or listeners envision the events described in the stories—they paint a vivid picture for readers. The following sentences are also colorful, interesting and vivid. Why? Because the college students who wrote them used descriptive verbs:

> A cargo door *popped* open, *tearing* a hole in the plane's side. Eleven passengers *sucked* out of the hole *plunged* 30,000 feet to their deaths.

> A gunman *jumped* behind the customer service counter of a department store Monday, *grabbed* a handful of money—then *fled* on a bicycle.

By comparison, the following sentences are weak and bland, yet it is easy to improve them. Simply add a strong verb:

> The murder suspect was taken into custody by police.
> REVISED: Police arrested the murder suspect.

> The man was killed when he was struck by the speeding car.
> REVISED: The speeding car struck and killed the man.

Strong verbs describe one specific action. Weak verbs cover a number of different actions. The first sentence below is vague and bland because it uses a weak verb. The last three use specific, descriptive verbs and are more informative:

His brother got a personal computer.
His brother bought a personal computer.
His brother won a personal computer.
His brother stole a personal computer.

Avoid the repeated use of forms of the verb "to be," such as "is," "are," "was" and "were." These verbs are overused, weak and dull—especially when a writer uses them in combination with a past participle to form a passive-voice verb, such as "was captured." Sentences using passive verbs are also wordier than those with active ones:

It is believed by the homeowners that the man broke into their homes. (13 words)
REVISED: Homeowners believe the man broke into their homes. (8 words)

The campaign was supported by the students. (7 words)
REVISED: Students supported the campaign. (4 words)

A sharp criticism of the plan was voiced by the mayor. (11 words)
REVISED: The mayor sharply criticized the plan. (6 words)

Police officers were summoned to the scene by a neighbor. (10 words)
REVISED: A neighbor called the police. (5 words)

AVOIDING PROBLEMS IN YOUR WRITING

Good writing requires thought and hard work. Reporters have to think about the best words to use to get their ideas across to their audience—and the best words may not be the first ones they write down. That's where the hard work comes in—reporters have to edit their work. Editing and rewriting can help reporters find better words. The following sections identify problem areas writers should watch for.

WORDS TO AVOID

Adjectives and Adverbs

Newswriters avoid adverbs and adjectives, since they tend to be less forceful, specific and objective than nouns and verbs. William Strunk Jr. and E.B. White, authors of the influential book "The Elements of Style," wrote, "The adjective hasn't been built that can pull a weak or inaccurate noun out of a tight place." Along the same lines, Mark Twain warned, "When you catch an adjective, kill it."

Most adverbs and adjectives are unnecessary. They waste space by stating the obvious, and they may unintentionally inject a reporter's opinion into the story. If you write about a child's funeral, you do not have to comment that the mourners were "sad-faced," the scene "grim" and the parents "grief-stricken." Nor is there reason to report that an author is "famous," a witness "alert" or an accident "tragic."

Adverbs and adjectives in the following sentences editorialize. Rather than simply reporting the facts, they comment on those facts:

It was not until Monday that university officials finally released the report.
REVISED: University officials released the report Monday.

Upon hearing about the frivolous lawsuit, the mayor made it quite clear that she plans to fight the outrageous suit.
REVISED: Upon hearing about the lawsuit, the mayor said she plans to fight it.

The word "finally" in the first sentence implies university officials were negligent and should have released the report sooner. Similarly, if you report the facts in the second story clearly and concisely, you should not have to add that the lawsuit was "frivolous" or "outrageous." Also avoid concluding that the mayor made anything "clear."

Clichés

Clichés are words or phrases that writers have heard and copied over and over. Many are 200 or 300 years old—so old and overused that they have lost their original impact and meaning. Clichés no longer startle, amuse or interest the public. Because they eliminate the need for thought, clichés have been called the greatest labor-saving devices ever invented.

The news media can take a fresh phrase and overuse it so that it quickly becomes a cliché. Presidential candidate H. Ross Perot opposed the North American Free Trade Agreement on the grounds that it would eliminate American jobs. He said the migration of jobs to Mexico would create a "giant sucking sound." The phrase was fresh and effective when Perot first said it in a presidential debate, but journalists and others soon nearly wore it out. After the U.S. military announced it would open the Second Gulf War with a bombing campaign that would "shock and awe" Iraqis, the phrase "shock and awe" started appearing in stories dealing with such topics as football, the economy and insect invasions. Soon, the phrase aroused only disgust and boredom. Other phrases The American Journalism Review has identified as clichés are "contrary to popular belief," "hand-wringing," "no laughing matter" and "own worst enemy."

Journalists employ clichés when they lack the time (or talent) to find words more specific, descriptive or original. So a reporter under deadline pressure may say that a fire "swept through" a building, an explosion "rocked" a city, police officers gave a suspect a "spirited chase" or protesters were an "angry mob."

Other clichés exaggerate. Few people are really as "blind as a bat," "cool as a cucumber," "light as a feather," "neat as a pin," "straight as an arrow," "thin as a rail" or "white as a sheet."

You are likely to be so familiar with clichés that you can complete them after seeing just the first few words. Want to try? The final word is missing from the following clichés, yet you are likely to complete all 10:

a close brush with ____________	has a nose for ____________
a step in the right ____________	last but not ____________
could not believe her ____________	left holding the ____________
evidence of foul ____________	lived to a ripe old ____________
fell into the wrong ____________	lying in a pool of ____________

Political reporting is especially susceptible to clichés. It seems as though candidates always are nominated in "smoke-filled rooms" or "test the waters" before "tossing their hats into the ring." Other candidates launch "whirlwind campaigns" and "hammer away" at their opponents, or they employ "spin doctors" to control unfavorable news. Some candidates "straddle the fence" on the "burning issues of the day." However, few "give up without a fight."

Some clichés are so closely associated with newswriting that they are called "journalese." The term identifies phrases reporters use to dramatize, exaggerate and sometimes distort the events they describe. In news stories, fires "rage," temperatures "soar," earthquakes "rumble" and people "vow." Rivers "go on a rampage." Third World countries are often "war-torn" or "much-troubled." Sometimes they are "oil-rich." Politicians who get in trouble are "scandal-plagued." If the scandal lasts long enough, reporters will create a name for it by tacking the suffix "gate" (which began with the Watergate scandal of the Nixon era) to the appropriate noun, as in "Irangate" (during the Reagan presidency), "Travelgate" and "Monicagate," also called "Zippergate" (during Clinton's presidency).

Journalese is common on sports pages. Sports reporters and copy editors fear overusing the word "won" to describe the outcomes of contests. Instead, especially in headlines, they report that one team "ambushed," "bombed," "flattened," "nipped," "outlasted," "scorched," "stunned," "thrashed" or "walloped" another.

Sometimes a cliché can be twisted into a fresh expression or used in a surprising way, as in this sentence from a New York Times story about a National Basketball Association cham-

CLICHÉS

There are thousands of clichés and slang phrases that reporters must learn to recognize and avoid. Some of the most common are listed here.

a keen mind
ambulance rushed
around the clock
arrived at the scene
at long last
at this point in time
baptism by fire
bare minimum
beginning a new life
behind the wheel
benefit of the doubt
bigger and better
blanket of snow
blessing in disguise
called to the scene
calm before the storm
came to their rescue
came to rest
came under attack
came under fire
cast aside
caught red-handed
clear-cut issue
colorful scene
complete stranger
complete success
coveted title
crystal clear
dead and buried
decide the fate
devoured by flames
dime a dozen
doomed to failure
dread disease
dream come true
drop in the bucket
dying breed
erupted in violence
escaped death
exchanged gunfire
faced an uphill battle
fell on deaf ears
few and far between
foreseeable future
gained ground
gave it their blessing
get a good look
go to the polls
got off to a good start
grief-stricken
ground to a halt
hail of bullets
heated argument
heed the warning
high-speed chase
hits the spot
in his new position
in the wake of
landed the job
last but not least
last-ditch stand
left their mark
leveled an attack
limped into port
line of fire
lingering illness
lodge a complaint
lucky to be alive
made off with
made their escape
made their way home
miraculous escape
Mother Nature
necessary evil
never a dull moment
no relief in sight
notified next of kin
once in a lifetime
one step closer
in the mix
opened fire
paved the way
pillar of strength
pinpointed the cause
pitched battle
police dragnet
pose a challenge
proud parents
proves conclusively
pushed for legislation
quick thinking
real challenge
reign of terror
see-saw battle
set to work
smell a rat
sped to the scene
spread like wildfire
start their mission
still at large
stranger than fiction
strike a nerve
sudden death
sweep under the rug
take it easy
talk is cheap
tempers flared
time will tell
tip of the iceberg
tipped the scales
took its toll
too late to turn back
tower of strength
tracked down
traveled the globe
tried their luck
under siege
under their noses
undertaking a study
up in the air
view with alarm
went to great lengths
won a reputation
word of caution
words of wisdom
word to the wise

pionship series between the New York Knicks and the Houston Rockets: "It is the city that never sleeps versus the city that never wins." Chief Justice William Rehnquist enlivened another cliché in an opinion he wrote for the U.S. Supreme Court upholding an Indiana law that prohibits totally nude dancing. "Indiana's requirement that the dancers wear at least pasties and a G-string is modest, and the bare minimum necessary to achieve the state's purpose" in protecting public morality, Rehnquist wrote. Such opportunities for the effective use of clichés are rare.

Clichés that journalists should recognize and avoid appear in the box on the facing page.

Slang

Journalists avoid slang, which tends to be more faddish than clichés. Some words that started out as slang have won acceptance as standard English. "Blizzard," "flabbergast" and "GI" (for soldier) are among such terms. Most slang never makes this transition, however.

Feature stories and personality profiles sometimes employ slang effectively, but it is inappropriate in straight news stories because it is too informal and annoying. Moreover, slang may baffle readers who are not of the right age or ethnic group to understand it.

Slang rapidly becomes dated, so that a term used in a story may already be obsolete. During the 1970s and 1980s, young people overused such terms as "cool," "freaked out," "heavy," "gnarly" and "radical." By the 1990s, young people found a whole new set of "slammin'" slang terms and "dissed" anyone still using the slang of the 1980s as a "Melvin." Youths in the 21st century "bounced" the old slang and now "chill" with their "homeys," show off their "tight" "bling-bling" and look for a "phat" girlfriend or boyfriend.

Slang also conveys meanings journalists may want to avoid. It often expresses a person's attitude toward something. Thus, slang terms such as "flaky," "ego trip" and "flatfoot" convey evaluations—often negative and stereotypical—of the things described. Reporters, however, should leave to editorial writers or readers and viewers the job of making evaluations.

Technical Language and Jargon

Nearly every trade or profession develops its own technical language or jargon. When professionals use jargon to impress or mislead the public, critics call it gobbledygook, bafflegab, doublespeak or bureaucratese. Most jargon is abstract, wordy, repetitious and confusing. For example, a government agency warned, "There exists at the intersection a traffic condition which constitutes an intolerable, dangerous hazard to the health and safety of property and persons utilizing such intersection for pedestrian and vehicular movement." That sentence contains 31 words. A good journalist could summarize it in four: "The intersection is dangerous."

Many sources reporters routinely use—doctors, lawyers, business people, press releases, technical reports, and police and court records—speak in jargon. Journalists must translate that jargon into plain English. Here are two examples:

> JARGON: Identification of the victim is being withheld pending notification of his next of kin.
> REVISED: Police are withholding the victim's name until his family has been notified.
>
> JARGON: Dr. Stewart McKay said, "Ethnic groups that subsist on a vegetarian diet and practically no meat products seem to have a much lower level of serum cholesterol and a very low incidence of ischemic diseases arising from atherosclerotic disease."
> REVISED: Dr. Stewart McKay said ethnic groups that eat little meat have low rates of coronary heart disease and related illnesses.

Americans expect teachers to set a good example for their students by writing clearly and accurately, but even teachers succumb to jargon. Some call themselves "educators" or "instructional units." Desks have become "pupil work stations"; libraries, "instructional resource centers"; hallways, "behavior-transition corridors"; and schools, "attendance centers." A principal in Houston sent this note home to parents:

> Our school's cross-graded, multi-ethnic, individual learning program is designed to enhance the concept of an open-ended learning program with emphasis on a continuum of multi-ethnic, academically enriched learning using the identified intellectually gifted child as the agent or director of his own learning.

This passage translates as "Our curriculum lets the gifted student learn at his or her own pace." Why do people use jargon unnecessarily? Probably they want to make themselves and everything they say seem more important.

Readers usually can decipher the jargon's meaning, but not easily. Sometimes jargon is almost impossible to understand:

> The semiotic perspective promotes a reflective mode of thinking that requires attention to specific contextual clues and relates them to one's understanding of the world with a kind of "informed skepticism" that the authors believe is fundamental to critical thinking.

This kind of technical language may be appropriate in some specialized publications written for the experts in a particular field. It is not appropriate in newspapers written for a mass audience.

Euphemisms

Euphemisms are vague expressions used in place of harsher, more offensive terms. Some etiquette experts say that good manners require the use of euphemisms. Prudishly, Americans often say that a woman is "expecting" rather than "pregnant," and that they have to "go to the washroom" rather than "go to the toilet." Other examples of euphemisms preferred by Americans are "donkey" for "ass," "intestinal fortitude" for "guts" and "affirmative action" for "minority hiring."

Whatever value euphemisms have for etiquette, they detract from good news writing, in which clarity and precision are the most important goals. Geneva Overholser, a former ombudsman at The Washington Post, has said journalists need to realize that they sometimes hurt or offend people when they report incidents involving sexist and racist speech. Nevertheless, she said, the fear of giving offense should not interfere with the journalist's obligation to report

Reprinted with permission of United Features Syndicate.

facts and situations readers need to know. The (New Orleans) Times-Picayune put that principle into practice when it covered the Louisiana gubernatorial campaign of David Duke, who had a history of involvement with the Ku Klux Klan. When Duke urged a return to "neighborhood schools," the Times-Picayune reported that Duke was using the phrase as a euphemism for "segregated schools."

Because newspapers are written for a general audience, words or phrases that could offend members of the audience are rarely, if ever, used. As Kelly Luvison, publisher of the Hornell (N.Y.) Evening Tribune and a group executive for Liberty Group Publishing, said, "It's not worth losing one subscriber just so a reporter can feel like he or she is titillating the audience with an obscene or offensive word." But sometimes news events force reporters to use descriptive words in place of confusing and awkward euphemisms. An example is the case of Lorena Bobbitt, the Virginia woman who used a kitchen knife to cut off her husband's penis in 1993 after he allegedly raped her.[1] The word "penis" rarely had appeared in news stories, and some news organizations were squeamish about using it, especially in headlines. Euphemisms like "member," "organ" or "offending organ" appeared instead. The widespread coverage the Bobbitt case received apparently diminished journalistic sensitivity to the word. A computer search found more than 1,000 news stories that used the word "penis" in the six months after the Bobbitt story broke, compared to only 20 mentions in the previous six months.

A similar phenomenon occurred with the Monica Lewinsky scandal during Bill Clinton's presidency, as many reporters and news anchors found themselves writing and talking about oral sex and semen stains.

As with sex, Americans often employ euphemisms when talking about death. They say that a friend or relative "passed on" or is "no longer with us," not that he or she has died and been buried. Hospitals report a "negative patient outcome," not that a patient died. Funeral directors object to being called "morticians"—a word that itself was originally a euphemism for "undertakers."

During a recession, major companies lay off thousands of employees. Few admit it, however. Instead, corporate executives say they are "restructuring," "downsizing" or "rightsizing" to get rid of "excess workers." Some executives insist such "reductions in force" offer their employees "career enhancement opportunities."

The prestigious titles that some Americans give their jobs are euphemisms. Garbage collectors call themselves "sanitation workers"; prison guards have become "corrections officers," and dogcatchers are "animal welfare officers."

War spawns grotesque euphemisms, perhaps, as some critics say, to hide the human pain and suffering every war causes. Killing the enemy has become "servicing the target." Airplanes no longer bomb enemy soldiers; instead they "visit a site." And if, while bombing enemy troops, soldiers kill some civilians, that is "collateral damage." The United States calls the largest of its land-based nuclear missiles "Peacekeepers." During the First Gulf War, the U.S. military rarely admitted that American soldiers captured by Iraqi troops were tortured. Instead, briefing officers said, "Allied personnel being forcibly detained appear to be under considerable duress." Finally, modern armies no longer retreat. Instead, they "move to the rear," "engage in a strategic withdrawal" or "occupy new territory in accordance with plan."

OTHER PROBLEMS TO AVOID

Avoid Stating the Obvious: Platitudes

Dull, trite, obvious remarks are called "platitudes," and journalists must learn to avoid them. Platitudes that have appeared in news stories include:

> As it has in most areas of modern life, science has entered the profession of firefighting in recent years.
>
> Superhighways, high-speed automobiles and jet planes are common objects of the modern era.

---

[1]The husband, John Wayne Bobbitt, was charged with marital sexual assault but was acquitted. Lorena Bobbitt was prosecuted for malicious wounding but was found innocent by reason of temporary insanity.

The second example appeared in a story about technological changes that had occurred during the life of a 100-year-old woman. The sentence would have been more interesting if it had described the changes in more detail and clearly related them to the woman's life, such as:

> Lila Hansen once spent three days on a train to visit relatives in California. Now, she flies there in three hours every Christmas.

Students have included these platitudes in their stories:

> Counselors help students with their problems.
>
> The mayor said she was pleased by the warm reception.
>
> The sponsors hope the art show will attract a large crowd.

The writers of these stories were quoting sources who were stating the obvious. Platitudes make for dull quotations, and dull quotations should be deleted:

> The newly elected mayor said, "I hope to do a good job."
>
> The committee chair said, "Homecoming weekend is going to be big and exciting."

When people stop reading a story, they rarely think about why it bored them. If they reexamine the story, they might realize it is just a series of platitudes. Platitudes say nothing that hasn't been heard before. Thus, people might quit reading the story because it is no longer interesting or newsworthy.

To avoid platitudes, reporters must be alert, particularly when conducting interviews. Sources often give obvious, commonplace answers to questions they are asked. If a bartender is robbed at gunpoint, there is no reason to quote him as saying he was scared. Most people confronted by guns are scared, and they often say so. If journalists wanted to quote the bartender—or any other source—they would have to ask more penetrating questions until they received more specific, interesting or unusual details.

Avoid First-Person References

Except in extraordinary circumstances, journalists should remain neutral bystanders. They should not mention themselves in news stories. Journalists should not use the words "I," "me," "we" or "us," except when they are directly quoting some other person.

Beginning reporters sometimes use "we" or "us" when referring to the community in which they work or the United States. Although USA Today has adopted that usage as its style, most newswriters refrain from using the first person. When first-person pronouns appear outside quotation marks, readers usually conclude the writer is editorializing about the subject:

> He said we must work harder to improve the city's schools.
> REVISED: He said parents must work harder to improve the city's schools.
>
> The governor said we are being hurt by inflation.
> REVISED: The governor said state residents are being hurt by inflation.

Avoid the Negative

For clarity, avoid negative constructions. Sentences should be cast in positive rather than negative form, as in the following examples:

> The student did not often come to class.
> REVISED: The student rarely came to class.
>
> The defense attorney tried to disprove her client's sanity.
> REVISED: The defense attorney tried to prove her client was insane.

Sentences containing two or three negatives are wordy and even more difficult to decipher. As you read the following examples, you may have to pause to determine their meaning:

> The women said they are not against the change.
> REVISED: The women said they favor the change.

The senator said she would not accept any campaign contributions from people who do not live in her district.

REVISED: The senator said she would accept campaign contributions only from people living in her district.

In most cases, you can correct the problem by changing just a word or two:

Most people are not careful readers.
REVISED: Few people are careful readers.

The financial planner said he could help people not go into debt.
REVISED: The financial planner said he could help people avoid debt.

Avoid an Echo

An echo is a redundancy or the unnecessary repetition of a word. Good writing avoids an echo by eliminating redundant words or phrases:

Her annual salary was $29,000 a year.
REVISED: Her annual salary was $29,000.

In Japan, cancer patients are usually not told they have cancer.
REVISED: In Japan, patients usually are not told they have cancer.

Writers sometimes repeat a key word or phrase for emphasis or to demonstrate an important similarity. If the repetition is needless, however, the result is likely to be awkward, distracting or confusing.

Avoid Gush

Reporters also avoid "gush"—writing with exaggerated enthusiasm. They write news stories to inform members of a community, not to please their sources. News stories should report useful information. They should not praise or advocate.

Two ways to avoid gush are to always use more than one source for a story and to demand that sources provide specific details to support their generalizations. Using multiple sources who are independent of one another prevents reporters from being misled or manipulated by sources seeking favorable publicity. And by insisting that sources provide details and specific examples to support their claims, reporters can minimize the tendency of sources to engage in the kind of self-praise found in these examples:

"We feel we are providing quality recreational programs for both adults and children," Holden said.

Police Chief Barry Kopperud said the city's mounted horse patrol, which began one year ago, has become a great success.

When a journalist finishes an article, it should sound like a news story, not a press release. Yet, one travel story gushed that Mexico is "a land of lush valleys and marvelous people." Other examples of gush include:

The fair will offer bigger and better attractions than ever before.

The event will provide fun and surprises for everyone who attends.

This gush cannot be rewritten, because there is nothing of substance to rewrite. It simply should be deleted.

There is a second type of gush—an escalation in modifiers. Columnist Donna Neely explains that what used to be called "funny" is now called "hilarious" and what used to be "great" is now "fantastic" or "incredible."

Exaggerations appear everywhere: in news stories, press releases, advertisements and everyday speech. Sportswriters call athletes not just "stars" but "superstars." Advertisers call their inventories "fabulous" and their sales "gigantic." Delete all such modifiers or replace them with facts and details and let readers and viewers decide for themselves what adjectives are appropriate.

Avoid Vague Time References

Unless your instructor tells you otherwise, do not use "yesterday" or "tomorrow" in print news stories to refer to a specific day, and use "today" and "tonight" to refer only to the day of publication. Instead, use the day of the week—Monday, Tuesday and so forth—to date events that occur within seven days before or after the day of publication. For events that are more than seven days in the past or future, use a specific date, such as July 23 or March 4. Using date or day of the week eliminates the confusion that might arise with the use of "today," "tomorrow" or "yesterday" in news stories that are written a day or more in advance of their publication.

For example, if a fire destroyed a home at 5 p.m. Tuesday, a reporter would write the story later that evening for publication in the Wednesday newspaper. If the reporter wrote that the fire happened "today," readers would think "today" means the day they are reading the story—Wednesday. If the reporter is writing about an event that will happen on the day of publication, the use of "today" is appropriate, as in this sentence: "The concert will begin at 3 p.m. today."

"Yesterday," "today" and "tomorrow" may be used in direct quotations, and they may be used to refer to the past, present or future in general and not to specific days. Journalists also avoid the word "recently" because it is too vague.

Avoid the Present Tense

Print journalists avoid the present tense and terms such as "at the present time" because many of the events they report end before readers receive the newspaper. A reporter working on deadline should not say, "A fire at the Grand Hotel threatens to destroy the entire block." Firefighters almost certainly would have extinguished the blaze before readers received the paper hours later. For the same reason, a reporter covering a fatal accident should not say, "The victim's identity is not known." Police might learn the victim's identity in a few hours, and local radio and television stations might broadcast the person's name before subscribers received their papers. Consequently, print journalists must use the past tense:

> A fire at the Grand Hotel threatens to destroy the entire block.
> REVISED: A fire at the Grand Hotel was threatening to destroy the entire block at 11:30 p.m.

> The victim's identity is not known.
> REVISED: Police were unable to learn the victim's identity immediately.

Avoid Excessive Punctuation

Journalists avoid excessive punctuation, particularly exclamation points, dashes and parentheses. Exclamation points are rarely necessary and should never be used after every sentence in a story, regardless of that story's importance. Parentheses interrupt the flow of ideas and force people to pause and assimilate some additional, often jarring, bit of information:

> She (the governor) said the elderly population (people 65 and older) had grown twice as fast as any other segment of the state's population during the last 20 years.
> REVISED: The governor said the percentage of people 65 and older had grown twice as fast as any other segment of the state's population during the last 20 years.

Sources use a lot of pronouns and vague references. Students often quote these sources, adding explanations within parentheses. If an explanation is necessary, then a direct quote is not a good idea. Instead, reporters use partial quotes or paraphrase what a source has said:

> "I wish they (school administrators) would quit fooling around," she said. "They say they don't have enough money (to hire more teachers), but I don't believe that. I know they have it (the money); it's just a matter of priorities—of using their money more wisely."
> REVISED: She said the school administrators should "quit fooling around." They say they do not have enough money to hire more teachers, but she does not believe that. "It's just a matter of priorities—of using their money more wisely," she said.

CHECKLIST FOR THE LANGUAGE OF NEWS

1. Choose words that convey your meaning as precisely as possible. Write your story with detail and explanation, so it answers all the questions one logically might ask about the topic.
2. Use active verbs and vivid nouns.
3. Prune adjectives and adverbs from your sentences.
4. Avoid clichés, journalese, slang and euphemisms.
5. Avoid loaded words and opinionated or artificial labels.
6. Avoid mentioning yourself in the story and using the words "I," "me," "we," "us" and "our," except in direct quotations from a source.
7. Avoid misleading statements about the time of the story. Use the specific day of the week or the date—not "yesterday," "today" or "tomorrow."
8. Avoid gush, exaggeration, contrived labels and excessive punctuation.
9. Avoid an echo: Do not unnecessarily repeat the same word in a sentence.
10. Avoid platitudes: Do not state the obvious, such as the fact that a government official was happy to be elected.
11. Avoid the present tense when writing for print media; most events you write about already will have occurred.
12. Cast your sentences in positive rather than negative form.

THE WRITING COACH

BECOME A POWER LIFTER WHEN PICKING VERBS

By **Joe Hight**
Managing Editor of The Oklahoman

Consider stronger verbs in your sentences if you want to become a Hercules—or Hemingway—of writers.

These are verbs that are specific, active and descriptive. They pace your sentence like a smoothly running engine in a Corvette. They strengthen your voice in writing. As Gary Provost writes in "100 Ways to Improve Your Writing," they are the executives of sentences—the primary source of energy in your sentences.

This means writers should avoid the passive voice whenever possible. In "On Writing Well," William Zinsser writes, "The difference between the active-verb style and the passive-verb style—in pace, clarity and vigor—is the difference between life and death for a writer."

Likewise, avoid weak linking verbs such as is (there is, for example) and has. Avoid verbal phrases that carry unnecessary prepositional phrases, abstract nouns or adjectives. Avoid extending verbs with the suffix "ize."

Often, reporters think they can strengthen their sentences by substituting longer verbs such as "purchase" for "buy" or "conclude" for "end." However, they're mistaken, writes Jeffrey McQuain in "Power Language." He quotes poet Oliver Wendell Holmes Sr., father of the Supreme Court justice, as saying a long word should never be used when a shorter word serves the purpose. McQuain, who also writes a column called "Our Language," adds that the most inspiring verbs often are the simplest.

(*continued*)

Watch how these three sets of verbs grow in power as they shrink in syllables:

initiate—introduce—begin—start.
accentuate—emphasize—highlight—stress.
communicate—dialogue—discuss—talk.

Long verbs are not necessarily strong verbs. Jack Hart, The Oregonian's managing editor who writes "Writers Workshop" for Editor & Publisher, recommends that writers devote part of their self-editing time to strengthen their verbs. He also recommends they use transitive verbs that create the most ruckus. Those are ones that require direct objects and generate casual flow: *Its claws raked her back.* Or, strong intransitive verbs such as *The skier plunged into empty space.*

"Nothing injects energy like action. And only verbs describe action. They deserve a lot of end-stage attention," Hart writes.

But the question remains: How do you develop the ability to strengthen verbs in your sentences? By practice. By reading. By exercising your language skills as a bodybuilder lifts weights.

Author John Gardner was a powerful fiction writer who was known for his passion for just about anything, including motorcycles—he died in an accident in 1982—and writing. A friend, Charles Johnson, tells a story in "On Writers and Writing" of how at dinner one evening Joan Gardner teased her husband about the archaic language he used in "Jason and Medeia." The upset Gardner then took a magnifying glass and pored over every word in a dictionary so he could find stronger words to revise his story.

Perhaps Gardner was a man of extremes, but the story about him does make a point: that writers must seek the right words—the right verbs—to rank among the strongest of all.

SUGGESTED READINGS

Brooks, Brian S., and James L. Pinson. *Working With Words: A Concise Handbook for Media Writers and Editors,* 3rd ed. New York: St. Martin's Press, 1997.

Cooper, Gloria, ed. *Red Tape Holds Up New Bridge: And More Flubs from the Nation's Press.* New York: Perigee, 1987.

Kessler, Lauren, and Duncan McDonald. *When Words Collide: A Media Writer's Guide to Grammar and Style,* 4th ed. Belmont, Calif.: Wadsworth, 1996.

Lewin, Esther, and Albert E. Lewin. *The Thesaurus of Slang.* New York: Facts on File, 1988.

Lutz, William. *Doublespeak.* New York: Harper & Row, 1989.

Neaman, Judith, and Carole G. Silver. *Kind Words: A Thesaurus of Euphemisms,* expanded and rev. ed. New York: McGraw-Hill, 1990.

Provost, Gary. *Beyond Style: Mastering the Finer Points of Writing.* Cincinnati, Ohio: Writer's Digest Books, 1988.

Rice, Scott. *Right Words, Right Places.* Belmont, Calif.: Wadsworth, 1993.

Safire, William. *On Language.* New York: Times Books, 1990.

Strunk, William Jr., and E.B. White. *The Elements of Style,* 4th ed. New York: Macmillan, 2000.

Urdang, Laurence. *The Dictionary of Confusable Words.* New York: Facts on File, 1988.

Zinsser, William. *On Writing Well: An Informal Guide to Writing Nonfiction,* 4th ed. New York: Harper-Perennial, 1990.

Name ______________________ Class ______________________ Date ______

EXERCISE 1

VOCABULARY

The following pairs or groups of words often cause confusion because, although they may look or sound similar, their meanings differ. You will be expected to know the words' meaning and use them correctly in all your work. On a separate piece of paper, define each of the words and explain how its usage differs from that of the other word or words. When a conflict or question arises, follow the recommendations of The Associated Press Stylebook.

1. about/around
2. above/more than/over
3. adapt/adept/adopt
4. advice/advise
5. affect/effect
6. aid/aide
7. alley/ally
8. allude/elude
9. altar/alter
10. alumna/alumnae/alumni/alumnus
11. among/between
12. anecdote/antidote
13. angel/angle
14. average/mean/median/mode
15. bazaar/bizarre
16. because/since
17. bloc/block
18. blond/blonde
19. born/borne
20. burglar/robber/swindler/thief
21. calendar/calender
22. canvas/canvass
23. capital/Capitol
24. censor/censure
25. choose/chose
26. cite/sight/site
27. complement/compliment
28. compose/comprise/constitute
29. confidant/confident
30. conscience/conscious
31. consul/council/counsel
32. convince/persuade
33. criteria/criterion
34. damage/damages
35. data/datum
36. decent/descent/dissent
37. desert/dessert
38. discreet/discrete
39. elusive/illusive
40. emigrate/immigrate

41. ensure/insure
42. entitled/titled
43. envelop/envelope
44. fair/fare
45. farther/further
46. fewer/less
47. fiance/fiancee
48. foreword/forward
49. forth/fourth
50. foul/fowl
51. hang/hanged/hung
52. imply/infer
53. incite/insight
54. it's/its
55. lay/lie
56. liable/libel/likely
57. loose/lose
58. marshal/marshall
59. media/medium
60. miner/minor
61. moral/morale
62. naval/navel
63. ordinance/ordnance
64. pedal/peddle
65. people/persons
66. personal/personnel
67. phenomena/phenomenon
68. plague/plaque
69. pole/poll
70. pore/pour
71. pray/prey
72. principal/principle
73. ravage/ravish
74. receive/suffer/sustain
75. reign/rein
76. role/roll
77. statue/statute
78. than/then
79. that/which
80. their/there/they're
81. to/too
82. trail/trial
83. trustee/trusty
84. waive/wave
85. weather/whether
86. who/whom
87. who's/whose
88. your/you're

Name ______________________ Class ______________________ Date ______

EXERCISE 2

VOCABULARY

Words with different meanings often look or sound similar. As a journalist, you should be familiar with these words and use them correctly. Cross out the wrong words in the following sentences, leaving only the correct ones. Consult The Associated Press Stylebook for preferred usage. Also correct errors in style and possessives. If you need help, the rules for forming possessives appear in Appendix C, and AP style rules are summarized in Appendix B.

1. The (cite/sight/site) chosen by the City for (it's/its) new office building could (affect/effect) parking in that part of town.
2. The United States army general was able to (envelop/envelope) the enemy in (fewer/less) than 24 hours, capturing (more than/over) 7,000 soldiers (who/whom/which) were (than/then) disarmed.
3. The fire (marshall/marshal) said it will cost (about/around) 100,000 dollars to repair the apartment complex, where a dozen (people/persons) lived before Fridays fire (burnt/burned) most of the building.
4. The elementary school (principal/principle) said Mister Smith is a man of high (principal/principle) and deserves the (reward/award) as teacher of the year.
5. The (blond/blonde) girl (complimented/complemented) her friend on the new shoes (that/which) she bought on sale for just ten dollars.
6. The Governors (aid/aide) said the rally on the steps of the state (Capital/Capitol) drew 10 thousand people despite the bad (weather/whether).
7. The mayor said city employee's (moral/morale) is very low and blamed it on (they're/their/there) recent pay cut, (that/which) was (adapted/adopted) by City (council/counsel) last month.
8. John and his (fiance/fiancee), (who/whom) he met at college, checked the (calendar/calender) and said (their/there/they're) sure they want to have the party on May 1st.

9. That (desert/dessert) was a tasty (complement/compliment) to our meals'.
10. He (adviced/advised) the investors to (altar/alter) their plans (because/since) it would be difficult to (ensure/insure) everyones cooperation.
11. Rather (than/then) (censor/censure) the 9 bank (trustees/trusties), he wants a new state (ordinance/ordnance) to govern (their/there/they're) behavior.
12. The woman (who/whom/that) came to my (aide/aid) when I fell on the sidewalk is a (alumna/alumnae/alumni/alumnus) of Princeton.
13. The antique carriage began to (role/roll) (foreword/forward) until a (loose/lose) wheel fell off, making it impossible to travel any (farther/further).
14. The (forth/fourth) group of veterans entered the (alley/ally), which veers south at a forty-five degree (angel/angle), (then/than) marched 7 more (blocs/blocks).
15. Mother helped to (canvas/canvass) the neighborhood today with (fliers/flyers) for dad's new store, and she said she needs to (lay/lie) down for a while before making dinner.
16. The book (entitled/titled) "Betrayal" estimates that the (trail/trial) will last (fewer/less) than 10 days, and (implies/infers) that the jury will find the defendent (innocent/not guilty).
17. They (hanged/hung) the controversial painting in a school hall way and want to know (who's/whose) side (your/you're) likely to favor.
18. The minister (prayed/preyed) for the swift recovery of the 8 (persons/people) (who/whom) (received/suffered/sustained) injuries during last nights storm.
19. The children said (their/there/they're) families (emigrated/immigrated) from Asia and are (liable/libel/likely) to move (farther/further) South.
20. The large (bloc/block) of voters opposed to the plan (convinced/persuaded) Board members to reread the (data/datum) and (altar/alter) the five (criteria/criterion) for (choosing/chosing) the schools architect.

Name ________________________ Class ________________________ Date ______

EXERCISE 3

VOCABULARY

Words with different meanings often look or sound familiar. As a journalist, you should be familiar with these words and use them correctly. Cross out the wrong words in the following sentences, leaving only the correct ones. Consult The Associated Press Stylebook for preferred usage. Also correct errors in style and possessives. If you need help, the rules for forming possessives appear in Appendix C, and AP style rules are summarized in Appendix B.

1. A (pole/poll) conducted by the candidates supporters showed 60 (per cent/percent) of the (persons/people) surveyed planned to vote for (he/him) in the Nov. election.
2. Her (fiance/fiancee) (implied/inferred) that her softball teams (moral/morale) was (effected/affected) when the coach was replaced.
3. The jogger became (conscience/conscious) of several cars behind her, and then decided to (alter/altar) her course, even though the new route took her up (to/too) many (ascents/assents).
4. I am (confidant/confident) that you will win the leading (role/roll) in this years' play, but Bill thinks (your/you're) likely to (lose/loose) it to Beth.
5. Nancys Mother will (lay/lie) out a blanket for her in case she wants to (lay/lie) down before Robert comes over to visit.
6. The woman, an (emigrant/immigrant) (born/borne) in Irelands (capital/capitol) of Dublin, said she wants to (aid/aide) the nine-member city (consul/council/counsel).
7. The companys new president is an (alumna/alumnae/alumni/alumnus) of the local university (who/whom) started her speech with an amusing (anecdote/antidote) to put the (personal/personnel) at ease about her hiring.
8. The teachers said they will need (more than/over) 100 volunteers to help with all the student's programs on this year's (calendar/calender), but the (principal/principle) warned that (fewer/less) than a dozen parents were likely (to/too) offer their assistance.

9. To (ensure/insure) (its/it's) success, the editors updated the (medias/mediums) content, thereby increasing its circulation and prestige.
10. In his report, the police officer said the (burglar/robber/swindler/thief) who broke into the home at 313 North Twenty-first St. (ravaged/ravished) only a closet, and added that the crime was the most (bazaar/bizarre) he has seen in his 6-yr. career.
11. George just joined the country club, but he already is (adapt/adept/adopt) at (convincing/persuading) the (trustees/trusties) to (waive/wave) the restrictions on guests using the facilitys.
12. The judges (complemented/complimented) all the teams but said the girls in the (forth/fourth) lane swam (farther/further) than any of their competitiors.
13. Barbara said the (foul/fowl) odor coming from the next room was (liable/libel/likely) to make other (people/persons) sick regardless of (weather/whether) they entered the room.
14. (More than/Over) fifty (persons/people) (comprised/composed) the team of volunteers (who's/whose) job it was to address and seal the (envelops/envelopes).
15. The reporters story about the bicycle (trail/trial) quoted several people who said (its/it's) (to/too) dangerous (since/because) they (received/suffered/sustained) injuries as they tried to (pedal/peddle) (farther/further) North.
16. Carla (dyed/died) her hair (blond/blonde) because she heard that (blonds/blondes) have more fun.
17. The (statue/statute) of a misshapen (angel/angle) on the church (altar/alter) caused a (miner/minor) controversy among the two-hundred member congregation.
18. Acting on the (advise/advice) of (they're/there/their) older sister, the twins bought prom dresses that (complemented/complimented) each other.

19. The (legislators/legislatures) vowed to fight the Governors budget, saying they have the (block/bloc) of votes needed to veto the spending plan.
20. (There/They're/Their) the ones who are trying to raise 1,000 dollars for a new (plaque/plague) on the (sight/site/cite) of the famous Civil War Battle, (that/which) occurred (about/around) 2 miles from the center of town.

Name ______________________ Class ______________________ Date ______

EXERCISE 4

VERBS

SECTION I: AVOIDING USE OF NOUNS AS VERBS

Rewrite the following sentences, eliminating the use of nouns as verbs.

1. She authored a new book on the Vietnam War.
2. The soldiers were headquartered in Kuwait City.
3. The class interfaced with the teacher by e-mail.
4. They inked a new contract with the record company.
5. They were shotgunned to death, and their bodies will be autopsied Friday.

SECTION II: USING STRONGER VERBS

List three stronger, more active and descriptive verbs that could replace the verbs in the following sentences.

1. The soccer goalie was able to prevent the last shot.
2. That art history book has many photographs.
3. She got a new car.
4. The politician did a survey of local voters.
5. More than 300 people are employed at the plant.

SECTION III: USING STRONGER VERBS

Rewrite the following sentences, using stronger verbs. Also use normal word order (subject, verb, direct object).

1. The car is in need of a new paint job.
2. He was planning to open a restaurant in Houston.
3. The professor was able to interest many students in his classes.
4. The preschool nutrition program is set up so that the cost is paid by the state.
5. A short circuit in the electrical wiring at the church was the cause of the fire.

6. The cost of a ticket for admission to the amusement park is $25.
7. A trip to the beach is what Karen and David are planning for this summer.
8. To obtain extra money to pay for college, John has picked up a second job.
9. It was suggested by the moderator that the panel participants may want to take a break.
10. The reservations she made at the hotel were for three rooms.

Name ______________________ Class ______________________ Date ________

EXERCISE 5

AVOIDING COMMON ERRORS

SECTION I: AVOIDING GRAMMATICAL AND VOCABULARY ERRORS

Rewrite the following sentences, correcting their wording.

1. The city council voted on the motion they made to accept the bids.
2. Police officers arrested the man that had broken into the store.
3. Saying the administration would support her, the professor said they wanted her to take the position.
4. The men and women that are members of the committee hope to settle the dispute soon.
5. The hospital board plans to attend the opening of the new wing of the hospital they approved last year.

SECTION II: KEEPING RELATED WORDS AND IDEAS TOGETHER

Rewrite these sentences, improving the word placement.

1. The construction workers saved the drowning boys who were working at the site.
2. The girl was taken to a hospital for observation by her parents.
3. The award was presented to the class which represents perfect attendance.
4. Robert Allen Wiese was sentenced to one year in prison after pleading guilty to violating probation by Circuit Court judge Samuel McGregor.
5. A suspect in the burglary case was arrested after a high-speed chase involving two lawnmowers stolen from a hardware store.

SECTION III: AVOIDING IMPRECISION

Rewrite the following sentences, making them as precise as possible.

1. The woman bought the dress she saw in the window walking down the street.
2. The man was killed instantly after he was struck by the train.
3. After paying a $325 fine, the dog was free to go home with its owner.
4. The judge sentenced the corporate executive to 10 years in prison after pleading guilty to five counts of fraud.
5. Minutes after the man left the bar, he collided with a car that totally destroyed his pickup truck.

SECTION IV: DEFINING AND EXPLAINING

Define or explain each of the large numbers or unfamiliar terms in the following sentences.

1. Their son has meningitis.
2. A single B-2 Stealth bomber costs $800 million.
3. Pioneer 10, a satellite launched on March 2, 1972, is 4.2 billion miles from the sun.

SECTION V: AVOIDING CLICHÉS

Rewrite the following sentences, eliminating clichés.

1. He said the cold soda really hit the spot on a hot day.
2. Police are trying to find the serial rapist and halt his reign of terror.
3. The mayor had won a reputation for trying to sweep problems under the rug.
4. The bicycle race got off to a good start with a see-saw battle between the two leaders.
5. The governor said he made a last-ditch stand to save the legislation he was proposing to the state senate.

SECTION VI: AVOIDING UNNECESSARY PARENTHESES

Eliminate the parentheses, and other errors, from the following sentences.

1. She (the mayor) said (in response to a question about property taxes) that she opposes any such proposal (to increase them).
2. Despite the loss (now estimated at $4.2 million) he said the company should be able to pay all their debts before the deadline (Dec. 30).
3. The governor predicted, "They (members of the Legislature) will approve the proposal (to increase the sales tax) within 60 days."

SECTION VII: AVOIDING THE NEGATIVE

Rewrite the following sentences in positive form.

1. Not until last year were they able to buy their new home.
2. The test was not that easy to finish in the allotted time.
3. The students do not have any limitations on which songs they can choose.
4. The car was parked not far away.
5. The mayor said she would not be disinclined to vote against the motion.

SECTION VIII: IMPROVING SENTENCES

Rewrite the following sentences, correcting all their errors.

1. He and she was planning to go to the concert.
2. The fire occurred Sunday night in a basement room used by the school band, causing an estimated $30,000 damage and destroyed 80 of their uniforms.
3. The physician, an alumni of the university, came under fire for his comments about the schools medical program.
4. The tragic accident was finally cleaned up by police and firefighters so traffic lanes could re-open.
5. She wants to establish a program where convicted juveniles would be required to perform some sort of community service and not go to jail.

Name ______________________ Class ______________________ Date ______

EXERCISE 6

REVIEW

SECTION I: AVOIDING SLANG AND CLICHÉS

Rewrite the following sentences, eliminating their slang and clichés. Answer key provided: See Appendix D.

1. The president of the company asked employees to give the benefit of the doubt to his restructuring plan, but his plea fell on deaf ears.
2. The crowd erupted in violence when the doors to the club were closed, leaving them outside.
3. The governor said the election had tipped the scales in favor of his party.
4. The students believed the program was doomed to failure because few supported it.
5. Soldiers fought a pitched battle with a group of guerrilla fighters.

SECTION II: IMPROVING VERBS AND SENTENCE STRUCTURE

Rewrite the following sentences, using stronger verbs and normal word order (subject, verb, direct object).

1. The final plans for the project will not be decided upon until later this year by officials.
2. With her re-election campaign coming this fall, the mayor noted that she will be making plans soon.
3. Their lawsuit complains that the bottle has an insect in it.
4. The file server would be not be able to provide enough space for the web site, the computer expert claimed.
5. Police were told by the witnesses that the suspect had approached the woman and asked for the keys to her car with a gun.

SECTION III: KEEPING RELATED WORDS AND IDEAS TOGETHER

Rewrite the following sentences, moving the related words and ideas as close together as possible. Correct any style or grammatical errors.

1. She sent her husband a letter about the birth of their baby boy who is in Iraq in the United States army.
2. In order to get the bill passed, the senator addressed her colleague's in a speech on the senate floor asking them to provide funding Monday afternoon.
3. Waiting until they had sufficient evidence, the police department decided to arrest the suspect before he could flee the country and put him in handcuffs.
4. She said that if a student fails two or more subjects, is frequently absent, has discipline problems, and show signs of low self esteem, loneliness or stress, that youngster is at high risk for dropping out of high school.
5. The accident victim was found with lacerations on his arms and legs trapped under the motorcycle.

SECTION IV: TESTING ALL YOUR SKILLS

Rewrite the following sentences, correcting all their errors.

1. The envelop containing there test scores was delivered at 8 am in the morning.
2. The mayor said we must all work to improve the cities streets and neighborhoods to make the city a cool place to live.
3. The policeman and the fireman both said they would vote in favor of the ban on smoking at they're stations.
4. The consensus of opinion among participants in the workshop is that a pay raise of 15 to 20 % should be received by the nurses.
5. The woman said she was not likely to purchase products at the disgusting supermarket ever again after she found a cock roach in her box of cereal.
6. It was stated by the writer of the article that bowling was a sport that could be learned by any one.

7. Whether or not they would be able to pay for the program, the city council decided to increase funding for the program to help expectant mothers by a vote of six to one.
8. Even though people were protesting her annual salary of 35000 dollars a year, it is believed by a lot of persons that they will support her being reappointed to the board of directors.

SECTION V: AVOIDING JOURNALESE

Rewrite the following sentences, eliminating slang and journalese.

1. She racked up $30,000 in medical expenses.
2. He gave an OK to spending the $26,000 figure for a car.
3. The program is geared toward helping high school students.
4. The new building will carry a price tag of about $6 million.
5. The proposal met with opposition from three council members.

SECTION VI: AVOIDING JARGON

Rewrite the following sentences, eliminating jargon.

1. Police said the perpetrators of the burglary would be arraigned later in the week.
2. Teresea Phillips, a/k/a Marie Phillips, testified that she entered the store and helped the defendant steal an unknown quantity of jewelry from the premises on or about the 9th day of last month.
3. The company said it would maximize efforts and utilize every department it had available to overcome the budget crisis.
4. The mayor said if the sanitation engineers went on strike, he would be forced to have other city workers drive the trucks.
5. Brown's lawsuit charges that, as a result of the auto accident, he suffered from bodily injury, disability, disfigurement and mental anguish. Browns lawsuit also charges that he has lost his ability to earn a living and that the accident aggravated a previous condition.

Name ______________________ Class ______________________ Date ______

EXERCISE 7

SPELLING AND VOCABULARY

Correct all the errors in the following sentences, which contain a number of words that cause confusion because they look or sound like other words. You were asked to define many of the words in Exercise 1.

The sentences also contain possessives that need correcting and errors in AP style. If you need help, the rules for forming possessives appear in Appendix C, and AP style rules are summarized in Appendix B. Answer key provided: See Appendix D.

1. She said she was an alumni of the university.
2. The stock holders recieved a 15 per cent dividend.
3. Police placed the envelop with the ransom money in the mailbox.
4. Legislators passed the statue that will add three thousand acres to the national park.
5. The principle said he plans to bloc parents from developing there own sports program.
6. She said the job was to hard for average persons to complete in 1 hour.
7. The portrait of the president hung in the rotunda of the capitol building.
8. The concept was to illusive to insure success.
9. She said she plans to lay on the beach all day.
10. At one time, Poland was a member of the Soviet block.
11. Police said it was only a miner acident, but the man sustained several injuries.
12. Joanne is not adverse to the trip, but thinks everyone should pay his own meals and hotel room.
13. He has blonde hair, but some persons say it is died.
14. She described the purse-snatching suspect as someone who prays on lone women.
15. The nurse gave the soldier a snake bite anecdote at the cite of the bite.
16. Bobs youngest sister is the only one who's advise he will take.
17. Do you know whom will be at the meeting?

18. The committee is comprised of four women and three guys.

19. Ellen should fair well in this years bike race.

20. The man was sentenced to prison because he insighted a riot which caused three deaths.

21. If she decides to go along, than the rest of they're journey will take longer.

22. She eluded in her testimony to the company's president having taken the funds.

23. The attorney said it was a bazaar incident that lead his client too sue the company.

24. The presidents confident said the president was willing two work with congress on the legislation.

25. The mayor stated the media is unfair and inferred that it has no right to offer descent of her programs.

CHAPTER 5

SELECTING AND REPORTING THE NEWS

The function of the press is very high. It is almost holy. It ought to serve as a forum for the people, through which the people may know freely what is going on. To misstate or suppress the news is a breach of trust.

(Justice Louis D. Brandeis, U.S. Supreme Court)

Sept. 11, 2001, dawned with a brilliant blue sky. By the thousands, workers from New York City and its surrounding suburbs in New York and New Jersey poured into Lower Manhattan to fill the vast complex of offices, retail shops and restaurants of the World Trade Center. The twin towers of the World Trade Center were the tallest buildings in the city and had, since 1976, served as the icons of American economic power. By the end of the morning, however, they would be a crumpled pile of twisted metal, debris and dead bodies.

At 8:48 a.m., a hijacked American Airlines Boeing 767—Flight 11 from Boston to Los Angeles—slammed into the north tower. The building belched smoke and flame as volatile jet fuel ignited on impact. Fifteen minutes later, United Airlines Flight 175, also a Boeing 767 bound for Los Angeles out of Boston, rocketed into the south tower with the same devastating results. Less than an hour later, the south tower collapsed, spreading terror and panic among the spectators gathered in the streets below the burning building. The north tower fell soon after.

At 9:40 a.m., American Airlines Flight 77, a Boeing 757 from Dulles Airport heading for Los Angeles, exploded through the north face of the Pentagon in Washington, D.C. A fourth jetliner—United Airlines Flight 93 from Newark, N.J., to San Francisco—crashed in rural Pennsylvania near Somerset. Officials believe the plane crashed when the passengers battled the hijackers for control of the aircraft.

As people in New York City and around the United States found themselves transfixed by the sight of the buildings' collapse, reporters struggled to contain their emotions as they went about the business of gathering the news. Over the next several months, reporters would unravel the story about the life and death of the World Trade Center and the people who worked there and died there. Reporters would also bring the story of those involved in the attack and the American response to the attack.

On Sept. 11 and Sept. 12, newspapers across the country relayed the stories of death and destruction in large, bold headlines that contained a similar theme and, in many, the same words. "Terror: United States Under Attack" announced The Journal News of Westchester County, N.Y. "Terror: Attack on American Soil" said The Los Angeles Daily News. "U.S. Attacked" said The Cincinnati Enquirer, while The Advocate of Newark, Ohio, proclaimed "American nightmare." "Day of Death" was the headline in The Indianapolis Star. "Bastards!" screamed the San Francisco Examiner.

The editors of these widely separated newspapers had no difficulty deciding what to put on the front page that day. On Sept. 11, there was only one news story. But even when the day lacks one compelling story, many editors across the country choose to emphasize the same stories on the same day because they all apply the same sets of news values—values they have developed through years of experience.

Selecting news stories to publish in a newspaper or air on a news broadcast is a subjective process—an art. No scientific test helps journalists measure a story's newsworthiness. Journalists have tried to define news, but no single definition has won widespread acceptance. Also, no definition acknowledges all the factors affecting the selection process. Walter Lippmann, a reporter and columnist, said news is "what protrudes from the ordinary . . . a picture of reality on which [people] can act." Another journalist, Nicolas Tomalin, defined news as "things that people don't want to be known." And television commentator David Brinkley said news is "what I say it is."

THE CHARACTERISTICS OF NEWS

Even if journalists cannot agree on a definition of news, they agree news stories possess certain characteristics or news values. Jack Hart, managing editor of The (Portland) Oregonian, says a good story should have the following characteristics: (1) an interesting central character who (2) faces a challenge or is caught up in a conflict and (3) whose situation changes as (4) action takes place in (5) an engaging setting. More traditionally, journalists have said that newsworthy events are those that possess timeliness, impact, prominence, proximity, unusualness and conflict or controversy. By either Hart's values or the more traditional ones, the terrorist attacks on the United States and the country's response to them were big news.

Timeliness

Journalists stress current information—stories occurring today or yesterday, not several days or weeks ago—and try to report it ahead of their competitors. Obviously, print journalism trails the electronic media in reporting the basic facts of a breaking news story. When reporting a story that occurred even hours earlier, journalists look for fresh angles and new details around which to build their stories. If some background is necessary, they usually keep it to a minimum and weave it throughout a story.

Impact

Reporters stress important information that has an impact on their audience: stories that affect, involve or interest thousands of readers or viewers. A plane crash that kills 180 people is more newsworthy than an automobile accident that kills two. Similarly, an increase in city property taxes is more newsworthy than an increase in dog license fees because the former affects many more people.

As reporters evaluate events, they must consider the impact or importance of those events for readers and viewers. News stories tend to focus on the most severe storms, the most damaging fires, the most deadly accidents, the most important speeches and the most interesting organizations because these are likely to affect the most readers and viewers and have the most serious consequences.

Prominence

If an insurance salesperson or a plumber catches a cold, no one cares, except that person's friends and family. If the president of the United States catches a cold, the stock market may lose 500 points. Even routine events become newsworthy when they involve prominent indi-

TUESDAY SPECIAL EDITION INSIDE

WEDNESDAY

THE SUN HERALD

www.sunherald.com

SEPTEMBER 12, 2001 50¢ COVERING THE MISSISSIPPI COAST VOL. 117, NO. 341

SPECIAL EDITION

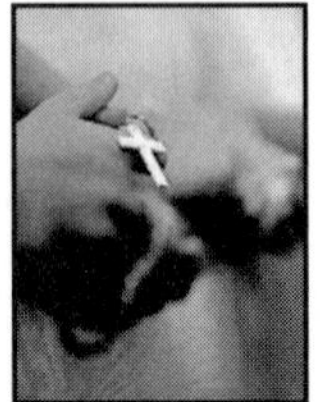

Prayer soothes hurting nation

Coast residents join a weeping nation in turning to prayer for solace. At offices, homes, schools and churches, people are gathering to pray, **A-3**

Gas stations are gouging

Gov. Ronnie Musgrove declares a state of emergency in response to stations hiking gas prices. The state is investigating price gouging and anti-trust violations, **A-6**

Gun owners grab ammo

"Some people think this could be the beginning of the end, and others think we might be getting ready to go to war," gun-shop owner says as customers flood store to stock up on ammunition, **A-3**

Donors line up

Hundreds of Coast residents turn out to give blood for victims of Tuesday's attacks. Collection hours have been expanded for today, **A-4**

Games halted

For the first time since 1945, the entire day's baseball schedule is canceled, World Cup soccer matches are postponed, racetracks are dark, and the NCAA and NFL are considering whether to go ahead with weekend games, **D-1**

SOUND OFF OF THE DAY

"As I watch the billowing clouds of smoke and debris issuing from the World Trade Center and the Pentagon, one image keeps coming to mind: Pearl Harbor. These attacks are cowardly acts equal to a declaration of war against the United States. Only this time, we are not certain who is the enemy. May God bless and protect this nation, the people of this nation, and bring comfort to those whose lives have been affected by this tragedy."

More Sound Offs, A-2

With thousands dead, friends and families grieve and a nation struggles with a devastating attack on native soil.

WHAT NOW?

THE ASSOCIATED PRESS

Firefighters make their way through rubble Tuesday after terrorists crashed two hijacked airliners into the World Trade Center in New York City, bringing the twin 110-story towers crumbling to the ground. The audacious attack on U.S. soil, coupled with an attack on the Pentagon, claimed the lives of thousands of people.

Tragedy reaches to Coast

An agonizing day waiting for word

By GEOFF PENDER
THE SUN HERALD

Coast families went through the depths of agony after Tuesday's terrorist attacks, waiting to hear from loved ones living in or visiting Manhattan or Washington, D.C.

For many, relief came in the form of a telephone call or an e-mail message that their family or friends were OK.

But for some the agony continued late Tuesday, and phone service into or out of each city remained hit-and-miss.

"We still haven't heard anything," Ronald Brown, a Gulfport physician, said of his son-in-law Stephen Poulos, who works for an insurance company on the 105th floor of the World Trade Center in Manhattan.

Please see **Coast,** *A-6*

DAVID PURDY/THE SUN HERALD

Biloxi firefighter Mike Watts puts up an American flag at the city's historical flag display next to the Biloxi Lighthouse on U.S. 90 Tuesday afternoon. Mayor A.J. Holloway ordered the display changed to eight U.S. flags; American flags at municipal buildings are being flown at half-staff. 'This is a time of national tragedy,' Holloway said. 'We must show unified support for our country. I encourage all citizens to show their support by flying the American flag, and praying for the victims and their families.'

Terror from air kills thousands

Intercepted calls point to bin Laden

By DAVID CRARY
and JERRY SCHWARTZ
THE ASSOCIATED PRESS

Emergency contact numbers, **A-6**

WASHINGTON — In the most devastating terrorist onslaught ever waged against the United States, knife-wielding hijackers crashed two airliners into the World Trade Center on Tuesday, toppling its twin 110-story towers. The deadly calamity was witnessed on televisions across the world as another plane slammed into the Pentagon, and a fourth crashed outside Pittsburgh.

U.S. officials began piecing together a case linking terrorist mastermind Osama bin Laden to the attack, aided by an intercept of communications between his supporters and harrowing cell phone calls from victims aboard the jetliners before they crashed on Tuesday.

U.S. intelligence intercepted communications between bin Laden supporters discussing the attacks on the World Trade Center and Pentagon, according to Utah Sen. Orrin Hatch, the top Republican on the Senate Judiciary Committee.

"They have an intercept of some information that included people associated with bin Laden who acknowledged a couple of targets were hit," Hatch said in an interview with The Associated Press. He declined to be more specific.

Hatch also said law enforcement has data possibly linking one person on one of the four ill-fated flights to bin Laden's organization.

Government and industry officials said at least one flight attendant and two passengers called from three of the planes as they were being forced down in New York and Washington.

The callers indicated hijackers

Please see **Terror,** *A-6*

INDEX

Ann & Abby	B-4	Living	B-1
Business	D-7	Movies	B-2
The Buzz	C-3	Obituaries	A-7
Classified	E-1	Opinion	C-4
Comics	B-5	Sports	D-1
Crosswords	E-3	Traffic Watch	A-9
Horoscope	B-3	TV	B-4

Printed in part on recycled paper; please recycle your newspapers.

TODAY'S WEATHER

Mostly sunshine
High: 88º
Low: 72º

Winds from NE at 10-20 knots
Relative humidity: 70%;
Weather, C-6

Storm in Gulf

A, large slow-moving storm system in the Gulf of Mexico off southwest Florida could become a tropical depression today, **A-9**

Hot college prospect

Harrison Central quarterback Jeremy Lee is making a name for himself with college recruiters. Lee is being courted by schools such as Stanford, Colorado, Jackson State and Southern, **D-4**

SPECIAL EDITION

SAN FRANCISCO

The Examiner.

Wednesday, September 12, 2001 Keeping San Francisco a two-newspaper town. (including tax) 25 cents

BASTARDS!

A CHANGED AMERICA

On Sept. 12, 2001, one story dominated the front pages of U.S. newspapers: the terrorist attacks on New York City and Washington, D.C. Different news organizations, however, emphasized different aspects of the tragedy. Some editors, like those of The SunHerald in Biloxi, Miss., wondered what effects the attacks would have and how the United States would respond. Others, such as the editors at The Examiner in San Francisco, vented their anger at the attackers.

viduals, such as governors, business leaders or celebrities. Almost everything the president does is news because he is the nation's leader.

Reporters should not cover celebrities to the exclusion of stories about ordinary people, but the American public seems to have an insatiable appetite for information about those who are famous. People magazine, for example, is successful because it fills its pages with facts and photographs about the lives of glamorous people.

TWO VIEWS OF 9/11

A HORRIBLE PLACE TO BE

By **Erin Schulte**

New York City on Sept. 11, 2001, was a horrible place to be as a human, an eye-opening place to be as an American and a once-in-a-lifetime place to be as a journalist.

About 8:30 that morning, I passed through the World Trade Center on my way to work as a reporter for The Wall Street Journal Online. Our office was across the street from the twin towers, and my window on the 11th floor looked out directly into the imposing gray columns of steel.

Minutes after I threw my bag at my desk, my coworkers and I heard a heavy boom. Ducking and looking out the window, we saw the top of the north tower in flames. We thought perhaps it was another bombing, like the one in 1993. I grabbed my bag, a notebook, a pen and my cell phone and got ready to head out the door. But being the stock market reporter, I was ordered to stay at my desk and work on the market story. At that time, we thought that was all the bombing would be—a little "shave off the Dow," as a co-worker of mine put it later.

Once the second plane hit, we knew it was more than a bombing or a small plane that had lost its way and hit the WTC by accident. We evacuated.

We scattered to start reporting. Just before the towers fell, I had ducked into a co-worker's nearby apartment to call our office in Brussels, Belgium, with news of what was happening in New York. It was then that we found out the Pentagon had been hit, and that all of America was truly under attack.

By about 11 a.m., 100 or so print Journal reporters had spread out as well, covering news from downtown Manhattan, Brooklyn, airports and bedroom communities in New Jersey, among other places, and filing by e-mail from anywhere they could find a working modem.

Later that afternoon, the online Journal's staff boarded ferries and boats to cross the river to safety, along with other workers and residents of lower Manhattan who clutched babies, dogs and cherished belongings—one even carried a parrot. That evening we arrived at corporate headquarters in New Jersey to help edit copy for the newspaper and Web site. We had no clothes, no toothbrushes, and many of us arrived in borrowed cars. Some of us still wore some of the dust and debris that covered lower Manhattan in a thick gray layer.

Top editors from the print side huddled at one apartment on the Upper West Side while other editors clustered at an apartment in Brooklyn. Both groups worked to come up with a strategy for the next day's paper and pull together reporters' accounts.

From a bare-bones backup newsroom at the corporate campus 50 miles away in South Brunswick, N.J., an editing staff of about 40 (compared with the normal 350) who already lived in New Jersey or had found a way to get out of the city and across the river frantically pushed to edit the thousands of inches of copy reporters in New York had filed. With help from the Washington bureau, the editors managed to get the print edition of the paper to nearly 90 percent of the Journal's 1.8 million subscribers despite communication and technical constraints caused by using the backup newsroom, decimation of our New York headquarters, scattering of the news staff and problems with telephone lines in New York.

Being journalists allowed us a certain level of separation from the events that day. Most of us had been in horrific situations before and had at least some experience with being witnesses to and recorders of disaster. While working in Arkansas, I saw families and homes destroyed by tornadoes, fires, shootings and airplane crashes. That experience helped me remain focused on reporting on Sept. 11 and not think too much about the horror I experienced personally.

Unlike reporters who prepared to cover the war in Iraq by heading to boot camp, learning things like getting a gas mask on in less than nine seconds, we had no preparation, physical or mental, for horrors of the magnitude we saw on Sept. 11.

Usually, the most shocking thing I see while reporting for WSJ.com is the Dow industrial average sliding 200 points, but on that day, men and women were jumping from the upper reaches of the trade center, more than 100 stories above ground. And everywhere there was carnage—body parts in the street, airplane seats scattered in parking lots, bloody, terrified people panicking and running with nowhere to go on the slender strip of island called Manhattan. Most of our staff had to run themselves as the towers fell and rained heavy debris and ash, leaving some of us vomiting and gasping for air.

If there is anything positive to say about working through a terrorist attack, it would have to be the knowledge that an entire nation was glued to CNN and frantically checking Web sites for updates on what was happening right in front of us. To know that our firsthand accounts, called in to overseas bureaus and immediately published online, would help America understand what was taking place in New York was a powerful incentive to stay focused on reporting, rather than to succumb to the more base instinct to flee and survive.

After I had time to process the day, I realized what a blessing it was to work for a news organization with global resources. The Wall Street Journal would later win a Pulitzer Prize for breaking news for the work it did that day, publishing some of the most riveting accounts of the attacks even though we had lost our permanent office (and would not work there again for nearly a year). Our online edition published some of the first accounts of the attacks, going by what we saw out our own windows and in the streets.

It is our hope, of course, that no other journalist will ever have to witness, or experience, such terror. For those of us who were there, our only option was to try to describe accurately and poignantly what was happening to the rest of the country and the world. Journalist friends of ours who were not there that day said they felt in some way as though they were "missing out," which sounded funny to a group of reporters who have suffered nightmares ever since.

As a business journalist, I spend much of my time at a bank of computers, watching numbers flash and deciphering their meaning. That day, my colleagues and I were in the thick of a story that has gripped the nation ever since and will define much of what will happen with U.S. foreign and domestic policy in the new century. In the end, I can see their point about missing out.

Erin Schulte is a reporter for The Wall Street Journal Online in New York City.

SMOKE RISING OVER THE POTOMAC

By **Jeff Zeleny**

The taxi driver looked at me with a disbelieving eye as I shouted that I must get to the Pentagon at once.

The massive building was on fire. People were running away. And there I was, headed toward the heavy clouds of black smoke that were quickly rising over the Potomac River and drifting into downtown Washington.

It was Sept. 11, 2001, about 9:45 a.m., and the gravity of the now-historic day had yet to sink in. The adrenaline, though, was running fast as I dashed out of the taxi cab

(*continued*)

and cautiously scaled down a freeway embankment to reach a main road leading to the Pentagon that had already been closed to traffic.

As I made my way toward the giant building, a steady stream of civilian and military employees rushed in the opposite direction. Reporting any spot news event requires on-the-spot decision making and stirs an instant rush of questions: Should I talk to the first people I can find? Should I try to creep as close to the site as possible? Should I be running away, too?

Even though I knew that two planes had crashed into the World Trade Center earlier that morning, I didn't immediately know the Pentagon also had been penetrated by a hijacked aircraft. It was clear that the smoke was coming from the far side of the building, so I decided that was my destination.

Witnesses, of course, are important to any story. But on the scene of a breaking news event, they are critical. So I decided I couldn't allow these people to pass by without trying to get a sense of what had happened.

Much to my surprise, several of the uniformed and civilian workers were willing to stop—even for a moment—to tell me what they had seen. Once again, a theory proved true: Don't assume people aren't interested in talking with you simply because you are a reporter.

At the Pentagon, just as at the floods, fires or even funerals that I have covered at newspapers around the country, several witnesses were more than willing to speak. In fact, some wanted to ask their own questions, and through our conversations came dialogue that told the story far better than I could have. One woman I approached was so desperate to reach her husband, I let her use my cell phone, an instance when setting aside the notebook for a few moments ultimately yielded a better interview. A simple act of humanity rarely hurts.

The moment a reporter arrives on the scene of a spot news event, every sense imaginable should come alive. A former editor of mine called it the vacuuming technique. What does the scene look like? What is the terrain like? What does the air smell like? What are people wearing? Is the grass green or brown?

Along the way, use any device available to better tell the story: Draw a sketch in your notebook. Ask a witness or a victim for a photograph or a letter that could enrich the story. Take down telephone numbers.

Creating a sense of place is one of the most essential—and often most difficult—tasks a newspaper reporter has while covering a spot-news event. At the Pentagon that day, as the morning unfolded, I scribbled page after page of notes as I watched chaos turn to order. In the end, the observations were boiled down to five simple sentences.

> On four lanes of Virginia Route 110 near the Pentagon, normally a bustling thoroughfare into Washington, hundreds of military officials, civilian employees and volunteers waited hours in the baking sun Tuesday to help in the rescue effort.
>
> They pitched tents on the road and set up a makeshift pharmacy. Dozens of stretchers were strewn along the road's shoulder. Doctors, in green scrubs, in military uniforms and in suit coats, converged on the area.
>
> They waited and they waited, but no patients came.

Gone are the days when most reporters had the luxury of spending all day in the field before coming back to the newsroom to leisurely sort through their notes and begin writing. On Sept. 11, 2001, I was constantly dictating material to a colleague who was hastily assembling a story for the afternoon EXTRA edition.

Laptop computers, mobile phones and text pagers are tremendous tools, but the modern technology barely functioned at all, I soon learned on that unforgettable day. Cellular towers were jammed and only about one of every 20 phone calls actually went through. The nearly lost skill of dictation, which I had learned years earlier while working for The Associated Press, is one that every reporter should be comfortable with.

That morning, as I was running along the side of the Pentagon, an F-16 fighter jet roared overhead, and thousands of employees ran for cover behind trees, a nearby overpass or parked cars. As I furiously tried to capture the scene in my notebook, my telephone rang. An editor finally managed to penetrate the overburdened phone system.

There was no time to jot my thoughts down on a laptop or even on a legal pad. So I performed the newspaper equivalent of a "live report" and quickly composed a story to a colleague who was typing at a furious pace on the other end of the phone.

An organized notebook helped me meet my deadline. Each time I interviewed someone that morning, I wrote that person's name on the back flap of a brown notebook. I also used a number system and a crude system of earmarking pages, which helped me quickly find details I wanted to share with the reader.

One month later, as I returned to the Pentagon for a memorial service with President Bush, I found myself furiously scribbling another set of names. On the morning of Oct. 11, 2001, as I stood at the site of where 189 people had died, it struck me that the ranks of the dead told the tale perhaps better than anything else. And from those pages of notes, came these two sentences:

> For eight minutes, as "Amazing Grace" swelled in the background, the name of each Pentagon victim scrolled across a giant screen. The names represented an alphabetic tapestry of America: from Dickens and Falkenberg, to Kincaid and Olson to Rasmussen and Whittington.

Jeff Zeleny is a reporter in the Chicago Tribune's Washington, D.C., bureau.

Proximity

The closer an event is to home, the more newsworthy it becomes. Murders are important news stories locally. Sometimes murder cases attract national attention. A gay University of Wyoming student, Matthew Shepard, died after he had been kidnapped, robbed, pistol-whipped and left tied to a fence near Laramie, Wyo. Because the attack on him apparently was motivated by his sexual orientation, his death ignited a national debate over hate crime laws. Near Jasper, Texas, a black man, James W. Byrd Jr., was chained to the back of a pickup truck and dragged to death by a trio of white men. The murder of Byrd reminded Americans of the enduring problem of racism. Most murders, however, lack such shocking or unusual circumstances, so they draw little national attention. Journalists explain that readers and viewers are most interested in and affected by stories about their own communities.

Henry Coble, a former editor with the Greensboro (N.C.) News & Record, often evaluated a story's proximity by its closeness to the Haw River, which flows through central North Carolina. When a story's dateline was distant, Coble was fond of saying, "It's a long way from Haw River." He meant News & Record readers would be less interested in a story the farther away it was from the Haw.

Proximity may be psychological. Two individuals separated by thousands of miles but sharing a characteristic or an interest may want to know more about each other. An American mother may sympathize with the problems of a mother in a distant country. American college students are likely to be interested in the concerns of college students elsewhere.

Singularity

Deviations from the normal—unexpected or unusual events, conflicts or controversies, drama or change—are more newsworthy than the commonplace. The murder of 13 students and teachers at a high school in Littleton, Colo., by two students who later committed suicide is more newsworthy than the routine school day experienced by hundreds of thousands of other students. Similarly, the fact that a city's mayor is squabbling with another city official is more newsworthy than the fact that two other officials are good friends.

Journalists must be alert for the unusual twists in otherwise mundane stories. Few newspapers will report a minor auto accident, but if a 6-year-old girl, a robot or a police chief was driving the car, the story could become front-page news.

The Ann Arbor (Mich.) News once published a front-page story about a birthday party. The host and guests were dogs—eight of them. Each dog received party favors and dined on ice cream.

Critics charge that the media's emphasis on the unusual gives their audiences a distorted view of the world. They say that the media fail to portray the lives of normal people on a typical day in a typical community. Editors respond that, because there is too much news to allow them to report everything, they report problems requiring the public's attention. However, reporters should write stories about things that work in a community: organizations or individuals who help a community improve its education or health care, programs that defeat domestic violence, efforts to reduce teen drinking or pregnancy.

Conflict or Controversy

Two people arguing about their divergent philosophies on a social issue is more newsworthy than two people who agree on everything. The tension between the subjects creates the conflict that often makes a story dramatic and interesting to read. While conflict between government officials or agencies, private organizations or private individuals can be viewed as negative news, it often provides readers and viewers with different opinions about policies and problems. Conflict can exist in any story. The single mother working her way through college faces the conflicts of time to care for her child and time needed to prepare herself for a better future. A young man fighting AIDS faces the conflict of trying to live his life. An athlete fighting to gain the edge against her competitors in a championship game faces the conflicts of the limits of her body's endurance and the talent and strength of her competition. In each of these stories, the conflict can be positive.

Other Characteristics

Dozens of other factors affect journalists' selection of news; however, most definitions of news acknowledge only a few of them. Reporters look for humorous stories—anything that will make the audience laugh. They also report straightforward events—fires, storms, earthquakes and assassinations—partly because such dramatic events are easier to recognize and report. Journalists are less adept at reporting complex phenomena, such as the causes and consequences of crime, poverty, inflation, unemployment and racial discrimination. Journalists also have difficulty reporting stories that never culminate in obvious events.

That is changing, however. The increased use of computers is allowing journalists to analyze information that in the past was difficult to gather and compare. Stories that report, analyze and explain are becoming more common at larger news organizations. Even small organizations attempt such projects. While technology has helped, editors still must publish a newspaper or air a broadcast every day, and they may need all their staff members just to accomplish that. Smaller budgets prevent smaller news organizations from hiring the staff necessary to spend time on big projects.

Another characteristic of news is that it varies somewhat from medium to medium. Daily newspapers emphasize events occurring in their communities during the last 24 hours. A few major dailies also strive to provide extensive national and international coverage. Weekly news magazines report events of national interest, often in more depth, and try to explain the events' significance. Television reports headline news—a few details about the day's major stories. Also, television news broadcasters favor visual stories—ones with strong, dramatic pictures—over stories that are complicated and difficult to illustrate.

A news organization's size and the size of the community it serves affect the selection of news. A news organization in a small town may report every local traffic accident; one in a medium-sized city may report only the accidents that cause serious injury; and big-city newspapers and television stations may report only the accidents that result in death. Similarly, newspapers in small cities often publish all wedding and engagement announcements and obituaries, whereas newspapers in larger cities publish only those of prominent citizens. Death announcements in some papers appear not as news stories, but as advertisements paid for by families.

The day of the week on which news occurs is important. Newspapers publish more advertisements on Wednesdays, Thursdays and Sundays, the days when readers plan their weekend shopping or have more time to spend reading. Most newspapers attempt to maintain a specific ratio of advertisements to news, often about 60 percent to 65 percent advertisements to 35 percent to 40 percent news. So on the days they publish more advertisements, newspapers also publish more news.

News organizations also develop tendencies and traditions to emphasize some types of news stories over others. The New York Post traditionally emphasizes crime, sex, sports and photographs. The New York Times, which appeals to a wealthier, better-educated audience than the Post, places a greater emphasis on political, business and foreign news. Similarly, some newspapers diligently investigate the problems in their communities, whereas others hesitate to publish stories that might offend their readers or advertisers.

Few publishers or station managers admit they favor any individuals or organizations. Yet, most develop certain "dos and don'ts" that reporters call "policies" or "sacred cows." Sacred cows reflect the interests of an organization's executives. In a few cases, news organization executives have used their power to distort the news, ordering their staffs to report only positive stories about the executives' favorite candidates, political parties, causes or organizations.

TYPES OF NEWS

Journalists recognize two major types of news: hard and soft. "Hard news" usually refers to serious and timely stories about important topics. The stories may describe a major crime, fire, accident, speech, labor dispute or political campaign. Journalists call hard news "spot news" or "straight news." "Breaking news," a similar label, refers to events occurring, or "breaking," now.

"Soft news" usually refers to feature or human-interest stories. Soft news entertains and informs. It may make readers laugh or cry, love or hate, envy or pity. While still newsworthy, soft news often is less timely than breaking news. Consequently, editors can delay soft stories to make room for more timely stories. Soft stories also may use a less formal style of writing, with more anecdotes, quotations and descriptions.

Nonjournalists are more likely to classify news as "good" or "bad." Many critics of the media claim news organizations focus too much on bad or negative news. Spiro T. Agnew, vice president to Richard Nixon, once called journalists "nattering nabobs of negativism." DeeDee Myers, former press secretary to President Clinton, said reporters have the philosophy that "good news is no news."

The late David Brinkley, who worked for decades as a reporter for NBC and ABC television news, criticized local newscasts for their emphasis on bad news. Brinkley complained:

> There's a tired old cliché that news is about a man biting a dog. That's silly. News is something worth knowing, something you didn't know already. I don't look at local news much. I'm tired of seeing stories about crime on the sidewalk: blood, knives, guns, death and destruction. I don't like the stories about bodies on sidewalks. It's of no interest except, of course, to the family of that body on the sidewalk.

Systematic studies have found, however, that most people exaggerate the amount of crime and violence reported by the media. Dozens of studies have examined the issue and found individual newspapers devote 2 percent to 35 percent of their space to violence. On average, one-tenth of newspaper content concerns violence.

Other critics claim that the news media are becoming detached from the audiences they are supposed to serve. James Fallows, former editor of U.S. News & World Report and author of "Breaking the News: How the News Media Undermines American Democracy," says the news

Things You Should Know About Readers

- About 54 percent of the nation's adults say they read a newspaper daily, compared to 74 percent who say they watch television news regularly.
- While 28 percent of the nation's adults read a magazine, only about 5 percent read a newsmagazine regularly.

The typical newspaper reader:

Spends an average of 26 minutes a day reading a paper.
Is about 35 years old.
Attended college.
Has a white–collar job.
Has a household income of $50,000 or more.
Is registered to vote.
Lives in an urban area.

Most popular news stories:

Wars, crime, disasters, weather, human interest, consumer information and scientific discoveries.

Least popular news stories:

Business, agriculture, religion, minor crimes, state government, art, music and literature.

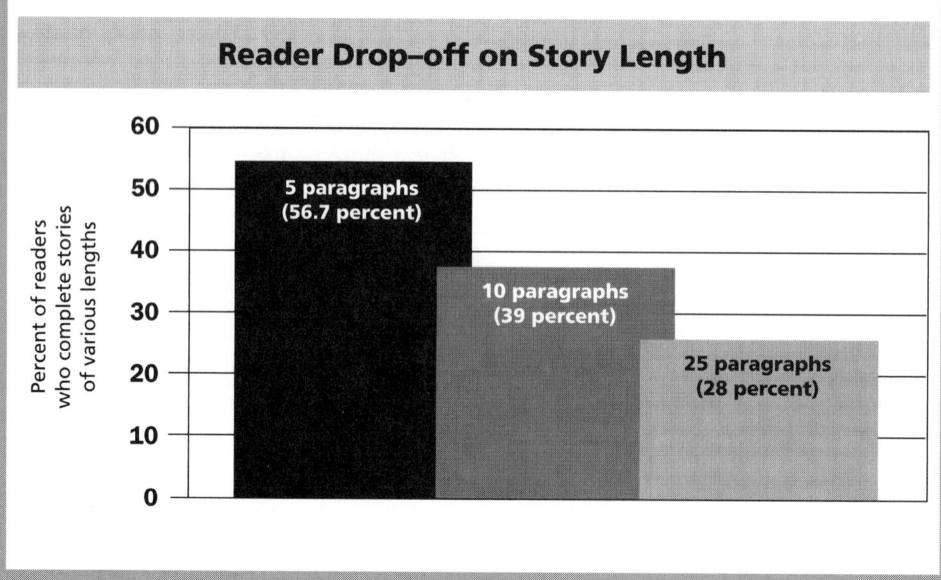

media "define the news in narrow and destructive ways." Fallows criticizes the media for focusing on the process rather than the news. In stories about public issues, the news media tend to cover the issues as feuds between political opponents instead of informing audiences about the issues. Such reporting tends to turn off audiences, Fallows claims, leaving them uninformed and cynical toward their government and bureaucratic officials, as well as the news media. He suggests making straight news stories more entertaining rather than filling space and air with entertainment. Fallows believes that to be successful in their role as the eyes and ears of the public, the news media need to make audiences feel less like spectators and more like participants in public life and the news.

PUBLIC/CIVIC JOURNALISM

Nearly 20 years ago, a movement began finding its way into many newsrooms—about 200 around the country today. That movement is influencing how journalists define and gather news. Proponents call it public or civic journalism. Professor Jay Rosen, a leading advocate of public journalism, says the movement is both a set of approaches to newsgathering and a philosophy about the proper task of the press.

The philosophy about the task of the press says this: If public life is in trouble in the United States, then journalism is in trouble. Therefore, journalists should do what they can to support public life. The press should help citizens participate in public life and take them seriously when they do, rather than treat citizens as spectators to a drama performed by professionals and technicians. And the press should nourish or create the sort of public talk some might call a deliberative dialogue. Most important, perhaps, journalists must see hope as an essential resource that they cannot deplete indefinitely without costs to the community.

Supporters base public journalism on a fundamental concept of democracy espoused by James Madison: By participating in the governing of themselves, people preserve democracy. To have the kind of democracy envisioned by Madison, the press must be a participant because a democracy needs an informed citizenry.

Americans have grown tired of the press because they believe the news is boring and biased. To combat the growing public disenchantment with the press and public life, public journalism offers a set of approaches for reporters to adopt. In political coverage, news organizations should turn away from the horse-race aspect of coverage—who's ahead, who's behind. Instead, journalists should conduct extensive interviews, polls and public forums with voters to find out what issues concern them. This process allows the public to decide what is important.

Proponents of public journalism say journalists cannot live in a vacuum as neutral observers. Reporters should listen to all voices, not just the loudest; and listen particularly to those people whose views on issues fall near the center, not just those on the extremes. Proponents of public journalism suggest that the routine five W's and H questions (who, what, when, where, why and how) work well but may not be the only ones that work. In public journalism, reporters should ask:

- Who—cares, is affected, needs to be included, has a stake, is missing from this discussion?
- What—are the consequences, does it mean to citizens, would this accomplish, values are at work?
- When—were things different, can things be different, should talk lead to action?
- Where—are we headed, is the common ground, should debate take place, is the best entry point for citizens?

A 13-year-old boy in Lakeland, Fla., was electrocuted while climbing a tree. The boy lost his footing, reached out and grabbed a high-voltage electric line. A Lakeland newspaper, The Ledger, published this photograph showing the victim's body being lowered from the tree, his legs hanging over the side of the bucket. Another photograph showed the boy's mother weeping and embracing a friend.

The Ledger's executive editor, Louis M. "Skip" Perez, defended the photos–but wondered how the mother felt. "Nothing you did made me angry," she told Perez. Nor was she offended by the photos. "I appreciate them now," she said. "They are the only photos I have of that day. You really couldn't see my son's face."

- Why—is this happening, do we need discussion, are things not happening, should we care?
- How—does it affect civic life, did the community do, does my story encourage action or help the public decide?

Reporters and editors at The Wichita (Kan.) Eagle created a foundation for tapping into a community's civic life that requires reporters to dig deeper into their communities. First, reporters need to explore the layers of civic life in their communities beyond the elected officials with whom they normally deal. They also must be aware of the different neighborhoods of their communities because people in different neighborhoods may have different experiences and opinions regarding issues. Finally, reporters need to identify the community leaders who can be engaged as sources on stories. Community leaders are not limited to elected officials; private citizens also can be knowledgeable sources regarding issues facing a community.

The Knight-Ridder Co., which owns the Eagle, surveyed more than 16,300 readers and nonreaders in the 26 communities where it publishes newspapers. The survey found that people with a real sense of connection to their communities are almost twice as likely to be regular readers of newspapers. While the result was not surprising, it was a message about what papers need to do. "Newspapers that immerse themselves in the lives of their communities, large or small, have the best prospects for success in the years ahead," James K. Batten, the late president of Knight-Ridder, once said. "And they have the best chance of drawing people in from the apathetic periphery to the vibrant center of community life. That will be good for the communities, and good for the newspapers."

APPLYING THE PRINCIPLES OF NEWS SELECTION

How do reporters find good news stories? Ken Fuson, an award-winning reporter for The Des Moines (Iowa) Register, has suggested, "Whenever you find yourself laughing at a situation, shaking your head or saying to someone 'Listen to this,' you've probably got a story." Fuson added that if an idea for a story is not a good one, "no amount of solid reporting or pretty writing can salvage it."

Some reporters can get story ideas from thinking about their own experiences. Things they see or hear about around town or around campus, events they attend, likes and dislikes, people who interest them all may become subjects for news stories.

Another approach is to ask other people for ideas. Reporters often ask people what they want to know, what puzzles them or what concerns them. Joseph Alsop, a Washington columnist for many years, said he asked 10 people a day for ideas for columns. By the end of the week, he would have 50 ideas. If only one in 10 proved usable, he still would have enough ideas to write his column for the next week. That type of digging is part of a reporter's job—perhaps the most important part.

THE CONCEPT OF OBJECTIVITY

A previous chapter noted that news stories must be objective, or free of bias. Journalists gather information and report it as factually as possible. They should not comment, interpret or evaluate. If an issue is controversial, journalists interview representatives of all the sides involved, then include as many opinions as possible. Some sources may make mistakes, and some may lie. Journalists may point out inconsistencies or inaccuracies in sources' statements, but they should not call them liars.

Journalists traditionally assumed, perhaps mistakenly, that if they reported all the information, their readers would think about the conflicting opinions and then decide which were most important and truthful. That has not always worked, so newspapers now publish separate stories analyzing major issues in the news. The stories, labeled "commentary" or "analysis," critically evaluate the news to help readers better understand it.

No human can be totally objective. Families, education, personal interests and religious and political beliefs all influence how reporters cover stories and what stories they see as newsworthy. Nevertheless, they strive to be as impartial and objective as possible. Routine newsroom practices encourage impartiality. News stories are rarely the work of a single individual. Normally, an editor assigns a story and a reporter writes it. Several other editors may then evaluate and change it. Each serves as a check on the others. If one expresses an opinion in a story, another has a chance to detect and eliminate that bias.

Biases, whether intentional or not, often appear in a story when a reporter covers only one side of an issue or gives one side disproportionately more space or time than others. Reporters may talk to more sources supporting an issue than those opposed. While it may be impossible for reporters to write about every conceivable side of an issue in their stories, they can provide readers with many sides rather than just one. By treating various sides of an issue equally and allowing partisans for each to state their case, reporters provide their audiences with facts they need to understand a story more fully. While total objectivity may be difficult to achieve, balance and fairness in a story can be achieved through thorough reporting and clear writing.

DETAILS NEWSPAPERS ARE RELUCTANT TO PUBLISH

Reporters must learn to recognize what information is not newsworthy. News organizations rarely mention routine procedures, such as the fact that a city council met in a city hall and began its meeting with the Pledge of Allegiance. Reporters delete the obvious and the irrelevant: the fact that police officers rushed to the scene of a traffic accident, or that an ambulance carried the injured to a hospital.

News organizations often must decide whether to use information about a crisis or threat. The so-called Unabomber, whose decades-long series of terror bombings baffled law enforcement authorities, sent a lengthy manifesto to The New York Times and The Washington Post. He promised that his killings would stop if the papers published his writings. The newspapers' executives decided to publish, knowing that the bomber might make good on his threat to continue bombing. Not all journalists agreed with that decision, but the publication of the manifesto led to the arrest of Theodore J. Kaczynski. One of his relatives, who noted similarities between the Unabomber manifesto and other anarchist writings by Kaczynski, alerted law enforcement agencies.

Offensive Details

Generally, editors omit material that is obscene, gruesome or in poor taste, usually on the grounds their newspapers or broadcasts reach children as well as adults. What would be the point, for example, of using grisly photographs or video, unless the material was highly newsworthy? Normally, news organizations avoid specifics about sexual assaults and omit most bloody details about accidents.

Different news organizations adopt different policies about what kinds of information they will use. Journalists must understand their employers' policies.

Sensationalism

Most news organizations avoid sensationalism, but not sensational stories. Historically, the word "sensationalism" has described an emphasis on or exaggeration of stories dealing with crime, sex and oddities. However, some events are inherently sensational—presidential assassinations, wars and other disasters. News stories do not make such events sensational, but the news media report on them because of their importance.

Journalists evaluating a potentially scandalous or sensational story must weigh several conflicting considerations and may ask themselves:

- Is the story newsworthy?
- Does the public need and have a right to this information?
- How seriously will this story harm the people it mentions?
- How will readers react to the information?

Some journalists might balance these interests by avoiding anything tasteless or sensational, but that approach can make reporting the news more difficult. A federal judge's ruling that the lyrics of a 2 Live Crew song were obscene contributed to a national furor about censorship and sexually graphic music. Ironically, it was impossible for most readers to decide for themselves whether the lyrics were offensive and obscene because newspapers refused to print the lyrics. The lyrics called women "bitches" and mentioned forcing anal sex on a woman, forcing a woman to lick feces and "busting" the walls of a vagina. Another controversy involved the work of the late photographer Robert Mapplethorpe. News organizations reported that some people objected to exhibits of Mapplethorpe's photographs because some were "homoerotic." Editors were hesitant to report that one photograph showed a man urinating into another man's mouth, that another photograph showed a finger inserted in a penis, and that three other photographs showed men with various objects inserted in their rectums. Now news organizations find themselves reporting stories about obscene words and images used on the Internet. Again, editors must decide what language to use to accurately report messages coming through cyberspace without offending readers and viewers.

There are no right or wrong answers to these problems; each is a matter of individual judgment. The examples, however, reflect journalists' dilemma. Journalists are reluctant to report graphic details likely to offend the public. Yet readers denied those details may consider them important.

Rumors

News organizations are reluctant to report rumors, especially harmful ones. Yet the failure to report some rumors may confuse, frighten or alienate the public. As a rumor spreads through a community, more people are likely to become interested in it and believe it. People who hear a rumor but see no coverage of it also are likely to believe journalists are deliberately suppressing the story.

Some rumors involve important issues, such as racial conflicts, and may cause widespread anxiety. Normally, responsible editors investigate the rumors and, if they find no evidence the rumors are true, conclude there is no story. Editors will consider a rumor's effects upon the community, and especially upon innocent people. They may decide a story exposing a rumor as untrue will be more helpful to the people involved—such as by clearing a person's reputation—than if the news organization remained silent.

A story on the Drudge Report, a Web site run by Matt Drudge, alleged that presidential candidate John Kerry had had an affair with a young woman. Most news organizations refused to pick up Drudge's report, which lacked sources or details, such as the name of the young woman. The rumor finally became a news story in major publications after radio talk show host Don Imus asked Kerry whether he had had an affair. Kerry denied it. News organizations also tracked down the young woman, who also vehemently denied the allegation, and the rumor quickly died. For major news organizations, however, what was newsworthy was not the rumor itself, but Kerry's denial of the rumor.

Rape

Most news organizations refuse to identify rape victims, even though they have a legal right to do so. Some journalists believe that publishing the names of victims may discourage women from reporting rapes. When professional basketball star Kobe Bryant was arrested on a rape charge, mainstream news organizations withheld his accuser's name. They continued to do so even after a number of Web sites unaffiliated with news organizations had identified her. Reporters should learn their organization's policy regarding the use of rape victims' names.

To help the media deal with issues concerning victims and survivors of rape and other violent crimes, the National Center for the Victims of Crime in Arlington, Va., has established several voluntary guidelines. Among other things, the guidelines advise reporters to:

- Give the public factual, objective information concerning the type of crime, where it occurred, the name or description of the alleged offender if appropriate, and facts that may prevent other crimes.
- Give equal coverage to the victim's and the criminal's perspectives when possible.
- Quote the victims, families and friends fairly and in context.
- Avoid photographing or filming lurid crime details, such as bodies or instruments of torture.
- Notify and ask permission from victims and their families before using pictures or photographs for documentaries or other news features.
- Refrain from publishing unverified or ambiguous facts about the victims, their demeanor, background or relationship to the offender.

Officials of the National Center for Victims of Crime say news reporters will get better stories about crime if they show sensitivity toward the victims.

Other Details Reporters Avoid

News organizations constantly search for humorous stories, but few make fun of another person's misfortune. Also, the news media generally do not identify juveniles accused or found guilty of a crime, unless they are tried as adults for a serious offense like murder. In many cases, names of the juveniles are not released until authorities have filed charges and prosecutors have decided to try juvenile defendants as adults. However, the high-profile shootings of students at elementary and high schools around the United States in the late 1990s received so much media attention that the juveniles involved often were identified before charges were filed.

Some editors hesitate to mention trade names, because they think publication of trade names is unnecessary and provides free advertising for the products. But detail is important to a story, and the use of specific names can add to that detail. However, unless a trade name helps readers understand a story, reporters should use generic names. "Soft drink" is an acceptable generic term for Coke or Pepsi. Similarly, a journalist should report that someone used a "tissue" rather than a Kleenex or made a "photocopy" rather than a Xerox.

Manufacturers encourage journalists to use trade names properly. They place advertisements in magazines read by journalists to remind them to capitalize all trade names. Manufacturers want journalists to use their trade names to describe the products made by their companies, not similar products made by competitors. If the public begins to use a trade name to describe every product within a certain category, the manufacturer may lose its exclusive right to use that trade name. Some trade names have become generic terms. Manufacturers lost the right to the words' exclusive use when the public repeatedly used the words to describe similar products. Examples include:

aspirin	escalator	raisin bran
brassiere	kerosene	shredded wheat
cola	lanolin	tollhouse cookies
corn flakes	linoleum	trampoline
cube steak	mimeograph	yo-yo
dry ice	nylon	zipper

If carried to an extreme, the media's policy of avoiding trade names can have unfortunate results. When a small airplane crashed during a snowstorm in a mountainous area of California, a family aboard the plane survived for three days by drinking melted snow and eating boxes of Cracker Jack. In reporting the family's ordeal and rescue, some newspapers pointlessly substituted the term "candied popcorn" for Cracker Jack. Similarly, a copy editor became disgusted because his paper refused to allow him to use the trade name Jeep in a story about several hundred people who had formed a caravan of Jeeps for a weekend camping trip (called a "Jeep Jamboree"). He substituted the phrase "small truck-type four-wheel-drive vehicles of various manufacture." He did not expect his newspaper to print this circumlocution, but it did.

Common sense should dictate whether a reporter uses a trade name. Include the trade name in the story if it seems pertinent.

THE IMPORTANCE OF ACCURACY

When Mark Twain began his career as a reporter, an editor told him never to state as fact anything he could not personally verify. Here is his account of a gala social event: "A woman giving the name of Mrs. James Jones, who is reported to be one of the society leaders of the city, is said to have given what purported to be a party yesterday to a number of alleged ladies. The hostess claims to be the wife of a reputed attorney."

Reporters should avoid taking the advice given to Twain as literally as he did, but accuracy is important. Errors affect the public's perception of the media and ultimately the media's credibility with the public.

Thomas E. Franklin captured the mood of the country with this photograph of three New York firefighters raising an American flag over the rubble of the World Trade Center. The photo was published in The Record of Hackensack, N.J., and has been compared to the famous 1945 photo by Joe Rosenthal of the Associated Press showing Marines raising the flag on Iwo Jima. (Reprinted in Editor & Publisher Oct. 29, 2001)

Accuracy in Facts

The information appearing in newspapers and on television news is more accurate than most Americans believe. Professionals who manage news organizations do their best to report the news as fairly and accurately as possible. Journalists, however, are not always able to convince the public of that fact. When reporters Bob Woodward and Carl Bernstein of The Washington Post investigated the Watergate scandal, their editors required that they confirm every important fact with at least two sources. This policy is not uncommon. Editors insist on accuracy.

Debbie Price, former executive editor of the Fort Worth (Texas) Star-Telegram, says it is critical to get everything right—names, streets, time—even the most obscure detail. Mistakes hurt the reputations of reporters and their news organizations.

Some reporting errors have been stupendous. In the rush to be first with a story, several news organizations reported that the bombing of a federal office building in Oklahoma City was the work of Middle Eastern terrorists. As a result, some angry people threatened Arab-Americans, their businesses and mosques. If news organizations had waited only a few hours, that mob reaction might have been avoided, for law enforcement agencies quickly identified two Americans as the likely bombers. Both of them—Timothy McVeigh and Terry Nichols—were eventually convicted of the bombing.

Other factual errors are embarrassing. A daily newspaper in Iowa was forced to publish a correction after one of its reporters mistakenly quoted a dead sheriff. The reporter had called the sheriff's office to obtain information about an accident and assumed the man who answered the telephone was the sheriff. He was the sheriff, but a new one; his predecessor had died a few weeks earlier. In writing a story about the accident, the reporter—who failed to ask the sheriff his name—attributed all the information to his dead predecessor.

Carelessness and laziness cause most factual errors. After finishing a news story, reporters must recheck their notes to be sure the story is accurate. If reporters lack some information, they should consult their sources again. If the sources are unavailable or unable to provide the information, reporters may have to delete portions of the story or, in extreme cases, kill the entire story. Reporters never should guess or make any assumptions about the facts; they are too likely to make an error.

Conscientious news organizations check their stories' accuracy. About 50 daily newspapers employ a proofreading affiliate in Lakeland, Fla. Employees there read each newspaper twice a year to find factual and grammatical errors. In 10 years the error rate has gone from an average of four per page to 2.5. Some papers assign staff members to monitor whether stories are factual, and some send sources copies of the stories in which they are mentioned, with letters asking for reactions. Copy editors double-check reporters' math by calculating percentages and statistics in stories. Many errors occur because reporters fail to check their stories' internal consistency. For example:

> Of the 10 men and women who were interviewed, five favored the proposal, three opposed it and three said they had not reached a decision.

Reporters also must understand a topic before they begin to write about it. Too often, when asked about a fuzzy sentence or paragraph, beginners respond, "I really didn't understand that myself." If reporters do not understand something they have written, neither will the audience. Reporters who are puzzled should go back to their source and ask for a better explanation or find a source who can explain it.

Accurate writing requires specifics instead of generalities. Getting specifics requires more effort, but in the end the story will be clearer, more accurate and more interesting to readers and viewers. The trick is to double-check, even triple-check, all the information, to ask for specifics, to ask for spellings, to ask whether the information you have is correct.

Sometimes inaccuracies appear in news stories because reporters fabricated quotations, sources or facts or plagiarized. News organizations usually fire reporters caught in such misconduct. The New York Times fired reporter Jayson Blair after discovering he had made up quotations, sources and other details in stories published over a seven-month period. A couple of senior editors at The Times resigned because they had continued to trust Blair even after doubts arose about his truthfulness. A news organization's most important asset is its credibility, and managers must protect that asset.

Accuracy in Names

News organizations are particularly careful in their handling of names. Spelling errors damage a paper's reputation and infuriate its readers, particularly when the misspelled names appear in wedding announcements, obituaries and other stories readers will save. Consequently, many newspapers require reporters to verify the spelling of every name that appears in local news stories. They can do so by consulting a second source, usually a telephone book or city directory.

Other errors arise because of a reporter's carelessness. A source may say his name is "Karl" and a reporter may assume his name is spelled with a "C" rather than with a "K." Dozens of other common American names have two or more spellings, such as Ann (Anne), Cathy (Cathie, Kathy), Cindy (Cyndi), Fredrick (Fredric, Frederic, Frederick), Gail (Gayle), John (Jon), Linda (Lynda), Steven (Stephen) and Susie (Suzy).

Obstacles to Accuracy

Absolute accuracy may be impossible. Because of the need to meet strict deadlines, reporters work quickly and sometimes lack the time to perfect their stories. Reporters also are vulnerable to misinformation. They get much of their information from sources. Some sources may not know all the facts, and others may lie. Reporters, however, may unknowingly report a source's misstatements. If a prominent person discusses a matter important to the public, that discussion is news and must be reported, even if reporters doubt the comments' validity. This definition of news required journalists to report President Lyndon Johnson's claims of victory in Vietnam, President Richard Nixon's claims of innocence in Watergate and President Bill Clinton's denials of his affair with Monica Lewinsky.

Historians often can be more accurate than journalists because they see more of a story before they begin to write. Journalists obtain stories piece by piece and cannot always predict the outcome or significance of the events they cover. Reporters sometimes will revisit a story at a key moment to put events into perspective and give them meaning. Such stories allow readers to get a complete picture of events that originally came in piecemeal fashion.

Journalists might eliminate even more errors by giving the people named in news stories an opportunity to read and correct those stories before papers publish them. The idea surfaces most often among science writers and other journalists who deal with complex issues. However, editors generally prohibit the practice. They fear that it will consume too much time and that sources may try to change the statements they disagreed with, not just factual errors.

Researchers who have analyzed sources' corrections have found that sources believe that about half the stories they are shown contain an error. However, many perceived errors are judgmental rather than factual. Sources may interpret some facts differently from reporters or want to include, emphasize or de-emphasize different facts. Sources also may complain that a story misquotes them or a headline distorts a story. Only about one-third of the errors sources point out are typographical or factual errors. And most factual errors involve misspelled names and inaccurate times, dates, numbers, addresses, locations and titles.

Most journalists agree a correction should appear in a paper or on the air as quickly as possible. Some believe it is healthy to go through the catharsis of admitting an error. By correcting errors, journalists show their willingness to respond to public concerns, improve their relationship with the public and improve their credibility. Others argue that admitting all errors, including the most trivial, harms a news organization's credibility.

Some news organizations identify the reporter or editor who made a mistake. Others believe public humiliation does not solve the problem or help an individual improve. Many news organizations fire journalists who consistently make errors, because errors affect the integrity of the organization.

SUGGESTED READINGS

Adam, G. Stuart. *Notes Toward a Definition of Journalism: Understanding an Old Craft as an Art Form.* St. Petersburg, Fla.: Poynter Institute for Media Studies, 1993.

A Free and Responsible Press (The Hutchins Commission Report). Chicago: University of Chicago Press, 1947.

Charity, Arthur. *Doing Public Journalism.* New York: Guilford, 1995.

Clark, Roy Peter. *A Call to Leadership.* St. Petersburg, Fla.: Poynter Institute for Media Studies, 1992.

Cronkite, Walter. *A Reporter's Life.* New York: Alfred A. Knopf, 1996.

Dahlgren, Peter, and Colin Sparks. *Journalism and Popular Culture.* Newbury Park, Calif.: Sage Publications, 1992.

Fallows, James. *Breaking the News: How the Media Undermine American Democracy.* New York: Pantheon Books, 1996.

Hachten, William A. *The Troubles of Journalism: A Critical Look at What's Right and Wrong With the Press.* 2nd ed. Mahwah, N.J.: Lawrence Erlbaum Associates, 2001.

Jensen, Carl. *Censored: The News That Didn't Make the News—and Why.* Chapel Hill, N.C.: Shelburne Press, 1993. (Published annually since 1976.)

Kaniss, Phyllis. *Making Local News.* Chicago: University of Chicago Press, 1991.

Kovach, Bill, and Tom Rosenstiel. *The Elements of Journalism: What Newspeople Should Know and the Public Should Expect.* New York: Three Rivers Press, 2001.

Merritt, Davis. *Public Journalism & Public Life: Why Telling the News Is Not Enough.* Hillsdale, N.J.: Erlbaum, 1995.

Miller, Edward D. *The Charlotte Project: Helping Citizens Take Back Democracy.* St. Petersburg, Fla.: Poynter Institute for Media Studies, 1994.

Reah, Danuta. *The Language of Newspapers.* 2nd ed. New York: Routledge, 2002.

Rosen, Jay. *Community Connectedness: Passwords for Public Journalism.* The Poynter Papers: No. 3. St. Petersburg, Fla.: Poynter Institute for Media Studies, 1993.

———. *Politics, Vision and the Press: Toward a Public Agenda for Journalism.* New York: Twentieth Century Fund, 1992.

Reese, Stephen D., Oscar H. Gandy Jr., and August E. Grant, eds. *Framing Public Life: Perspectives on Media and Our Understanding of the Social World.* Mahwah, N.J.: Lawrence Erlbaum Associates, 2003.

The Harwood Group. *Timeless Values: Staying True to Journalistic Principles in the Age of New Media.* Reston, Va.: American Society of Newspaper Editors, 1995.

———. *Tapping Civic Life: How To Report First, and Best, What's Happening in Your Community.* Washington, D.C.: Pew Center for Civic Journalism, 1996.

Zelizer, Barbie, and Christopher Benson, eds. *Journalism After September 11.* New York: Routledge, 2002.

Name ______________________________ Class ______________________ Date ______

EXERCISE 1

SELECTING AND REPORTING THE NEWS

NEWS JUDGMENT

Every day, journalists make difficult decisions involving matters of importance, interest, taste, ethics and myriad other considerations. The following questions ask you to make those types of decisions. After deciding which stories to use and emphasize, compare your decisions with your classmates'.

1. As editor of your local daily newspaper, you have space for one more photograph on Page 1. Circle the photograph in each of the following pairs that you would select.

   A. A photograph showing the first lady visiting an elementary school in your city.

   B. A photograph of college students protesting an increase in tuition and fees at a university in your city. The increase is the fourth in five years.

   A. A photograph showing two students from one of your city's high schools participating in the semifinal round of a national spelling bee.

   B. A photograph of three high school seniors being led away in handcuffs after being charged with vandalizing school property over the weekend. The three students caused nearly $80,000 in damage to a computer room and the main office. They sprayed foam from fire extinguishers onto computers and into file cabinets and smashed computer monitors and other equipment.

   A. A photograph of a young child in Iraq handing a bunch of flowers to a U.S. soldier.

   B. A photograph of the bodies of an Iraqi father and his four children killed in a suicide bombing near an American compound in Iraq.

2. Rank the following nine stories by their newsworthiness, starting with "1" for the most newsworthy:

   A. ______ The U.S. Department of Education released a report today that said high school students in your city have reached an all-time high in scoring on their SAT exams.

   B. ______ The state approved a plan to build a six-lane bypass around your city that will cost $284 million and destroy thousands of acres of prime agricultural and developable land.

   C. ______ A city man was charged in an arson fire that destroyed an apartment building and killed eight people, including five children.

   D. ______ FBI investigators visited the public libraries in your city to check on the reading records of several local residents who the FBI believe may be linked to terrorism.

E. ______ Three Israelis and 10 Palestinians were killed in a suicide bombing at a bus stop in a suburb of Tel Aviv.

F. ______ The parents of quintuplets in your city saw their five children off to school for the first time, as the three boys and two girls were picked up by a bus that took them to kindergarten.

G. ______ More than 100 people were killed and another 800 injured when a runaway passenger train collided with a freight train in Tanzania.

H. ______ Tennis star Andre Agassi today announced that he is retiring from tennis and plans to become a sports announcer.

I. _______ City officials agreed at their Tuesday night council meeting to spend $128 million to build a new trash incinerator that would burn trash from the city as well as from six surrounding counties.

3. Rank the following nine stories by their newsworthiness, starting with "1" for the most newsworthy:

A. ______ The driver of a compact car escaped injury early today when her car was struck by a freight train at a railroad crossing.

B. ______ A chest containing manuscripts of music written by Johann Sebastian Bach was discovered today in Russia, more than half a century after it was lost during World War II.

C. ______ Police and prison officials in your city were conducting a mock prison escape when three inmates walked out of the prison and disappeared.

D. ______ A new senior citizens' center opened on the east side of the city offering nearby residents a place to get a hot meal at lunch time, participate in games and educational programs, and to pass time with friends.

E. ______ A 14-year-old city girl who had been missing for six months was found safe in Mexico with a man she met on the Internet who turned out to be a convicted murderer.

F. ______ An Arkansas woman was convicted in the deaths of her four children who were drowned in the family's bathtub. She was found guilty of four counts of second-degree murder.

G. ______ Your state's Department of Labor and Industry announced today that the unemployment rate rose to 7.5 percent despite a rally that saw significant increases in the stock market.

H. ______ A city police officer was arrested and charged with aggravated assault and using undue force after he broke the leg of a man who was attending a concert. The officer who was on duty patrolling the stadium parking lot mistook the man for a scalper and got into an argument with him and threw him to the ground.

I. _______ A group of teenagers from a nondenominational church youth organization volunteered to help two elderly sisters maintain their home so that they would not be fined by the city for having a blighted property. The youths mowed grass, trimmed hedges and painted the sisters' house.

4. Patricia Richards, a 52-year-old business woman in your city, today announced that she is running for mayor. You know and can prove all the following facts, but have

never reported them because she was a private citizen. Mark the facts you would report today.

A. ______ Richards has been divorced three times.

B. ______ At the age of 17, Richards and two friends were charged with stealing a car. The charges were dropped because the car was recovered undamaged and the car's owner, a neighbor, declined to prosecute.

C. ______ Richards has diabetes.

D. ______ Richards has had two abortions.

E. ______ Richards is a recovered alcoholic; she has not had a drink in 20 years.

F. ______ Before going into business for herself, she was fired from two other jobs because of her drinking.

G. ______ Her campaign literature says she attended the University of Iowa, yet she never graduated.

H. ______ She established, owns and manages the city's largest chain of furniture stores.

I. ______ Various tax and other public records reveal that her chain of furniture stores is valued at $20 million and, last year, earned a profit of $2.3 million.

J. ______ Each year, Richards donates more than $1 million to local charities that help troubled young women, but always avoids publicity, insisting that the charities never mention her donations.

5. Your state representative, Constance Wei, was involved in a traffic accident that resulted in the death of another driver and his passenger. Which of the following details would you use and which would you discard?

A. ______ Wei is married and has two children.

B. ______ As an attorney, Wei successfully defended two people who had been accused of vehicular manslaughter.

C. ______ Wei was speeding and ran a red light.

D. ______ A woman, who didn't want to be identified, called your newsroom and said the minivan she and her children were riding in was almost struck at an intersection one time by a car driven by Wei.

E. ______ Friends of Wei said she often joked about having a "lead foot."

F. ______ Police said Wei refused to cooperate with them when they arrived at the scene of the accident.

G. ______ Wei has had five tickets in the past four years for speeding and reckless driving.

H. ______ Wei was first elected to office nine years ago.

I. ______ Wei was driving on an expired driver's license.

J. ______ Wei once sponsored a bill to eliminate the point system used to penalize drivers stopped for motor vehicle law violations. Drivers would lose their licenses after accumulating a certain number of points.

CHAPTER 6

BASIC NEWS LEADS

Freedom of speech is a right to be fought for and not a blessing to be wished for.
(Kofi A. Annan, secretary-general of the United Nations)

The first paragraph or two in a news story is called the "lead." The lead (some people spell it "lede") is the most important part of a story—and the most difficult part to write. Like the opening paragraphs of a short story or novel, the lead of a news story attracts the reader and, if it is well-written, arouses a reader's interest. It should tell the reader the central point of the story, not hide the subject with unnecessary or misleading words and phrases.

THE SUMMARY NEWS LEAD

Every news story must answer six questions: Who? How? Where? Why? When? and What? The lead, however, is not the place to answer all of them. The lead should answer only the one or two questions that are most interesting, newsworthy and unusual. For example, few readers in large cities know the ordinary citizens involved in news stories, so the names of those people do not have to appear in leads. Also, the exact time and place at which events occurred may also be unimportant.

To determine which questions are most important for a story, consider the following points:

1. What is the most important information? What is the story's central point?
2. What was said or done about the topic? What happened or what action was taken?
3. What are the most recent developments? What happened today or yesterday?
4. Which facts are most likely to affect or interest readers?
5. Which facts are most unusual?

Each of the following leads emphasizes the answer to only one of the six basic questions—the question that seems most important for that particular story:

> **WHO:** DAVOS, Switzerland—Microsoft billionaire Bill Gates pledged $100 million to the search for an AIDS vaccine and challenged the rich and powerful at the World Economic Forum to pitch in as well.
>
> *(The Associated Press)*

HOW: A postal worker at a mail processing center walked up to his boss, pulled a gun from a paper bag and shot him to death today, the authorities said.

(The Associated Press)

WHERE: BEIJING—A strong earthquake shook northeastern China early today and was felt as far away as Beijing, the official Xinhua News Agency reported. There were no immediate reports of deaths.

(The Associated Press)

WHY: WASHINGTON—New home sales shot up 8.1 percent in May, the biggest advance in six months, as low mortgage rates motivated buyers.

(The Associated Press)

WHEN: Before Friday, Kishan Garib, 12, had never been away from his family.

(The Chambersburg [Pa.] Public Opinion)

WHAT: WASHINGTON—About 1.7 percent of U.S. college women were raped during the 1996–97 school year and an additional 1.1 percent were victims of attempted rape, according to a Justice Department study that suggested the government is underestimating the number of rapes in America.

(The Associated Press)

When writers try to answer all these questions in one paragraph, they create complicated and confusing leads. Here's an example of an overloaded lead and a possible revision:

Charles E. Vickers, 47, of 1521 Yarmouth Drive, died and John Aston Walters, 39, of 1867 Colonial Ave., was severely injured Sunday afternoon when the bicycles they were riding were struck near the intersection of Weston and Falmouth roads by a car driven by a man police said had a blood alcohol count of nearly .23 percent and was driving without a license because it had been revoked last year after his fourth conviction for driving under the influence of alcohol.

REVISED: One Mechanicsburg man is dead and another severely injured after the bicycles they were riding were struck by a drunken driver Sunday afternoon near the intersection of Weston and Falmouth roads.

Because people and what they do are central to many news stories, some journalists recognize two variations on the summary news lead: the immediate-identification lead and the delayed-identification lead. Reporters use the immediate-identification lead when the identities of the major subjects in the story are important or are well known:

Federal Reserve Board Chairman Alan Greenspan delivered a mixed message to Congress on Wednesday, saying the country has made economic progress but warning, "we are not out of the woods yet."

(The Detroit News)

A judge sentenced former Harris County Sheriff's Deputy John Lawrence, 28, to four years in prison Friday for using and buying drugs while on duty.

In many stories, the names of the main subjects are not as important as what those people did or what happened to them. For those stories, reporters use leads that withhold complete identification of the people involved until the second or third paragraph. The following leads are examples of delayed-identification leads:

An east Philadelphia man held his girlfriend's baby at knifepoint for more than two hours Saturday night before police officers captured him after shooting him with a stun gun.

An 82-year-old Dallas woman is slowly recovering from a gunshot wound to the head, and police say they may be on the verge of charging a suspect with attempted murder.

Leads that hold back details so the reporter can get to the central point of the article more quickly are called "blind leads." Beginners should not misinterpret the terminology. A blind lead does not hide the central point of the story, only information that the reader does not need immediately. Blind leads let the reporter tell readers what the story is about to pique their interest and get them into the story.

A "catchall graf" usually follows the blind lead to briefly identify sources and answers questions created by the lead. Missing details appear in subsequent paragraphs. Here's an example of a blind lead:

> It was an Altoona company that lost its appeal to Commonwealth Court, but it's the state agency charged with overseeing construction matters that's feeling the pain.
>
> *(The [Harrisburg, Pa.] Patriot-News)*

In its second paragraph, the article identified the company and what the case involved. In the third paragraph, the article identified the state agency involved and what it had done wrong.

Before reporters can write effective leads, however, they must learn to recognize what is news. Leads that fail to emphasize the news—the most interesting and important details—are worthless. After deciding which facts are most newsworthy, a reporter must summarize those facts in sharp, clear sentences, giving a simple, straightforward account of what happened. Examine these leads, which provide clear, concise summaries of momentous events in the nation's history:

> NEW YORK—President Bush promised swift retaliation for the attacks that crumbled the World Trade Center's twin towers and shook the Pentagon yesterday, assaults that killed or injured thousands in the worst act of terrorism against the United States in history.
>
> *(The [Westchester County, N.Y.] Journal News)*

> DENVER—Timothy McVeigh, the once-honorable soldier who turned his killing skills against the people of Oklahoma City, was condemned Friday to die.
>
> *(The Dallas Morning News)*

> DALLAS, Nov. 22—A sniper armed with a high-powered rifle assassinated President Kennedy today. Barely two hours after Mr. Kennedy's death, Vice President Johnson took the oath of office as the thirty-sixth President of the United States.
>
> *(The Associated Press)*

SENTENCE STRUCTURE IN LEADS

Most leads are a single sentence, and that sentence must follow all the normal rules for punctuation, grammar, word usage and verb tense. If an event occurred in the past, the lead must use the past tense, not the present. Leads must be complete sentences and should include all the necessary articles—the words "a," "an" and "the."

Some problems with sentence structure arise because beginners confuse a story's lead with its headline. The lead is the first paragraph of a news story. The headline is a brief summary that appears in larger type above the story. To save space, editors use only a few key words in each headline. However, that style of writing is not appropriate for leads:

> HEADLINE: Crash in Pa: 'We are being hijacked!'
>
> LEAD: STONY CREEK, Pa.—An investigation will continue today into whether the deadly crash of a United Airlines jet here yesterday was linked to two acts of apparent terrorism that destroyed the World Trade Center and damaged the Pentagon.
>
> *(The [Philadelphia] Inquirer)*

Reporters usually write leads that use subject-verb-object word order. Most leads begin with the subject, which is closely followed by an active verb and then by the object of the verb. Reporters deviate from that style only in the rare case that a different sentence structure better tells the news. Leads that begin with long qualifying clauses or phrases lack the clarity of simpler, more direct sentences. Long introductory clauses also clutter leads, burying the news amid a jumble of less significant details. Writing coach Paula LaRocque calls these "backed-into leads." She describes them as "one of the most pervasive and uninviting habits a writer can fall into":

> WASHINGTON—In the most significant court case dealing with money and politics since 1976, a special three-judge panel today upheld several major provisions of a sweeping new law limiting political donations but found that some of its measures were unconstitutional.
>
> *(The New York Times)*
>
> REVISED: A special three-judge panel today upheld major portions of a new federal law limiting political campaign contributions, but it also found some parts of the law unconstitutional.

Before it was revised, the lead delayed the news—information about the court's decision—until after a 13-word introductory phrase containing information that could probably be delayed until the second or third paragraph.

GUIDELINES FOR WRITING EFFECTIVE LEADS

Be Concise

Newspapers' concise style of writing makes it easy for the public to read and understand leads, but difficult for reporters to write them.

Two- or three-sentence leads often become wordy, repetitious and choppy, particularly when all the sentences are very short. Like most multisentence leads, the following example can be made more concise as a single sentence:

> Two women robbed a shopper in a local supermarket Tuesday. One woman distracted the shopper, and the second woman grabbed her purse, which contained about $50.
>
> REVISED: Two women stole a purse containing $50 from a shopper in a local supermarket Tuesday.

The original lead was redundant. It reported two women robbed a shopper, then described the robbery.

Reporters use two-sentence leads only when the need to do so is compelling. Often, the second sentence emphasizes an interesting or unusual fact of secondary importance. Other times, the second sentence is necessary because it is impossible to summarize all the necessary information about a complex topic in a single sentence. The following example from The Washington Post uses a second sentence to illustrate and explain the first:

> In 1988, Joseph I. Lieberman took a calculated political risk. He was Connecticut's popular Democratic attorney general, but he decided to challenge the state's imperious U.S. senator, Republican Lowell P. Weicker Jr.

Sometimes professionals do a poor job of keeping their leads concise. A recent study of news sources and the average number of words in their leads produced these results:

Source	Average length of leads in words
The Washington Post	39
Los Angeles Times	34.6
The New York Times	33
United Press International	30.5
The Associated Press	30
Scripps Howard News Service	25.5

Many readers find a 25-word lead "difficult" to read and a 29-word lead "very difficult." A better average would be 18 to 20 words. Reporters should examine their leads critically to determine whether they are wordy or repetitious, or contain facts that could be shifted to later paragraphs.

Reporters shorten leads by eliminating unnecessary background information—dates, names, locations—or the description of routine procedures. Leads should not contain too many names, particularly names few readers would recognize or the names of people who played minor or routine roles in a story. If a lead includes someone's name, it also may have to identify that person, and the identification will require even more words. Descriptive phrases can substitute for names. Similarly, the precise time and location of events can be reported in a later paragraph. A lead should report a story's highlights as concisely as possible, not all its minor details:

> A former Roxbury woman, who has eluded federal law enforcement authorities since she allegedly hijacked a flight from San Juan to Cuba using a plastic flare gun in 1983, was arrested Wednesday as she stood alone on Union Street in Boston, according to the Federal Bureau of Investigation.
>
> REVISED: The FBI on Wednesday arrested a former Roxbury woman who has eluded authorities since 1983, when she was accused of hijacking an airplane.

Although leads can be too long, they cannot be too short. An effective lead may contain only four, five or six words: "The president is dead" or "Americans landed on the moon" or "There's new hope for couch potatoes."

Be Specific

Good leads contain interesting details and are so specific that readers can visualize the events they describe. As you read the following lead from The Tampa (Fla.) Tribune, you should be able to imagine the dramatic scene it describes:

> At 59, she'd never touched a gun—until someone held one to her head.

The following lead is less interesting because it is abstract and contains vague generalities. Reporters can easily transform such leads into more interesting ones by adding more specific details:

> The city council passed an ordinance that will affect all parents and teenagers living within city limits.
>
> REVISED: The city council ignored the objections of the mayor and numerous parents and voted 6-1 Monday to enact a dusk-to-dawn curfew to keep youngsters off city streets.

Some leads use worn-out clichés—a lazy way of summarizing a story. Avoid saying that "a step has been taken" or that someone has moved "one step closer" to a goal. Present specific details:

> University officials moved one step closer to increasing tuition and fees for the upcoming school year, leaving students up in the air.
>
> REVISED: The university's Board of Governors voted Tuesday to increase tuition and fees 10 percent next year to offset cuts in state funding.

An anxious American soldier watches outside Red Cross headquarters in Baghdad, Iraq, shortly after an attack by a suicide bomber, one of five such attacks that day. Just as photographer Michael Kamber captured the emotion of this situation, so should lead writers strive to capture the emotion of the events they describe.

Avoid "iffy" leads that say one thing may happen if another happens. In addition to being too vague, "iffy" leads are too abstract, tentative and qualified. Report the story's more immediate and concrete details.

Use Strong, Active Verbs

A single word—a descriptive verb—can transform a routine lead into a dramatic one. As you read the following lead, for example, you may be able to picture what happened:

> Vincente Chavez Sr. said he didn't feel the high-velocity police bullets tear into his body, shattering bones, cutting nerves and severing a finger on his left hand.
>
> *(The [Sioux Falls, S.D.] Argus Leader)*

The following lead uses several colorful verbs to describe the capture of a wayward Angus steer that escaped his handlers:

> The suspect tore through a homeowner's fence, ripped the wires from a satellite dish with his teeth, slammed head-on into a travel trailer, then bolted down the street on his way to a weird encounter with a canoe.
>
> *(The Orlando [Fla.] Sentinel)*

Avoid passive-voice constructions. Strong, active-voice verbs are more colorful, interesting and dramatic:

> One person *was killed* and four others *were injured* Sunday morning when their car, which *was traveling* west on Interstate 80, *hit* a concrete bridge pillar and *was engulfed* in flames.
>
> REVISED: A car *traveling* west on Interstate 80 *swerved* across two eastbound lanes, *slammed* into a concrete bridge pillar and *burst* into flames, *killing* one person and *injuring* four others Sunday morning.

Writers can easily convert passive voice to the active voice. Simply rearrange the words, so the sentence begins by reporting (1) who . . . (2) did what . . . (3) to whom. Instead of reporting: "Rocks and bottles were thrown at firefighters," report: "Rioters threw rocks and bottles at firefighters."

Emphasize the Magnitude of the Story

If a story is important, reporters emphasize its magnitude in the lead. Most good leads emphasize the impact stories have on people. When describing a natural disaster or man-made catastrophe, such as airplane crashes, tornadoes or major fires, reporters emphasize the number of people killed, injured and left homeless. They also emphasize the dollar cost of the damage to buildings or other objects. When describing a storm, reporters may emphasize the amount of rain or snow that fell. The following lead from an Associated Press story does not deal with a disaster or catastrophe, but it shows how magnitude can be emphasized in a story:

> NEW YORK (AP)—Secondhand cigarette smoke will cause an estimated 47,000 deaths and about 150,000 nonfatal heart attacks in U.S. nonsmokers this year, a study says. That's as much as 50 percent higher than previous estimates.

Stress the Unusual

Leads also emphasize the unusual. By definition, news involves deviations from the norm. Consider this lead from a story about two men who shot each other in a dispute over a repossessed vehicle:

> MIAMI—Two men died Monday over a repossessed 1987 Chevy with a wheel that was about to fall off.
>
> *(Knight-Ridder Newspapers)*

A lead about a board of education meeting or other governmental agency should not report "the board met at 8 p.m. at a local school and began its meeting with the Pledge of Allegiance." Those facts are routine and not newsworthy. Most school boards meet every couple of weeks, usually at the same time and place, and many begin all their meetings with the Pledge of Allegiance. Leads should emphasize the unique—the action that follows those routine formalities.

Bank robberies are so common in big cities that newspapers normally devote only a few paragraphs to them. Yet a robbery at the Burlington National Bank in Columbus, Ohio, became a front-page story, published by newspapers throughout the United States. A story transmitted by The Associated Press explained:

> A 61-year-old man says he robbed an Ohio bank with a toy gun—he even told the FBI ahead of time when and where—because he wants to spend his golden years in federal prison.

After his arrest, the bank robber insisted he did not want a lawyer. Instead, he wanted to immediately "plead guilty to anything." The man explained he recently was divorced, had no family ties and was disabled with arthritis. He had spent time in at least three federal prisons and wanted to return to one of them. "I knew what I was doing," he insisted. "I wanted to get arrested, and I proceeded about it the best way I knew how."

Reporters must learn to recognize and emphasize a story's unusual details:

> LONDON—A Dutch driver who watched movies and ate dinner while 58 Chinese immigrants slowly suffocated in the back of his sweltering tomato truck was convicted Thursday of manslaughter and sentenced to 14 years in prison.
>
> *(The Associated Press)*

Localize and Update

Reporters localize and update their leads whenever possible by emphasizing their communities' involvement in stories. Readers are most interested in stories affecting their own lives and the lives of people they know.

Reporters also try to localize stories from other parts of the world. When a bomb exploded in a Pan Am plane over Lockerbie, Scotland, newspapers across the United States not only ran the story of the bombing, but localized the story on the basis of where the passengers had lived. The Gazette in Delaware, Ohio, focused on the death of a student from Ohio Wesleyan University, which is located in the town. Similarly, when the FBI reports on the number of violent crimes committed in the United States, reporters stress the statistics for their communities:

> The FBI reported Tuesday that the number of violent crimes in the United States rose 8.3 percent during the last year.
>
> LOCALIZED: The number of violent crimes committed in the city last year rose 5.4 percent, compared to a national average of 8.3 percent, the FBI reported Tuesday.

Reporters update a lead by stressing the latest developments in the story. If a breaking story appears in an early edition of a newspaper, a reporter will gather new information and rewrite the story for later editions. The same thing happens with a television news broadcast. Instead of reporting that a fire destroyed a store the previous day, reporters may stress that authorities have since learned the fire's cause, identified the victims, arrested an arsonist or estimated the monetary loss. Stories are updated so they offer the public something new—facts not already reported by other newspapers or by local radio or television stations. Major stories about such topics as economic trends, natural disasters, wars and political upheavals often remain in the news for months and must be updated regularly.

Not every lead can be updated or localized. If a story has no new or local angles, report it in a simple, straightforward manner. Do not distort the story in any way or fabricate any new or local angles.

Be Objective and Attribute Opinions

The lead of a news story, like the rest of the story, must be objective. Reporters are expected to gather and convey facts to their readers, not to comment, interpret or advocate. Reporters may anger or offend readers when they insert their opinions in stories.

Calling the people involved in news stories "alert," "heroic" or "quick-thinking" or describing facts as "interesting" or "startling" is never justified. These comments, when they are accurate, usually state the obvious. Leads that include opinion or interpretation must be rewritten to provide more factual accounts of the news:

> Speaking to the Downtown Rotary Club last night, Emil Plambeck, superintendent of the City Park Commission, discussed a topic of concern to all of us—the city's park system.
>
> REVISED: Emil Plambeck, superintendent of the City Park Commission, wants developers to set aside 5 percent of the land in new subdivisions for parks.

The original lead is weak because it refers to "a topic of concern to all of us." The reporter does not identify "us" and is wrong to assert that any topic concerns everyone.

Here are other examples of leads that state an opinion or conclusion:

> Adult entertainment establishments have fallen victim to another attempt at censorship.
>
> Recycling does not pay, at least not economically. However, the environmental benefits make the city's new recycling program worthwhile at any cost.

To demonstrate that both leads are statements of opinion, ask your friends and classmates about them:

- Do all your friends and classmates agree that the regulation of adult entertainment establishments is "censorship"?
- Do all your friends and classmates agree that recycling programs are "worthwhile at any cost"?

Although reporters cannot express their own opinions in stories, they often include the opinions of people involved in the news. A lead containing a statement of opinion must be attributed so readers clearly understand the opinion is not the reporter's.

A lead containing an obvious fact or a fact the reporter has witnessed or verified by other means generally does not require attribution. An editor at The New York Times, instructing reporters to "make the lead of a story as brief and clear as possible," noted: "One thing that obstructs that aim is the inclusion of an unnecessary source of attribution. . . . If the lead is controversial, an attribution is imperative. But if the lead is innocuous, forget it." Thus, if a lead states undisputed facts, the attribution can be placed in a later paragraph:

> Sidney Baylis, a 38-year-old musician who grew up in Ann Arbor, was killed Friday in a freak traffic crash on a Nebraska expressway.
>
> *(The Ann Arbor [Mich.] News)*

Strive for Simplicity

Every lead should be clear, simple and to the point. Here is an example:

> In a torrent of tears, John Eric Armstrong's gruesome secrets spilled out one by one.
>
> The prostitutes he choked to death. The bodies he dumped and then returned to violate.
>
> *(The Detroit News)*

Here is an example of a lead that suffers from far too much detail:

> Officials of the city and the Gladstone School District are breathing sighs of relief following the Clackamas County Housing Authority's decision to pull out of a plan to build an apartment complex for moderate-income people on 11 acres of land between Southeast Oatfield and Webster roads.

The lead could be rewritten any number of ways. The reporter must decide what the important point is. Here are two versions of a simple blind lead for the same story:

> Several city and school district officials applauded the county's decision to scrap plans for a subsidized housing complex.

> A new subsidized housing complex will not be built, and city and school district officials are relieved.

AVOIDING SOME COMMON ERRORS

Begin with the News

Avoid beginning a lead with the attribution. Names and titles are dull and seldom important. Moreover, if every lead begins with the attribution, all leads will sound too much alike. Place attribution at the beginning of a lead only when it is unusual or significant or deserves that emphasis:

> At a press conference in Washington, D.C., today, Neil A. Schuster, spokesperson for the U.S. Bureau of Labor Statistics, announced that last month the cost of living rose 2.83 percent, a record high.
>
> REVISED: The cost of living rose 2.83 percent last month, a record high, a U.S. Bureau of Labor Statistics official said Friday.

Originally, the lead devoted more space to the attribution than to the news. As revised, it emphasizes the news—the information revealed by the Bureau of Labor Statistics. The attribution has been condensed and can be reported more fully in a later paragraph.

Emphasize the News

Chronological order rarely works in a news story. By definition, news is what just happened. The first events in a sequence rarely are the most newsworthy. Decide which facts are most interesting and important, then write a lead that emphasizes these facts regardless of whether they occurred first, last or in the middle of a sequence of events:

> The O.J. Simpson trial started with the selection of jurors, which was a long and arduous process. After opening arguments by the prosecution and defense, the prosecutors began calling their witnesses and started building their case against the former football star. After months of legal maneuvering and bickering, prosecutors rested their case.
>
> Now O.J. Simpson's attorneys plan to call their first witness Monday morning. The next few weeks promise a lineup of Simpson's friends, family and golf chums testifying about his demeanor before and after the murder.
>
> REVISED: Now O.J. Simpson has the ball.
>
> With the prosecution case finished after five months of testimony, Simpson's lawyers are about to begin presenting his side of the story.
>
> *(The Associated Press)*

> The City Council began its meeting with the Pledge of Allegiance, then approved the minutes from its last meeting, approved paying omnibus budget bills and examined a list of proposed ordinances.
>
> REVISED: City Council voted 6-1 Monday night to increase the city's police department budget by 15 percent in order to hire more officers and buy new weapons.

Look for a story's action or consequences. That's what should be emphasized in a lead. The following lead, as revised, stresses the consequences of the accident:

> A 15-year-old boy learning to drive his family's new car struck a gasoline pump in a service station on Hall Road late Tuesday afternoon.
>
> REVISED: A 15-year-old boy learning to drive created a fireball Tuesday. The family car he was driving struck a gasoline pump at a Hall Road service station, blocking traffic for three hours while firefighters extinguished the blaze.

Avoid "Agenda" Leads

An opening paragraph that places too much emphasis on the time and place at which a story occurred is called an "agenda" lead. While agenda leads are used to announce an upcoming event—public relations news releases use them to promote an organization's product or event—they should never be used in a news story about something that occurred the previous day. A lead should focus on the news, as the following lead, after revision, does:

> James Matthews, president of International Biotech Inc., a company that manufactures recycling and composting machinery, was the keynote speaker at Monday night's opening ceremony of the Earth Preservation Society's annual conference at the Lyceum Center.
>
> REVISED: There's gold in the garbage society discards, the president of a company that manufactures recycling and composting machinery said, staking his claim on the future of recycling.

The revised lead focuses on what the speaker said, something the original lead failed to do. Other leads place too much emphasis on the time at which stories occurred:

> Last weekend the women's volleyball team participated in the regional playoffs.
>
> REVISED: The women's volleyball team won five of its seven games and placed second in the regional playoffs last weekend.

Avoid "Label" Leads

"Label" leads mention a topic but fail to reveal what was said or done about that topic. Leads should report the substance of a story, not just its topic. A good lead does more than report that a group met, held a press conference or issued a report. The lead reveals what the group did at its meeting, what was said at the press conference or what was written in the report.

Label leads are easy to recognize and avoid because they use similar words and phrases, such as "was the subject of," "the main topic of discussion," "spoke about," "delivered a speech about" or "interviewed about." Here are two examples:

> The City Council Tuesday night discussed ways of regulating a new topless club in the city.

> Faculty and staff members and other experts Thursday proposed strategies to recruit more minority students.

The first lead should summarize the city council's discussion, clearly explaining how the council plans to regulate the topless club. The second lead should summarize the experts' strategies for recruiting more minority students.

Avoid Lists

Most lists, like names, are dull. If a list must be used in a lead, place an explanation before it, never after it. Readers can more quickly grasp a list's meaning if an explanation precedes it, as the following lead and its revision illustrate:

> The company that made it, the store that sold it and the friend who lent it to him are being sued by a 24-year-old man whose spine was severed when a motorcycle overturned.
>
> REVISED: A 24-year-old man whose spine was severed when a motorcycle overturned is suing the company that made the motorcycle, the store that sold it and the friend who lent it to him.

Avoid Stating the Obvious

Avoid stating the obvious or emphasizing routine procedures in leads. For a story about a crime, do not begin by reporting police "were called to the scene" or ambulances "rushed" the victims to a hospital "for treatment of their injuries." This problem is particularly common on sports pages, where many leads have become clichés. For example, stories that say most coaches and players express optimism at the beginning of a season report the obvious: The coaches and players want to win most of their games.

The following lead, before its revision, is ineffective for the same reason:

> The Colonial Park school board has decided to spend the additional funds it will receive from the state.
>
> REVISED: The Colonial Park school board voted Monday night to rescind the 5 percent cut in spending it approved last month after learning the district will receive more money from the state.

Avoid the Negative

When writing a lead, report what happened—not what failed to happen or what does not exist:

> Americans over the age of 65 say that crime is not their greatest fear, two sociologists reported Friday.
>
> REVISED: Americans over the age of 65 say their greatest fears are poor health and poverty, two sociologists reported Friday.

Avoid Exaggeration

Never exaggerate in a lead. If a story is weak, exaggeration is likely to make it weaker, not stronger. A simple summary of the facts can be more interesting (and shocking) than anything that might be contrived:

> A 78-year-old woman left $3.2 million to the Salvation Army and 2 cents to her son.

> A restaurant did not serve a dead rat in a loaf of bread to an out-of-town couple, a jury decided Tuesday.

Avoid Misleading Readers

Every lead must be accurate and truthful. Never sensationalize, belittle or mislead. A lead must also set a story's tone—accurately revealing, for example, whether the story that follows will be serious or whimsical:

> The party went to the dogs early—as it should have.
>
> Parents who host parties for their children can understand the chill going up Susan Ulroy's spine. She was determined guests wouldn't be racing over her clean carpeting with their wet feet. "This could be a real free-for-all," she said.
>
> Even though only seven guests were invited, eight counting the host, that made 32 feet to worry about.
>
> This was a birthday party for Sandi, the Ulroys' dog.
>
> *(The Ann Arbor [Mich.] News)*

Break the Rules

Reporters who use their imagination and try something different sometimes can report the facts more cleverly than the competition.

Edna Buchanan, who won a Pulitzer Prize for her police reporting at The Miami Herald, consistently made routine stories interesting. Here's a lead she wrote with some imagination. Notice the active verbs and description she incorporates into her writing:

> Gary Robinson died hungry.
>
> He wanted fried chicken, the three-piece box for $2.19. Drunk, loud and obnoxious, he pushed ahead of seven customers in line at a fast-food chicken outlet. The counter girl told him that his behavior was impolite. She calmed him down with sweet talk, and he agreed to step to the end of the line. His turn came just before closing time, just after the fried chicken ran out.
>
> He punched the counter girl so hard her ears rang, and a security guard shot him—three times.

Remember Your Readers

While writing every lead, remember the people who will read it. Leads must be clear and interesting to attract and keep readers. The following lead, until revised, fails both tests:

> Two policy resolutions will come before the Student Senate this week.
>
> REVISED: Two proposals before the Student Senate this week would raise student parking and athletic fees by more than $100 a year.

Is the first lead interesting? Why not? It emphasized the number of resolutions the Student Senate was scheduled to consider. Yet almost no one would care about the number of resolutions or, from the lead, would understand their significance: the fact that they would affect every student at the school.

Rewrite Leads

Critically examine all leads and rewrite them as often as necessary. First drafts are rarely so well-written that they cannot be improved. Even experienced professionals often rewrite their leads three or more times.

APPLY THE GUIDELINES TO OTHER KINDS OF LEADS

The guidelines in this chapter are for effective writing of all kinds of openings, not just leads for news stories. Good writing does not vary from one medium to another. You may want to work in public relations, to write for a radio or television station, to become a columnist or to write a book. Regardless of your goal, the guidelines will help you achieve it.

Begin to analyze everything you read. You are likely to find some surprising similarities among books, magazines and newspapers. Also watch the opening scenes in movies and on television. Most, like a good lead, begin with a detail (or a story or scene) likely to capture your attention.

These, for example, are the opening sentences of two newspaper columns:

> Ozzie E. Garcia has a shaved head, a crooked grin and three tiny dots tattooed in the shape of a triangle near his right eye.
>
> *(Bob Herbert)*
>
> A 13-year-old girl was jumped in Cleveland last month. Last week, charges were filed against her alleged assailants—all 18 of them.
>
> *(Leonard Pitts Jr.)*

Similarly, these are the opening sentences from four books:

> The small boys came early to the hanging.
>
> *(Ken Follett, "The Pillars of the Earth")*
>
> On the 26th of July, my best friend decided he wanted to kill me.
>
> *(Wyatt Wyatt, "Deep in the Heart")*
>
> In a hole in the ground there lived a hobbit.
>
> *(J.R.R. Tolkien, "The Hobbit")*
>
> I did not realize for a long time that I was dead.
>
> *(Alice Walker, "Possessing the Secret of Joy")*

CHECKLIST FOR WRITING LEADS

1. Be specific rather than vague and abstract.
2. Avoid stating the obvious or the negative.
3. Emphasize the story's most unusual or unexpected developments.
4. Emphasize the story's most interesting and important developments.
5. Emphasize the story's magnitude and its impact on its participants and readers.
6. Use complete sentences, the proper tense and all the necessary articles—"a," "an" and "the."
7. Be concise. If a lead exceeds three typed lines, examine it for wordiness, repetition or unnecessary details and rewrite it to eliminate the problems.
8. Avoid writing a label lead that reports the story's topic but not what was said or done about it.
9. Begin leads with the news—the main point of the story—not the attribution or the time and place the events occurred.
10. Use relatively simple sentences and avoid beginning leads with a long phrase or clause.
11. Use strong, active and descriptive verbs rather than passive ones.
12. Avoid using unfamiliar names. Any names that require lengthy identification should be reported in a later paragraph.
13. Attribute any quotation or statement of opinion appearing in the lead.
14. Localize the lead, and emphasize the latest developments, preferably what happened today or yesterday.
15. Eliminate statements of opinion, including one-word labels such as "interesting" and "alert."
16. Remember the readers. Write a lead that is clear, concise and interesting and that emphasizes the details most likely to affect and interest readers.
17. Read the lead aloud to be certain that it is clear, concise and easy to understand.

THE WRITING COACH

OH WHERE, OH WHERE DOES THE TIME ELEMENT GO?

By **Joe Hight**
Managing Editor of The Oklahoman

You've just finished your lead and something is missing. The day. Oh, the dreaded time element. Where to place the day so it doesn't tarnish your fine lead or be criticized by your editor.

I recently received an e-mail from an editor frustrated by the many ways that the day is haphazardly placed in sentences. The editor sent these variations of how the placement of the day can change the sentence's meaning.

> He wondered Thursday where to place a time element in a sentence.
>
> He wondered where Thursday to place a time element in a sentence.
>
> He wondered where to place Thursday a time element in a sentence.
>
> He wondered where to place a time element Thursday in a sentence.
>
> He wondered where to place a time element in a sentence Thursday.

The editor wrote, "I see too many variations, and a lot of them are pretty darn convoluted. Break up the subject and verb? The verb and object? Insert between prepositional phrases? Tag at the end of the sentence?"

In his column, "Writers Workshop" in Editor & Publisher, Jack Hart wrote, "Faulty time element placement produces much of the strange syntax that often taints newspaper writing. We regularly come up with oddities such as 'A federal judge Monday approved' or 'Secretary of State Warren Christopher threatened Monday . . .' "

If you have problems—and most of us do—with the time element trap, here are six tips from Hart, the AP Stylebook and others:

1. The most natural place to put the day is immediately after the verb or the main clause. Thus, you follow the basic formula for writing a lead, especially in a hard news story: who, what, time, day or date and place.

   The robber was killed Friday at the convenience store.

2. Avoid placing the time element so it appears that it's the object of a transitive verb. If this occurs, use "on" before the time element.

   Awkward: The city council postponed Thursday a resolution. . . . (This makes it seem that the council postponed Thursday. The better way would be: The city council postponed on Thursday a resolution. . . .)

   Awkward: Deputies arrested Thursday a man wanted . . . (The better way to write it would be: Deputies arrested on Thursday a man wanted. . . .)

3. Use "on" before the principal verb if it seems awkward after the verb or main clause.

(*continued*)

Awkward: The embassy Friday expelled several diplomats. (The better way would be: The embassy on Friday expelled several diplomats.)

4. And use "on" to avoid an awkward juxtaposition of the day and a proper name.

Awkward: Police told Smith Tuesday. . . . (This makes it seem that the name of the person is Smith Tuesday. The better way would be: Police told Smith on Tuesday.)

(Please remember, however, that you do not use *on* if the time element would not confuse the reader: The council meeting will be Wednesday.)

5. Hart recommends breaking the tradition of always putting the day or time element at the beginning of the sentence. However, he adds that it's occasionally the best place, especially when considering the example he provided:

Richard "Joe" Mallon received the phone call this week he had dreaded for 19 years.

The day or time element can be used properly as a transitional expression, but probably should not be used in your lead.

6. Place your time element in a different sentence. Don't think that the time element must be in the lead, especially when you're writing a profile or issue, trend or feature story. In many cases, the time element can be effectively delayed for later paragraphs.

As always, my best advice is that you read your sentence out loud or to another person to ensure that the time element doesn't sound or seem awkward. This will ensure that your Mondays, Tuesdays and so on are in their proper place today.

SUGGESTED READINGS

Baker, Bob. *Newsthinking: The Secret of Making Your Facts Fall Into Place.* Boston: Allyn and Bacon, 2002.

Buchanan, Edna. *The Corpse Had a Familiar Face.* New York: Random House, 1989.

Cappon, Rene J. *Associated Press Guide to News Writing.* New York: The Associated Press, 1991.

Clark, Roy Peter, and Christopher Scanlan. *America's Best Newspaper Writing: A Collection of ASNE Prizewinners.* Boston: Bedford/St. Martin's, 2001.

LaRocque, Paula. *The Book on Writing: The Ultimate Guide to Writing Well.* Oak Park, Ill.: Marion Street Press, 2003.

Schwartz, Jerry. *Associated Press Reporting Handbook.* New York: McGraw-Hill, 2002.

Zinsser, William. *On Writing Well: The Classic Guide to Writing Nonfiction.* New York: HarperResource, 2001.

Name ______________________ Class ______________________ Date ______

EXERCISE 1

LEADS

EVALUATING GOOD AND BAD LEADS

Critically evaluate the following leads. Select the best leads and explain why they are effective. In addition, point out the flaws in the remaining leads. As you evaluate the leads, look for lessons—"dos and don'ts"—that you can apply to your own work.

1. A 24-year-old Greeley man was charged with multiple counts of first-degree murder and arson in the deaths of his wife and three children who died in an early morning fire in their home.
2. City Council has to return a grant it received last year to fix deteriorating road conditions on Main Street.
3. People are jumping into swimming pools and switching buttons to high on air conditioners as temperatures in the Midwest soared to record numbers over the past three days.
4. University administrators say they are considering imposing the largest tuition and fee increases in a decade because of state budget cuts.
5. A petition filed by city council member William Bellmonte to force the council into a special session to reduce local property taxes was thrown out in court Monday after it was discovered that half the names listed on the petition were dead people.
6. An 85-year-old woman stepped off the curb and into the path of a moving car. She was struck by the car and tossed 50 feet into the air. She died instantly.
7. Ray's Mini-Mart at 2357 S. Alderman St. was the location of a burglary sometime Friday night.
8. Police Chief Barry Kopperud is concerned that crime is rising in the city.
9. This weekend will offer the best chance yet to see a brilliant performance of "My Fair Lady" at the Fairwood Community Theater, so reserve your tickets now.
10. Loans become popular way to cut college costs.
11. The right of students to freely express themselves may soon be cast aside if the board of governors votes to restrict access to campus public areas.
12. The tree-lined campus is home to many wild and stray animals.
13. Two men suspected of burglarizing five churches, two homes and a pet store all in one night were captured Wednesday during another burglary attempt.
14. The union representing university secretaries and maintenance workers reached a tentative agreement Friday that will give members a 6.5 percent raise over three years.
15. Distance education classes offer alternative to classroom.
16. Fingerprints on a candle led the FBI to a man accused of blowing up the building he worked in to hide the shooting deaths of the man's boss and three co-workers.
17. Around 10 a.m. Wednesday a savings and loan at the intersection of Marion and State streets was the scene of a daring daylight robbery by three armed gunmen.
18. A teenage driver lost control of his car Wednesday night killing himself and a female passenger, while a 14-year-old friend who was riding in the back seat walked away with only scratches and bruises.

Name ______________________ Class ______________________ Date ______

EXERCISE 2

LEADS

WRITING LEADS

SECTION I: CONDENSING LENGTHY LEADS

Condense each of these leads to no more than two typed lines, or about 20 words.

1. Roger Datolli, 67, of 845 Conway Road, a retired attorney and husband of Mayor Sabrina Datolli, who is serving her fourth term as mayor, was injured in a three-vehicle accident Thursday afternoon around 3:20 p.m. at the intersection of Warren and Davidson avenues, suffering a broken leg and several broken ribs when the car he was driving was struck broadside by a pickup truck driven by Jerry R. Harris, 31, of 2245 Broadway Ave., and then was pushed into the path of another vehicle.
2. The city Planning and Zoning Commission met Thursday for its regularly scheduled meeting and voted 3-2 to approve a joint plan by the citys Council of Government and the local Chamber of Commerce to renovate the core downtown business district by building a convention center and sports arena complex that will serve as a site for business meetings and conferences as well as possibly host a minor league hockey team on the Olympic-size ice rink planned for the site.

SECTION II: USING THE PROPER SENTENCE STRUCTURE

Rewrite the following leads, using the normal word order: subject, verb, direct object. Avoid starting the leads with a long clause or phrase. You may want to divide some of the leads into several sentences or paragraphs. Correct all errors.

1. Wondering whether or not it was legally possible and if they could muster enough votes to support their desire to see changes implemented in the downtown historic section of the city, city council members Sandra Gandolf and Alice Cycler at the regular monthly city council meeting raised the issue of having the city's planning and zoning commission look into the possibility of creating a local board to oversee changes to buildings within the six-block downtown historic district.
2. Because the victim contributed in large measure to his own death by refusing medical attention that might have saved his life after the incident, James K. Arico, the 47-year-old man accused of stabbing him in the chest during an argument seven months ago, was allowed to plead guilty to assault today and was sentenced to six months in the county jail. He had been charged with murder.

SECTION III: EMPHASIZING THE NEWS

Rewrite the following leads, emphasizing the news, not the attribution. Limit the attribution to a few words and place them at the end, not the beginning, of the leads.

1. At a news conference held at the Department of Energy in Washington, D.C., Monday afternoon the head of the agency told reporters that the Senate's approval of

a plan to store nuclear waste material in the Nevada desert near Las Vegas will provide a safe haven for more than 77,000 tons of radioactive waste.

2. Tracy Tibitts, Lisa Drolshagen and Dorothy Brayton, all members of the Tau Rho Nu sorority at Iowa State University, appeared in a local courtroom this morning and testified that the defendant, Steven House, appeared drunk when he got into his car to leave the party moments before he struck and killed the pedestrian.

SECTION IV: COMBINING MULTISENTENCE LEADS

Rewrite each of the following leads in a single sentence, correcting errors if necessary.

1. Mildred Berg, the former president of City College, is a professor of economics at the college now. Berg got a call Monday from David DeBecker, president of the Harrison County Board of Education. BeDecker offered Berg the job of superintendent of Harrison County Schools, a position Berg interviewed for two months ago.
2. At 10:41 a.m., two police detectives saw two men enter Barneys Liquor Mart in the Oak Hill Shopping Center. The shopping center is located in the 1300 block of Oak Hill Avenue. The men were acting suspiciously. When the detectives entered the store to investigate, they saw one of the men pointing a gun at the clerk and the other taking money from the register. The officers pulled their weapons and shot the man with the gun. There have been seven robberies at the shopping center in the past month.

SECTION V: STRESSING THE UNUSUAL

Write only the lead for each of the following stories, correcting errors if necessary.

1. The city is sweltering under a heat wave. Temperatures have hit 100 degrees-plus for the past week and humidity levels have hovered between 75 and 90 percent each day. Authorities have been cautioning people, especially the very young and the elderly to stay inside in air conditioning and avoid exerting themselves outside in the sun. City Health Department officials held a press conference this morning to announce that three people had died over the past two days because of the heat. All three were elderly people who lived in the downtown area. Two of the three were a married couple. The one victim was identified as Betsy Aaron, 86, of 410 Hillcrest Street, Apartment 302. Aaron was a retired teacher who had taught elementary school for more than 30 years. The other two victims were Jeffrey Ahsonn, 84, and his wife, Teresa Ahson, 79, both of 49 Groveland Avenue. Ahsonn was a retired mechanical engineer who had worked for the city for many years. Police and health department officials were alerted to the deaths in each case by relatives who discovered the bodies. When they entered the dwellings, police told officials that they found a pair of fans and an air conditioner in each dwelling. The fans and air conditioners had been delivered by city workers to disabled elderly people to help them cope with the heat wave. But authorities found the fans and air conditioners still in their boxes. They had never been installed.
2. Destiny Schfini is a vice president with SunBank. Schifini is divorced and the mother of two children—a 10-year-old girl and an eight-year-old boy. The children visit her once a month. Schifinis son, Ronald, was visiting this weekend. Schfini is 36 years old and lives at 3260 Timber Ter. Ronald was injured in an accident Saturday afternoon around 2 p.m. The boy was struck by a train. Police said Schifini and her son were riding bikes along Fremont Avenue when the mother decided to take a

shortcut across the railroad tracks that run along Fremont Avenue. The boy is on life support in Mercy Hospital and listed in critical condition. He was struck by a train. Witnesses said the mother saw the train coming and crossed anyway and encouraged her son to cross. The boys bike got caught on the tracks and as he tried to free it, the train struck him. Ronald was thrown through the air and sustained broken ribs, a broken pelvis and a bruised heart. Police charged Destiny Schifini with aggravated assault, reckless endangerment, endangering the welfare of a child and failure to obey a train signal. Police said they charged Schfini after they learned from witnesses that Schifini did not help the boy, but taunted him as the train approached.

3. Tuesday was election day in your city. Voters were deciding on a new mayor, four new council members and a referendum to increase the local income tax half a percent to finance a new wing for the public library. Diedre Morsberger, the city's supervisor of elections, asked the county attorney Ronald McNally to file fraud charges against Herbert J. MacDonald, 53, of 1842 Hazel Lane, the owner of Tastee Popcorn. McDonald came to vote on Tuesday. When he arrived at the polls, he had his dog Sandy with him. Sandy is a three-year-old female black Labrador retriever. The city passed an ordinance last year at the urging of Morsberger that requires eligible voters to show identification—a voter registration card or photo identification card—when they come to vote. McDonald had protested at the time the ordinance was passed that it was an infringement of voters rights. MacDonald applied for and received a Social Security card and driver's license for Sandy. McDonald claims that Sandy is 21-years-old in human years and thus is old enough to vote. She also has the proper identification papers to vote. Election officials refused to allow either to vote. McDonald plans to sue the city for preventing him from voting.

4. The police department in your community are investigating a two-vehicle accident. The accident occurred at 5:38 p.m. Thursday during rush hour. The accident occurred at the busy intersection of Huron Avenue and Timber Trail Road. Police said a blue Toyota Camry driven by Cheryl Nicholls, 25, of 1287 Belgard Avenue, ran into the rear of a pickup truck driven by Ronald Dawkins, 44, of 1005 Stratmore Drive. Dawkins is a bricklayer. Nichols Toyota suffered severe damage, but she sustained only bruises and a laceration on her leg. Police said the car was a total loss. Police charged Nicholls with inattentive driving and operating a cell phone while driving. The cell phone law was passed last year by the state legislature and banned the operation of a cell phone while driving. Nicholls was talking to her car insurance company about an error on a car insurance bill when she struck the rear of Dawkins pickup truck.

5. A home at 2481 Santana Avenue was burglarized between the hours of 1 p.m. and 4 p.m. yesterday afternoon. The owner of the home is Dorothy R. Elam, a sixth-grade teacher at Madison Elementary School. She said no one was home at the time. Neighbors said they saw a truck parked in the driveway but thought some repairmen were working at the home. The total loss is estimated at in excess of $8,000. The items stolen from the home include a color television, a videocassette recorder, stereo, sewing machine, computer, 2 pistols and many small kitchen appliances. Also, a stamp collection valued at about $1,000, some clothes, silverware and lawn tools were taken. Roger A. Elam, Mrs. Elams husband, died 2 days ago. The robbery occurred while she was attending his funeral at 2:30 p.m. yesterday at the Powell Funeral Chapel, 620 North Park Avenue. Elam died of cancer after a long illness.

SECTION VI: LOCALIZING YOUR LEAD

Write only the lead for each of the following stories, correcting errors if necessary. Emphasize the information that would have the greatest local interest.

1. The U.S. Department of Justice is calling identity theft the crime of the 21st century. Identity theft is the illegal appropriation of another persons personal information—Social Security card number, driver's license number, credit card numbers, etc. —and using them to drain bank accounts or go on a buying spree. Justice Department officials say it is the fastest-growing crime in the United States. Criminals can get access to peoples personal information by going through their trash or stealing their mail. The Federal Trade Commission estimated the dollar loss to businesses and individuals last year was in the billions. The number of victims nationally is running as high as 750,000 a year. The rate of identity theft complaints nationally is averaging 22 victims per 100,000 people. Justice Department officials say that is too high. But the rate of identity theft complaints in your city is 77 victims per 100,000 people. State Representative Constance P. Wei is sponsoring a bill that would establish a web site that would allow credit card holders check to see if their numbers have been stolen. The bill also would increase the penalties for identity theft and raise the crime from a misdemeanor to a felony.

2. Your state's department of education announced that it is awarding more than 30 million dollars in federal grant money to 53 school districts throughout the state. The money is to be used to offset recent cutbacks in state funds given to school districts for educational programs and materials. Among the programs eligible for grant money are innovative programs to help identify and support at-risk youth who are not receiving the help they need. At-risk youth are more prone to failing in school and dropping out, becoming involved with drugs, becoming involved in crime or gang-related activity, and ending up in prison. The states Commission on Crime and Delinquency identified your local school district as a leader in the effort to help at-risk youth with its Community Helping Hands program. The program identifies at-risk youth at an early age and then engages teachers, community members and other students to help at-risk youth through academic tutoring, social activities and counseling. The state Commission on Crime and Delinquency through the state department of education is providing $1.2 million to your school districts at-risk program. The funds will help support the programs operation for at least three years.

SECTION VII: UPDATING YOUR LEAD

Write only the lead for each of the following stories, correcting errors if necessary.

1. William MacDowell, 28, a house painter who lives at 1429 Highland Drive, is being tried for the murder of a cocktail waitress, Ethel Shearer. His trial opened last Thursday, and witnesses last Friday said a ring found in MacDowells home belonged to the murder victim. MacDowell took the stand today and said he knew the victim and had bought the ring from her for $60 for a girlfriend. If convicted, MacDowell could be sentenced to life in prison. He is currently on parole after spending 8 years in prison on an armed robbery charge.

2. There was a grinding head-on collision on Cheney Road yesterday. Two persons were killed: Rosemary Brennan, 27, and her infant daughter, Kelley, age 2, both of 1775 Nairn Dr. The driver of the second car involved in the accident, Anthony Murray, 17,

of 1748 North 3 Street, was seriously injured, with multiple fractures. Police today announced that laboratory tests have confirmed the fact that Brennan was legally drunk at the time of the accident.

3. The state Legislature passed a law which prohibits doctors from performing abortions on girls under the age of 16 without the consent of their parents or guardians. The law specifies that doctors found guilty of violating the law can be fined up to $5,000 and can lose their licenses to practice medicine in the state. The law, which was signed by the governor, will go into effect at midnight tonight. The Legislature adopted the law after news media in the state revealed that girls as young as the age of 11 were given abortions without their parents knowledge or consent. The law is intended to prevent that. The parents consent must be in writing. The law stipulates that the girl who is pregnant must also agree to the abortion so her parents cannot force her to have one unwillingly.

Name ______________________ Class ______________________ Date ______

Pro Challenge

EXERCISE 3

LEADS

WRITING BASIC NEWS LEADS

Write only a lead for each of the following stories. As you write your leads, consult the checklist on Page 158. A professional has been asked to write a lead for each of these stories, and the leads appear in a manual available to your instructor. You may find, however, that you like some of your own and your classmates' leads better. As you write the leads, correct spelling, style and vocabulary errors. Also, none of the possessives have been formed for you.

1. Researchers from the Centers for Disease Control conducted a major study of American marriages and announced their results at a press conference today. Of couples that marry, the researchers found that 43% break up within fifteen years, according to their study of 50,000 women. It helps if women are wealthy, religious, college-educated, and at least 20 years old when they marry. They are less likely to divorce. The CDC found that half of U.S. women had lived with a partner by age 30. And 70% of those couples that lived together for at least five years eventually walked down the aisle. But their marriages were most likely to break up. After 10 years 40% of the couples that had lived together before marriage had broken up, compared with 31% of those couples that did not live together. That's because people who choose to live together tend to be younger and less religious and have other traits that put them at a greater risk for divorce, the CDC concluded.

2. Your citys downtown businessmen want something done immediately about the problem of panhandling and vagrants, especially on downtown city streets. Some vagrants sleep at night in parking lots or on doorsteps. Passersby they approach for money find them scary, and business leaders don't like them in front of their stores, saying they scare away good customers and give the downtown a seedy image. Businessmen say vagrants also eat, urinate, and sleep in parks, in unlocked vehicles, and elsewhere. So mayor Datolli said today she will introduce a new panhandling ordinance to the city council at its regular meeting at 8:00 pm next Tuesday night. The ordinance calls for the establishment of a program to offer homeless people one-way bus tickets to a town where they have family. A critic, Sandra Gandolf, says it is heartless, since many of the homeless have long-lasting problems including mental illness and/or drug or alcohol addiction and need real help. She favors providing programs to feed and house the homeless and to guide them toward mental health treatment, substance abuse counseling, and job assistance. However, the mayor said today the citys police now charge vagrants with minor crimes such as indecent exposure and shoplifting, that vagrants clog the jails and the court system, and that they end up right back on the streets. Downtown businessmen have promised to raise all the money needed for bus tickets.

3. Erik Barsh is the son of Margaret and Michael Barsh of 2498 Hazel Lane. He was hit by lightning at a municipal swimming pool last summer. A friend was killed and Erik was injured. Now, Erik is suing the city for his injuries: for the cost of his mounting medical bills that total thousands of dollars each and every month. He says the citys lifeguards knew a storm was coming and were gathering their own equipment but failed to warn swimmers of the danger. He is 17 yrs. old, has dropped

out of high school where he was to be a senior this school year, and now takes pain medication daily and says he cannot work or even muster the strength to go to church or to a mall or to a movie theater with friends. He says he can't stand for more than ten minutes at a time. He says his body was set in a slow, painful decline of lightning-induced brain and nerve injuries that he and his lawyers contend may eventually leave him in a wheelchair and destroy his sight and memory. He adds that before the unfortunate incident he was his high schools top male tennis player, earned As in all his classes, and planned to begin playing tennis and studying engineering next year at Notre Dame. Alan Farci, your City Attorney, said, "Our position on this is that we didn't have any greater knowledge than he did. The problem was obvious. It had started raining, and we've got a dozen witnesses who heard the thunder approaching and said the lifeguards had, in fact, ordered everyone to immediately get out of the pool, but this kid was horse playing with his friend. Its tragic, but they just didn't listen, and lightning hit before the lifeguards could do anything else."

4. Cynthia Lowrie of 118 Hillside Dr., Apt. 74, was arrested today by policemen. She was charged by them with grand theft and with defrauding an adoption agency. She had said she was pregnant. She received $12,000 from the Hope Agency to pay all her medical and other expenses while pregnant and had signed a contract to give her unborn child up for adoption. Medical tests given her today showed she isn't pregnant and never has been. She admits submitting at one point to the adoption agency test results from a friend who was pregnant. After all the money, the entire amount, was spent, she cut off contact with the agency and the prospective adoptive parents. A private detective hired by the couple tracked her down. She then said at first that her baby was born dead. Based on the results of todays tests, medical doctors concluded she was not recently pregnant, and she was arrested.

5. Construction workers for a new apartment complex were digging a trench for some underground utilities today. They hit by accident a major water main, shattering it, leaving major parts of the city with low or no water pressure. It may not be fully restored for 24 hours, authorities say. Now, water officials warn everyone living North of Hanson Avenue to boil their cooking and drinking water for the next three days. All water used for drinking and food preparation should be boiled vigorously for at least 3 minutes. The boil-water notice affects about 25,000 customers. The break occurred in a 24-inch pipe, a major line running from the citys main water plant. The area was flooded as a fountain of water gushed an estimated fifty feet upward, flooding the entire construction site near the intersection of Colonial Ave. and Chapman Rd., and the intersection also had to be closed due to being under 3 or more feet of water. During the repair process dirt is likely to get into the lines and will have to be flushed out.

6. A policeman yesterday arrested an 8 yr. old boy. Today police are conducting an internal investigation. The charges have been dropped but the boys mother is upset, saying officer Roger Temple who arrested her son should have simply separated the 2 children who were squabbling on a playground. The boys mother, Audrey W. VanPelt, said the girls mother was out of control and hysterical, insisting that she wanted to press charges. The boys mother said, "That dumb cop that gave my son a ticket reacted to the womans feelings instead of acting as an officer of the law and trying to calm her down." The incident happened at about 4 p.m. at Riverview Park. The boys mother had taken him there to play with several friends. A girl was trying to use a swing when the children began squabbling, and the boy slapped her on the face leaving a red mark. The girls mom immediately called police and insisted that

charges be filed, so officer Tempel took the boy to a juvenile detention facility on a battery charge. An internal investigation will be done to examine the decision to take the boy to the juvenile lockup says the Police Chief. The name of the boy was not released because he is a juvenile.

7. Elizabeth Anne Daigel was 102 years old and apparently in perfect health. She never used her Medicaid benefits. Federal investigators called at her home yesterday to find out her secret for good health and longevity. They found she had been dead twenty years. She apparently died of natural causes and her body had been wrapped in blankets and hidden in a trunk in a locked room in the basement of her home at 431 Central Boulevard. Her granddaughter, Annette, told police her grandmother died in her sleep and she hid the body in order to keep collecting her monthly social security check which Annette said she desperately needs as a divorced mother with four children to support. The government routinely compares the names of those receiving social security checks to the rolls of Medicaid users. Today police charged Annette with grand theft. She could not be charged with improper burial or failure to report a death because the crimes are beyond the statute of limitations. If convicted she could be sentenced to five years in prison and ordered to make full restitution for all the money she collected after her grandmothers death, a total well in excess of 200,000.00, plus interest.

8. Your city needs more money to eliminate a 6 million dollar deficit. So mayor Datolli at a press conference today proposed a fire tax. The tax would put the financial bite on all property owners, without exception, including churches, schools, and nonprofits as well as residences and businesses. Under the proposal by mayor Datoli, the city would charge homeowners a \$134.00 fee each year regardless of a propertys value. Apartment owners would pay \$89.00 per unit. Churches, businesses, and schools would have various rates based on square footage. Datolli noted that for the past seven years there has been no tax rate increase in the city. Council member Nyad called the idea "bizarre." Nyad said, "We already pay for fire protection through our property taxes. This would tax citizens twice for the same thing. It's the dumbest thing I've ever heard of. You don't tax schools. Where would they get the money from?" But the mayor on the other hand stated, "Its painful but ultimately a good thing. We have to be fiscally responsible. We have to solve our financial problems and provide essential services. I don't want to cut back on them."

9. There's a new program to help your citys teachers. They aren't paid much. Many can't afford a down payment for a house. So local school officials today unveiled a new program that will offer mortgages with below-market interest rates to teachers and administrators in public schools. Its designed for first-time buyers and would offer eligible educators up to 10,000 dollars to help cover down payments and closing costs. They will not have to repay any of that amount provided they both continue to teach and remain in the home for a minimum of the next five consecutive years. Helping teachers buy or rent is becoming a popular incentive across the nation as teacher shortages and attrition continue to plague schools. Cash for the down payments will come from Federal funds already used to help low to moderate income residents buy homes. Program rules have been tweaked so teachers qualify, said school supt. Gary Hubard. There are limits on applicants income and on a homes purchase price, mostly depending on exactly where a home is located.

10. Your citys Fire Chief announced today that the fire department is ending a tradition at least a hundred years old. It's the tradition of sliding down a pole to get to a fire engine. The city, he explained, is phasing poles out as it builds new one-story

stations to replace older multistory firehouses. Going down the pole too fast and hitting a concrete floor can cause injuries and was therefore never a good tradition, he said. He explained that fire department records show over the past 20 years at least 12 firemen suffered injuries, especially sprained or broken ankles or legs. Still, crews improved their response time to fires by bypassing staircases from their upstairs living quarters, by cutting holes in the floors of firehouses, and by installing and using the brass or steel poles. The last multi-story firehouse with a pole is slated for demolition sometime early next year.

11. There's a deadly problem at Kennedy High School. Two more students tested positive for tuberculosis last week, indicating they likely picked up the germ from a student with an active case of TB, city health officials announced today. The two students are not yet ill and can not pass the infection on to anyone else but will be given antibiotics to make sure they never develop TB. The two were among 170 persons tested at the school last week. The tests were necessary because health officials determined that one student has active TB, which is contagious. The Health Department last week tested every student and staff member who was in a class or rode a school bus with the ill student. The ill student is no longer in school, having dropped out for the year. The health officials said there is little danger to the schools nearly 3000 other students. TB is spread when an ill person coughs, but only after prolonged exposure and in poorly ventilated areas. A high school campus isn't likely to be a place for TB transmission. Those two who tested positive will be given a chest x-ray and medication to be sure they don't develop active TB.

12. Community leaders wanted to know who are the homeless in your city, so they raised 50,000 dollars to fund a grant for researchers in the sociology dept. at your institution to study them. The researchers who issued their report today found, "Most thought these people in our community were chronically homeless, that they came here from someplace else and that they had mental health or substance abuse histories. When interviewed, less than 30% informed us of mental health or substance abuse histories. Sixty-seven percent claimed this was their first time homeless. Sixty-eight percent had been homeless for less than six months. Almost 55% had been living in the city when they became homeless because of a job loss, eviction, marital breakup, domestic violence, victimization or having been jailed. Just 14% became homeless while living in another state before moving here. Many were married or unmarried couples with children. Thus, we conclude that homelessness is a local problem. Our citys homeless are mostly neighbors who've temporarily fallen on hard times."

Name ______________________ Class ______________________ Date ______

EXERCISE 4

Pro Challenge

LEADS

CITY, STATE AND NATIONAL LEADS

Write only a lead for each of the following stories. As you write your leads, consult the checklist on Page 158. The first set of stories involves events in your city; the second set involves events in your state; and the third set involves events in the nation. A professional has been asked to write a lead for each of these stories, and the professionals' leads appear in a manual available to your instructor. You may find, however, that you like some of your own and your classmates' leads better. As you write the leads, correct spelling, style and vocabulary errors. Also, none of the possessives have been formed for you.

CITY BEAT

1. Two researchers at your school today announced the results of an important study they conducted. Both are psychologists. Their study involved 50 children, all boys between the ages of ten to twelve who attend the University Learning Center. One by one, the boys were sent into a laboratory furnished to look like a playroom. They were told they could open all the drawers and look on all the shelves and play with whatever toys they found. Among the items under clothes in one drawer was a genuine pistol. The 2 researchers watched and filmed each child. One of the researchers, Aneesa Ahmadd, said many boys found the pistol and played with it and even pulled the trigger without knowing whether or not it was loaded. "They did everything from point it at each other to look down the barrel," said Prof. Ahmadd. About seventy-five percent, or 37 found the gun, and 26 handled it. At least 16 clearly pulled the trigger. Many, when questioned later, said they did not know if the gun was real. None knew it was unloaded and that the firing pin had been removed so it could not possibly be fired. All the childrens parents had given the researchers permission for their offspring to participate in the important study, and Ahmadd said many were horrified by the results, especially since all said they had warned their children never to play with guns. Ahmadd said the studys real significance is that it reveals that simple parental warnings are ineffective.

2. For the last 62 years, Olivida Saleeby has lived with her husband, Wesley, in their home at 1961 Elizabeth Lane, a structure originally built by her parents. The couple has been married all 62 of those years, immediately moving in with her parents after their honeymoon and later inheriting the house. Last week Wesley died, and his body remains unburied in a funeral home. Olivida last night asked the citys Zoning Board at its regular weekly meeting for permission to bury her dead husband in their back yard. By a vote of 7-0, board members refused. Olivida explained that she has no other living relatives, deeply loved her 81-yr.-old husband, and wanted her beloved husband to remain near her. He died suddenly and unexpectedly of a heart attack. Board members rejected her plea and explained burial in a residential neighborhood would set a bad precedent and bring down property values.

3. Susan Carigg of your city was forty-two years old and the mother of 4 kids, 3 girls and 1 boy. She was in a serious and tragic car accident 7 months ago. Since then, she's been in a coma at Mercy Hospital in your city. Her husband, Craig, now wants

to remove the feeding tube that has kept his comatose spouse alive. Susans parents oppose the idea. They are Elaine and Vernon Sindelar, and they appealed to a Superior Court judge to issue an injunction to stop their son-in-law from removing the tube. The judge today ruled that Craig can proceed, clearing the way for the tubes removal by doctors. Three doctors who have treated the woman testified unanimously that she is brain dead with no hope of recovering. Mr. Carigg said he will wait until he receives final paperwork and consults again with his wifes doctors. Without the tube Mrs. Carigg will die of starvation and dehydration, probably in a period of approximately five to seven days.

4. A Circuit Court judge today issued an important decision that involves your citys school board. A gender-discrimination lawsuit was filed against the school board by girl softball players parents. Judge McGregor ruled that the school district violated state and federal gender-discrimination laws by providing better baseball fields for boys than for girls. Two girls high school softball teams in your district have to travel up to 4 miles to practice while boys teams have fields on their high school campus. Parents complained the girls fields are unsafe and substandard, with dirty bathrooms and open-air dugouts. The judge ordered the district to bring the girls softball fields up to par with the boys fields. Like the boys fields, the new fields for the girls must have 6 foot high fencing with backstops, bleachers, dugouts with refrigerated water for each team, electronic scoreboards, batting cages and 8-by-12 foot storage sheds. The School Board estimates that all that will cost approximately $600,000 to build new fields adjacent to the boys fields at the two schools involved, and the board said it does not know where the money will come from.

5. Some people in your city don't like billboards, considering them an urban blight. The issue was brought before the citys Planning Board last night. By a unanimous vote of 7-0 its members recommended banning any new billboards within the city limits and also taking down all existing billboards within seven years. Its recommendations will go to the city council for final consideration, and council members have already said they will hold two public workshops to give interested parties an opportunity to provide their input. There are currently about 180 billboards within the city. A spokesman for the citys billboard companies responded that any edict to remove existing signs is akin to stealing from legitimate businesses. She said the city government must legally pay fair market value for existing signs which are worth millions of dollars, and that local billboard companies will sue, if necessary, to protect their property rights.

6. Deer Creek Park is normally a popular city park but thousands of winged mammals have made their home in the rafters of the parks three picnic pavilions. People who had reserved the pavilions for picnics over the next several days have been notified the areas are now off limits. People can picnic elsewhere in the park but not in the pavilions. "In a general sense, bats are good people to have around," said Carlos Alicea, an epidemiologist for the City Health Department. "They do a wonderful job of insect control, but the flip side of that is that if you have a one-on-one encounter, there could be a risk of rabies, and there's also a problem with their droppings." The city is waiting to hear from state experts about relocating the bats elsewhere in the park. One option is to erect bat houses elsewhere to provide shelter during daylight hours when the bats are inactive, but there is no guarantee the bats would use them.

STATE BEAT

1. There was a daring daylight robbery in your state capital. It involved an armored car. It was owned and operated by Brinks. Police say it is unclear whether a second person was involved, but about 400,000 dollars were taken. There were no signs of struggle or foul play, and they are looking for the trucks driver, Neil Santana, age 27. He is suspected of taking the cash while his partner went into a supermarket for a routine money pickup. He is still at large. Officials searched in and around his home and checked airports and are looking for his car. The heist occurred shortly after 4:10 p.m. yesterday afternoon when Santana drove his partner to the supermarket. As his partner went inside to pick up a bag of cash, witnesses said the driver drove off. When his partner returned, the truck was gone and remains missing. The incident occurred at the end of their route, which included a total of 22 stops and pickups. The co-worker called the police. Company officials said the driver started working for the company about five weeks ago and had no arrest record.

2. Your state legislature acted today. Its members want to end a serious problem. Each year, a dozen or more little helpless newborn babies in the state are found abandoned, and some are dead. Often, their mothers are unwed and young and don't want the babies or know how to care for their babies, so they abandon them, and some die before being found. Some mothers and some fathers kill some unwanted newborn infants. To end the problem, the legislature today adopted a law that will allow anyone to leave an unwanted newborn at any manned hospital or fire station in the state, no questions asked and with no criminal liability whatsoever. Your governor has endorsed and promised to sign the bill.

3. Jennifer Pinccus, a member of the state legislature elected from your district, is troubled. She says there are too many motor vehicle accidents, and too many of those accidents involve the elderly some of whom, according to her, "are no longer fit to drive." So she today introduced a controversial bill that would require senior motorists to take an extra test, and it is a controversial piece of legislation which will, to be passed, have to be approved by both the House and the Senate and then signed by your Governor. Under her plan, drivers age seventy-five and older would have to renew their licenses in person every three years, and would have to submit proof of hearing and vision tests by their physician when doing so. Those eighty-one and older would have to take a road test every 3 years as well as pass the screenings. Now, any driver over age seventeen can renew a six-year license two consecutive times by mail. So it is possible to hold a valid license for 18 years before having to actually walk into a state licensing bureau which Pincus thinks is too long for seniors whose health can change dramatically in a short time. Seniors are expected to actively oppose the proposal, yet 18 other states have additional testing or renewal requirements for seniors. Many require a doctors vision or hearing certification. Only 2 other states require regular road tests.

4. Your State Supreme Court acted today. It ruled unanimously that Jason Perez of your city can be kept in a state prison even though Perez has completed his sentence and has not been charged with a new crime. Health officials believe he is a public health risk, and a lower court judge who heard the case brought by the health officials concluded Perez cannot be trusted to participate willingly in a treatment program. So the 46-year-old tuberculosis patient sits in an isolated 6-by-10 foot cell eight days after his sentence to a state prison for assault with a deadly weapon ended and he was supposed to be a free man. His attorney wants Perez freed on his own recognizance. But before his incarceration for assault, Perez fled three times in violation of court

orders and failed to get complete treatment for his drug resistant form of TB, a highly communicable and potentially deadly disease. That's why the state Dept. of Health considers him a public health risk. His attorney says he belongs in a hospital, but the Supreme Court today concurred with the lower court that he can be detained so long as he remains a clear and present health threat to others.

5. The Humane Society of your state announced today a new policy. All its city and county affiliates will immediately stop providing homeless cats to paramedic students. In the past the affiliates provided the cats so the students could practice inserting breathing tubes into humans. For as long as anyone can remember, the Humane Society allowed its city and county affiliates to provide cats scheduled to be euthanized for practice by students in emergency-medical-technician, paramedic, emergency-medical-service, and related programs. The society said it has received lots of complaints since PETA last week denounced its policy as unnecessary, gruesome, and potentially painful to the cats. People for the Ethical Treatment of Animals urged its members to withdraw all funding from the Humane Society and to encourage others to do so as well. A spokesman for the society today said no cats suffered but PETA's criticisms led to a reconsideration of the program. "We concluded there was not a need for us to be involved, and so we're out of it," she said. The cats were anesthetized but still alive when students practiced sticking breathing tubes down their throats. After the class, the cats were given a final, lethal shot. Students say they are losing an important training opportunity, especially for dealing with babies and infants, and that some young children may die since no alternatives for practicing helping them have been developed.

6. There's a new trend in your state. The population is aging, with more people over the age of 65 than ever before. So throughout your state, new hospitals are being built and old hospitals are being expanded. State health officials calculate that, across the state, the aging and inadequacy of mature buildings has fueled an unprecedented multi-billion dollar rush of construction by hospitals. Of all existing hospitals in the state, 31% are currently in the process of expanding or renovating. Two dozen of those hospitals are spending at least $25 million, and 14 are known to be spending more than $50 million each. Two dozen hospitals are enlarging crowded emergency rooms to ease overcrowding. Growing numbers of people who are uninsured or don't have family doctors go to ERs for any medical problem, sharply increasing patient volumes at ERs. Many other hospitals are expanding operating rooms, adding outpatient centers, and building physician offices to handle increased businesses. Expansions also are bringing new or larger speciality medical services such as highly profitable heart surgery centers and cancer programs needed primarily by the elderly.

NATIONAL BEAT

1. Each year the Institute for Highway Safety located in Washington D.C. gathers a variety of statistics about highway safety. It analyzes data gathered throughout the nation. Today it announced the results of a study of young drivers. It found that, of all young drivers, 16-year-old boys remain the most risky drivers on the road. 16 yr. old boys have more accidents than any other age group, and that's been true since the Institute began analyzing highway data 32 years ago. But this year the institute found that 16-year-old girls are gaining. For every 1000 licensed 16-year-olds girls, 175 were in car accidents last year. That's up 9 percent from just 10 years ago when 160 girls crashed per 1000 drivers. Accidents for 16-year-old boys decreased slightly during the same period, from 216 to 210 per 1000 licensed drivers. A spokesman for

the institute said boys are crashing less because of safer vehicle designs and less drunk driving.

2. Some men kill their wives and girlfriends. They've been the subject of a major national study. Those men typically have a long history of domestic violence. They own handguns and use them "in a final act of rage against a woman perceived to be their property," concludes the first national review of domestic violence deaths conducted by the national Centers for Disease Control. The CDC today announced that, nationally, about 19 percent of all murders are domestic related. Sixty-two percent involve the spouse or live-in girlfriend of the alleged killer. Children were the victims in roughly 11% of the cases of domestic deaths. In all, about 27% of all violent crimes reported to the FBI including murder, forcible rape, aggravated assault, and stalking involve domestic issues. And in the vast majority of cases, victims have had plenty of advance warning, as the violent behavior of their partners escalated over time. Many of those killed had received death threats from spouses who felt betrayed and jealous, the CDC concluded. Guns were the weapons of choice.

3. Its another national study, this one of married men and women. It found that many married Americans admit keeping a major secret from their spouses, but most secrets have nothing to due with an affair or fantasy. Of those married men and women with a secret:

 —48% said they had not told their spouse the real price of something they bought.
 —About 40% of the wives and 30% of the husbands said they wish they could persuade their spouses to be less messy.
 —About a quarter of each sex said they cannot get their partners to lose weight.
 —About 20% of the nations marrieds have dreams or aspirations they haven't mentioned to a spouse, ranging from living somewhere else (50%) to getting a dog (8%).
 —16% of both men and women admitted that, at least once during their marriage, they wished they could wake up and not be married any more.
 —About 15% had not told their spouse about a failure at work.
 —About 15% had not told their spouse about a childs misbehavior
 —14% kept quiet about being attracted to another person.
 —Only 9% of the respondents, equally split among men and women, said they had an extramarital affair that remains a secret.

The poll was conducted last month by the Centers for Disease Control, which interviewed by phone 700 husbands and 700 wives.

4. A startling new study shows how difficult it is to be a parent. When teens start dating new problems arise. The Harvard School of Public Health conducted a comprehensive study of 1,977 high school girls and found that 1 in 5 reported being a victim of physical or sexual violence in a dating relationship. Girls reported being hit, slapped, shoved, or forced into sexual activity by dates. Since this was the first study of its kind its not clear whether such abuse is on the rise. The report concluded that high school girls think they can handle situations they're not ready for. The researchers add that the pressures and status of having a boyfriend can propel girls into unhealthy relationships. And many of these girls never tell their moms and dads about dating violence.

5. Ralph Wick is 5 feet, 5 inches tall and weighs 342 pounds and lives in Denver. He blames fast-food restaurants for his excessive weight. He is suing 4, saying they contributed to his obesity, heart disease, and diabetes. He filed the 4 suits this week and explained at a press conference today he wants 1 million dollars from each. He is only twenty-eight years old and worked as a barber but says he's no longer able to work. He said millions of other Americans also should sue the companies which sell products loaded with saturated fats, trans fats, salt, cholesterol, and other harmful dietary content. He says he wants to warn everyone of the adverse health effects that could cause obesity, diabetes, heart disease, high blood pressure, and elevated cholesterol levels. A spokesman for McDonalds, one of the companies he's suing, called the suit "frivolous." The other restaurants he's suing include Pizza Hut, Wendys, and Burger King, since he says he ate at them an average of once or more a day.

6. Kimberley Mchalik, one of Harvards most prominent Sociologists, focuses on marriage and family life as her primary area of study. Today she spoke to 6000 delegates attending the national convention of the Association of University Women in San Francisco and said: "As women age, more and more who never married or lose a spouse complain there are no good men left. But instead of griping, women should increase their pool of prospects. As women become more successful, independent, and confident, they're better able to dump societys old rules and create new ones. No longer are younger men out of the question. Each generation becomes more tolerant and progressive. Plus, men usually are the ones putting the moves on older women. What attracts them are the older womens accomplishments, sophistication, and self-assurance. And the fact that older women are looking much younger. You've got to realize that women now take much better care of themselves. We eat more healthfully, go to the gym, and spend more time taking care of ourselves. Sure, there can be problems. If the age difference is more than 10 or 15 years, it becomes a little edgy. As you approach a decades difference, you have men and women born in different social contexts that affect their attitudes about marriage and relationships. Whether these relationships work out generally depends on the individuals involved. Couples need to share common values and to figure out whether they're at the same stage of life. Differences in incomes, the desire for children, and decisions about when to retire can be problems. But couples who iron out those differences can go the distance."

Name ______________________ Class ______________________ Date ______

EXERCISE 5

Pro Challenge

LEADS

EMPHASIZING THE UNUSUAL

Write only a lead for each of the following stories. As you write your leads, consult the checklist on Page 158. A professional has been asked to write a lead for each of these stories, and the leads appear in a manual available to your instructor. You may find, however, that you like some of your own and your classmates' leads better. As you write the leads, emphasize stories' unusual details. Correct the stories' spelling, style and vocabulary errors. Also, none of the possessives have been formed for you.

1. Scott Forsythe is 22 years old. He was killed in a car accident today. Police in your city say the accident occurred at about 8:45 AM this morning on Kirkmann Rd. Forsythe was driving a ford mustang. Police estimate the vehicle was traveling at least 100 m.p.h. and witnesses told police it was passing slower traffic when a large dog walked into his path. As Forsythe veered to avoid the dog he lost control of his car and hit two trees and a fence before coming to a complete stop, police said. The accident occurred about a half mile from the church where he was to be married to Sara Howard of 812 Bell Av. at 9:00 a.m. today He was alone in the vehicle. No one else was hurt.

2. Your city needs more money. Its in a financial crisis and trying to trim its expenses. So today city officials announced that every time someone is arrested and the police take mug shots and fingerprints, the jail will charge them $25 for the service. Police chief Barry Kopperrud said he wants to make criminals pay a price for their actions. "They have to learn there's a cost for their behavior," Kopperrud said today. "Decent citizens shouldn't have to pay for this. Let the crooks and other bad guys pay the full cost what it costs to arrest and incarcerate them." The fee will go into effect immediately but will be refunded to people who are arrested and later acquitted.

3. Larry Chavez, a detective with your citys police dept., went to a football game at Kennedy High School last Saturday to watch his son play at 2:00 PM. He then recognized a player on the opposing team, a sixteen-year-old from Colonial High School. Chevez arrested him several months ago for armed robbery. The youth is currently under house arrest yet allowed to play football. He robbed a pizza delivery woman at gunpoint. He was charged with armed robbery and released from juvenile detention under house arrest. He was ordered not to leave his house except to attend school, and an electronic bracelet was attached to his ankle. Still, Tony Guarino, coach of the Colonial High School football team, allows him to play for the team. "We just taped the bracelet up real good," Guarino said in an exclusive interview with you today. The deputy was amazed, saying today, "I was amazed to see someone charged with an armed robbery with a handgun playing on the field." School Supt. Gary Hubard said juveniles on home detention are allowed to participate in school functions and that students are not always suspended for crimes committed off campus.

4. There's been a national survey involving a random sample of the nations High School students. It contradicts many negative images or stereotypes. The survey of 2400 High School students paints a largely upbeat picture of American teenagers, showing they are very directed, very motivated, very serious. When asked to rank various pressures:

   —26% said the need to get good grades and go to college was a major problem.
   —16% cited that a pressure to look a certain way was their major problem.
   —15% cited financial problems.
   —14% had a major problem getting along with their parents.
   —12% cited pressure to do drugs or drink alcohol.
   —10% spoke of pressure to have sex.
   —9% listed loneliness and a feeling of being left out as their worst pressure.

   So overall, students said the greatest pressure in their lives was a pressure to take tough courses, earn high grades, score well on college-entrance exams and load their resumes with all sorts of athletic and extracurricular activities in an attempt to succeed in college and in life, according to researchers in the College of Education at the University of Wisconsin in Madison, Wisc.

5. Stephanie Courhesne is 9 years old and fought city hall and today won. Stephanie lives at 1186 N. Highland with her parents, Mr. and Mrs. Adolph Courhesne. On Saturdays and Sundays each summer she makes money selling lemonade from a stand in front of her house. She charges a quarter a cup. She also sells water at a dime a cup. She said she typically make $3 to $5 a day, earning more when its hot. She says 10% of her profits go into savings and 10% go to her church. She must reimburse her mother for the ingredients, but that leaves her a tidy profit which she said she uses "to buy toys, clothes, candy, and stuff." A city code enforcement officer noticed and shut down the stand yesterday, forcing her to pack up her cups, cooler, cardboard sign, table, chair, and shade umbrella. Her father immediately called councilman Alyce Cycler, to complain. Cycler said the ruling was preposterous and promised to get it taken care of right away. Today the code enforcement officers supervisor overruled her and said it was all a mistake, an error in judgment, and Stephanie is welcome to sell as much lemonade as she can. Then, just a few minutes ago, the mayor announced she intends to become a regular customer. The young girls spot is a prime selling spot because people jog, roller skate, and walk on Highland Drive, which borders Lake Clarity.

6. Maria Deyo is 17 years old and a Senior at Kennedy High School. Three months ago she was involved in a serious car accident. Just minutes before the crash a policeman had given her a ticket for speeding 72 miles per hour in a 35 mile per hour zone. Minutes after getting the ticket she collided with a tree, suffering serious injuries that left her paralyzed from the waist down. Today she and her parents, Ashley and Ralph Deyo, sued the city, charging that the policeman was negligent for failing to arrest her and take her into custody for drunken driving, thus preventing the accident. Their suit says her medical bills now exceed 250 thousand dollars and will continue for the duration of her life. Police department officials would not comment. The familys lawsuit alleges that Maria had been drinking to excess and had numerous open beer cans visible in the vehicle which the officer negligently failed to notice and act upon. No one else was in the car at the time and, fortunately, no one else was hurt.

7. It was a shocking discovery. Myron Hanson died more than a year ago. Friends and neighbors thought it odd they weren't invited to Myrons funeral. But Myrons son, Brandon, said he had honored his dads last wishes by having him cremated and sprinkling his ashes over his favorite golf course. Today, authorities learned Myron was buried in his back yard at 880 6th Street. Police said they got an anonymous tip that a body was buried in the back yard. Armed with a search warrant and a dog trained to detect human remains, they found the body of an elderly man buried behind the modest house shared by Myron and his son. Police are now awaiting a report from the medical examiner to determine whether Myron, age 67, died of natural causes. Family members said he was a heavy smoker, smoking two to three packs of marlboros a day, and had been diagnosed with lung cancer. No charges have been filed yet and no one has been arrested yet. Other family members who live out of state said they are furious. Family members were suspicious because there was no obituary in your local paper and no funeral services. Plus, no one could locate a death certificate. Police found that Myron continued to receive his social security and Veterans benefits, having served in the United States army twenty-three years, thereafter working as a carpenter. Brandon said he didn't have the money to bury his father, but another son said, "The only reason we can think of is that he didn't want our dads social security checks to stop. He was a freeloader. We all knew that, but we thought he was taking good care of dad."

8. Brandon Chenn is a 9 year old boy. He attends Washington Elementary School. He's lucky to be alive. He lives at 91 Melrose Av. and, yesterday, was walking to school. He was crossing Bell Ave. when a truck hit him. Minutes after the crash the police gave him a jaywalking ticket. "I was in shock," Brandon's mother Ann Chen said. "He was dazed and bleeding and what he needed was help and love, not stupidity." A police spokesman said an officer wrote the ticket because Brandon was at fault since he "ran out in front of the vehicle." The Police Chief explained: "If we find someone involved in an accident at fault, as a matter of policy we write them a ticket. In this case it was a boy who skinned his knees and was crying, but that doesn't change the fact he was responsible for the accident. What's more, we've learned that he'd previously been warned at least twice for doing the same thing, for jaywalking. These tickets are mostly for insurance purposes, to assign fault in motor vehicle accidents." The normal fine for jaywalking is $25.00.

9. Margaret Jones of 1152 Darlington Av. appeared in court today. She was convicted of shoplifting in Municipal Court by Judge Marci Hall. The judge noted that it was her 5th conviction and ordered her, when in any store during the next year, to wear a red badge that says in 4 inch letters "Convicted Shoplifter." In addition, judge Hall sentenced Jones to one year of probation and ordered her to seek counseling. Jones, a mother of 5, said to you in an exclusive interview today after her conviction and sentencing, "I admit I have a problem, but what that bitch did wasn't right, wasn't right at all to try to humiliate me like that. She's the one who should be in jail."

10. Samuel Pinckney is 84 four years old. He married his bride, Teresa, when he was 22. She was younger than he, then being age 17. They had five children. Last night Samuel shot Teresa in the back of the head with a pistol. In a statement he gave police today, he said, "She begged me to kill her. She suffered for years. Everything was wrong with her, arthritis, cancer, diabetes, blindness, everything." Samuel added in a formal statement to police that he shot her with his .22-caliber revolver and was supposed to then use the revolver on himself after he shot her. They wanted to die together, he said, but after shooting her he found himself traumatized and unable to shoot himself and called police for help. In court today his attorney, Enrique Diaz,

asked that he be released without bail. "What danger does he pose to anybody?" his attorney asked. "There's none. He's been nothing but a model citizen for eighty years and should be freed without bail because he's not a threat to anyone. He loved his wife, everyone knows that. They've been going through hell, and there's no sense in putting him in jail. He's just way too old to be in there." The judge disagreed and ordered Pinckney to post 100,000 dollars bail. His attorney said he does not have that kind of money but that the couples 4 surviving children "are in the process of posting the bail as they understand and respect their parents decision."

11. Denise Abondanzio is the spokesman for the Salvation Army in your city. Three weeks ago, while vacationing in Orlando, Florida, and sightseeing at Disney World, Raymond Cross and his wife, Dana, of 101 Charow Lane in your city bought several $1 Florida lottery tickets. They won a $28,000,000 jackpot. They elected to receive the money in 30 annual payments spread over the next 30 years. Yesterday they received the first payment, a check for $933,333. The couple immediately paid off the $87,213 mortgage on their home. They then gave each of their four children $25,000 to buy a new car. They then divided what remained of their first payment and gave half to their church and half to the Salvation Army. Today Abondanzio announced that the Salvation Army will return the entire amount it received. "We don't accept money associated with gambling," Abondanzio explained. "The Salvation Army counsels families who face homelessness and bankruptcy because of gambling. We really believe that, if we accepted this money, that we'd be hypocrites talking out of both sides of our mouth. We do everything we can to discourage gambling, and we want to set a good example." Tyrone Burns, pastor of the United Methodist Church, when interviewed by you today, said, "Of course we've accepted the familys gift. Our ministry helps feed and clothe the needy, getting them back on their feet. We have the opportunity here to do good, and I'm not going to deny the needy services they need because of some philosophical debate over the moneys source. This is a wonderful Christian family, and we respect their generosity."

12. Tourists take carriage rides through your citys historic district. Typically, the rides last a half-hour ride, with most people riding at night, especially weekend nights. Some couples think it's a romantic adventure over picturesque cobblestones and gas-lit streets. Today PETA appealed to your Mayor and to all of your citys councilmen to stop the rides, saying they expose horses to air pollution, traffic hazards, hoof damage, and other afflictions. Letters People for the Ethical Treatment of Animals members sent to the Mayor and all your city councilmen warn, "Vehicle fumes and the constant pounding on rough cobblestones make life inhumane and dangerous for horses in the carriage business. They are overworked and lead a nose-to-tailpipe existence." Interviewed by you, Minnie Cosby, President of the chapter of PETA in your community, added, "Whether the rides create a pretty picture for tourists doesn't really matter to us. There are a lot of things from bygone days that we've eliminated as a society because they were cruel." A carriage owner who doesn't want his name used responded that carriage owners in the city have adequate safeguards which include plenty of rest for their horses, custom-made feed, and "shoeings" specifically designed to protect their animals hooves. Also their carriages have back lights, reflectors and "Slow Moving Vehicle" signs. He added that his two 2,000-pound Belgian draft horses are plenty strong enough to pull a small carriage.

CHAPTER 7

ALTERNATIVE LEADS

The art of writing, like the art of love, runs all the way from a kind of routine hard to distinguish from piling bricks to a kind of frenzy closely related to delirium tremens.

(H.L. Mencken, journalist)

Chapter 6 described basic summary news leads. Summary leads are more common than any of the alternatives—and probably easier to write. While reading your local newspaper, you may find that most stories begin with a summary lead. Yet increasingly, experienced reporters are using alternative types of leads, sometimes known as "soft leads."

Journalists employ at least a dozen variations of soft leads, but most begin with a story's most interesting details—often an anecdote, description, quotation or question. Stories with soft leads, which may run four or five paragraphs, usually have a nut paragraph immediately after the lead. The "nut graph" states the central point of the story and serves some of the same functions as the summary news lead.

Writing an alternative lead requires thought and imagination as well as the ability to recognize and convey an interesting idea uniquely. It does not require an unusual story. In the example below, the lead first appears as a routine report of a news release. The alternative lead captures the news better:

> TYPICAL SUMMARY: The number of people filing for bankruptcy has nearly doubled in the past 10 years, according to the U.S. Department of Commerce.
>
> ALTERNATIVE LEAD: Business is great—in the nation's bankruptcy courts.
>
> More people are filing for bankruptcy than ever before, driven into insolvency by layoffs, high credit-card debt and even divorce.
>
> *(The Orlando [Fla.] Sentinel)*

Here is another example in which creativity lends freshness to a story about a young man waiting for a heart transplant:

> Kyle Bennett poured his heart into becoming this year's valedictorian at Sam Houston High School. Now the 18-year-old honors student is patiently awaiting a new one.
>
> *(Houston Chronicle)*

Good reporters can write many kinds of leads, choosing the appropriate type of lead for each story. This versatility allows reporters to avoid the trap of blindly following a particular trend in newswriting. According to Paula LaRocque, who coaches writers, "Compelling leads are as individual as writing, and writing is as individual as thinking." In other words, reporters will write better leads if they use their intelligence, inventiveness and imagination—their thinking skills—instead of trying to put their writing into a formula.

When reporters finish a story, their editors expect it to be well-written: clear, concise, accurate and interesting. If a story meets these criteria, editors are unlikely to object if its lead uses an alternative form. Nor are they likely to object to a summary lead that creatively and freshly captures the essence of a story.

Members of a Bronx street gang crashed a christening party. A fight broke out, someone fired shots, and a 10-year-old girl was killed. The New York Post, the Daily News and The New York Times all covered the incident. The Post and the Daily News stories use summary leads; the Times story used an alternative lead that linked the killing to the shooting of another girl in Brooklyn. Here are the leads from the three stories:

> A 10-year-old altar girl was killed by stray bullets outside her Bronx church yesterday after a gang of armed street thugs crashed a christening party and began arguing with guests.
>
> *(New York Post)*
>
> Little Malenny Mendez went to church to celebrate a new life, but instead she lost her own.
>
> *(New York Daily News)*
>
> Malenny Mendez, a 10-year-old girl from the Bronx, loved to strap on her in-line skates and smile at anyone who sauntered past her parents' grocery story. Katherine Crisantos, a 4-year-old girl from Brooklyn, loved the connotation of the word Friday, because it meant a trip with her big sister to Burger King for fries and soda.
>
> Early yesterday morning, both girls, children of Mexican immigrants, were shot in the head less than an hour apart at parties given by friends and relatives.
>
> *(The New York Times)*

CRITICISMS

During the 1940s, The Wall Street Journal became one of the first daily newspapers to use soft leads. Since then, other dailies, including the Los Angeles Times, The Miami Herald and The Boston Globe, have given their reporters more freedom to experiment with their writing, becoming known as "writers' newspapers." Proponents of soft leads say whether the lead works is what matters, not whether it is hard or soft. They disparage the traditional summaries as "suitcase leads." In the past, they explain, newspapers tried to jam too many details into leads, like a traveler trying to jam too many clothes into a suitcase. They say summary leads are unnatural and make it more difficult for reporters to write good stories. They further explain that summary leads eliminate the possibility of surprise and make all stories sound alike.

The more literary style of soft leads also may help newspapers compete with television. The style's proponents concede that television can report the news more quickly than newspapers, but by using soft leads, newspapers can make their stories more interesting.

Critics call the use of alternative leads "Jell-O Journalism." They complain that soft leads are inappropriate for most news stories: too arty, literary, dangerous and unprofessional. Critics add that soft leads are too long and fail to emphasize the news. If a story begins with several paragraphs of description or quotations, for example, its most important details may be buried in a later paragraph. Critics also complain that some reporters strain to write fine literature, and many lack the necessary ability.

The following example illustrates how poorly constructed alternative leads can confuse readers and make them impatient. You have to read more than 145 words before getting to the news—the main point of the story:

> Eleanor Lago considers herself an intelligent, educated woman.
>
> She's read the information provided her by the Grand Rapids Township Board. She's talked to friends and neighbors. And she intends to vote Tuesday in a special election that could determine the township's future.
>
> "I just want to do what's best," says Lago.
>
> Like many residents, though, she's not sure what that is.
>
> An unusual battle is being fought in this smallest of Kent County townships, a raggedy-shaped 16 square miles set cheek to jowl against the cities of Grand Rapids, East Grand Rapids and Kentwood.
>
> The battle is not about zoning, the more typical flash point of local politics. Nor is it about leaf burning ordinances or other grass-roots laws in this suburb of nearly 11,000 people.
>
> This battle is about what the community can do to keep from being nibbled to pieces by annexation.

The writer's intention was good: describing an intelligent voter who is confused about an important issue. The introduction would have been more effective, however, if cut in half. The writer could have eliminated some description, cut the clichés and avoided saying what the election was not about.

The following sections describe different types of alternative leads and offer examples of each.

"BURIED" OR "DELAYED" LEADS

A "buried" lead is the most common type of alternative lead. Some reporters call it a "delayed" lead. Typically, a buried lead begins with an interesting example or anecdote that sets a story's theme. Then a nut graph—perhaps the third or fourth paragraph—summarizes the story and provides a transition to the body. The nut graph states the central point of the story and moves it from a single example or anecdote to the general issue or problem. Like a traditional lead, it summarizes the topic. In addition, it may explain why the topic is important.

Here are two examples of buried leads. The first is by Walter R. Mears, a special correspondent for The Associated Press, who takes a different approach to writing about a company filing for bankruptcy. The second is by Sabra Chartrand of The New York Times, who wrote about a business side of athletics most people rarely think about:

> WASHINGTON (AP)—Time was, writing meant typewriting. Words like these—written on a television screen—were composed on the solid keyboard, banged noisily onto a piece of paper, XXXXd out when they weren't quite right, ripped out and scrapped when the paragraphs just didn't work.
>
> It's easier and faster with the computer, a reality that pushed Smith Corona Corp., the last big-name American typewriter manufacturer, into bankruptcy on Wednesday.

> Cal Ripken, Jr., less than two months from breaking Lou Gehrig's streak of 2,130 consecutive games, is famous for his endurance on the baseball field. For a less celebrated example of his stamina, consider the more than 10,000 autographs he will sign this year.
>
> The vast majority will not be the old-fashioned face-to-face kind. Rather, Mr. Ripken signs balls by the boxload, hundreds at a time, in his hotel room or at home, to be sold at a big profit.

After giving some details about how Ripken signs the balls, how much an autographed ball costs and what Ripken makes from the sale of each, Chartland gets to the point of the story in the fourth paragraph:

> Ten years ago, mass-autographed merchandise was a rarity. Today, these balls, helmets, jerseys and athletic shoes are a $500 million industry.

The delayed lead can introduce a complex or abstract problem by showing how the problem affects a single individual—someone your readers may know or identify with. Or an anecdote can illustrate a problem and arouse readers' interest in the topic.

Some buried leads surprise their readers with an unusual twist. If a story is only three or four paragraphs long, journalists may save the twist for the last line. If a story is longer, they use the twist to lure readers to the nut graph, which then provides a transition to the following paragraphs.

MULTIPARAGRAPH LEADS

Other newswriters think of a lead as a unit of thought. Their summary leads consist of two or three paragraphs that flow into each other as if they were one:

> STARKE—Gone were the painted, manicured fingernails and the fashionable dark hair. Gone was the tough-edged woman who drove around Pensacola in a Corvette and told bigger-than-life stories about her life, her businesses and her Chanel perfume.
>
> Judy Buenoano walked shakily to Florida's electric chair Monday, her head freshly shaved. Guards had covered it with gel—highlighting every bump, every vein—to conduct the electricity better. She wasn't the same person who had boasted that Florida would never execute her. She was simply an old, frightened woman.
>
> And by 7:13 a.m. Buenoano, 54, had become the first woman executed in the state in 150 years and the first woman to die in the chair.
>
> *(The Orlando [Fla.] Sentinel)*

> NEW YORK—It seemed like a perfect night for a mugging. The street was dark, the hour late, the Brooklyn neighborhood rough.
>
> But the teenage boys who stalked Arthur Boone as he left a corner market missed one thing: the .44-caliber Magnum in his belt.
>
> One of the muggers, nicknamed "B-Boy," put the barrel of a BB gun to Boone's head. The other, "Taz," reached for his wallet.
>
> Then Boone fired three shots heard 'round the city.
>
> *(The Associated Press)*

USING QUOTATIONS

Reporters usually avoid using quotations in leads. Sources rarely provide quotes that meet three criteria for leads: (1) They summarize the entire story (not just part of it), (2) they are brief, and (3) they are self-explanatory. Some editors prohibit the use of quotation leads because they lack clarity and often are too long and complicated. As with the use of any quote in a story, the source's statement should be so effective the reporter cannot improve it. When used in the first line of a story, a quote also must tell the reader the point of the story:

> "I wanted to slam the plane into a mountain so I could die with my husband," said Betty Smith, whose husband died at its controls. But then she thought of her children on the ground.

> "Our children can't read, add or find countries on a map," the nation's teacher-of-the-year said at a congressional hearing Wednesday.

If a quote is only sensational, then it does not meet the criteria noted above. It may be suitable to use in the story, but not in the lead. Reporters have other ways of writing leads that will startle readers or grab their attention. Remember that the lead provides the organization for the rest of the story. If the quote does not lead readers into and set the stage for the rest of the story, then it will only confuse and discourage them. Even within the body of a story, a quote should be brief. In the lead, brevity is a virtue because a complicated, long quote will raise unnecessary questions.

Avoid quotations that begin with words needing identification or explanation, words like "he," "she," "we," "they," "it," "that" and "this." If such words open a story, readers have no way of knowing to whom or what the words refer. When the subject's identity is revealed later in a story, readers may have to reread the quotation to understand its meaning.

Leads using a quotation often can be rewritten with a brief introduction placed before the quotation to enhance its clarity:

> "The water was rising so fast and the bank was so muddy and slippery I just didn't think I could get away from that torrent of water." That's how a Bremerton man described his ordeal just before rescue workers used a utility truck to pluck him out of a tree hc had climbed to escape a flash flood during Monday night's thunderstorms.
>
> REVISED: A Bremerton man who was rescued from a tree he had climbed to escape a flash flood Monday night said, "The water was so fast and the bank was so muddy and slippery I just didn't think I could get away from that torrent of water."

USING QUESTIONS

Questions occasionally make effective leads. Some editors, though, prohibit question leads because they believe news stories should answer questions, not ask them. Also, question leads often run the risk of being clichés.

To be effective, question leads must be brief, simple, specific and provocative. The question should contain no more than a dozen words. Moreover, readers should feel absolutely compelled to answer it. Avoid questions if the readers' responses may discourage them from continuing with the story:

> Are you interested in nuclear physics?

A few readers might be interested in nuclear physics, but many would think the story too complicated. This question lead also fails because readers can answer "yes" or "no," possibly ending the reader's interest in the story.

A question should concern a controversial issue that readers are familiar with and that interests and affects them. Avoid abstract or complicated questions requiring a great deal of explanation.

The following question is ineffective because it is too abstract, long and complicated. Moreover, it fails to ask about issues that everyone is certain to care about:

> If you were on vacation miles from your house, and you thought the mechanics at a service station deliberately damaged your car, then demanded an exorbitant fee to repair it, would you be willing to file criminal charges against the mechanics and return to the area to testify at their trial?

The following questions also fail, but for different reasons. The first question asks about an issue unlikely to concern most readers. The second question is unanswerable and flippant, treating a serious topic as a trivial one:

> Have you thought lately about going to prison?
>
> Someone was swindled today. Who'll be swindled tomorrow?

The following questions make more effective leads. Notice that immediately after asking a question, the reporter answers it:

What's in your wallet—or trash?

For most people, a wallet contains a handful of credit cards, retail store cards, ATM card, driver's license, health insurance card, video rental card, Social security card and a few blank checks.

(Chambersburg [Pa.] Public Opinion)

CHEBOYGAN—When every second counts, why pay by the minute?

Representatives of the fifth largest long-distance service in the United States are asking telephone users this very question.

(The Cheboygan [Mich.] Daily Tribune)

SUSPENSEFUL LEADS

Some reporters write leads to create suspense, arouse readers' curiosity or raise a question in their minds. By hinting at some mysterious development explained in a later paragraph, this type of lead compels readers to finish a story:

LEESBURG—No funerals. No headstones. No sympathy cards.

Just a body, found without identification and buried without ceremony.

(The Orlando [Fla.] Sentinel)

NEW YORK—When Aaron Stansbury of Baltimore ordered almost $500 worth of California chardonnay this spring, three well-known wineries quickly filled his telephone request.

They made a $55,000 mistake.

(USA Today)

The first story focused on the life and death of transients in a Florida city. The second story reported on a police sting operation targeting wineries that mail wine directly to consumers.

DESCRIPTIVE LEADS

Other leads begin with descriptive details that paint a picture for the reader before moving gradually into the action. The description should be colorful and interesting, so that it arouses readers' interest. The description should also help summarize the story.

The following examples show the effectiveness of descriptive leads. Notice the use of concrete images and active verbs in the first lead: "wounded animal," "warm asphalt" and "slender frame"; "twisted," "heaving" and "streaming":

Tina Volker crouches like a wounded animal on the warm asphalt, her face twisted in fear, her shoulders heaving as sobs rack her slender frame.

"I just want him to leave me alone," she shouts, tears streaming down her cheeks. "I just want to get on with my life."

Handcuffed in the back of a Sacramento County Sheriff's department squad car, agitated and drenched with sweat, is the man she has loved and hated for five years.

(The Sacramento [Calif.] Bee)

TRINIDAD, Texas—With holsters strapped to their hips, three bearded men wearing camouflage hats and torn jeans sit in folding chairs at the end of a dirt driveway.

Homemade signs hang on the gate, barbed-wire fence and trees: "We are militia and will live free or die!" "Disobedience to tyranny is obedience to God!" "Notice to all public servants. No trespassing—survivors will be prosecuted."

(The Associated Press)

The second lead describes the scene of a police standoff near a small Texas town near Waco and how events in Waco shaped the events in this standoff.

SHOCKERS—LEADS WITH A TWIST

Reporters like "shockers"—startling leads that immediately capture the attention of readers. The following examples have an unusual twist that adds to their effectiveness:

Driving a car is a rite of passage for teenagers in the United States. And for an enormous number of them, it is a passage to the graveyard.

(The Washington Post)

MANAGUA, Nicaragua—She had been raped. She was pregnant. And she was poor. And Rosa was 9. That gave her one more reason to want an abortion.

(The Los Angeles Times)

IRONIC LEADS

Closely related to shockers are leads that present a startling or ironic contrast. The use of striking details is likely to arouse readers' curiosity:

She earned $27,000 a year but owned 300 pairs of shoes. Now she's paying for it.

The 24-year-old former manager of an Ann Taylor boutique plans to file for bankruptcy—one of a growing number of young adults who are so in over their heads financially that they've resorted to bankruptcy to bail themselves out.

(Los Angeles Times)

When union activist Oliver French goes on trial today on charges of killing two auto plant colleagues and wounding two others, he likely will be portrayed as the victim.

(The Detroit News)

DIRECT-ADDRESS LEADS

Reporters occasionally use a form of direct address, speaking directly to their readers:

PHOENIX—Picture this scenario. You're walking along when you notice a poster for a Springsteen concert. "The Boss is coming here!!!???" So you grab your cell phone, aim it at a bar code on the poster, and are wirelessly connected to an online ticket agent.

(USA Today)

WASHINGTON—Consider the penny. Or rather, consider what it can buy, which is—well, what is it even worth these days?

(Atlanta Journal Constitution)

The image of a man dressed in the garb of a 12th-century Scottish warrior talking on a cell phone presents the kind of startling contrast that is likely to attract attention. Good leads often use stark contrasts or irony to grab and hold readers.

WORDS USED IN UNUSUAL WAYS

A clever reporter with a good imagination (or a good grasp of literature) can use a common word or phrase in an uncommon way:

> FOUNTAIN VALLEY, Calif.—The Internal Revenue Service is playing hardball with the Fountain Valley Girls' Softball League, and the players, ages 4 to 14, are crying foul.
>
> *(The Washington Post)*

> Perhaps it was God's joke on a newly ordained priest when the Rev. Jim Farnan, former class clown and no stranger to the detention room, was asked to speak with the occasional clone of his former self at Our Lady of Fatima School.
>
> *(The Pittsburgh Post-Gazette)*

This style is difficult, because what seems funny or clever to one person may seem corny or silly to another. Also, the subjects may be too serious for such a light touch:

> Oakland County Prosecutor Richard Thompson wants to be known by the criminals he keeps.
>
> *(The Detroit Free Press)*

The story was about the high costs a prosecutor was creating for the county by refusing to plea bargain with criminals.

OTHER UNUSUAL LEADS

The following leads are difficult to categorize. All the leads are unusual yet effective. Notice their simplicity, brevity and clarity. Also, notice the leads' emphasis on the interesting and unusual. The first lead introduces a story describing the effects of unusually cold weather on the economy. The second lead reports the death of actress Audrey Hepburn, who played Eliza Doolittle in the movie "My Fair Lady." The third lead introduces the man in charge of demolishing Three Rivers Stadium in Pittsburgh, Pa.

> WASHINGTON—Jack Frost is nipping at our growth.
>
> *(The Wall Street Journal)*
>
> Audrey Hepburn was the fairest lady of them all.
>
> *(The Detroit News)*
>
> Circuses have ringmasters. Military boot camps have drill sergeants. The Three Rivers Stadium implosion has Greg Yesko, who's a bit of both.
>
> *(The Pittsburgh Post-Gazette)*

THE WRITING COACH

TOO MANY WORDS CAN MUDDLE WRITING

By **Joe Hight**
Managing Editor of the Oklahoman

You've just heard that familiar voice from the copy desk say, "We're not going to make it!" Your stomach quivers.

You're writing or editing that masterpiece for the next day's paper. But the inevitable deadline awaits, and you have another story to write, an assembly line of stories to edit or someone on the phone wondering when you're coming home.

You know the names and facts are correct. But check again. Your Mona Lisa has a handlebar mustache that must go—your story has too many words.

And you only have a few minutes left.

This situation faces many writers and editors daily. Those few minutes that you have to complete your editing—to trim those excessive words—may help keep a few more readers.

Here are four reasons why excessive words should concern you:

- Despite increased emphasis on graphics, technology and design, the major part of any paper is words. "Like the trucks that carry other products to market they are part of the delivery system we use to reach readers with news, advertising and entertainment," wrote Jack Hart, managing editor of the Oregonian, in his "Writers Workshop" column for Editor & Publisher. "But words not only carry freight, they also ARE freight. Nobody much cares about the color of the truck that delivered yesterday's canned corn. But every reader reacts to the way words, sentences and paragraphs come together to deliver the news. One bad word choice can cost a subscription."
- A Poynter Institute study indicated that 75 percent or more of the participants processed or looked at the artwork and photos and more than 55 percent read the headlines. But only 25 percent read text.

(continued)

- Seventy-three percent of the regular and occasional newspaper readers "feel extremely time pressured," according to a recent report prepared for the American Society of Newspaper Editors. That means many readers think they have less time to read your stories.
- American Press Institute studies have shown that 90 percent of readers easily understand sentences averaging 16 to 19 words. But the same 90 percent cannot understand sentences that average 30 words or more. "The higher the word count, the more difficult it is for the reader," writing consultant Don Fry has written.

That is why long sentences and leads of 44, 48, 59 words should be discouraged. Sure, some well-written sentences that contain details can be longer. And stories should have a range of short, medium and longer sentences.

But those extra and abstract words, the ones that lengthen your story or harm its clarity, must be trimmed. Thus, you should develop habits that will help you make those quick fixes.

So after you've checked the names and facts, remember these tips to trim the excess:

- The *ofs:* Prepositions are good connectors, but they can add excessive words. So look for ways to trim prepositions: *a native of Oklahoma City* should be *an Oklahoma City native, member of the planning commission* should be *planning commission member* and *the mayor of Tulsa* should be *Tulsa mayor.* Also, look for prepositional phrases or clauses at the end of sentences that repeat information in your story.
- Quotes: I know many reporters complain that their good quotes are cut first. But I maintain that quotes should be cut if they don't add emphasis to your story or help the flow. Cut or recast quotes with excessive ellipses or parentheses, repetitive information or that simply don't add to your story.
- Background: Seek to trim unneeded or excessive background about the story's topic.
- *There, it's, it is* and *to be:* All of us put too many of these in our first drafts. Sentences that are rewritten without these words usually are shorter and clearer.
- Active, not passive: Subject, strong verb and object are preferred unless you want to emphasize the sentence's object.
- Repetition: Scan your story to see if you've repeated a full name, age, title or time reference. Also, look for parallel prepositions, ones that repeat a preposition: City council members were concerned *about* the new road and *about* its effect on nearby residents. The sentence should have been: City council members were concerned *about* the new road's effect on nearby residents.
- Know your weaknesses: Even experienced writers and editors have trouble in certain areas. This could include the use of *its* and *it's,* using *for example* or *of course* too many times, misspelling *separate* or *similar* or being too wordy. Rick Wilber, in his book "Writer's Handbook for Editing & Revision," says that good writers recognize their trouble areas

and develop tricks to overcome them. Wilber says he has learned to do a computer word search for *you* so he can ensure that he's used *your* and *you're* correctly.

- Simpler ways: This can be the most difficult on deadline. But you should seek simpler words and ways to replace clauses with phrases and phrases with single words.

Here are some other ways recommended by Paula LaRocque, writing coach: Trim vague qualifiers *(very, really, truly, extremely, somewhat, quite* and *rather).* Avoid excessive use of *a, an, the, this, these, those* and *that.* Cut unneeded infinitives and *who, which* and *that* clauses.

LaRocque adds that your goal should not be to cut for no reason or write short. She recommends you use the right words and compress instead of cut. "Brevity is a companion of good writing, not its cause," she says.

"Compression means being able to say everything while still making our work as solid, concrete and terse as possible."

Well, your time is up. Your story is due. But you've done the improbable. By developing habits for quick fixes, you've improved parts of your story—and helped you and the readers feel better about it the next day.

Name ______________________ Class ______________________ Date ______

EXERCISE 1

ALTERNATIVE LEADS

EVALUATING ALTERNATIVE LEADS

Critically evaluate the following leads, each of which uses one of the alternative forms discussed in this chapter. Select the best leads and explain why they succeed. Point out the flaws in the remaining leads. As you evaluate the leads, look for lessons—"dos and don'ts"—that you can apply to your own work.

1. Are you ready for a big change?
2. "I saw the train coming at us and I knew it would never get stopped."
3. No shirt! No shoes! No service!

   Unfortunately, the 350-pound black bear that wandered into the city limits and pried open a window to break into the Oakhill Restaurant couldn't read. The bear was captured by state game commission officers after it had ransacked the restaurant's kitchen and helped itself to a variety of treats.
4. Amy Clauch sat beside the rough hewn pine fence, her fingers rubbing the worn knuckles of the knots in the rope she held in her hand.

   The sweet scent of clover hay wafted on the light breeze that blew through the barn. She sucked in a deep breath and held it. The scent lingered. She wished it always would.

   The sun hung in the early morning cobalt blue sky like a spotlight in a theater, illuminating her, the actor on this stage. This is where she wanted to be—free from the confines of the four pale beige walls that surrounded her in clinical sterility for months.

   She tugged at her jeans. Her lips pursed. "You can do this," she whispered in prayer to herself.

   Clauch rocked the wheelchair to the left and reached for the stirrup hanging limply from the saddle. Pulling herself upright, she grimaced as she felt the braces tighten on her legs. The muscles in her arms clenched as she pulled herself into the saddle. The chestnut mare flinched at the load and Clauch grabbed the worn leather saddle horn to steady herself. Her smile stretched her cheeks to their limit. She was back where she belonged.

   It had been eight months since a riding accident left Clauch temporarily paralyzed from the waist down.
5. Too much work. Too many demands. Too many responsibilities. Not enough time.

   Stress is killing Americans, the American Medical Association said in a report released Monday.
6. Should high school students have to take a competency test before receiving their diplomas?
7. The state's motorcycle riders won the right today to have the wind in their hair and bugs in their teeth. The state Legislature passed a bill eliminating the state's helmet requirements for riders 18 and older.
8. How much would you pay for, say, a triple heart bypass? Or gallbladder surgery?

   As government officials struggle to rein in health care costs without sacrificing the quality of care, they find themselves confronted with the question of who should pay how much.

9. "If we can't solve the state budget crisis today, the students of tomorrow will suffer the consequences," school Superintendent Gary Hubbard said about the state's failure to pass a budget before the start of the school year.
10. The Freedonia County Fair begins today and if you want to catch all the action this week, you better get to the fairgrounds.
11. Billy Lee Anderson pushes the blond hair away from his blue eyes, exposing the dusting of freckles on his forehead.

    The 12-year-old sits in a chair that is a bit too adult for his small frame, his feet, clad in gleaming white athletic shoes, dangling several inches above the floor.

    There is an air of innocence surrounding the boy that will make it hard for any jury to believe that he could have set the fire that killed his parents and baby sister. But that is what prosecutors will attempt to do as Anderson's murder trial gets under way today.
12. You're driving down a tree-shaded city street when a child runs out from between two parked cars. Could you stop in time?
13. Thompsontown hit a grand slam over the weekend as all four of its Little League teams won their championship games.
14. When Jim and Suzanne Baker left the mall, they were loaded down with Christmas presents and laughing about the surprises they had in store for their children.

    Half an hour later, they were dead.
15. It actually was a dark and stormy night when Sharon Murphy sat down in front of her typewriter to start writing her first novel.
16. A 60-year-old Salem man who was rescued Monday from a burning building said, "I could hear the sirens of the fire trucks, but they just seemed so far away. I decided that I needed to make peace with the fact that I was going to die."

EXERCISE 2

ALTERNATIVE LEADS

WRITING ALTERNATIVE LEADS

Using techniques you studied in this chapter, write an alternative lead for each of the following stories. You may want to use complete or partial quotations, questions, descriptions, buried leads, multiparagraph leads, suspense or chronological order. Or, you may want to try a shocking lead, ironic lead, direct-address lead or a word used in an unusual way. Correct any errors you may find.

1. The Steak & Ale is a restaurant in your town. It is a favorite eating spot for many families in the area. Three people were injured while eating at the restaurant Saturday evening. The injured were Chester Garland, 48, of 2008 North 21st street and his wife, Charllotte, also of 2008 North Twenty-First street. Chester Garland is a city health inspector who was celebrating his birthday at the restaurant. The third person injured was Sarah Kindstrom, 23, of 4828 N. Vine St., who is a waitress at the Steak & Ale. They were injured by flying glass, plates of food and silverware when a car crashed through the brick wall and plate glass window at the front of the restaurant at 8:13 p.m. The car, a blue Buick Park Avenue was driven by Lois Zarrinfare, 81, of 411 Wisconsin Avenue. Zarrinfair is a retired elementary school teacher. Zarrinfair was planning on joining some friends for dinner when the accident occurred. According to police, Zarrinfair was parking her car at the front of the restaurant when her foot missed the brake pedal and hit the gas pedal, propelling the car through the front of the restaurant. The car hit several empty tables, pushing them into the table occupied by Mr. and Mrs. Garland. The Garlands and Kindstrom suffered minor injuries that were treated by paramedics who responded to the scene. Zarrinfair, who was wearing a seatbelt and whose airbag deployed, was not injured. "I'm usually concerned about the safety of the food at a restaurant, not the safety of the front wall," Chester Garland said.

2. Police in your city are completely baffled by the robbery of a clothing store in an outlet mall. The crime occurred in the broad daylight on a Sunday afternoon while thousands of shoppers were enjoying a beautifully sunny day of shopping. Police said Cynthia Lowrie, 118 Hillside Drive Apartment 74, assistant manager of the Tommy Hilfiger store in the Oakland Hills Outlet Mall, 2457 Mall Boulevard, reported the crime. Lowrie called the police at 4:30 p.m., half an hour before the store closed to report the robbery. Lowrie told police that nearly $4,000 in merchandise was pilfered from the store between noon when the store opened and 4 p.m. when store employees found a pile of security tags hidden under some clothing in a dressing room. The security tags are attached to apparel to foil shoplifters. The devices emit a loud beep when they pass through an electronic field at the store's entrance. The robbers apparently used a special tool to remove the devices and hide them. Police have no idea how the robbers escaped with the merchandise. The robbers made off with 57 women's shirts, 28 women's polo shirts, 32 men's polo shirts and 20 pair of men's shorts. The total loss was $3,788.63. According to police, the store was very busy, and was packed with customers throughout the day.

3. It was just one of those days for Representative Constance P. Wei. Wei is the representative for the 86th District. Wei, who lives at 206 North Wabash Avenue, is a proponent of limited government. State representatives have been trying to pass a ban on using cell phones while driving. Wei thinks it is an infringement on individual rights. "All this is is Big Brother telling you what to do," she said. Advocates of the ban say it is an issue of safety. They point to a recent accident in which five people were killed in a two-car accident. The driver who caused the accident was a 48-year-old man who was talking on his cell phone while trying to pass another car on a two-lane stretch of road. Witnesses said the man swerved into the path of the other car and the two vehicles collided head-on. Two of the five people killed were children. The state legislature has never backed a ban on cell phone use, but other states have instituted successful bans. Opponents of the ban, including Wei, claim the ban will not affect safety because forcing people to pull off the road and get out of their cars to talk on the phone could be more hazardous. In addition, opponents say that the state cannot ban all distractions drivers create, such as eating, reading or applying makeup while driving. Proponents of the ban want it to take affect in January of next year. Wei was on her cell phone Wednesday as she was driving home. She was talking to State representative Peter Mackey, 89th District, about postponing a vote on the bill banning cell phone use while driving when her Cadillac Sedan de Ville struck the rear of a car driven by Michael Jeffreys, 41, of 2781 Collins Ave. Jeffreys suffered minor injuries and was taken to Mercy Hospital. He was treated and released. Police said the accident occurred at 5:37 p.m. at the intersection of 29th Street and Melrose Avenue. Jeffreys was stopped at a traffic light. Wei did not see the red light or the cars stopped in front of her and rammed the rear of Jeffreys Toyota Camry. Police said the Camry suffered severe damage. Weis Cadillac sustained an estimated $8,000 in damage.

4. It's a unique idea. School board members and school administrators in your local school district are considering changing the school week to cut costs. The state announced that it does not have enough money to fund schools because of the slow economy and schools will have to cut their budgets. Superintendent of schools Gary Hubbard told school board members at Monday night's meeting that the district has cut all the fat out of the budget that it can. "We've cut out after-school programs and eliminated all but the essential teacher's aides positions," Hubbard said. "We've even raised the price of school lunches, but we are still coming up short." Hubbard and school board members are proposing to go to a four-day school week to help the district save money. The school day, which now runs from 8 a.m. to 2:30 p.m. would be lengthened by two hours, running from 8 a.m. to 4:30 p.m. to make up for the loss of one day during the week. Hubbard and the board say the district could save more then one million dollars in transportation, food service and janitorial costs. The board voted 7-0 in favor of the proposal.

5. Your city officials received a gift on Tuesday. Attorney Richard Cycler handed a check for over $2 million to Mayor Sabrina Datolli. The money will be used to build the Willie Hattaway Center in an annex of City Hall. Plans to develop the annex into a community center, senior citizens center, a historical exhibit hall and meeting and conference rooms had been postponed for several years because of a lack of funds to complete the project. The city had built the annex with money from a federal grant but could not raise enough money to complete the project. The building has been an empty shell for more than seven years. City officials were using the space to store boxes of old water bills and other papers. Willie Hattaway gave the money to the city in his will. Hattaway died last year. He was 98. He was a widower. His wife, Estelle, died 10 years ago. Everyone, including his neighbors, was surprised that Willie had

that much money in the bank. Willie lived in a modest two-story, white clapboard house on Virginia Avenue for more than 60 years. Flowers surrounded the house. Hattaway loved to work in his garden and flower beds. He was particularly fond of roses and grew several assorted varieties. He had entered Sunnyview Retirement Home on Wisconsin Avenue last year, shortly after his 97th birthday. Neighbors said he could no longer take care of himself after he fell and broke his hip. Neighbors said Hattaway drove a car that was 40 years old and never traveled very far from home. The car, a green Chevrolet Impala, is still parked in the garage. Hattaway did not want to sell the car even though he had not been driving since he was 90. He enjoyed sitting on his porch and talking to neighbors or giving neighborhood children treats of candy or fruit. He did not live extravagantly. "It just goes to show that you never really know your neighbors. Willie was such a wonderful, friendly gentleman. He was so generous with his time helping neighbors and playing with the neighborhood children. It doesn't surprise me that he would be so generous with his money, too," said a former neighbor Marilyn Boudinot, 41, of 4340 Virginia Ave. Hattaway and his wife had no children. He was a retired construction worker who had invested his money in the stock market for many years.

6. Officials in your county are trying to deal with an environmental problem. The county landfill is scheduled to receive 3,700 tons of 16-year-old incinerator ash. The ash is from incinerated household trash destroyed in a facility near your state capital. The ash was supposed to be buried in the county's landfill 16 years ago, but the county has been waging a legal battle to prevent the ash from being buried in its landfill because county officials say the ash is contaminated with lead, mercury and other contaminants. The county lost its final battle last month when the state Supreme Court ruled that the county cannot prohibit the state from dumping the ash in the landfill. Because county officials refused to accept it 16 years ago, the ash has been sent to many places during the court battle with the state. The ash spent two years on a ship touring the Caribbean Sea looking for a country that would accept it, 12 years on a deserted stretch of beach in Puerto Rico and two years on a barge in Louisiana. The ash will be unloaded from the barge and placed in special metal containers before being trucked over land to the landfill. State officials said the delay in disposing of the ash and the cost to store it for 16 years cost the state more than $2 million. "I don't care if it cost the state $20 million to get rid of the stuff. Its the states trash. That incinerator ash didn't come from the people of this county and we don't want it dumped in our landfill," said County Commissioner Valerie Dawkins. State officials say the ash contains nothing that is hazardous to humans. "If that ash is so safe, why doesn't the governor and the states legislators bury it in their back yards?" Dawkins said.

Pro Challenge

EXERCISE 3

ALTERNATIVE LEADS

WRITING ALTERNATIVE LEADS

Professionals have written alternative leads for the following stories. Write an alternative lead for each of the stories. When you finish, you can compare your work with the professionals'. Their leads appear in a manual available to your instructor. You may find, however, that you like some of your own and your classmates' leads better.

1. There was an announcement made today by officials at the United States Census Bureau. The announcement was made at a press conference in Washington, D.C. The news was a surprise to many people. The Census Bureau conducted a survey of 7,898 people ranging from age 25 to 64—which demographers identify as a typical work-life period. The survey was a special project separate from the census taken every 10 years by the bureau. Officials said that college graduates could expect to earn more than $1 million more than workers with just a high school diploma. A college graduate can expect to earn more than two million dollars during his or her work-life period. A college graduate with a master's degree can expect to earn $2,500,000. Someone with a doctoral degree can expect to earn 3.4 million dollars. Someone with a professional degree—such as a doctor or lawyer—can expect to earn $4.4 million. On the other hand, a high school graduate will earn around 1,200,000 dollars, while a high school dropout can expect to earn around 850 thousand dollars. The survey was conducted last year and is based on last years salaries. The salary figures were not adjusted for inflation. Census Bureau officials said the study will help the public understand the connection between getting an education and having the opportunity for higher earning power. Having a higher earning power can improve ones standard of living, a bureau official said. "Going to college can cost a lot of money, but if you look at it as an investment, it is worth it," said Judith Wheatly, Census Bureau spokesperson. Wheatly said that the survey indicated that more Americans are staying in school longer. Of those surveyed, eighty-four percent had at least a high school degree, while 26 % had a bachelor's degree or more, both records for the U.S.

2. It was just another car theft in your city. Police were startled when the car thief called them and told them where he would be leaving the vehicle. The vehicle in question was a white 2003 Chevrolet cargo van. The van belonged to Hertz Rent A Car car rental agency. Chief of police Barry Kopperud said the man who stole the van was frantic when he called police around 11 P.M. Thursday. "He jumped in that van and roared off. He didn't know he had a passenger," Kopperud said. Police said the van was stolen while it was parked in front of a residence in the 4000 block of New Orleans Ave. It was stolen at 9:35 p.m. The driver of the van said he was in the residence talking to the homeowner when he heard the door of the van slam shut and the engine being gunned. By the time he got to the front door, the van was speeding down the street. The driver said he had left the keys in the van because he only had to get some paperwork he left in the residence. The van had been rented earlier in the day by Parsons Funeral Home. A spokesperson for the funeral home said both hearses they normally used were in the shop being repaired and the funeral home rented the van to pick up bodies during the day until the hearses were repaired. The driver of the van, William Thomas, 38, of 2838 Vermont Ave., an employee of Parsons Funeral

Home, said he was at the residence picking up the body of an elderly man who had died that evening. Thomas was talking to the son of the man who died when the van was stolen from in front of the son's house. The man who stole the van called police to tell them he had just stolen the van he was driving, but he didn't know anything about the body in the back of the van. He said he had nothing to do with the man's death. Police recovered the van shortly after midnight in the 3000 block of Eastland Drive. They believe the thief must have gotten curious about what was in the big black bag in the back of the van because the body bag was partially unzipped when police opened the back of the van.

3. Its an idea that many people are praising. Beginning next year, aspiring doctors will have to take a test. The National Board of Medical Examiners created the examination. The exam will be required of all medical students who want to practice medicine in the United States. While clinical skills are already tested, this examination will test the would-be doctors bedside manner. Medical students will be required to examine 20 people who will have fictional illnesses. The "patients" will be trained to act like they are sick and complain of various symptoms. They will be trained to test the students patience and communication skills, such as how they listen to the patient and how well or thoroughly they question the patient. Each of the fictional patients will be examined for 15 minutes. After the examination, they will fill out a report on how the would-be doctor handled the examination. The test will cost $1,000 and students will have to travel to major cities, where test sites will be set up. Students who fail the test will be able to repeat the test after 90 days. During that time the students who fail will be offered counseling in developing better people skills.

4. Patricia Richard, 23, of 42 Tusca Trail, got married Saturday. It was a lovely ceremony. Her new husband is Grady Smith, 22, of 8213 Peach Street. Richards was arrested Saturday night and charged with disturbing the peace, criminal mischief, simple assault and resisting arrest. Police handcuffed Richards and put her in jail. She was released Sunday and left for her honeymoon on Monday after posting a $25,000 bond. Richards said it was all a misunderstanding. The reception was held at the Downtown Club at the intersection of Washington and Virginia avenues. More than 200 guests had been invited to the reception. When the reception dinner was served, it was discovered that the wrong meal had been prepared. Instead of prime rib au jus and salmon almondine as entries, the reception party was served baked ham and stuffed chicken breasts. Richards said she had already paid the bill and wanted a refund. She got into an argument with Walter Morton, the manager of food service at the Downtown Club. Richards picked up a stuffed chicken breast and threw it at Morton, striking him in the face. She then grabbed a serving plate of ham and threw it at a waiter. The waiter picked up some of the ham and threw it back at Richards. The ham struck Richards in the chest. Grady Smith tried to stop Richards, to calm her down, and Richards struck him on the head with a serving platter. Richards began throwing food and wine glasses at other waiters and waitresses. By the time police arrived, Richards was throwing hunks of her wedding cake at Morton and staff members of the Downtown Club. Several officers were struck by cake when they tried to take Richards into custody. Richards kicked one of the officers during the struggle. Police said alcohol was a factor in the incident.

5. There was an attempted burglary at the Wendys Old Fashion Hamburgers restaurant, 1853 Huron Ave. The attempted burglary occurred between 2 a.m. and 8 a.m. Tuesday. Police said the burglary was discovered by the store manager, Jenna Adams, 31, of 550 S. Highland Ave. Police said the burglar attempted to enter the fast-food

restaurant through the drive-thru window on the north side of the building. Adams is the day manager. She usually arrives at work around 8 a.m. to begin preparations for the restaurants opening at 11 a.m. Police said her normal routine is to go directly to her office located behind the cooking and serving area of the restaurant. Adams told police she did not notice anything unusual when she first entered the restaurant. Nothing seemed to be missing. About 30 minutes after arriving at the restaurant, Adams heard a noise. She said it sounded like a whimpering animal. She began to look around the restaurant to locate the noise. What she found shocked her. A man was stuck in the drive-thru window of the restaurant. His belt and a belt loop of his pants were hooked on a metal peg used to open and close the window. The upper half of his body was inside the restaurant and the lower half was outside the restaurant, his feet dangling a foot off the ground. Adams said the man apparently had been hanging there for hours. Adams called police and officers managed to free the burglar. Police charged the suspect, Thomas C. Ahl, 19, of 2634 6th Street, Apartment 382, with burglary and indecent exposure. Ahl had torn the seat of his trousers while trying to free himself from his predicament. "I surrender. Now please get me out of here," Ahl said when police arrived at the restaurant.

CHAPTER 8

THE BODY OF A NEWS STORY

Always, when time permits, read your story before submitting it. If you can't cut out at least a couple of words, you're not doing a sufficiently critical job of reading. One of the toughest things in the writing trade, and one of the best for a writer, is to cut your own copy.

(Morton Sontheimer, journalist)

The portion of a news story that follows the lead is called the "body." It contains the information a reporter believes readers need to know. The information can be presented in several styles: inverted pyramid, hourglass, focus or narrative. No technique works best with all readers, all stories or all reporters. All require thorough reporting. And all require reporters to organize the facts and present them effectively.

Think of writing a news story as driving a train along a track. The rails are the story's central point and give the story direction. The railroad ties—who, what, when, where, why and how—provide a foundation. The train's engine is the lead; it must be powerful enough to pull the rest of the story. Like the whistle of the engine, a story's lead must capture the reader's attention. Each car that follows the lead represents a paragraph containing information and providing structure. The cars (paragraphs) can be arranged in any sequence—for example, from most important to least or chronologically—that seems most effective. The train is strengthened when research, verification, multiple sources, quotes, anecdotes and descriptions fill the cars. The amount of information needed to complete the story decides the number of cars in the train. Holding the train cars together are couplings, which represent the transitions between paragraphs of information. Without strong transitions, the paragraphs disconnect from one another.

This chapter discusses the writing styles and the techniques reporters often use to write effective bodies for their news stories.

THE INVERTED-PYRAMID STYLE

Inverted-pyramid stories arrange the information in descending order of importance or newsworthiness. The lead states the most newsworthy, important or striking information and establishes the central point for the rest of the story. The second paragraph—and sometimes the third and fourth paragraphs—provides details that amplify the lead. Subsequent paragraphs add less important details or introduce subordinate topics. Each paragraph presents additional information: names, descriptions, quotations, conflicting viewpoints, explanations and background. Beginning reporters must learn this style because it helps them decide what is most important and what is least important. It also helps reporters discover "holes" in their information—details that have not been collected and need to be found.

The primary advantage of the inverted pyramid is that it allows someone to stop reading a story after only one or two paragraphs yet still learn the newest, most newsworthy and most important facts. The inverted pyramid also ensures that all the facts are immediately understandable. Moreover, if a story is longer than the space available, editors can easily shorten it by deleting paragraphs from the end.

The inverted-pyramid style also has several disadvantages:

- Because the lead summarizes facts that later paragraphs discuss in greater detail, some of those facts may be repeated in the body.
- A story that follows the inverted pyramid rarely contains any surprises for readers; the lead immediately reveals every major detail.
- The inverted pyramid-style evolved when newspapers were readers' first source for breaking news; now radio, television and the Internet fill that role.
- Readers with less than a high school education cannot easily understand stories written in this style.
- The inverted pyramid locks reporters into a formula and discourages them from trying new styles.

Many writing coaches discourage the use of the inverted pyramid, saying it is overused, confusing and often irrelevant. The inverted pyramid remains a common form for organizing news stories, however, partly because of its inherent advantages, partly because using it is a difficult habit to break. Daily deadline pressures also encourage its use because other news-story formats require additional thinking and, perhaps, more rewriting.

Organizing the Information

If two cars collide and several people are injured, an inverted pyramid story about the accident might contain the following sequence of paragraphs:

Lead	Summarizes the story
Paragraph Two	Identifies the injured
Paragraph Three	Explains how the accident occurred
Paragraph Four	Reports charges filed against driver(s)
Paragraphs Five, Six, Seven	Quotes driver(s), police officer(s) and witness(es)
Paragraph Eight	Describes unusual damage to the cars
Paragraph Nine	Describes traffic problems caused by the accident
Paragraph 10	Presents minor details

Normally, reporters emphasize people: what they do and what happens to them. Consequently, in the example above, the injuries to the people are described early in the story. Damage to the cars is less important and reported later. If the damage was not unusual, the story might not mention it. Paragraph three describes the accident itself—the recent action and main point of the story. Quotations, such as those used in paragraphs five, six and seven, add detail and color as well as a pleasing change of pace. Paragraphs eight, nine and 10 are less essential and might be deleted if space is limited.

The exact organization of a story will vary depending on the story's unique facts and most newsworthy points. The second, third and, maybe, fourth paragraphs should provide details that develop and support the lead.

Notice how the leads in the following stories summarize their topics, and how the second and third paragraphs present their most important details. Neither story ends with a summary or conclusion; instead, the final paragraphs present the least important details. The stories are cohesive because their leads summarize the main topics and because each of the subsequent paragraphs presents additional information about those topics:

> SALT LAKE CITY (AP)—Burglary and theft charges were filed Thursday against a handyman who once worked in the home of Elizabeth Smart.
>
> Police said the charges against Richard Ricci are not related to the disappearance of 14-year-old Elizabeth. On June 5, the teen was taken from her bedroom at gunpoint as her younger sister watched.
>
> Ricci faces one count of theft for allegedly stealing $3,500 worth of items—jewelry, a perfume bottle and a wine glass filled with sea shells—from the Smarts' home in June 2001. They were found during a search of Ricci's home last month, according to charging documents.

> MACON, Ga. (AP)—Two men who illegally plucked the tail feathers from two golden eagles were sentenced to work in a chicken processing plant.
>
> "You'll have your fill of feathers—and, hopefully, you'll never want to be around another feather in your life," U.S. Magistrate Claude Hicks told them Wednesday.
>
> The two men, John Kevin Cooper, 24, and Douglas Grant Rustay, 25, were also placed on 18 months' probation, fined $500 each and ordered to make $600 in restitution.
>
> Cooper, a student, and Rustay, a convenience store manager, were ordered to work a 40-hour week at a chicken plant to help them pay the fine and restitution.
>
> In 1993, the men broke into an eagle cage at a wildlife center and stole the feathers. Possession of golden eagle feathers is a federal offense.
>
> Lawyers for Cooper and Rustay said they were interested in nature and Indian culture and stole the feathers for themselves.
>
> Golden eagle feathers are sacred to Indians.
>
> "It's like going into a church and stealing the altar," said Ernie Dockery, a member of the Northern Cheyenne Tribe and commander of the Native American Veterans Warrior Society.

Many of the facts reported in longer news stories are of approximately equal importance. Those stories are more likely to resemble the diagram shown below rather than the perfect triangle shown on Page 201.

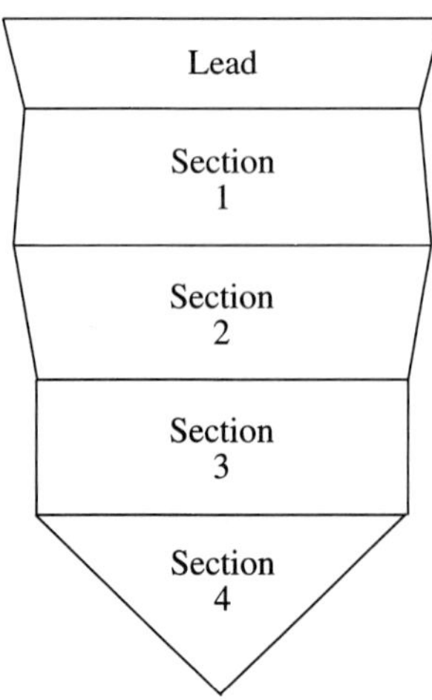

Immediately after the diagram's summary lead, Section 1 presents several paragraphs that contain information of roughly equal importance. Those paragraphs may present some additional information about a single topic, or information about several different but related subtopics. Section 2 may describe a somewhat less important aspect of the story. Section 3 presents more facts of about equal importance to one another but of less importance than the facts in Section 2. Section 4 contains the least important details, perhaps routine procedures, background information or a reminder of related or similar incidents that occurred in the past.

Writing the Second Paragraph

The second paragraph in a news story is almost as important as the lead—and almost as difficult to write. Like the lead, the second paragraph should emphasize the news. In addition, the second paragraph should provide a smooth, logical transition from the lead to the following paragraphs.

While writing their stories' second paragraphs, some reporters fail to emphasize the news. Other reporters fail to provide smooth transitions. As a result, their stories seem dull or disorganized. The following pages discuss both these problems and present some solutions.

Avoid Leapfrogging

Reporters often refer to an individual in their lead and begin their second paragraph with a name. However, many reporters fail to say clearly that the individual referred to in their lead is the person named in their second paragraph. Readers are forced to guess, to make that assumption. They will usually guess right—but not always.

This problem is so common that it has a name: "leapfrogging." To avoid it, provide a one- or two-word transition from the lead to the name in the second paragraph:

> LEAPFROGGING: ALLENTOWN (AP)—A man rammed his car into his wife's car, then shot her in the arm and leg before bystanders tackled him, police said.
>
> Police expressed gratitude to the bystanders who helped bring Felipe M. Santos, 53, of Allentown into custody Monday.
>
> REVISED: ALLENTOWN (AP)—A man rammed his car into his wife's car, then shot her in the arm and leg before bystanders tackled him, police said.
>
> Police expressed gratitude to the bystanders who helped bring the man suspected of the attack, Felipe M. Santos, 53, of Allentown, into custody Monday.

Continue With the News

After providing a smooth transition between the lead and the second paragraph, continue with information about the topic summarized in your lead. Mistakenly, some reporters shift to a different topic, a decision certain to confuse their readers:

> The mayor and city council agreed Monday night to freeze wages and make city workers pay more for benefits in an effort to close a budget deficit that is now larger than officials expected
>
> Mayor Sabrina Datolli, who has been a lifelong resident of the city, is in her fourth term as mayor. She has seen many ups and downs over her years as mayor, but hopes the city can overcome its problems.
>
> REVISED: The mayor and city council agreed Monday night to freeze wages and make city workers pay more for benefits in an effort to close a budget deficit that is now larger than officials expected.
>
> Mayor Sabrina Datolli said the wage freeze and other measures are needed to prevent layoffs of city employees, cuts in programs and more drastic fiscal surgery to balance the city's budget.

Before revision, the story seems to discuss two different topics. The lead summarizes a problem that confronts city officials everywhere: balancing budgets. The second paragraph shifts to the mayor's career and hopes. It fails even to mention the problem of balancing the budget.

Names, Names—Dull, Dull

Reporters sometimes place too much emphasis on their sources' identities. As a result, their second paragraphs lack interesting facts. Note how the following example can be revised to emphasize the news—what the source said, saw or did, not who he is:

> A highway engineer was killed Wednesday at an Interstate 95 construction site when a tractor-trailer owned by Shearson Trucking Inc. plowed through a concrete barrier and struck him.
>
> A materials engineer, Riley Patterson of Independent Testing Laboratory Inc., was killed in the mishap.
>
> Jonathan Martin, a site manager for Baldini Construction Co., saw the accident happen.
>
> REVISED: A tractor-trailer plowed through a concrete barrier at an Interstate 95 construction site Monday, killing a highway engineer.
>
> The force of the crash pushed the concrete barrier into a piece of road equipment, crushing the engineer, Riley Patterson. Patterson had been using a core-drilling machine to bore a sample hole in the concrete roadbed when the accident occurred. He was pronounced dead at the scene.
>
> Jonathan Martin, a worker at the site, said he saw the truck crash through the barrier, but could not warn Patterson because of the noise of the drilling machine.

Background: Too Much, Too Soon

Avoid devoting the entire second paragraph to background information. The second paragraph in the following story is dull because it emphasizes routine, insignificant details:

> Local Red Cross officials expressed alarm Wednesday that blood supplies are dangerously low prior to the beginning of the long holiday weekend.
>
> Nancy Cross, executive director of the Broward County Chapter of the American Red Cross, said the Red Cross strives to maintain an adequate blood supply for emergency situations. "The role of the Red Cross since it was founded is to help people during times of need," she said.

The story shifts from the news—the lack of adequate blood supplies—to the organization's purpose. Yet that purpose has not changed since the Red Cross was established. Thus, the second paragraph says nothing new, nothing likely to retain readers' interest in the story. Fortunately, the problem is easy to correct:

> Local Red Cross officials expressed alarm Wednesday that blood supplies are dangerously low heading into the long holiday weekend.
>
> Restocking those supplies will require a 50 percent increase in blood donations over the next three days, said Nancy Cross, executive director of the Broward County Chapter of the American Red Cross.
>
> "Holiday periods are often a problem because people are traveling or have other plans and don't think about the need for blood," Cross said. "But the holiday period is also a busy time for emergency rooms and trauma centers, which increases the demand for blood."

The revised second and third paragraphs describe the solution to the blood supply problem and explain the reasons for the problem—details central to the story.

Complex Stories

Stories that contain several major subtopics may be too complex to summarize in a brief lead. The U.S. Supreme Court, when it is in session, may in one day take action in several cases. Two or three of those actions may be important, but to save space, most newspapers report them all in a single story. Reporters can mention only the one or two most important actions in their leads, so they often summarize the remaining ones in the second, and sometimes the third, paragraphs of their stories.

After summarizing all the major actions, reporters discuss each in more detail, starting with the most important. By mentioning all the cases in their stories' opening paragraphs, reporters alert readers to their entire contents. Readers interested in the second or third case immediately learn that it will be discussed later in the story. If the lead and following paragraphs mention only the most important action, readers might mistakenly assume that the entire story concerns that one case. Many might stop reading before reaching the story's account of other cases that might be of greater interest to them.

The following story begins with the Supreme Court's most newsworthy action and then, in subsequent paragraphs, summarizes other actions taken the same day:

> WASHINGTON—The Supreme Court Monday refused to overturn a ban on the private possession of machine guns. A National Rifle Association lawyer called it "the first ban on firearms possession by law-abiding citizens in American history."
>
> In a defeat for the NRA, the justices refused to hear a Georgia gun manufacturer's argument that the Second Amendment "right of the people to keep and bear arms" allows him to make or possess a fully automatic weapon.
>
> The Court also decided cases involving anti-abortion protests, the sanctuary movement, libel and local regulation.
>
> NRA lobbyist Jack Lenzi said his organization was "disappointed but not surprised." He said the federal ban is "an infringement on the rights" of about 100,000 Americans who collect automatic weapons.
>
> Gun control and law enforcement groups told the high court that the NRA's argument would permit private persons to have "bazookas, hand grenades, Stinger missiles and any other weapon of mass destruction. . . . The public safety implications of such a position are truly staggering."
>
> In other matters, the court:
>
> - Refused to lift limits on demonstrations by opponents of abortions at a Dayton, Ohio, abortion clinic and a ban on protests by the opponents at the homes of the clinic's staff and patients.
> - Left intact the criminal convictions of eight sanctuary movement members who helped Central American aliens smuggled into this country.
> - Heard arguments in a libel case in which a psychologist says a New Yorker magazine staff writer made up quotes attributed to him.
> - Agreed to decide whether communities may regulate the use of pesticides or whether such local regulations are pre-empted by federal law.

Reporters often use lists in news stories that involve several ideas, subtopics or examples. If all the ideas or examples are important, reporters may begin a news story by summarizing one or two main points, adding a brief transition and presenting the other ideas or examples in a simple, orderly list:

> Assailants attacked three women in the college's parking lots, and Police Chief Alvin Schwab today warned other students that the attacks may continue.
>
> To protect themselves, Schwab recommended that women:
>
> - Avoid dark areas.
> - Park in areas that will be lighted when they return.
> - Tell friends where they are going and when they will return.
> - Keep their car doors locked and windows rolled up when driving alone.
> - Check their car's floor and back seat for intruders before getting into the vehicle.
> - Report any suspicious activities to the campus police.

Later in a story, reporters can discuss each point in greater detail. The initial summary may contain all the essential information about a topic; in that case, it need not be mentioned again.

Each item in a list must be in parallel form. If the first item is an incomplete sentence that begins with a verb, then the rest must have the same structure.

Reporters also use lists to summarize less important details placed at the end of news stories. Lists are particularly useful when the details are minor and concern several diverse topics that would be difficult to organize in any other manner:

> Donald M. Schoen, a Republican candidate for governor, last night promised to cut the state's budget and taxes by a "minimum of 10 percent."
>
> Schoen, mayor of Madison for the past eight years, also promised to dismiss 10 percent of the state's employees.
>
> "People complain that the government has become too big and that it imposes too many taxes and places too many restrictions on their lives," he said at a fund-raising dinner held last night at Pine Hills Country Club.
>
> On other subjects, Schoen said:
>
> EDUCATION—School budgets should be frozen until educators trim administrative costs and improve students' test scores.
>
> CRIME—Only 19 percent of the serious crimes committed in the state are solved. Fewer than 2 percent of the criminals responsible for those crimes are convicted and sentenced to prison. Penalties should be harsher, and criminals should be kept in jail until they have served their full terms, without parole.
>
> MEDIA COVERAGE—News media devote too much attention to staged campaign activities and "have failed to critically analyze candidates' qualifications and positions on major issues."

Some newspapers number each item in a list. Others mark each item with a dash, bullet, asterisk, check mark or some other typographical symbol.

THE HOURGLASS STYLE

Roy Peter Clark, the writing coach at the St. Petersburg (Fla.) Times, observed that the inverted pyramid often forced writers to tell their stories in unnatural ways. It also homogenized the news so stories about bank robberies and congressional debates sounded the same. At the same time, writers who were experimenting with narrative structures for their stories often were losing sight of the news. The most important and newsworthy information might be buried so far down that frustrated readers never saw it. Clark offered the hourglass style of story writing as one that combines the strengths of the inverted pyramid and the narrative format.

Organization of the Hourglass Story

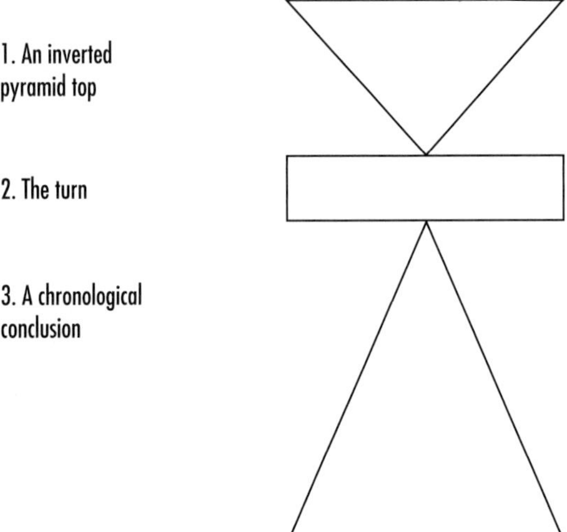

The hourglass story begins in typical inverted pyramid fashion. But after four or five paragraphs stating the central point and most newsworthy facts, the story switches to a chronological narrative. The key to the success of the hourglass format is the turn paragraph which makes the transition between the inverted pyramid and narrative styles.

The hourglass story has three parts: an inverted pyramid top that summarizes the most newsworthy information, a turn or pivot paragraph and a narrative. The inverted pyramid top, which may be only three to five paragraphs, gives readers the most newsworthy information quickly. The narrative allows the writer to develop the story in depth and detail, using the storytelling power of chronology. The key, Clark says, is the turn or pivot, which makes the transition between the two formats. Here's an excerpt of a story illustrating the hourglass style:

> NEW YORK (AP)—An aspiring politician strolled past a metal detector at tightly guarded City Hall—escorted by the councilman he once hoped to replace—then pulled a gun in the crowded balcony of the council chamber and shot his rival to death.
>
> The attack Wednesday turned New York City's seat of government into a crime scene, with screaming political aides and terrified visitors diving for cover. A security officer fired up at the gunman, killing him with five bullets.
>
> Councilman James Davis, 41, a former police officer and ordained minister who campaigned against urban violence, was struck several times in the torso and died at a hospital. He had planned to introduce legislation on workplace violence that afternoon.
>
> His killer, Othniel Askew, 31, died a short time later at the same hospital, police said. For a time before emergency workers arrived, the two fatally wounded men were lying side by side in the balcony.
>
> Mayor Michael Bloomberg said the attack "strikes at the very essence of democracy." He was startled at his desk in City Hall when the gunfire erupted but was unharmed.
>
> Askew had filed papers to oppose Davis in a three-way council race in this fall's Democratic primary, Bloomberg said. But he was not an official candidate because he had not filed enough petition signatures.
>
> Davis spokeswoman Amyre Loomis said Davis and Askew had recently called a truce, and had met three times in recent weeks. When Askew showed up Wednesday at Davis' office in Brooklyn and asked if they could go to City Hall together, Davis agreed.
>
> Three hours before the shooting a man identifying himself as Askew called the FBI's New York office to allege that Davis was harassing him over the upcoming primary election, FBI spokesman Joe Valiquette said.
>
> Both men arrived together at 1:45 p.m. Wednesday at City Hall, where Davis planned to introduce legislation on workplace violence, Councilman Charles Barron said.
>
> Barron said Davis introduced him to Askew, saying, "This is the guy who was once against me, but now he's with me." Askew offered a firm handshake and an intense stare, Barron said.
>
> A short time later, Barron stood staring into the balcony as the gunman shot down at Davis' prone body with a .40-caliber pistol. "He wasn't shooting randomly," Barron said.
>
> Davis, who was black, joined the police department in 1993, a decade after he was allegedly beaten by two white officers. He founded a not-for-profit organization, Love Yourself Stop the Violence, denouncing violent music lyrics and stores that sold realistic toy guns.
>
> He was elected to City Council in 2001, becoming active on public-safety issues and working to keep a check on excessive behavior by police.
>
> On Wednesday, the councilman was carrying a licensed gun, but police said he never had time to remove the weapon from its holster.
>
> As many as 14 bullets rattled around the second floor of City Hall during the gunfire. City Council members and reporters in a nearby press room took cover under their desks.
>
> "I heard bang, bang, bang, bang," said councilman Mike Nelson. "I thought it was firecrackers. Then I heard people screaming, and then I saw people ducking."
>
> Outside, police in riot gear swarmed nearby streets, and police tape blocked sidewalks. Sirens screamed, and confused downtown workers ran from the building.

The first five paragraphs tell this story in traditional inverted pyramid fashion, reporting the newsworthy facts that a New York City councilman had been shot and killed by a political rival. The sixth paragraph is the turn. It tells the reader that Askew had filed papers to run against Davis, but that his candidacy had been rejected because of a lack of signatures. The seventh paragraph begins the rest of the story, which adopts a more narrative style, using quotations, details and anecdotes to enhance the story.

The hourglass style will not work for all stories, as Clark admits. For stories that have no meaningful chronology, such as an account of a city council meeting in which topics are discussed in no particular order, the hourglass style is useless. But for stories about many newsworthy events—sports contests, criminal investigations, natural disasters and political campaigns—the hourglass can be an effective way of organizing information.

THE FOCUS STYLE

The focus style has been used for years by The Wall Street Journal. Its front-page news feature stories usually employ this format. Many other newspapers and their reporters have been using the focus style as well. The focus style, like the hourglass style, tries to incorporate storytelling techniques in news writing. But unlike the hourglass, the focus story begins with a lead that focuses on a specific individual, situation or anecdote and uses that to illustrate a larger problem.

The focus story has four parts. The first is the lead, which, unlike the lead for an inverted pyramid story, may run three, four, five paragraphs or more. Also, unlike the hard-news lead, the focus lead describes a person, place, situation or event that may not be newsworthy by itself but exemplifies a larger problem that is newsworthy.

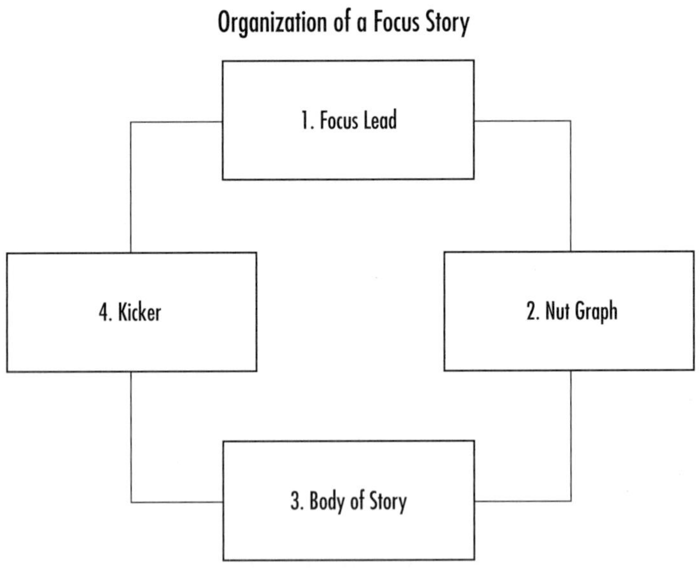

The focus story begins with a lead that focuses on a particular individual, place or situation. A nut graph tells how that individual depicts a more general problem and states the central point of the story. The body of the story develops the central point in detail. The kicker concludes the story and ties it back to the individual in the focus lead.

The second part of the focus story is a nut graph—which may actually be two or three paragraphs—stating the central point of the story and how the lead illustrates that point. The third part of the story is the body, which develops the central point in detail. And the final part is a one-, two- or three-paragraph close, or kicker, that brings the story to a conclusion. The kicker often relates to the person, place or situation described in the focus lead. Here's an example of a focus story from The Washington Post:

> NEW YORK—An hour before dawn, bleary-eyed Frank Colasuonno rolled his Kenworth dump truck for the third time into Lower Manhattan's smoking valley of blight.
>
> The 16-acre debris field where twin towers had soared, a hellscape by day, felt altogether otherworldly in darkness. Diesel-powered halogen beams plowed through clouds of dust. Outside their blinding white cones lurked an inky black not known here since the collapse of the city's power grid in 1977.
>
> Heaped across the disfigured terrain is a dumbfounding 2 billion pounds or more of rubble in a massive crime scene. Today began in earnest the labor of excavating and removing it, of sifting for human remains and evidence.
>
> Colasuonno and three trucker buddies, unpaid volunteers all, hauled three loads each of wreckage across the empty Verrazano Narrows Bridge to FBI collection fields on Staten Island. Great caches of evidence in past cases, such as the 1988 downing of Pan Am Flight 103 over Lockerbie, Scotland, might be assembled inside an aircraft hangar. The rubble from this apocalypse will cover the southeast quadrant of the 3,000-acre Fresh Kills Landfill, closed in March and reopened on Wednesday with a dreadful new significance in its name. Numbered barrels spread across the landscape mark the wreckage according to its point of origin at the blast site. Agents in white moon-suits sift every load by hand.
>
> Colasuonno rolled through a heavily guarded gate off Muldoon Road and paused at a weigh station. There, without comment, an inspector from the New York City Department of Sanitation handed him an improvised receipt for 19,700 pounds of debris. It will take more than 100,000 such truck loads to shift the bulk of the wreckage. The Washington Post counted 23 trucks coming in and out before law enforcement authorities ordered the count to cease.
>
> "Oh, yeah, it's going to take months," Colasuonno said, bumping back toward Lower Manhattan along a lane of Route 440 North reserved for emergency traffic. "That's what they told me, too."
>
> The sheer mass and volume of the rubble is daunting by any standard of human enterprise. It would take 568,828 Plymouth Voyagers to match the weight of aluminum, glass and steel fabricated into the doomed skyscrapers. Parked bumper to bumper, the vehicles would line the 1,673 miles of roadway from Tijuana, Mexico, to the Canadian border.
>
> And even so, there is less in the debris field than might have been. About 425,000 cubic yards of concrete were poured during construction, from 1966 to 1973, according to the lead architects at Minoru Yamasaki Associates in Rochester Hills, Mich. The cataclysmic plunge on Tuesday crushed that concrete to powder and sent thousands of tons back up into the air as boiling silicate clouds. Those, in turn, caught an easterly breeze and flew away.
>
> All of which helps explain how twin towers of 1,353 feet each could collapse into piles the height of a tall oak tree. The World Trade Center, or much of it, is now in Brooklyn and Queens, being washed off cars and draining into sewers miles away.
>
> "The building was pulverized, and the winds were blowing to Brooklyn Heights," said Bill Bouchey, the design director who escaped the 21st-floor South Tower headquarters of Mancini Duffy, an interior design and architecture firm.
>
> Concrete and steel, of course, constitute a fraction of the debris field at Ground Zero, as emergency workers are calling the implosions' core.
>
> The pile is foremost a tomb for thousands of men and women presumed dead, with about 4,700 numbered thus far among the missing. Of no less importance to authorities, the pile holds vital clues—somewhere—to the identities of those who had brought about the twin structures' demise. FBI technicians from the Evidence Response Team formed in 1993 are looking particularly for the remains of the two jetliners that slammed

into the towers Tuesday morning. The flight recorders, if recovered intact, could reveal essential facts obtainable no other way.

Somewhere in the pile is a television mast, the pencil-shaped hat of the destroyed North Tower, that by itself rose nearly as high as the Washington Monument. Somewhere is a 2 1/2-acre refrigeration plant. Somewhere are thousands of bottles of vintage wine from the cellar of Windows on the World. Somewhere are plantations of carpeting—an acre on every floor of each tower—and enough electrical wire to stretch from here to Los Angeles. Somewhere are 208 elevators, 7,000 toilets, 40,000 door knobs.

All that is merely the building. Heaped in the sodden valley, heavy with seawater from the 68,000 gallons a minute pumped by fireboats in New York Harbor, are the labors and personal effects of more than 50,000 financial workers.

At the South Cove Esplanade below the towers, strollers are scattered where parents left them, panicked, while evacuating by boat on Tuesday. A Maclaren side-by-side has a swaddling blanket, a stuffed fish and a tub of cheese cubes moldering in the sun. Flowers bloom. A wrecked stretcher stands beside a plate glass window with two children's handprints in the ash. Next to the handprints: the compressed image of a face from the side, a jawline and an ear.

Bouchey, who ran down the fire stairs when jumpers from the top floors began raining past his window, stopped to lock his office before departing, mindful of the pilfering that had taken place during the panicky retreat after the garage bombing of the twin towers in 1993. Today the jangle of a key chain was audible during his telephone interview from Brooklyn. "I have my keys to my office and to the men's room that says 'WTC,'" he said. "I'm about to throw them out."

The first thing Colasuonno noticed when he reached the site Wednesday night was a woman's white pump. The next was a baseball cleat. "He must have played softball after work," he said.

Colasuonno's mud-crusted maroon truck circled Ground Zero and then backed up to the rubble that had been 5 World Trade Center, one of seven major structures on the ground. A loader with a scoop and bucket dropped in aluminum facing, papers, wet soot, mangled fire hoses and hunks of sheered steel. Colasuonno hoped silently that he would not find half a body when he reached Fresh Kills, as his friend had on the load before.

This morning, just before leaving on his last trip to Staten Island, Colasuonno joined an impromptu group around a canted flagpole outside Building No. 5.

"We found a pry bar and snapped open the little box" that encloses the pulley, "and one of the guys had an American flag, and we raised it," he said. "Everybody just stood there and looked at it for a minute. And then we had to go."

The first two paragraphs of the story describe the focus, one of the many workers cleaning up debris at Ground Zero after the terrorist attack that destroyed the World Trade Center. The writer introduces Frank Colasuonno and describes the site and the work that is taking place there. Those facts are moderately interesting, but paragraph three—the nut paragraph—reports the beginning of the massive clean-up effort. The last four paragraphs of the story provide the kicker—tying the end of the story back to the beginning and providing a sense of conclusion to the story.

The success of the focus story depends on the selection of the lead. Some beginners start their stories with interesting anecdotes or descriptions that have little or no connection to the central point of the story. If the focus has no connection to the central point, it is likely only to confuse and frustrate readers.

The focus style also has flexibility. The body of the story can be developed in any number of ways. If the story has several subtopics, they can be arranged in descending order of importance. Or if the material lends itself to a narrative structure, the information can be arranged chronologically.

THE NARRATIVE STYLE

A narrative has two components: a story and a storyteller. A storyteller writes as a playwright or novelist would, depicting people interacting with other people and within their surroundings. To write in the narrative style, a reporter must find people who are crucial to the story and record their actions. This technique requires more than just interviewing sources, recording quotes and reporting numbers. It requires observation.

Observation does not mean reporters are free to interject their opinions into a story. It means that reporters observe people, places and events important to a story and describe them in vivid detail. Through those details readers get a better sense of what is occurring. But to paint a picture with words, reporters must be specific. Notice the difference between the following sentences:

> Students are angry about the board of trustees' decision.
>
> Students gathered in the administration building lobby waving signs protesting the board of trustee's decision.

The first sentence presents an opinion. Without using attribution it says the students are angry at the board's decision. The reader does not know whether the opinion is the writer's or not. The second sentence, however, shows the student's negative behavior in response to the board's decision.

The narrative approach allows reporters to be more creative. Reporters can describe the drama—even if it is not high drama—at a school board meeting, for example. What happened? What did they see? Were people shouting? Were people laughing? Did the participants exchange views? Reporters cannot answer these questions and others unless they take extensive notes.

Long-time writing coach Don Fry describes the style this way:

> Narrative writing requires narrative thinking, narrative reporting and narrative forms.
>
> Narrative thinking means seeing the world in terms of people doing things, not as piles of disparate facts. Actions connect to one another to create meaning, mostly based on human motives. The best journalistic storytellers let their curiosity lead them into stories, because they want to find out why real people do things.

A story written in narrative style may still lead with the news—the most important part of the story—but then quickly switch to using chronology, flashbacks, dialogue and other storytelling techniques. Generally, such stories have a beginning, a middle and an end, each of relatively equal importance. It is more difficult to cut the final paragraphs of narrative stories than of stories written in the inverted pyramid style.

The following excerpts from a story about ranching in Montana by Great Falls Tribune regional editor Karen Ogden illustrate the narrative style:

> EDEN—Scanning the pasture through a spotting scope, Karl Anderson looks for telltale signs of labor. He stops on a cow with the number "989" branded on her side.
>
> "She's definitely not long for it," he says of the wide, red cow. Now and then, Anderson checks her progress through the scope in his mudroom. She lies down, lumbers to her feet, paces, lies down again and, after half an hour, slides a gelatinous cocoon onto the ground—a perfect delivery.
>
> But the calf lays still, its amniotic sack stuck over its head.
>
> Anderson, 49, jams on his boots and bolts for the door.
>
> "Keep going, honey!" yells his wife, Donna, as he sprints through ankle-high snow to free the calf before it suffocates.
>
> The Andersons are deep into calving season, the busiest time of year for Montana's $966 million-a-year cattle industry. As townsfolk spend weekends on the ski slopes or snuggle up with a good book, ranchers pull all-nighters to deliver this spring's calf crop into the world. Subzero wind chills at 2 a.m., angry cows in labor and wet, slimy gloves come with the territory.

Most of Montana's roughly 12,000 ranches time their calving from late January through mid-April. The season lasts about six weeks on the Andersons' spread in Eden, a close-knit community of farms and ranches 17 miles south of Great Falls.

They live in the sturdy rock home Donna's great-grandfather, an Austrian stone mason named Gallus Wuerl, built in the 1890s. The stone barns and corrals could have leapt from the English countryside, except for the sweeping view of the Big Belt Mountains.

In the end, Karl's dash through the pasture is for naught.

The newborn—a healthy bull calf—breaks out of his sack before Karl can reach him. He stands back to watch as the shivering creature stretches his spindly legs and blows amniotic fluid from his nostrils.

Ninety percent of the births are normal, Donna says. But a calf is worth roughly $500. A cow fetches $1,000 or more at market. Ranchers leave nothing to chance this time of the year.

Since the arrival of the season's first calf Jan. 27, the Andersons have lived like sleep-deprived new parents, waking every two hours at night to hustle wet new calves into the barn or pull a calf for a struggling mother cow.

It's Donna's favorite time of the year.

Growing up on a ranch near Sand Coulee, her father never gave her a curfew during calving season.

"He said, 'If you get home by midnight, go check the calves,'" Donna recalled. She was never late.

These days, the long nights, the blizzards, the bitter winds blur together.

On an unseasonably warm night, Donna and Karl stroll through the pasture before dinner, getting a last look at the herd before darkness falls.

Karl is a slight, quiet man with a weathered face and soft blue eyes. He swings his legs over corral fences with the ease of a gymnast.

Donna, 45, is small and sturdy—a bundle of energy. When the kids were young, they knew mom was going to town when she appeared wearing makeup. On the ranch she favors coveralls, her blond hair tucked under a headscarf.

"873 is close," she says as the sun slips behind the mountains. The Andersons watch for cows kicking at their bellies or kinking their tails. Sometimes they look uncomfortable, as if they're standing on eggshells.

"Women can usually tell better than men," Donna says. "It's kinda like—I remember that feeling."

They pay special attention to the heifers, or first-time moms. Not yet full grown, they're most likely to have complications.

By Montana standards, the Andersons' ranch is small, with 112 head of red angus cows. Montana ranches often run herds of 400 or 500. The Andersons have never handled more than nine births in one day.

"We baby our cows a lot more than most people do," Donna says. On bitter cold nights, calves sometimes end up in the kitchen near the wood stove. Dangerously cold critters are treated to a few minutes under Donna's hairdryer.

Ninety-eight percent of the Anderson's calves survive until weaning, when the cattle are shipped to feedlots in the Midwest or held back to become next year's mother cows.

Heading back to the house, Donna checks on a casserole in the oven and reaches for a blue binder on top of the refrigerator.

Here she meticulously records the details of each birth—weather conditions, birth weight and, later, vaccinations, antibiotic treatments and any other work done on the animals.

"If the house ever caught on fire, this is the first thing I'd grab," she says.

The binder includes careful notes on how each cow treats her calves.

Occasionally a heifer is afraid of her baby, kicking it when it tries to nurse. After a shot of sedative, she'll usually accept the calf. Once it sucks, her hormones kick in and she'll bond with her baby.

But come fall, troublesome cows go to market with the calves.

* * * *

After dinner, Karl steps out into the starless night for one last check.

Ruby, the Andersons' cattle dog, leaps from her rug in the mudroom, ready for business, as he pulls on his jacket.

The closest thing the Andersons have to a ranch hand, the black-and-white border collie never misses a beat. The Andersons can't hire human help because the state-required workers compensation is too expensive.

The pasture is inky black and the cow's eyes glint in the beam of Karl's flashlight. He spots a lone cow along the fence line.

"Sometimes when they're standing out by themselves like that it means they're doin' somethin'," Karl says, striding off in her direction.

Coming closer, he sees a wet calf standing next to her.

He heads back to the house to tell Donna, who consults her record book. Last year this cow's delivery was breech and she was a nervous mom. She'll need to be watched with this calf.

"Her mother was plum ornery," Donna says. "She comes from a long line of ornery stuff. If this wasn't our son's cow she'd be gone, but he needs the money for college."

Kal, 20, is pursuing an agriculture degree at Northwest College in Powell, Wyo. He plans to take over the ranch someday.

But first he'll have to find a job in town. Karl and Donna have only been on the land 15 years and may work another 20 before retiring.

Their daughter Heather, 24, lives in a home on the ranch with her husband and works in town.

Karl works as an outfitter to supplement the ranch income. But the Andersons are fortunate their land is paid for. Many take jobs in town to make ends meet.

"There's an awful lot of our neighbors whose wives are teachers," Donna said.

Kal's cow lives up to her reputation as Karl and Donna coax her to the barn, one step forward, two steps back.

Karl scoops up the calf in his arms and starts a kind of tango with the snorting mom, luring her toward the barn with her baby.

One minute she looks ready to charge, the next she wanders in another direction, as if she's forgotten her calf.

The newborn's tiny moo brings her back.

"Keep bellowing, baby," Donna says as she prods the cow from behind. "C'mon, squirtie."

In the barn, Karl wraps a small chain attached to a scale around the kicking calf's feet while Donna throws the other end over a rafter and hoists the creature off the ground—he weights in at a hearty 78 pounds.

With mom and baby tucked safely under a red heat lamp, Karl heads back to the house and straight to bed. He's been up since 5 a.m. Donna's on call until 1 a.m. tonight.

She passes the time with a jigsaw puzzle or snoozes between cow checks.

Sometimes she worries.

Most years the Andersons grow enough hay to feed their cattle through the winter with extra to sell.

Last summer, drought wilted 75 percent of their alfalfa crop, barely enough for their cows, whose rations are slimmer this year.

Springs that flowed during the Dust Bowl have quit and there's no grass left in the pastures.

One more dry year, and the Andersons will start culling their herd.

"It's gonna be tough decisions," Donna says. "We've worked 15 years to get the herd to this point."

A cow bellows and Donna jumps to her feet. It's 12:30 a.m. She was supposed to check the cows at midnight.

Donna throws on her coat, grabs her box of calving supplies and heads out the door with Ruby at her heels.

"By George we've got a little baby . . . nice and dry," Donna says as she spots a cow and new calf close to the house. The calf is healthy and the mom reliable. This pair will stay outside tonight.

"Hi, mama," Donna coos to calm the concerned cow as she turns the calf over. She squirts iodine in its belly button—a safeguard against infection—and shoots a syringe-full of vitamins down its throat.

Donna keeps one eye over her shoulder as she works. Last week a cow affectionately licked her hair as she tended to its baby.

But if ever a cow is dangerous, it's when she has a brand new calf. Bumps and bruises are part of ranch life.

"I always told our kids, 'Unless you see blood or there's bones sticking out just shut up and take it,'" she said. "The term is 'cowboy up.'"

Back at the kitchen table, Donna enters the new calf in her record book and writes Karl a note with the temperature and details on the latest birth. She's been up since 7 a.m.

Karl and Donna spend their nights alone during calving season.

"You get up in the morning and think, "Hmmm, 20 years of marriage reduced to a weather report at 2 o'clock in the morning," she says with a dash of wry humor.

She disappears to the bedroom and bleary-eyed Karl stumbles out, sets a small alarm clock and settles down on his bear skin rug on the living room floor.

* * * *

Donna wakes just in time for bacon and eggs and the couple starts another round of loading and unloading hay, moving calves, vaccinations and barn cleaning.

Two weeks later, even Ruby is slowing down.

"She's getting tired cause she lays out there on her rug when you're getting ready to go out and she just looks at ya," Donna says.

For the first time in years, the Andersons lost a cow and calf last week.

They knew the cow was in trouble when they felt the calves' tangled legs inside. They called a neighbor for help, but in hindsight, should have called the vet as well, Donna says.

"It just breaks your heart. And it never gets easier, at least for me."

But she doesn't cry as much as she used to. Donna prefers to focus on the bright spots. One of their cows delivered a set of twins this season.

"Just to watch them being born, to me it's a miracle every time."

She starts this workday watering the cows.

"Hello mom," she says to the first cow to plunge her head in the water trough.

Despite the numbing cold Donna wears no gloves. She ties the cold hose to the edge of the trough—to keep the cows from knocking it out—with a piece of rough twine.

"One of the things I admire about people who work in town is the ladies with beautiful hands and long fingernails," she says.

The brilliant, sunny morning gives way to a cloudy evening. A snowstorm is pushing over the mountains so Donna and Karl usher the newest arrival and its mother into the barn.

Before nightfall they check on a cow that showed signs of labor more than an hour ago, but isn't making any progress.

> They herd her into a "head-catch" in the barn—a metal gate that shuts around the back of the cow's head so they can work on her.
>
> "That was our Valentine's Day present to each other a few years ago," Donna says of the shiny green contraption.
>
> "Boy, was that a blessing," Karl adds. They used to corner cows behind a barn stall gate. One worked on the cow while the other held the rope around her head.
>
> This mom-to-be is OK, just taking her time.
>
> The Andersons walk back to their home, which, like the barns, is steeped in memories and family history, birth and death.
>
> They pass by the old stone barn, where Gallus Wuerl carved "1905" above the door.
>
> Occasionally Donna thinks about him as she does her chores.
>
> "I sometimes wonder," she says. "If Grandpa would be pleased with what we're doing."

Notice how the writer has used quotations, dialogue and description to give readers a sense of life on the ranch and of each source's distinctive personality. The details are ones that easily bring images to the mind of the reader. One can imagine the calf as a "shivering creature" or the Andersons as "sleep-deprived new parents." Notice, too, the length of the story. Stories using the narrative style tend to be longer, and yet the rich detail and concrete imagery make them easier to read than many shorter straight news stories.

While narrative style can be a refreshing change from the inverted pyramid, it is not appropriate for all stories. Stories about breaking news events, speeches or most government meetings, for instance, often make more sense to readers when told in traditional inverted-pyramid fashion. Narrative touches, such as dialogue and colorful descriptions, can make any story more readable, however. Regardless of the occasion, the success of a narrative story depends on the depth of the reporting. A writer who has not attentively gathered details and quotations will have difficulty constructing a narrative story.

USING TRANSITIONS

Transitions help stories move from one fact to the next in a smooth, logical order. Again, think of the story as a train. The engine is the lead, and each car that follows is a paragraph. The couplings that hold the cars together are transitions. Reporters introduce ideas by relating them to ideas reported earlier in a story. Often, the natural progression of thought, or sequence of facts and action, is adequate. Or reporters may repeat a key name or pronoun:

> School board member Diana *Maceda* voted against the proposed cuts in the school lunch program. *Maceda* said cuts would hurt low-income families that rely on the program.

> State police *Capt. Virginia Detwieler* said the accident occurred when a car cut in front of the tractor-trailer, causing the rig to jackknife when the driver slammed on his brakes.
>
> *She* added that police investigators had gotten a description of the car and a partial license number and were searching for the vehicle to question the driver.

The first example repeats the name of the school board member. In the second example, the pronoun "she" refers to the captain mentioned in the preceding paragraph. Reporters can also repeat other key words, ideas or phrases:

> Richard *Nolles,* editor of the Weekly Outlook, said the *newspaper* tries to report the truth even when its *readers* do not want to hear it.
>
> "A *newspaper* that reports only what its *readers* want to hear is dodging its moral obligations," Nolles said.

In a speech Wednesday, *Nolles* added that many *readers* want to avoid unpleasant news, and threaten to cancel *their* subscriptions when he reports it.

"But if a problem exists, *they* need to know about it so *they* can correct it," he said. "Ignorant citizens can't make wise decisions."

Transitional Words

Sometimes a single word can lead readers from one idea to the next. Many transitional words refer to time: words such as "earlier" and "later," "before" and "after," "promptly" and "tardy." Other common transitional words are:

Time

delayed	meanwhile	once
eventually	next	seldom
finally	now	sometimes
formerly	occasionally	soon
frequently	often	then

Using the hour, day of the week, month, season, year, decade or century ("an hour later," "the previous Saturday" and so on) can also provide a transition.

Other types and examples of linkage words include:

Addition

again	beyond	new
also	extra	other
another	furthermore	together
besides	moreover	too

Causation

accordingly	hence	then
because	since	therefore
consequently	so	thus

Comparison

agreeing	identical	opposite
conflicting	inconsistent	related
contrary	like	separately
different	objecting	similarly

Contrast

although	however	still
but	if	until
conversely	nevertheless	while
despite	simply	without
exactly	solely	yet

Dozens of phrases can move a story from one idea to another. Examples include:

along with	for instance	in other business
as a result of	for that reason	on the contrary
aside from	in addition	on the other hand
at last	in an earlier	until then
at the same time	in another	years earlier
due to	in contrast	with the exception of
for example	in other action	

Transitional Sentences

Transitional sentences link paragraphs that contain diverse ideas, but the sentences should do more than report that another idea was "introduced" or "discussed." They should present some interesting details about the new topic so readers want to finish the story. Mistakenly, beginners often use vague generalities. A good transitional sentence often serves the same purposes as a lead, summarizing the topic it introduces and revealing what was said or done about it. The following paragraphs then discuss the topic in more detail:

She also commented on the legislators' overriding of the governor's veto.

REVISED: She said the legislators' overriding of the governor's veto would anger supporters of the death penalty.

He also discussed the budget proposal.

REVISED: He said the budget had been cut as much as possible.

Questions as Transitions

Transitional sentences occasionally take the form of questions. The questions should be short and, as in the following examples, should be immediately followed by their answers—the new details or topics that reporters want to introduce:

How does he manage to play the piano so well at such a young age?

"Practice," he said, the freckles blossoming with the smile that spread across his 7-year-old face. "I practice four hours a day—every day. I practice even when I don't feel like it."

Forty-seven percent of the students enrolled in the university will earn a degree within the next six years, according to Robert McMahon, director of the Office of Institutional Research.

What about the other 53 percent? They will drop out or transfer to another institution.

Why? A study just completed by McMahon found that most students who drop out of school accept full-time jobs, get married, have children or say they lack the money needed to continue their education.

EXPLAIN THE UNFAMILIAR

Reporters should avoid words that are not used in everyday conversation. When an unfamiliar word is necessary, journalists must immediately define it. Stories that fail to define unfamiliar terms may annoy as well as puzzle readers and listeners. A story about a 19-year-old Olympic skater who collapsed and died before a practice session at the University of Texas reported she died of clinical terminal cardiac arrhythmia. The journalist placed the term in quotation marks but failed to define it. Yet many people would be interested in the death of an Olympic skater and would wonder why an apparently healthy young athlete had died. Because the story failed to define the term, it failed to satisfy their curiosity about the cause of the young woman's death.

Here are three techniques journalists can use to define or explain unfamiliar terms:

1. Place a brief explanation in parentheses:

   The law would ban accessory structures (sheds, pool houses and unattached garages) in new subdivisions.

2. Place the explanation immediately after the unfamiliar name or term, setting it off with a colon, comma or dash:

   Amy and Ralph Hargis of Carlton Drive filed for bankruptcy under Chapter 13, which allows them to repay their creditors in monthly installments over a three-year period.

About 800 foreign students at the university are on F-1 student visas—which means that they are allowed to stay in the United States only until they complete their degrees.

3. Place the explanation in the next sentence:

The major banks raised their prime rate to 12.5 percent. The prime rate is the interest rate banks charge their best customers.

Instead of using an unfamiliar term and then defining it, journalists may eliminate the term and use the definition or explanation instead:

She said the school will have K-6 facilities.
REVISED: She said the school will accept children from kindergarten through the sixth grade.

Journalists using these techniques can make even the most complicated stories understandable. For example, an environmental reporter for The Arizona Daily Star in Tucson wrote about several wells contaminated by trichloroethylene. The topic was complex, yet reporter Jane Kay's stories were clear and dramatic. Kay explained that the chemical, also called "TCE," is an industrial degreaser that may cause cancer in humans. The wells contaminated by TCE were closed, and government officials assured people their drinking water was safe. But after hundreds of interviews, Kay discovered, "For 10 to 30 years, many South Side Tucson residents unknowingly got minute quantities of TCE almost every time they turned on the tap water." As many as 20,000 people "drank TCE at home, inhaled it in the shower and absorbed it through their skin when they washed the dishes."

TCE is a tasteless, odorless, colorless—and very toxic—chemical. It is volatile, meaning that it evaporates quickly, much like common household cleaning fluids.

Only a teaspoon of it poured into 250,000 gallons of water—about the amount used by five people in an entire year—would create a taint slightly beyond the 5 parts per billion suggested as a guideline for safety by the state Department of Health Services.

Apparently as a result of the TCE contamination, residents of Tucson's South Side suffered from an unusual number of serious illnesses, including cancer.

Large numbers—millions, billions and trillions—also need explaining. For example, few readers who saw a story reporting that failing savings and loan companies cost the nation $500 billion would really comprehend that number. Reporters can help audiences understand large numbers by converting them into something related to everyday life.

The Washington Post reported that an investment bank offered to pay $20.6 billion to take over RJR Nabisco Inc. (The company has split since then into R.J. Reynolds Tobacco Co. and Nabisco.) At the time, the conglomerate made Oreos, LifeSavers and Camel cigarettes. RJR Nabisco rejected the offer, saying it wasn't big enough. If $20.6 billion cannot buy a cookie company, what is it good for? A writer at The Post calculated it could:

- Provide shoes for every American for a year.
- House 2 million criminals in prisons for a year.
- Sponsor 80 million destitute children around the world for one year.
- Match the combined fortunes of the six richest people in the United States.
- Cover the cost of every movie ticket bought in the United States in the past four years.
- Buy every advertisement in every magazine published in the United States for the past four years, or every radio ad for the past three years.

When a sentence must explain several items in a list, the explanation should precede the list, not follow it. If the explanation does not appear before the list, people may not immediately understand the relationship between the items or the significance of the list:

> To provide children with better nutrition, better health care and better educational opportunities were the reasons the senator voted for the bill.
>
> REVISED: The senator said he voted for the bill to provide children with better nutrition, better health care and better educational opportunities.

THE IMPORTANCE OF EXAMPLES

Examples make stories more interesting, personalize them and help audience members understand them more easily. A story about a teenager who became an alcoholic and flunked out of college might include examples of the problems she experienced:

> She said school became unimportant, adding: "I can remember staying up all night before my public health final. When I took the test I was smashed. And if that wasn't bad enough, then I ran the entire 10 blocks back to my apartment so I could drink some more. Of course, I flunked public health."

Examples are especially important in stories about abstract issues. Sometimes numbers help put those issues into perspective. A story about the lives of people who drop out of college might include the percentage of U.S. students who drop out, their reasons for dropping out and what they do afterward: join the military, get married or find a job. In addition to reporting the general trends, a good writer would illustrate the story by describing the lives of two or three dropouts—specific examples of the trend.

Unfamiliar concepts can be made clearer by comparing them to things that are familiar. Many readers find business and finance hard to understand, and stories of financial fraud can be extraordinarily complex. Paul Krugman, a columnist for The New York Times, used the following analogy to help readers understand how mutual fund managers and major investors were cheating ordinary investors.

> You're selling your house, and your real estate agent claims that he's representing your interests. But he sells the property at less than fair value to a friend, who resells it at a substantial profit, on which the agent receives a kickback. You complain to the county attorney. But he gets big campaign contributions from the agent, so he pays no attention.
>
> That, in essence, is the story of the growing mutual fund scandal.

THE USE OF DESCRIPTION

Descriptions, like quotations, make stories more interesting and help people visualize scenes. But many journalists are reluctant to use descriptive phrases; they summarize whatever they hear but are less likely to describe what they see, feel, taste and smell. For instance, a student who attended a speech by an expert in communications technology handed her instructor a story that said:

> The speaker, John Mollwitz, showed some examples of electronic newspapers and talked about how they fit into the newspaper industry.

The student failed to describe what the electronic newspapers looked like and how they "fit into the newspaper industry." She also neglected to mention that the crowd intermittently applauded Mollwitz, who has developed some profitable electronic newspapers.

When told to describe something, most students rely too heavily on adverbs and adjectives. Nouns and verbs are more effective. Nouns and verbs are less redundant and less opinionated than adverbs and adjectives.

The following descriptive passage is an excerpt from a story written by Barton Gellman in The Washington Post two days after the World Trade Center was destroyed:

> Two World Trade Center, the southern tower, had thrust 110 stories and 1,353 feet into the New York skyline since 1976. Today what remained stood no higher than the fifth floor of the adjacent, grievously damaged, former Dow Jones headquarters at 90 West Street. The second tower, just north, barely reached the eighth floor of the Verizon building it so recently dwarfed.
>
> These compact piles defied comprehension. Where were the 950,000 tons of concrete poured less than three decades before? The 200,000 tons of steel? Where were the conference tables, the desks, the water coolers? Where were the people?
>
> Three large sections of the South Tower's latticed aluminum skin stood in the center of West Street opposite Liberty walkway. They blossomed outward like peeling bark from a log split by a wedge. The only other distinct chunks to be seen were the steel I-beams—61 to a side—that had been built to keep the tower erect through explosion, fire or 200 mph winds.
>
> Ironworkers cut the girders in 40-foot lengths with acetylene torches, then loaded them with two huge Lumma cranes onto flatbed trucks for removal. The flatbeds labored around the block to Rector Place and Thames Street, where two smaller Tadano cranes strained to offload the girders, one crane at each end, and stacked them like cut lumber atop a crushed Chevy van and a sleek black Jaguar that had been parked in the wrong place.

Reporters who want to describe an object must learn to use concrete, factual details as opposed to trite phrases and generalities. Readers should be able to visualize the scene in their minds:

> VAGUE: There were about 50 men and women working in the area.
>
> BETTER: About 50 men and women worked in the area, and most wore hard hats, some yellow, some white and others red. Four of the workers had tied nail pouches around their waists. Others smoked cigarettes and looked weary in their dirty white T-shirts, jeans and sunglasses.

Vagueness also becomes a problem when reporters attempt to describe other people. Some reporters mistake generalities or their personal impressions for factual detail:

> She spoke with authority.
>
> She seemed to enjoy talking about her work.

Neither sentence is an actual description. The first concludes the woman spoke "with authority" but fails to explain why the writer reached that conclusion. The second sentence reports she "seemed to enjoy" talking about her work, but does not specifically describe either the speaker or what she said.

Generalities are often inconsistent among observers. One student reported a woman "seemed relaxed and very sure of herself." Everything about her "conveyed calmness." Yet, another student concluded, "She seemed nervous." The students could have avoided the problem by reporting specific details as opposed to their impressions, opinions and conclusions.

Reporters must learn to observe and describe specific details. If they are important to the story, include descriptions of people's voices, mannerisms, facial expressions, posture, gestures and surroundings. Include details about or descriptions of their height, weight, age, clothing, hair, glasses, jewelry and family, if they help to bring an image alive. Each factor can be described in detail. For example, a journalist might describe a man's hands by mentioning their size, calluses, nails, smoothness or wrinkles or veins, and jewelry. Avoid generalities and conclusions:

VAGUE: He is a large man.
BETTER: He is 6 feet tall and weighs 210 pounds.

VAGUE: Butler looked as though he had dressed in a hurry.
BETTER: Butler's shirt was buttoned halfway, his socks were mismatched, his shoelaces were untied and his hair was not brushed.

Descriptions help the audience see the situation or person through the eyes of the reporter. When describing people, however, reporters should not write anything about a woman that they would not write about a man in the same situation and vice versa. Don't note, "The woman had long slender legs" if you wouldn't write in the same situation, "The man had long slender legs."

THE USE OF HUMOR

Editors constantly look for humorous stories and often place them on Page 1. But humorous stories are particularly difficult to write. Journalists should not try to inject humor into stories that are not obviously humorous. If a story is funny, the humor should be apparent from the facts. Journalists should not have to point out the humor by labeling it "funny" or "comical." Author and economist John Kenneth Galbraith has explained: "Humor is an intensely personal, largely internal thing. What pleases some, including the source, does not please others."

A story about the peculiar laws in some cities never called the laws "peculiar" or "funny." Instead it simply listed them so people could judge the humor of the laws for themselves. The laws made it illegal to:

- Take a cow on a school bus.
- Take a bath without a bathing suit.
- Break more than three dishes in a single day.
- Ride a horse not equipped with a horn and taillight.

If you were writing about Ann Landers, you might give an example of her famous wit so audience members could judge it for themselves:

While attending an embassy reception, Landers was approached by a rather pompous senator.
"So you're Ann Landers," he said. "Say something funny."
Without hesitation Landers replied: "Well, you're a politician. Tell me a lie."

Humor, when it is appropriate, makes news stories more interesting, but remember understatement is more effective than exaggeration. Simply report the facts that seem humorous and hope others will laugh.

THE NEED TO BE FAIR

Regardless of how a story is organized, it must be balanced, fair and accurate. Reporters who write about a controversy should present every significant viewpoint fully and fairly. They must exercise particular care when their stories might harm another person's reputation. A reckless or irresponsible charge may destroy an innocent person's reputation, marriage or career.

If a story contains information critical of an individual, that person must have an opportunity to respond. It is not enough to get the person's response after a story has been published and report it in a later story, because not everyone who read the original criticism will see the second story. The New York Times has an unbreakable policy requiring that a person criticized in a news story have an immediate chance to respond. If the person cannot be reached, editors and reporters should consider holding the story. If the story cannot be held, it must describe the efforts made to reach the person and explain that those efforts will be renewed the next day.

When the subject of a negative story is unavailable or refuses to respond, that fact should be mentioned. A brief sentence might explain:

> Repeated attempts to reach a company employee were unsuccessful.
> OR: A vice president at the company declined to comment about the charges.
> OR: Company officials did not return phone calls made by reporters.

THE FINAL STEP: EDIT YOUR STORY

After finishing a story, edit it ruthlessly. Author Kurt Vonnegut recommends, "If a sentence, no matter how excellent, does not illuminate your subject in some new and useful way, scratch it out." Vonnegut also urges writers to have mercy on their readers, explaining: "Our audience requires us to be sympathetic and patient teachers, ever willing to simplify and clarify—whereas we would rather soar high above the crowd singing like nightingales."

Good reporters will reread and edit their stories. Lazy reporters immediately submit their stories to an editor, thinking their stories need no editing or expecting the editor to correct any mistakes. That attitude involves some risks. If an editor misses the errors, the reporters will be the ones who suffer the embarrassment and bear the responsibility. Or, an editor may decide the stories require extensive changes, perhaps even total rewriting. When that happens, reporters often complain about the changes. Reporters who correct their own errors will develop reputations as good writers and earn better assignments, raises and promotions.

CHECKLIST FOR WRITING NEWS STORIES

Use the following checklist to evaluate all your stories.

1. Place the most important details in your lead.
2. Throughout the story emphasize the details most likely to interest and affect your readers.
3. Include details from your observations to create a picture your readers can visualize.
4. In the story's second paragraph, continue to discuss the topic initiated in your lead.
5. Do not leapfrog. If your lead mentions an individual, and your second paragraph begins with a name, provide a transition that makes it clear you mean the same person.
6. Make your sentences clear, concise and to the point. (Avoid passive verbs. Also, use the normal word order of subject, verb, direct object.)
7. Vary your sentence structure.
8. Avoid overloading your sentences.
9. If your story discusses several major subtopics, mention all the major subtopics in your story's opening paragraphs so your readers know what to expect.
10. If you use a list, make sure each item is in parallel form.
11. Provide transitions to lead your readers from one sentence or paragraph to another smoothly and logically.
12. Make your transitional sentences specific; say something intriguing to sustain readers' interest in the topic.
13. If you use a question as a transition, make it clear, short and simple.
14. Avoid generalities that have to be explained in a later sentence or paragraph. Be specific.
15. Resist the temptation to end your story with a summary, conclusion or opinion.
16. After finishing your story, critically edit and rewrite it.

THE WRITING COACH

HOW TO FIND THE ENDINGS TO STORIES

By **Joe Hight**
Managing Editor of The Oklahoman

Reporters sometimes ask this question about their stories: How do you know when you have a good ending?

Gary Provost, author of "100 Ways to Improve Your Writing," offers the advice I've heard the most: "Look at the last sentence and ask yourself, 'What does the reader lose if I cross it out?' If the answer is 'nothing' or 'I don't know,' then cross it out. Do the same thing with the next to last sentence, and so forth. When you get to the sentence that you must have, read it out loud. Is it a good closing sentence? Does it sound final? Is it pleasant to the ear? Does it leave the reader in the mood you intended? If so, you are done. If not, rewrite it so that it does. Then stop writing." I suggest that you end with a quote or phrase that leaves an impression on a reader. Ask yourself, someone who sits near you or an editor if your ending solves a problem, stirs an emotion (for example, it takes the reader back to a significant moment in a person's life) or makes a point about an issue. If it did, then the ending is appropriate.

In her story about Larry Jenkins turning the So Fine Club into a church, The Oklahoman's Religion Editor Pat Gilliland's ending made a point because it assured readers that Jenkins would remain firm in his decision:

"There is only one person that has never lied to me, and that is Jesus," Jenkins said. "My faith is stronger now than when I started. I started on blind faith; now I have deep-rooted faith."

I say hallelujah to Pat's ending, hallelujah to powerful endings and hallelujah to editors who don't automatically whack good ones!

SUGGESTED READINGS

Anderson, Douglas A. *Contemporary Sports Reporting,* 2nd ed. Chicago: Nelson-Hall, 1993.
Cappon, Rene J. *Associated Press Guide to News Writing,* 3rd ed. Stamford, Conn.: Thomson/Arco, 2000.
Jackson, Dennis, and John Sweeney, eds. *The Journalist's Craft.* New York: Allworth Press, 2002.
LaRocque, Paula. *Championship Writing: 50 Ways to Improve Your Writing.* Oak Park, Ill.: Marion Street Press, 2000.
Lewis, Anthony. *Written into History.* New York: Times Books, 2001.
Schwartz, Jerry. *Associated Press Reporting Handbook.* New York: McGraw-Hill/Contemporary Books, 2001.
Sims, Norman, ed. *Literary Journalism in the Twentieth Century.* New York: Oxford University Press, 1990.
Woods, Keith, ed. *Best Newspaper Writing 2002.* Chicago: Bonus Books, 2002.
Zinsser, William. *On Writing Well.* New York: HarperResource, 2001.

Name ______________________ Class ______________________ Date ______

EXERCISE 1

THE BODY OF A NEWS STORY

SECOND PARAGRAPHS

SECTION I: GRADING SECOND PARAGRAPHS

Second paragraphs are almost as important as leads. Like leads, second paragraphs must help arouse readers' interest in a topic. Critically evaluate the second paragraphs in the following stories. Judge which of the second paragraphs are most successful in: (1) providing a smooth transition from the lead; (2) continuing to discuss the topic summarized in the lead; and (3) emphasizing the news—details that are new, important and interesting. Give each second paragraph a grade from A to F.

1. A Pinkerton courier was robbed at gunpoint and fatally wounded on Tuesday while leaving Merchants Bank with the day's daily transaction records.

   Edwin James, 59, of 826 Bell Drive, was following standard bank procedures and carrying no money. (Grade: ________)
2. A 41-year-old teacher who fell and broke an ankle while stopping for a cup of coffee on her way to work sued a convenience store Monday.

   The teacher, Tina Alvarez, has worked at Washington Elementary School for 21 years. (Grade: ________)
3. Two young men are presumed dead after falling off a 30-foot rock formation into the Pacific Ocean at a California park Saturday.

   The men remain unidentified, and their bodies have not been recovered. (Grade: ________)
4. Police responding to a 911 call about a shooting at 10 p.m. Sunday discovered Ralph Beasley on Bennett Road with a gunshot wound to his head.

   County sheriff's deputies arrived at about the same time in response to a radio request for assistance. An ambulance was already at the scene, as were fire department paramedics. (Grade: ________)
5. A 32-year-old woman who said she smoked marijuana to ease the pain of a rare intestinal disease was charged Tuesday morning with possessing illegal drugs.

   Ruth Howland was stopped at the Municipal Airport after a K-9 dog singled out her suitcase. She and her husband, Terry, were returning from Mexico. (Grade: ________)
6. Three gunmen who entered a restaurant on Wilson Avenue at 10:30 p.m. Tuesday held four employees and 12 customers at gunpoint while taking more than $3,000 from several cash registers.

   Peggy Deacosti, the restaurant's hostess, was on duty when the robbery occurred. (Grade: ________)
7. Eileen Guion, 38, a food and beverage coordinator at Walt Disney World for 18 years, died at her home Tuesday of unknown causes.

   Although she was offered many other jobs at restaurants, she never accepted them. She once said, "I've loved working at Disney because I get to work with people from all over the world, and I think that is very neat." (Grade: ________)
8. Police are searching for a man who attacked a woman outside the Bayside Bar & Grill Thursday night.

Terry Smythe, a bartender at the restaurant, said he heard a woman screaming outside the entrance at 9 p.m. Smythe darted to the foyer, where he saw the woman trapped in the entryway. Smythe said it was "kind of like a tug of war," with the assailant trying to pull the woman outside while waitresses tried to pull her inside. (Grade: ________)

SECTION II: TRANSITIONS

Critically evaluate the following transitions. Which would be most likely to entice you to continue reading the stories? Which provide a smooth, specific, informative and interesting introduction to the next idea? Give each transition a grade of A to F.

1. ________ Other students said they would tell their teachers about cheaters because cheating is not fair to those who take the time to study.

2. ________ But what should happen when a husband and wife disagree about having a baby?

3. ________ A concerned citizen then addressed the commission about the fence.

4. ________ Next, the task force presented its plan for preservation and renovation of the downtown.

5. ________ In a flat, emotionless voice, Howard responded that he and Jackson stole a red Mustang convertible on the night of June 3, picked up the two 14-year-old girls and took them to the motel.

6. ________ Gary Hubbard, superintendent of schools, then addressed his concerns about security in the city's schools.

7. ________ Police Chief Barry Kopperud said his department is trying to combat juvenile crime by changing the way officers interact with children.

8. ________ He then discussed prejudice as a problem that plagues society.

9. ________ She also spoke about the different religious celebrations and rituals.

10. ________ Parents who love, care for and respect their children don't raise delinquents, she said.

Pro Challenge

EXERCISE 2

THE BODY OF A NEWS STORY

WRITING COMPLETE NEWS STORIES

Write complete news stories based on the following information. Be thorough; use most of the information provided. Because much of the material is wordy, awkward and poorly organized, you will have to rewrite it extensively. Correct all errors in your rewrite.

When you finish, you can compare your work to a professional's. Experienced reporters have been asked to write stories for each set of facts, and their work appears in a manual available to your instructor.

1. A family that owns a farm about 2 miles outside your town has decided to sell it. It has been in they're family for four generations. They often bring fresh eggs, produce and other items to the farmers market in town to sell, which is held once a month on the first Saturday. The father of the family told you they are selling because their children are nearly grown and don't want to farm, and that they will be moving to another state to be closer to other family members, but he declined to say any more than that. A real estate developer is buying the property, and he wants to subdivide it for single-family homes and town houses. There would be a total of five hundred new homes as the developer, Eugene McIntry, President of McIntry Realty, has planned it. McIntery has submitted his subdivision plan to the county commissioners. The commissioners and the County Planning Commission are extremely worried about this giant new development. They don't believe their roads and their water and sewer systems can handle all those people. In fact, right now the water system and sewer system don't even run to the farm. The family that lives on the farm have a well and a septic tank for their house and another well for their barn. But, the county doesn't have any zoning, so the supervisors don't think they can keep McIntry from buying the farm and building all those homes. Plus, McIntry has threatened to file a lawsuit if the township tries anything to keep his plans from going through. He said he has a lot of money invested and doesn't want to lose it. Some nearby residents, however, are going to file a lawsuit of their own to keep him from building the houses. They are angry that they're peaceful, quiet stretch of road just outside the city will soon be filled with cars and their view will be ruined by hundred's of new houses. The residents attorney, Hector Salvatore, says he is finishing up the suit and will file it in County Court next week. He said the residents also are afraid they will be forced to hook up to the water and sewer systems if they are expanded out to the farm, which means several hundred dollars out of each of their pockets, which he said is unfair and possibly illegal.

2. A bad accident happened this morning on the intestate highway that runs right along the western edge of your city. It is Interstate 790. Apparently two tractor trailers collided and started a chain reaction crash. The citys Police Department is not done investigating the accident, which happened at 6:45 a.m. in the morning, but that is what they believe preliminarily. A total of 4 tractor-trailers and fourteen cars were involved, according to Sgt. Albert Wei of the police department. One of the tractor-trailers was a tanker hauling diesel fuel; it was very lucky, Wei said, that it didn't roll over or dump any fuel or catch fire. The truck part of the tanker was damaged when a

car hit it, but the truck driver managed to get it stopped along the side of the road. He wasn't hurt, Wei said, but 2 people driving cars were killed and twenty other people were injured and taken to the hospital, four of them seriously hurt. The fire chief, Tony Sullivan, said those seriously hurt people had injuries that were life-threatening. One of the ambulance drivers told him that. Sulluvan said his firefighters had to cut the roofs off three of the cars to free the drivers and passengers that were trapped inside. All five of the fire department's ambulances were on the seen, along with ambulances from four nearby citys' fire departments. Also, the "Life Flight" helicopter from Memorial Hospital in you're city was called to the scene and flew two of the worst injuries to the trauma center in Statesville, 50 miles away. Sullivan said the crash scene looked like something from a war zone when he arrived, with bodies laying along the road, people covered with blood sitting next to their cars, emergency workers running from place to place trying to help the injured, and sirens wailing in the distance as more fire trucks and ambulances were called. He had never seen anything that bad in the 18 and a half years he's been with the fire department. Wie said the police officers on the scene were having trouble figuring out which people were from which vehicles, and who were the drivers and who were the passengers. According to Wei, the accident, which happened in the northbound lanes, closed the entire highway, north and south. The interstate was still closed at 10 a.m., the deadline for your story, and Wei had no idea when it would be open again. It created quite a mess for the rush hour traffic today, since people who normally would have used Interstate 790 had to go on Interstate 690, on the eastern side of the city, and that backed up traffic on 690 for three hours.

3. It seems to be turning into a controversy in your local school district. The School Board is considering implementing random drug testing of all student athletes at the high school. Students and parents on both sides of the issue plan to attend tomorrow night's board meeting, which was to be in the library at Wilson Elementary School but has been moved to the cafeteria at Kennedy High School to accommodate the expected large audience. The 5 school board members you were able to talk to this morning before your deadline, David DeBecker, Mimi Lieber, Judie Lu, Diana Maceda and Jane Tribitt, were reluctant to say anything before the meeting that might give away their positions on the issue. Gary Hubbard is the Superintendent of schools. He didn't really want to say much either when you called him, but then did admit that he was the one who asked the board to consider the new policy. He believes there are members of the football and boys basketball teams that are using steroids and other performance-enhancing drugs, and said some players on those teams have come to him and complained. The school can't test only certain athletes, Hubberd said, so they have to test players in all sports. DeBecker referred you to the school boards attorney, Karen Bulnes. She said she has drafted a proposed policy for the board to consider, but said she doesn't know how they will vote. She said such a policy is legal based on past United States Supreme Court decisions. You were able to talk to some students at the high school this morning before classes started. Hazel Beaumont was dropping off her son, Roger, in front of the school. Roger is a tenth-grader who is playing soccer this fall. He thinks drug testing is a violation of his privacy, but then admitted that he really likes playing soccer and probably would take the test. His mother said she would make him take the test, and said she'll be at the school board meeting. Two girls who play field hockey, Ann Capiello and Amy Deacosti, don't like the idea either, but said they don't have anything to hide and would take the test if required. Both girls are seniors, and when you asked them about the football players taking steroids, Ann said she has heard that. James Carigg and Diana Nyer are seniors who both play basketball, and both are opposed to drug testing. In fact, they plan to go to the meeting and voice they're opinions against the idea. Lu called you

back after you had talked with her and said she decided to publicly say that she is in favor of the idea because she thinks it will be a deterrent for students who might be thinking about taking drugs. The meeting will start at 7 p.m.

4. Fire destroyed two businesses downtown last night, and police think it was arson. They also think they know who set the fire, which caused an estimated five hundred thousand dollars' damage. The businesses that were destroyed were Kalani Brothers Bakery and Barton School of Dance. The fire started in the bakery and spread to the dance studio. Fire chief Tony Sullivan said an automatic alarm at the bakery sounded at 11:35 p.m. When the first fire truck arrived on the scene, flames were shooting out the front of the bakery, where a large picture window had burst, and fire was visible on the 2nd floor, where the dance studio was located. The city fire department was assisted by fire companies from two neighboring towns. A total of 75 firemen and other emergency personnel responded to the call. The first fireman on the scene was Eddy Muldaur, a student at Lake Community College and a volunteer with the city fire department. He told you last night at the scene that there was a lot of smoke and flames coming from the building when he got there. About ten minutes later, the first truck arrived. You were very surprised this morning to find out that Police chief Barry Kopperud issued a news release saying that Muldaur had been arrested and charged with arson for allegedly setting the fire and damaging the sprinkler system so it wouldn't work. He was placed in the city jail on $1 million dollars bail. Eileen Barton, the owner of Barton School of Dance, was inconsolable when you talked to her this morning. She started the dance school 8 years ago. It was the only thing she ever wanted to do. She invested all her savings to start the school; that was the money that her grandfather left her when he died. She has no idea what she'll due because she doesn't think her insurance payment will be enough to start over. The president of the Kalani Brother's Bakery, Charles Kalani said he and his brother, Andrew, will re-open eventually, but in a different location, although he didn't know where yet. He was very angry to learn that the fire had been started intentionally. The two businesses were located at 338 North Fifteenth St. It took firefighters 1 and a half hours to get the fire under control. A business in the building next door, at 340 North Fifteenth Street, Bon Voyage Travel Agency, suffered some smoke and water damage. The manager there, Wayne Morell, said they would be closed today but hoped to open again tomorrow. Chief Sullivan said he found gasoline soaked rags in the back room of the bakery, which they believe were used to start the fire. When he heard that Muldaur was the first one on the scene, he said, he was surprised because he lives on the other side of the city, further away than the fire companys headquarters. Police found a can of gas and a bag of rags in Eddy's pick-up truck. No one was in the building at the time of the fire, and no one was injured fighting it.

5. A magic act at an outdoor childrens festival in your city over the weekend turned out to be no treat for 3 youngsters that had to be taken to the hospital after they were scratched by a rabbit who then disappeared into some bushes. The children were started on a series of rabies shots just to be sure they weren't infected by the rabbit, which could not be found. The magic act was performed by Maggie the Magician, who travels to festivals through out the state with her act, which is aimed at little children and includes small animals like rabbits and turtles that the children can touch and hold. Maggie said nothing like this had ever happened before in the 4 and a half years she's been doing her act. The accident came at the end of her act, when she made the big white rabbit in question, who she called Buster, appear out of a tophat. The children watching her act gathered around to pet Buster when he apparently was frightened by a baby's crying and tried to get away. The 3 children he scratched tried to grab Buster but couldn't hold on. Harriet Ruiz, Director of Public Affairs at

Regional Medical Center, where the 3 youths were taken for treatment, said they will have to have two additional shots unless the rabbit is found and it can be determined that it is not rabid. She declined to give you they're names, but said 2 of the 3 were brother and sister, ages 5 and 4, respectively, and the other was a four-year-old boy. Kim Rybinski, owner of Kim's Pets, who sells rabbits along with numerous other small animals, said it was highly unlikely that Buster had rabies because he was in captivity and never got exposed to wild animals. Michael Jeffreys, director of the Humane Society, said several society volunteers helped Maggie search for Buster, but to no avail. He agreed with Rybinksi that Buster probably didn't have rabies, but said you can't take chances with someone's life. Maggie was uncertain how Buster would survive by himself, but said she had to leave to go to another festival the next day. The festival was held from 10 a.m. to 2 p.m. Saturday at the city park. Maggie's act was on from 10:30 to 10:45. The children were taken by their parents to the hospital right after the accident. A paramedic from the city ambulance department, Julius Povacz, who was volunteering at the festival, cleaned up the children's scratches and advised the parent's to take them to the hospital. He said the wounds were minor. Just as you are approaching deadline on your story, you get a call from Emil Plambeck, Superintendent of the city parks commission. A city worker, Carlos Alicea, was picking up trash in the park this morning when he spotted Buster sitting under a tree and captured him. Now Buster can be quarantined and checked for rabies, and the children hopefully can avoid furthur shots, Ruiz said when you called her back.

6. Your State Legislature is considering a bill that would change the state law requiring motorcyclists to wear helmets. Many physicians in your city are opposed to the bill. About fifty of them held a press conference yesterday afternoon. They unveiled a petition to legislators asking them not to pass the bill. Doctors from Memorial Hospital, Mercy Hospital, Regional Medical Center, Sacred Heart Hospital, St. Nicholas Hospital and the Medi-First Clinic were present at the press conference. In the audience also were over a hundred nurses, paramedics and other healthcare professionals supporting the doctors. The press conference was held on the front lawn of Memorial Hospital, the largest of the citys hospitals, and while it was going on, 2 ambulances came racing into the parking lot and pulled up to the Emergency Room doors with victims from a two-vehicle accident. Ironically, one of the victims injured in the accident had been on a motorcycle. The doctors have gotten nearly four hundred signatures so far on they're petition and hope to have at least five hundred by the time they send it to the legislature. The number of serious head injuries caused by motorcycle accidents in your state is over 70% less now then when the helmet law was adopted 25 years ago, according to Dr. Karl .Sodergreen. He said that reduction is directly related to passage of that law. Dr. Hector Rivera said a study from last year about health-care costs related to motorcycle riding by the state medical society showed that emergency room costs alone could go up by more than 45 percent if the helmet law is repealed. The motorcyclist injured in the accident was 19-year-old Grady Smith of 8213 Peach Street. Smith suffered a broken arm and several broken ribs. In the report from city police, his doctor was quoted as saying Smiths injuries would have been much worse if he had not been wearing a helmet. Dr. Sodergreen said the physicians plan to send their petition to the legislature on Monday. The bill is to be considered by the Legislature next Wednesday.

EXERCISE 3

THE BODY OF A NEWS STORY

WRITING COMPLETE NEWS STORIES

Write complete news stories based on the following information. Critically examine the information's language and organization, improving it whenever possible. To provide a pleasing change of pace, use quotations in your stories. Go beyond the superficial; unless your instructor tells you otherwise, assume that you have enough space to report every important and interesting detail.

1. Your county's Industrial Development Authority made an announcement today. A local company that manufactures automobile parts received a $250,000 grant to retrain some of its workers. The training is required because the company won a contract with the United States government to manufacture replacement parts for military vehicles. The money was provided through your state's Critical Job Training program. The program was designed two years ago to help keep critical and high-paying manufacturing jobs in the state. State and county officials had said too many manufacturing jobs were leaving the state. Only about 16 percent of the jobs in the state involve manufacturing. The rest are professional, service-related or agricultural jobs. The company receiving the training funds is TCB Manufacturing Company Incorporated. The money will allow the company to train 50 current employees, as well as the 150 additional employees that will be hired to work on the new contract. The training will begin next month and continue for 8 to ten weeks. TCB is one of the largest manufacturing companies in your county, employing nearly 2,500 workers at two plants in the county. TCB recently recalled 300 workers that had been laid off last year because of the downturn in the economy that had affected car sales. TCB manufactures high-quality steering gear, transmission and brake assembly parts for several automotive manufacturers. "These training funds will help 50 of our employees to keep their jobs and will enable us to hire 150 new people. This program is a benefit for the people of this county and the state and shows how government and business can work together to improve the economy," said TCB vice president of human resources Jonathan Seiler. At one time TCB employed nearly 4,000 people in manufacturing, but the introduction of robotic welding and assembly machines three years ago eliminated some jobs. "This training program will give me a new lease on my work life. Without it I might have been laid off because I don't have the skills necessary to run the new machines needed for this new contract we got from the military. I would never be able to find another job in the county with the pay and benefits that this job has," said Frank Peacock. Peacock has worked for TCB for 25 years. He is 47 and went to work for TCB after serving four years in the Army. "These funds will allow TCB to remain a major economic force in the county. Keeping manufacturing jobs is important to the local community, the state and our country," said state Representative Constance Wei. Wei was at the 11 a.m. press conference announcing the awarding of the grant. Wei helped the county apply for the money and worked with state officials to get the funds approved.

2. Researchers at the U.S. Department of Health and Human Services are puzzled. A report released Monday in Washington, D.C., by the U.S. Census was unexpected,

researchers said. The census is collected every ten years. The last one was in 2000. The Census Bureau data shows that median income for a single-parent household run by a mother is about $25,000. The median income for a single-parent household headed by a father is $35,000. Yet HHS researchers found that children in single-father households are more likely not to have health insurance. Researchers found that 40% of the 2.5 million single-parent families headed by the father had children without health coverage while only 19% of the 4.9 million single-parent households headed by the mother had children without coverage. Researchers found that only 12 percent of the nation's 10.8 million married couple homes had children without health care coverage. HHS spokesman Jenna Olivetti declined to speculate during Monday's press conference on any government action regarding the trend. She did comment on what she thought may be causing it. "This is something we have never seen before in our research. I'm wondering if single-dad households are less aware of the help they can get from public programs that are available to them," Olivetti said. In the one million homes where a single father raised two or more children, nearly 20 percent had all children uninsured compared to just 10% of the single-mother households with two or more children. The 2000 Census found that the number of single-parent households headed by the father increased 65 percent since the 1990 census. The research was based on a national HHS survey of 110,000 households conducted last year. Programs to cover children in low-income families include Medicaid, which covers 30 million people in low-income families. Medicaid currently covers one in five children in the United States. The HHS research was part of a study to gather more detailed information about children with and without health insurance. Previous research had shown that about 9.2 million children, or 12.1 percent of all children lacked health coverage. The new research found that 15.4 percent of all children, or 9.6 million children, lacked health care coverage.

3. A bizarre situation finally came to a conclusion Wednesday. Minnie Cosby, 43, of 487 Jamestown Drive, is happy the episode is concluded. She wants to get on with her life. Local police are happy, too. Cosby was constantly calling police. In fact, she had called them 163 times over the past six months. The calls to police were complaints about vandalism, crank calls or prowlers. Cosby also complained that someone was stalking her. Police could never find any evidence to arrest anyone in any of the alleged crimes. Cosby told police someone had turned her gas outdoor grill on several times and left items burning on the cooking surface. Graffiti had been spray painted on the aluminum siding of her home and on her driveway several times over the six-month period. The driveway also had been strewn with broken glass, nails and screws on several occasions. On several other occasions, litter and garbage had been strewn about Cosbys yard. In another complaint, Cosby told police someone had sliced a 50-foot garden hose to pieces. Several times, Cosby complained to police that someone tampered with her car and she had to make mechanical repairs to the vehicle. Cosby also complained of numerous crank and harassing calls. Cosby complained about the calls to the telephone company, which put a trace on her telephone line. However, the calls were always made from pay telephones around the city. Cosby told police she thought the vandalism was being done by her neighbor or her neighbor's children. She told police that she has had strained relations with her neighbor for several years. Police staked out Cosbys house on several occasions, but were unable to catch anyone. "This has been a case that has stumped the department for a long time. We spent a lot of time and effort trying to track down leads but didn't have a lot of success," said police Chief Barry Koperud. Police didn't have success until Monday night when patrol officers caught a man prowling around Cosbys house. The man was dressed in black and wore a ski mask. He had a screwdriver, a utility razor knife and a can of spray paint in his possession. The color

of the spray paint matched the color that had been sprayed on Cosbys house on several occasions. When police arrested the man, he had allegedly flattened three tires on Cosbys car and was attempting to flatten the fourth tire. Police charged Randall Cosby, 47, of 5845 South Conway Road, with more than 150 counts of criminal mischief, loitering and prowling, harassment, stalking by communication, possessing instruments of crime, criminal trespass and defiant trespass. The suspect, Randall Cosby, is the ex-husband of Minnie Cosby. They have been divorced for four years. Police said that Randall Cosby was angry with his ex-wife after she had requested money from him to make repairs to the house they had once shared. Minnie Cosby said the repairs were supposed to have been made to the house as part of their divorce agreement, but Randall had refused to abide by the agreement. Cosby is a 20-year veteran of the citys police department. During that time he was awarded several commendations for public service for his work as a patrol officer. Randall Cosby responded to several of the vandalism calls and twice was on the stakeout unit watching the former Mrs. Cosbys home. "I'm just glad this is over. The police probably thought I was crazy making all those calls to them about the things that were happening to me. But I wasn't crazy. I feel sorry for Randall. This wouldn't have happened if he just would have done what he was supposed to do. Maybe some time in prison will let him cool off and think about what he's done. I hope he goes to jail because at least in jail, he won't be able to hurt me anymore," Minnie Cosby said.

4. County sheriff's deputies were in for a bit of a surprise Wednesday. Your county implemented a new program nine months ago. The program requires inmates at the county prison to perform "service" work to help pay for their incarceration. The program is part of the county probation departments pre-release program that gives county inmates an opportunity to qualify for work release and earn credit for early release from incarceration. The service work can vary, but often includes picking up litter along highways or working as laborers on county road crews trimming grass and weeds along county roads. Sheriff's deputies had a road crew picking up litter along Collins Road Wednesday afternoon at 3:10 p.m. There were 18 prisoners working on the litter collection crew and two sheriffs deputies and a corrections officer guarding them. Marvin Kehole, 28, of 182 West Broadway Avenue was one of the inmates. Kehole was serving time for driving under the influence of alcohol, public drunkenness and possession of marijuana. The prison inmates were dressed in bright orange shirts and bright orange and white striped pants. Suddenly there was a loud boom and a 1998 Ford Taurus struck the back of the box van that the corrections officer was driving. The passenger box van is used to transport the inmate workers to and from the job site. Paula Andrews, 65, of 4030 New Orleans Ave., told police she reached down to adjust the volume on the cars radio. When she looked back up, the van was there and she could not get stopped. Andrews was not injured in the crash. When the sheriffs deputies checked the prison inmates after the commotion, they were missing one inmate. Keyhole had escaped. Officers called for help and 20 police and corrections officers, including a K-9 unit responded to the scene. Police and corrections officers found Keholes prison uniform behind a storage shed at a nearby house. Police called in a helicopter to aid in the search. The K-9 unit tracked the scent trail of Kehole for nearly 2 miles to the door of Jim's Lounge, located in the 4700 block of Collins Road. Police found Kehole inside, sitting at the bar drinking a beer. "He was sitting there just as cool as you please when we came into Jim's. He didn't offer any resistance when we arrested him. He had slipped away when our attention was diverted by that accident. He ran to a nearby house and stole some clothing off a clothesline, then walked down a couple of back streets to Jim's. Kehole told us he just wanted a drink. He must have been really thirsty because this is going to cost him when he gets in front of that judge," said sheriff's deputy Roger Horan.

Kehole was charged with escape, theft of property and violation of prison regulations regarding consuming alcohol.

5. It was a potential tragedy that your citys police, rescue and fire officials say was just barely averted. James Shanahan, his two daughters Alyssa and Adrienne, and his wife, Mary, were traveling from Grand Rapids, Mich. They were flying near your city when the plane they were in had to make an emergency landing. James Shanahan is a licensed pilot. He has been flying for 30 years. He has never had a problem in all that time. No one was seriously injured, but James Shanahan was admitted to Mercy Hospital for observation. Mrs. Shanahan was treated for a broken wrist and a laceration on her forehead and released. Adrienne suffered minor cuts and bruises. Alyssa was not injured. The plane was a four-passenger Mooney Executive 21 propeller-driven, fixed-wing aircraft. The undercarriage of the plane sustained minor damage. There was a small fuel spill, according to the fire department. "They were very fortunate. It could have been much worse than it was. There were a lot of startled people when that plane came at them," said Fire Chief Tony Sullivan. Police Chief Barry Kopperud said the Shanahans left Grand Rapids early in the morning. The flight was proceeding normally until the plane was 100 miles east of the city. The plane began to wander off course and was contacted by the control tower at City Regional Airport. A girls voice responded to the control tower. "The girl I talked to on the radio told me the pilot was having problems. She told me he had slumped in his seat and was unconscious. I could hear the passengers screaming in the background. It was really confusing. I think they were getting a bit panicky up there," said control tower flight manager Peter Jacobs. Police said James Shanahan lost consciousness as he was about to contact the tower to request an emergency landing. His wife, Mary, told police her husband began complaining about not feeling well. He told her that he felt dizzy and couldn't get his breath. She said he suddenly slumped over in his seat and the plane went into a shallow dive. "There was nothing I could do. I was in the back passenger seat with my daughter Adrienne. I couldn't reach the controls. And even if I could have, I don't think I could have helped because I never learned how to fly. I hate flying," Mrs. Shanahan said. Kopperud said Aylssa Shanahan was seated beside her father. It was she who responded to the towers call about the plane wandering off course. Alyssa pulled her fathers arms away from the controls and his legs off the rudder pedals. She then took over the controls of the aircraft and called the tower for help to land the plane. Jacobs stayed in contact with Alyssa and gave her instructions on what to do. He talked to her the entire time and directed other aircraft away from the airport until the emergency was over. Alyssa was able to locate the airport and brought the plane down. When the plane landed, it overshot the runway and skidded across an open field. The landing gear of the plane collapsed and the plane plowed through a chain-link fence and came to a stop just 10 feet from the northbound lane of Interstate 51. The interstate was crowded with traffic at the time of the accident. The accident occurred at 4:05 p.m., police said. No one on the ground was injured. Alyssa is 12 years old, 4 feet 3 inches tall and weighs 88 pounds. "I've been flying with my Daddy since I was a little girl. He taught me all about flying and even let me handle the controls sometimes. I was a little scared because I couldn't reach the rudder pedals very well. But I couldn't be too scared because I want to be a pilot like my Daddy someday. I was more worried about my Daddy because I didn't know what happened to him. I just wanted to get on the ground and get help for him," Alyssa said. Doctors at Mercy Hospital said Mr. Shanahan was in satisfactory condition after suffering an allergic reaction to a prescription medicine he had begun taking that morning.

EXERCISE 4

THE BODY OF A NEWS STORY

REPORTING CONTROVERSIAL STORIES (QUOTING OPPOSING VIEWPOINTS)

Write complete news stories about the following controversies. As you write the stories, present both sides of each controversy as fully and as fairly as possible. Also, try to integrate those conflicting viewpoints. Instead of reporting all the opinions voiced by the first source, and then all the conflicting opinions voiced by the second source, try—when appropriate—to report both opinions about the story's most important issue, and then both opinions about the second, third and fourth issues.

STORY 1: SCHOOL BOARD BAN

FACTS: The school board in your town made a unanimous decision Tuesday night. It wasn't a popular decision with some students and parents. But school board members said they made the decision for the safety of athletes participating in sports in the school district. The vote was 9 to nothing. The board voted to ban boys from playing on girls' teams. The policy was implemented after four boys tried out for and made the high schools girls field hockey team last year. The boys played on the team last fall and helped the team make the state playoffs. The policy banning boys from girls teams says the size, speed and power of male athletes poses a hazard for female players. Several schools that played your towns high school team last year forfeited their games rather than take a chance of fielding their girls against the boys on the team. The policy takes affect immediately. The policy will ban boys from playing on the girls field hockey, volleyball and softball teams

ONE SIDE: High school athletic director Hugh Baker told the board that such a blanket policy could hurt the schools athletics program because the school would have to forfeit games to other teams. "If safety is the issue of concern for the board, then our girls teams would have to forfeit games if there are boys on the opposing teams. If we can't have boys on our teams because the board is afraid girls will get hurt, then our teams can't play against teams that have boys on their teams. Our girls field hockey team would have had to forfeit at least ten of their 18 games last season because we played other schools that had boys on their teams. It would be unfair to force our field hockey team to have a losing record every year because it has to forfeit all those games. Some of the schools we play are smaller schools and they wouldn't be able to field enough players if they didn't allow boys and girls to play on the same team." Jacob Stevens is a senior at the high school. He played on the girls field hockey team last year. He was looking forward to playing on the team his senior year. He spoke to the board during the meeting. "I don't think it is fair. There are countries in the world where men's field hockey is a recognized sport. Not every guy wants to play football, basketball or baseball. Field hockey is a fast and exciting sport that requires a lot of skill. I enjoy playing the game and I haven't had any of the other female players on the team complain about my being there. If we can't play with the girls, we wouldn't be able to play. There are not enough boys interested to create a mens field hockey team."

THE OTHER SIDE: School board member Jane Tribitt voted for the policy. She proposed the ban after receiving complaints from parents in both the home district and away districts. "I just don't believe the sexes should be mixed in this case. The boys are just too big and physical and it intimidates the girls on the team. It is a matter of safety. And there are other teams that have no boys on their teams that do not want to play our school for whatever reason because there are boys on the team. I think other schools will adopt policies similar to this one and ban boys from their teams as well. The question of forfeiting games will then become a moot point." Sandra Adler is a parent whose daughter was a senior on last years team along with the four boys. Adler also was an all-state consensus pick as player of the year during her senior year on the girls field hockey team thirty years ago. Her husband is Stuard Adler, minister of the Church of Christ. "I just don't think it is healthy mentally or physically to have the boys and girls playing on the same team. There probably are girls who want to play on the boys football or baseball teams, but they are not allowed. So I don't think the boys should be allowed to take over the girls team sports. Just because there are not enough boys interested in the sport to field their own team is not justification for their being allowed to join the girls team."

STORY 2: PAINT CAN PROJECT

FACTS: It is a debate that has been raging for weeks. Your City Council voted last night on a motion to approve a controversial sale and improvement project. The vote, which was 4-3, was a close one. The meeting drew a large crowd of supporters and opponents to the proposal. The city owns an old metal water tank. The tank can hold 200,000 gallons of water. The city no longer uses the water tank because it is obsolete. It has sat empty for the past seven years. The city stopped using the tank because of state government regulations regarding open sources of water and possible contamination. The city now uses completely enclosed water storage facilities. The tank is 50 feet tall and 25 feet in diameter. More than 100 residents attended the meeting, which was held at 7:30 p.m. in City Hall. A local businessman who owns a paint manufacturing plant near the site offered to buy the water tower. He wants to clean up the tower, which is scarred by corrosion and peeling paint. He wants to repaint it so it resembles a giant can of paint and put his company logo on it. Residents in the area want the city to tear the water tower down because they claim it is an eyesore. They also claim that the tank poses an environmental hazard because lead in the peeling paint is leaching into the ground around the tank. It would cost the city 483 thousand dollars to demolish the water tank and haul it away. The paint company has offered $50,000 to buy the tank from the city.

ONE SIDE: William Krueger, 284 Erie Ave., is the president of Alladdin Paints. Kruegar said at the meeting: "This is in the best interest of the town and will be a novel way to promote my business. The city would have to spend nearly half a million dollars to tear that tank down and I'm offering to provide the city with some extra revenue instead. The promotional value of that tank painted up as a giant paint can is invaluable to my company. It also will promote the city as a business-friendly city because news organizations from all over the country will want to do stories on it. The American Paint Manufacturers Association is ready to help pay some of the cost to clean up the tank and paint it. I think it is a win-win situation for the city." Barton Masters, executive director of the Chamber of Commerce attended the meeting in support of the proposal. "This is a unique way to deal with that water tank, which has been an eyesore for years. It shows that business and government can work cooperatively to solve problems in a community. When it is renovated and painted, I'll bet money that residents in the area will be surprised at how attractive it looks."

THE OTHER SIDE: Amanda Blake, 3314 Santana Blvd., lives near the water tank. She can see the top of it from the back porch of her house. "If Mr. Masters thinks that can will look so attractive, why doesn't he put one in his backyard. Santana Boulevard residents have had to put up with a lot of neglect by city officials over the years. We have requested, begged and threatened to sue to have that tank removed. It is an eyesore and a potential environmental hazard. Tests have shown that the original paint on that tank contains lead and that lead is leaching into the ground. Kids play near that area. What is going to happen to them? Do city officials think that a new coat of paint is going to solve that problem? It may sound like a bargain to sell the problem to someone else, but selling the tank is not going to solve the real problem—how to enhance life for the residents of Santana Boulevard. The city should tear the tank down and clean up the site." Roger Ellam, 2481 Santana Blvd., opposes the idea: "Four years ago the city promised us that it would tear the tank down. And four years later it is still sitting there. I drive by that thing every day on my way to work. You don't have to drive by it because you don't live near it. The residents of Santana Boulevard deserve better from their elected officials. You're trying to save money at our expense." City council member Alice Cycler voted against the proposal: "I can't support this proposal because we promised residents that we would clean up that section of Santana Boulevard and provide funds for residential revitalization. I don't think a giant paint can will provide a symbol of neighborhood revitalization."

STORY 3: HOUSING PROJECT

FACTS: Your City Council voted last night on a proposal to locate a low-income housing project in the 4200 block of Forest Boulevard, which is part of the Creekside Village subdivision. The project would consist of 14 two-story brick buildings. Each building would house 6 to 8 families. The project would cost $6 million and would be federally subsidized. It would serve the elderly, the handicapped and low-income families. After last nights meeting, at which many people loudly and vigorously objected to the plans, the City Council vetoed the proposal by a unanimous vote of 7 to 0. The plans were presented to the City Council by the Tri-County Housing Authority, which is a semi-autonomous public body but which needs the approval of local governing boards to locate its projects within the boundaries of their jurisdictions.

ONE SIDE: The director of the City Housing Authority, Tom Chinn Onn, told the City Council before the vote: "I'm really disappointed in the opposition here tonight. We have a backlog of over 900 applicants waiting to find public housing. This would go a long way toward meeting that need. Low income people are the ones who'll be hurt, badly hurt, if this isn't approved. Everyone seems to be saying they want to help the poor, but no one wants them in their own neighborhoods. Everyone complains when we try to place them in a nice neighborhood. And a lot of what you're hearing tonight about this project is emotional rather than factual. Its all scare tactics. Studies done by Don Brame (the citys traffic operations engineer) show that the project would add only 600 to 800 additional vehicles on the areas roads on a daily basis, and thats a very liberal estimate considering that about a third of the units would be occupied by older people who probably wouldn't drive much. The elderly also wouldn't need other city facilities, like schools. Now, we've already spent more than $160,000 planning this project, and all the money will be wasted, just totally wasted, if you reject this proposal, and we've got nowhere else to go with it. Everyone says they want to help the poor, but they want to help them somewhere else. Thats real hypocrisy. This is a chance for the members of this council to be real statesmen and do some real good for some needy people. This means a lot to them, so I ask you to approve these plans."

THE OTHER SIDE: Residents of the neighborhood voiced the following complaints during the council meeting. Frank D. Shadgett of 8472 Chestnut Drive said, "This thing would cause all sorts of problems: crowded roads, crowded schools, more kids in the streets. We don't have enough parks, and there's only one junior high school and one high school that serve our neighborhood, and both have been filled for years. Now, if you dump this project on us, you'll have to bus some of our children out of their neighborhood schools, or you'll have to bring in some portable classrooms. There are other places that could handle the project better. It just doesn't fit in our neighborhood. You should come out and look at the area before coming up with an idea like this. A lot of our homes cost $185,000 or $230,000 or more. You put this project in the middle of them, and it'll hurt our property values." Another person, James Lasater of 374 Walnut Drive said: "The area is zoned for single-family homes and thats why we invested here. We've got our life savings in our homes, and this will hurt us. We've got no lack of compassion for the cause, but it just doesn't belong here. We want to protect our neighborhood and keep our neighborhood the way it is. We object to this bunch of bureaucrats coming in and changing its character. Its a good area to live in, and we don't want that to change." An attorney representing the neighborhood, Michael Perakis, said: "The area is one of the most stable and beautiful single-family neighborhoods in the city, and these people are only interested in maintaining that status. Right now, you're in danger of violating your own laws if you put this project in Creekside Village. There's been no proper hearings to rezone the land, and this project doesn't fit its current zoning restrictions. The zoning laws are intended to prevent this very kind of thing, this invasion of a residential neighborhood with a nonconforming project of any type."

STORY 4: BANNING FREE SPEECH

FACTS: There was a protest in your city over a new law passed by city officials that bans smoking in all public places. The new ordinance passed by City Council late last year even banned smoking in restaurants and bars. The ordinance was passed over the objections of restaurant and tavern owners and a group called Stop Making Ordinances; Keep Every Right Safe, or SMOKERS. Last week a group of SMOKERS led a protest against the law. The eight men and five women walked into the Steak & Ale Restaurant and chained themselves to the bar. They then lit cigarettes and cigars and began smoking them. The restaurant's manager called police, who had to use bolt cutters to free the protesters from the bar and then carry each of the protesters out of the bar to waiting patrol cars. City officials figure it cost several thousand dollars to arrest and process the 13 protesters. The city is now considering another ordinance. This one would require protesters who get arrested to pay the cost of the time and effort it takes police to place them in custody. City officials say it costs the city too much money to arrest and process the protesters. To offset the cost, protesters who get arrested would have to pay a $300 processing fee in addition to any fines or court costs for charges filed against them. City council member William Belmonte proposed the ordinance and made a motion to have city attorney Allen Farci explore the legal aspects of such an ordinance. Belmonte wants the city to vote on the proposed ordinance next month. City council approved

Belmonte's motion to explore the need for and legality of such an ordinance by a vote of 5-2.

ONE SIDE: In interviews this morning after Tuesday night's meeting, city council member William Belmonte said: "This is not about taking away the people's right to protest. It is a matter of trying to stretch scarce city resources. I support the people's right to free speech, but I don't support their right to be arrested for free. Someone has to bear the cost of securing public safety and it shouldn't always be the public. These people who protest are trying to disrupt our community and make a spectacle of themselves. They're like spoiled children who can't get their way so they want to scream and shout about it. They think if they disrupt our city and our lives and hurt us economically, we'll cave in to their demands. Well I've got news for them, this city is not going to be held hostage by a bunch of hooligans." In a second interview with city attorney Allen Farci, Farci said: "I think the city is on solid legal ground here. I think the state and federal courts would allow us to add a fee to someone being arrested as a protester. We impose fees on criminals all the time to generate revenue to support the courts, and I see this as no different. We are not stopping people from protesting. They can still protest in a peaceful manner. It is when people break the law and try to get themselves arrested in order to tie up law enforcement and disrupt life in the city that it becomes a problem financially for the city."

THE OTHER SIDE: In a follow-up interview later that day, Lydia Hanson, 880 6th St., a lawyer and member of your states Civil Liberties Union, said: "We don't live in a dictatorship. Protesting government policies and actions is as American as apple pie. This is a tactic that totalitarian regimes use to control their people. They make the people pay for the cost of prosecution so people are afraid to protest onerous government policies. If the city council is going to treat SMOKERS like this, are they going to treat all protesters the same. What about those who demonstrate about issues the city council supports? Are they going to have them arrested and make them pay the processing fee? I think this crazy idea by city council should be challenged all the way to the Supreme Court." Alan Macco, 503 29th St., a musician whose band plays many of the bars in the city, had this to say: "Belmonte is a former smoker and he is the one who proposed the original no smoking ban that prompted all this. Now he even wants to take away the ability of people to speak out. He won't admit he was wrong about the no smoking ban; he just wants to silence those who don't agree with him." In a telephone interview, Beverly Cheng, executive director of the State Restaurant Association, said: "This is an example of government taking a good thing too far and then compounding the problem. I see nothing wrong with having separate areas in a restaurant or bar for smokers and non-smokers. That is fair to everyone. But to ban a whole segment of society from doing something they enjoy is unfair. And then to persecute them even more by taking away their right to voice their opinion is adding insult to injury."

CHAPTER 9

QUOTATIONS AND ATTRIBUTION

It's hard for a wire editor staring into a computer in Louisville to evaluate the motives and credibility of people who whisper to reporters in Washington corridors.

(Linda Raymond, newspaper editor)

The Children's Gallery of the Wichita, Kan., Art Museum displayed the reactions some of its young patrons had to the art they saw and made. One young art critic, identified only as "Garrett," said, "If we didn't have art, we would all look like puddles of black and white paint."

Garrett's remark is both funny and provocative. It also reveals something of his personality and makes those who read his remark want to know more about him. People reveal themselves through their words. Part of the joy of meeting new people is discovering how they speak and how they view the world. And one way readers meet new people is through news stories.

Quotations add color and interest to news stories by allowing readers to hear many voices rather than just the voice of the writer. Weaving those many voices into one coherent news story, however, can be difficult. Experienced writers follow certain customs and guidelines to help them handle the difficulties.

QUOTATIONS

Reporters incorporate in their stories information they have obtained from other people in one of three forms: (1) direct, (2) indirect or (3) partial quotations. Direct quotations present a source's exact words and, consequently, are placed entirely in quotation marks. Indirect quotations are not placed inside quotation marks because reporters use their own words to summarize, or paraphrase, the source's remarks. Partial quotations take key phrases from a source's statement and quote them directly:

> DIRECT QUOTATION: Ambrose said: "Journalism students should be dealing with ideas of a social, economic and political nature. There's too much of a trade-school atmosphere in journalism schools today. One spends too much time on minor technical and mechanical things, like learning how to write headlines."

PARTIAL QUOTATION: Ambrose criticized the "trade-school atmosphere" in journalism schools and said students should study ideas, not mechanical techniques.

INDIRECT QUOTATION: Ambrose said journalism students should deal with ideas, not mechanical techniques.

When to Use Direct Quotations

Reporters use direct quotations when their sources say something important or controversial and state their ideas in an interesting, unusual or colorful manner. When The Kansas City Star profiled Bo Gritz, a controversial right-wing political figure and activist, the story included this quotation: "I'm proud of people in Missouri. They're hard, like woodpecker lips." Probably nobody but Gritz would have expressed that thought in that way.

Direct quotations are so much a part of news stories that reporters and editors may think a story is incomplete without its quota of quotations. But reporters who merely decorate their stories with quotations are not using them effectively.

Jack Hart, managing editor for staff training and development at The Oregonian in Portland, has identified several instances when direct quotations are appropriate:

- Use quotations to let the sources talk directly to the reader.
- Use quotations when you cannot improve on the speaker's exact words or cannot match the speaker's wit, rhythm, color or emotion.
- Use quotations to tie a controversial opinion to the source.
- Use quotations as evidence for a statement.
- Use quotations to reveal the speaker's character.

John Aloysius Farrell, Washington bureau chief for The Denver Post, wrote a story about increasing partisanship in state legislatures. One of Farrell's sources was Grover Norquist, head of Americans for Tax Reform and a leading Republican strategist. Norquist said one of the GOP's goals was to make politics in state capitals more partisan and bitter. "Bipartisanship is another name for date rape," Norquist told Farrell. His remark fit many of the criteria for direct quotations.

The best direct quotations usually are short and full of emotion. Four words spoken by President Richard M. Nixon during the Watergate scandals captured public attention not only because the president said them but also because he felt the need to say them: "I'm not a crook."

Using Direct Quotations Effectively

Direct quotations should illustrate a point, not tell an entire story. Stories composed entirely of quotations seem poorly organized because they lack natural transitions. The following story contains a pleasing combination of quotations and paraphrases:

The most important thing women's basketball coach Vance Coleman carries in his briefcase is not a sketch of a new defensive scheme, a game plan for the upcoming opponent or even the phone number of a basketball colleague.

It's a crumpled, yellowed piece of paper with a list full of scratches and re-dos. It's his list of five life goals. Coleman lists living a long and healthy life, playing the role of a good father and husband and earning a million dollars as his top three goals. The other two, he said, constantly change as he ages.

But the point, Coleman said, is to always have them.

"There is an equation I use that works on the basketball court, on the playing field, in business and in life," Coleman said, "and that is performance equals ability times motivation. You may have all the ability in the world, but with no motivation, you won't accomplish anything. Zero times anything is nothing.

"No matter what you do in life, you have to have goals. And you have to stick to those goals."

Coleman, now in his second year at the university and his 17th year of coaching, spoke about goals and motivation to nearly 300 students at the Student Alumni Association Conference Friday.

"The first thing you need is a good attitude," Coleman said. "When you get up at 7 a.m., do you say, 'Good morning, God,' or 'Good God, morning'? Same words, big difference in attitude."

Next, the coach shifted gears to the importance of beliefs.

"When someone asks you what you believe in, tell them with conviction," Coleman said. "Say, 'I believe in myself and what I think with my whole heart and nothing less.'"

Reporters often summarize a major point, then use a direct quotation to explain the idea or provide more specific details about it. But the quotation should provide new information. Here's an example of how a quotation can effectively support a point. It's from a story about a speech given by a 34-year-old African-American corporate executive to a group of college students. He advised students to establish personal advisory boards:

Gather five people in your life who helped to shape your views. Whether it's a mentor, a parent, a preacher or a friend, advisory board people can provide support and confidence, Johnson said.

"My mom is part of my advisory board. As a person of color, it really wasn't popular to be nonwhite in my elementary school," he said. "My mom had to come to school everyday because I was picked on. She'd say, 'Art, you are the best. Always remember that.' She instilled a sense of self-confidence in me that I still have today."

A quotation should not repeat, or echo, facts reported earlier in a story:

Company officials said they are not worried about the upcoming audit.

"We're not expecting anything to worry about," treasurer Peter VanNeffe said.

Quotations can also help describe a story's dramatic moments. Because of their importance, those moments should be described in detail and placed near the beginning of a story. The following quotations are so interesting and dramatic that they compel readers to finish the story:

"I'm a taxpayer and I'm a business woman," Hilt said. "This is bad for taxes, and this is bad for business. The only ones who stand to gain from this are the 12 to 18 rich white men who own the town."

"We had four guys with their heads painted in school colors, and some people were so excited I thought they were gonna wet their pants before the game started," she said.

"The mayor thought we were not in a position to ask a question like that," Combs said. "He was livid—livid, livid, livid—that we would do that."

When to Use Indirect Quotations

Some sources are more quotable than others, and even colorful sources say things that are not quotable. Reporters may be tempted to use whatever quotations happen to be available. Yet a weak quotation is worse than none. If a quotation bores or confuses people, many will immediately stop reading a story. Compare the interesting quotations above with these:

"It's something that's pretty unique here," she said.

"We're here for many reasons," he said.

"The positive response was tremendous," Wesely said.

In none of these quotations are the speaker's words interesting or remarkable. Each would be better paraphrased or omitted entirely.

Reporters use indirect quotations when their sources fail to state their ideas effectively. Indirect quotations allow reporters to rephrase a source's remarks and state them more clearly and concisely. Reporters also can emphasize the source's most significant remarks and revise or eliminate remarks that are unclear, irrelevant, libelous, pretentious or otherwise unprintable:

> ORIGINAL STATEMENT: He said, "I fully intend to resign from my position as mayor of this city."
>
> PARAPHRASED: The mayor said he plans to resign.

> ORIGINAL STATEMENT: Edna Czarski said, "Women do not get the same tax and insurance benefits that men receive, and they do not receive maternity benefits that even start to cover what they should."
>
> PARAPHRASED: Edna Czarski said women receive neither the same tax and insurance benefits as men nor adequate maternity benefits.

Reporters can never justify a weak quotation by responding, "But that's what my source said." They should use their interviewing skill and judgment to elicit and report strong quotations—quotations that are clear, concise, dramatic and interesting.

Sometimes sources give reporters only routine, boring quotations such as, "I really love to play football." By continuing the interview and asking better questions, reporters can get better responses. Here's the type of quotation reporters want:

> "I really love football," Joe Lozado said. "I've been playing since I was 7 years old, and I would feel worthless if I couldn't play. There's no better feeling than just before a game when you run out on the field with all your buddies and see the crowd. You can feel the excitement."

Asking questions that encourage the source to elaborate on her or his ideas or reactions often will produce good quotations.

Some reporters go further and dream up what they think sources should say and then try to get them to say it. James Carville, the political consultant who directed Bill Clinton's first presidential campaign, has written: "There's no one who has dealt with the national media who has not gotten any number of phone calls saying, 'I'm writing a story and I want to say this. Can you say it for me?'" This practice is unethical and it distorts the news. Let the source say what is on his or her mind; the good reporter, who should also be a good listener, usually will find plenty of things to quote.

Avoid quotations—direct or indirect—that state the obvious. The following quotations are likely to sound familiar because they appear dozens of times every year. You may see these quotations in newspapers or hear them on radio and television:

> "We really want to win this game," coach Riley said. (Readers already know this. Does any coach want to lose?)

> "If we can score some points, we can win this game," Tran Ogbondah said. (A team that does not score points obviously cannot win.)

Equally weak are self-serving quotations in which sources praise themselves and their programs:

> Lyons called her program a success. "We had a terrific crowd and a particularly good turnout," she said.

Reading or listening to someone's self-praise is as interesting as watching a videotape of someone else's vacation.

When to Use Partial Quotations

Sometimes reporters—especially beginners—try to get around the problem of weak or confusing quotations by directly quoting only a few words from a sentence. In fact, most partial, or fragmentary, quotations are awkward, wordy or unnecessary. Sentences that contain several partial quotations are particularly distracting. Usually, the quoted phrases can be turned into indirect constructions, with the quotation marks simply eliminated:

> PARTIAL QUOTATION: He said the press barons "such as William Randolph Hearst" created "an amazingly rich variety" of newspapers.
> REVISED: He said the press barons such as William Randolph Hearst created an amazingly rich variety of newspapers.

Reporters also should avoid using "orphan" quotes—that is, they should not place quotation marks around an isolated word or two used in an ordinary way. The addition of quotation marks to emphasize individual words is inappropriate. Similarly, there is no reason to place quotation marks around profanities, slang, clichés or grammatical errors:

> INCORRECT: He complained that no one "understands" his problem.
> REVISED: He complained that no one understands his problem.

> INCORRECT: She said that having to watch her child die was worse than "hell" could possibly be.
> REVISED: She said that having to watch her child die was worse than hell could possibly be.

At worst, an orphan quotation may be libelous. A New York newspaper included this sentence in a story about a murder case: "As police delved into his tangled business affairs, several women described as 'associated' with Brenhouse (the victim) were questioned at Hastings Police Headquarters." One of those women, who was named in the story, sued for libel. She argued—and the court agreed—that readers would infer from the quotation marks around "associated" that she had been having a love affair with the victim.

Reporters may use partial quotations to more clearly attribute to a source phrases that are particularly controversial, important or interesting:

> Phil Donahue accused the television critic of "typing with razor blades."

> The petition urged the City Council to ban the sale of Penthouse and Playboy magazines "for the sake of our wives and children."

BLENDING QUOTATIONS AND NARRATIVE

Every news story must have a central point, and everything in the story must bear on that point. The sources whom the reporter interviewed, however, may have spoken about a number of topics, some of which may bear only slightly on the story's central point. Reporters must blend the quotations and the narrative they write to create a coherent, well-focused news story. This blending of narrative and quotations presents several problems and dilemmas for reporters.

Explaining Quotations

Sometimes reporters use a quotation, then realize readers need background information to understand it. They might try inserting explanatory material in parentheses. Or they might tack on the explanation after the attribution. Still others might put a large block of background information high in the story, hoping that it will give readers the information they need to understand the quotations and new facts reported elsewhere in the story. None of these approaches works well.

Lazy writers solve the problems of providing explanatory material by inserting it in parentheses in the quotation. When reporters pepper their stories with parenthetical explanations, the stories become difficult to read. Each bit of parenthetical matter forces readers to pause and absorb some additional information before moving on with the rest of the sentence. The occasional use of parentheses to insert brief explanations may be acceptable, but reporters should paraphrase quotations that need several parenthetical explanations. And if reporters find themselves using parentheses repeatedly, they should consider reorganizing their stories.

INCORRECT: "When (head coach Tom) Whitman decides on his starter (at quarterback), the rest of them (the players) will quit squabbling," the athletic director said.
REVISED: The football players will quit squabbling when head coach Tom Whitman selects a starting quarterback, the athletic director said.

ACCEPTABLE: Dr. Harold Termid, who performed the operation, said, "The technique dates back before the 20th century, when it was first used by the French to study ruminants (cud-chewing animals)."

Adding the explanatory information after the quotation or attribution is little better than using parentheses. Such backward constructions force readers to complete the sentence before they can figure out what the topic is. Here's an example:

"We're mobilizing for an economic war with other cities and states," the mayor said of his plan for attracting new businesses to the city.

Instead of using this "said-of" construction, turn the sentence around and use an indirect quotation. For example:

The mayor said his plan for attracting new business amounted to mobilization for an economic war with other cities and states.

Beginning reporters sometimes think they must report their questions so that readers can understand the source's answers. The news is in the answers, however, not the questions. The use of both questions and answers is unnecessary, repetitive and dull. Reporters usually omit the question. If the question provides important context, reporters incorporate it in the answer:

INCORRECT: The president was asked whether he plans to seek a second term, and he responded that he would not announce his decision until next winter.
REVISED: The president said he would not announce his decision regarding a second term until next winter.
OR: In response to a question, the president said he would not announce his decision regarding a second term until next winter.
OR: During a question-and-answer session after his speech, the president said he would not announce his decision regarding a second term until next winter.

To Change or Not to Change Quotations

Sometimes the exact words a source uses may be inappropriate to use in a news story. To make a quotation usable, reporters may be tempted to alter the words the speaker used. Whether writers should ever change a quotation is a matter of debate among journalists. Many journalists accept making minor changes in quotations to correct grammatical errors or delete profanity. Other journalists say reporters should never change quotations. And still others accept extensive changes in quotations, so long as the altered quotations are faithful to the speaker's meaning.

Correcting Grammatical Errors

Many reporters routinely correct the grammatical errors in direct quotations. An editor at The New York Times has explained: "Cultured people are not expected to maintain in conversation the rigid grammatical standards normally applied to writing, so we delete their false starts and grammatical lapses. Failing to do so would make those we quote seem illiterate by subjecting their spoken language to the standards of writing." Reporters are most likely to correct grammatical errors for ordinary citizens who are not accustomed to dealing with journalists.

GRAMMATICAL ERROR: An usher said, "The people started pouring in, and there weren't no way to stop them."

REVISED: An usher said, "The people started pouring in, and there wasn't any (or *was no*) way to stop them."

When the source is a public official or a sports or entertainment celebrity, reporters are less likely to correct grammatical or other errors. If the quotation is newsworthy, journalists will report the speaker's words unchanged. They assume people in the public spotlight are experienced enough to know what to say and how to say it.

Some sources are so well known for the way they misuse words or create confusing sentences that reporters should not clean up their statements. The late Casey Stengel, a baseball manager, was famous for sentences like this one describing an unusually lucky player: "He could fall in a hole and come up with a silver spoon." A more recent example is President George W. Bush, whose malapropisms, mispronunciations and fractured syntax often have been made fun of, even by Bush himself. When during his first presidential campaign Bush mispronounced "subliminal" as "subliminable," many news reports noted the slip. Bush later made fun of it by intentionally mispronouncing the word. Other linguistic flubs by Bush were widely reported:

"I am a person who recognizes the fallacy of human beings."

"I know how hard it is to put food on your family."

"Rarely is the question asked: 'Is our children learning?'"

Although correcting grammatical errors is a widely accepted practice in journalism, some oppose it. The Associated Press Stylebook says: "Never alter quotations even to correct minor grammatical errors or word usage. Casual minor tongue slips may be removed by using ellipses but even that should be done with extreme caution." If a speaker's words are unclear, the AP admonishes, seek a clarification or don't use them.

Other reporters refuse to alter quotes under any circumstances. Carol McCabe, who won national writing awards as a reporter for the Providence (R.I.) Journal-Bulletin, finds poetry in the natural speech patterns of ordinary people and says reporters who correct the grammatical errors in their sources' quotations are being condescending. For reporters such as McCabe, correcting grammatical errors presents readers a false view of life and flattens the individuality of the people described in news stories.

A U.S. Supreme Court decision in a libel suit over the alteration of quotations lends support both to those who oppose altering quotations and to those who accept some changes. Psychoanalyst Jeffrey Masson sued journalist Janet Malcolm and The New Yorker magazine over a profile of him. The profile was based on extensive interviews of Masson that Malcolm had tape-recorded, but Masson said Malcolm had made up some defamatory quotations and attributed them to him. One of the disputed quotations was on tape, but Masson said it had been taken out of context. The other quotations were not on the tapes, but Malcolm said Masson made some of the controversial statements when the tape recorder was broken or not present. She said she had made handwritten notes of those conversations but lost them after she made a typed version. (Malcolm found her handwritten notes after a trial jury had decided the case in her favor.) The question the Supreme Court considered was whether the deliberate alteration of quotations may be evidence that the author knowingly published a falsehood about a libel plaintiff. The Supreme Court refused to say that all alterations of quotations are evidence of deliberate falsehood. The court recognized that quotations do not always present the exact words of the speaker, and evidence that a reporter simply cleaned up grammar and made other stylistic changes is not going to be enough for a plaintiff to win a libel suit. Only if the reporter intentionally changed the meaning of the source's words and the change is defamatory can it be the basis for a libel suit, the court said.

Using the source's exact words eliminates questions about accuracy. It also is the approach most news organizations require. Reporters who are uncertain about the source's exact words (or think a statement needs rewriting) should use indirect rather than direct quotations. Doctoring a quotation could lead to a mistake that would injure the reputation of the source and the career of the reporter. Whether using direct or indirect quotations, a reporter always has an obligation to present a source's views as faithfully as possible.

Even those who oppose altering quotations recognize a few instances where changes are necessary. They usually involve the deletion of unnecessary words, grammatical errors and profanities:

ORIGINAL STATEMENT: He said, "Look, you know I think nuclear power is safe, absolutely safe."

REVISION: He said, "Nuclear power is safe, absolutely safe."

Reporters may use an ellipsis (three periods) to show where they deleted a word, phrase or sentence. An ellipsis that appears at the end, rather than the middle, of a complete sentence should have four periods. Policies vary from news organization to news organization, and some journalists do not use ellipses in reporting ordinary interviews. Reporters are more likely to use them when quoting formal statements or documents.

Deleting Profanities

Reporters delete most profanities. Editors and news directors explain that children as well as adults read their newspapers and view their programs. Not only may profanities be inappropriate for children, but some adults also may find four-letter words offensive. News organizations are becoming more candid, however, and some publish mild profanities that are essential to a story. Casual profanities—those used habitually and unnecessarily by many people—remain forbidden in most newsrooms:

UNNECESSARY PROFANITY: "Shit, I wasn't going to try to stop that damned idiot," the witness testified. "He had a knife."

REVISED: "I wasn't going to try to stop that idiot," the witness testified. "He had a knife."

Editorialization

Avoid unintentional editorials. If worded carelessly, partial quotations, and even the form of attribution used, can express an opinion:

EDITORIALIZATION: The mayor made it clear that the city cannot afford to give its employees a raise.

REVISED: The mayor said the city cannot afford to give its employees a raise.

EDITORIALIZATION: Each month, Sen. William Proxmire presented the Golden Fleece Award "for the biggest, most ironic or most ridiculous example of wasteful government spending."

REVISED: Each month, Sen. William Proxmire presented the Golden Fleece Award for what he considered "the biggest, most ironic or most ridiculous example of wasteful government spending."

Before revision, the first sentence editorializes by saying the mayor "made it clear," which implies that she stated a fact in a convincing manner. Others might regard the statement that the city cannot afford pay raises for employees as an opinion or political posturing. The second sentence reports as fact the claim by Proxmire, who was a U.S. senator from Wisconsin, that all the recipients of his "award" wasted the government's money. Many of the recipients disagreed, and some provided convincing evidence that Proxmire was wrong.

ATTRIBUTION

The Purpose of Attribution

Reporters are experts in finding things out. They rarely possess expertise in the topics they write about, such as city planning, health care, finance or international relations. Instead, reporters must rely on the expertise of their sources. Attribution lets the readers know who the reporter's sources are. Ideally, all direct quotations, opinions, evaluations and secondhand statements of fact should be attributed to specific individuals. This information lets readers draw their own conclusions about the credibility of the story.

Reporters can attribute information to people, documents or publications, but not to places or institutions. For example, reporters can quote a hospital official, but not a hospital:

> INCORRECT: The hospital said the epidemic had ended.
> REVISED: A hospital spokesperson said the epidemic had ended.

> INCORRECT: Atlanta announced that all city offices would be closed next Monday.
> REVISED: The mayor of Atlanta announced that all city offices would be closed next Monday.

Statements That Require Attribution

Reporters do not have to attribute statements that report undisputed facts, such as the fact that World War II ended in 1945, that Boston is in Massachusetts or that three people died in an accident. Nor must reporters attribute things they witness. However, reporters must attribute the information they get from other people, especially: (1) statements about controversial issues, (2) statements of opinion and (3) all direct and indirect quotations. News stories that fail to attribute such statements appear to present the reporter's personal opinions rather than the opinions of the sources. Two or three words of attribution are usually adequate:

> UNATTRIBUTED: The Birthing Center is an alternative for pregnant women who prefer more personalized care.
> ATTRIBUTED: Director Sally Malone said the Birthing Center is an alternative for pregnant women who prefer more personalized care.

Reporters must attribute statements that criticize a person or organization. Readers should immediately recognize that a story reports what someone else said—not the reporter's opinions or those of the news organization:

> UNATTRIBUTED: Congress has failed to deal effectively with the problem of unemployment.
> ATTRIBUTED: The House Democratic leader said Congress has failed to deal effectively with the problem of unemployment.

News stories should also attribute statements that assign blame. For example:

> UNATTRIBUTED: Acting in self-defense, the deputy shot the teen three times in the chest.
> ATTRIBUTED: The deputy said she was acting in self-defense when she shot the teen three times in the chest.

Statements that imply carelessness or recklessness or culpable conduct can provoke lawsuits. Careful attribution, particularly if the statements can be attributed to official sources, will reduce the risk of being sued.

Guidelines for the Placement and Frequency of Attribution

Attribution may be placed at the beginning or end of a sentence, or at a natural break within it. However, it should never interrupt a thought:

> INCORRECT: "I shall," Gen. MacArthur said, "return."
> REVISED: Gen. MacArthur said, "I shall return."

> ACCEPTABLE: "Some men are killed in a war and some men are wounded," President Kennedy said, "and some men never leave the country. Life is unfair."

Readers and listeners should be told who is speaking as soon as conveniently possible; they should never have to guess. If a quotation is long, the writer should place the attribution at the beginning or end of the first sentence or after the first meaningful clause in that sentence. The attribution should not be delayed until the end of the second or third sentence. Similarly, if a quotation contains only one sentence, but that sentence is long, the attribution should come at or near the beginning of that sentence—not at the end:

> "However close we sometimes seem to that dark and final abyss, let no man of peace and freedom despair. For he does not stand alone. If we all can persevere, if we can in every land and office look beyond our shores and ambitions, then surely the age will dawn in which the strong are just and the weak secure and the peace preserved," the president said.
>
> REVISED: "However close we sometimes seem to that dark and final abyss," the president said, "let no man of peace and freedom despair. For he does not stand alone. If we all can persevere, if we can in every land and office look beyond our shores and ambitions, then surely the age will dawn in which the strong are just and the weak secure and the peace preserved."

Attribution should come at the beginning of any quotation where there is a change of speakers. If reporters fail to provide transitions from one speaker to another, particularly when the statements are contradictory, readers may not understand who is speaking:

> The newspaper's editor said he no longer will accept advertisements for X-rated movies. He explained: "These movies are worthless. They contribute nothing to society and offend our readers. They're depressing and pornographic."
>
> "Newspapers have no right to pass judgment on matters of taste. If they do, they should also ban the advertisements for other products considered harmful: cigarettes, liquor and pollutants like automobiles," a theater owner responded.

These two paragraphs are confusing. Readers beginning the second paragraph might mistakenly assume the editor has begun to contradict himself. The writer can avoid the confusion by placing a brief transition at the beginning of the second paragraph, such as the following: "However, a local theater owner responded, 'Newspapers have no right. . . .' "

Direct Quotations

A direct quotation should be attributed only once, regardless of the number of sentences it contains:

> INCORRECT: "I'm opposed to any laws that prohibit the sale of pornography," the attorney said. "The restriction of pornography infringes on Americans' First Amendment rights," he said. "I like to picture myself as a good guy defending a sleazy thing," he concluded.
>
> REVISED: "I'm opposed to any laws that prohibit the sale of pornography," the attorney said. "The restriction of pornography infringes on Americans' First Amendment rights. I like to picture myself as a good guy defending a sleazy thing."

Even when a direct quotation continues for several paragraphs, it needs attribution only once:

> Capt. Bonventre eliminated the Police Department's motorcycle squad.
>
> "The main reason is that there are more injuries to motorcycle officers," he said. "I want to protect my officers. They think there's no danger on a cycle. Well, that's just optimistic thinking; there's a real danger.
>
> "Officers have much more protection in a car. I think that's pretty obvious. If an officer gets in a hot pursuit and crashes, he stands a better chance of escaping injury when he's in a car.
>
> "Also, almost any situation, even traffic, can be handled better in a patrol car than on a motorcycle. There are some places a motorcycle can go more easily, but a car certainly commands more respect."

Reporters also must avoid "floating" quotations: direct quotations that lack clear attribution to a speaker. Direct quotations need attribution only once, but that attribution must be clearly attached to the quotation. Careless writers sometimes name a source in one sentence and then deliver an unattributed quotation in the following sentence or paragraph. The reader then must figure out whether the quotation comes from the person just named or someone who will be identified later. The uncertainty halts the reader. Several such delays can cause the reader to put down the newspaper. Clear attribution makes the reader's work easier:

> INCORRECT: Wendy Mitchell, a sociologist, said there is a trend toward vocationalism on college campuses.
>
> "Many students now demand from college not a chance to think, but a chance to become qualified for some job."
>
> REVISED: Wendy Mitchell, a sociologist, said there is a trend toward vocationalism on college campuses.
>
> "Many students now demand from college not a chance to think," she said, "but a chance to become qualified for some job."

Another confusing practice is reporting a quotation and then attributing it in the following paragraph:

> INCORRECT: "I was scared to death. I knew I was hurt, and I needed help."
>
> These were the words today of an 18-year-old student trapped in her wrecked car.
>
> REVISED: "I was scared to death," said an 18-year-old student who had been trapped in her wrecked car. "I knew I was hurt, and I needed help."

Partial Quotations

On the rare occasions when writers quote part of a sentence, they take care to separate it from complete sentences that are also being quoted. Combining partial and complete quotations sometimes causes confusing pronoun shifts, which can be avoided by (1) placing attribution between the partial quotation and the full-sentence quotation or (2) paraphrasing the partial quotation:

> INCORRECT: Ross said he expects to find a job "within a few weeks. And when I do get a job, the first thing I'm going to buy is a new car."
>
> ACCEPTABLE: Ross said he expects to find a job "within a few weeks." He added, "And when I do get a job, the first thing I'm going to buy is a new car."
>
> BETTER: Ross said he expects to find a job within a few weeks. "And when I do get a job, the first thing I'm going to buy is a new car," he added.

The original passage is confusing because of a shift in pronouns. The first sentence uses the third person, referring to Ross as "he." But in the second sentence, which is the full quotation, Ross refers to himself in the first person. Rewriting the partial quotation eliminates the confusion.

Indirect Quotations

Indirect quotations (or paraphrases) need more frequent attribution than direct quotations. Every opinion or unverified fact in an indirect quotation—sometimes every sentence—must be attributed:

> INCORRECT: The police chief insisted that the death penalty must be retained. The death penalty, harsh as it may seem, is designed to protect the lives and rights of law-abiding citizens. Without it, criminals' rights are overly protected. Because of the almost endless mechanisms of the appeal system, it is unlikely that an innocent person would be put to death.
>
> REVISED: The police chief insisted that the death penalty must be retained. The death penalty might seem harsh, he said, but it is designed to protect the lives and rights of law-abiding citizens. Without it, criminals' rights are overly protected, he said. Because of the almost endless mechanisms of the appeal system, he said, it is unlikely that an innocent person would be put to death.

If the police chief's remarks have been paraphrased, the reporter cannot attribute them by placing the paragraph within quotation marks because it does not contain the police chief's own words. Similarly, editors cannot convert an indirect quotation written by a reporter into a direct quotation. However, editors can take a statement out of quotation marks and reword it, provided they do not change its meaning.

While every sentence of indirect quotation should have attribution, writers should avoid inserting phrases that may attribute a quotation twice. For example, the following sentence reports that a fire chief made an announcement, then adds that he "said":

> INCORRECT: In making the announcement, the fire chief said arsonists caused 20 percent of the blazes reported in the city last year.
>
> REVISED: The fire chief said arsonists caused 20 percent of the blazes reported in the city last year.

Whether reporting direct or indirect quotations, the writer should strive to vary the location of the attribution. Writing becomes dull if every sentence begins with "she said" or some variation. Moving the attribution to the end or middle of the sentence keeps writing interesting. Often the most effective location for attribution is after the first natural pause in the sentence.

Word Choice in Attributing Statements

The verbs used to attribute statements must be accurate and impartial. For straight news stories, they also should be in the past tense. For feature stories, present tense attribution may be acceptable.

Some form of the verb "to say" best describes how sources communicate information. For variety, reporters sometimes use such verbs as "comment," "reply," "declare," "add," "explain," "state," "continue," "point out," "note," "urge," "suggest" and "warn." Each has a more specific meaning than "say" and can be used only when that meaning accurately reflects how the source spoke. "Explain," for instance, means to make something comprehensible or less obscure. Unless the source was discussing a complicated or unclear topic, "explain" would not be an appropriate verb for attribution:

> UNACCEPTABLE: The city council meeting will begin at 8 p.m., he explained.
>
> ACCEPTABLE: She explained that tort law requires that the injurious consequences of a person's actions be foreseeable before that person can be held liable for damages.

The statement in the first sentence is obvious and needs no explanation; the most appropriate verb of attribution is "said." In the second example, the source talks about a point of law that may be confusing or unclear to the average reader. The source's explanation increases understanding of the issue.

Many editors object to the use of verbs such as "hope," "feel," "believe," "want" and "think." Editors say reporters know only what their sources tell them, not what those sources hope, feel, believe, want or think.

Other words are even more inappropriate. People speak words—they do not "grin," "smile," "chuckle," "laugh," "sigh" or "cough" them. Reporters should rephrase such sentences as this:

> "It's a wonderful movie," she smiled.
>
> REVISED: "It's a wonderful movie," she said.
>
> OR: "It's a wonderful movie," she said with a smile.
>
> OR: Smiling, she said, "It's a wonderful movie."

The words "claimed" and "admitted" are especially troublesome. The word "claimed" casts doubt on a source's remarks. It suggests that the remarks are controversial and possibly wrong. Similarly, the word "admitted" implies that a source conceded some point or confessed to an error, charge or crime. By comparison, the word "said" is almost always appropriate. It may sound awkward at first, but "said" is a neutral term and can be used any number of times in a story.

Attribution should also be concise. Each of the following phrases (which have actually appeared in news stories) can be replaced by either "said" or "added":

made it clear that	said that he feels that
further stated that	brought out the idea that
went on to say that	went on to say that in his opinion
let it be known that	in making the announcement said that
also pointed out that	continued the speech by urging that
emphasized the fact that	responded to the question by saying that
stated in the report that	concluded the speech with the comment that

Levels of Attribution

Ideally, every source should be fully identified, but sometimes sources want their identities withheld. Experienced reporters and sources have worked out a shorthand for describing how much of the source's identity may be revealed and how much of what the source says may be published. This shorthand system recognizes four levels of attribution: on the record, on background, on deep background and off the record.

On the record attribution means that everything the source says may be published and quoted directly, and the source may be fully identified by name and title. Reporters should try to keep as much as possible of every interview on the record. This allows readers to see or hear the source's exact words and know who the source is.

On background, which is sometimes referred to as *not for attribution,* means the reporter may quote the source directly but may not attribute the statements to the source by name. The reporter may describe the source by her or his position. Patrick E. Tyler of The New York Times used on-background sources for a story exposing U.S. military assistance to Iraq during its war against Iran. Tyler reported the United States had covertly provided intelligence and battle plans to Iraq even though U.S. officials knew Saddam Hussein was using chemical weapons against both Iranian troops and civilian rebels inside Iraq. Much of Tyler's story was attributed to "senior military officers with direct knowledge of the program" or "former Defense Intelligence Agency officers" who were willing to talk only on the condition that they not be identified. When reporters use on-background information, they try to describe the source as fully as possible. To say the information came from "a government employee" is meaningless. Saying the source is "an aide to the speaker of the House" gives readers more information. Sources often will try to keep the identification as vague as possible; reporters try to make it as specific as possible.

On deep background is a variation of the backgrounder. This level of attribution is sometimes called the Lindley Rule, named after Ernest K. Lindley, a Newsweek reporter who used it to get U.S. military leaders to talk about their strategy and objectives during World War II. A source on deep background may not be quoted directly and may not be identified in any way. A reporter must publish the information without any attribution or with a phrase like, "It has been learned that. . . ." Unless reporters have a high degree of confidence in the source and the information—and the approval of their supervisors—they should stay away from information given on deep background.

Off the record is the final level of attribution. It generally means a source's information cannot be used, but that is often misunderstood. Some people say they are speaking off the record when they really mean they are speaking on background. Also, reporters and sources sometimes disagree as to exactly what "off the record" means. The U.S. State Department's Office of Press Relations says reporters may not use "off the record" information in any way. Reporters, however, sometimes use off-the-record information as leads to other sources. Almost every "secret" is known by several people, sometimes hundreds of people. Once reporters know what they are looking for, they usually can locate public records or sources who can verify the information on the record or on background. Some reporters refuse to listen to off-the-record statements. If one cannot publish or broadcast the information, why listen to it? Others see it as an opportunity to gain insight into official thinking. Or it may help them put the information they can publish in a more accurate context.

Anonymous Sources

If reporters want sources on the record, why do so many stories use anonymous sources? Sometimes sources want to remain anonymous for legitimate reasons. (See the box on this page for guidelines on when to use anonymous sources.) Corporate or government officials who want to blow the whistle on waste, fraud or other illegal or unethical conduct at their workplace may fear retaliation. Many have lost jobs or been demoted because they disclosed truths that made their supervisors uncomfortable.

The Seattle Times made effective use of anonymous sources when it published a story saying U.S. Sen. Brock Adams had sexually harassed several women over a period of 20 years. The investigation began after Kari Tupper, a congressional aide, publicly accused Adams of having drugged and molested her. Although Tupper took her story to prosecutors, no charges were brought because the federal district attorney concluded the case had no merit. The Times, however, started getting phone calls from women who reported similar experiences with Adams but did not want to be publicly identified. Eventually, the Times agreed to publish a story detailing the women's charges so long as the accusers signed affidavits and promised to come for-

GUIDELINES FOR USING ANONYMOUS SOURCES

Editors are becoming more reluctant to use anonymous sources. Journalism critics say reporters can get more information on the record by threatening to ignore all information from sources who demand anonymity. If some sources insist on remaining anonymous, reporters might seek the same information from other sources who are willing to be identified. On the rare occasions when justification exists for using anonymous sources, news directors and editors tell their reporters to follow guidelines like these:

1. Do not use anonymous sources without the approval of your supervising editor or news director.
2. Be prepared to disclose the identities of anonymous sources to your editors or news directors and, possibly, to your news organization's lawyer.
3. Use anonymous sources only if they provide facts that are essential to the story, not just interesting quotations or opinions. Be sure the source is appropriate for the story and that she or he is in a position to give authoritative information. Even then, information from anonymous sources should be verified.
4. Be sure you understand the motives of the anonymous source, such as whether the source is carrying a grudge or trying to puff a program or an agency. The motives help you evaluate the reliability of the information.
5. Identify sources as specifically as possible without revealing their identities so that readers can judge their importance and reliability. For example, instead of attributing information to "an informed source" or "a key official," you might attribute it to "an elected city official." This tells the reader the level of government in which the official works and alerts the reader to the fact that the official may have political interests. Never include any misleading information about the identity of a source, even if your motive is to protect the source.
6. Explain in the story why the source does not want to be identified.
7. Never allow a source to engage in anonymous attacks on other individuals or groups. Anonymous attacks risk involving you and your employer in a libel suit and are inherently unfair to the person attacked.

ward if Adams sued the Times for libel. Adams abandoned his re-election campaign but denied the sexual harassment charges.

Anonymous sources often pose threats to the independence, accuracy and credibility of journalists. Benjamin Bradlee, the former executive editor of The Washington Post, deplored the continued abuse of unattributed information and said: "Why, then, do we go along so complacently with withholding the identity of public officials? I'm damned if I know. I do know that by doing so, we shamelessly do other people's bidding: We knowingly let ourselves be used. . . . In short, we demean our profession."

Anonymous sources often try to influence the way journalists cover the news. In Washington, high-level government sources often demand that their briefings be on background or on deep background. The officials use these briefings to place administration policy in the best possible light. They think they can do that most effectively when their identities and their political motives are hidden from the general public. Reporters abide by the background rules officials set because of the competitive pressures they face to get the story.

Anonymous sources also may provide inaccurate information. Whether they do so intentionally, their anonymity protects them from the consequences of their mistakes. The same is not true of the news organizations that publish the information. Several newspapers that covered the inmate riots at the Southern Ohio Correctional Facility at Lucasville received inaccurate information from anonymous sources. For instance, the Cleveland Plain Dealer said 19 had been killed in the riots, and the Portsmouth (Ohio) Daily Times said between 50 and 150 were dead. Both newspapers relied on unidentified sources, and both were wrong. In fact, nine inmates and one guard died in the riots.

A final problem with anonymous sources is that under some circumstances a promise to keep a source's identity secret can be enforced in court. The U.S. Supreme Court has ruled that a source whose identity is revealed after confidentiality was promised may sue for damages. The court said the law protects people who are injured when they rely on an explicit promise and that promise is broken. That law applies to everybody, the court said, including news organizations.

GUIDELINES FOR CAPITALIZING AND PUNCTUATING QUOTATIONS

The Use of Quotation Marks

Use double quotation marks to set off quotations. Only the quotation—never the attribution—should appear within the quotation marks:

> INCORRECT: "The motorcycle slid sideways and skidded about 100 feet, she said. The driver was killed."
>
> REVISED: "The motorcycle slid sideways and skidded about 100 feet," she said. "The driver was killed."

If a quotation continues for several sentences, all the sentences should be enclosed within a single set of quotation marks; quotation marks do not have to be placed at the beginning and end of each sentence in the quotation:

> INCORRECT: She said: "I did not see the car when I stepped out onto the street." "But when I saw the headlights coming at me, I knew it was going to hit me."
>
> REVISED: She said: "I did not see the car when I stepped out onto the street. But when I saw the headlights coming at me, I knew it was going to hit me."

Like any other part of a news story, a long quotation should be divided into short paragraphs to make it easier to read. New paragraphs should begin at natural breaks in the quotation, usually at changes in topic, however slight. Place quotation marks at the beginning of a long quotation and at the start of each new paragraph. Place closing quotation marks only at the end of the entire quotation, not at the end of every paragraph:

The senator added: "Perhaps the most shocking example of the insensitivity of the Bureau of Indian Affairs' educational system is the manner in which boarding school dormitories have been administered.

"Psychiatrists familiar with the problems of Indian children have told us that a properly run dormitory system is the most crucial aspect of boarding school life, particularly in elementary schools.

"Yet, when a 6-year-old Navajo child enters one of the boarding schools and becomes lonely or homesick, he must seek comfort from an instructional aide who has no training in child guidance and who is responsible for as many as 100 other unhappy children.

"The aide spends most of his time performing custodial chores. At night, the situation worsens as the ratio of dorm aides to children decreases."

When a quotation includes another quotation, use double quotation marks to identify the overall quotation and single quotation marks (or an apostrophe on the keyboard) to indicate the quotation within the quotation:

During the 1960 presidential campaign, Republicans were accusing John F. Kennedy of using his family's wealth to buy the election. Kennedy joked, "I got a wire from my father that said: 'Dear Jack, Don't buy one vote more than necessary. I'll be damned if I'll pay for a landslide.'"

If the passage has a quotation within a quotation within a quotation, use double quotation marks to indicate the third level of quotation, as in this example:

The senator said, "I had a voter tell me, 'I'm fed up with tax cheats. They get away with "murder."' And I had to agree with her."

Other Punctuation

If the attribution comes before a quotation that contains just one full sentence, a comma should follow the attribution. If the attribution precedes a quotation that contains two or more sentences, it should be followed by a colon. Do not use a period after attribution that comes before the quotation:

CORRECT: James Thurber said, "It is better to know some of the questions than all of the answers."

CORRECT: Mark Twain said: "I apologize for writing a long letter. If I'd had more time, I'd have written a shorter one."

INCORRECT: The council member said. "We need to raise the speed limit."

REVISED: The council member said, "We need to raise the speed limit."

When reporters place the attribution after a quotation, they use a comma—not a period—at the end of the quotation and place a period after the attribution to punctuate the entire sentence:

INCORRECT: "I'm feeling better." she said.

REVISED: "I'm feeling better," she said.

The comma or period at the end of the quotation should always be placed inside the quotation marks. This rule has no exceptions. Colons and semicolons should be outside the quotation marks. Whether a question mark or an exclamation point should appear inside or outside the quotation marks depends on the meaning. If the quotation is a question or exclamation, put the question mark or exclamation point inside the quotation marks. Otherwise, leave it outside the quotation marks:

CORRECT: The senator asked, "How much will the program cost?"

INCORRECT: Why did you say, "It's time to leave?"

REVISED: Why did you say, "It's time to leave"?

Capitalization

The first word in a quotation that is a complete sentence is capitalized, but the first word in a partial quotation is not:

INCORRECT: He said, "life is just one damned thing after another."
REVISED: He said, "Life is just one damned thing after another."

INCORRECT: He called journalism "Literature in a hurry."
REVISED: He called journalism "literature in a hurry."

Word Order for Attribution

Journalists put the name of or pronoun for the speaker and the verb of attribution in their normal order, with the subject appearing before the verb. That is the way people talk, and it is usually the most graceful way to write:

INCORRECT: Said Ronald Reagan, "I've noticed that everybody who's for abortion has already been born."

REVISED: Ronald Reagan said, "I've noticed that everybody who's for abortion has already been born."

INCORRECT: "Hard work is good for you," insisted the executive. "Nobody ever drowned in sweat."

REVISED: "Hard work is good for you," the executive insisted. "Nobody ever drowned in sweat."

However, if you place a long identifying or descriptive phrase after the name of the speaker, the normal word order may be awkward. In that case, place the verb first and the subject second:

AWKWARD: "It will cost $2 million," Smith, a 29-year-old architect employed by the California firm, said.

REVISED: "It will cost $2 million," said Smith, a 29-year-old architect employed by the California firm.

CHECKLISTS FOR QUOTATIONS AND ATTRIBUTION

Quotations

1. Use quotations sparingly—to emphasize a point or change pace rather than to tell the entire story.
2. Place only the exact words of the source within quotation marks.
3. Each quotation should serve a purpose, such as reveal the source's character, describe or emphasize a point or present additional details.
4. All direct quotations should be clear, concise, relevant and effective.
5. Avoid awkward combinations of partial and complete quotations.
6. Report only the source's answers, not the questions you asked.
7. Eliminate orphan quotations and floating quotations.
8. Make sure the quotations do not repeat facts reported elsewhere in the story.
9. For a one-paragraph quotation that includes two or more sentences, place the quotation marks only at the beginning and end of the entire quotation, not at the beginning and end of each sentence.
10. Capitalize the first letter of all quotations that are full sentences but not of partial quotations.
11. Divide long quotations into shorter paragraphs; place quotation marks at the beginning of each paragraph, but at the end of only the final paragraph.
12. Use single quotation marks for quotations that appear within other quotations.

Attribution

1. Attribute all second-hand information, criticisms, statements about controversial issues, opinions and all direct and indirect quotations. (Do not attribute undisputed facts.)
2. Punctuate the attribution properly. Put a comma after attribution introducing a one-sentence quotation and a colon after attribution introducing two or more sentences of quotation.
3. Put the attribution at or near the beginning of a long quotation.
4. Attribution that appears in the middle of a sentence should come at a natural break rather than interrupt a thought.
5. Vary sentences and paragraphs so that all do not begin with attribution.
6. Place the attribution outside the quotation marks.
7. Attribute each direct quotation only once.
8. Attribute each separate statement of opinion in indirect quotations.
9. Attribute statements only to people, documents or publications, never to places or institutions.
10. Provide transitions between statements from different sources, particularly when a quotation from one source immediately follows a quotation from a different source.
11. Select the verb of attribution that most accurately describes the source's actual meaning and behavior.
12. Do not use such verbs as "hope," "feel," "believe," "think," "laugh," "cough" and "cry" for attribution.
13. Make the attribution as concise as possible.

A Memo From the Editor

DESCRIPTIVE WRITING: TURNING A GOOD STORY INTO A GREAT STORY

By **Tommy Miller**

Good writing has four basic elements: dialogue, background, observation and description.

Dialogue is traditional in journalistic writing, reporting what people say, either indirectly or with direct quotations. Background information provides perspective and context for a story. It pushes the past into the future. Observation conveys what a reporter perceives in the moment. Good observation leads to good description.

Unfortunately, good description is too often overlooked in journalistic writing. This limits writing, because it is description that lifts a story beyond the ordinary.

Most of what I've learned about description comes from David McHam, my former journalism professor at Baylor University who now teaches at the University of Houston. Much of what I've put together here is drawn from his unpublished manuscript "Notes on Writing."

I've also learned about description by reading good descriptive writing. McHam taught me that, too!

Description, more than other basic elements of good writing, challenges the writer's creative skills. Sensory images of quantities, colors, sounds, occasions and settings are descriptive. These perceptual associations help make reading a vicarious experience.

Journalistic writers should take full advantage of all literary and artistic techniques available to them. Too much writing is flat and poorly developed.

Newspaper writing is often produced under urgent deadline pressure, which tends to curtail creativity. But when deadlines aren't a factor, writers may nonetheless be tempted to take shortcuts, use clichés, or rely on cuteness instead of focusing on expressive descriptive writing.

Here are some reasons why writers fall short on description:

- They have not trained themselves to observe, to concentrate carefully on the events or people they are writing about.
- They have not worked at building a vocabulary for description.
- They have not worked at deciding when to use description, how much to use, and where to use it.
- They have not read enough.
- They have not thought enough about imagery, metaphors, timing and pacing.

While occasional stories won't benefit from any description at all, most do. Good description is needed in both long and short stories. Description often can be just a word, or just a sentence, properly placed to give even a three-paragraph story a special touch.

Here are some guidelines for getting good description in your stories:

PRACTICE OBSERVATION. PRACTICE DESCRIPTION. CONCENTRATE ON OBSERVING PEOPLE OR EVENTS.

In his "Monologue to the Maestro" in "By-Line Hemingway" (1967), Ernest Hemingway described how to get good description. The setting for the story was a deep-sea fishing trip and a young writer asked how he could train himself to write description. Hemingway said:

> Watch what happens today. If we get into a fish see exactly what it is that everyone does. If you get a kick out of it while he is jumping remember back until you see exactly what the action was that gave you that emotion. . . . Remember what the noises were and what was said. Find what gave you the emotion; what the action was that gave you the excitement. Then write it down making it clear so the reader will see it too and have the same feeling that you had.

WORK AT FINDING OUT WHAT THINGS ARE, SPECIFICALLY.

Don't write that the patient was rolled into his room on a hospital bed. Use a more specific, descriptive word—gurney. If you don't know what something is, find out.

Be selective and careful about which words to use and which words not to use. Be careful about which words stand alone and which words may need explanation. Words that require no explanation are within the reader's experience.

But infrequently used words like veranda, gargoyle, sluice, trotline, and cotter pin may be outside the realm of ordinary experience. They may need some explanation so that the reader can visualize them. For example: Small children's eyes widen and their steps slow as they spot the sleeping gargoyles atop columns guarding the entrance to the reptile house. *These gargoyles are sculptures of mythical stone reptiles that seem to have escaped from the pages of Maurice Sendak's book of wild things.*

(*continued*)

READ AND THINK ABOUT THE USE OF IMAGERY AND METAPHORS.

Be alert to fresh, powerful descriptive phrases in others' writing, not to recycle cliches but to stimulate creative thinking. Reading a phrase like "black-and-gray tabby-striped clouds shot through with lightning" broadens one's ability to think about the unique qualities different rain clouds can have (from an unpublished journal, 2003, by Leah Quin, Peace Corps volunteer and former Austin American-Statesman reporter).

BE SPECIFIC. BUT BE CAREFUL ABOUT BEING JUDGMENTAL.

Description, by its nature, will require some judgment by the writer. But emphasis on precise, explicit description will lessen the danger of subjectivity. For example, don't write: He had an ugly scar on his face. Describe the scar more specifically, such as. . . . He had a 3-inch, bulging scar down the side of his right cheek. (Remember the show me, don't tell me rule.)

REMEMBER THAT DESCRIPTION AND DIALOGUE CAN MIX EFFECTIVELY.

Often, people can describe events or scenes better than the writer can. Ask news sources to describe what happen. Don't ask, for example, "Mrs. Jones, how did it feel when the gunman forced you and your son into the car and told you to drive to Los Angeles?" Instead, ask: "Mrs. Jones, would you describe what happened when the gunman told you and your son to get in the car?"

REMEMBER THAT DETAILS LEAD TO GOOD DESCRIPTION.

This description of a professional baseball pitcher preparing for a game is an excellent example of how specific details paint a picture for readers.

From "Hats Off to You, Nolan Ryan," Bruce Newman, Sports Illustrated:

> The sun was still high above Disneyland's Space Mountain last Friday, tracking steadily across the sky toward Sleeping Beauty's Castle, when Nolan Ryan, about to face the New York Yankees, took a surgeon's scalpel from his locker in Anaheim stadium and began to whittle away at the fingers on his right hand. In the cool of the California Angels' clubhouse, Ryan went about his work slowly, drawing the blade painstakingly down each of the fingers as if he were peeling grapes. With each stroke the knife shaved away a layer of the pitcher's skin, removing his fingerprints, as if Ryan were a thief determined to leave no clues behind. Having prepared himself this way, Ryan knew that a baseball clutched in his right hand would feel as smooth as a bullet. And bullets are what the Yankees would see.

Adapted from "Good Writing's Great, But It's Not Enough," published in September 1988, in The Write Stuff, an in-house publication of the Houston Chronicle.

Tommy Miller holds the Roger Tatarian Endowed Chair of Professional Journalism at California State University, Fresno. He is a former managing editor of the Houston Chronicle.

SUGGESTED READINGS

Clark, Roy Peter, and Christopher Scanlan, eds. *America's Best Newspaper Writing: A Collection of ASNE Prizewinners*. Boston: Bedford/St. Martin's, 2001.

Kovach, Bill, and Tom Rosenstiel. *The Elements of Journalism: What Newspeople Should Know and the Public Should Expect*. New York: Three Rivers Press, 2001.

Wicker, Tom. *On the Record: An Insider's Guide to Journalism*. Boston: Bedford/St. Martin's, 2002.

USEFUL WEB SITES

American Society of Newspaper Editors: http://www.asne.org
The Journalist's Toolbox: http://www.journaliststoolbox.com/newswriting/onlineindex.html
The Power of Words: http://www.projo.com/words/past.htm
The Poynter Institute: http://www.poynter.org
Society of Professional Journalists: http://www.spj.org

EXERCISE 1

QUOTATIONS AND ATTRIBUTION

IMPROVING QUOTATIONS AND ATTRIBUTION

SECTION I: AVOIDING DOUBLE ATTRIBUTION

Rewrite the following sentences, attributing them only once. Correct any other errors.

1. A report issued Tuesday by the U.S. Department of Justice said the number of serious crimes committed in the United States declined 3% last year.
2. Speaking to more than 3,000 people in the Municipal Auditorium, she continued by stating that only the Democratic Party favors universal health care.
3. The Census Bureau issued a report today stating that, according to data it gathered last year, 5.2 million people in the U.S. are homeless, including 620,000 children.

SECTION II: CORRECTING PLACEMENT ERRORS

Correct the placement of the attribution in the following sentences. Correct any other errors.

1. People under 18, she said, should not be allowed to drive.
2. Another important step is to, she said, lower the books prices.
3. "The average shoplifters are teenage girls who steal for the thrill of it, and housewives who steal items they can use. They don't have to steal; most have plenty of money, but they don't think its a crime. They also think they'll get away with it forever," Valderrama said.

SECTION III: CONDENSING WORDY ATTRIBUTION

The attributions in the following sentences are too wordy. They appear in italics and contain a total of 76 words. How many of the words can you eliminate? Rewrite the attribution, if necessary. Correct any other errors.

1. *She concluded her speech by telling the scouts that* the jamboree will be held August 7-13.

2. *He was quick to point out the fact that, in his opinion,* the president has "failed to act effectively to reduce the federal deficit."
3. *She expressed her feelings by explaining that she believes that* all those convicted of drunk driving should lose their licenses for life.
4. *She also went on to point out the fact that the results of federal studies show that,* by recycling 1 ton of paper, you can save 17 trees.
5. *In a speech to the students Tuesday, he first began by offering them his opinion that* their professors should emphasize teaching, not research.
6. *He continued by urging his listeners to remember the critical point that* the countrys energy policy has failed: that the U.S. is not developing alternative fuels, nor conserving existing fuels.

SECTION IV: IMPROVING ATTRIBUTION

Correct all the problems in the following attributions and quotations and any other errors.

1. He said: "after a certain number of years, our faces become our biographies".
2. Andy Rooney declared "if dogs could talk, it would take a lot of fun out of owning one".
3. "Because that's where the money is" Willie Sutton answered when asked why he robbed banks.
4. He continued by claiming that there are "two" types of people who complain about their taxes: "men" and "women."
5. "Blessed is he" said W. C. Bennett "who expects no gratitude, for he shall not be disappointed". explained Bennett.
6. Mother Teresa then spoke to the youths, telling them that. "The most terrible poverty is loneliness and the feeling of being unwanted."
7. "My views on birth control" said Robert F. Kennedy "Are somewhat distorted by the fact that I was the seventh of nine children".

8. Being a police officer is not always fun and exciting, says Griffith. “Some things you’d just as soon forget.” “Some things you do forget.”
9. “The art of taxation.” claimed a French statesman long ago “Consists in so plucking the goose as to obtain the most feathers with the least hissing”.
10. Dr. Hector Rivera said they test for AIDS at the clinic “but do not treat the disease.” “People come in to be tested scared to death.” “Some leave the clinic relieved, and some don’t.” he said.
11. Her friendships, home, and family are the most important things in her life. “My husband is my best friend.” “Maybe that’s why we’ve lasted so long.” “You really need to be friends before you’re lovers”.
12. “I cheat because professors give too much work.” It’s crazy, he said. “They don’t take into consideration that some people have jobs, families and other outside interests.” continued the history major. He then continued by adding that he’s never been caught.
13. “My son thinks I’m old.” “But I’m actually in good health for my age.” “Of course, I have the usual aches and pains of an 80-year-old.” “But I can still take care of my own house, and I still enjoy it.” “My son thinks I should move into one of those retirement apartments and watch Wheel of Fortune all day.” said he.
14. Jo Ann Nyez, a secretary, grew up in Milwaukee and described a childhood fear: There was this house at the end of my street and none of us would dare go near it on Halloween. It was supposed to be haunted. The story was that the wife had hung herself in the basement and the husband killed and ate rattlesnakes.

EXERCISE 2

QUOTATIONS AND ATTRIBUTION

WORDING, PLACEMENT AND PUNCTUATION

Make any changes necessary to improve the attribution in the following sentences and paragraphs. Also correct style, spelling and punctuation errors. Answer Key Provided: See Appendix D.

1. "Our goal is peace". claimed the president.
2. Benjamin Franklin said: "death takes no bribes".
3. She said her son refers to her literary endeavors as, "moms writing thing".
4. He is a scuba diver and pilot. He also enjoys skydiving. "I like challenge, something exciting."
5. "The dangers promise to be of indefinite duration." the president said referring to the Mideast crisis.
6. "Freedom of the press is not merely freedom to publish news." "It is also freedom to gather the news. We cannot publish what we cannot gather." said columnist Jack Anderson during a speech last night.
7. Jesse Owens expressed the opinion that "I think that America has become too athletic." "From Little League to the pro leagues, sports are no longer recreation." "They are big business, and they're drudgery." he continued.
8. The man smiled, "It's a great deal for me." "I expect to double my money," he explained.
9. When asked what she likes most about her job as a newspaper reporter, the woman responded by saying—"I'm not paid much, but the work is important. And it's varied and exciting." She grinned: "Also, I like seeing my byline in the paper."
10. The librarian announced to reporters that the new building "will cost somewhere in the neighborhood of about $4.6 million."

11. "Thousands of the poor in the United States," said the professor, "die every year of diseases we can easily cure." "It's a crime," he said, "but no one ever is punished for their deaths."
12. Thomas said students should never be spanked. "A young boy or girl who gets spanked in front of peers becomes embarrassed and the object of ridicule."
13. The lawyer said, "He ripped the life-sustaining respirator tubes from his throat three times in an effort to die. He is simply a man" the lawyer continued "who rejects medical treatment regardless of the consequences. He wants to die and has a constitutional right to do so."
14. Bobby Knight, the basketball coach at Texas Tech University, said. "Everyone has the will to win." "Few have the will to prepare." Knight added that. "It is the preparation that counts."
15. She said she firmly believes that the federal government "must do more" to help cities "support and retrain" the chronically unemployed.

EXERCISE 3

QUOTATIONS AND ATTRIBUTION

USING QUOTES IN NEWS STORIES

Write complete news stories based on the following information. Use some quotations in each story to emphasize its highlights, but do not use quotations to tell the entire story. Use the most interesting, important and revealing quotations, not just those that happen to appear first.

1. Carlos Vacante is a police officer who has worked 3 years for your city's police department. Last night he had an unusual experience. This is his story, as he told it to you in an interview today: "I remember his eyes. They were cold, the eyes of a killer. He was pointing a gun at me, and it fired. I smelled the gunpowder and waited for the pain. I thought I was dead. The whole thing had started at about 11 p.m. This man was suspected of stealing from parked cars, and I'd gotten his description by radio. Then I spotted him in a parking lot. This morning we learned he's wanted in the robbery and murder of a service station attendant in Tennessee. There's no doubt in my mind he wanted to kill me last night just because I stopped him. I was an object in his way. I'd gotten out of my car and called to him. He started turning around and I spotted a handgun in his waistband. As he drew the gun and fired, I leaned to the right and dropped to one knee. It was just a reflex that saved my life. When I heard the shot, I thought he hit me. I couldn't believe it was actually happening to me. I thought I was going to cash everything in. Then I was running—zig-zagging—behind some cars. He fired another shot, but my backup arrived, and he fled. Maybe 60 seconds had passed from the time I spotted him. Five minutes later, we found him at the back door to a house, trying to break in and hide. I ordered him to stop, and he put his hands up and said, 'You got me.' I still smell the gunpowder this morning. I thought I was dead."

2. The city's Ministerial Alliance spoke out today against the death penalty. A copy of a resolution it adopted will be sent to the governor and to every member of the state legislature. As its spokesman, the Rev. Stuart Adler declared: "None of us is soft on crime. There must be just punishment for those who commit violent crimes, but what we are saying is we stop short of taking another persons life. We object because several independent studies have concluded that the death penalty is no deterrent to crime, rather the violence of the death penalty only breeds more violence. Also, the method of sentencing people is inconsistent. There is a great disparity between the victim being black or white. Defendants accused of killing black victims often are not sentenced to death, but when the victim is white, the death penalty is often imposed. People are frightened by the amount of violence in our society, and they've been sold a bill of goods. They've been told that the death penalty is a deterrent, and yet every major study disproves that reality. We're not getting at the deeper causes. We're a violent society, and getting more violent. Half the households in this city have guns, and its inevitable some are going to use them. If we're really serious about stopping crime and violence, we have to recognize and correct its root causes: poverty, racial and sexual discrimination, broken homes and unloved children. Also drugs and alcohol. That's what's responsible for most crimes. And television. Studies show the average child in America witnesses, on television,

200,000 acts of violence by age 16. So we're against the death penalty. Its not going to solve our problems, and its not fair, not fairly applied. It'll take time, but we intend to abolish it, and we'll persist. We're already beginning to stimulate discussion, and we expect that discussion to spread."

3. A rise in insurance rates is being blamed for a rise in hit-and-run motor vehicle accidents within the state. Richard Byrum, state insurance commissioner, discussed the problem during a press conference in his office today. He said, "The problem is serious. At first, we thought it was a police problem, but police in the state have asked my office to look into it. There has been a dramatic increase in hit-and-run accidents in the state, particularly in big cities where you find the higher insurance rates. I'm told that last year we had nearly 28,000 motor vehicle accidents in the state, and 4,500 were hit-and-run. People are taking chances driving without proper insurance coverage, or they're afraid of a premium increase if they have insurance and stop and report an accident. They seem to think, 'What the heck, no one saw it, and I won't get caught,' and they just bug out of there. If you look at the insurance rates in the state, its practically impossible for some people to pay them, and as insurance rates go up, the rate of leaving the scene of an accident increases. Drivers with the worst records—those with several accidents and traffic citations—pay as much as $3,600 a year in insurance premiums, and they may pay even more than that if they are young or have a high-powered car. Even good drivers found at fault in an accident may find their rates going up several hundred dollars for the next three to five years. So leaving the scene of an accident is definitely tied to the economic situation, yet the insurance company people I've talked to say they can't do anything about it. Its just not realistic to expect them to lower their rates; they aren't making that much money. Right now, I'm not sure what we'll do about the situation. In the meantime, we can expect more hit-and-run accidents and more drivers going without any insurance coverage because of its high cost."

EXERCISE 4

QUOTATIONS AND ATTRIBUTION

USING QUOTES IN NEWS STORIES

Write complete news stories based on the following information. Use some quotations in each story to emphasize its highlights, but do not use quotations to tell the entire story. Use the most interesting, important and revealing quotations, not just those that happen to appear first.

1. Michael Ernest Layoux, 22, is a clerk at a convenience store at 1284 East Forest Boulevard. He was robbed late yesterday. Here is his account of the incident: "First, you have to understand where the store is. Its located in a remote area in the northeast corner of town. There's nothing around that's open at night, so I'm all alone in the store. I started carrying a gun to work last year after I read where two clerks at another convenience store in the city were robbed and killed. Carrying a gun is against company policy, but I figured I had to protect myself. We're open 24 hours, and the store has a history of holdups, particularly at night when there aren't any customers in the store. But it never happened to me personally before. Just after 11, when the store was empty except for me last night, this guy walks in and asks for a pack of Winston cigarettes. I handed him a pack, and then he pulled a gun and says, 'You see what I got?' He had a pistol, and he held it low, level with his hip, so no one outside the store could look in and see it. Then he asked me for the money, and I gave it to him. We never have more than $30 in cash in the register. Its company policy. We put all the big bills we get into a floor safe we can't open. So he didn't get much, maybe $20. Then he motioned for me to move toward the cooler. We have a big cooler in the back for beer and soda and other stuff we have to keep cold. When he started shoving me toward the cooler I really got scared. There's no lock on the cooler, so he couldn't lock me in while he was getting away. There's no reason for him to put me in the cooler; I could walk right out. The only thing I could figure was that he wanted to shoot me, and he wanted to do it in some place where no one could see what was happening. That's where the two other clerks were shot last year, in a cooler in their store. Since they were killed, I've kept a .25-caliber pistol under the counter, and when he motioned for me to get into the cooler I shot him. He'd started turning toward the cooler, and then he must have heard me cocking the pistol because he started jerking his head back around toward me. I shot him 3 times in the chest and side, but I didn't know right away that I hit him. He just ran out through the front door. He didn't even open it. He ran right through the glass. I called the police, and they found his body in a field about 200 yards away. He was dead, and now I've lost my job. But I wouldn't do it any different. The police talked to me for almost two hours, and they said it was OK, that I acted in self-defense. Then this morning, just after 8, I got a call at home from my district manager, and he said I'm fired because it's against company policy to have a gun in the store. Its a real shame, because I'm still a college student, and I need the job. I can attend classes during the day and then work at night at the store. I've been doing it for 4 years now, and I want to graduate in a couple more months. But I can understand the companys rules. Most people don't know how to handle guns. I do. I've been around them and using them all my life. Company officials refused to comment about the robbery or the firing."

2. Lillian Shisenaunt is a pharmacist. She was elected president of your County Pharmacists Association at a meeting held last night. During an interview with you today, she talked about an issue of concern to pharmacists, one that the pharmacists talked about at their meeting last night, along with possible solutions. She said: "We find that we've got an awful lot of older people taking three or four or five different drugs all at once. If they think that's going to do them any good, they're fooling themselves. We find that, in many cases, the medicine—the dosage and the way its taken—are all wrong. Patients, especially the elderly, sometimes get all their different drugs confused, and then they take two of one and none of the others. Even when the elderly take all the right pills, sometimes the different drugs nullify each other. Different doctors these people see give them prescriptions without knowing what else a patient is taking for some other problem. So some of these oldsters become real junkies, and they don't even know it. As they get older and have more problems, they take more and more medication. After a few years, their children think their minds are going because they're so heavily sedated all the time. But if they get a good doctor, or a good druggist, they probably can stop taking some of the medicines, and then they don't actually have all the problems people think they have. A lot of these older people aren't senile; they just take too many different drugs, and then it hits them like senility. Drug companies don't help. If you look at most drug companies, they test their products on healthy young adults, a 25-year-old, 180-pound male. Then the companies set a normal adult dosage based on the clinical tests with these young adults. But the things that determine how drugs affect you change with age, so what the drug companies set as a normal daily dosage doesn't always fit an older person with a number of conditions. If you look at studies of hospital emergency rooms, you'll find that people over 60 are admitted twice as often for adverse drug reactions as the young. Most people don't know that. They think about all the problems of the young, not the old. But most of the problems can be solved, and without too much effort. People should talk to a good pharmacist or physician. Unfortunately, we find that most people are scared of their doctors and don't ask them enough questions and don't understand what their pharmacists have to offer. Patients also should make a list of all their different medicines and dosages each time they go to a doctor and tell him what they're taking. Then when they get a new prescription, they should write down the doctors instructions, and they should get all their prescriptions from just one pharmacist so the pharmacist knows everything they're taking and can watch for any problems. If they ask, the pharmacist can color code their pill bottles so they can't be confused. But patients also have a responsibility for their own health care. Each morning, they should sort out all that days pills ahead of time, and then they'd be less likely to make a mistake."

CHAPTER 10

INTERVIEWS

Censorship can never be the solution. The only thing worse than an out-of-control press acting with no regard for decency would be restricting that very same press.

(George Clooney, actor)

Reporters interview people to gather newsworthy information and opinions. Some interviews provide facts about events reporters were unable to witness. Other interviews provide opinions or colorful quotations about people, problems or happenings. How successfully reporters obtain information depends on how well they have prepared. Just as every news story must answer six questions—Who? What? When? Where? Why? and How?—reporters must answer similar questions for themselves as they prepare for and conduct interviews.

WHY AM I INTERVIEWING?

Reporters beginning the process of gathering information for a news story should ask themselves, "Why am I conducting this interview? What kind of story will I write from this information?" Their answers will determine what kinds of questions they ask, what kinds of sources they seek and how they conduct themselves during an interview. The reasons for interviewing may be as varied as stories themselves, but most often the reporter will be seeking information for one of three types of stories: the news story, the feature story or the investigative story.

Reporters who cover a news story, such as a crime or a city council action, usually need to interview several individuals to gather all relevant information. From each individual, reporters may seek no more than a few specific facts, but from the sum of the interviews, reporters construct a complete narrative. This means reporters must interview sources who will provide the following:

- Facts and details, including dates, names, locations and costs.
- A chronology showing the unfolding of events.
- Relationships among the people or interests involved.

- Context and perspective, including the significance of the event or issue, its relationship to other issues and its historical significance.
- Anecdotes that illuminate the event or issue and make it more dramatic and understandable for readers or viewers.

Reporters interviewing sources to write a feature story, such as a personality profile, need everything they would need to write a news story plus descriptions of the following:

- The environment in which the subject lives or works.
- How the subject appears and dresses.
- The subject's mannerisms.
- Smells, sounds and textures associated with the subject's home or work, using every sense to create an image of the interview subject.

Interviews for personality profiles may consume many hours for reporters and subjects, but often they are enjoyable experiences for both. In-depth interviews conducted for investigative stories produce more tension. The purpose of the investigative story often is to expose wrongdoing, and sources may fear losing their careers and reputations. Reporters working on the investigative story must obtain the same information as those working on more routine news stories or personality profiles plus some additional data:

- The subject's version of events, which may differ from that of other sources and records.
- Explanations of contradictions. If the subject of the story tells a version of events that differs markedly from that of other sources, reporters must ask for an explanation. The subject's explanation may be reasonable and may resolve the conflict—or it may not.
- Replies to charges and allegations. During an investigation, reporters may gather charges and allegations against the subject of the story. Those charges and allegations should be presented to the subject, who should have the opportunity to reply to them.

WHOM SHOULD I INTERVIEW?

Once reporters know the purpose of the interviews, they must decide whom they should interview. Sometimes the answer is obvious. If reporters are preparing a personality profile of a prominent person, the subject of that profile and his or her friends, enemies and co-workers should be interviewed. For reporters working on feature stories or investigative pieces and who don't have a deadline looming, the rule is simple: Talk to everyone. Think of everyone who might have relevant information and interview each person. Ask every interview subject for the names of more people who might contribute information, and keep doing this until the list of sources has been exhausted. And then go back and reinterview sources to fill in gaps and clear up discrepancies in their stories.

Reporters working on deadline must be more selective in whom they interview. The basic principle reporters follow is to seek the best available source. Such a source possesses knowledge, expertise or insight relevant to the story. Sources also should be articulate; they should be able to make complicated matters clear and interesting. They also should be accessible. If the best source is ill or backpacking in the Himalayas, reporters must be able to find an alternative. Reporters should remember that sometimes the best available source is not a person but a document or record. Reporters can save themselves and the people they interview time and trouble if they begin by searching for documents or public records that provide the factual background for a story. Finding sources who can provide insights and information can challenge a reporter's skill. A number of resources can help reporters locate the people they need to talk to.

Many of the most frequently used sources work in local governments: cities, counties and school districts. Some of these sources can be found through the telephone book. In some communities, local chapters of the League of Women Voters publish directories of local officials. And many local governments now operate Web sites that can lead reporters to sources.

State governments annually publish directories of their agencies. Those directories describe each agency's responsibilities and identify its top personnel. The directories are available in most community libraries. States also put much of the same information on the World Wide Web.

The federal government publishes the U.S. Government Manual every year. Most libraries have a copy. Like the state directories, the U.S. Government Manual identifies all federal agencies, their responsibilities and their top personnel.

Some excellent news sources work not for government but for private organizations. The Encyclopedia of Associations, a reference work found in most college and university libraries, lists thousands of organizations and interest groups. Each organization is described in a paragraph accompanied by its address and phone number and the name of its top official. Many of these organizations have helpful information and are eager to share it with reporters.

Local colleges and universities can provide helpful sources for many stories. The faculty members can provide background, explain complex issues and offer insights. College and university public relations offices usually help reporters identify and contact the faculty members who can provide the most useful information.

Finding sources in private businesses may be more challenging than finding government sources. One resource is the directories of members published by local service clubs, like Rotary and Lions. Many club members are local business leaders who will be identified by company and title. Some companies publish internal phone books, and reporters may be able to get copies. Most businesses have to file documents and reports with local, state and federal governments. Financial statements for companies whose stock is traded publicly are filed with the U.S. Securities and Exchange Commission and are available on the World Wide Web. State agencies may have the names of principal officers of companies incorporated or doing business in that state. Local governments often issue business licenses, which may name key executives.

Reporters should never let any organization, governmental or private, allow its public relations person to be the fall guy. Tony Kovaleski, an investigative reporter for Channel 7 News in Denver, says the job of the reporter is to hold the real decision maker accountable. The PR person usually is not the best source.

How Many Sources Are Enough?

Beginning reporters sometimes wonder how many sources they need for a story. The answer depends on at least four factors: deadline pressure, the expertise of the sources, the degree of controversy raised by a topic and the complexity of a topic.

When stories involve breaking news, which must be published or broadcast as soon as possible, reporters cannot afford the luxury of searching widely for sources and information. They must construct a story from the materials readily available. Still, reporters should get as complete an account of the event and include as many points of view as possible. If a reporter cannot interview a key source before the deadline, the story should say so clearly.

If reporters' sources possess broad expertise in a topic, three or four might be enough. If they have more limited experience, reporters might need to speak to dozens. A reporter writing a story about the economic health of a city, for instance, might be able to produce a complete and accurate picture after talking to just a few people with broad expertise, such as academic and government economists, chamber of commerce officials, bank executives or union leaders. The reporter would have to interview dozens, if not hundreds, of individual business owners for the same story. The individual business owners may know the conditions for their own businesses, but they probably don't know the economic health of the community as a whole.

The degree of controversy also affects the number of sources reporters should speak to. If a topic is not controversial—the cause of polio, for example—then one source may be sufficient. But if the topic is global warming—about which experts disagree vigorously—then a reporter must be sure the story includes all reasonable points of view.

As a story becomes more complex, the number of sources needed will grow. A story about a particular crime committed by a particular teenager probably would be fairly straightforward. Reporters could get a complete picture from only a few sources. A story about the causes of teenage crime in general is much more complicated and would require talking to dozens of sources from such fields as law enforcement, criminology, psychology and social work.

No matter how many sources reporters talk to, they must evaluate those sources. Journalists should do more than simply pass along quotations from other people, even those considered experts. The obligation to evaluate information increases as the complexity of the story increases. Evaluating sources requires reporters to ask two questions: What is the basis of the source's knowledge? How credible or reliable is the source? The first question calls on reporters to find out and weigh the manner in which the source obtained the information. Water-cooler gossip is not as valuable as information from an eyewitness. When a source makes an assertion, ask "How do you know that?" The credibility and reliability of the source require asking about the source's credentials and cross-checking information from one source with that from others. The process is not simple or easy, but it is essential if reporters are going to produce sound, accurate news stories.

WHEN SHOULD I CONDUCT MY INTERVIEWS?

Social scientists have observed that many reporters are reluctant to use documents or library resources. Reporters much prefer to interview sources. The preference is understandable. Interviews with human sources make reporters feel as if they are getting as close as possible to the events and issues they write about. Also, reliance on human sources is a habit built from years of covering breaking news stories where time may not allow library or documentary research. Nevertheless, all interviews, especially in-depth interviews, are more productive when reporters do their research first.

To prepare for an in-depth interview, reporters may spend hours, days or even weeks learning all they can about their sources and about the topics to discuss with them. Their research may lead them to a library, where they might read everything published about a person or an issue. It might also lead them to public records, such as those showing what property a person owns or who controls a business. Research often leads reporters to secondary sources, people who are familiar with the main source and who may have insights and information that will help reporters interview the main source. Pat Stith, an investigative reporter for The Raleigh (N.C.) News & Observer, said the reporter's goal is to know more about the small portion of the subject's job the reporter is interested in than the subject herself knows.

Reporters should always conduct their research before they interview the main source or subject of their stories. Thorough research gives reporters at least seven advantages:

- They will not waste time by asking about issues that have already been widely publicized.
- They will have leads for asking productive, interesting questions.
- They will not embarrass themselves by appearing ignorant. On the other hand, reporters sometimes want to feign ignorance about a topic to elicit more in-depth, revealing explanations.
- They are more likely to recognize newsworthy statements and ask intelligent follow-up questions about them.
- They are more likely to spot inconsistencies and evasions in a source's responses.

- They are less likely to have to reinterview their main source. If they interview the main source before doing their research and interviews with secondary sources, their subsequent research may uncover important topics they failed to cover in the initial interview.
- They encourage their sources to speak more freely, because sources are more likely to trust reporters who seem knowledgeable.

Reporters who fail to prepare for an interview will not know what to ask or how to report the information they get. Some sources will try to manipulate ignorant reporters or avoid difficult topics. Sometimes, sources will immediately end an interview—and scold unprepared reporters.

When conducting the interview in person, reporters should arrive early for their appointments and keep the interview within the agreed-upon time. They also should ask when the source might be available to answer follow-up questions.

WHERE SHOULD I CONDUCT THE INTERVIEW?

The prospect of being interviewed creates anxiety for some sources. Their nervousness will interfere with their ability to answer questions in a natural manner. To reduce the anxiety, reporters conduct interviews in places where sources are comfortable and will talk freely, usually their homes or offices. Reporters can learn more about a source by seeing that person's home or office. Eric Nalder, a reporter for the San Jose (Calif.) Mercury News, advises reporters to survey the source's office or home, looking for clues and details. By asking about photos, lapel pins, items clipped from newspapers and other decorations, reporters may gain insights and anecdotes about their sources.

Newsrooms are poor places for interviews. They are noisy and chaotic. News sources unfamiliar with newsrooms may find them intimidating.

Reporters should also avoid luncheon appointments. Although the idea of a leisurely interview over lunch sounds pleasant, restaurants have several drawbacks as interview locations. Crowd noise and interruptions from waiters may interfere with the conversation. Reporters who tape interviews may find that the background noise drowns out the interview. Lunch itself will distract both reporter and news source. Also, reporters or their news organizations should pay for lunch to avoid any appearance that they can be influenced by a generous source. Thus, the practice of interviewing people over lunch can become expensive.

Reporters conduct many interviews by telephone. Telephone calls save enormous amounts of time, since reporters do not have to drive to a source's home or office, wait until the source is free, conduct the interview, then drive back to their offices.

Experienced reporters wear telephone headsets, keeping their hands free to type notes directly into a computer as they interview their sources. Some sources become upset when they hear the clicking of the keyboard and realize that reporters are typing everything they say; they begin to speak more cautiously or try to end the interview. If a source cannot be soothed, reporters can take notes more quietly in longhand. Sources used to dealing with reporters become accustomed to the noise.

Despite their advantages, telephone calls are an unsatisfactory means of conducting in-depth interviews about controversial or complex issues and personalities. It is difficult to cultivate sources known only by telephone and never seen face-to-face. Sources are reluctant to talk on the phone for a long time and answer questions about embarrassing or personal matters. Thus, telephone interviews tend to be brief and superficial. If reporters want to conduct longer, in-depth interviews, they must visit the source in person.

E-mail has opened up another way of interviewing sources. Sources who won't take phone calls and are too distant to interview in person may respond to e-mail questions. An advantage of e-mail is that it provides the reporter an accurate record of sources' responses. It also allows sources to develop their thoughts in more detail than they might in a telephone or even in a face-to-face interview. A drawback, however, is that e-mails do not convey sources' facial expressions or vocal inflections, which may help reporters understand what sources are trying to say.

WHAT QUESTIONS SHOULD I ASK?

The preparation of good questions may be the most important step in the interviewing process. Every story has a unifying central point. Interviewers should have a tentative central point in mind as they plan their stories. That central point will help them decide whom they should interview and what questions they should ask. Say a reporter is planning a profile of a local bank executive who has won several marathon races. The central point for the story may be that long-distance running enhances the bank executive's personal and professional life. That idea suggests certain questions the reporter may ask the bank executive and his friends and family. If the reporter is investigating the bank's treatment of minorities, however, the reporter may want to interview the same bank executive, but the central point will be different. It may be the way the bank's lending practices affect minorities who want to buy homes or start businesses. The questions reporters would ask to develop a story about treatment of minorities would be much different from the questions they would ask for a feature about running in marathons.

Once reporters have selected a central point and have researched the topic, they should write their questions in advance. As they interview sources, they should check off each question as they ask it to make sure they do not forget one.

The questions should be arranged in a logical order, so that a source's answer to one question will lead into the next. Reporters may structure interviews in a variety of ways, depending on the nature of the interview and the reporters' preferences. Some organize their interviews to begin with general questions and gradually move to more specific issues. Others go in the opposite direction, starting with specifics and building to general matters. Still others may remain at roughly one level of specificity but organize their questions to cover an entire issue systematically. With all these strategies, reporters usually ask their most important questions first so that if they run out of time for the interview they will still be able to produce a good story.

Reporters save their most embarrassing or difficult questions for the end of interviews. By then, their sources should be more comfortable answering questions. Moreover, if a source refuses to answer embarrassing questions and abruptly ends an interview, the reporter will have already obtained most of the information needed for the story.

Regardless of how they organize the questions, reporters should craft all of them to elicit as much information as possible. This means asking open-ended rather than closed-ended questions. A closed-ended question is one that sources can answer with a yes or no: "Will the state's new tax lid hurt schools?" If reporters want more information, they have to ask follow-up questions. An open-ended question would be, "What will be the effect of the state's new tax lid on schools?" The question pushes the source to provide an analysis of the problem with some supporting facts.

John Sawatsky, an investigative reporter from Canada renowned for his interviewing skill, advises journalists to ask short, neutral questions that begin with "what," "how" and "why" and to a lesser extent "who," "when" and "where." Questions that begin with those words encourage interview subjects to tell their stories and reveal their feelings. Questions like "Are you angry?" or "Were you scared?"—besides inviting only yes or no answers—suggest that the interviewer has a preconceived notion about how the subject should have acted or felt. The subject may not want to tell her story to a reporter who appears to have already decided what happened.

Reporters also should choose questions that will elicit anecdotes, examples and quotations. Here are examples of such questions:

- What crime was the most difficult for you to solve in your career as a detective?
- What television shows do you consider most harmful for children?
- What do you fear the most when you perform before a live audience?

Anytime news sources generalize or give vague answers, reporters should ask for anecdotes and examples that support the generalizations or make the vague responses clearer and more specific. Reporters can use the anecdotes, examples and quotations to make their stories more colorful, interesting and understandable.

HOW SHOULD I CONDUCT INTERVIEWS?

Live interviews with celebrities or important officials appear so often on television that students may think them typical of all journalistic interviews. Live interviews, however, are probably the worst model for journalistic interviewing. Even the few people who do them well—ABC's Ted Koppel is one—recognize their limitations. The live interview usually lasts just a few minutes and allows little chance to ask challenging questions. Taped interviews, such as those on CBS's "60 Minutes" and ABC's "Prime Time Live," are better examples of journalistic interviews. Even with those shows, viewers see only a few minutes of interviews that might have lasted hours. Also, some of the questions TV interviewers ask are calculated for dramatic effect, not for eliciting information. Canadian journalist John Sawatsky often uses television interviews to show reporters what they should not do, which is to approach an interview as a contest or combat. Sawatsky instead urges interviewers to act more like therapists, leading their interview subjects through the material.

Reporters should start an interview with a clear statement of its purpose, if that's not already understood. For brief news interviews, reporters usually try to get right to the main questions. For longer interviews, reporters often begin with a few minutes of small talk to put a source at ease.

Once the serious questioning begins, reporters should take charge of the conversation, decide what questions to ask, keep the interview on track and make sure the source fully answers every question. If a source wanders or tries to evade questions, reporters should bring the conversation back to the central topic and politely but firmly ask the source to respond to the questions.

Successful interviewers are good listeners. The principle of good listening means a reporter does not interrupt, argue with or lecture the source. Sources do not want to be badgered, and reporters who do so are likely to find their sources reluctant to speak. Reporters also need to give their sources time to develop their thoughts. Usually, the reason for interviewing sources is to let them tell a story in their own words.

The principal of listening to and not arguing with sources applies even when reporters think a source is lying. Eric Nalder of the San Jose Mercury News lets sources he suspects of lying spin out their tales. He interrupts them only to ask for elaboration or more detail. Once he has the source's entire story, he can begin to use the facts he has already gathered to pick the source's story apart and get that person to tell the truth.

Reporters should ask for clarification when they do not understand things sources say. Sometimes that means asking a question that might appear naive or silly. Reporters should not be afraid to ask those questions, however. Reporters who assume they understand what a source said or who fail to ask a critical question out of fear of appearing naive or ignorant may make serious and embarrassing mistakes when they write their stories.

Reporters also must be alert to unexpected but newsworthy developments in an interview. Well-prepared reporters enter an in-depth interview with a list of questions and a central point they wish to develop. But sometimes sources reveal information or ideas reporters do not expect. When that happens, reporters must abandon their plans and pursue new angles.

Reporters interviewing sources for radio or television have problems print reporters don't face. In an interview with American Journalism Review, Terry Gross, host of the National Public Radio program "Fresh Air" and one of the best interviewers in the business, explains the difference this way: "For most print journalists the interview is the raw material for the piece, along with everything else the reporter has seen and heard in researching the story. For me the interview is the piece." Gross tries to arrange her questions so that the answers produce a pleasing narrative, rather than something that sounds like answers to a random questionnaire. Although Gross's program is not broadcast live, giving the program staff time to check and edit responses, the production deadlines are tight enough that extensive editing is impractical.

Television reporters need to plan their interviews in advance with the technicians who will be operating the cameras and sound equipment, especially if the interview needs to be shot quickly for broadcast that day or if the source does not want to appear on camera. They also may want to show the interview subject doing more than talking. Where possible, television reporters may want the subject to demonstrate an activity or respond to a video or another source.

Most sources cooperate with reporters because they welcome the opportunity to tell their side of a story; however, a few are hostile and refuse to talk to reporters. They may fear that a topic is too difficult for reporters to understand; they may have been embarrassed by reporters in earlier interviews; or they may fear that the resulting story may portray them in a bad light. Reporters who encounter a reluctant source should try to learn why the source is hesitant to speak to them. After learning the reason, they may be able to overcome that specific objection. Or reporters may argue that sources will appear ashamed or evasive if they refuse to comment about an issue, whereas if sources explain their side, a story may be less damaging. In another technique, reporters obtain as much information as possible from other people, including a source's critics. Then they confront the source and ask for a comment on the information. Alternatively, reporters may pretend that they have already obtained all the information they need for a story. If reporters possess or appear to possess enough facts to prepare a story, the reluctant source may talk in the hope of portraying those facts in as favorable a light as possible.

Reporters should never try to bully or intimidate hostile sources or try to deceive them about the purpose of an interview. Information obtained from a source who has been intimidated may be unreliable. And sources who have been led to believe an interview will be about one topic when, in fact, the reporters want information about something else will feel unprepared to respond fully and accurately.

At the end of an interview, reporters should always ask sources if they have anything to add. Sometimes the most surprising and newsworthy information emerges in response to that question. Reporters should also ask sources for the names of other people to interview or for documents that might provide additional information or verification. They also should ask the best time to call sources back if they have follow-up questions. Finally, reporters should thank sources for granting the interview.

Taking Notes

Reporters conducting interviews must balance the tasks of note-taking and questioning. Unless reporters take detailed notes, they probably will forget much of what is said. Most interviewers take copious notes, writing down much more information than they can possibly use. During an interview, reporters may not know which facts they will need or want to emphasize in their stories. If they record as much as possible, they are less likely to forget an important point or make a factual error. They can easily ignore notes that later prove to be unimportant or irrelevant.

Few reporters know shorthand, but most develop their own shortcuts for taking notes. They leave out some words, abbreviate others, and jot down names, numbers, good quotations and key ideas. When sources speak too rapidly, reporters can ask them to slow down or repeat important statements. Note-taking makes some sources nervous. Reporters should explain that the notes will help them write more accurate and thorough stories.

After completing interviews, reporters should review their notes immediately, while everything is fresh in their minds. They may want to fill in some gaps or be certain that they understand everything a source said. Reporters should write their stories as soon as possible after their interviews. The longer they wait, the more likely they are to forget some facts or distort others.

Tape-recording interviews frees reporters to concentrate on the questions they want to ask and sources' responses to those questions. Tapes also provide verbatim and permanent records, so reporters make fewer factual errors, and sources are less likely to claim that they were misquoted. And when reporters replay the tapes, they often find important statements they failed to notice during the interviews.

Tape-recording has drawbacks, too. After recording a one-hour interview, reporters may have to replay the entire tape at least once, and perhaps two or three times, before writing the story. They also may have difficulty locating a particular fact or quotation on the tape. By comparison, reporters may need a minute or less to find a fact or a quotation in their handwritten notes from a one-hour interview.

As a third possibility, reporters may record major interviews but augment tapes with written notes. The reporters can consult their notes to write the stories, then use the tape recordings to verify the accuracy of important facts and quotations. If a tape recorder has a counter that indicates how much tape has played, reporters can use that to note the location of important or interesting quotations.

Although tape recorders have become commonplace, some sources still refuse to be taped. Recorders are small enough now that reporters can easily hide them in their pockets or handbags, but taping a conversation without the other party's consent is unethical and sometimes illegal. Laws in 12 states (California, Connecticut, Florida, Illinois, Maryland, Massachusetts, Michigan, Montana, Nevada, New Hampshire, Pennsylvania and Washington) prohibit recording a conversation without the consent of all parties to the conversation. In all other states, one may record a conversation with the consent of only one party. In the case of an interview, the consenting party would be the reporter doing the taping. But even where it is legal, taping a conversation without the other party's consent raises ethical questions. Undisclosed tape recording seems manipulative and invasive. Readers, viewers and jurors (if a story results in a lawsuit) may consider tainted any information reporters obtain through secret recording.

Final Thoughts

Interviewing is an art form that requires practice. Journalists who are most successful at interviewing have done it for years and have developed insights into the sources they interview and into their own strengths and weaknesses in relating to other people. NPR's Terry Gross told American Journalism Review: "My theory of interviewing is that whatever you have, use it. If you are confused, use that. If you have raw curiosity, use that. If you have experience, use that. If you have a lot of research, use that. But figure out what it is you have and make it work for you." Student journalists often lack the experience and the maturity to be excellent interviewers, and their initial attempts at interviewing may yield disappointing results. Young reporters should not become discouraged, however. With time and persistence, they, too, can become excellent interviewers.

WRITING THE INTERVIEW STORY

Writing a story based on an in-depth interview, such as a personality profile, is little different from writing any other news story. An interview story does raise a couple of unusual problems, however.

One option reporters have when writing an interview story is to use a question-and-answer format. Few do so, however, because it requires too much space and makes it difficult for readers and viewers to grasp quickly a story's highlights. Instead, reporters begin most interview stories with a summary lead that presents the story's central point. Reporters then present the highlights in the following paragraphs. Reporters also may use an alternative lead, such as an anecdote or description that introduces a nut paragraph containing the central point. Information in the body of the story usually is organized by topic, and facts and quotations are presented in the order of their importance, not the order in which the source provided them. Reporters must be sure, however, that in rearranging information they keep every direct and indirect quotation in its proper context. Background information is kept to a minimum and usually presented in later paragraphs. Also, reporters vary their style of writing so that sentences and paragraphs do not always begin with a source's name.

Making sure an interview story adheres to its central point can be difficult. A student interested in the U.S. space shuttle program interviewed a representative of the National Aeronautics and Space Administration. The NASA source overwhelmed the student with facts about the technological benefits of the Apollo and Skylab projects. Those were the facts that filled the reporter's story. They were accurate but irrelevant to the student's purpose of writing about the space shuttle program. Had the student kept the interview focused on the shuttle program, the story would have kept its focus, too.

Another problem is the overuse of quotations. Some writers think they have done their job simply by stringing together quotations from their sources. Quotations should be used only for emphasis and impact. Reporters should tell most of the story in their own words and use only those quotations that show strong emotion or phrase a point in a particularly effective way.

THE WRITING COACH

FIGURE IT: POETRY CAN BE IN NEWSPAPER STORIES

By **Joe Hight**
Managing Editor of The Oklahoman

Some journalists hate poetry. Sissy stuff, they say. Never in a hard-hitting paper of worth.

But figures of speech often used in poetry can enhance well-written stories. Among them are similes and metaphors.

Before giving you examples, here are definitions of the two:

- *Similes* compare unlike entities by using *as* or *like.*
- *Metaphors* are words or phrases used to compare unlike objects or ideas.

Mary Goddard, the late writer, editor and writing coach for The Oklahoman, said similes and metaphors enliven reading.

"Nothing can match a simile when it comes to drawing verbal pictures for a reader, especially if it is a brand-fresh one coined from a writer's imagination," she wrote in 1986 when poetry was even more taboo in newspapers.

Here are two examples of similes that appeared in The Oklahoman:

> Berry Tramel:
> Raymond Cato's fork would leave his plate like an elevator, straight up, before a 90-degree turn toward his mouth.
> Covey Bean:
> The smooth surface of a lake shatters like a mirror when hungry white bass slam into a school of shad.

Each of these similes added personality to the story by giving readers specific images through figurative language.

As for metaphors, Daryl Moen, a University of Missouri professor, says they are "a splash of cold water on a hot day; it jerks the reader to attention." He describes his favorite, one from Associated Press writer Saul Pett about a former New York mayor: "Ed Koch is a seltzer with a lifetime fizz." Another is one used by Charles Schulz in the Peanuts comic strip: "Happiness is a warm puppy."

Author John McPhee is known for using metaphors. In "Coming Into the Country," he writes how "a pedestrian today in Juneau, head down and charging, can be stopped for no gain by the wind." McPhee then describes Anchorage as a "city that has burst its seams and extruded Colonel Sanders. It has come in on the wind, an American spore. A large cookie cutter brought down on El Paso could lift something like Anchorage into the air. Anchorage is the northern rim of Trenton, the center of Oxnard, the ocean-blind precincts of Daytona Beach. It is condensed, instant Albuquerque."

Similes or metaphors will add life to your stories, but writers should beware: Don't throw them into your stories the way some people throw trash along the roadways.

"The key word is 'occasionally,' because the overuse . . . makes words sound overworked. Slip in a simile or personification rarely, and weak words may gain power," Jeffrey McQuain writes in "Power Language."

Personification, another figure of speech, gives human traits to something that's not human.

Similes and metaphors can be used to add that personality, that touch of poetry, to your writing. As Moen writes, "They don't decorate; they engage the readers' senses.

"When properly used, similes and metaphors invite us to see, hear, smell, taste or touch familiar things in unfamiliar ways and unfamiliar things in familiar ways."

SUGGESTED READINGS

Best Newspaper Writing. St. Petersburg, Fla.: Poynter Institute for Media Studies. (This book, published every year since 1979, contains prize-winning articles, followed by the editors' comments and question-and-answer sessions with the writers. Several of the writers have published exceptional interviews, and some discuss their interviewing techniques.)

Biagi, Shirley. *Interviews That Work: A Practical Guide for Journalists,* 2nd ed. Belmont, Calif.: Wadsworth, 1992.

Killenburg, George M., and Rob Anderson. *Before the Story—Interviewing and Communication Skills for Journalists.* New York: St. Martin's Press, 1989.

Kunkel, Thomas. "Interviewing the Interviewer." *American Journalism Review.* July/August 2001, pp. 56–60.

Sincoff, Michael Z., and Robert S. Goyer. *Interviewing.* New York: Macmillan, 1984.

Stewart, Charles J., and William B. Cash Jr. *Interviewing Principles and Practices,* 3rd ed. Dubuque, Iowa: William C. Brown, 1985.

Paterno, Susan. "The Question Man. *American Journalism Review.* October 2000, pp. 50–57.

Yates, Edward D. *The Writing Craft,* 2nd ed. Raleigh, N.C.: Contemporary, 1985.

USEFUL WEB SITES

Biography.com: http://www.biography.com

CIA Chiefs of State and Cabinet Members of Foreign Governments:
http://www.odci.gov/cia/publications/chiefs/index.html

The Journalist's Toolbox:
http://www.journaliststoolbox.com/newswriting/onlineindex.html

Power Reporting: http://powerreporting.com (Links to a variety of Web sites arranged by beat)

The Power of Words: http://www.projo.com/words/past.htm

The White House: http://www.whitehouse.gov

U.S. Congress: http://thomas.loc.gov

EXERCISE 1

INTERVIEWS

DISCUSSION QUESTIONS

1. How would you respond to a source who, several days before a scheduled interview, asked for a list of the questions you intended to ask?
2. Do you agree that reporters have an obligation to inform their sources when they plan to record an interview even when it's legal to do so?
3. If a story's publication is likely to embarrass a source, do reporters have a responsibility to warn the source of that possibility? Does it matter whether the source is used to dealing with reporters?
4. Would you be willing to interview a mother whose son just died? Would it matter whether her son drowned in a swimming pool, was slain or was a convicted killer executed in a state prison?
5. Imagine that you wrote a front-page story about students' use of marijuana on your campus. To obtain the story, you promised several sources that you would never reveal their identities. If, during a subsequent legal proceeding, a judge ordered you to identify your sources, would you do so? Or would you be willing to go to jail to protect your sources?

CLASS PROJECTS

1. List 10 interviewing tips provided by other sources.
2. Interview an expert on body language or nonverbal communication, perhaps someone in your school's psychology or speech department, then report on the information's usefulness to journalists. You might also invite the expert to speak to your class.
3. Interview an expert on interviewing, perhaps a faculty member in your school's psychology department. You might also invite the expert to speak to your class.
4. Interview government officials who frequently deal with reporters. Ask those officials what they like and dislike about the interviews and how they try to handle the interviews and the reporters conducting the interviews.
5. Ask several government officials which local reporters are the best interviewers, then interview those reporters about their interviewing techniques. You might invite one of those reporters to speak to your class.
6. Ask every student in your class to write one paragraph about each of the three most newsworthy experiences in his or her life. Then select the students with the most interesting experiences and have your entire class interview them, one by one, and write news stories about their experiences.

EXERCISE 2

INTERVIEWS

INTERVIEW WITH AN INJURED BICYCLIST

Write a news story based on the following interview with Marsha L. Taylor, conducted this morning, two days after she was released from a hospital after being injured in a bicycling accident. "Q" stands for the questions that Taylor was asked during the interview at her home, and "A" stands for her answers, which may be quoted directly. Taylor manages a McDonald's restaurant and lives at 2012 Lincoln Blvd. in your city.

Q: How long have you been bicycling?
A: I started when I was in college, but I didn't do any serious cycling until after I had graduated. I spent that first summer looking for work, and cycling was a way of filling in time and keeping fit while I waited for interviews. Eventually I got involved with some groups of cyclists and participating in weekend rides and even some races. Since then its been a major part of my life. I can't imagine what my life would be like without bicycling.

Q: How active have you been in bicycling recently?
A: I rode a lot this year. Um, I guess I must have ridden at least maybe 3,500 miles because in the spring I rode in the annual Governors Bicycle Tour, which goes across the state. And in the fall I rode in a tour across the United States.

Q: How did your accident happen?
A: Well, a lot of it is hazy to me, but it happened shortly after I finished the U.S. tour. I had been back in town about two weeks and I was just out for a short ride of an hour or so. I was riding down 72nd Street almost to Southland Boulevard when a car hit me from behind and sent me flying off my bike. That's all I remember until I was in the hospital.

Q: What were your injuries?
A: Gee, you might as well ask what wasn't injured. I had a mild concussion, a broken neck, six broken ribs, a broken arm, and a broken pelvis.

Q: Were the doctors worried about your condition?
A: Yeah, somewhat. They didn't think there was anything they couldn't control, but there was a lot of stuff broken. They were especially concerned about the broken neck. One doctor said I had what they call a hangman's fracture. She said it was a miracle that I wasn't paralyzed.

Q: Was your recovery pretty smooth?
A: No. In fact I got worse at first. After a couple of weeks, they sent me to a rehabilitation facility, but then I developed complications. The doctors discovered I had some internal injuries. My intestine was perforated and my liver and gall bladder were injured. All that caused my skin to change color, start turning bright orange. When my mother saw me she said I looked like a Halloween pumpkin. I had to go back to the hospital because of those complications. But for that, I probably would have been out in two months instead of four. I still have to go back for rehabilitation three times a week.

Q: Have you changed your attitude about cycling since your accident?
A: No. I still want to ride. If I could, I'd be out there right now, but its hard to ride a bike when you have to use crutches. If you, you know, take precautions and are careful, bicycling's pretty safe.

Q: What kind of precautions?
A: Well, the main thing, you know, is protective clothing, especially the helmet. I never ride unless I have my helmet. It probably saved my life this time.

Q: How long have you lived here?
A: Let's see, ah 15, years now, ever since I started work for McDonald's.

Q: How long have you been manager there?
A: Four years.

Q: How old are you?
A: Ah, 37. Old enough, yeah.

EXERCISE 3

INTERVIEWS

INTERVIEW WITH A ROBBERY VICTIM

Write a news story based on the following interview with Michele Schipper, a sophomore majoring in journalism at your college. The interview provides a verbatim account of a robbery that occurred yesterday. "Q" stands for the questions Ms. Schipper was asked during an interview this morning, and "A" stands for her answers, which may be quoted directly. (This is a true story, told by a college student.)

Q: Could you describe the robbery?

A: I pulled up into the parking lot of a convenience store on Bonneville Drive, but I pulled up on the side and not in front where I should have, and I was getting out of my car, and I was reaching into my car to pull out my purse when this guy, 6 foot tall or whatever, approached me and said, "Give me your purse." I said, "OK." I barely saw him out of the corner of my eye. And then, I, um, so I reached in to get my purse. And I could see him approaching a little closer. Before then, he was 4 or 5 feet away. So I turned around and kicked him in the groin area, and he started going down, but I was afraid he wouldn't stay down, that he would seek some kind of retribution. So when he was down, I gave him a roundhouse to the nose. I just hit him as hard as I could, an undercut as hard as I could. And I could hear some crunching, and some blood spurted, and he went on the ground, and I got in my car, and I went away. I called the cops from a motel down the street. They asked where he was last I seen him, and I said. "On the ground."

Q: Did the police find him?

A: No, he was gone.

Q: Had you taken judo or some type of self-defense course?

A: No, but I used to be a tomboy and I used to wrestle with the guys, my good friends, when I was young. It was a good punch. I don't know, I was just very mad. My dad, he works out with boxing and weightlifting and everything, and I've played with that, so I've got the power.

Q: Could you describe the man?

A: I didn't see him well enough to identify him, really, but I hope he thinks twice next time.

Q: What time did the robbery occur?

A: This was about 4 in the afternoon, broad daylight, but there were no other cars parked around, though.

Q: Did you see the man when you drove up, or was he hiding?

A: There was a dumpster, and I guess he came from behind the dumpster, like he was waiting there, just like he was waiting there. And I guess he was waiting around the dumpster, because no one was standing around when I pulled up, I remember that.

Q: Were there any witnesses who could describe the man?

A: There was no one around, there were no cars parked. The clerks were inside the store. I didn't see any pedestrians around and, after I did it, I didn't wait to find if there were any witnesses because I wanted to leave right away.

Q: Was the man armed?
A: Out of the corner of my eye I realized I didn't see any weapon. And I guess I thought he was alone. You register some things; you just don't consciously realize it.

Q: What was your first reaction, what did you think when he first approached and demanded your purse?
A: I didn't think of anything, really, you know. I just reacted. I was very, really indignant. Why, you know, just because he wanted my purse, why should he have it? There was really only $10 in there, and I probably wouldn't really do it again in the same situation. And my parents don't know about it because they would be very angry that I fought back.

Q: Had you ever thought about being robbed and about what you would do, about how you would respond?
A: It just came instinctively, and after the incident, you know, I was shaking for about an hour afterwards.

Q: About how long did the robbery last?
A: It really only lasted a second, just as long as it would take for you to kick someone and then to hit them and then drive away in the car. It really only lasted a second.

EXERCISE 4

INTERVIEWS

SLEEP SHORTAGE

Write a news story based on the following interview with Diana Gant, a member of the psychology faculty at your institution. Gant is recognized as one of the nation's leaders in the study of sleep. The interview provides a verbatim account of an interview you conducted today in her office. "Q" stands for the questions that you asked Gant, and "A" stands for her answers, which may be quoted directly.

Q: You're a professor in the Psychology Department?
A: That's right, for 17 years now. That's how long I've been here, ever since I finished graduate school.

Q: Have you been studying sleep all that time?
A: Even earlier. I started when I was a graduate student and wrote my thesis, then my dissertation, about sleep.

Q: How much sleep have you found most people need a night?
A: Most people need 9 to 10 hours a night to perform optimally. Some should be taken in afternoon naps.

Q: I read somewhere that most people need only 7 or 8 hours of sleep a night, and that there are people who need only 4 or 5.
A: Nine hours is better. I know not everyone agrees with me, but that's what I keep finding. Think of sleep like exercise. People exercise because its healthy. Sleep is healthy.

Q: How much sleep does the average person actually get?
A: About seven hours.

Q: If most people need more sleep, why aren't they getting it?
A: Believe it or not, some people think that going without sleep is the big, sophisticated, macho thing to do. They figure they don't need it, that the rules don't apply to them, that they can get more done. It may work for them for a while, but sooner or later they begin to suffer the consequences. Then you can have some real problems.

Q: How can the average person tell if he's getting enough sleep?
A: Its easy. Ask yourself: Do you usually feel sleepy or doze off when you are sitting quietly after a large lunch?

Q: What else happens if people don't get enough sleep?
A: Going without enough sleep is as much of a public and personal safety hazard as going to work drunk. It can make people clumsy, stupid, unhappy.

Q: Can you give some examples of the problem?
A: I look at a lot of disasters, really major disasters like the space shuttle Challenger, the accident at Russias Chernobyl nuclear reactor and the Exxon Valdez oil spill. The element of sleeplessness was involved in all of them, at least contributed to all of them, and maybe—probably—caused all of them. The press focused on the possibility that the captain of the Exxon Valdez was drunk, but undershifting and long shifts on the ship may have led to the third mate's falling asleep at the wheel.

Q: How did you get interested in sleep?
A: When I started I wanted to write about people who got little sleep and remained productive. The problem was, when my subjects arrived in laboratories and got a chance to sleep in dark, quiet rooms, they all slept for about nine hours. That and other work convinced me that most people suffer from sleep deprivation.

Q: How do you gather your data?
A: Partly laboratory studies and partly statistics, statistics on the connection between sleeplessness and accidents. One thing I've done is study the number of traffic accidents in the state right after the shift to daylight savings time in the spring, when most people lose an hours sleep. Theres an 8% increase in accidents the day after the time change, and there's a corresponding decrease in accidents in the fall when people gain an extra hour of sleep.

Q: Why's that?
A: What we're looking at when people get up just an hour early is the equivalent of a national jet lag. The effect can last a week. It isn't simply due to loss of sleep, but complications from resetting the biological clock.

Q: How else can a lack of sleep hurt people?
A: You feel as if your clothes weigh a few extra pounds. Even more than usual, you tend to be drowsy after lunch. If, say, you cut back from 8 to 6 hours, you'll probably become depressed. Cut back even further, to 5 hours, and you may find yourself falling asleep at stoplights while driving home.

Q: If people aren't getting enough sleep, or good sleep, how can they solve the problem? What do you recommend?
A: That's easy. Almost everyone in the field agrees on that. First, you need someplace that's dark and quiet. Shut off all the lights and draw the shades. Second, its good to relax for an hour or so before going to bed. Watch TV, read a good book. Don't drink or eat a lot. That'll disturb your sleep, especially alcohol and caffeine. Plus, it should be cool, about 65 is best for good sleep. Tobacco, coffee and alcohol are all bad. As their effects wear off, your brain actually becomes more alert. Even if you fall asleep, you may find yourself waking up at 2 or 3 a.m., and then you can't get back to sleep. Also avoid chocolate and other foods that contain a lot of sugar. Finally, get a comfortable bed, and keep your bed linens clean and fresh.

EXERCISE 5

INTERVIEWS

INTERVIEW AFTER A MURDER

Write a news story based on the following interview with a bookkeeper at the North Point Inn. "Q" stands for the questions she was asked during an interview at her home this morning, and "A" stands for her answers, which may be quoted directly. (The interview is based on an actual case: a robbery and murder at an elegant restaurant.)

Q: Could you start by spelling your name for me?
A: N-i-n-a C-o-r-t-e-z.

Q: You work as a bookkeeper at the North Point Inn?
A: Yes, I've been there seven years.

Q: Would you describe the robbery there yesterday?
A: It was about 9 in the morning, around 7 or 8 minutes before 9.

Q: Is that the time you usually get there?
A: At 9 o'clock, yes.

Q: How did you get in?
A: I've got a key to the employee entrance in the back.

Q: Was anyone else there?
A: Kevin Blohm, one of the cooks. He usually starts at 8. We open for lunch at 11:30, and he's in charge.

Q: Did you talk to him?
A: He came into my office, and we chatted about what happened in the restaurant the night before, and I asked him to make me some coffee. After he brought me a cup, I walked out to the corridor with him. That was the last I saw him.

Q: What did you do next?
A: I was just beginning to go through the receipts and cash from the previous night. I always start by counting the previous day's revenue. I took everything out of a safe, the cash and receipts, and began to count them on my desk.

Q: About how much did you have?
A: $6,000 counting everything, the cash and receipts from credit cards.

Q: Is that when you were robbed?
A: A minute or two or less, a man came around the corner, carrying a knife.

Q: What did you do?
A: I started screaming and kicking. My chair was on rollers, and when I started kicking, it fell. I fell on the floor, and he reached across my desk and grabbed $130 in $5 bills.

Q: Did he say anything?
A: No, he just took the money and walked out.

Q: Was he alone?
A: I don't think so. I heard someone—a man—say, "Get that money out of there." Then someone tried to open the door to my office, but I'd locked it. Three or four minutes later, the police were there.

Q: Is that when you found Mr. Blohm?
A: I went into the hallway with the police and saw blood on a door in the reception area. It was awful. There was blood on the walls and floor. Kevin was lying on the floor, dead. He had a large knife wound in his chest and another on one hand.

Q: Can you describe the man who robbed you?
A: He was about 5 feet 10, maybe 6 feet tall, in his early 20s, medium build.

Q: What was he wearing?
A: Blue jeans, a blue plaid button-up shirt and blue tennis shoes.

Q: Did you see his face?
A: He had a scarf, a floral scarf, tied around the lower part of his face, cowboy style. It covered the bottom half of his face.

Q: Did the man look at all familiar, like anyone you may have known or seen in the restaurant?
A: No.

Q: Did you notice anything unusual that day?
A: I saw a car in the parking lot when I came in, one I didn't recognize. It didn't belong to anyone who worked there, but that's all I remember.

Q: Do you have any idea why someone stabbed Blohm?
A: No. Kevin might have gotten in his way or tried to stop him or recognized him or something. I don't know. I didn't see it. I don't know anything else.

EXERCISE 6

INTERVIEWS

HOSPITAL BILL

Write a news story based on the following interview with Carmen Foucault, 1425 Penham Ave., the mother of a 23-year-old son, James, who died last week. The interview provides a verbatim account of an interview you conducted today in the family's home. "Q" stands for the questions you asked Foucault, and "A" stands for her answers, which may be quoted directly.

Q: Can you tell me what happened, why you're so upset?
A: You're damn right I will. I'm mad, mad as hell, and I want everyone to know it, to know about that damn hospital.

Q: Which hospital?
A: Mercy Hospital.

Q: When you called, you said your son died last week. Can you tell me what happened?
A: Its hard, so hard, for me to talk about it now. Its not just the sorrow, its the anger that makes it hard. I tried to do the right thing, they told me it was the right thing, and I thought my son would want it.

Q: What happened to your son?
A: I worried about him. It was that Harley of his. I loved him but hated that Harley, told him he'd kill himself on it some day. Then two officers came ringing the bell last Wednesday, saying a car hit him and I'd better ride to the hospital with them.

Q: What did the doctors at Mercy Hospital tell you?
A: That I should agree to let them keep Jimmy alive long enough to donate his organs, that even though he was dying, just barely alive then, he could help save other lives.

Q: What happened then?
A: He died. We knew he was dying, maybe he was dead, I don't know. That wasn't what upset me so bad, its what happened next.

Q: Did he ever regain consciousness after the accident?
A: I don't know, I'm not sure. A nurse told me there was a flicker of brain activity, the nurse said, and they were keeping him alive. I really didn't understand that, if he was dead, why they'd do that. Then they started asking me if I would consider donating his organs. I knew its what he would want. He was always helping other people, so I agreed. I stayed there, at the hospital, until about noon Thursday. That's when they said he was gone, that they'd gotten everything they'd wanted and turned off the machines, let him die. A nurse told me it was over, that I should go home.

Q: Did the doctors tell you why they couldn't help him?
A: They said he was brain dead, that he had real serious head injuries and would never regain consciousness.

Q: What happened next?
A: They had him all cut apart, just butchered him. They didn't say it was going to be like that. Then they didn't thank me or anything. Can you believe it? My son dies, they take his parts, and then they send me a bill.

Q: A bill for what?
A: For keeping him alive an extra day, $41,000 for keeping him alive an extra day while they took his organs.

Q: Had they told you that you'd have to pay that much, or anything, to help keep him alive?
A: No, no one said anything about it, not ever.

Q: So you weren't told anything about the cost?
A: Maybe. I don't think so. I can't remember them saying anything about it. But I wasn't understanding everything, wasn't, couldn't, listen too good. He's my only son, and all I remember was them telling me he was dead, that there wasn't anything they could do for him.

Q: What's happened since then?
A: They've put a lien on his estate.

Q: A lien?
A: Oh yeah, that's what they said, but now their story's changing. Now they say they're re-examining my bill, like I should be grateful or something. Its bad enough dealing with my son's death without having to deal with this, too.

Q: Tell me more about the lien.
A: It was Thursday. He died, the day after his motorcycle was hit. And, uh, we had a funeral on Saturday. I made it Saturday so more of his friends could come. So then, uh, it was yesterday I got a notice, a registered letter, that those thieves put a lien on my son's estate for $41,000. Today, in the mail, I got the bill for $41,000 listing all the stuff the hospital did to keep Jimmy alive. I couldn't believe it! They kept him alive to get his organs, then they send me the bill for keeping him alive.

Q: Have you been told whether your son's organs helped anyone?
A: Oh yeah, that was in another of their letters. Got it from the donor bank, not the hospital. They said his organs—his heart, kidneys, liver and pancreas—saved five lives. Plus his eyes. His eyes helped someone too.

Q: What are you doing now?
A: Got myself a good lawyer, one I saw on television saying she can help people like me. She's giving 'em hell, getting things right. They're apologizing all over the place now, since she called them, the doctors and other people at the hospital, saying it was all a mistake.

Q: Did Jimmy have enough insurance to pay for his bills?
A: Yeah, I managed to talk him into that, but I can't use it now, can't pay for the funeral for my own son, can't get a gravestone, a good stone for my son. There's still that damned lien on Jimmys estate, so I can't pay for his funeral, can't use his money, and I don't have enough of my own.

Q: Is there anything else you'd like to add?
A: I'd like to meet whoever got his organs but the donor bank says it doesn't allow that. I just want to meet them, touch their chest and see who Jimmy saved.

OTHER SOURCES

Christina Snyder, a spokeswoman for the hospital, told you early today: "The lien is standard procedure to ensure a bill is paid. I agree the bill needs to be re-examined, and the donor bank will pay most of it. But Mrs. Foucault will have to pay for her sons initial treatment, and right now I don't know what that will be. Legally, we have to file a lien within 10 days after a patient dies or is discharged. Its standard practice because 50% of the trauma patients we get don't have any insurance."

Irwin Greenhouse, the hospitals chief administrator, returned another of your calls just minutes ago and said: "Its a mistake the bill went to Mrs. Foucault. We're dreadfully sorry that happened and hope to learn from our mistake. The bill should have gone to the Division of Transplantation for review. We're looking at our billing procedures to make certain this never happens again. It's embarrassing, and we've already had our attorney remove the lien, told him to make it his number one priority. Normally, Mrs. Foucault would be billed the cost of normal emergency care, but the donor bank has agreed to pick up everything in this case, everything, and we'd like to apologize to Mrs. Foucault. I called her twice today to apologize, just hung up again a minute ago, and told her what we're doing, that she should be proud of her son—he's helped save several lives—and that we're sorry for our mistake, terribly sorry."

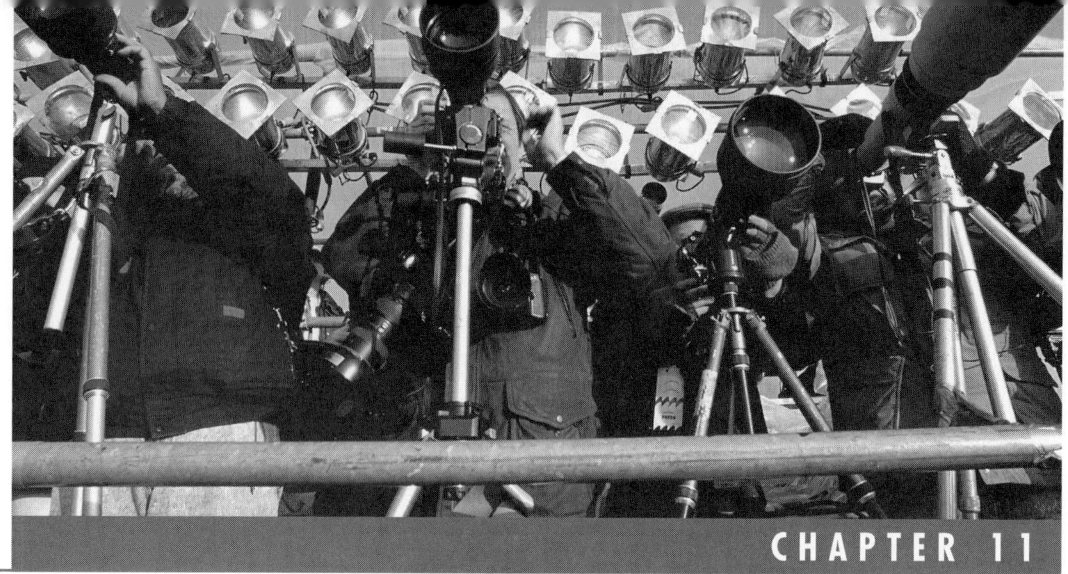

CHAPTER 11

WRITING OBITUARIES

I have never killed a man, but I have read many obituaries with a lot of pleasure.
(Clarence Darrow, attorney)

Obituaries—descriptions of people's lives and notices of their deaths—produce one of the most popular sections of the newspaper, both in print and online. Relatives scrutinize obituaries; townspeople inspect them, and others who have moved away but still read their hometown newspaper peruse them.

Obituaries are popular because of their importance to the people involved. Few other stories are as likely to be laminated, pasted in scrapbooks, fastened to refrigerators or mailed to friends. Also, obituaries are well-read because only newspapers report them. Radio and television stations may mention the deaths of celebrities, but only newspapers publish obituaries for everyone in their communities.

Obituaries are reports on the lives of people who have died. For most journalists, writing an obituary is the art of capturing a person's personality. Obituaries convey the feeling the people they describe possessed unique personalities and sets of experiences. Well-written obituaries make the person who died seem warm or lively.

In some respects, an obituary resembles a feature profile—it describes a person's life and work. Thus, journalists report and write obituaries as they would news stories about living people. Although they may be reluctant to question grieving relatives and friends, they soon discover most family members are willing to talk about the deceased.

Some critics contend obituary writing requires the best writer on the staff—the one with the most life experiences and who understands what a death means to the family and to the community. Unfortunately, at some newspapers, the newest reporter is assigned to write obituaries, and the obits tend to follow a standard formula, with little regard to the deceased's character and no quotes from family and friends. Often, obituaries are poorly written because newspapers devote inadequate resources to them. A single reporter may be assigned to write all the obituaries before deadline and must assemble the facts for the report without leaving his or her desk. As a result, obituaries may seem detached or unfeeling because journalists lack the time to go into depth.

Newspapers try to publish an obituary for everyone who lived in their circulation area and for well-known community members who may have moved away from the area. Newspapers in smaller communities usually publish longer obituaries, because everyone in a small community knows almost everyone else. In large cities, a smaller percentage of readers will know any of the people described on the obituary page. Thus, the amount of space devoted to obituaries varies with the size of the newspaper. Other decisions about space arise because newspapers have limited room for obituaries. The addition of headlines and perhaps photographs leaves even less room for each obituary.

At one time, obituaries were free in all newspapers. That standard has changed in recent years because many family members want much longer obituaries than newspapers can afford to publish. And, whereas reporters write objectively, family members want to include words that subjectively describe the deceased.

Newspaper policies on charging for death notices and obituaries vary. For example, the Orlando (Fla.) Sentinel does not charge for short death notices. However, an obituary, which includes more detailed accounts of people's lives, costs about $5 a line and the addition of a photo is $75. Some newspapers offer free obits, while other newspapers merge free obit copy with paid copy, and still others publish only paid obits. For example, a seven-line obit in the Charlotte (N.C.) Observer is free of charge. Beyond that, the paper charges $2 a line. Different newspapers charge to publish obituaries written by a family member or friend.

Charging for obits gives everyone who can afford them the opportunity to have an obit in the newspaper. In addition, when family members write obits, thc printed record is precisely as they want. A criticism of paid obituaries, however, is that newspapers lose their ability to check the obit for accuracy and completeness.

Obituary databases have become a popular part of online newspapers. Many newspapers, such as the Richmond (Va.) Times-Dispatch, offer death notices, archives, a search engine and notices by e-mail. Visitors may also write in a "guest book" for friends and family.

TYPES OF DEATH REPORTS

Death or funeral notices, biographical obituaries and feature obituaries are different types of articles that cover someone's death. Death or funeral notices include only basic information—name, age, city of residence, date of death and funeral home. Biographical obituaries include more, such as lists of accomplishments and survivors. Feature obituaries are full articles on the news pages and cover noteworthy individuals whose names are familiar to most readers.

Death or Funeral Notices

Usually, funeral directors write and place short death or funeral notices, and the fee for publishing them is added to the cost of funerals. Sometimes the newspaper prints death notices for free. Newspapers publish funeral notices in alphabetical order usually near the obituaries or among the classified advertisements. Most are one paragraph long. A paid funeral notice ensures publication of information about someone's death. Thus, everyone with some type of memorial observation usually has a funeral notice, and some will have both an obituary and funeral notice (and perhaps a feature story, as well).

All death or funeral notices indicate the person's name, age, when he or she died and the funeral home that is handling the arrangements. Thus, at a minimum, readers see the announcement of someone's death and the funeral home to call for more information. Funeral directors may also include the cause of death, the deceased's profession and the times of the memorial or burial. The following is an example of a paid funeral notice:

> Lizzanne Baker, 22, died Friday while on a mission in Kirkuk, Iraq. Services 10 a.m. Saturday at St. Gerard Catholic Church. Arrangements by Tiffany Funeral Home.

Biographical Obituaries

The difference between a funeral notice and biographical obituary is that the funeral notice announces who died and the funeral home making the arrangements. The obituary written by a newspaper reporter focuses on how people lived their lives.

Obituary Characteristics

Information commonly presented, and its approximate order, in an obituary includes:

1. Identification (full name, age, address).
2. Unique, outstanding or major attribute.
3. Time and place of death.
4. Cause or circumstance of death.
5. Major accomplishments.
6. Chronology of early life (names of parents, place and date of birth, moves, education).
7. Place and date of marriage.
8. Occupation and employment history.
9. Honors, awards and offices held.
10. Additional interests and accomplishments.
11. Memberships in churches, clubs and other civic groups.
12. Military service.
13. Surviving relatives (spouse, children, grandchildren, etc.).
14. Religious services (location, officiating clergy, pallbearers).
15. Other burial and funeral arrangements.

Gathering Facts

Funeral directors give newspapers much of the information they need to write obituaries. Funeral homes obtain the information when families arrange services. Some funeral directors have the families fill out forms provided by the newspapers and immediately deliver the completed forms to the papers. Just before their daily deadlines, reporters may call the funeral homes to be certain they have not missed any obituaries.

If the person who died was prominent, reporters may learn more about the person by going to their newspaper's library and reading previous stories published about him or her. Journalists may also call the person's family, friends and business associates to obtain additional information and a recent photograph. Most people cooperate with reporters; they seem to accept the requests for information as part of the routine that occurs at the time of death. Also, people want their friends' and relatives' obituaries to be accurate, thorough and well-written.

The Lead

After reporters have gathered the details they need, they begin the obituary by establishing as the central point the unique, most important or most interesting aspect of the person's life or some outstanding fact about that person, such as a major accomplishment. The lead also includes the person's name and identification:

> Arizona D. Markham of North 13th Street died when a car hit her while she was jogging two miles from her home Saturday. She was 42.
>
> REVISED: Arizona D. Markham, who never missed a trip in 23 years to gamble at the Kentucky Derby, died Saturday at the age of 42.

> Michael J. Jacobs, 68, of Eastwood, died Wednesday at his home surrounded by family and friends.
>
> REVISED: Michael J. Jacobs, who was an award-winning fisherman and avid sportsman, died Wednesday at the age of 68.

The original leads contained dull, routine facts: the people's ages, addresses and causes of death. Dull, routine facts make dull leads. The revisions contain more specific and interesting facts about the lives of the people who died and their accomplishments. Other good leads might describe a person's interests, goals, hobbies, philosophy or personality.

The Body

An obituary's second and third paragraphs should immediately develop the central point stated in the lead. For example, if the lead reports that the deceased was an electrician who also won ballroom dancing contests, the next two or three paragraphs should describe that person's work and hobby.

Mistakenly, inexperienced journalists quickly shift to chronological order and, in their second paragraph, report the earliest and least interesting details of the person's life: the dates of birth, graduation from high school or marriage. Instead, if time and space are available, reporters should include anecdotes about the person's life and recollections of friends and relatives, as well as other biographical highlights.

Direct and indirect quotes make obituaries more interesting, as shown here in the first few paragraphs of the obituary appearing in the Lansing State Journal for Michigan's former lieutenant governor:

> Martha Griffiths, the matriarch of Michigan politics and one of the nation's greatest advocates for women's rights, has died.
>
> Griffiths, 91, died Tuesday night at her home in Armada in Macomb County. The 10-term U.S. House member led the fight to pass the Equal Rights Amendment in Congress and added language banning sex discrimination in the 1964 Civil Rights Act.
>
> She continued spearheading women's rights as the state's first female lieutenant governor.
>
> "I would not be determining legislation today if it were not for all the women who went to jail so that all of us could vote and for women who have worn their shoes out getting me into office," Griffiths once said in explaining why she pushed to outlaw gender bias in the Civil Rights Act.
>
> Described as crusty, passionate, saucy, unpredictable, firecely independent, outspoken and controversial, Griffiths had a way of persuading people.

The following obituary illustrates how facts are generally ordered in obituaries:

> Flags flew at half-staff Thursday morning near the family home of Charleston High School graduate Jimmy John North, who died while on a mission in northern Iraq on Tuesday.
>
> The 24-year-old Army infantryman was killed near Kirkuk, the third-largest city in Iraq, when North's unit, the 74th Long Range Surveillance Detachment, parachuted into Northern Iraq to survey the area and encountered combat with Iraq loyalists.
>
> "He always thought for himself," his mother, Linda Bowen, said. "He wanted to make things right in the world, and joining the military was his way of doing that."
>
> She described her son as a kind, self-disciplined man, who always managed to stay close to the family. "He kept saying they'd have to build new telephone poles because he was wearing out the old ones with all his calls and e-mails home."
>
> Margaret Mead High School counsclor Micah Reeves recalled being impressed that North knew he wanted to join the military so early in life. He called North an outgoing student with many friends. "He did a lot of laughing and was popular with the other students."
>
> North was an independent movie buff who introduced family and friends to the work of film directors before they became well-known. He was a fan of country music, despite growing up with a brother who played in a rock 'n' roll band.
>
> North was born in Charleston on July 20, 1970, and graduated from high school in 1998 before going into the military. North also served in Afghanistan. His unit was attached to the 173rd Airborne Brigade, part of the elite Army Rangers.
>
> His father had marched with the Rev. Martin Luther King and died in 2000. North's survivors include his mother, Linda Bowen, and two siblings, Isabella and Tommy Lynn, all of Charleston.
>
> The family will receive visitors from 1 to 3 p.m. Saturday at the Skyline Funeral Home, 2340 Murrin Road in Charleston. The funeral service will be 3 p.m. Sunday at the First Presbyterian Church of Charleston with the Rev. Lacy Gray officiating. Burial will follow immediately in Memory Gardens in Charleston, where North will be placed beside his father.
>
> The family asks that friends donate to the local chapter of the YMCA Children's Scholarship Fund instead of sending flowers. Condolences may be sent to www.skylinehome.com.

Cause of Death

Why a person died is often newsworthy information, so some newspapers try to report the cause of every death. However, other newspapers do not because that information is difficult to obtain. Family members and funeral directors may be reluctant to announce a cause of death. Some causes of death have social stigmas attached to them. People used to be reluctant to mention cancer, so obituaries said people "died after long illness" or "died after a lingering illness." Now, people are reluctant to admit that a relative died of AIDS, because the disease frequently is associated with homosexuality and sexual promiscuity, although a victim may contract the disease in other ways. They prefer the euphemism "complications from pneumonia." Cirrhosis is another disease that is not named because it is often associated with alcoholism.

Suicides and drug overdoses also are delicate issues. Some newspapers consider suicide a family matter and never report it in an obituary as the cause of death. Because family members clip and keep obituaries, they may not want a reminder that a relative committed suicide. Drug overdoses sometimes are suicides, or they may be accidental overdoses of illegal drugs. In either case, the information may upset family members. When newspapers report suicides and drug overdoses, they carefully attribute the determination of the cause of death to some authority, usually the coroner. Even when the cause of death is known and reported, the obituary rarely includes details of how a person died because its central point is a review of the person's life.

Survivors

Most newspapers no longer print the specific street address of the deceased or the survivors. One reason for the omission is that burglars assume the house will be empty during funeral services. Another reason is that swindlers often prey upon a deceased person's relatives. Also, journalists try to preserve the privacy of survivors.

Newspapers usually name the deceased's immediate family members who have already died to establish lineage. The list of survivors normally includes only an individual's immediate family. It begins with the name of the person's spouse and continues with the names of parents, brothers and sisters, and children. Many newspapers list the number but not the names of grandchildren and great-grandchildren. Few newspapers list more distant relatives, such as nieces, nephews and cousins, unless they are the only survivors or are themselves people of note. Some newspapers list the names of other survivors—nonrelatives, such as live-in friends who played an important role in the person's life.

Normally, the names of surviving relatives and the times and places for the religious services and burial appear at the end of an obituary. The information should be as specific as possible so that mourners will know when they can call on the person's family, and when and where they can attend the funeral and burial.

When writing obituaries, journalists remember that they are describing a person, not merely a subject or event.

> Jenna Mae Hollingsford Merryman, a community activist who championed equal opportunities for children, died of cancer Saturday. She was 86.
>
> She was a force in the community, an advocate for improving the region's schools, said former mayor Miriam Cauldron. "She just had a passion for it, and it all began with families and children," Cauldron said.
>
> "She enjoyed being active in the community, right up to the end," said her son, Josiah Merryman, a trustee of Delaware University.
>
> Merryman was born in Travis County to Maria (Bassett) and Jacob Hollingsford. She was graduated cum laude in education at Delaware University, where she met her husband, John K. Merryman. They moved to Cedar Falls the following year.
>
> From 1958 to 1962, Merryman served as the first female president of the local branch of the National Association for the Advancement of Colored People. In 1993, she received the Star Award, presented by the Cedar Falls City Council, for her dedication to the city.
>
> Merryman was the first minority person to act as secretary for the Delaware Legislature, and she was secretary for DU's College of Education and a DU specialist on

training minorities and women. In addition, she held many volunteer leadership positions with civic, church and human-service organizations. She was a a charter member for DU's presidential Women's Steering Committee, Black Faculty and Administrators Association and the non-academic Women's Advisory Committee.

Merryman is survived by her husband, John, and her daughter, Angela Beckett of Chicago, and two sons, Robert of Grand Haven, and Satchel of Cedar Falls. She has four grandchildren.

Friends may call from 2 to 4 and from 7 to 9 p.m. Tuesday at the Pine Woods Chapel, 540 E. Pine Woods Drive. The funeral will be held at 4 p.m. Wednesday at the Pine Woods Chapel, with the Rev. Donna Johnson officiating. Burial will follow in Pine Woods Cemetery.

The family requests that memorial contributions be made to the American Cancer Society or to the education department of Delaware University for a scholarship in Merryman's name.

JIM NICHOLSON: NO. 1 IN OBITUARIES

Jim Nicholson started working on the obituary page for the Philadelphia Daily News in 1983.

Earlier, Nicholson worked as an investigative reporter and was nominated for a Pulitzer Prize. While working for the Daily News, Nicholson has become famous and been honored as the nation's best obituary writer.

While most newspapers publish long obituaries only for celebrities, Nicholson writes colorful obituaries of ordinary Philadelphians. Nicholson writes about bus drivers, school crossing guards, sanitation workers and retirees. He calls these people the real heroes in our society:

> Most people never make the paper because they never murdered anybody, dealt in narcotics, got locked up or elected to public office. But what I write about are the most important people in the world—[those] who make your water run, your streetcars and buses operate, deliver the vegetables. Who would you miss more when he goes on vacation, the secretary of state or your garbage man?

A colleague at the Philadelphia Daily News adds:

> On Jim's obit page, you read about laborers, plumbers, pastors, housewives; you read about their pride and their small kindnesses. You read about the security guard who died with no survivors and few possessions who was a World War II hero. You read about the elderly storekeeper who gave away as much as she sold, and listened to her customers' troubles.

Nicholson calls his job "the most rewarding I've ever had." He explains that, as an obituary writer, he has "touched more lives positively than I have with anything else I've done." In addition, an obit "is the last—and sometimes only—time we can say someone lived a life and their being here mattered."

> Any one of my obits will outlive any investigative thing I've ever done. People save these forever. Some people will Xerox 200 to 300 copies and take them to the funerals. They'll put them next to the register and people will sign in and take a copy. People laminate my obits and give them to friends.

Feature Obituaries

If a newsworthy individual dies—someone most readers know—newspapers will publish a feature story in their news pages about events in the person's life and circumstances surrounding his or her death.

Obituaries for national celebrities emphasize different types of information from that in obituaries for ordinary people. Newspapers almost always report cause of death when a celebrity dies. Politicians, athletes and entertainers have lived their lives before the public, and the public usually wants to know what caused their death. When the celebrity's family tries to withhold the cause of death—for instance, when the celebrity dies of a drug overdose or of AIDS—reporters will work to uncover it.

Because few readers are likely to know a national celebrity personally and attend the funeral and burial, the obituary may not mention those services. Instead, it will emphasize the celebrity's personality and accomplishments. Sometimes, journalists repeat what the person had said on earlier occasions to show the character of the individual. Sometimes the person's personality will come through in quotes from family and friends.

Here are the first few paragraphs of the obituary for Ann Landers that appeared in the Chicago Tribune. These paragraphs describe Landers' major achievement, relate the cause of death and include quotes from Landers and her daughter to give readers a sense of Landers' personality.

> CHICAGO—Ann Landers, who for more than 40 years was the world's most widely syndicated newspaper columnist, died Saturday in her home of multiple myeloma, a bone-marrow disease. She was 83.
>
> Her column offered a daily snapshot of a society in transition to some 90 million readers in 1,200 newspapers.
>
> Frank, feisty, funny, with a voice as brash as her advice, Landers—whose real name was Eppie Lederer—had a ready answer for people who wondered why strangers turned to her for help with their most intimate problems.
>
> "Well, they don't consider me a stranger," she once said, with sacks of letters to back her up. "I'm the lady next door, their best friend, the mother they couldn't communicate with before, but they can now. Most of all, I'm a good listener."
>
> "She was like America's mother, and I'm not alone in my sadness," said her daughter Margo Howard, who pens her own column, "Dear Prudence," for the online magazine Slate. "She was about fixing the world. She really wanted to make things better. She really cared about the people."

Todd Spangler of The Associated Press began his obituary for Fred Rogers with these paragraphs. The journalist summarized Rogers' outstanding work, showed his cause of death and used quotes to describe his traits:

> Fred Rogers, who gently invited millions of children to be his neighbor as host of the public television show "Mister Rogers' Neighborhood" for more than 30 years, died of cancer early Thursday. He was 74.
>
> Rogers died at his Pittsburgh home, said family spokesman David Newell, who played Mr. McFeely on the show. Rogers had been diagnosed with stomach cancer sometime after the holidays, Newell said.
>
> "He was so genuinely kind, a wonderful person," Newell said. "His mission was to work with families and children. . . . That was his passion, his mission, and he did it from day one."

The Boston Globe's Bob Hohler opened his feature obituary about Ted Williams by retelling his greatest accomplishment and describing his illness and death.

> Ted Williams, an American icon who rose from the sandlots of San Diego to realize his dream of being recognized as "the greatest hitter who ever lived," died yester-

day at a hospital in Inverness, Fla. The Red Sox legend, who hit .406 in 1941 to become the last player to break the .400 barrier, was 83.

Mr. Williams died at 8:49 a.m. at Citrus Memorial Hospital, a few miles from his home in Hernando. He suffered cardiac arrest upon arrival at the hospital, and doctors were not able to revive him.

In the winter of his life, Mr. Williams battled an array of ailments, including a debilitating bout of congestive heart failure. The Hall of Famer suffered two strokes in the 1990s that impaired his once-remarkable vision and sapped his energy. Surgeons operated on his heart for 9 1/2 hours on Jan. 15, 2001, after implanting a pacemaker two months earlier.

No funeral is scheduled, but the Red Sox are considering holding a service at Fenway Park July 22.

"Baseball has lost one of its very best today with the passing of Ted Williams, someone I considered a great hero and a close friend," said George H.W. Bush, father of the current president. "The entire Bush family, as did so many baseball fans, loved Ted. On and off the field he believed in service to country and indeed he served with honor and distinction . . . I will miss him."

The Splendid Splinter, as he was known in baseball's Golden Age when he and Joe DiMaggio ranked as the biggest stars on the national stage, whispered a mournful goodbye to friends and former teammates in his last public appearance, a ceremony Feb. 17 at the Ted Williams Museum near his home.

Sandy Grady, writing for USA Today, began Williams' obituary with the following paragraphs. Readers get a better sense of Williams' personality and his background, but less about the circumstances surrounding his death:

> Ted Williams loved to watch John Wayne movies. By some peculiar osmosis, as he grew older, he began to look and talk like Wayne—same arrogant, big-shouldered swagger, same booming voice, same flashes of combativeness.
>
> But, as others remarked when he died at 83 this past weekend, there was a difference: Williams did everything in life that Wayne merely faked on the screen.
>
> After all, Wayne hadn't racked up all of the hitting records in what was arguably baseball's greatest era. He hadn't been a pilot in two world wars. He hadn't flown as John Glenn's wingman in Korea. Or crash-landed a flaming F-9 Panther jet. Or managed in the major leagues. Or become a world-renowned fisherman.
>
> Yep, Williams was the real—as opposed to reel—John Wayne.

Reporting the Good and the Bad

Newspapers and magazines devote a lot of space to a celebrity's obituary. Obituary writers may recall anecdotes or tales that will reveal more about the person's life and character. They often describe the hurdles that the celebrity overcame. And, many journalists insist that obituaries should not simply praise individuals, but should report their lives: both the good and the bad.

An obituary in Time magazine for Queen Mother Elizabeth recalled an anecdote during World War II to describe her conduct:

> During the war, the couple (the king and queen) became highly visible symbols of the nation's resolve, climbing over rubble as they visited bombed-out areas of London. The queen defiantly insisted on staying by her husband's side even during the Blitz, prompting Adolf Hitler to call her the most dangerous woman in Europe. Her sense of duty and steadfastness never waned, even when Buckingham Palace itself was bombed. On VE Day, when she stood waving on the balcony, the palace's windows were still obscured by blackout shutters.

Obituaries reported the hurdles Katharine Meyer Graham overcame in her personal life as she transformed a mediocre newspaper, The Washington Post, into one of the world's most important media companies. Newsweek published that "Katharine Meyer grew up in a kind of chilly grandeur. She was surrounded by governesses and private tutors, but once had to make an appointment to see her mother. Agnes Meyer was a self-dramatist who fed her own ego by trampling on her daughter's." The New York Times reported that her father had invited her husband, Philip, to become publisher at 31 and later gave him the newspaper. "Eugene Meyer also arranged for him to hold more stock in the company than his daughter because, he explained to her, 'no man should be in the position of working for his wife.'" U.S. News & World Report reported: "Manic-depressive illness turned Phil into an erratic, abusive husband who played upon his wife's insecurities. Taunting her before friends with the nickname 'Porky,' he briefly abandoned her for another woman."

An obituary in USA Today included good things about Princess Margaret, but also some less-than-complimentary ones: "For much of her life, Margaret was considered the quintessential party girl—something many believe stemmed from her doomed affair with divorced air force Capt. Peter Townsend. Her marriage a few years later, in 1960, to photographer Anthony Armstrong-Jones lasted nearly 20 years, but many of those were spent separate from her husband, hanging out with entertainment figures such as Frank Sinatra and Rudolf Nureyev. She rocked Britain when it was disclosed in 1978 that she was having an affair with a gardener 17 years her junior."

Another example of reporting the bad happened years ago in Europe—with good results. Alfred Nobel was born in Stockholm in 1833 and became a chemist and engineer. Nobel invented dynamite and other explosives, became an armaments manufacturer and accumulated an immense fortune. In 1888, Nobel's brother died, and a newspaper in Paris published an obituary for Alfred by mistake. The newspaper's obituary called Alfred "a merchant of death." Nobel was so shocked by the obituary's description of him that, when he died in 1896, he left the bulk of his estate in trust to establish the Nobel Prizes for peace, literature, physics, chemistry and physiology or medicine. Thus, Nobel used his wealth to honor people who have done the most to advance humanity.

Newspapers are more likely to publish negative information about public figures than about private citizens. Also, national dailies are more likely than smaller daily and weekly newspapers to mention a person's indiscretions. Smaller newspapers tend to be more protective of their communities and of the people living in them. Journalists in smaller cities may know the people who died and find that the critical information will anger friends and relatives and disturb the entire community.

Preparing Obituaries

The Associated Press and other news services prepare some celebrities' obituaries in advance and update them periodically. When that person dies, a reporter adds final information to the lead, and the news service disseminates the obituary across the country. The prewritten obituary is stored in a computer system until it is needed. Years before Bob Hope died, his canned obituary was miscoded and inadvertently appeared on the AP's Web site for 45 minutes. The headline on the obit copy read: "Bob Hope, Tireless Master of the One-Liner, Dead at XX." The lead said: "LOS ANGELES (AP)—Bob Hope, the master of the one-liner and tireless morale-booster for servicemen from World War II to the Gulf War, xxxxxxxxxxxxxxxxxxxx. He was xx (born May 29, 1903)." His death was announced on the floor of the U.S. House of Representatives. A Hope spokesperson declared the lawmakers were misinformed. "Well, Congress has been wrong before," he said.

Journalists need to be careful when strangers call with obituaries. The callers may provide all the necessary information. They also may explain that a funeral home will not be announcing a service or burial because the deceased's body will be cremated by a private burial society or donated to medical research. Or callers may say the deceased had been a member of the community but moved to another town. Most such calls are genuine, but sometimes they are hoaxes. Later, the people described in these obituaries call the newspaper, insisting that they are not dead. Because of the possibility of a hoax, editors often require their reporters to call a second source and confirm the details in every obituary before it is published. Author Mark

Twain experienced the problem while traveling in Europe. After learning that newspapers in the United States had reported he was dead, Twain sent a cable saying, "Reports of my death have been greatly exaggerated."

Even the information provided by funeral directors should be checked for errors. Survivors may be upset and flustered about the death of their friend or relative. Thus, when they make funeral arrangements, they may be mistaken about some of the information they give to funeral directors. They may not know or remember some facts and may guess at others. Furthermore, funeral directors may make some mistakes while recording information and may misspell names, especially names of unfamiliar individuals and cities.

Obituary writers must be especially careful and accurate. Obituaries are usually the last stories written about a person. If a reporter makes an error, it is likely to infuriate the person's friends and relatives. The error may also be difficult to correct.

OBITUARY WRITING CONSIDERATIONS

1. Obituaries become more interesting when reporters go beyond the routine and do more than list the events in a person's life—that is, when they take the time to include additional details and to explain their significance. For example, instead of just saying a woman owned a flower shop, the obituary might include what inspired her to buy or open the shop and how her shop differed from others. In addition to reporting that a man enjoyed playing chess during his retirement, the obituary might describe his favorite spot to play, how often he played and whether he was any good at the game. The reporter might describe the person's character and physical appearance. If the person who died was young, his or her goals or hobbies might be reported.
2. The addition of anecdotes and quotes from family and friends gives a personality to the person in the obituary.
3. Reporters should avoid euphemisms for "died," such as "departed," "expired" or "succumbed." Airplanes depart, driver's licenses expire and dieters succumb to the desire for chocolate, but people die. Obituary writers must also avoid the sentimental language used by funeral directors and by grieving friends and relatives—terms such as "the loved one." And they should resist the temptation to write eulogies—speeches praising the deceased.
4. Obituary writers encounter some problems other reporters rarely face. Many people are reluctant to reveal a deceased relative's age, particularly if the relative had falsified or kept it a secret. Reporters should always double-check ages by subtracting the date of birth from the date of death. Also, obituary writers may prefer to report that someone died in a hospital, but not identify the hospital because the information may unfairly harm its reputation.
5. A woman is survived by her husband, not her widower. Similarly, a man is survived by his wife, not by his widow.
6. A Catholic funeral Mass is celebrated or sung, and the word "Mass" is capitalized.
7. Because burglars sometimes break into surviving relatives' homes while they are attending a funeral, most newspapers no longer print survivors' addresses in obituaries.
8. Many editors object to reporting that a death was "sudden," explaining that most deaths are sudden.
9. Medical examiners conduct autopsies to determine the cause of death. When that happens, simply report, "an autopsy will be (or has been) conducted." If you report, "an autopsy will be conducted to determine the cause of death," you will be stating the obvious—and thus wasting your readers' time and your newspaper's space.
10. Avoid suggesting one relationship is inferior to another. Unless the family requests that you do so, do not create separate lists of natural children and adopted children, or of sisters and half-sisters, for example.

CHECKLISTS FOR REPORTING AND WRITING OBITUARIES

1. Gather basic information about the individual's life: Name, age, occupation, area of residence, activities (hobbies and organizational memberships), honors and awards, survivors, funeral arrangements.
2. Find the unique trait or ability of the individual that makes this person stand out from all other individuals, and that can be expanded into another paragraph or two.
3. Paint a picture of this person, using character traits and personality and, perhaps, physical characteristics.
4. Gather quotes from family and friends. Maybe repeat something the deceased had said, if it reflects the person's personality.
5. Consider the good and not-so-good. People have flaws and it is often their quirks that make them human or give them character.
6. Add some historical context to give readers a better feel for what it was like to grow up or live as this person did.
7. Remember that the obituary is about a life, not a death.

SUGGESTED READINGS

Ball, John C., and Jill Jones. *Fame at Last: Who Was Who According to the NY Times*. Kansas City, Mo.: Andrews McMeel Publishing, 2000.

Calhoun, Chris, ed. *52 McGs: The Best Obituaries from Legendary New York Times Writer Robert McG. Thomas Jr.* Secaucus, N.J.: The Citadel Press, 2003.

Hume, Janice. *Obituaries in American Culture*. Oxford, Miss.: University Press of Mississippi, 2000.

O'Boyle, Jane. *Cool Dead People: Obituaries of Real Folks We Wish We'd Met a Little Sooner*. Plume, 2003.

Siegel, Marvin. *The Last Word: The New York Times Book of Obituaries and Farewells: A Celebration of Unusual Lives*. New York: William Morrow, 1997.

See also The New York Times obituaries for good examples.

USEFUL WEB SITES

The International Association of Obituarists Web Site. http://www.obitpage.com

Goldstein, Gerry. "Making Obits Anything But Routine." http://www.projo.com/words/tip325.htm

Scanlan, Chip. "Summing Up a Life: Meeting the Obituary's Challenge." http://www.Poynter.org/column.asp?id=52&aid=29333

Starkey, Shawn M. "Obits: A Lasting Tribute / One of the Most Important Things We Do." http://www.sharon-herald.com/localnews/obituaries/smsobits.html

Archived Poynter Institute online discussion on interviewing friends and family and a summary of two great obituary writers, Jim Nicholson of the *Philadelphia News* and Robin Hinch of the *Orange County Register*. http://www.notrain-nogain.org/listarc/obit.asp

For good examples of obituary leads, see The Spokesman-Review.com. http://www.spokesmanreview.com/news/allcat.asp?cat=Notable_Obits

EXERCISE 1

WRITING OBITUARIES

Write obituaries based on the information given below. Use your judgment, based on what you have read in this chapter, in deciding whether to use the most controversial details. Be sure to check facts in the City Directory.

OBITUARY 1: CATHY VERNEL

Identification: Cathy S. Vernel. Born in July 29, 1963. Address: 1010 Vermont St.

Circumstances of death: Died at 4 p.m. today in Roosevelt Hospital. Vernel was admitted to the hospital almost three weeks ago and very slowly died from the AIDS virus.

Funeral services: A memorial service at All Faiths Church will be held at 4 p.m. Saturday. Burial immediately following at Clover Field Cemetery. There will be no viewing of the body. The family will receive visitors Friday from 5 p.m. to 7 p.m. They request no flowers and that expressions of sympathy be in the form of contributions to All Faiths Church.

Survivors: an ex-husband from years ago, Joe Simmons of Hawaii; an adopted daughter, Raynelle of this city; parents, Barbara and Paul Wyman of this city; lots of cousins.

Accomplishments: Born and attended elementary and high schools in this city. Was graduated with honors from State University with a degree in accounting about 20 years ago. Worked as an accountant for IBM in Chicago for about 15 years, the last five as a senior accountant, and the last two as head of the department.

Additional Information: Quit accounting to become a cab driver in this city. Bought a horse farm. Got into debt and had to sell some of the horses. Was trying to save money to open a horse riding business for little kids. This was something she had always wanted to do.

OBITUARY 2: JOEL FOULER

Identification: Joel Fritz Fouler. Born March 13, 1984. Address: 2006 Hillcrest St.

Circumstances of death: Taken to the emergency room at Mercy Hospital at 1 a.m. yesterday, where he died shortly thereafter. An autopsy will be conducted because police found some drugs in his residence, which he shared with another student.

Funeral services: The family will see people at Safe Haven Funeral home from 2 to 4 p.m. tomorrow and the funeral follows at 5 p.m. Burial immediately following at Glenn Acres Cemetery. Donations can be made to the school for a scholarship in Fouler's name.

Survivors: His parents, Barbara and Fritz of 88 Eastbrook Avenue.

Three sisters, Wendy, Sierra and Regina, all at home. A brother, Frederic, a soldier stationed in Germany. Also, his college roommate of the last two years: Timothy Bolankner, also of 2006 Hillcrest St.

Accomplishments: In the top 10 percent of his graduating class at Central High School, where he was a member of the baseball, basketball and soccer teams, a member of the student council, a member of the National Honor Society. Now, a sophomore studying veterinerary medicine in hopes of becoming a veterinarian someday. He maintained a 3.8 gpa in college and was on the Dean's List. He was also on the baseball team.

EXERCISE 2

WRITING OBITUARIES

Many newspapers give blank obituary notice forms to funeral homes and ask the people working there to fill out the forms when friends and relatives come in to arrange a funeral. The system makes it easy for newspapers to obtain all the information needed to write most obituaries. Use the information in these forms to write obituaries for the individuals they describe.

OBITUARY NOTICE

Please supply the information asked for below and send to the newspaper office as quickly as possible after death. Relatives, friends and neighbors of the deceased will appreciate prompt reporting of this news so that they may attend funeral services or send messages of condolence.

Full Name of Deceased Terrence C. Austin **Age** 81

Address 418 Cottage Hill Rd.

Date and Cause of Death Died late last Sunday of cancer of the throat

Place of Death Mercy hospital

Time and Date of Funeral 4 p.m. Friday afternoon so his entire family have time to travel here for the funeral.

Place of Funeral St. Mark African Methodist Episcopal church

Place of Burial All Saints Cemetery with a reception afterwards at the family home.

Officiating Cleric The Rev. James J. Burnes

Place of Birth Chicago

Places and Length of Residences Mr. Austin moved here as an infant with his family and lived in the city all his entire life except 3 years service in the marines during the Korean war.

Occupation Retired. Former chef at Deacosta's Restaurant

Did Deceased Ever Hold Public Office (When and What)? None

Name, Address of Surviving Spouse Wife Anna Austin, 418 Cottage Hill Rd.

Maiden Name (if Married Woman) ____________________

Marriage, When and to Whom Married to his widow the former Anna L. Davis 56 years

Names, Addresses of Surviving Children 3 sons. Walter J. Austin and Terrence L. Austin both of Atlanta. Also James K. Austin of Chicago. Two daughters who live locally, Heather Kocembra of 388 31st St. and Betty Sawyer of 2032 Turf Way Apt. 512.

Names, Addresses of Surviving Brothers and Sisters Brothers Edward John Austin of Chicago and Robert Wesley Austin of Montreal in Canada.

Number of Grandchildren (Great, etc.) 14 grandchildren, 27 great grandchildren and 2 great great grandchildren.

Names, Addresses of Parents (if Living) Mother Lulu T. Austin died ten years ago and his father Frank died 27 years ago.

Other Information Mr. Austin was a retired chef for Deacosta's Restaurant for more than 25 years. He was also a member of the New Day Singers male chorus and a member of St. Mark African Methodist Episcopal church. After retiring from the restaurant he and his wife catered for weddings and other social gatherings. He learned to cook as a child from his mother, and was further trained as a cook in the marines but then was moved to rifleman, winning two purple hearts and a bronze star during service in Korea. After returning home he got a job in a restaurant kitchen and learned more via on-the-job training. In recent years he never tired of playing with his grandchildren and great grandchildren. He said he missed spending as much time with his own children as he wanted since he often went to work at 11am or 12 noon and didn't get back home until after midnight.

Reporter's Additional Notes—Interviews with Friends, Relatives and Co-workers:

His wife said, "He worked hard cooking all week at work and then relaxed by cooking at home, but he refused to do the dishes which was fine with us. Until he retired his job didn't often allow him to be with the family for the holidays. Those were the times he worked 12 hours a day preparing other people's feasts. Since he retired he just loved singing at church. But he smoked those damn Camels, 2 or more packs a day, and that's what killed him, caused his cancer. I wanted him to stop but he was hooked, really hooked on 'em ever since Korea."

His son Walter said, "Dad loved to cook, and he loved working with people. During the holidays and family gatherings he'd cook up a storm. As soon as we stepped in the door we'd smell the hams, turkeys, greens, and baked pies. He liked Deacosta's because they let him use his imagination to create new dishes and they gave him a big bonus every Christmas. He always went right out and spent every penny of it on toys for us kids and things for the house and Mom, which made Christmas a really happy time for our family."

Peggy Deacosta said, "His specialty was creating dishes filled with edible colors and designs using fresh fruits and vegetables. Plus desserts, he made the best desserts in town."

OBITUARY NOTICE

Please supply the information asked for below and send to the newspaper office as quickly as possible after death. Relatives, friends and neighbors of the deceased will appreciate prompt reporting of this news so that they may attend funeral services or send messages of condolence.

Full Name of Deceased Anne "Kitty" Capiello **Age** Twenty

Address 8210 University Boulevard, Apartment 311

Date and Cause of Death Police say apparent suicide via overdose of prescription drugs

Place of Death Corpse found at 7:40AM this morning on a bench in Riverside Park.

Time and Date of Funeral Not yet scheduled. Body awaiting autopsy. Coroners report on cause of death is due in a few days.

Place of Funeral University Chapel

Place of Burial Body to be cremated/no burial

Officiating Cleric Campus ministry/The Reverend and Professor Mildred Berg

Place of Birth Mercy Hospital in this city

Places and Length of Residences A life-long resident of the city.

Occupation College student currently in her 2nd year of study, major in pre-med.

Did Deceased Ever Hold Public Office (When and What)? no

Name, Address of Surviving Spouse Parents said she was committed to her boyfriend, Jorge Alberto Coto. The two shared a college apartment.

Maiden Name (if Married Woman) ______________________________

Marriage, When and to Whom Never married

Names, Addresses of Surviving Children gave up her only child for adoption 3 years ago, a baby girl.

Names, Addresses of Surviving Brothers and Sisters a brother, Burt, age 17, and a younger sister, Amy, age 15, both still living with their mother and stepfather.

Number of Grandchildren (Great, etc.) none

Names, Addresses of Parents (if Living) Mother Sara Knoechel and stepfather Alvin Knoechel; father and stepmother Otto and Sandra Capiello.

Other Information An honors student at Kennedy high school in this city and on the deans list at your college with a 3.92 gpa (only 1 B and all her other grades As) during her first completed semesters of college. The winner of several scholarships. Enrolled in your colleges Honors Program. Not a member of a sorority or any church. Secretary of the Pre-Med Club. To help pay her college expenses she worked part time, twenty hrs. a week, as a clerk in the Student Health Center.

Reporter's Additional Notes—Interviews with Friends, Relatives and Co-workers:

Friend Thomas Alvarez said, "She was a top student, got As in everything. She was very giving, caring, and I think that's why she wanted a career in medicine. She was a smart, beautiful person, but never very secure. She'd do anything for you and never ask anything in return."

Sue DaRoza, another friend, said, "At first she wanted to major in engineering, then switched to pre-med, but wasn't always certain if she wanted to be a nurse or a doctor. She loved kids and wanted to help them, kids with special needs. I think she really wanted to be a doctor, but her family couldn't afford to send her to med school, and she didn't want to be a burden."

Friend Patricia Richards said, "Ann was very serious, very competitive, always pushing herself, trying to do better, to be Number One. We've been friends since elementary school. She was 14 when her parents got divorced, and that really hurt her. I'd gone through the same thing and we were always talking about it, trying to understand it. She wanted to marry Jorge but he said he wanted to wait until they finished college, and then they started having problems a couple months ago, and she caught him with someone else. They'd been going together since high school, and it was hard, so hard for her."

OBITUARY NOTICE

Please supply the information asked for below and send to the newspaper office as quickly as possible after death. Relatives, friends and neighbors of the deceased will appreciate prompt reporting of this news so that they may attend funeral services or send messages of condolence.

Full Name of Deceased Kevin Barlow **Age** 34

Address 3365 Andover

Date and Cause of Death Cycle accident yesterday

Place of Death In the city—the intersection of Cortez Av. and Alton Rd.

Time and Date of Funeral 2 p.m. Saturday afternoon with visitation at the funeral home from 7-9pm Friday evening and 10-12 noon Saturday

Place of Funeral Woodlawn Funeral Home

Place of Burial Body donated for transplants, with remains to be cremated & scattered.

Officiating Cleric Friends and fellow members of the Resurrection Life Center

Place of Birth Regional Medical Center in this city

Places and Length of Residences Mr. Barlow was a native of the city, attending Hawthorn elementary school and Kennedy high school then served 3 years in the marines. He attended college a year, didn't like it, and joined the police dept. 11 years ago.

Occupation City police officer

Did Deceased Ever Hold Public Office (When and What)? Elected Secretary, then Vice President, and was currently serving in the latter position of the local Police Officer's Benevolent Assn.

Name, Address of Surviving Spouse See below

Maiden Name (if Married Woman) ____

Marriage, When and to Whom See below

Names, Addresses of Surviving Children No children

Five years ago Mr. Barlow celebrated an "Eternal Commitment" ceremony at the Resurrection Life Center with Seth Bernaiche with whom he shared his home.

Names, Addresses of Surviving Brothers and Sisters 3 older sisters. Molly Palomino, 374 Douglass Rd. Jennifer Haself, 544 Beloit Rd. Dorothy Moravchek, 1487 14th St.

Number of Grandchildren (Great, etc.) none

Names, Addresses of Parents (if Living) Stephen and Harriot Barlow, retired to Fort Lauderdale, Florida

Other Information 3 years ago Mr. Barlow was named the police dept.'s "Officer of the Year". He was 2nd runnerup in the competition for the states "Officer of the Year" since that year he pulled a woman and her 4 children from a badly burning house he spotted while on routine patrol, saving their lives while himself receiving some painful 2nd and 3rd degree burns. For his action he received the dept's "Medal of Valor," its highest decoration. He was a member of the dept's Emergency Response Team and was also a Training Field Officer. He loved motorcycles and, while riding with friends yesterday, was hit by an apparently drunk driver who went though a stop sign. He idolized his grandfather, a policeman in the city, served as an MP in the marines, then returned to the city to become a police officer. Raised a Catholic, he left to join the Resurrection Life Center.

Reporter's Additional Notes—Interviews with Friends, Relatives and Co-workers:

His sister Dorothy said, "It made perfect sense for him to become a police officer. When he was growing up he always like to see things done right. He expected everyone to do the right thing. He saw his job as a way of helping the community—putting the bad guys away, keeping the streets safe for children, mothers, and the good guys."

His mother said, "He was big, 6 feet 4 and 200 pounds, He always liked lifting weights and working out. He lived with us before we retired to Florida, and he'd come home with his uniform all torn and dirty after chasing someone. It scared me, but he always laughed and said there wasn't anyone who could get away from him. He liked tackling. To him it was a game, like when he played football in high school."

Chief Barry Koperud said, "Officer Barlow was very committed to the community. All in all, he was an excellent officer. A better person you'll never meet."

His partner Manual Cortez said, "It was hard for Kevin, especially at first, being a gay cop. He never tried to hide it, and some officers, even today, gave him a hard time, were real asses about it. But most of us admired him, his courage and all. When you needed help Kevin was always the first one there, always."

EXERCISE 3

WRITING OBITUARIES

1. Write an obituary for another student in your class. Assume the student died of unknown causes early today and the student's funeral arrangements have not yet been made. Do not write a news story about the person's death, but an obituary about his or her life. Include the student's philosophy and goals and interesting experiences or major accomplishments. You might also describe the student's physical traits. Avoid generalities and clichés.
2. During a two-hour class period, go out onto your campus and look for two people together, both strangers to you. With their consent, interview one of those persons in order to write an obituary about the other person. Continue the interview until you obtain some good quotations and specific details about the "deceased." Then return to your classroom and write an obituary before the end of the period. Assume the person died of unknown causes early today and the funeral arrangements have not yet been made.
3. Write an in-depth obituary for a celebrity. Briefly report the person died of unknown causes at home last night and the funeral has not been scheduled. Do not make up any other facts or report only what you remember about the person. Instead, use your campus library to thoroughly research the person's character and accomplishments. (Consult and, on a separate page, list a minimum of 10 sources you used while writing the obituary.)

   After your lead, immediately report additional highlights—interesting and important details—that help describe the person's life, character and accomplishments. Avoid dull lists, and avoid reporting the information in chronological order. More routine details (such as the person's place of birth, education and survivors) should be placed near the end of the obituary, not near the lead.

   Celebrities about whom you might write an obituary include musicians, athletes, political figures, journalists, entertainers and authors. You might write an obituary on your mayor, governor, senator or representative.

CHAPTER 12

SPEECHES AND MEETINGS

Freedom of speech is not about good speech versus bad; it's about who holds the power to decide which is which.
(Robyn E. Blummer, editorial writer and columnist)

Many news stories report what important or interesting people say in speeches or the actions people take at public meetings. Even in small towns, dozens of speeches and meetings happen every week. In large cities, there may be thousands. Some speeches and meetings involve government agencies. Others are sponsored by clubs, schools, churches, business and professional organizations. Journalists cover only the speeches and meetings most likely to affect or involve large numbers of people.

News organizations often publish two stories about major speeches and meetings: an "advance" story before the speech or meeting and a "follow" story, which reports on the speech or meeting itself.

ADVANCE STORIES

Advance stories alert readers, listeners and viewers to coming events they may want to attend, support or oppose. Most advance stories are published the same day a speech or meeting is announced, or shortly thereafter. As a reminder to their audiences, news organizations may publish a second advance story a day or two before the speech or meeting occurs.

News organizations publish several advance stories about events of unusual importance. If, for example, the president of the United States announced plans to visit your city, local newspapers and radio and television stations would immediately report those plans. As more information became available, news organizations would publish additional advance stories about the president's schedule, companions and goals—and about opportunities the public would have to see the president.

All advance stories emphasize the same basic facts:

- What will happen.
- When and where it will happen.
- Who will be involved.

The advance stories for speeches identify the speakers, report the times and places they will speak and describe their topics. The advance stories for meetings identify the groups scheduled to meet, report the times and places of the meetings and summarize the agendas. Advance stories also may mention the event's purpose or sponsor, whether the public is invited, whether those who attend will have an opportunity to participate and whether there will be a charge for admission. Some news organizations publish advance stories for only those events open to the general public.

The leads for advance stories should emphasize what is important and unusual, not just the fact that someone has scheduled a speech or meeting. Often, leads mention celebrities who will be involved in the events or the topics that will be discussed. For example:

> Singer and actress Barbra Streisand has agreed to perform in Washington, D.C., at a dinner expected to raise more than $5 million for the Cancer Society.

> Members of the American Civil Liberties Union will meet at 8 p.m. Friday at the YMCA to discuss charges that the Police Department refused to hire an applicant because he is a homosexual.

Advance stories are short and specific. They often contain only three or four paragraphs:

> The last time the City Commission discussed Memorial Hospital there was standing room only.
>
> The city planner's advice for Tuesday's meeting? Come early if you want a seat.
>
> The commission will meet at 4:30 p.m. to discuss a 10-year master development plan that would change the hospital from a community to a regional facility.
>
> The commission will also discuss spending $10,810 for signs, installing speed bumps in hospital parking lots and driveways and the proposed closing of Eddy Drive.

Because of time limitations, broadcasters usually carry advance stories for only the most important speeches and meetings. Newspapers run more advance stories, but to save space, they may publish them in roundups or digests (often called "Community Calendars") that list all the newsworthy events for the coming week.

COVERING THE SPEECH OR MEETING

Speeches and meetings quickly become routine assignments for most reporters, but covering them effectively requires perfecting some basic reporting skills: advance preparation, sound news judgment, accuracy, an ear for interesting quotations and an eye for compelling details.

Reporters may cover speeches about topics with which they are unfamiliar or meetings about complicated issues. Meetings of some public agencies can be particularly confusing. In larger communities, a city council might vote on issues without discussing them at its regular meeting because all the discussion occurred in committee meetings days or weeks earlier. Unless reporters are familiar with the committee action, they might misunderstand the full council's action or fail to recognize newsworthy developments.

Planning and preparation help reporters cover speeches and meetings. Reporters usually try to learn as much as possible about the participants and issues before a speech or meeting. As a first step, reporters may go to their news organization's library and research the topic for the speech or meeting, the speaker or the group.

Reporters who cover meetings should learn all the participants' names beforehand in order to identify the people who are speaking or making decisions. So they understand everything that is said, reporters should also learn as much as possible about every item on the agenda. Reporters can get agendas before many meetings. The agendas identify what topics the group will consider, and reporters can research those issues.

In some cases, agendas provide more than just lists of topics. The agenda may be a small packet with supporting information on each item coming before the board or council. For instance, if a school board is considering a pay increase for substitute teachers, the agenda packet might include the superintendent's rationale for the increase, projections of its impact on the budget or comparisons with the pay rates for substitutes in other nearby districts. Even if the published agenda lists only the topics to be considered, additional documents and information presented to board and council members are public records under most state laws, and reporters can get copies simply by asking and paying for them.

Sometimes, unexpected or confusing issues arise during a meeting. Reporters prepare for those situations by arranging to see the leading participants after a meeting adjourns to ask follow-up questions.

Reporters who cover speeches often try to talk to a speaker so that they can clarify issues or get additional information. The groups that sponsor speeches will sometimes accommodate reporters by scheduling press conferences with speakers before or after the speech. If no formal press conference is arranged, reporters may ask to see speakers for a few minutes immediately after their appearances. Reporters also like to get advance copies of speeches, when speakers make them available. Then, instead of having to take notes, reporters can follow the printed text and simply record any departures from the prepared remarks.

Some steps reporters take are common to covering both speeches and meetings:

- They arrive early and find seats that will allow them to hear and see as much as possible. Some public bodies that news organizations regularly cover set aside seating for reporters. The U.S. Supreme Court provides 19 seats for reporters who cover the court regularly. When the court hears a highly newsworthy case, several times that number of reporters may attend. Those who arrive late find themselves relegated to seats behind columns and draperies from which they can see little of the attorneys or the justices.
- They introduce themselves to speakers, if possible, or the participants in the meeting, if they have never covered the group before. They may also ask a few quick questions or arrange to talk with speakers or meeting participants later.
- They take detailed notes. Thorough notes will help them recall and understand what was said or done and reconstruct it for their audience.
- As they listen to a speech or meeting, they try to think of groups or individuals who might have different points of view or who might be affected by any actions taken. Reporters will try to speak to these individuals or groups later so they can provide readers or viewers with as complete a news story as possible.

FOLLOW STORIES

Follow stories are published after speeches or meetings and report on those events in detail. Therefore, they are much longer than advance stories. They are also harder to write.

Speech and meeting stories need a central point as much as any other news story, but the fragmented nature of most meetings and some speeches makes identifying that idea difficult. An expert on economic development in rural areas might describe the obstacles such areas face in attracting new businesses and their resources for overcoming the obstacles. Should the central point be the obstacles or the resources? Or should it be broad enough to cover both and, therefore, vague and difficult to understand? A school board might at one meeting adopt a set of achievement standards for district pupils, announce a major expansion of the district's soccer facilities and hear a report on why construction of a new high school has been delayed. All are important issues, and none is related to the others. How can a writer work all three issues into a single coherent news story?

Organizing the Story

Usually reporters select one idea or issue from a speech or meeting as the central point for the story. Which idea or issue they emphasize will depend on their news judgment about what is going to be most important and interesting to their readers or viewers. If a speech or meeting involves several important topics, reporters usually focus on the most newsworthy in the lead and summarize the others in the next two or three paragraphs. Reporters then develop each topic in detail, starting with the most important. If the opening paragraphs mention only one topic, readers or listeners will think the story discusses only that topic. If that topic fails to interest them, they may stop paying attention.

Here are three solutions to the problem of organizing a story about a speech or meeting:

Solution 1

If a speech or meeting involves several major topics, select the one or two most important topics and summarize them in the lead. Summarize the remaining topics (rarely more than two or three) in the second and third paragraphs. Then discuss the topics in the order of their importance:

> The Board of Education gave final approval Tuesday night to its annual budget—two weeks after the new school year had started.
>
> Members also approved instructions to a subcommittee that will represent the board as it intervenes in a lawsuit over the formula for state aid to schools.
>
> And the board set a special meeting to plan for hiring a search firm to find a new superintendent of schools.

Solution 2

If a speech or meeting involves several major topics, select the most important and summarize it in the lead. Provide a brief transition, and then briefly describe the meeting's other major topics, using numbers, bullets or some other typographical device to introduce each item. Remember that such lists must be parallel in form: If the first element in a list is a complete sentence, the following elements must also be complete sentences and use the same verb tense.

Normally, reporters will return later in the story to each topic, discussing it in more detail:

> Carlos Diaz, a Democratic candidate for governor, promised last night "to cut the state's taxes by at least 20 percent."
>
> Diaz said the state can save billions of dollars a year by:
>
> - Eliminating at least 10 percent of the state's employees.
> - Hiring private companies to build and operate the state's prisons.
> - Establishing a "workfare" system that will require every able-bodied adult on the state's welfare rolls to either work or go to school.
> - Reforming the state's school system by abolishing tenure and reducing the number of administrators.

Solution 3

If a speech or meeting involves one major topic and several minor topics, begin with the major topic and, after thoroughly reporting it, use bullets or numbers to introduce summaries of the minor topics in the story's final paragraphs:

> In response to questions asked after her speech, LeClarren said:
>
> - Most colleges are still dominated by men. Their presidents, deans, department chairs—and most of their faculty members, too—are men.
> - A subtle, often unintentional, discrimination steers women away from fields traditionally dominated by men—from mathematics, business and engineering, for example.
> - When two college students marry, the husband rarely drops out to support his wife. Rather, the wife drops out to support her husband.

- Some parents discriminate against their college-age daughters by giving them less help and encouragement than they give their sons.

Never simply report in a story's final paragraph that a speaker or group "discussed" or "considered" another topic. If a topic is important enough to mention, give readers meaningful information about it. As specifically as possible, summarize the discussion or action:

VAGUE: Finally, Commissioner Cycler expressed concern about the Senior Citizens Center on Eisenhower Drive.

REVISED: Finally, Commissioner Cycler said several people have called her to complain that the staff at the Senior Citizens Center on Eisenhower Drive is arrogant and unhelpful.

Writing Effective Leads

Inexperienced reporters often err by beginning their follow stories for speeches and meetings with leads so broad they contain no news. The overly broad lead may say that a speaker "discussed" a topic or "voiced an opinion" or that a group "considered" or "dealt with" an issue. Here are examples of overly broad leads:

FOLLOW STORY LEAD (SPEECH): The president of the Chamber of Commerce discussed the dangers of higher taxes in a speech Tuesday night.

FOLLOW STORY LEAD (MEETING): The City Council considered the problems of billboards and panhandlers in an eight-hour meeting Monday.

Neither lead contains any news. The advance stories for these events would already have informed readers and viewers of the topic of the chamber president's speech and of the bill before the Senate committee. The news is what was said or done about these issues. The leads might be revised as follows to emphasize the news:

REVISED LEAD (SPEECH): If the city continues to raise its property taxes, major businesses will begin moving elsewhere, throwing thousands of people out of work, the president of the Chamber of Commerce warned Tuesday night.

REVISED LEAD (MEETING): The City Council voted to ban most billboards and to restrict panhandling to about two dozen zones downtown during a meeting that lasted eight hours Monday.

Usually leads for follow stories emphasize the most newsworthy information to emerge from a speech or meeting. Often that is the speaker's main point or the most important action taken or issue discussed at a meeting. Sometimes, other aspects of the story are more newsworthy:

FOLLOW STORY LEAD (EMPHASIS ON MAIN POINT): NEW YORK—Wall Street securities companies should be barred from allocating sought-after shares in initial public offerings to executives of investment banking clients, New York Attorney General Eliot Spitzer said.

(The Albany [N.Y.] Times Union)

Although state attorneys general are newsworthy people, the most newsworthy point here is the call for a reform in the way brokerages do business, not the fact that the recommendation came from the New York attorney general. At other times, who said something is more important than what was said:

FOLLOW STORY LEAD (EMPHASIS ON SPEAKER): Attorney General Janet Reno said on a television program yesterday that she would not have approved the raid on the Branch Davidian cult near Waco, Texas, if she had known it would end with more than 80 deaths.

(The Washington Post)

Here's a speech story that illustrates how a description of a dramatic part of the speech can make an effective lead.

INTERNET BRINGS PORNOGRAPHY TO CHILDREN, RESEARCHER SAYS

"I sit down as a 14-year-old and type in a few words and let the mouse roam where the mouse will roam," said Edward Donnerstein as he started to demonstrate what's available on the Internet.

And roam the mouse did.

Donnerstein, a professor of communication and dean of the division of social science at the University of California at Santa Barbara, typed the words "free porn" into the computer search engine he was using. The program responded with a list of dozens of Web sites offering pornographic images.

Donnerstein clicked on a few of the links as his audience of university students and faculty watched, and he brought to the screen still and moving pictures of naked women and men, vaginas, erect penises and couples having intercourse. And then he moved on to the rough stuff.

From sites that specialized in bondage and sadomasochism, Donnerstein opened photographs of women tied up and tortured. One image showed a naked woman with what appeared to be cigarette burns covering her breasts, belly and thighs.

"That's a 14-year-old not being asked age, not paying a cent and getting some pretty violent things," Donnerstein said.

Sex, violence, hate-group messages, bomb-building instructions and promotions for tobacco and alcohol are just some of the culturally nonconformist messages children have access to over the Internet, Donnerstein said Monday during a lecture on children and the Internet at the student union. And the most frequently mentioned solutions to the problem—government regulation, blocking software, ratings systems and safe sites for children—have weaknesses. The lecture was part of a 2000 lecture series on media and children sponsored by the university's Family Research and Policy Initiative.

Some parents may decide the best solution is to keep children off the Internet all together, but Donnerstein said that was wrong.

"The solution is not to pull the plug. In fact, it's just the opposite," he said. Children need to be online to access valuable educational information, Donnerstein said, adding that he cannot image writing a scholarly paper without using the Web. And Internet access is likely to become more important, he said, as people conduct online more and more of their daily business, from trading stocks to seeking medical advice.

Children have embraced the Internet, Donnerstein said, but parents have little knowledge or understanding of what their children are doing.

Of children between 9 and 17, Donnerstein said, 79 percent say they are online daily and prefer using their computers to television or the telephone. And 44 percent of those children say they have found X-rated material; 25 percent say they have seen hate-group sites; and 14 percent have seen bomb-building materials.

By comparison, parents are ignorant of computers, the Internet and what their children are doing with them, he said. The Internet is the first mass medium, Donnerstein said, where children and parents are at opposite ends in terms of their use and knowledge of the medium. Most parents, he said, don't know what sites their children visit, don't have rules for using the Internet and haven't installed blocking software, even if they own it, because it's too complicated for them.

(*continued*)

Every new medium—movies, radio, television—has raised concerns among parents about how it will affect children, but the Internet is different, Donnerstein said. The sex and violence in the movies and on television, even cable, are benign compared to what is on the Internet, he said.

"The Internet is whatever you want. Things that have no other media correlation are available," Donnerstein said. Also, the interactive nature of the Internet may heighten any arousal the user experiences. Theoretically, he said, the effects of the Internet may be much stronger than those of older media.

Parents are justified in worrying about what effects exposure to Internet sex and violence may have on their children, he said, but the most frequently mentioned solutions have shortcomings.

Government regulation won't work, he said, in part because of the First Amendment, which allows government to prohibit only messages that meet the stringent legal definition for obscenity or that are child pornography. Even if the First Amendment allowed greater regulation of the Internet, it would not stop access to sex and violence. Many of the most salacious sites, Donnerstein said, are based overseas, beyond the reach of U.S. law.

Ratings systems suffer a similar defect. They rely on the content providers to rate content as to its level of sex and violence, Donnerstein said. The systems are voluntary and would not bind content providers from other countries.

Parents can buy computer programs that block access to certain Web sites. But Donnerstein said studies of these programs show that sometimes they fail to block pornographic sites. Other times, he said, they may blocks access to valuable information, such as sites that deal with breast cancer or AIDS.

Web sites specifically designed for children can provide a safe environment. Donnerstein mentioned Yahooligans, Dig (a Disney site) and Apple Kid Safe as sites that allow children to see educational materials but not pornography, violence and hate. Such sites are not likely to satisfy older children, he said.

The best approach, Donnerstein said, may be for parents to learn more about the Internet and what their children are doing with it. Parents can teach their children "critical viewing," he said, in which the children and parents view Web sites together and discuss what they see.

Children are aware of computer technologies and will make use of them, Donnerstein said; parents need to teach children how to use those technologies productively and safely.

Many people criticized the government's decision to use force to end the standoff at the Branch Davidian complex, but the fact that the person who ordered the attack has second thoughts makes this story newsworthy. Sometimes, the most important news is not made in the speech or the meeting but in reaction to it:

> FOLLOW STORY LEAD (EMPHASIS ON REACTION): IOWA CITY, Iowa—At every mention of the word "spoiler," the crowd groaned.
>
> The students and others who packed a hall at the University of Iowa on Friday night to hear Ralph Nader, the Green Party's presidential candidate, justify his campaign simply did not want to hear any more about the possibility that they would throw the election to Gov. George W. Bush. They were so upset at being confronted with the evil of two lesser candidates, they said, that they refused to vote again for the lesser of two evils.
>
> *(The New York Times)*

Candidates say the same things over and over in campaign speeches, so often the more interesting story is how the audience responds. In this case, the response was particularly important because the size of the vote for Ralph Nader was likely to affect—and did affect—the race between George W. Bush and Al Gore.

Yet another approach to the follow story uses a lead that might be an anecdote from the speech, a description that sets a scene or a bit of dialogue from a meeting to introduce a nut paragraph that states the central point:

> FOLLOW STORY LEAD (ANECDOTAL): Cheetos may be a popular snack food in the United States, but they were a flop in China, Roger Enrico, chief executive officer of PepsiCo, said Friday.
>
> When PepsiCo's Frito-Lay subsidiary tried to introduce Cheetos in China, the company discovered that Chinese consumers don't like cheese and they don't like snack foods that leave yellow dust on their fingers, Enrico told an audience in the university's College of Business Administration. Now Frito-Lay is marketing to Chinese a steak-flavored cheese puff.
>
> Companies engaged in international business often experience frustration and setbacks, as PepsiCo did with Cheetos, Enrico said, but for those organizations willing to be flexible and realistic, doing business overseas offers excitement and rewards.

Anecdotal or other delayed leads offer an opportunity to hook readers with a bit of narrative or description. But the anecdote or description must clearly lead into and support the nut paragraph. (See the sidebar on pages 317–318 for an example of a speech story that uses a descriptive lead to engage readers.)

Quotations also can hook readers with a colorful phrase, but they rarely make good leads. As a rule, writers should use a quotation in the lead only if it accurately and succinctly states the most newsworthy point of the meeting or speech. In practice, few quotations will satisfy that standard.

Solving Problems of Sequence and Attribution

Two common weaknesses in speech and meeting stories are reporting events in chronological order and failing to vary the location of the attribution.

Some beginners report events in the order in which they occurred, as if the sequence were somehow important to readers. The agendas for meetings rarely reflect the importance of the topics discussed. Major issues may be taken up early or late, but news stories should not make readers or viewers endure descriptions of minor actions before learning about important ones. While speeches usually have a more logical order, speakers rarely put their most important points at the beginning. Rather, they save them for the middle or end of the speech.

Experienced reporters write most follow stories in the inverted-pyramid style, presenting information in the order of its importance—not in the order in which it arose during a speech or meeting. Reporters can move statements around and may begin their stories with a statement made at the end of a one-hour speech or meeting, then shift to a topic discussed midway through the event. If topics brought up early are unimportant, reporters may never mention them at all.

Beginners also tend to start every paragraph with the speaker's name and attribution. As a result, their stories become dull and repetitious.

Reporters should look at the paragraphs of their finished stories. If they see this pattern or something like it, they need to rewrite:

> City Manager Faith An-Pong began by discussing the problems that recycling is creating for the city.
>
> Next, An-Pong said. . . .
>
> Turning to a third topic, An-Pong said. . . .
>
> She then went on to add that. . . .
>
> Continuing, An-Pong said. . . .
>
> In conclusion, she added. . . .

Writing Transitions

Transitions shift a story from one idea to another. A good transition will show readers how two ideas connect and will arouse readers' interest in the topic being introduced.

Transitions should be brief. The repetition of a key word, phrase or idea can serve as a transition to a related topic, or it can shift the story to a new time or place. If the change in topic is more abrupt, a transitional sentence or question may be necessary. The transition should not, however, simply report that a speaker or group "turned to another topic." Instead, the transition should function as a secondary lead, summarizing the new topic by giving its most interesting and important details:

WEAK TRANSITION: The board also considered two other topics.
REVISED: The board also considered—and rejected—proposals to increase students' health and athletic fees.

WEAK TRANSITION: Hunt then discussed the problem of auto insurance.
REVISED: Hunt then warned that the cost of auto insurance rose 9.6 percent last year and is expected to rise 12 percent this year.

REMEMBER YOUR READERS

Reporters should write with their readers in mind, clarifying issues so that readers can understand how events will affect them and their neighborhood, city or state. Sometimes reporters forget this rule and try to please the people they are writing about instead of the people they are writing for. One news report of a city council meeting began by saying three employees received awards for working for the city for 25 years. Placing the presentation of the awards in the lead probably pleased the city officials, but few readers would care about that. Readers were likely to have a greater interest in a topic presented later: plans for the city government to help people with low incomes buy their own homes.

Reporters also need to clarify jargon, especially the bureaucratic language used at government meetings, so that readers and viewers can understand their stories. A story reported that a county commission had imposed "stricter signage requirements" for adult bookstores, theaters and clubs. Instead of repeating such jargon, reporters should give specific details. In this case, the commissioners limited the size and location of outdoor signs advertising adult entertainment businesses.

Check Facts

The reporter has an obligation to go beyond what is said or done at the speech or meeting to check facts, find opposing points of view and get additional information and comments.

People say things in speeches that may not be true or may be largely opinion. And because a speech represents the views of only the speaker, a reporter who does nothing more than report the speaker's words may be presenting a one-sided and inaccurate view of a topic. In the 1950s, Sen. Joseph McCarthy built his political career by accusing individuals and organizations of being sympathetic to the Communist movement. Reporters at that time rarely tried to check statements made by speakers, especially U.S. senators. But as journalists came to understand McCarthy's tactics, many realized they had an obligation to check his statements and to point out his falsehoods.

Now, news organizations are more likely to expect reporters to check controversial statements of fact or opinion made in speeches. How much checking a reporter does will depend on how much time the reporter has before the deadline and how controversial the speech is. Certainly, reporters should check personal attacks and give the target of the attack an opportunity to respond, preferably in the same story in which reporters summarize the attack.

Participants in public meetings may make controversial statements, and reporters should check them. Reporters who cover meetings also have an obligation to get reactions to any decisions made. When President George W. Bush announced a compromise plan that allowed federal funding of some research using embryonic stem cells, anti-abortion groups complained Bush had broken his campaign promise to prohibit any funding of such research. Supporters of stem-cell research, however, said the plan would undermine efforts to find cures for such diseases as Alzheimer's and diabetes. News organizations included both criticisms of Bush's policy in their initial stories, in sidebars or in follow-up stories published a day or two after the speech.

Double-checking personal attacks and getting responses from the targets may help avoid libel suits. If a defamatory personal attack is made at a speech or meeting that is not an official government proceeding, a person who is attacked may sue for libel both the speaker and any news organizations that report the statement. The fact that news organizations accurately quoted a speaker is not a defense. Even if a personal attack is not defamatory or is made in an official government meeting—and therefore cannot be the basis for a libel suit—the journalist still has an ethical obligation to check facts, get opposing points of view and give people who have been attacked a chance to respond.

ADDING COLOR

Report What You Hear

Quotations, direct and indirect, help the writer describe debates that take place in a public meeting. The people who read and view the news need to know why certain actions were taken or why their elected representatives voted a certain way. Simply recording votes and actions will not give readers and viewers the information they need to make informed judgments. They also need to know the competing points of view.

Before the fall of the Soviet Union, a school board considered an exchange program that would allow 32 American high school students to spend a semester there studying and traveling. Two men objected to the program, complaining that it would expose students to Soviet propaganda. The following story uses quotations to describe the participants and illuminate the issues:

> "This is a sneak attempt at changing the students' values," said LeRoy DeBecker of the John Birch Society. "The students will never be shown any of the negative aspects of communism, only propaganda promoting the system."
>
> Erik Lieber, chair of the Pro-Family Forum, agreed that the program should be rejected. "Russia wants only one form of peace," Lieber said. "It wants to completely dominate the world, and this trip will help it."
>
> Catrina Weinstein, a teacher at Colonial High School, disagreed. Weinstein said that she has led students from other high schools on similar trips, and that the trips made the students more patriotic, not pawns of the Communists.
>
> "When the students got home they realized how fortunate they were, so they were more motivated to study our political system," Weinstein said. "All these other comments you've heard are nonsense. These trips introduce students to the Soviet people, not Soviet ideology. The closest we ever came to propaganda was a guide's speaking with pride of his country's accomplishments."
>
> The board voted 6-1 to establish the program, and board member Anna Nemechek explained, "If we're going to be afraid every time our children cross a border, then perhaps we should lock them up in cages and make sure they're well-fed."

Describe What You See

Vivid descriptions of participants, audiences and settings add drama to speech and meeting stories. The descriptions can appear anywhere. The following example shows how vivid description can enliven a meeting story:

A public hearing on an ordinance that would limit the number of animals allowed in homes drew a standing-room-only crowd to a County Commission meeting Thursday.

Some of the spectators wore T-shirts inscribed with pictures of their pets, primarily cats and dogs.

A combination of quotations and descriptions can make stories even more interesting:

Baker loudly objected to each vote in favor of the project.

"We're citizens," she yelled. "You should consider us."

After all the votes were cast, she threw her petition to the floor and stormed out of the room, shouting: "This is not a dictatorship! You should listen to us."

CHECKLISTS FOR REPORTING SPEECHES AND MEETINGS

Advance Stories

1. Report what speech or meeting will happen, when and where it will happen, and who will be involved.
2. Keep advance stories short—normally no more than three or four paragraphs.

Covering the Speech or Meeting

1. Get background information on the group or speaker, including a copy of the agenda or the speech, if it's available.
2. Learn the names of all participants.
3. Find out if there will be an opportunity to interview the speaker or the participants before or after the event.
4. Arrive early and find a seat where you can see and hear as much as possible.
5. Introduce yourself to the speaker or the participants in the meeting if they do not know you.
6. Take detailed notes, making sure you record colorful quotations, information about the setting of the event and the responses of the participants and observers.
7. Identify and seek responses from people who may be affected by what happens or who may have views or interests different from those expressed at the speech or meeting.

Follow Stories

1. Identify the issue or decision that is most likely to interest your readers and viewers and make that your central point. If other important issues or decisions arose in the speech or meeting, be sure to mention them early.
2. Focus the lead on specific actions or statements to keep it from being overly broad.
3. Organize the story in inverted-pyramid fashion, not according to the order in which statements were made or topics considered.
4. Vary the location of the attribution in direct and indirect quotations so that the story does not become monotonous.
5. Provide transitions from one topic to another.
6. Avoid generalities and eliminate or explain jargon or technical terms.
7. Check controversial facts and give any person or group who has been attacked in the speech or meeting an opportunity to respond.
8. Include color in speech and meeting stories by providing direct quotations and descriptions of speakers, participants, settings and audience responses.

THE WRITING COACH

GO BEYOND THE STICK

By **Joe Hight**
Managing Editor of The Oklahoman

Reporters sometimes treat people as if they were drawing stick people. Name, address, age and past job experience. That's all. This tells the reader basic information—the stick—but not what the person is really like.

So to go beyond the stick people approach, you must realize that people have:

- Personality/character (each person is different).
- Beliefs (religious, personal, political).
- An environment (surroundings, friends, family, hobbies, etc.).
- Likes/dislikes.

Use the interview process to determine these qualities in people—to make them whole, much more than a stick person.

SUGGESTED READINGS

Readership Issues Committee. *The Local News Handbook.* Reston, Va.: American Society of Newspaper Editors, 1999.

Aldrich, Leigh Stephens. *Covering the Community: A Diversity Handbook for Media.* Thousand Oaks, Calif.: Pine Forge Press, 1999.

Baker, Bob. *Newsthinking: The Secret of Making Your Facts Fall Into Place.* Boston: Allyn and Bacon, 2002.

Paulos, John Allen. *A Mathematician Reads the Newspaper.* New York: Anchor Books, 1995.

USEFUL WEB SITES

American Press Institute: http://www.americanpressinstitute.org
American Society of Newspaper Editors: http://www.asne.org
The Journalist's Toolbox: http://www.journaliststoolbox.com/newswriting/onlineindex.html
Power Reporting: http://powerreporting.com (Links to a variety of Web sites arranged by beat)
The Poynter Institute: http://www.poynter.org
Society of Professional Journalists: http://www.spj.org

Name ______________________ Class ______________________ Date ______

EXERCISE 1

SPEECHES AND MEETINGS

EVALUATING SPEECH AND MEETING LEADS

Critically evaluate the following speech and meeting story leads, giving each a grade from A to F. Then discuss the leads with your teacher and classmates.

1. The County Commission voted unanimously Tuesday against raising the county tourism tax by one cent to pay for a new baseball stadium. (Grade: ________)
2. A spokesperson for Citizens Against Crime warned parents Wednesday night about violent crime and its impact on families in the city. (Grade: ________)
3. By a vote of 5-4, the City Council rejected on Monday night a proposal to build an apartment complex near Reed Road and State Road 419. (Grade: ________)
4. A heated debate took place at the City Council meeting Thursday night over the need for police dogs. (Grade: ________)
5. Fifty percent of the drug abusers entering treatment centers go back to using drugs within a year, Mimi Sota told an audience here Monday. (Grade: ________)
6. In a speech Monday, reporter Samuel Swaugger talked to journalism students about his past as a journalist and his experiences with the two largest newspapers in the state. (Grade: ________)
7. During a speech to the American Legion last night, former Marine Lt. Col. Oliver North discussed his work in the Reagan White House. (Grade: ________)
8. County commissioners heard testimony from more than 20 people Tuesday morning on plans to license and regulate snowmobiles. (Grade: ________)
9. The County Commission reviewed a resolution Wednesday to create a committee that will identify conservation and recreation lands within the county. (Grade: ________)

10. Blasting opponents of the plan, Mayor Sabrina Datoli last night defended a proposal to establish a police review board. (Grade: ________)
11. Traveling by airplane has never been more dangerous, Ramon Madea charged in a fiery speech Sunday night. (Grade: ________)
12. The City Council voted unanimously Monday to change the zoning along three streets from residential to commercial. (Grade: ________)
13. The business before the School Board flowed smoothly Tuesday night as the board proceeded through the agenda. (Grade: ________)
14. The county commissioners continued to struggle with the issue of protecting the water quality in Butler Lake at their meeting Monday. They eventually denied a petition to build a new boat ramp on the lake. (Grade: ________)
15. The County Commission unanimously passed an ordinance that makes it illegal for anyone to possess an open container of alcohol in a vehicle. A previous law made it illegal to drive while drunk, but legal to drink while driving. (Grade: ________)

EXERCISE 2

SPEECHES AND MEETINGS

SPEECHES

Write separate advance and follow stories about each of the following speeches. Because the speeches are reprinted verbatim, you may quote them directly. Correct the stories' grammatical and spelling errors, including all possessives. You may want to discuss with classmates the problem of handling speakers' errors in grammar and syntax and statements that seem sexist.

1. AMERICANS' WORK

Information for advance story:

Leslee D'Ausilio will speak this forthcoming Saturday night to the Chamber of Commerce at the organizations annual meeting. The affair will start with an open bar at 6:30, dinner at 7:30, and the speech to begin promptly at 8:30 PM, all in the spacious Grand Ballroom of the Downtown Hilton Hotel. Cost for the dinner and speech: $39.00 for members and their guests, $49.00 for nonmembers.

Tickets are conveniently available at the Chamber of Commerce office until Noon Saturday. The speaker, a famous celebrity and frequent TV guest commentator, is the author of 3 best-selling books, all about American workers, their jobs, their characteristics, their problems. She received her B.A. and M.A. from the University of Wisconsin in Madison Wisconsin where for both degrees she majored in Sociology, and Ph.D. from Harvard where she majored in Management with a speciality in Labor Relations. She currently teaches at Harvard, serves as a consultant for the UAW-CIO, and was Assistant Secretary of Labor in the Clinton administration. Her announced topic will be "Today's Workers, Workweeks, And Productivity."

Speech for follow story:

"Today, the U.S. ranks Number One in the world in productivity per worker. That has both advantages and disadvantages for workers, their families, and employers.

"On the upside, American families are enjoying more prosperity, but not due solely to rising wages. More family members are working, especially among Black and Hispanic families. During the last 10 years, the average middle-class familys income rose 9.2% after inflation, but the typical familys wage-earners had to spend 6.8 percent more time at work to reap it. Without increased earnings from wives, the average middle-class familys income would have risen only 3.6%. The share of married women working full-time rose from 41 to 46%. Plus, the average workers workweek has risen from about 38 hours for full-time workers to slightly more than 41 hours a week. Executives, on average, work 47 hours a week.

"On the downside, workers complain they're working harder and that they're having difficulty balancing their jobs and personal lives. American workers seemed to be squeezed during both booms and busts. In expansions, companies keep giving their workers more work, and in recessions companies downsize. Then, with fewer employees, those that remain have to work longer and harder to get everything done. So its not surprising that American workers are sometimes frustrated. Forty-one percent feel they do not have enough time to accomplish all their tasks each day.

"Its a complex issue, and there're also other culprits. One is technology. More than ever before, technological advances keep people tethered to their office by cell phone and computer. Think about it! It doesn't matter where you go: to a movie, a nice restaurant, or even a golf course or your church. People carry telephones everywhere and, while some calls are social, many are business.

"There's also the American psyche and culture. Much of the increase in time spent at work is voluntary. Workers want to earn more and to move up economically. They're eager to make a good impression: to impress their boss and co-workers. Also, work is important to them, sometimes the most important thing in their lives. Many are ambitious, even obsessed, with getting ahead. Increasingly, then, some Americans work even on holidays and are forgoing vacations and time with their families and friends.

"During the past decade, Americans added nearly a full week to their work year, working on average 1,978 hours last year. That's up 36 hours almost a full week from ten years ago. That means Americans who are employed spent nearly 49 weeks a year on the job. As a result, they worked longer than all other industrial nations last year. Americans work 100 more hours (2 weeks per year) than Japanese workers. They work 250 hours (about 6 weeks) more per year than British workers, and 500 hours (12 weeks) more per year than German workers.

"Why? Among the reasons for the differences are the fact that Europeans typically take 4 to 6 weeks of vacation each year while Americans take only 2 to 3 weeks. Also, while American employers offer or require lots of overtime, the French government has reduced that countrys official workweek to 35 hours. That's because the unemployment rate in France is high, and the government wants to pressure companies to hire more workers.

"Clearly, all these trends, whether good or bad, have contributed to our countrys outstanding economic performance, which translates into more income for employees and more profits for employers. So, no one can deny that Americans are working harder, and I don't like that, but I don't see the situation as all bad. Our economy is booming. There are good jobs for most workers, and incomes are going up along with our productivity."

2. COLLEGE ATHLETICS

Information for advance story:

Erik Nieves, your schools Athletic Director for the past twenty-four years, has previously announced his retirement, effective at the end of next month. Before then, he's planning a farewell speech and today he told you it will be "a candid discussion about some serious problems in athletics, primarily college athletics." Its all free this coming Saturday night at the annual meeting of members of your schools Athletic Boosters Club. The speech is being held in the beautiful Grand Ballroom of your Student Union with only Booster Club members and their guests invited. Each member of the club donates $500 or more annually to your schools Athletic Foundation. Bronze Key Club members donate $1000 or more, Silver Key Club members $5000 or more, and Gold Key Club members $10000 or more. There's an open bar at 6:30, dinner at 7:30, and the speech at 9:00pm, with good fellowship for all. "Its my farewell address to the club," Nieves said. (Press kits will be available, with free seating available to the press. No radio or TV tapings or broadcasts of any type will be permitted, all such rights being exclusively retained by the Athletic Boosters Club.)

Speech for follow story:

"As I look around this room, I see many familiar faces: good people, generous people who've been friends and supporters for as long as I've been here. Now, all of you know I'm retiring at the end of next month. I'm 64, and its time. What you don't know is that I've decided to devote the time I have left to increasing public awareness of a serious problem for our athletes and athletic programs. I'll continue with that effort after I retire. What I'm going to say isn't going to be popular, but its something I feel I have to say, something eating my heart out. The fact is, its no longer fun to play college football; its become a fatiguing grind. Its a full-time job, a year-around job, and that's true of every college football program across the country.

"The insanity has to stop. Coaches demand more, colleges demand more. Alumni demand more, so college football has turned into a 12-month-a-year job that never ends. We've got fall games and winter workouts. There's spring practice, and there're summer conditioning drills. So our players work and work and work during the season. Then, when the season ends, they work even more. They push harder and stay longer, and it doesn't matter what time of the day or what month of the year.

"You've got wonderful young players some still teenagers literally working themselves to death, dying so you can have a winning season. Eleven college football players died in the past 12 months year, and its a tragedy we have to stop.

"Heatstroke is a part of the problem, especially during those damned summer drills. Heatstroke can cause your body temperature to soar to 108 degrees, cause a heart attack, and induce a coma. On college teams its hard to help people 50 to 100 pounds sometimes even 150 pounds above the ideal weight for their height. With people who are so overweight, often deliberately, you're going to have problems. We tell our players on a hot day he should drink 16 to 20 ounces of fluid and then continue to drink every 15 minutes whether he's thirsty or not. You can't depend on your thirst mechanism. The center of the brain doesn't click on and tell you that you're thirsty until a long time after all your fluids are gone. If you're a coach, whether in high school or college, and your kids aren't getting water every 15 or 20 minutes, you shouldn't be coaching.

"Actually, heat stroke is one of the easier problems we deal with. Some of our players have pre-existing conditions we don't know about. We require players to have physical exams before letting them play. Still, right here in our state, we had a freshman die after a series of early-morning agility drills. He was just 19, 6 feet 4, and 230 pounds, with no history of heart problems. When he reported to campus doctors detected no heart abnormalities during his physical exam. That non-detection is no surprise. Many cardiologists say arrhythmia can be difficult to find.

"Cardiac arrhythmia is an irregular heartbeat. The heartbeat is not constantly out of kilter, so the problem is not likely to be detected even in an athlete undergoing a yearly physical. But at some point under exertion, the heart is pushed beyond its limits, and there's no way of knowing when or why it will happen. There are a number of causes for this problem, including defects in the heart structure. People are born with these defects but often show no outward signs of the problems. Including high school teams and all sports, about 100 to 200 young athletes die each year from the condition.

"Now, some of this is the coaches fault and some the fans fault. Coaches work their players too hard. They work themselves too hard. And players give every last drop of their time, energy and effort. They sacrifice way too much for far too little. They have tremendous pride and ambition, and they all want to be drafted into the professionals, so they push themselves through heat and pain.

"To solve the problems, our coaches at every level need more sports medicine knowledge. We don't have a system of coaching certification in this country. In other countries, especially Europe, you have to have expertise and take courses and pass tests. In this country I could be an accountant who never took a course in first aid, and so long as I can win football games, it doesn't matter.

"Other things are just common sense. If you're a coach, you take your team out at 7:00 in the morning or 5:00 or 6:00 in the evening. On hot days, you don't work outside at noon. Somehow, we also have to cut back on off-season drills. They take way too much of our athletes time, so an awful lot of these young men never graduate. There's just no time left for their studies.

"We also need better physicals. That will cost several hundred dollars for every player every year but should be a priority, and schools can afford it.

"Plus, fans put way too much pressure on their coaches, forcing coaches to put more pressure on their players. You see it in every game, high school, college, and professional. You see coaches send too many injured players back into games before they're ready. We've also got fans who like to brag their teams linemen average 250 or 300 pounds. That's not healthy for young men to gain an extra 50 or 100 pounds. I'd rather have fans brag about how many of our athletes graduate. To get this awful pressure off coaches, give them tenure just like you give faculty members. No coach should be fired after just one or two losing seasons.

"Now all this isn't going to happen soon, and it can't happen at just one or two schools. It has to be a national effort. Football is a game. Enjoy the game whether your team wins or loses. A few more victories aren't worth risking a players life."

EXERCISE 3

SPEECHES AND MEETINGS

SPEECH: THE POLICE AND THE PRESS

Write separate advance and follow stories about the following speech. Because the speech is reprinted verbatim, you can use direct quotations. Correct any spelling or grammatical errors.

Information for advance story:

Barry Kopperud is scheduled to speak to the local chapter of the Society of Professional Journalists Monday of next week. The club meets for dinner the second Monday of every month at the Blackhawk Hotel. Both the dinner and the speech are open to the public.

The dinners are $17.50 per person. Those wishing to hear the speech only may attend free. The evening begins with a social hour and cash bar at 6 p.m. Dinner starts at 6:30 p.m., and Kopperuds speech will begin at 7:30 p.m. Anyone wishing to attend the dinner must make reservations in advance by calling LeeAnn Verkler at the university.

Kopperud is the chief of police, and he will speak about issues regarding press coverage of crime and the police.

Speech for follow story:

Good evening, ladies and gentlemen. I've met most of you before. A couple of you I've seen just within the last hour. I'm glad we have this opportunity to talk under conditions that are more pleasant than when we usually meet.

The police beat is among the most active beats for any reporter. I've noticed that a good share of the content of the news broadcasts and the newspaper comes from the police.

This heavy reliance by the media on the police probably accounts for a situation police and news people have observed in many towns and cities. There is a symbiotic, co-dependent, love-hate relationship between cops and reporters that develops about everywhere.

Obviously, reporters rely on the police to provide information about some of the most important and dramatic events of the day. But police need reporters to get out information on the things they want to promote. Police understand that people read and watch news stories about crime. One of the first places people turn to when they get their daily paper is the police blotter.

Although the police department has had generally good relations with the press, there are some common problems—points of friction, you might call them—that arise from time to time. One of these points of friction involves the release of information through unofficial channels.

The police department has lots of information, some of it secret that it doesn't want released to the public. A classic example is information relevant to a homicide, such as autopsy information and details about the scene of the crime. Why do we want to keep this information secret? Because doing so helps us investigate the crime. A few years ago we had a homicide in which a man was bludgeoned to death with a tire iron. The killer then doused the body with gasoline and tried to set it afire. The body was in a wooded area and not discovered for several weeks. We got a lot of tips about that murder. We also had a couple of people show up trying to confess. Because we withheld the details about the crime scene and cause of death, we were able to distinguish the real culprit from the cranks and the real sources from the phony ones. Because the details were never published in the media, we could trace leads back to the one person with firsthand knowledge—a person who is now serving a life sentence. But those details are exactly the kind of thing reporters most want.

One of the banes of my existence is that there are people in the police department who like to release that kind of information. Maybe these leaks are intentional—from disgruntled officers—or maybe the leaks are unintentional, where an officer tells a friend who tells a reporter. Either way, reporters will call us back asking for confirmation of these leaks, but the police department will never confirm or deny anything.

That brings me to some ethical questions. Both police and reporters deal with ethical issues. Sometimes we err and release information that we shouldn't. Sometimes we wonder why you folks in the media publish what you do. I just want to share with you some recent incidents that raise ethical issues and ask you to consider them.

A few weeks ago, a police dog bit its handler's daughter. The dog was retired from service but had been living with its handler. As a result of the incident the girl needed stitches. Somehow a TV reporter got onto the story and wanted to do an on-camera interview with someone from the department. We refused. The reporter suggested it was because the story would embarrass the department or suggest irresponsibility or create problems with the city council. But none of those was correct. We refused because the dog had been put down, and the little girl didn't know that. She was fond of the dog, and the dog had meant a lot to her. Her mom and dad asked that the story not be released, and we agreed.

In another recent case, we had an accidental death of a graduate student in a university dorm. The man had suffocated to death, and the newspaper reported—correctly—that he had died while practicing autoerotic asphyxiation. I read that article and thought, "How crass!" Imagine how that must have made that students mother and father feel. I'd like to think that reporters would take that kind of thing into account before they publish a story. Sometimes the feelings of the family outweigh the publics need to know.

The case that for me presented the most searing ethical problem was the Wendy Ray case. You all remember that Wendy was a university student who was abducted from just outside her parents apartment one night, repeatedly raped, tortured and then murdered.

For weeks she was just missing, and no one knew where she was. We got our first break in the case when we arrested a couple of men for burglarizing an electronics store. After we had charged them, Donald Hendricks, the assistant county attorney, called and said one of them, Scott Reed, wanted to cut a deal: He'd tell us about Wendys murder if we promised not to seek the death penalty for him. Reed told us where to find Wendys body.

At this point, I went to Bill and Liz Ray, Wendys parents, and told them we had remains and believed them to be Wendys, pending a dental match. I also told them that we knew a lot more about how she had died and that I would tell them as much as they wanted to know when they wanted to know it. They understood that I meant there were grisly details about Wendys death. A few hours later, we had a positive dental match, but before I could get back to Wendy's parents, one of the radio stations had aired a news story with all the gory details. I can't tell you how devastated the Rays were. I think it was not a good way for the family to learn those details.

I guess the moral of these stories is a simple one: People really are affected by news stories. I hope reporters have enough humanity not to get caught up in the competitive practices of the business and realize how they may hurt others. I understand some people may reach different decisions about how to handle these ethical issues. I have no problem with someone who disagrees with me. I have a real problem, however, with reporters who won't consider other points of view.

EXERCISE 4

SPEECHES AND MEETINGS

SURGEON GENERAL'S SPEECH

Write a news story that summarizes the following speech given by the surgeon general of the U.S. Public Health Service. Assume that the surgeon general spoke at a state PTA convention in your city at 8 p.m. yesterday. This is a verbatim copy of a speech actually given by the surgeon general and can be quoted directly. As you write the story, assume that it is just a few days before Halloween. Correct any spelling or grammatical errors.

I am pleased to be here today with representatives of several organizations who recognize that alcohol is the nations number one drug problem among youth and who share my concern that the alcohol industry has targeted Halloween, a traditional holiday for children, as their latest marketing opportunity.

Just as Saman, the ancient Keltic Lord of the Dead, summoned the evil spirits to walk the earth on October 31, Americas modern day distilleries, breweries and vineyards are working their own brand of sorcery on us this year. On radio and television and even at supermarket check-out counters we are being bombarded with exhortations to purchase orange and black 12-packs and even "cocktails from the Crypt."

Well, as your surgeon general I'm here today with my own exhortation: Halloween and hops do not mix.

Alcohol is the number one substance abuse problem among Americas youth. In fact, it is the only drug whose use has not been declining, according to our most recent National High School Senior Survey. The National Institute on Alcohol Abuse and Alcoholism reports that, currently, 4.6 million teen-agers have a drinking problem.

Why do so many of our young people drink? There are no easy answers to this question, but clearly the availability of alcohol and its acceptance, even glamorization, in our society are factors. The National Coalition on Television Violence reports that before turning 18, the average American child will see 75,000 drinking scenes on television programs alone.

In just two days many of our young people will be celebrating Halloween. Many children look forward to this day as much as they do Christmas and Hanukkah. Who among us can forget the excitement of dressing up as ghosts and goblins and going from door to door shouting "trick or treat," and coming away with a fistful of candy?

Trick or treat.

This year the alcohol industry has given new meaning to those innocent words of childhood. They are serving up new treats—and new tricks.

They are saying: "It's Halloween, it's time to celebrate, it's time for a drink!" Beer companies offer free Halloween T-shirts, bat sunglasses, and glowing cups. Halloween parties sponsored by a major brewer are being held in nearly 40 cities.

What I say is scary is the possibility of increased carnage on our highways, the real specter of more binge drinking by our young people, and the absolute reality of those smaller, less dramatic cases of health and emotional problems caused by alcohol consumption.

Last year alone, we lost 3,158 young people in alcohol-related crashes, over 60 in every state in the union. Fully 40 percent of all deaths in young people are due to crashes—6,649 last year, and, as you can see, about half are related to alcohol.

What is also scary to me is the encouragement of "binge drinking" by our young people.

Some of these Halloween ads encourage the purchase of 12 or 24 packs of beer, and who will drink all that beer? 43 percent of college students, 35 percent of our high school seniors and 26 percent of 8th grade students have had five or more drinks in a row during the past two weeks. And beer and wine coolers are their favorite alcoholic beverages.

I also find it scary that we continue to think of beer and wine as "soft liquor." There's nothing "soft" about ethyl alcohol. And there's just as much ethyl alcohol in one can of beer or one glass of wine as there is in a mixed drink. That is the hard fact.

Finally, as the nations doctor and as a pediatrician, what I find scariest of all is that alcohol affects virtually every organ in the body. Alcohol consumption is associated with medical consequences ranging from slight functional impairment to life-threatening disease states—among them, liver disease, cancer of the esophagus, and hypertension.

Where the organs of the body are concerned, alcohol is an equal opportunity destroyer.

The alcohol industry and its hired guns, the advertising agencies, know these facts. I hope that parents and other concerned adults do, too. For if the alcohol industry has chosen to be part of the problem, it is up to you to be part of the solution.

In closing I would like to speak on behalf of those who have no voice in this debate—Americas children and adolescents. Let us not make this year, the year they robbed the kids of Halloween. For their sake and our own, let us keep Halloween sane, safe—and sober.

EXERCISE 5

SPEECHES AND MEETINGS

PRESIDENT GEORGE W. BUSH'S SPEECH AT THE END OF IRAQ WAR

This is a transcript of President George W. Bush's address May 1, 2003, announcing the end of major combat operations in Iraq. The speech was delivered on the deck of the aircraft carrier Abraham Lincoln at sea off the coast near San Diego, Calif. President Bush had flown to the Abraham Lincoln in an S-3B Viking jet piloted by Lt. Ryan Phillips.

THE PRESIDENT'S SPEECH

Thank you all very much. Admiral Kelly, Captain Card, officers and sailors of the USS Abraham Lincoln, my fellow Americans: Major combat operations in Iraq have ended. In the battle of Iraq, the United States and our allies have prevailed. (Applause.) And now our coalition is engaged in securing and reconstructing that country.

In this battle, we have fought for the cause of liberty, and for the peace of the world. Our nation and our coalition are proud of this accomplishment—yet, it is you, the members of the United States military, who achieved it. Your courage, your willingness to face danger for your country and for each other, made this day possible. Because of you, our nation is more secure. Because of you, the tyrant has fallen, and Iraq is free. (Applause.)

Operation Iraqi Freedom was carried out with a combination of precision and speed and boldness the enemy did not expect, and the world had not seen before. From distant bases or ships at sea, we sent planes and missiles that could destroy an enemy division, or strike a single bunker. Marines and soldiers charged to Baghdad across 350 miles of hostile ground, in one of the swiftest advances of heavy arms in history. You have shown the world the skill and the might of the American Armed Forces.

This nation thanks all the members of our coalition who joined in a noble cause. We thank the Armed Forces of the United Kingdom, Australia, and Poland, who shared in the hardships of war. We thank all the citizens of Iraq who welcomed our troops and joined in the liberation of their own country. And tonight, I have a special word for Secretary Rumsfeld, for General Franks, and for all the men and women who wear the uniform of the United States: America is grateful for a job well done. (Applause.)

The character of our military through history—the daring of Normandy, the fierce courage of Iwo Jima, the decency and idealism that turned enemies into allies—is fully present in this generation. When Iraqi civilians looked into the faces of our servicemen and women, they saw strength and kindness and goodwill. When I look at the members of the United States military, I see the best of our country, and I'm honored to be your Commander-in-Chief. (Applause.)

In the images of falling statues, we have witnessed the arrival of a new era. For a hundred of years of war, culminating in the nuclear age, military technology was designed and deployed to inflict casualties on an ever-growing scale. In defeating Nazi Germany and Imperial Japan, Allied forces destroyed entire cities, while enemy leaders who started the conflict were safe until the final days. Military power was used to end a regime by breaking a nation.

Today, we have the greater power to free a nation by breaking a dangerous and aggressive regime. With new tactics and precision weapons, we can achieve military objectives without directing violence against civilians. No device of man can remove the tragedy from war; yet it is a great moral advance when the guilty have far more to fear from war than the innocent. (Applause.)

In the images of celebrating Iraqis, we have also seen the ageless appeal of human freedom. Decades of lies and intimidation could not make the Iraqi people love their oppressors or desire their own enslavement. Men and women in every culture need liberty like they need food and water and air. Everywhere that freedom arrives, humanity rejoices; and everywhere that freedom stirs, let tyrants fear. (Applause.)

We have difficult work to do in Iraq. We're bringing order to parts of that country that remain dangerous. We're pursuing and finding leaders of the old regime, who will be held to account for their crimes. We've begun the search for hidden chemical and biological weapons and already know of hundreds of sites that will be investigated. We're helping to rebuild Iraq, where the dictator built palaces for himself, instead of hospitals and schools. And we will stand with the new leaders of Iraq as they establish a government of, by, and for the Iraqi people. (Applause.)

The transition from dictatorship to democracy will take time, but it is worth every effort. Our coalition will stay until our work is done. Then we will leave, and we will leave behind a free Iraq. (Applause.)

The battle of Iraq is one victory in a war on terror that began on September the 11, 2001—and still goes on. That terrible morning, 19 evil men—the shock troops of a hateful ideology—gave America and the civilized world a glimpse of their ambitions. They imagined, in the words of one terrorist, that September the 11th would be the "beginning of the end of America." By seeking to turn our cities into killing fields, terrorists and their allies believed that they could destroy this nation's resolve, and force our retreat from the world. They have failed. (Applause.)

In the battle of Afghanistan, we destroyed the Taliban, many terrorists, and the camps where they trained. We continue to help the Afghan people lay roads, restore hospitals, and educate all of their children. Yet we also have dangerous work to complete. As I speak, a Special Operations task force, led by the 82nd Airborne, is on the trail of the terrorists and those who seek to undermine the free government of Afghanistan. America and our coalition will finish what we have begun. (Applause.)

From Pakistan to the Philippines to the Horn of Africa, we are hunting down al Qaeda killers. Nineteen months ago, I pledged that the terrorists would not escape the patient justice of the United States. And as of tonight, nearly one-half of al Qaeda's senior operatives have been captured or killed. (Applause.)

The liberation of Iraq is a crucial advance in the campaign against terror. We've removed an ally of al Qaeda, and cut off a source of terrorist funding. And this much is certain: No terrorist network will gain weapons of mass destruction from the Iraqi regime, because the regime is no more. (Applause.)

In these 19 months that changed the world, our actions have been focused and deliberate and proportionate to the offense. We have not forgotten the victims of September the 11th—the last phone calls, the cold murder of children, the searches in the rubble. With those attacks, the terrorists and their supporters declared war on the United States. And war is what they got. (Applause.)

Our war against terror is proceeding according to principles that I have made clear to all: Any person involved in committing or planning terrorist attacks against the American people becomes an enemy of this country, and a target of American justice. (Applause.)

Any person, organization, or government that supports, protects, or harbors terrorists is complicit in the murder of the innocent, and equally guilty of terrorist crimes.

Any outlaw regime that has ties to terrorist groups and seeks or possesses weapons of mass destruction is a grave danger to the civilized world—and will be confronted. (Applause.)

And anyone in the world, including the Arab world, who works and sacrifices for freedom has a loyal friend in the United States of America. (Applause.)

Our commitment to liberty is America's tradition—declared at our founding; affirmed in Franklin Roosevelt's Four Freedoms; asserted in the Truman Doctrine and in Ronald Reagan's challenge to an evil empire. We are committed to freedom in Afghanistan, in Iraq, and in a peaceful Palestine. The advance of freedom is the surest strategy to undermine the appeal of terror in the world. Where freedom takes hold, hatred gives way to hope. When freedom takes hold, men and women turn to the peaceful pursuit of a better life. American values and American interests lead in the same direction: We stand for human liberty. (Applause.)

The United States upholds these principles of security and freedom in many ways—with all the tools of diplomacy, law enforcement, intelligence, and finance. We're working with a broad coalition of nations that understand the threat and our shared responsibility to meet it. The use of force has been—and remains—our last resort. Yet all can know, friend and foe alike, that our nation has a mission: We will answer threats to our security, and we will defend the peace. (Applause.)

Our mission continues. Al Qaeda is wounded, not destroyed. The scattered cells of the terrorist network still operate in many nations, and we know from daily intelligence that they continue to plot against free people. The proliferation of deadly weapons remains a serious danger. The enemies of freedom are not idle, and neither are we. Our government has taken unprecedented measures to defend the homeland. And we will continue to hunt down the enemy before he can strike. (Applause.)

The war on terror is not over; yet it is not endless. We do not know the day of final victory, but we have seen the turning of the tide. No act of the terrorists will change our purpose, or weaken our resolve, or alter their fate. Their cause is lost. Free nations will press on to victory. (Applause.)

Other nations in history have fought in foreign lands and remained to occupy and exploit. Americans, following a battle, want nothing more than to return home. And that is your direction tonight. (Applause.) After service in the Afghan—and Iraqi theaters of war—after 100,000 miles, on the longest carrier deployment in recent history, you are homeward bound. (Applause.) Some of you will see new family members for the first time—150 babies were born while their fathers were on the Lincoln. Your families are proud of you, and your nation will welcome you. (Applause.)

We are mindful, as well, that some good men and women are not making the journey home. One of those who fell, Corporal Jason Mileo, spoke to his parents five days before his death. Jason's father said, "He called us from the center of Baghdad, not to brag, but to tell us he loved us. Our son was a soldier."

Every name, every life is a loss to our military, to our nation, and to the loved ones who grieve. There's no homecoming for these families. Yet we pray, in God's time, their reunion will come.

Those we lost were last seen on duty. Their final act on this Earth was to fight a great evil and bring liberty to others. All of you—all in this generation of our military—have taken up the highest calling of history. You're defending your country, and protecting the innocent from harm. And wherever you go, you carry a message of hope—a message that is ancient and ever new. In the words of the prophet Isaiah, "To the captives, 'come out,'—and to those in darkness, 'be free.'"

Thank you for serving our country and our cause. May God bless you all, and may God continue to bless America. (Applause.)

EXERCISE 6

SPEECHES AND MEETINGS

PRESIDENT BILL CLINTON'S MEMORIAL ADDRESS FOR OKLAHOMA CITY BOMBING VICTIMS

This is a transcript of President Bill Clinton's address at the memorial service held on April 23, 1995, for the people who died in the explosion that destroyed the Alfred P. Murrah Federal Building in Oklahoma City. The service was held at the State Fairgrounds Arena in Oklahoma City and was attended by more than 10,000 people. Oklahoma Gov. Frank Keating and the Rev. Billy Graham also spoke at the service. Write a news story that summarizes its content. Because the speech is reprinted verbatim, you may quote it directly. Correct errors if necessary.

BACKGROUND

This information is what was known to the public on the day President Clinton gave this speech.

The Oklahoma City federal building had been destroyed by a bomb, made from fertilizer and fuel oil, that exploded the morning of April 19. The number of people known at this time to have died in the blast is 78. In addition, 432 people have been injured, and 150 are still missing. Soon after the explosion, FBI agents announced they were seeking two white men whom they were calling John Doe No. 1 and John Doe No. 2. The agents now suspect Timothy James McVeigh of Kingman, Ariz., is John Doe No. 1 and have charged him with destruction of federal property. Just hours after the bombing, McVeigh was arrested by an Oklahoma trooper for driving without a license plate and carrying a concealed knife. The search for John Doe No. 2 is continuing. FBI agents have been questioning Terry Nichols of Herington, Kan., and his brother James of Decker, Mich. Neither Terry nor James Nichols is suspected of being John Doe No. 2. But federal agents say in affidavits filed in court that the Nichols brothers and McVeigh are involved in right-wing militia organizations and know one another. Other court papers described McVeigh as angry with the federal government because of the assault by federal agents on the Branch Davidian complex in Waco, Texas, on April 19, 1993.

THE PRESIDENT'S SPEECH

Today our nation joins with you in grief. We mourn with you. We share your hope against hope that some may still survive. We thank all those who have worked so heroically to save lives and to solve this crime, those here in Oklahoma and those who are across this great land, and many who left their own lives to come here to work, hand-in-hand, with you.

We pledge to do all we can to help you heal the injured, to rebuild this city and to bring to justice those who did this evil.

This terrible sin took the lives of our American family, innocent children in that building only because their parents were trying to be good parents as well as good workers; citizens in the building going about their daily business; and many there who served the rest of us, who worked to help the elderly and the disabled, who worked to support our farmers and our veterans, who worked to enforce our laws and to protect us.

Let us say clearly they served us well and we are grateful.

But for so many of you, they were also neighbors and friends. You saw them at church, or the P.T.A. meetings, at the civic clubs or the ball park. You know them in ways that all the rest of America could not. And to all the members of the families here present who have suffered loss, though we share your grief, your pain is unimaginable and we know that. We cannot undo it. That is God's work.

Our words seem small beside the loss you have endured, but I found a few I wanted to share today. I have received a lot of letters in these last terrible days. One stood out because it came from a young widow and a mother of three whose own husband was murdered with over 200 other Americans when Pan Am 103 was shot down. Here is what that woman said I should say to you today.

"The anger you feel is valid but you must not allow yourselves to be consumed by it. The hurt you feel must not be allowed to turn into hate, but instead into the search for justice. The loss you feel must not paralyze your own lives. Instead, you must try to pay tribute to your loved ones by continuing to do all the things they left undone, thus ensuring they did not die in vain."

Wise words from one who also knows.

You have lost too much but you have not lost everything, and you have certainly not lost America, for we will stand with you for as many tomorrows as it takes.

If ever we needed evidence of that, I could only recall the words of Governor and Mrs. (Cathy) Keating, "If anybody thinks that Americans are mostly mean and selfish, they ought to come to Oklahoma."

If anybody thinks Americans have lost the capacity for love, and caring, and courage, they ought to come to Oklahoma.

To all my fellow Americans beyond this hall I say, one thing we owe those who have sacrificed is the duty to purge ourselves of the dark forces which gave rise to this evil.

There are forces that threaten our common peace, our freedom, our way of life. Let us teach our children that the God of comfort is also the God of righteousness. Those who trouble their own house will inherit the wind. Justice will prevail.

Let us let our own children know that we will stand against the forces of fear. When there is talk of hatred, let us stand up and talk against it. When there is talk of violence, let us stand up and talk against it. In the face of death let us honor life.

As St. Paul admonished us, "Let us not be overcome by evil, but overcome evil with good."

Yesterday Hillary and I had the privilege of speaking with some children of other federal employees, children like those who were lost here. And one little girl said something we will never forget. She said, "We should all plant a tree in memory of the children." So this morning before we got on the plane to come here, at the White House, we planted that tree in honor of the children of Oklahoma.

It was a dogwood with its wonderful spring flower and its deep enduring roots. It embodies the lesson of the Psalms that the life of a good person is like a tree whose leaf does not wither.

My fellow Americans, a tree takes a long time to grow, and wounds take a long time to heal, but we must begin. Those who are lost now belong to God. Some say we will be with them, but until that happens, their legacy must be our lives.

Thank you all and God bless you.

EXERCISE 7

SPEECHES AND MEETINGS

COUNTY COMMISSION MEETING

Assume that your county commission held a meeting at 2 p.m. yesterday. Write a news story that summarizes the comments and decisions made at this meeting. Correct all errors.

The members of your county commission began their meeting by listening to plans for a luxury condominium development on Elkhart Lake. The new development will be called "Sun-Crest." The property is owned by The Roswell Development Corporation, headquartered in Pittsburgh. Carlos Rey, a spokesman for the company, said: "We are planning a series of 10-story buildings overlooking the lake. None will exceed 100 feet in height. They will contain a total of 715 units. Estimated selling price of a unit will be $250,000 and upwards, perhaps to a top of $750,000 for the larger penthouse units. The development is about 5 miles from the nearest town, and we intend to promote it as a vacation and recreation center. We'll have our own well and our own sewer system, with an extensive recreation system centered around the lake. We know that fire protection is a concern. The township fire department serving the area doesn't have a ladder truck capable of reaching the top of a 10-story building. We'll donate $600,000 for the purchase of one." The commission voted 5-2 to approve the plans and to rezone the land from agricultural to PUD: Planned Unit Development.

Next, at 3 p.m., the commission honored and presented plaques to two 15-year-old girls. The girls, Doreen Nicholls and Pamela DeZinno, were walking along a river in a county park last week and saw a young child fall from a boat. Both girls dove into the river and pulled her out. While Doreen then proceeded to administer CPR, Pamela called for help, thus saving a life.

Appearing next before the commission, Sheriff Gus DiCesare asked it to require a three-day wait before a pistol could be bought from any gun dealer in the county. "I do not think that 72 hours is too long for someone to wait to buy a handgun," Sheriff DiCesare said. "There are a lot of cases where people went out and bought a gun with criminal intent and used it right away to shoot or rob someone. We want a cooling off period." Under the proposed ordinance, a customer would have to provide the dealer with his name, address, date of birth and other information, then wait 72 hours before picking up the pistol. The dealer would mail the information to the sheriffs department, where it would be kept on a computerized file. Sheriff DiCesare said it would speed the identification of the owner of a pistol found at a crime scene. A majority of the commissioners said they favor such a proposal but want to get more information and possibly hold a public hearing to give every citizen an opportunity to speak his mind. They promised to seriously consider it at their next meeting.

The commissioners then decided not to give themselves a raise, rejecting a proposed pay raise on a 4-3 vote. It has been five years since the last pay raise for them. Then their salary went from $47,500 to $51,000 a year. Yesterday, the majority, led by Commissioners Roland Graumann and Anita Shenuski, argued that a raise was "inappropriate." Faith Ellis argued a proposed increase to $56,500 was not out of line because commissioners in other counties earn more. "This is not asking too much," she said. "The county is getting a good deal for the time we put in." Anne Chen responded, "Our work should be done for community service, not just for how much we make."

EXERCISE 8

SPEECHES AND MEETINGS

SCHOOL BOARD MEETING

Assume that your school board held its monthly meeting at 7:30 p.m. yesterday. Write a news story that summarizes the comments and decisions made at this meeting. Correct all errors.

The school board opened its meeting by honoring seven retiring teachers: Shirley Dawsun, Carmen Foucault, Nina Paynich, Kenneth Satava, Nancy Lee Scott, Lonnie McEwen, and Harley Sawyer. Paynich worked as a teacher 44 years, longer than any of the others. Each teacher was given a framed "Certificate of Appreciation" and a good round of applause.

The school board then turned to the budget for next year. The budget totals $618.7 million, up 5% from this year. It includes $9.3 million for a new elementary school to be built on West Madison Ave. It will be completed and opened in two years. The budget also includes a 4.5% raise for teachers and a 6% raise for administrators. Also, the salary of the superintendent of schools was raised by $10,000, to $137,000 a year. The vote was unanimous: 9-0.

The school board then discussed the topic of remedial summer classes. Board member Umberto Vacante proposed eliminating them to save an estimated $2.1 million. "They're just too expensive, especially when you consider we serve only about 900 students each summer. A lot of them are students who flunked their regular classes. Often, if they attend the summer classes, they don't have to repeat a grade. If we're going to spend that kind of money, I think we should use it to help and reward our most talented students. They're the ones we ignore. We could offer special programs for them." Supt. Greg Hubbard responded, "Some of these summer students have learning disabilities and emotional problems, and they really need the help. This would hurt them terribly. Without it, they might never graduate." The board then voted 7-2 to keep the classes one more year, but to ask its staff for a study of the matter.

During a one-hour hearing that followed, about 100 people, many loud and angry, debated the issue of creationism vs. evolution. "We've seen your biology books," said parent Claire Sawyer. "I don't want my children using them. They never mention the theory of creationism." Another parent, Harley Euon of 410 East Third Street, responded: "Evolution isn't a theory. Its proven fact. Creationism is a religious idea, not even a scientific theory. People here are trying to force schools to teach our children their religion." A third parent, Roy E. Cross of 101 Charow Lane, agreed, adding: "People can teach creationism in their homes and churches. Its not the schools job." After listening to the debate, the board voted 6-3 to continue using the present textbooks, but to encourage parents to discuss the matter with their children and to provide in their individual homes the religious training they deem most appropriate for their families.

Finally, last on its agenda, the board unanimously adopted a resolution praising the school systems ADDITIONS: adult volunteers who contribute their spare time to help and assist their neighborhood schools. Last year, Supt. Greg Hubbard reported, there was a total of 897 ADDITIONS, and they put in a total of 38,288 hours of volunteer time.

EXERCISE 9

SPEECHES AND MEETINGS

CITY COUNCIL MEETING

Assume that your City Council held a meeting at 8 p.m. yesterday. Write a news story that summarizes the comments and decisions made at this meeting. Correct all errors.

BACKGROUND

For 10 years, a downtown church in your city (the First United Methodist Church at 680 Garland Avenue) has provided a shelter for the homeless, allowing them to sleep in the basement of its fellowship hall every night and feeding them both breakfast and dinner. The church can house 180 people each night and relies on a staff of more than 200 volunteers. In recent years, they've been overwhelmed, and the church, by itself, is unable to continue to afford to shoulder the entire burden. It has asked for help: for donations and for more room, especially in winter, for the homeless to sleep. Civic leaders have formed the Coalition for the Homeless, Inc., a nonprofit organization, and hope to build a new shelter. The coalition has asked the city to donate a site, valued at $500,000. Coalition leaders said they will then raise the $1.5 million needed to construct the shelter. The coalition leaders say they will also operate the shelter, relying on volunteers; a small, full-time professional staff; and donations from concerned citizens.

FIRST SPEAKER

Ida Levine, president of the Coalition for the Homeless, Inc.:

"As you, uh, know, what we're trying to do here is raise $1.5 million to build the shelter. We're approaching everyone that might be able to help and, so far, have collected about $200,000 and have pledges of another $318,000, and thats just the beginning, in two months. So we're certain that if you provide the land, we'll be able to, uh, come up with all the money for this thing. The site we have in mind is the old fire station on Garland Avenue. The building is so old that its worthless, and we'd tear it down, but its an ideal location for our purposes."

SECOND SPEAKER

Lt. Luis Rafelson:

"I'm here officially, representing the police department, to say that we're all for this. It costs the taxpayers about $350,000 a year to arrest homeless people for violating city ordinances like trespassing on private property and sleeping at night in parks and such. During the average month last year we arrested 300 homeless people, sometimes more. It takes about 2 hours to arrest a person and do all the booking and paperwork, while taking five minutes to transport them to a shelter. So you're wasting police time, time we could be spending on more important things. So if the city spends $500,000 on this deal, it'll save that much in a year, maybe more."

THIRD SPEAKER

Banker Irvin Porej:

"The people who stay in shelters are just like you and me. The difference is that we have a place to go. They're good people for the most part, just down on their luck. This would provide a temporary shelter for them, help them get back on their feet. Until now, we've had churches doing this, and the Salvation Army has a shelter, too, but we should put an end to the church shelters. Its not fair to them because the churches are burdened by a problem that everyone should be helping with, and the problem is getting too big for them to handle."

FOURTH SPEAKER

Council member Sandra Bandolf:

"We have to address this problem. It's not going to go away. And with this solution, it really won't cost the city anything. No one's asking us for money or anything, only for a piece of land that's been lying unused for years."

FIFTH SPEAKER

Council member William Belmonte:

"I suppose I'm going to be the only one who votes against this. Why should taxpayers suddenly start paying for this, people who work hard for their money and are struggling these days to support their families? And what happens if the coalition doesn't raise all the money it needs for the shelter, what happens then? What happens if they breach the agreement? Then we'll be left holding the bag, expected to pay for this damn thing and to support it for years. That'll add a whole new bureaucracy to the city, and where'll the money come from then?"

SIXTH SPEAKER

Trina Guzman, president of the Downtown Merchants' Assn.:

"The members of my association are strongly opposed to this. We agree that the city needs a shelter, that we have an obligation to help the people who are really homeless and needy, but not on Garland Avenue. That's just a block from downtown, and we've been having trouble with these people for years. Some of them need help, have all sorts of problems like alcoholism and mental illness that no one here's talking about. Remember too that these people aren't allowed to stay in the shelters during the day. Theoretically, they're supposed to go out and work, or at least look for work. What some of them do is hang around Main Street, panhandling and annoying people and using our parking lots and alleys for toilets. We've got customers who tell us they won't come downtown any more because they're afraid of being approached and asked for money and being mugged or something. Let's feed these people and help them, but put them out somewhere where they can't hurt anyone."

OUTCOME

The council voted 6-1 to donate the land. Belmonte cast the single vote against the proposal.

CHAPTER 13

SPECIALIZED TYPES OF STORIES

I make an earnest plea to my profession to seek ways of reporting the positive. In a sense I guess I am only saying that we should tell it like it is, and it is often better than we say it is.

(Howard K. Smith, news commentator)

A new reporter told to write a speech or a meeting story would immediately understand what was asked of her. But someone who has never worked in a newsroom might scratch her head when asked to write a bright, a follow-up, a roundup or a sidebar. Yet all are common assignments for beginning reporters.

BRIGHTS

Brights are short, humorous stories that often have surprise endings. Some brights are written in the inverted pyramid style: They begin with a summary lead, then report the remaining details in descending order of importance. Other brights have unexpected or bizarre twists, and reporters may try to surprise readers by withholding those twists until the stories' final paragraphs. Brights that have surprise endings are called "suspended-interest stories" and, to keep their endings a surprise, usually begin with intriguing or suspenseful facts—some details likely to interest readers—but withhold the most newsworthy or interesting facts until the end. A suspended-interest story cannot begin with a summary lead, because it would reveal the surprise ending.

Editors and news directors search for humorous stories and display the best ones prominently in their newspapers and news broadcasts. Brights entertain viewers and readers, arouse their emotions and provide relief from the seriousness of the world's problems. Here are examples of summary leads for brights:

> NEW YORK (AP)—"Hello, ma'am. Drop the gun, please."
>
> New York's finest are getting a manners lesson from Mayor Rudolph Giuliani, who wants police officers to be a little more civil, professional and courteous.

> MARTINSBURG, W.Va. (AP)—Police are looking for the naughty person who stole Santa's wallet and pants from the Martinsburg Mall last week.

> Clarence Esser, 68, of Winchester, Va., had his wallet and navy blue work pants stolen from the break room Thursday as he listened to children's holiday wishes while playing Santa Claus, police said Saturday.

The suspended-interest story that follows begins so routinely that at first it may mislead the audience; its bizarre twist is not revealed until the final paragraphs:

> Police killed an intruder after he set off a burglar alarm in a clothing store on Main Street shortly after 1 a.m. today.
>
> Police entered the store after customers in a nearby tavern heard the alarm and surrounded the building until the officers arrived.
>
> Police found the intruder perched on a counter and killed it with a fly swatter.
>
> "It was my third bat this year," declared a police officer triumphantly.

Here are two more brights. The one on the left begins with a summary lead. The one on the right does not, and its ending may surprise you:

> College students often complain about sloppy roommates, and Oscar—the first pig to be evicted from an apartment in the city—may be the sloppiest of all.
>
> Oscar is a 6-week-old, 20-pound Hampshire pig. His owners claim that Oscar is only slightly different from other pets that live in the Colonial Apartments on University Boulevard. But the complex's owners say Oscar has to go.
>
> "He's dug up the entire back yard," co-owner Sean Fairbairn said. "Besides that, he's noisy, and he stinks. We've gotten all sorts of complaints."
>
> Oscar has lived in an old hay-filled refrigerator in Todd Gill's patio for a week. The patio is fenced in, but neighbors complained to the owners. The owners then told Gill and his roommate, Wayne Brayton, that Oscar has to go by noon Saturday.
>
> "I don't think it's fair," Gill said. "People love Oscar. He runs around and grunts and squeals, but nothing too obnoxious. We've only let him out a couple times, and he's dug a hole under the fence once or twice, but no one's complained to me."
>
> Gill and Brayton bought Oscar last week at a livestock auction.

> The briefcase was on the floor near the Police Department's information desk for about 45 minutes. A clerk got suspicious. Maybe it contained explosives, she thought.
>
> She called the department's bomb squad, and it evacuated the building. Members of the bomb squad then carried the briefcase outside and blew it up in a vacant lot.
>
> That's when they learned that the briefcase belonged to their boss, Police Chief Barry Kopperud. He left it at the information desk while visiting the mayor.
>
> "It's my fault," Kopperud said. "I should have mentioned it to someone. My officers did a good job, and I'm proud of them. They did what they were trained to do: to be alert and cautious."
>
> Kopperud added that his son is likely to be upset, however. Today is the boy's seventh birthday, and Kopperud had his present in the briefcase.

Animals are a favorite topic for brights. The New York Times tracked down rumors that a cat had made its home in the Fulton Street subway station. The rumors were true, and the cat had been surviving on mice and tins of cat food left by subway passengers. Other brights draw their humor from the stupid things even smart people may do. An Akron, Ohio, rookie police officer left his patrol car running with a suspect handcuffed in the back seat while he investigated a domestic disturbance. The suspect climbed into the front seat of the car and drove away.

Writers of brights need to walk a fine line, however. A story that seems to make fun of a tragedy is tasteless, not funny.

Stories about people who love unusual occupations or who have overcome difficulties make great brights. A story about this woman, Lucy Hinkle, had both qualities. Hinkle owns a business that cleans animal waste from the lawns of her customers. She started her business after she contracted a rare muscle disease that ended her career as a dental assistant.

FOLLOW-UPS

"Follow-ups," which are also called "second-day" and "developing" stories, report new developments in stories that were reported earlier. Follow-up stories differ from the follow stories we described in Chapter 12. Follow stories on speeches and meetings are simply the stories written after those events.

Major stories rarely begin and end in a single day, and news organizations prepare a fresh article or package each time a new development arises. So stories about a trial, a legislative session, political campaign or flight to the moon may appear in the media every day for weeks. The Sept. 11 terrorist attacks on the World Trade Center in New York City and the Pentagon in Washington, D.C., remained top news stories for weeks after the events. Follow-up stories described such things as rescue efforts, identification of the terrorists who carried out the attacks, the disruption of American air transportation, and plans to increase airport security. Although the follow-up story is tied to a past event, its lead always emphasizes the latest developments. Follow-ups may summarize previous developments, but that information is presented as concisely as possible and placed later in the story.

Follow-up stories about disastsers are especially common. On Monday, news organizations might report that a hurricane devastated areas of the Gulf Coast, killing 34 people and causing hundreds of millions of dollars in damages. Stories on Tuesday might report that several people missing in the storm have been found dead and others have been rescued. Wednesday's stories might describe relief efforts and report that the number of people known to have died in the storm had reached 42. Follow-up stories published on Friday might describe what people who had fled the storm find when they return to their homes and businesses. And weeks later, an investigative follow-up might report that many of homes destroyed in the hurricane had been shoddily built. Still later follow-up stories might report on civil and criminal court cases brought against the builders of the poorly constructed homes.

The following leads from The Associated Press trace developments over the days immediately following the flooding of a Pennsylvania coal mine that trapped nine miners:

SOMERSET, Pa. (AP)—Nine coal miners were trapped in a flooded shaft Thursday after they apparently ruptured a nearby abandoned mine that was filled with water, officials said. Sounds from the mine indicated at least some were alive as rescue crews scrambled to help them.

SOMERSET, Pa. (AP)—Encouraged by a tinny tapping sound coming up from the depths, rescuers drilled an escape hole Thursday in a race to save nine coal miners trapped 240 feet underground in a dark shaft filling up with millions of gallons of frigid water.

SOMERSET, Pa. (AP)—After a day of frustration caused by a broken drill bit, rescuers said Saturday they were getting closer to nine miners trapped deep underground in a cramped, flooded mine shaft.

SOMERSET, Pa. (AP)—Nine coal miners who were miraculously rescued from a cramped, flooded shaft Sunday morning decided early in their 77-hour ordeal that they were going to "live or die as a group," scrawling last messages to loved ones and tying themselves together so that if they drowned rescuers would find all the bodies.

HARRISBURG, Pa. (AP)—Gov. Mark S. Schweiker said Monday he will appoint a special state commission to examine mine safety in Pennsylvania and recommend changes to prevent a recurrence of the accident that left nine miners trapped deep underground for more than three days.

Nearly two months after the miners were rescued, the Associated Press carried a story with this lead:

GREENSBURG, Pa. (AP)—Two state lawmakers are seeking $4 million in state money to update and computerize maps of existing and abandoned coal mines.

State Rep. Robert Bastian, a Republican who represents the Somerset County district where nine miners were trapped for more than three days, said he plans to introduce legislation later this year to fund an effort to make maps more accurate and increase miner safety.

And four months after the rescue, this story ran on the AP wire:

SOMERSET, Pa. (AP)—The Quecreek miners gave nine thumbs up to a TV movie that will air on ABC Sunday night, chronicling the 77 hours they spent trapped in the flooded Somerset County mine in July.

Because each new development in a newsworthy situation prompts a follow-up story and each follow-up story recapitulates earlier stories, some viewers and readers grow weary of the repetition and believe the news media do it only to sensationalize stories. People who were unhappy with the amount of coverage given to the murder trial of O.J. Simpson often expressed such views. And yet news organizations cover trials, wars and disasters intensely because large numbers of readers and viewers are interested. Americans were so enthralled with the Simpson trial that the audiences for the nightly network news broadcasts were down as much as 10 percent because people were watching live coverage of the trial on cable channels CNN and Court TV.

Sometimes a follow-up story does not report new events but adds information unavailable earlier. The Federal Bureau of Investigation's arrest of a notorious computer thief who had stolen thousands of data files, including more than 20,000 credit card numbers, received front-page coverage in The New York Times. The next day, The Times followed up the initial story with another that described how the computer thief's work exposed the vulnerabilities of the Internet.

Follow-up stories are becoming more common as news organizations devote more resources to making sure important stories are followed to their conclusions. Some organizations have established regular columns or segments for follow-ups. In the past, critics complained that journalists, like firefighters, raced from one major story to the next, devoting most of their attention to momentary crises. Critics added that when one crisis began to subside, reporters moved on to the next. Older stories disappeared from the news before all the questions they raised had been answered. To address this complaint, news organizations now regularly return to important topics and tell readers what has happened since the topics dropped out of the headlines. Follow-ups may report that an area devastated by a hurricane has been rebuilt or that victims of an accident are still suffering from its consequences.

ROUNDUPS

To save space or time, news organizations summarize several different but related events in roundup stories. Traffic roundups are most common; instead of publishing separate stories about each traffic death that occurs in a single weekend, newspapers and broadcast stations may summarize several fatal accidents in a single story. Or news organizations may report all the weekend crimes, fires, drownings, graduation ceremonies or football games in roundup stories.

Another type of roundup story deals with a single event but incorporates facts from several sources. Reporters may interview half a dozen people to obtain more information about a single topic, to verify the accuracy of facts they have obtained elsewhere or to obtain new perspectives. For example, if a city's mayor resigned unexpectedly, reporters might ask her why she resigned, what she plans to do after she leaves office, what she considers her major accomplishments and what problems will confront her successor. They might then (1) ask other city officials to comment on the mayor's performance and resignation, (2) ask the city clerk how the next mayor will be selected and (3) interview leading contenders for the job. All this information could be included in a single roundup story.

The lead for a roundup story emphasizes the most important or unique developments and ties all the facts together by stressing their common denominator, as in the following example from the Associated Press reporting on Christmas Day happenings around the world:

> LONDON (AP)—Bloodshed marred some of the world's Christmas celebrations and social tensions shadowed others. A grenade killed a girl and two other worshipers at a church in Pakistan, bombs exploded at a church in India, protesters blocked church doors in Yugoslavia.

The story not only included the details of the violence, but it also reported on the Christmas message from the Vatican urging countries to avoid war, celebrations by U.S. troops at Bagram Air Base in Afghanistan, and year-end remarks by Britain's Queen Elizabeth II.

After the lead, roundup stories usually organize facts and quotations by topic, starting with the most newsworthy accident, crime, fire or drowning and moving on to the second, third and fourth most important.

Some beginning reporters make the mistake of organizing their material by source. For example, they might write a crime roundup by reporting first all the information they got from the police chief and then all the information they got from the county prosecutor. Stories organized by source are disjointed and repetitious. Each source is likely to mention the same events, and comments about a particular event will be scattered throughout the story.

SIDEBARS

Sidebars are related to major news stories but are separate from them. Sometimes, news organizations use them to break long, complicated stories into shorter, more easily understood ones. Other times, sidebars report information of secondary importance. Sidebars may give readers additional information about the main topic, usually from a different source or perspective. They may provide background information, explain a topic's importance or describe the scene, emphasizing its color and mood. If fire destroys a nightclub, news organizations may publish or broadcast a sidebar in which survivors describe how they escaped. When a new pope is selected, sidebars may describe his personality, past assignments, philosophy and trips to the United States. Other sidebars may describe problems confronting Catholic churches throughout the world.

When a company called Clonaid announced it had cloned a human, most news organizations led with a story that reported the claim, which was announced at a press conference, and the organization's plan to have DNA samples from the baby and her mother tested to verify the claim. The stories also reported that Clonaid had been founded by a religious sect called the Raelians, who believe human life was created by extraterrestrials. News organizations also published a variety of sidebars focusing on other aspects of the story. New York Times reporter Gina Kolata wrote a sidebar quoting experts in cloning who doubted that such a feat was possible. A sidebar by Tina Hesman of the St. Louis Post-Dispatch explained why cloned cats and cows and sheep may be genetically identical to their parents but may differ in appearance. Another Post-Dispatch sidebar reported that the U.S. Food and Drug Administration had launched an investigation to determine whether Clonaid had violated agency regulations by conducting any of the cloning work in the United States. The Associated Press published a sidebar in question-and-answer format that included an explanation of the cloning process, background information on Clonaid, and descriptions of the physical problems clones may have.

News organizations also use sidebars to report local angles to national and world stories. After the terrorist attacks of Sept. 11, news organizations across the country were finding local angles.

> Two of the hijackers, Mohammed Atta and Abdulaziz Alomari, began their journey Sept. 11 in Portland, Maine. The Portland Press Herald/Maine Sunday Telegram reported the details of their activities the night before the attack.
>
> The Fayetteville, N.C., Observer, located near Fort Bragg, reported a week after the attacks that some soldiers had "disappeared"; they had been called to duty and ordered to tell no one where they were going or why.
>
> And the East Valley Tribune reported on the murder of a Sikh man who owned a filling station in Mesa, Ariz. The murder was the first reported post-Sept. 11 hate crime.

Sidebars are usually briefer than the main news stories and are placed next to them in a newspaper or just after them in a newscast. If, for some reason, the sidebars must run on a different page of a newspaper or later in a newscast, editors or producers will tell the audience where or when the related stories will appear. Because some people read or view only the sidebars, most briefly summarize the main stories even when the two stories are close together.

CHECKLISTS FOR WRITING SPECIALIZED STORIES

Brights

1. Choose either an inverted-pyramid style or a suspended-interest style for the story.
2. If you use a suspended-interest approach, write a lead that will intrigue readers without revealing the bizarre or amusing twist the story takes at the end.

Follow-ups

1. Write a follow-up each time something newsworthy develops in a continuing story.
2. Stress the new developments in the lead and body of the story.
3. Summarize the important background and earlier developments.

Roundups

1. Emphasize the most important or unique incident or development in the lead.
2. Explain in the lead what is common to all the incidents reported in the roundup.
3. Organize facts and quotations by topic, not by source.

Sidebars

1. Focus the lead on background, color, mood or some other aspect of the story different from the one emphasized in the lead to the main story.
2. Summarize the news event described in the main story.

A Memo From the Editor

HISTORY, TRADITIONS AND CULTURE: OLD GLORY AND NOODLE

By **Tommy Miller**

On my first night as a newspaper reporter, I almost met my journalistic Waterloo because of Old Glory and Noodle.

The distressing moment came in 1963, when I was a freshman at Hardin-Simmons University in Abilene, a west Texas town about 500 miles from my east Texas home in Beaumont.

On the first day of my newswriting class, the professor told me to report for work on Friday night at the Abilene Reporter-News. My job: take information from phone callers and write stories about high school football games.

On Friday night, during my brief instructions from one of the sports reporters, I was told about six-man football. (For you non-football-junkies, six-man football was, and still is, played in small Texas towns that don't have enough players for an 11-man team. Scores in six-man games are unusually high.)

"Get everybody who scores in the story, but keep it to three paragraphs," the sports reporter said.

I nodded as if I knew exactly what he was talking about, but, in fact, I didn't have a clue. In East Texas, as far as I knew, we played with 11 players or we didn't play at all.

In a few minutes, phones started ringing throughout the newsroom. They were ringing loudly and often, and sports reporters and editors were yelling at each other with questions about games and stories. The best way I can describe it now is to compare the newsroom scene with the television show "ER", but without the gurneys and surgery.

After I had survived several callers, usually a home-team coach or student assistant, I got a caller who said he had a six-man game. He began listing names of players who scored. He listed four or five players. Then four or five more. He kept listing them, and even though he was well into the 20s with names, I continued to write the names along with information about how these names scored.

Then, I noticed a couple of people behind me were laughing. I turned around and saw that quite a few people were laughing. Then I realized that my caller was a sports staffer who had called me from another phone in a corner of the room.

After the laughter subsided, a veteran staffer mumbled that I had fallen for a traditional rookie-initiation rite. "Now you can really get to work," he said.

More phones rang. I kept taking callers. Several calls later, I answered the phone and a man said: "I've got the Old Glory-Noodle game."

I paused and said, "OK. You got me the first time. But I know there can't be any towns named Old Glory and Noodle."

(*continued*)

The caller protested, but I hung up, confident that I had averted another embarrassing initiation rite.

The phones kept ringing. I kept answering them. A few minutes after I hung up on the earlier caller, sports editor Fred Sanner, a huge, gruff man, stood at his desk and growled (yes, he really growled), "Who was taking the Old Glory-Noodle game?"

It is at about this point, as you might expect, that my memory has grown fuzzy about the events that night, primarily because I think I may have lost consciousness for a moment.

But I seem to recall that the newsroom became very quiet. Sports writers and others around me shook their heads. I felt a bit sick to my stomach. I figured that if I admitted what happened, my journalistic career would be over. But I think I did walk to Sanner's desk and say something like, "Mr. Sanner, I think someone called with that game a few minutes ago, but I kind of had a bad connection."

He looked at me and said, "Well, the coach is on the phone. Talk to him." I did, and as you might expect, the coach was not happy. He yelled something to me about how he couldn't believe I didn't know of Old Glory and Noodle. I told him I had just arrived in town about a week earlier and hadn't had a chance to check out the area. But I assured him that I would visit both Old Glory and Noodle soon.

Of course, had I been given a quick primer on the towns in the Abilene area, things might have been much better that night. But that was a time when young journalists were often thrown into newsrooms and expected to sink or swim. I didn't sink, although I never told Sanner what really happened.

Two years later, after transferring to Baylor University, I was back on Friday night football duty at the Waco Tribune-Herald. This time, I studied the names of the surrounding towns before the phones started ringing, and I didn't hang up on the caller who said he was from West, as in West, Texas, a small town a few miles north of Waco.

Six-man football games are still being played in Texas, but Old Glory and Noodle scores are no longer in the Saturday morning Abilene Reporter-News. Both towns closed down their schools a number of years back, I'm told. I never visited Old Glory and Noodle, as I assured the coach I would. Maybe one of these days I will.

Here is a list of things you can do on your first job to avoid the Old Glory-Noodle trap:

1. Read books and articles about the area where you will be working.
2. Prepare a thumbnail profile of the area, with information about the population, ethnic breakdown, economy, and so forth.
3. Take a long, leisurely drive through the area, paying particular attention to suburban towns and major streets.
4. Ask a veteran staffer to go for a drive with you to identify local landmarks and point out various communities' changing cultural and economic trends.
5. Study the newspaper's stylebook, if it has one. If not, prepare your own local stylebook, focusing on spellings and historical information.
6. If the city has a university, invite a local history professor to lunch.
7. Go to city and county government meetings to get the flavor of local government.
8. Ask several veteran reporters or editors for names of the city's most influential or interesting people. Talk with some of them.
9. Have lunch with one of the newspaper's best copy editors and ask for a list of the most common mistakes regarding local information.

10. And, finally, two old standbys—ride a bus to the end of the line and back and just listen to people talk. Or, take a cab and visit with the driver.

Adapted from The Local News Tool Kit, published in 2001 as a supplement to The Local News Handbook by the American Society of Newspaper Editors.

Tommy Miller is the Roger Tatarian Endowed Chair of Professional Journalism at California State University, Fresno. He is a former managing editor of the Houston Chronicle.

SUGGESTED READINGS

Hart, Jack. "Brites." *Editor & Publisher,* June 7, 1997, p. 3.
Hennessy, Joan. "Small Paper, Big Story." *American Journalism Review,* December 2001, pp. 44-48.

USEFUL WEB SITES

American Press Institute: http://www.americanpressinstitute.org
American Society of Newspaper Editors: http://www.asne.org
The Journalist's Toolbox: http://www.journaliststoolbox.com/newswriting/onlineindex.html
Power Reporting: http://powerreporting.com (Links to a variety of Web sites arranged by beat)
The Poynter Institute: http://www.poynter.org
Society of Professional Journalists: http://www.spj.org

EXERCISE 1

SPECIALIZED TYPES OF STORIES

BRIGHTS

Use the following information to write "brights," a series of short, humorous stories. Write some brights with a summary lead and others with a surprise ending.

1. SQUIRRELS

University officials are blaming squirrels for a rash of problems students, teachers and staff members have been experiencing with their cars. One person whose car has been damaged by squirrels is Oliver Brooks, an associate professor of English, 5402 Andover Dr. One of the headlights in his van went out a few weeks ago. He replaced it, but it still didn't work. When he opened the hood, however, he was surprised to find a squirrels nest. "There was a big squirrels nest in the corner where the light wires were," he said. Brookes spent $184 to get the wiring replaced. Linda Kasparov, university dietitian, 9301 Lake St., had a similar experience. She was driving home one night when the headlights, speedometer and oil-pressure gauge on her new sedan all quit working. She pulled into a service station and asked the attendant what was wrong. She said, "The attendant put up the hood and then jumped back exclaiming, 'My God, what have you got in there!'" She said there was a nest made of sticks, string and plastic bags. One of the bags started moving, and when the attendant pulled it out, he discovered three baby squirrels. The squirrels had chewed through every wire in the engine compartment except two. The repair bill for Kasparov was $425. Laura Ruffenboch, a wildlife professor at the university, said the insulation on many electrical wires is made from a soybean derivative, and the squirrels may find that attractive. She also said it was unusual for squirrels to make nests in cars that are used regularly.

2. MISDIRECTED LOVE

Joseph R. DeLoy told the judge today that he's in love. DeLoy, 26, said he loves a 29-year-old woman, Patty McFerren. DeLoy met McFerren while they were both shopping at a supermarket in the city. DeLoy asked McFerren for a date. McFerren refused. "But she was wonderful, and I could tell she really liked me, so I called her," DeLoy said. In fact, DeLoy tried to call McFerren more than 200 times, sometimes in the middle of the night. However, it wasn't really her number that he called. By mistake, he got the wrong number and called Patrick McFerren instead. The two McFerrens are unrelated and do not know each other. Their listings in the phone book are very similar. Patty is listed as "P. McFerren." Patrick is listed as "P.J. McFerren." Patrick informed DeLoy that he was dialing the wrong number. DeLoy said he didn't believe him and continued to call. "I was hoping that she'd answer," DeLoy said in court today. Patrick installed an answering machine so he could screen the calls, and the machine got a heavy workout. Finally, Patrick called the police, and they told DeLoy to stop making the calls, but no charges were filed against him. The calls continued, so Patrick sued, accusing DeLoy of intentional infliction of emotional distress and invasion of privacy. The calls were a costly mistake for DeLoy. In court today, DeLoys attorney explained that his client was acting "on his heart and hormones, not his head." A jury of 5 men and 7 women decided that his calls were worth $25 each—for a total of $5,000. The jury ordered DeLoy to pay that sum—$5,000—to Patrick. "I'm satisfied," Patrick said.

3. UNDERAGE DRIVER

Charles Todd Snyder was charged with drunk driving following a traffic accident in your city one week ago. He was also charged with driving without a drivers license in his possession. He was scheduled to appear in court at 9 a.m. this morning. He failed to appear in court. As a consequence, Judge Edward Kocembra ordered police to go to Snyders home and to haul Snyder into court. Police went to the address Snyder had given officers at the time of the accident: 711 Broadway Avenue. The police returned to the court at approximately 10:15 a.m. and appeared before Judge Kosembra with Snyder. Snyder was in his mothers arms. He is a 13-month-old child, and his mother insisted that he drinks only milk and that the only vehicle he ever drives is a stroller. So the judge apologized for the inconvenience and told the officers to give Snyder and his mother a ride back to their home. Snyder, apparently frightened by the unfamiliar surroundings and people, cried. Police said that whoever was stopped had falsely given the arresting officers Snyders name and address when he signed the drunken driving ticket and the ticket for driving without a drivers license in his possession. They told the judge that they have no idea who that person might be.

4. TRUCK THEFT

There was a motor vehicle theft which occurred in the city at some time in the middle of last night. The vehicle was taken from a building located at 7720 Avonwood Dr. The building was unlocked at the time, and 12 occupants sleeping in an upstairs room said they heard nothing unusual. They were all in bed by midnight and the first got up at 6 a.m., discovering the theft at that time. Police describe the missing vehicle as a bright canary-yellow fire truck, marked with the name of the city fire department. The custom-made truck cost a total of $192,000 and was delivered to the city just three months ago. Firemen said it had a full tank of gas, about 50 gallons. However, it gets only $1\frac{1}{2}$ miles to the gallon. It contained enough clothing and equipment for six firefighters, a dozen oxygen tanks, 1,000 feet of hose, four ladders (each up to 60 feet tall), plus miscellaneous other equipment. The people sleeping upstairs were all firefighters and the building was a fire station. The firefighters suspect that someone opened the stations main door, then either pushed or towed the truck silently outside and started its engine some distance away from the building. It is the first time in its history that the city fire department has reported that one of its trucks has been stolen. It was not insured. The keys are always left in the truck to reduce the response time when firefighters receive a call for help.

5. INHERITANCE

The will of a local man, Benjamin Satterwaite, 74, of 307 E. King Boulevard was filed in Probate Court today. Satterwaite died on the twentieth of last month of cancer. He had lived alone in his home, neighbors said, for at least the past 20 years. He was a retired postal clerk. According to the will, Satterwaite left a total estate of $1,471,400.38. Much of the money was earned in the stock market. Neighbors said they were surprised by the amount. Satterwaite was not a miser but lived frugally, and neighbors said they did not suspect that the deceased was a millionaire. Satterwaite left the entire estate to the U.S. government, explaining that, "Everybody seems to be living off the government, so maybe someone ought to help it out." He had no known relatives.

6. BANK REGULATIONS

Abraham Burmeister is president of the First National Bank, the largest bank in your community. Each year, in accordance with new federal laws, the bank is required to send all its customers copies of some complex new federal rules concerning the regulation of banks and the procedures followed for money transfers by means of electronic banking. Consequently, the First National Bank prepared a 4,500-word pamphlet describing and summarizing those new federal rules and then sent copies of the rules to all its 40,000 regular depositors and customers. Like many other bankers, Burmeister objected to the federal law, saying it imposed a needless burden and needless expense on bankers since the federal laws that banks are being forced to explain are too complicated for the average person to understand and too dull and uninteresting for people to spend time trying to read. To prove his point, on the last page of 100 of the 40,000 copies of the rules he took a gamble and inserted a special extra sentence. The sentence said, "If you return this pamphlet to any of the banks tellers within the next 30 days, they will give you $50." The 30 days passed yesterday and not one person turned in a single copy of the 100 special pamphlets and requested the $50 due on demand, apparently because no one read the pamphlets. Bank officials calculated that it cost somewhere in the neighborhood of $25,000 to prepare, print, address and mail the pamphlets to the 40,000 bank customers, and they said that is a waste of money, yet they must do it every year, even though obviously no one reads the things, as they have just proven with their interesting little experiment.

7. DRUNKEN RIDER

Lynita L. Sharp admits she was intoxicated last night but says she should not be charged with drunk driving. Sharp, 5836 Bolling Dr., was riding her 2-year-old filly horse along a state highway when Scott Forsyth, a corporal in the sheriffs department, came along. Forsyth said he saw Sharp sitting on her horse in the middle of the road. He said the rider looked to be sick or asleep. He turned on the blue lights on his cruiser, and the horse bolted off. Sharp said she was spending the weekend with her friends who own the farm where her horse is stabled. She had spent part of the evening at the local tavern and was riding home. Sharp said the cruisers light spooked the horse and caused her to lose control of it. Forsythe issued Sharp a ticket for operating a vehicle while under the influence of an intoxicating substance. Sharp said her horse, Frosty, is not a vehicle. "Vehicles can't think, but Frosty can think for herself," Sharp said. "I've fallen asleep in the saddle before, but it doesn't matter because Frosty knows the way home." Donald Hendricks, the assistant county attorney, said the state law does not require that a person be operating a motorized vehicle in order to be cited for drunk driving. The law was changed in 1991, he said, and since then 23 people who were not operating motorized vehicles, including a bicyclist and a man in a wheelchair, have been arrested for driving while intoxicated.

EXERCISE 2

SPECIALIZED TYPES OF STORIES

FOLLOW-UP STORIES

Write a story summarizing the initial set of facts and then just the lead for a follow-up story about the later developments. Or your instructor may ask you to write a complete news story about each day's developments.

YESTERDAY

Two boys were playing in Nichols Lake in Lakeside Park in your town. They were wading along the shore of the lake at about 12 noon at a point where the bottom drops off steeply. The two boys were Randy Stockdale, age 9, son of George and Lillian Stockdale, 472 Bolling Dr., and Edward McGorwan, age 10, son of Karen McGorwann, 4320 Elsie Drive, Apt. Six. Edward waded too far from shore, lost his footing and was unable to get back to shore. He and Randy started to yell for help. A man whose name has not been released by police heard their screams and ran to the lake to help. James Kirkman, a cab driver who was taking his lunch break in the park, heard the screams, too. He radioed his dispatcher who called 911. Kirkman said later that the unidentified man waded out as far as he could and tried to reach out to Edward, but the boy had drifted too far from shore. "When the boy went under and didn't come back up for air, this guy dove under to find him. But he didn't come back up, either," Kirkman said. Police Officers Kevin Barlow and Eddie Linn arrived on the scene at 12:18. Barlow immediately stripped to his shorts and started diving into the lake to find the victims. After several dives, he came back up with Edward McGorwan, who was unconscious. Linn tried to resuscitate the boy, but he was still unconscious when he was taken by ambulance to the Regional Medical Center. Barlow continued to search for the unidentified man for another 20 minutes until Dorothy Heslin, a scuba diver who assists the police on a volunteer basis, arrived. She pulled him from the water about 1:15 p.m. Wayne Svendson, a paramedic, tried to resuscitate the man. Svendson said the water was unusually cold and hypothermia had set it, which was indicated by the fact the mans skin had started to turn blue. The man was taken to the Regional Medical Center. Dr. Catrina Lowrie, a physician at the Medical Center, said the man was pronounced dead when he arrived. She also said that Edward McGorwan was in critical condition. Officer Barlow also was treated at Regional Medical Center for minor shock caused by the long period of time he spent in the water looking for the victims. He was released that afternoon.

TODAY

This morning, the police department released the name of the man who died trying to save Edward McGorwann from Nichols Lake. His name is William McDowell and he is an unemployed housepainter. He was 30 years old and he had lived at 1429 Highland Dr. Police Chief Barry Koperud said, "McDowell risked his life without hesitation to try to save someone in trouble. He was a real hero." Also this morning, Dr. Lowrie at the Regional Medical Center announced that Edward McGorwann had died. "He spent the night on a respirator, but his condition did not improve. This morning, at his mothers request, we took Edward off the respirator. He died less than half an hour later." McDowells sister lives in your town. Her name is Janice Carson and she lives at 2197 Marcel Av. She said her brother had dropped out of Colonial High School one year before graduating and joined the navy. He spent six years in the navy, and after he left he held a succession of jobs, including electronics technician, cook, construction worker and painter. She said he always enjoyed his jobs but was too restless to stay at one for more than a couple of years. "I guess some people would call him a drifter, but to me he was a free spirit. He loved people but he didn't want to be tied down with a house and a mortgage and all of that. There were only two things he never learned how to do. He couldn't hold a job for more than two years and he could never say no to anyone who needed help," she said with tears in her eyes.

EXERCISE 3

SPECIALIZED TYPES OF STORIES

FOLLOW-UP STORIES

Write a story summarizing the initial set of facts and then just the lead for a follow-up story about each of the later developments. Or your instructor may ask you to write a complete news story about each day's developments.

BACKGROUND

Years ago, tuberculosis ranked among the worlds most lethal diseases, and it remains a serious health problem in developing countries. The number of Americans with tuberculosis has declined dramatically over the last half century. Only approximately 23,000 new cases were reported in the U.S. last year, about 1,000 of them in your state. Basically, TB is a bacterial infection. It usually affects the respiratory system. It is spread through coughing, sneezing, singing or talking. Because of advances in the field of medicine, it is rare for a death to occur because of TB. Modern treatment succeeds virtually 100 percent of the time. Doctors can prescribe medications to stop the disease if the infection is detected early enough. However, TB can be fatal if undetected. Symptoms include a prolonged and unexplained cough, night sweats, and sudden weight loss. To test for TB, a small amount of dead bacteria is injected into the skin of the upper arm of a person. Health workers know there is an infection when natural anti-bodies, formed to fight the illness, respond to the dead bacteria, and harden the skin around the test area.

ORIGINAL STORY

Maureen Verdugo, principal of Kennedy High School, called a special assembly at the beginning of classes at the school today and made a startling announcement. Verdugo revealed to the students that a 16 year old student enrolled at the school, whose exact identity she in no way revealed, other than as a tenth grader, has been diagnosed as suffering from the disease tuberculosis. Verdugo continued on by announcing that city health officials were notified by the students doctor and will be available at the school all five days of classes next week to give free TB tests to every student enrolled in one of the 16 yr. olds classes, as well as to students known to be the victims friends. "Anyone else—students, faculty members, and school personnel—who fears they may have been infected will also be tested free of charge. The tests will be administered in the school clinic, and students will be excused from their study halls and other free periods to take the tests," Verdugo said. The clinic will be open from 7 am to 5 pm and people can also visit it before or after their classes. "I've been working in high schools for 30 years," Verdugo went on to say, "and this is the first time I've had a problem like this. But I want to reassure you that there's no reason for panic. We're taking all the necessary precautions and have the situation well under control."

WEDNESDAY OF THE NEXT WEEK

On Monday and Tuesday of this week the citys Public Health Dept. had its personnel at the school, busily testing for tuberculosis students that may have come in contact with the infected 16 yr. old student enrolled in Kennedy High School. Initial tests were given free of charge at the school clinic. About 250 of the schools students were singled out by school authorities as having regular contact with the infected teen, either by being enrolled in the kids classes or by having some other close contact with the guy. Other students and teachers went in on their own. The testing is continuing and the final results will be announced sometime during the course of next week.

Of approximately three hundred students tested Monday and Tuesday, six showed signs of infection and were advised to have more testing done on them. "Infected students are being advised to undergo chest X rays and possibly sputum tests to determine whether they have developed TB," said Cathleen Graham, head of the citys Public Health Dept. "Those who are merely infected with the bacteria will be prescribed an antibiotic to prevent the onset of the disease. If the disease has progressed further, students will have to undergo more extensive drug therapy."

Some parents were frightened and dissatisfied. Tanaka Holland, mother of Sophomore Andrea Holland, said during an interview today: "When I called the school with some questions they were totally uncaring, and their procedures stink. Every student in the whole school should be tested. Just because a child wasn't in a class with the carrier doesn't mean they didn't come in contact with the disease," Mrs. Holland said. A second parent, James R. Waundry, agreed, adding, "This isn't anything to mess with. I've heard that people can die of tuberculosis, and how do we know that, uh, it's not going to come back? We've told our son, Paul, to stay home this week, and we're thinking of putting him in a private school."

FRIDAY OF THE FOLLOWING WEEK

In all, 581 Kennedy High School students were tested after learning that a 10th grade schoolmate had TB, Kennedy High School Principal Maureen Verdugo announced today. A total of 23 of the 581 students have tested positive for exposure to tuberculosis but none of the 23 have developed the disease. "The students are not contagious but must take antibiotics for six months to prevent the disease," said Joseph Perez, a health official employed by the city.

Greg Hubbard is the citys superintendent of schools. Hubbard said during a press conference today that he believes that this TB outbreak was the worst in the citys entire history. Hubbard said there is nothing the district can do to prevent occasional health problems like this one. "You're always subject to this kind of thing with the number of kids we have," he said. Health officials added that no one will ever know exactly how the outbreak started.

EXERCISE 4

SPECIALIZED TYPES OF STORIES

FOLLOW-UP STORIES

Write a story summarizing the initial set of facts and then just the lead for a follow-up story about each of the later developments. Or your instructor may ask you to write a complete news story about each day's developments.

DAY 1

Twelve people have been selected to hear the murder trial of Sara Kindstrom, 27, of 4828 North Vine Street. She is charged with the first-degree murder of her live-in boyfriend, Frederick C. Taylor, 25. If convicted of the charge, she could be sentenced to life in prison and would have to serve at least 25 years before becoming eligible for parole. Taylors death occurred last summer, on August 4 at about 7 p.m. Taylor was killed by shots from a .22 caliber pistol. This morning, assistant county attorney Donald Hedricks and Kindstroms attorney, assistant public defender Marilyn Cheeseboro, spent several hours questioning 42 potential jurors before selecting an 8-man, 4-woman panel to hear the case. The trial will begin at 9:00 a.m. tomorrow before Circuit Court Judge Randall Pfaff.

DAY 2

A neighbor, Martha Rudnick, testified: "My husband and I heard her screaming, but that wasn't unusual. They were always fighting over there. The police had been there a dozen times, but it never seemed to do any good. This time I heard the gun. Right away, I knew they were shots, but I thought he was shooting her. He was always threatening to kill her. I ran next door to see if I could help Sara. But when I got outside, Freddy was crawling out their front door, and she was coming after him with the gun, still shooting him. She was shooting him in the back, and he was just lying there, bleeding on the sidewalk. She kept pulling the trigger, but the gun must have been out of bullets and was clicking every time she pulled the trigger. I could see her face was all red and swollen and bleeding where he'd hit her, and it wasn't the first time I'd seen her like that."

Police Sergeant Michael Barsch said: "I interrogated her as soon as we got her to the police station. She told me she'd shot him and that she hoped she'd killed him. It was his gun, but we checked and found that she'd used it before. He'd taught her how to shoot it. He'd taken her target shooting and hunting with him. We also found a box of shells in her purse, with 9 shells missing, and found that she'd bought the box herself at a sporting goods store near her home about a week earlier."

DAY 3

Jurors seemed to be spellbound as they listened to the fascinating testimony of Sara Kindstrom today. She told a tearful story of bloody beatings and verbal, physical and sexual abuse at the hands of her live-in boyfriend, whom she is accused of killing. During her $5\frac{1}{2}$ hours of testimony today, Kindstrom said: "He was going to kill me. It wasn't a matter of whether he'd kill me, but when he was going to do it. I met him a year ago, and he moved right in with me, and at first it was really nice. Then he lost his job and got sicker and sicker. We could sleep together for a month and not have sex. Then we'd fight and he'd force himself on me. I work as a waitress, and when I got home Aug. 4 he was waiting for me. He started calling me names and hitting me and accused me of running around with other men, and that's not true. I'd never do that, but he was always jealous. I tried to keep quiet and make supper, but he started drinking. Later, we started arguing again. He was telling me that if I left, he'd move someone nice in. I said it was my house, and he said I'd be dead and then it would be his house. He was hitting me really hard, and I was bleeding. Then we were in the bedroom, and I just couldn't take it anymore. He kept a pistol in a bedroom closet, and I had it in my hand. I don't remember getting it out, but I must have, and it started going off. I don't remember pulling the trigger. He looked surprised and then he just fell to the floor without saying anything. I knew I'd hurt him, but I didn't think he was dead. I didn't mean to kill him."

DAY 4

In his closing arguments, the prosecuting attorney said: "The defendant did not have to murder Fredrick Taylor. She could have called the police for protection. She could have charged Taylor with assault, and she could have forced him to leave her house. But she never sought help and consistently returned to the man who beat her. She may regret it now, but she killed him. If she only wanted to protect herself, she could have shot him once, possibly twice, and escaped. But she fired 9 bullets, and all nine hit him—mostly in the back. She continued firing those bullets even after Taylor was down on the ground, trying to crawl to safety. That's murder in the first degree."

In her closing arguments, the public defender said: "This woman acted in self-defense. She was repeatedly and brutally beaten by Fredrick Taylor during their 12-month relationship. We also know Sarah Kindstrom believed that Taylor eventually would have killed her. She killed him to protect herself from rape and murder. Imagine yourself in that situation. You're being beaten, badly beaten. Dazed, confused, in need of protecting yourself, you pick up a gun and begin to shoot. You're acting in self-defense, to protect your own life, and you may not be entirely rational at a moment like that."

DAY 6

After two days of deliberation, the jury announced that it found the defendant guilty of murder in the second degree rather than of murder in the first degree. The maximum penalty for a conviction of that type is from 5 to 18 years in prison.

DAY 10

The judge today sentenced the defendant, Sara Kindstrom, to a term in a state prison of the minimum sentence of 5 years. In sentencing Kindstrom to the minimum prison term the judge noted the extenuating circumstances in the case, including her brutal treatment at the hands of her victim and her apparent effort to defend herself. However, the judge complained that she used excessive force in that defense. She will be eligible for parole in as short a time as a period of 18 months, with time off for good behavior.

EXERCISE 5

SPECIALIZED TYPES OF STORIES

ROUNDUPS—MULTIPLE SOURCES

Write a single news story that summarizes the following information. Organize the information in a clear, logical, cohesive manner. As you write the story, correct the spelling, style, grammatical and vocabulary errors. Also be thorough; report every issue in depth. Notice that the sources' comments appear in quotation marks, so you can quote them directly.

BACKGROUND

The Sunnyview Retirement Home is an 8-story brick building located at 410 Hillcrest Street in your community. The building is a former hotel. Ten years ago it was renovated and turned into apartments for retirees. It is privately operated, for profit, with 110 apartments, including 30 for a single resident and 80 for two residents, often couples, sharing an apartment. About 175 people were living there when a fire broke out at approximately 7:10 a.m. this morning. As many as 150 firefighters from throughout your region, including nearby communities, were called in for assistance in battling the blaze and assisting in rescuing all the victims from their peril.

FIRE CHIEF TONY SULLIVAN

"Its the worst damn fire I've ever seen. We've got seven dead we know of and maybe 20 more that've been taken to hospitals with various injuries, some pretty serious. We just can't tell for sure. There could be lots more in the building, people who couldn't get out. I can't send my men in yet to look for them, not at this point, because its not safe. We've got the fire out, but it was a fierce one, and some floors and walls were weakened and are liable to collapse at any time. We may have to pull them down or they could fall on my men. It may be another day before we're able to make a thorough search and recover all the bodies."

RESCUE WORKER JOHN CHARLTON

"People I've talked to say the fire started on the first or second floor. The fire itself wasn't so bad, except on the first couple of floors. Everything on those floors is gone. The fire didn't spread to the upper floors, but most of the deaths occurred up there. It was the smoke that did it. People said they couldn't breathe, and then a lot of them were old and in bad shape to begin with. We've taken the survivors that weren't hurt none to a church just across the street, and they're mostly resting there now. I don't know where they'll go tonight, where they'll sleep. The Red Cross is setting up an information center for relatives at the church. We've, uh, got all sorts of relatives that've been in and out all morning, looking for their people and apparently bringing them home with them, so we don't know who's missing or dead or home safe with their families."

RETIREMENT HOME DIRECTOR MILDRED ANCHALL

"We don't know how the fire started, just that it started somewhere on the second floor, and our alarms sounded at 7. It happened so fast, it spread so fast, that all we could do was try and get everyone out. No one had time to stop and get a list of all our residents, and now they've been taken a half-dozen different places. We don't have any way of knowing who's safe and who's missing. Besides our residents, I've got my staff to worry about, and some visitors who were in the building. It's a tragedy, a real tragedy, something like this. You hear about things like this happening but never think it could happen at your home."

BUILDING INSPECTOR RALPH SCHWEITZER

"We inspected the building just a couple weeks ago, and it satisfies all our codes. When it was remodeled 10 years ago we didn't require sprinklers, and they would have saved everyone, would have put the fire out in a minute or two, so they would have really prevented a tragedy like this. Anyone building a nursing home today is required to put in sprinklers, and this is what we have in mind to prevent, a real serious tragedy like this one."

SURVIVOR STEVEN MINH

"I'm 82, and I've been living here since it opened 10 years ago. Nothing like this ever happened here before. Its like I was back in World War II or something. I lived on the eighth floor, and people up there were screaming for help. The smoke was real bad, and some of us don't move so quick anymore. The firemen got up there real fast and led us down the stairs. There were some real heroes up there. I saw firemen carrying a half-dozen people down 6 or 8 flights of stairs when they could hardly breath themselves, and a lot of us would be dead without them. We couldn't have lasted much longer with the smoke and all. I'd just like to know what started the fire because it spread so fast. One minute everything was OK, then we were all choking on the smoke."

SURVIVOR BETSY AARON

"It was terrible in there. We began hearing fire alarms, but they weren't loud enough. By the time we realized what it was and went out into the hall it was full of smoke. I had a third-floor apartment, so I was able to get right out. I just took an elevator downstairs. Other people said they weren't working, but that must have been later, after I was out, that the elevators stopped working. When I got out on the street and looked up I saw people I knew leaning out their windows and shouting, 'Help me! Help me!' I couldn't do anything for them, not anything at all."

FIRE MARSHAL R.J. HILTON

"We haven't pinpointed the cause of the fire yet. It's too early, but my personal feelings are, strictly on a preliminary basis, it seems to have been an accidental fire that started in one of the apartments. It'll be at least a day or two before we have anything official on that."

EXERCISE 6

SPECIALIZED TYPES OF STORIES

ROUNDUPS—MULTIPLE EVENTS

Write a single roundup story that summarizes all three of the fires described below.

FIRE 1

Two police officers patrolling Main St. reported a fire at Frishe's Bowling Alley, 4113 Main St., at 3:32 a.m. today. They smelled smoke, got out of their squad car and traced the smoke to the bowling alley. Firefighters said the fire was confined to an office, where it caused an estimated $10,000 damage. Firefighters found evidence of arson and notified police that the office apparently had been set on fire after it was burglarized. Two cigarette machines, a soft-drink machine and a door leading to the office had been pried open. Police said the thieves probably set the fire to hide the robbery. Art Mahew, manager of the bowling alley, estimated that $20 was missing from the three machines and $50 was taken from a cash box in the office. He added: "That's all the money we keep in the building at night. Except for some change for the next day's business, we just don't keep any money in the building at night. It's too risky. This is the third robbery we've had since I started working here four years ago."

FIRE 2

Firefighters were called to 1314 Griese Drive at 8:23 a.m. today. They found a fire in progress on the second floor of the two-story home. The home is owned by Mr. and Mrs. Timothy Keele. Mr. and Mrs. Keel and their four children escaped from the home before firemen arrived. Firefighters extinguished the blaze within 20 minutes. The fire was confined to two upstairs bedrooms and the attic. Smoke and water damage were reported throughout the house. No one was injured. Damage was estimated at $20,000. Mrs. Keel told firemen she had punished one of her children for playing with matches in an upstairs closet earlier in the morning. Fire marshals said the blaze started in that closet and attributed the fire to the child playing with matches. Mrs. Keel added that she was not aware of the fire until a telephone repairman working across the street noticed smoke, came over and rang her doorbell. When she answered, he asked, "Do you know your house is on fire?"

FIRE 3

Firefighters responded to a call at the Quality Trailer Court at 10:31 a.m. today after neighbors were alerted by screams from a trailer occupied by Mrs. Susan Kopp, age 71. Flames had spread throughout the trailer by the time firefighters arrived at the scene. The firefighters had to extinguish the blaze, then wait for the embers to cool before they were able to enter the trailer. They found Mrs. Kopp's body in her bedroom in the trailer. A spokesman for the Fire Department said she had apparently been smoking in bed, then awoke when her bedding caught fire. She died of suffocation before she could get out. Neighbors who heard her screams were unable to enter the trailer because of the flames, smoke and heat.

EXERCISE 7

SPECIALIZED TYPES OF STORIES

SIDEBARS

Use the following information to write two separate stories: first a news story reporting the fire, then a sidebar based on the interviews with Mrs. Noffsinger.

MAIN STORY

The Grande Hotel is located downtown at the corner of Wisconsin and Barber Avenues. It is a seven-story structure with a total of 114 rooms. It was constructed and opened for business in the year 1924. In recent years the hotel has been in an obvious state of decline, unable to compete with new facilities in the city and with the convenience of motels located along highways which now bypass the city. Many of the hotel rooms have been rented on long-term leases, often to elderly persons who like its downtown location, which is more convenient for them, since many facilities they use are in walking distance and buses are easily available for other trips they want to make. Three persons died in a fire at the hotel last night. The cause of the fire is undetermined. It started in a third-floor room. It spread and also destroyed the fourth, fifth, sixth and seventh floors before it was brought under control at 4:30 a.m. today. At about 11 p.m. a guest called the lobby to report the odor of smoke. A hotel employee used a passkey to enter the third-floor room where the fire originated and found it totally engulfed in flames. The room is believed to have been vacant at the time. The employee sounded a fire alarm in the hotel and called firefighters. It was the first five-alarm blaze in the city in more than 10 years. Every piece of fire equipment in the city was rushed to the scene, and off-duty firefighters were called in to assist. Fortunately, said Fire Chief Tony Sullivan, no other fires were reported in the city at the same time or he would have had to send a truck and men from the scene of the hotel blaze. Hotel records indicate that 62 persons were registered in the hotel at the time the blaze initiated; 49 had long-term leases and 13 were transients. All the transients were located on the second floor and escaped safely. The dead, all of whom had long-term leases, have been identified as Mildred Haserot, age 58; Willie Hattaway, age 67; and Pearl Petchsky, age 47. The bodies of all three victims were found on the fourth floor, where they lived. Fire Chief Tony Sullivan said this morning the hotel is a total loss and that some walls are in danger of collapse. He said: "The fire was already out of hand when our first units reached the scene. I was called from home, and by then the flames were breaking out through the third- and fourth-floor windows. We were really lucky there weren't more people killed, but the hotel people knocked on the door of every room that was occupied to get everybody out. Most guests used a back stairway, and we were lucky the elevators kept working for awhile even after my men got into the building, otherwise the loss would have been worse. I'm also told that the top two floors were empty, and that helped keep down the loss of lives."

The Red Cross is caring for survivors, finding them new rooms and providing clothes and emergency allocations of cash, a total of $250 per person. Five people were injured, including one fireman who suffered from smoke inhalation. The others suffered from burns, some serious, and also from smoke inhalation. Three are being treated at Mercy Hospital. Two have been released, including the fireman. Their names and conditions are unknown at this time.

SIDEBAR

Nora Noffsinger, 74, has been a resident of the Grande Hotel for the past nine years. She paid $880 a month rent for one room on the fifth floor. A retired bookkeeper, she said afterward: "It was dreadfully expensive, but it was a charming old building and I had lots of good friends living there. I was asleep last night when I heard someone pounding on my door. I don't know who it was, but he told me to get out fast, and I did. All I had on were my pajamas and a robe, but I could see the smoke, even up there on the fifth floor, and I was scared; I knew right away that it was bad. Everyone else was scared too, but we all knew what to do. We'd talked lots about what we'd do if there was ever a fire because you hear so often about fires in old hotels, and we wanted to be prepared. We all kept flashlights in our rooms and planned to go down the back stairway unless the fire was there, and it wasn't. The lights were still on, so we didn't even need our flashlights. Now the Red Cross put me in a motel room a few blocks away, and I guess I should be happy I'm safe, but I lost everything—my clothes, a little money I'd kept hidden in a secret place, all my photographs. My husband's dead, you know, and I lost all my pictures of him. I don't know what I'll do now; I don't have any children. I'm all by myself, except for my friends, and they all lived at the hotel with me."

EXERCISE 8

SPECIALIZED TYPES OF STORIES

SIDEBARS

Use the following information to write two separate stories, first a news story reporting the Senate's action and then a sidebar based on the interview with the sheriff.

MAIN STORY

The state Senate today approved a bill overwhelmingly. The bill has already been approved by the house and now goes to the Governor, who has indicated that she will sign it. The bill was passed almost unanimously by angry lawmakers who want inmates housed in jails throughout the state to help pay the costs of their room and board. There were only 2 votes against the measure in the senate and none against it in the house. The bill will go into effect next January 1st. It will require persons housed in a jail within the state to reveal their incomes and, if they can afford it, to pay the entire cost of their room and board behind bars, or whatever share of the cost they can reasonably afford. The bill requires the State Department of Offender Rehabilitation to draw up guidelines on how prisoners will disclose their finances and how much they will be required to pay. The department will consider a number of relevant variables, such as whether a prisoner must support a family and devote all his or her income to that family. The idea for the bill arose a number of months ago when lawmakers touring a state prison were told that some inmates received Government benefits (mostly Social Security and veterans' benefits). The lawmakers were told that some of the prisoners opened bank accounts in the prisons and that the money they received piled up so they had thousands of dollars accumulated in the accounts when they were released. A subsequent survey requested by legislative leaders found 19,000 inmates in the state and that, of that total, 356 received government payments of some type. The same survey found that the inmates had a total of $8.1 million in inmate accounts at state prisons. Prison officials cautioned that the prisoners may have more money deposited in banks outside the prison system and that it would be difficult to locate those accounts. To enforce the new bill, lawmakers stipulated that prisoners who refuse to disclose their finances cannot be released early on parole. Officials have not yet determined how much each prisoner will be charged. Lawmakers also noted that some inmates may have other assets, such as farms, homes, automobiles, and stocks and bonds, and that those prisoners can also be expected to help defray their prison expenses.

SIDEBAR

Gus DiCesare is the county sheriff. He has held that position for 11 years. To retain the position, he must run for re-election every four years. As sheriff, DiCesare is in charge of the county jail, which has a capacity of 120 inmates, mostly men but also a few women. Criminals sentenced to terms of less than one year in prison usually are sentenced to the county facility rather than to a state prison. Despite its capacity of 120 persons, the county jail usually holds 140 to 150 persons—20 or 30 more than its rated capacity. When interviewed today about the legislatures approval of the bill in question, DiCesare said: "Hey, I think its a great idea. Some of these prisoners got more money than I'll ever have. When we pick them up, they're driving fancy cars, living in big homes and carrying a thick wad of money. Not most of them, but there're always a few in here, mostly drug dealers. We sentence them to jail as punishment, but it punishes honest taxpayers who pay to keep them in here—pay for this building, their food, clothes, jailers and all the rest. A couple of years ago, we calculated that it cost about $55 to keep one prisoner here one day. Hell, if they can afford it, prisoners should help pay for it all; that could be part of their punishment. I'll bet our costs are up to nearly $90 a day apiece now, and they're still rising. It'd help me too. I've got a damned hard problem trying to run this place on the budget the county gives me. With a little more money, I could improve the food, come up with more recreational facilities and maybe even try to rehabilitate a few prisoners—bring in some teachers and counselors and that type of thing. Now, all I really do is keep them locked behind bars all day, and that's not going to rehabilitate anyone."

CHAPTER 14

FEATURE STORIES

We journalists don't have to step on roaches. All we have to do is turn on the kitchen light and watch the critters scurry.
(P.J. O'Rourke, humorist and newspaper columnist)

Most news stories describe recent events—meetings, crimes, fires or accidents, for example. News stories also inform the public about topics that are important, local or unusual.

Feature stories, by contrast, read more like nonfiction short stories. Many have a beginning, a middle and an end. They inform readers and viewers, but they also amuse, entertain, inspire or stimulate. Because of these emphases, they are also called "human interest" stories.

Features may describe a person, place, process or idea rather than an event. Their topics may be less timely, less local and less earthshaking than those of news stories, but producers and editors find time and space to run them because they are newsworthy and appeal to audience members.

Reporters use no single formula, such as the inverted pyramid. And, in general, features explore their topics in greater depth than news stories.

When writing a feature story, journalists may borrow techniques from fiction writers, often using description, sensory details, quotations, anecdotes and even personification. They may use characterization, scene setting, plot structure and other novelistic elements to dramatize a story's theme and to add more details.

Feature stories, however, are journalism, not fiction or "creative writing." Nothing is made up. Like news stories, features must be factual and original. They must be fair and balanced, based on verifiable information. They also must be objective—they are not essays or editorials.

SELECTING A TOPIC AND GATHERING INFORMATION

Feature story ideas are everywhere. Almost everything one sees or does has a story behind it—journalists just have to open their eyes and ears. CBS News correspondent Steve Hartman has built a career on finding stories about ordinary people selected "at random" from a phone book. The most crucial step in writing a good feature story is making the topic fresh, dramatic, colorful and exciting. Reporters use all their senses—seeing, hearing, touching, smelling and sometimes tasting. They record how people move, speak and dress. They use descriptive verbs instead of adjectives and adverbs. They give audience members a reason to care about the subject.

Feature writers find story ideas by being curious and observant. News stories may provide spin-off topics for features. An earthquake, plane crash, international incident or other news event can spark human-interest stories about the reactions of victims, heroism in crises and other "people" angles that bring the event into sharper focus.

Features about major events or social problems can be localized through personal interviews and background research on the event or issue. For instance, a college student read several news stories about the street people in her community and noticed that none of the stories quoted the homeless. Instead, reporters relied on the authorities in their community. Police blamed the homeless for a series of minor crimes. Welfare agencies wanted more money to care for the homeless. Church leaders wondered about their responsibilities to the homeless. The student drove to the area where homeless people congregated, sat on a curb and began to interview one of the homeless people. Others gathered around her, and in a few hours, she was able to complete a dozen interviews. Her feature story revealed that the homeless were not primarily men—or bums and criminals. Rather, families with small children had become homeless. For years, many of the families had lived in their own homes. Then a husband or wife became ill or lost a job, often because a factory closed or moved. The couples came to the city looking for work, but were unable to find new jobs or low-cost housing and ended up living on the streets.

Successful feature writers experience their story first-hand, instead of just relying on the interviews of others. For example, a newspaper reporter trained as a telemarketer and sold newspapers for about a day. She wrote about being on the other end of the telephone call, the work it takes to sell and the reactions of potential customers. Another journalist spent several hours at a tattoo and body piercing shop instead of just interviewing shop owners and people who had tattoos. Both reporters filled their stories with details that made the topic so much more interesting to readers.

Some feature stories are inspired by the personal experiences of reporters or their friends. If, after little or no training, a reporter's friend is given a gun and hired as a guard, the reporter might ask about the training and qualifications of other "rent-a-cops," who outnumber the police in some cities. Reporters also have written about unwed fathers, student suicides, child care for single parents in college, unusual classes, unusual teachers or a professor's latest research project.

After selecting a topic likely to interest a large audience, reporters must narrow the subject and find a central point that emphasizes, perhaps, a single person, situation or episode. For example, a profile cannot summarize a person's entire life, so a reporter might discuss just one aspect: a single experience, trait or achievement that sums up the person's character. If reporters fail to identify a central point, their stories become long, disorganized and superficial. This can leave readers and viewers confused, and they will quit the story.

While gathering the information for feature stories, reporters normally consult several sources, perhaps a half-dozen or more, to obtain a well-rounded account. Good reporters gather two or three times as much information as they can use, then discard all but the most telling details.

The concept of "universal needs" can help a reporter choose a topic. Everyone is interested in the needs all human beings have in common and the ways of satisfying those needs. Many people are attracted to such topics as food, clothing, shelter, sex, health, approval, belonging, self-esteem, job satisfaction and entertainment. The following exercise demonstrates how reporters can use universal needs to find a story idea: Write the universal needs down one side of a piece of paper. Write some current topics from the news, such as the new school year or unemployment, across the top. Then, where each line and column intersect, write in a "hybrid" topic combining the two, such as medical clinics that offer free services to students or loss of self-esteem among the jobless.

Al Thompkins of the Poynter Institute offers 50 story ideas, ranging from "caffeine kids" to "slum lords." These ideas, listed on the Poynter Web site, can trigger other interesting topics.

The Census Bureau has another helpful Web site to ignite the imagination on story ideas. Its "special topics" areas and its "press releases" offer history and statistics on many subjects.

TYPES OF FEATURE STORIES

Feature stories come in a wide variety. Here are a few of the most common types.

Profiles or Personality Features

Profiles describe interesting people. These people may have overcome a disability, had an interesting hobby, pursued an unusual career or become famous because of their colorful personalities. To be effective, profiles must do more than list an individual's achievements or important dates in the individual's life. They must reveal the person's character. To gather the necessary information, feature writers often watch their subjects at work; visit them at home; and interview their friends, relatives and business associates. Some profile subjects may surprise reporters by revealing their most personal and embarrassing secrets. Completed profiles quote and describe their subjects. The best profiles are so revealing that readers and viewers feel as though they have actually talked to the people. Here's a profile of late-night television star Dick Cavett written by Matthew Hansen for the Lincoln (Neb.) Journal Star:

> Dick Cavett has tired of this story.
>
> He's told it so many times, to so many people, that nearly all the funny has been harvested from the once-fertile comedic soil.
>
> But the question has been asked. A deep sigh, and the Lincoln lad who would be a late-night TV king begins:
>
> A 2-year-old boy recites passages from "A Midsummer Night's Dream." His mother gently prods him along. The assembled house guests listen in amazement.
>
> Then the punchline: "Afterwards I would encourage them to 'crap! crap!' Crap, of course, being my substitution for clap."
>
> Finally, the insight: "I think I kept saying crap even after I learned clap, because people were laughing."
>
> Cavett, now 65, has never stopped seeking that laughter. The ensuing decades have seen him on ABC's "Dick Cavett Show" from 1969 to 1975. He's had turns as a Broadway actor and a stand-up comedian, a writer and a pitchman. He's hosted several other talk shows and countless television specials. He's made cameos in "Annie Hall" and "Forrest Gump." He's even the voice you hear on University of Nebraska promotional commercials.
>
> In earlier days, he won a state gymnastics championship and a regional magician's grand prize, both before graduating from Lincoln High School in 1954. At 18, he was on scholarship at Yale, near New York City, the metropolis of his dreams. By 26, he was writing jokes for another Nebraska boy, the king of all late-night TV kings.
>
> And so it's gone.
>
> Money and fame have appeared before him. Groucho and Woody have been befriended. A beautiful Broadway actress has been wed. Depression has muted life's colors. A postcard-perfect house has burned to the ground. Senior-citizen status has been achieved. A life has been led.
>
> But before all that, after it, and even now, the unwavering constant: He tries to make you laugh. To make you think. To get your attention.
>
> To be The Show.
>
> Today, his stage is a canopied outdoor cafe on Manhattan's swanky Upper East Side. Across the street, patrons mill around the entrance to the Metropolitan Museum of Art.
>
> Cavett makes fun of the French toast. He cracks jokes to the waiter, then about the waiter. He muses on the possibility that a man on crutches may, in fact, be a terrorist, and at any second drop his disguise and firebomb the Stanhope Hotel.
>
> As the meal ends, he approaches a table of Asian-American girls and begins speaking Japanese (yes, he speaks fluent Japanese). They are supposed to be amazed. They are supposed to laugh.

But, the hitch: The girls turn out to be Korean-American. They look annoyed. No laughter here.

And Dick Cavett, after trying to salvage what's left of the joke, sneaks away.

"That bombed, didn't it?" he asks through a thin smile.

This brings him to a story . . .

"I met Groucho Marx right down the street from here. I went up to him and said, 'I'm a big fan.' He said, 'If it gets any hotter, I might need a big fan.'

"Then we walked down Fifth Avenue. The Puerto Rican Day Parade was going on. Groucho would go up to people and say, 'To think, just a few years ago, you were cutting sugar cane.'

"And they would smile, but only because they had no idea what he had just said."

Dick Cavett does not believe in God. He believes in Groucho, a belief system extending outward from the most famed Marx brother, and backward into the middle of the 20th century. Prophets like Fred Allen. Jack Benny. Laurel. Hardy. Bob Hope. And Sid Caesar.

Picture a teen-aged Cavett in front of the television on Saturday night, having chosen that spot instead of a date ("I didn't really need to try not to get a date in high school," he says. "It was pretty easy.")

He is watching Caesar and Imogene Coca on "The Show of Shows." He's hanging on every punch line.

"They were his heroes," said his stepmother, Dorcas Cavett, a retired schoolteacher who still lives in Lincoln. "They were his educators, too."

Dick Cavett has been putting his comedic education to practice for most of his 65 years. Born Nov. 19, 1936, in Gibbon, he moved quickly to Grand Island and then to Lincoln, where his father, Al, and mother, Ira, taught English in the public school system.

Then Ira got sick. It was cancer. She died when Dick was 10.

"I don't think he ever really got over that," said Dorcas. "He loved her so deeply. She was truly a wonderful lady."

The 10-year-old stepson Dorcas inherited had the deep voice and vocabulary of a grown man. He loved to talk to his parents' friends, who often filled the Cavett home with food and laughter.

If young Cavett was impressed by the group, they were more impressed with him.

"He would come back from Yale on break, and we would look at this kid and go 'wow,' " said Ron Hull, executive director of Nebraska Educational Television and a longtime Cavett family friend. "You just knew he was going to do something, be somebody special."

Just a decade after his Yale graduation, the boy marvel was hosting his own show. Groucho arrived as a guest, and the two bantered like best friends.

"There were plenty of times you could have convinced me that I wasn't really there, doing the stuff I was. I worked as hard as anybody, and then it just happened."

He walks down a New York street, crimson dress shirt rolled up at the sleeves, a tan fedora pulled low over his face. A certain group of people notice. They are mostly white, middle-aged. Their eyes look, and look again. If this were a cartoon, and if their thoughts were displayed in balloons, those balloons would say, "Isn't that . . . ?"

Cavett does not understand fame beyond one, simple fact: He always wanted it.

He returned for Christmas break after a semester at Yale and paraded around Lincoln in his college jacket ("Just sickening," he says now.) A decade later, he took to the streets of New York the morning after his early appearances on the "Tonight Show," head up, hoping people would recognize the face they'd seen next to Johnny's the night before.

At first, not many did. Then his own show spawned a devoted following. Suddenly, according to a 1970 Life magazine cover story, he was, "The Brightest Face on Television."

But times changed. Ratings waned. And fame peaked. Cavett made the gradual move from the brightest face to another respected one in television's old guard. Not Joe DiMaggio, but not Dom, either.

"Woody Allen said to me the other day, 'Cavett, remember when we looked up to guys like Groucho and George Kaufman? Isn't it strange that we're those guys now?' I had to agree."

Yet, even at those gratifying moments of recognition, he still is several million head jerks away from The King, still only the second-most famous late-night talk show host to hail from Nebraska.

One day, a young boy tells his parents he'd like to attend a magician's performance in the basement of Westminster Church. His father agrees to take him. Upon returning home, the boy asks his stepmother if he can use an old military trunk she has stored in the basement. She agrees.

The next morning the trunk is newly emblazoned with the title, "The Great Cavetti."

"Why that name?" she asks.

"Because the magician I saw last night, his name was the Great Carsoni."

Johnny Carson and Dick Cavett have been intertwined ever since.

While Cavett's flame arguably burned brighter, Carson's burned much longer. Carson had mass appeal; Cavett enjoyed critical and avant-garde fame. In real terms, this means that while more 18- to 34-year-olds know the name Johnny Carson, that 48-year-old standing behind you in the supermarket checkout line may have worshipped Dick Cavett.

"To a certain type of people, mainly educated types, Dick Cavett was it," Hull said. "He offered things that Carson didn't. To us, he was the best thing on TV."

Part of the popularity stemmed from a witty intellectualism, a brand of humor very much in sync with the educated, 20-something Baby Boomers of the late 1960s and early 1970s. In-depth interviews with unusual literary figures like Nebraska poet laureate John Neihardt ("Black Elk Speaks") and successful shows with reluctant superstars like Katharine Hepburn earned him the title, "The Thinking Man's Johnny Carson."

Another, equally important part of Cavett's success was his willingness to challenge The Man, a wildly popular idea with the Boomers.

"I think I was probably the first guy to take someone to task for Vietnam on the air," Cavett said. "All I had to do was say something like 'You realize that your good friend LBJ once said that this was a war for little Asian boys, don't you?' and the crowd just went nuts. They loved it," Cavett said of a 1968 interview with a friend of President Lyndon Johnson's.

Many noteworthy slams followed. In a famous 1971 show, he told a drunken, surly Norman Mailer to "fold it five ways and put it where the sun don't shine." He told LSD guru Timothy Leary that he was "full of crap."

He said things that ratings champion Carson never would have dreamed of.

Some viewers loved it. Others hated it.

"My favorite letter was the one that began 'you little sawed-off faggot Communist shrimp,'" Cavett said. "A great salutation. I always wanted to write back 'I'm not sawed off.'"

"I was in Tiananmen Square in China. Our tour guide says, 'Here comes some Americans,' and points at some distant figures. I ask him how he can tell from so far away. All he did was put his hands out at his sides and puff out his cheeks."

Dick Cavett cannot stop talking about fat people.

"If everyone were that big, there would be no sex in this world," he deadpans after four overweight women walk by.

From there, he opines on the epidemic proportions of obesity in the United States. He wonders about anorexia, and then males and anorexia. He expounds on the body image issues of both males and females.

He's deeply worried about all of this.

"My wife says I'm obsessed. Probably because I am."

It is just the largest obsession in a stockpile including, but not limited to: Indian wars in Nebraska, the degeneration of the family unit as a result of television, Willa Cather, Broadway, Japan, aging and its effect on the memory, and the Pima Indians, a tribe in the American Southwest afflicted with terrible obesity.

This feverish brain made it feasible for him to parry and thrust with hostile intellectuals like Mailer. It also makes him impossible to interview.

Dick Cavett does not answer questions. Instead, he uses them as a starting point, molds them to fit and creates a work of conversational art—insight the plaster, humor the finish. It is this way that one simple question about what he's up to leads from character actor Jerry Orbach to Minnesota Fats to Willa Cather to Mark Twain's connection with Thomas Edison to Twain impersonator Hal Holbrooke to senior citizen status to the "Sixth Sense" to the "Rocky Horror Picture Show," and finally, thankfully, to ticks.

He hates ticks.

"How did we get here?" asks Cavett, knowing full well how.

Dorcas says her stepson has always been interested in everything around him. Most passions fade in and out, sparked by a new book on the subject, or a discussion with a stranger.

Three have endured.

"He's always been interested in American Indians. Comedy, of course. And New York. For as long as I've known him, practically, he's wanted to go there."

"Did Dorcas tell you about the time we went to the Sandhills, laid down on the highway and watched the stars? It wasn't unsafe, of course. There were no cars in the world. If there were, you could've seen them coming for 20 minutes."

It was hard to imagine a New York City existing that day. The world was open sky and prairie grass, cattle and wind.

"And no people," he says. "(The Sandhills) are kind of nice for that reason, too."

It is true that Manhattan and the Sandhills are as different as two places can be. It is also true that, discounting his summer home in Montauk, N.Y., they are also his two favorite places.

"I think they balance me, you know? The two extremes."

Almost every time Cavett returns to Lincoln, he disappears for a day or two, traveling west into the vast emptiness of the undeveloped Great Plains. Sometimes he finds a spot and just sits and thinks. Other times, he chats up strangers like they are talk show guests.

"I was talking to this guy at a gas station one day in the middle of nowhere," Cavett said. "He was a young kid, late teens probably. I asked him 'Where's the farthest from here you've ever been?'

"The kid pointed west and said, 'I've been to Gordon.' He must have gone to see the bright lights."

Maybe, he says, it's better to be isolated. To know less of the world's problems.

"One day, Woody asked me, 'Cavett, can you think of anything that's getting better?' I'm still working on my answer. I haven't thought of anything yet."

Says Dorcas: "If I have to pinpoint one thing that's changed about Dick, I'd say he's gotten more pessimistic, more negative."

If it's sometimes gray now, Dick Cavett has known much darker.

"The crazy thing about depression is, there could be a magic wand over there, just across the room, that could cure you. And, for the life of you, you wouldn't have the energy to go pick it up."

The worst came in 1983. It had hit before, but this time it hit harder, and longer. He wasn't interested in work or play. He lost all confidence in his ability behind the mike. He convinced himself he had no talent as a performer.

Publicly, the show went on as normal. But, privately, Dick Cavett saw himself evaporating into silence, a punchline gone horribly wrong.

"I always hated it when people came up to me and said, 'You know just what you're doing. You're unflappable.' I would think, 'You should see inside me.' "

Depression had first plagued him at Yale. Subsequent episodes would last several days and then lift. Often, only he would know that a storm had come and passed.

But the storm that gathered in '83 was far more severe.

"Everything seemed to be growing gray," Cavett told Time magazine in 1992 .

So he fought to regain the color. He endured a five-week hospitalization during which an experimental antidepressant gradually took effect. He entered therapy.

And then he did what he does best—he talked, to friends and at depression symposiums, to the press, to whomever would listen. He offered humor and insight. He lent his famous voice to an anonymous, misunderstood sickness.

And people loved him for it. They still come up to him on the street and tell him how his honesty helped their father or their best friend. How the stigma associated with depression disappeared because Dick Cavett had it, and he was *talking* about it.

"God, it took incredible courage to talk about it when he did," ETV's Hull said. "It wasn't like today, when everybody talks about it. But he wasn't scared. He wanted to help people in the same boat."

He's still talking about depression today as he sits on a couch at his home in the Hamptons, on Long Island's tip. In the kitchen, three dogs wait to greet newcomers. Carrie Nye, his wife of 38 years and an acclaimed Broadway actress, offers some leftover fried chicken to a guest.

The couple has spent summers and weekends on this sublime patch of seashore for more than three decades.

Their original house burned to the ground in 1997, but the couple rebuilt it back to the original Stanford White-designed specifications.

Climb the porch steps and the waves of the Atlantic appear. The view is layered, with green trees melding into navy ocean which blends into powder blue of a cloudless sky. The perfectly white house sits atop a hill, centered and stunning in the three-tiered panorama.

"It's beautiful, isn't it?" Cavett says.

This is his sanctuary. A place to reminisce, a place to plan.

The new plan is to pen a third book (his first two, both biographical, were co-written with Time magazine editor Christopher Porterfield). He wants another shot at Broadway. Maybe another shot on television.

In the meantime, he wants to learn everything he can about aging, its effect on the body and the brain. "It's my new fascination," he said.

No, he isn't aging gracefully, quietly. He is aging honestly, uniquely, a one-liner at a time.

"In every situation, Dick is his own man," a friend told Life in 1970.

It's still true today.

"That thing, nobody knows what it is. It takes over for you and fills you up as you walk onstage into the bright lights and the people applauding and you say 'I know what I'm doing here, even if I don't anywhere else.

"This is what I do.' "

Cavett's latest turn in the spotlight occurs on a sweltering August afternoon. The Broadway hit "Frankie and Johnny" has just ended with a standing ovation.

After hugging Edie Falco (of "Sopranos" fame) backstage, he enters the street through a gate holding back the usual array of autograph seekers, tourists and hangers-on.

"That's Dick Cavett!" someone shouts.

The performer straightens up. A mock salute triggers spontaneous applause. He's shaking hands. He's cracking jokes.

"Aren't you my sister? How's mom?" he fires at a middle-aged woman.

It's there, it's building. Everyone can feel it now.

> Someone calls out: How are the actors doing?
> "They're all falling down drunk," he yells.
> They press closer and closer. They laugh louder and louder.
> And then it's over.
> He's standing alone, fedora in hand, sweat beads on his forehead.
> All around him—half a continent from the Sandhills silence—taxis honk and the snippets of a thousand conversations swirl.
> He doesn't notice. Dick Cavett is lost in a late-summer night's dream.

Not every subject of a personality profile is a celebrity. Often reporters profile people who are involved in newsworthy situations or confronting problems other readers might share. For example, instead of interviewing the police about a drug problem, or faculty members about students who cheat, reporters may interview the drug users and cheaters themselves—specific individuals who seem to be representative of a larger issue.

Historical Features

Historical features commemorate the dates of important events, such as the attack on Pearl Harbor or the bombing of Hiroshima. News organizations also publicize the anniversaries of the births and deaths of famous people.

Other historical features are tied to current events that generate interest in their topics. If a tornado, flood or earthquake strikes the city, news organizations are likely to present stories about earlier tornadoes, floods or earthquakes.

Historical features may also describe famous landmarks, pioneers and philosophies; improvements in educational, entertainment, medical and transportation facilities; and changes in an area's racial composition, housing patterns, food, industries, growth, religions and wealth.

Every region, city and school has experienced interesting events. Some students get ideas for stories by reading newspapers that publish "On This Date in History" columns, by interviewing the historians of clubs and by visiting historical societies. A good feature writer will learn more about those events, perhaps by consulting historical documents or by interviewing people who witnessed or participated in them.

The following historical feature is about a War of 1812 relic. The writer lets the old cannon speak in a first-person narrative:

> I was left to rot. And, rot I did for 180 years or more on the bottom of the Grand River.
> It seemed I might be rescued in 1992, when I was hauled up from the muck, but I was again left to rust, this time in a museum storage room, my story untold. Now, finally experts at the State Historical Museum want to know my secrets. Because my history is your history.
>
> *(Lansing [Mich.] State Journal)*

The writer educates readers in three ways as she weaves her story. Readers learn about the area and its people's involvement with the War of 1812. They are treated to a lesson in early weaponry and warfare, and they are invited to experience the ways in which scientists clean and preserve early relics, such as this British cannon, and piece together their history.

Adventure Features

Adventure features describe unusual and exciting experiences—perhaps the story of someone who survived an airplane crash, climbed a mountain, sailed around the world, served in the Peace Corps or fought in a war. In this type of feature story, quotations and descriptions are especially important. After a catastrophe, for example, feature writers often use the survivors' accounts to recreate the scene. Many writers begin with the action—their stories' most interesting and dramatic moments:

> "It was the 10th of July 1969, approximately 5 p.m.," said Steve Jefferson, one of the Vietnam veterans attending classes here. "Myself and two sergeants were driving down the road in a Jeep. Theoretically, we shouldn't have been in this situation. We

> should have been accompanied by more men in another Jeep, but I always thought that when my time was up, it was up. It was going to happen no matter what.
>
> "There was a white flash and a pop, and the next thing I knew I was lying in the middle of the road.
>
> "I crawled over to the side of the road, away from the Jeep, and hollered for the other guys. There was no answer. . . ."

Seasonal Features

Editors and news directors often assign feature stories about seasons and holidays: Christmas, Easter, St. Patrick's Day, Friday the 13th and the first day of spring. Such stories are difficult to write because, to make them interesting, reporters must find a new angle. International holidays also are informative and entertaining:

> Taiwan's leader marked the first day of the Chinese Lunar New Year on Thursday by giving out 15,000 red envelopes stuffed with cash to people in his hometown.
>
> President Chen Shui-bian handed out the equivalent of $5.80 in every envelope, totaling about $87,000 in the southern farm village of Kuantien. He ran out of envelopes before he got to the end of a line that stretched about two miles.
>
> *(The Associated Press)*

The journalist continued her story by tracing the traditional rituals for celebrating the holiday.

Explanatory Features

Explanatory features are also called "local situation" or "interpretive" features or "sidebars." In these, reporters provide more detailed descriptions or explanations of organizations, activities, trends or ideas in the news. After news stories describe an act of terrorism, an explanatory feature may examine the terrorists' identity, tactics and goals. After a bank robbery, an explanatory feature may describe the training banks give their employees to prepare them for robberies or may reveal more about a typical bank robber, including the robber's chances of getting caught and probable punishment.

One follow-up won a Pulitzer Prize for meritorious public service. An explosion killed 111 men in an Illinois mine, and Joseph Pulitzer II, publisher of the St. Louis Post-Dispatch, asked his staff to thoroughly review the tragedy. Pulitzer wanted to know what would be done to improve mine safety. What would be done to help the miners' families? Also, who was responsible for the tragedy, and were they likely to be punished for it? Notice that the story starts with the action. Also notice the reporter's use of detail:

> The clock in the office of the Centralia Coal Company's Mine No. 5 ticked toward quitting time on the afternoon of March 25. As the hands registered 3:27 and the 142 men working 540 feet underground prepared to leave the pit at the end of their shift, an explosion occurred.
>
> The blast originated in one of the work rooms in the northwestern section of the workings. Fed by coal dust, it whooshed through the labyrinth of tunnels underlying the town of Wamac, Ill., on the southern outskirts of Centralia.
>
> Thirty-one men, most of whom happened to be near the shaft at the time, made their way to the cage and were brought out alive, but the remaining 111 were trapped. Fellow workmen who tried to reach them shortly after the explosion were driven back by poisonous fumes.

How-to-Do-It Features

How-to-do-it features tell readers how to perform some task. They may describe a tangible project like building a house, planting a garden or training a puppy. They may focus on psychological issues, such as strengthening a marriage or overcoming shyness. Or they may explain how to find a physician or organize receipts for tax time.

Inexperienced reporters tend to preach or dictate to their audience, presenting their own opinions. Veteran reporters gather facts from several sources, including books and magazine articles. They also interview experts and get tips from people who have done what their stories describe. In addition, good reporters try to observe or participate in the "how-to-do-it" procedure itself, such as building a bird feeder or winterizing a car, to better understand their topic.

Reporters divide the task into simple, clear, easy-to-follow steps. They tell viewers and readers what materials are needed and the cost in money and time. Often they conclude such stories with a list or summary of the process, such as "eight ways to build self-confidence in children."

The following paragraphs are the beginning of a how-to story on taxes, published two months before the tax deadline. The story continues as a guide to help people decide what option is best for them.

> There used to only be one way to do taxes: hunker down for a long weekend at the kitchen table with the forms and a calculator.
>
> Today, there are a variety of options:
>
> - Computer software.
> - Certified public accountants.
> - National tax-preparation companies.
> - Or, still do it yourself.
>
> Once you know about the options, you can decide what is the best way for you to go.

Occupation or Hobby Features

Reporters may prepare features stories about occupations that are dangerous (fire fighter), highly specialized (cleaning up oil spills) or glamorous (personal fitness trainer to movie stars). Or they may report on a job many people think is boring (sorting clothes at Goodwill) and turn it into something exciting (such as when workers find something unusual that people drop off). Reporters can show that workers find even stereotyped jobs rewarding, such as this one:

> Twenty-nine-year-old Jordyn James is going through a lot of eggs this morning.
>
> "Eggs are the easiest to do," James said, barely looking up from the yellow batter on the stove top to glance at the seven tickets dangling in front of her. "With eggs, you can do a lot of things at one time. I can work on about six orders simultaneously."
>
> James cracks one after another, and carton after carton is tossed out.
>
> Her hands are working at lightning speed; turning the eggs into scrambled, over easy, Benedict, and poached.
>
> "You know, I've done a lot of other things with my time, . . ." James pauses to place a basket of hash browns on the counter, "but there wasn't anything that makes me as happy as this."
>
> *(The Associated Press)*

Collectors and crafts enthusiasts often make good subjects for feature stories because they are passionately involved and often eccentric, quotable and entertaining. Strange or trendy hobbies, such as body art, make good topics, too, because they tend to involve colorful characters.

To find story ideas, reporters scan newspaper notices of hobby club meetings, senior citizens' activities, church and school events and speeches on unusual topics. They ask other people what they do to relax. They read classified ads and seek out magicians, storytellers, psychic readers, basement cleaners and unicycle instructors.

Personal Experience Features

News stories are usually written in the third person, with the reporter as a neutral observer or outsider. Feature stories can be written in the first person, with the reporter appearing in the story. Feature stories can also be written in the second person, addressing audience members directly. Each style can be effective.

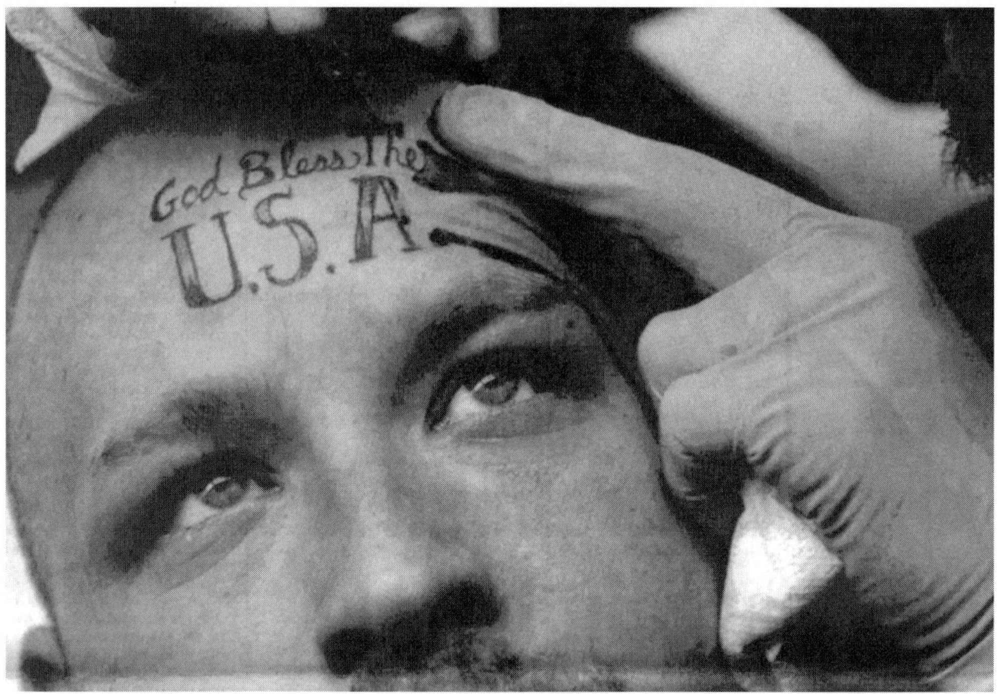

After Sept. 11, Jack Hansen of St. Petersburg, Fla., put his patriotic feelings where everyone could see them. People with unusual hobbies, habits or occupations often make good feature stories.

Beginning reporters may feel tempted to write about their own experiences because it seems easy. They do not have to interview anyone or dig out facts from the library or public records. But reporters should use the first person cautiously, especially in their first feature stories. They run a greater risk of selecting poor topics and dwelling on insignificant details and dull generalities when they describe their own experiences, as in the following example:

> During the summer, 20 ardent cyclists (I among them) biked through 300 miles of the Canadian Rockies. In the course of our journey, we encountered many exciting experiences.

Behind-the-Scenes Features

Behind-the-scenes stories take readers backstage for an inside view of some event. Reporters often find such ventures fascinating and are able to convey the excitement. Behind-the-scenes stories are based on personal interviews with such people as stage managers, rock group "roadies," library catalogers, night street cleaning crews, caterers, convention decorators and the like.

The venerable police ride-along story, in which a reporter accompanies a police officer on a shift and then describes what happened, is a common variation of the behind-the-scenes feature. So many news organizations and so many reporters have done ride-along stories that they have become a journalistic cliché, but Walt Harrington lifted the genre out of the routine when he spent several days following Washington, D.C., homicide detectives. The story he wrote for The Washington Post magazine, "Against the Tide," is a long, richly detailed, insightful look at what homicide detectives in major cities face every day. Here is a short excerpt:

> Everything squeaks. The heavy doors squeak. The metal swivel chairs squeak. The drawers in the metal desks squeak. The file drawers squeak. The keys of the old manual upright squeak. The room—No. 5058, dubbed Homicide North because it is isolated two floors above D.C.'s other homicide offices in the city's Municipal Center—

> is a concerto of squeaks. Its other noises—the hollering voices, the clamoring phones, the electric typewriters, "Gilligan's Island" laugh-tracking on the beat-up TV, the two coffeepots spitting mud, the hand-held walkie-talkies, belching static—all add layer upon layer of volume, creating finally a kind of jangled symphony.
>
> What will stop this din and turn the entire room of nine men prayerfully silent are three words their ears are tuned to as if they were set on a private frequency: "stabbing" or "shooting" or "homicide." When the police radio dispatcher speaks any of these words, everything stops, hands reach for tiny volume knobs on radios and everybody waits. Usually, it's a false alarm and, just as abruptly, the noise once again envelops the momentary silence like a stadium cheer after the crack of a long ball.
>
> The men in Homicide North are tonight "on the bubble"—cop talk meaning that their squad of detectives is on call to investigate the city's next murder. Detective Jeff Mayberry, a short, wiry, close-cropped, jet-propelled 34-year-old in a tight blue sports coat, is riding the top of the bubble in his rotation as lead investigator on whatever horror is next offered up from the bowels of the city. He has ridden the bubble aloft for four duty days now—and no murder. At least none on his 3-to-11 shift.

Reporters look for people who perform jobs out of the public eye but essential to many citizens. They interview sources, visit them on location and use the source's own words to tell the story. They also include details they observe, such as atmosphere, working conditions, physical appearance of people and their workspace, specialized terms and conversations between workers.

Behind-the-scenes features convey a sense of immediacy, allowing readers to see, feel, taste, touch, smell and understand the "backstage" work that goes into a public event.

Participatory Features

Participatory features give another kind of inside view, this time through the senses of a reporter who is actually experiencing an event or situation. If reporters lack the time and money to immerse themselves totally in the world of the subject, they might spend an afternoon shadowing—with permission—an attorney, a retail clerk, a parent of preschoolers or an elderly person.

Reporters usually arrange such experiences with the person they are shadowing or that person's supervisor, making it clear that they are reporters and will write or broadcast a story about the experience.

Undercover, cloak-and-dagger approaches, like getting arrested in order to expose jail conditions, are ethically questionable and expose reporters and their employers to civil and criminal liability. News organizations that have sent reporters undercover into private businesses to report on allegations of misconduct have been sued for fraud and trespass. And reporters who engage in criminal activities, such as trafficking in drugs or pornography, have been criminally prosecuted, even though they were only gathering information for a news story.

Medical Features

Some news organizations have medical reporters. However, general-assignment reporters can find good medical features in any community. Illness and health are vitally interesting to the public, and subjects abound: the cost of devastating illnesses, new and radical treatments for common ailments, ethical issues surrounding medical advances, pregnancy, child rearing, mental illness, death and the grief process, new equipment and what it does, support groups, workshops for patients with a chronic disease and volunteer programs.

Reporters gather facts from medical experts, people with a particular condition, relatives and friends. They use quotes, allowing subjects to tell about their experiences and feelings. Stories based on interviews with people dissatisfied with their medical treatment pose the threat of libel suits. Reporting a statement like "She's obviously a money-grubbing quack" can provoke a lawsuit, even if the subject did say it. It helps to balance complaints with experts' points of view.

Business Features

Many business features highlight one person or aspect of local commerce. Reporters find ideas by looking for the human interest in stories of promotions, new businesses, the local economy and even the election of club officers. Business features may have a side effect of promoting a particular business, service or product, but reporters should be sure that each story has enough news value to justify its inclusion in a newspaper or news broadcast.

A wealth of business stories exists in any town. Fad businesses like message balloons and flavored popcorn rise and fall. Dating bureaus, computer software merchants and shopping services for working parents respond to new needs in society. Stories on old, established firms, perhaps focusing on the personality of a founder or dynamic leader, are also of perennial interest.

TYPES OF FEATURE LEADS

Many features begin with summary leads. However, features also may begin with quotations, anecdotes, questions, action, descriptions, shocking facts or a combination of these techniques. The only requirement is that the leads interest people, luring them into the stories.

The following leads demonstrate some of the different approaches to beginning a feature story:

> SUMMARY: The annual 4-H llama show has become a highlight of the summer for Jess Winters and his family.

> ANECDOTES AND EXAMPLES: Josie Chi's first day on the job was his last.
>
> A few hours into the morning shift at a Pennsylvania metal stamping plant last week, the 17-year-old football star got his hands caught in a power press; both had to be amputated. He was one of about 500 teenagers injured at work every day.
>
> Neddie Scholaski was on her seventh day at work at a country club in Houston when the golf cart she was driving slammed into the side of a shed, crushing her chest.
>
> At 16, too young to be driving even a golf cart under Texas law, Scholaski was one of 73 teens killed on the job in 2000—one about every five days.
>
> The Labor Department says about 4 million 15- to 17-year-olds earn paychecks in the summer. And, eight in 10 teens will work at some point during high school.
>
> "We're finding that some employers don't do all they could to keep teens safe. We're also finding that teenagers are not entering the workplace with an understanding of the law that's there to protect them," said a leader of the national Child Labor Coalition.
>
> *(The Associated Press)*

> ACTION OR NARRATIVE: Janie Stevens stood in front of a microphone Tuesday, script in hand, waiting in alert anticipation.
>
> "Look, up in the sky! It's a bird!" the nine-year-old exclaimed, leaning forward as she delivered her part of an old Superman television show.

> DESCRIPTION: On Thursday, Jim Donaldson woke up and prepared for work. He took a shower, brushed his teeth and shaved. Jim then put on his makeup: a little blush here and a little eyeliner there. Afterward, he looked to his wife, Lara, for her approval.
>
> Lara inspected her husband. "You need a little more lipstick, honey." Jim put on some more lipstick while his daughter, Judy, added a bright red bow to her father's hair. That was the perfect touch. His family all agreed that he looked "absolutely marvelous." Jim kissed his family good-bye, grabbed his bow and arrow and headed off to another day at the office.
>
> As a member of the Activities Committee at Roubidoux Regional Medical Center in Baltimore, Jim has many annual rituals. On Christmas, he's Santa and on Halloween, he's Dracula. On Valentine's Day, he's a tall, dark and handsome Cupid.

No matter what type of lead writers choose for a feature story, they should try to make it as fresh and distinctive as possible. Dick Thien, an editor-in-residence at the Freedom Forum, notes that some leads, such as questions, figures of speech and shockers generally sound trite and should be used sparingly. ACES, the American Copy Editors Society, has on its Web site a list of cliché leads to avoid.

Every lead should either state the central point of the story or lead the reader to such a statement. Summary leads, like the first one in the series of examples above, contain the central point of the story. Delayed leads, whether they are quotations, anecdotes or description, prepare the reader for the central point, which is stated in a nut paragraph. In the example above illustrating descriptive leads, the nut paragraph is the third paragraph.

THE BODY OF A FEATURE STORY

Like the lead, the body of a feature story can take many forms. The inverted-pyramid style may be appropriate for some features and chronological order for others. Regardless of the form chosen, every feature must be coherent. All the facts must fit together smoothly and logically. Transitions must guide the audience from one segment of the story to the next and clearly reveal the relationship between those segments. Transitions should be brief. They may ask a question, announce shifts in time or place or link ideas by repeating key words or phrases.

Reporters should be concise and never waste their audience's time. Features should emphasize lively details—the action. And they should provide an occasional change of pace. A good reporter never writes a story consisting only of quotations or of summaries. Instead, the reporter might use several paragraphs of summary, then some quotations to add emphasis or emotion, then some description and then more quotations or summary. Bill Bergstrom of The Associated Press wrote this story about a World War I veteran who died hours before receiving a medal:

> Charles Fackler, 98, of Allentown, died in a nursing home, his 68-year-old son at his side, as relatives, friends and fellow veterans prepared to attend an award ceremony in his honor in the home's reception room.
>
> "He missed it by two hours. He was waiting for it. I think it kept him going this long," son Bill Fackler said. "It was a sad occasion. We had everything organized for that day. The presentation was to be at 2 p.m. He died at quarter to twelve."
>
> The elder Fackler, who served in the Meuse-Argonne offensive of September 1918, had been named a Chevalier of the National Order of the Legion of Honor by the president of France. That nation decided last year on the 80th anniversary of the 1918 armistice to honor Allied soldiers who fought in France. This is France's most distinguished award.
>
> Among "a bunch of medals" he received, Fackler considered the Purple Heart his highest honor. He was founder and past president of the Lehigh Valley chapter of the Military Order of the Purple Heart, his son said.
>
> Before offensives were waged with electronics and long-range missiles, Charles Fackler's war was fought up close and on the ground, often with bayonets. He was wounded by bullets and shrapnel and gassed several times as he slogged through the fields and forests as part of the Army's Company D, 112th Regiment, 28th Division.
>
> "It was called the Bucket of Blood. We survived like animals in the tall grass, weeds, bushes and the likes of that," he recalled in a September interview.

Good reporters bring characters to life. Instead of saying a person is generous or humorous, reporters give specific examples of the subject's generosity and humor. Instead of saying President Calvin Coolidge was a taciturn man, it would be better to illustrate his reluctance to speak by quoting Coolidge himself:

> A woman meeting President Coolidge for the first time said to him, "My friends bet that I couldn't get you to say three words." The president replied, "You lose."

Successful feature writers also use elements such as characterization, setting, plot and subplot, conflict, time, dialogue and narrative.

Reporters reveal character by using quotations and describing speech patterns, mannerisms, body language, appearance, dress, age, preferences, prejudices, use of personal space and a host of other traits. The setting reveals the subject's character and provides context for the audience to understand the subject. Geography shapes physical and mental traits, determines life span, influences ways of earning a living. Reporters should tell where a subject grew up, what the person's surroundings are now and how these factors contribute to what he or she is. Such touches of description sprinkled throughout a story show what the subject is like.

The plot of feature stories is often a description of the obstacles that lie between the subjects of the stories and their goals. The resolution of conflict (frustration induced by the obstacles) presents the theme of every human-interest story. The main variations of the plots are the conflicts between humans and nature, humans and humans, and humans and the inner self. As reporters interview people and ask them about events in their lives, plots naturally emerge. Often a subplot emerges, a secondary line of action that runs in counterpoint to the main action, sometimes helping and sometimes hindering the progress. If reporters listen and identify plot and subplot elements as the subject tells the story, a natural order emerges.

Time can be handled in a variety of ways. To organize some types of features, reporters can use a dramatic episode in the present as an opener, then flash back to the beginning of the story and bring it forward in chronological order. Reporters can foreshadow the future or build in a series of flashbacks, arranged in the order in which they happened. Whatever form reporters choose, they should be sure to use transitional words—"now," "then," "in 2002"—to let the audience know when events are taking place.

Feature stories need dialogue. Reporters use dialogue to show temperament, plot, events, time, customs, color or continuity. They must be careful to choose only the best, most revealing quotes.

Reporters use narrative to weave a story together. It summarizes, arranges, creates flow and transitions and links one idea to the next. Narrative should be unobtrusive and subtle.

THE ENDING OF A FEATURE STORY

A feature should have a satisfying conclusion, perhaps an anecdote, quote, key word or phrase repeated in some surprising or meaningful way. Reporters should avoid ending a feature story with a summary. Summary endings are too likely to state the obvious, to be repetitious, flat or boring.

Some endings come back around to the lead. For example, the following story is about ironworker volunteers, who have been assisting in rescues almost since the Golden Gate Bridge was opened in 1937. The story begins with a description of a suicide attempt and a call to an ironworker for help in the rescue. The writer then gently drops the narrative and weaves in the history and estimates of bridge suicides and rescues. After 20 paragraphs, the journalist retrieves the thread of the narrative:

> When the suicidal young man in the trench coat climbed over the railing, he tied a nylon rope around his neck and fastened the other end to the bridge. After all the talk, he never said why he wanted to die. The exhausted ironworker finally made a move to untie the rope from the bridge. Then came the 30-second ultimatum—and the leap.
>
> Polanski vaulted over the railing after him, landing on a beam. He and several other workers hoisted the man up by the rope he had tied around his neck and laid him on the road, unconscious but alive.

After finishing a feature, a professional is likely to edit and rewrite it many times. A professional will also angle the feature for a particular audience, publication or news program, emphasizing the story's relevance and importance to it.

WHAT DOES IT TAKE TO BE A TOP-NOTCH FEATURES WRITER?

By **Bryan Denham**
Assistant Professor
Clemson University

- **Descriptive writing skills.** The features writer should be able to "paint a picture" and capture the essence of a subject.
- **Good reporting skills.** Without the ability to gather information in an efficient manner, the writer will have nothing to discuss.
- **Good interviewing skills.** It's one thing to conduct a basic interview; it's quite another to draw from a source sensitive or controversial information.
- **Good research skills.** What, if anything, has been written about the subject you are addressing?
- **Respect for sources.** Treat people with respect and dignity.
- **Ethics.** Always use good judgment and attribute quotes carefully.
- **Persistence.** Good writers don't give up on a story if it gets off to a slow start.
- **Confidence.** Sources have faith in people who appear confident and professional.
- **Experience.** The more experiences you have in life, the more perspective you will bring to your writing.
- **Curiosity.** Great writers are curious about the social world and can distinguish good story ideas from bad ones.
- **Eagerness to explore.** The best writers crave "small adventures."
- **Broad-mindedness.** Keep your mind open to new perspectives.
- **Appreciation for cultural diversity.** Embrace individuals who can offer you insight into different cultural values, traditions.
- **Familiarity with trends in popular culture.** Always keep "an ear to the ground" and stay attuned with what's going on around you.
- **Vision.** Great writers can picture how their articles will look in print, and they create the articles to fit in the space allotted for newspaper features.
- **Reliability.** As with hard news reporting, failure to show up for an interview or return a phone call will undermine your ability to produce good work.
- **Appreciation for subtlety.** Sometimes the most interesting aspects of an individual do not "leap out" at the writer. Students of the social world and human behavior can observe things that go straight by others.
- **Ability to seek out sources apart from the primary source.** If you're profiling someone, for instance, you should talk to a few people who know the person.

SUGGESTED READINGS

Friedlander, Edward Jay, and John Lee. *Feature Writing for Newspapers and Magazines: The Pursuit of Excellence,* 4th ed. Boston: Allyn & Bacon, 1999.
Franklin, Jon. *Writing for Story: Craft Secrets of Dramatic Nonfiction by a Two-Time Pulitzer Prize Winner.* New York: Plume, 1994.
Garland, David, ed. *Pulitzer Prize Feature Stories: America's Best Writing, 1979-2003,* 2nd ed. Ames, Iowa: Iowa State University Press, 2003.
Garvey, Mark, ed. *Writer's Market: Where & How to Sell What You Write.* Cincinnati, Ohio: Writer's Digest Books. (An annual guide.)
Jacobi, Peter P. *The Magazine Article: How to Think It, Plan It, Write It.* Bloomington, Ind.: Indiana University Press, 1997.
Stewart, James B. *Follow the Story: How to Write Successful Nonfiction.* New York: Simon & Schuster, 1998.

USEFUL WEB SITES

Al Thompkins of the Poynter Institute has listed 50 story ideas: http://www.poynter.org/content/content_view.asp?id=3779
The Census Bureau offers history and statistics for story ideas: http://www.census.gov
Tips on Feature Writing from the U.S. Air Force: "10 Don't of Feature Writing": http://www.Afnews.af.mil/primer/corea7c.htm "Top 10 Tips": http://www.Afnews.af.mil/primer/corea7.htm
Cliché leads to avoid: http://www.copyesk.org/clicheleads.htm

EXERCISE 1

FEATURE STORIES

GENERATING IDEAS AND SELECTING A TOPIC

A. List some universal needs noted in the chapter (such as food, clothing, shelter, love, health) across the top of a piece of paper.

Down the left side, list some pressing social issues (concerns of the elderly, health care, unemployment and teen suicide). Draw lines to form a grid. Fill in the spaces in the grid with story ideas created by combining the two topics.

B. Listen and observe to find a feature topic. Ride a city bus to the end of the line, sit in the student union or in a cafeteria. Watch what people do, and listen to what people are talking about. Make a list of potential feature topics.

C. Pair up with another student. Set a timer and write for 10 minutes, completely free and uncensored, about one or more of the following topics: pet peeves; things I avoid writing about; things I am curious about; favorite places in my hometown; a specific holiday, such as Christmas or Thanksgiving; my biggest problem as a child (or teenager).

Take turns reading your papers aloud to your partner. Discuss how you could conduct research and interviews to make a story from one of the ideas you generated.

EXERCISE 2

FEATURE STORIES

IDEAS FOR CAMPUS FEATURES

Here are 32 ideas for feature stories that you can write on your campus. Interview some students affected by the issues as well as authoritative sources.

1. Interview at least five faculty members who have written textbooks. Describe their work, problems, profits and attitudes.

2. Describe the tenure and promotion system at your college. How easy is it for faculty members to obtain tenure? What must they do? Typically, how many succeed and how many fail? What happens to those who fail?

3. Write about your favorite teacher, a successful coach or another interesting personality on your campus. Interview other students, friends, relatives and colleagues so you have enough information for a well-rounded portrait of the person.

4. Find a campus club that helps people, such as Alcoholics Anonymous or Gamblers Anonymous. Interview club members about their problem and how it affects their lives.

5. What are the best part-time jobs for students on your campus? Who earns the most money and enjoys the best hours and benefits? (Students who earn tips—bartenders, baggage handlers, waiters and waitresses—often earn hundreds of dollars during weekend shifts.)

6. Write about your institution's use of adjuncts (part-time faculty members). Are adjuncts well paid? What are the advantages and disadvantages of employing them? Why do they teach and, compared to your full-time faculty members, how qualified are they?

7. What are the excuses your faculty members hear most often from students who miss classes, assignments and tests—or simply do poorly in a class?

8. What are students' primary health (physical or mental) problems? Or financial problems? Or housing problems? More students seem to be complaining about a stress disorder, for example.

9. Do students on your campus ever complain about faculty members they have difficulty understanding, especially faculty members from other countries? How serious is the problem, what's being done to correct it and how successful is the effort? Also, why does your college employ faculty members with language problems?

10. To obtain more practical experience, many students complete internships, and some students must do so. Typically, many interns are not paid, and some companies seem to exploit interns, using them as free labor. Discuss the advantages and disadvantages of internships and any abuses you find on your campus.

11. What are students' options if they have a grievance against a faculty member, perhaps a complaint about a racist or sexist comment, a low grade or a test that was never returned? How and where can they obtain help?

12. Write about the problems and perceptions of the international students on your campus (or the handicapped students). You might look specifically at the problems of students who are blind or use wheelchairs.

13. Write about faculty members and students who date each other or marry.

14. Write a historical feature that describes your college's establishment and early years.

15. If some buildings on your campus are named after individuals, write about several of these individuals, explaining who they were and why they were honored.

16. What, if any, are the advantages to being an athlete (or an honors student) at your institution? Do athletes have to meet the same entrance requirements as other students? Do they enjoy special housing, food or financial aid? Do they have special tutors or registration times?

17. Describe the wildlife on your campus, anything from bats to rats, cats, snakes and raccoons.

18. Write about cheating on your campus. How often are students caught? How are they punished? What are faculty members doing to avoid the problem?

19. How easy is it for the students on your campus to obtain credit cards, how many overspend and where do they find help?

20. Talk to the people who monitor your campus library. What problems do they encounter? For example, do they find people eating, talking, fighting, romancing, sleeping, smoking or stealing?

21. What percentage of the incoming students at your institution are required to complete remedial courses? Describe the courses, the cause of the problem that prompts remedial courses and its ramifications.

22. If you have heard horror stories about difficult roommates, write about the problem. What causes the problem, how common is it and how is it resolved? Cite some of the worst examples.

23. If you have heard horror stories about blind dates, write about the problem. What causes the problem, and how common is it? Cite some of the worst examples.

24. Do you have any cults on your campus? If so, describe the cults and their members.

25. Talk to people who come to your campus to interview and hire graduating seniors. What do they look for? What common mistakes should job seekers avoid? What advice would they give students interviewing for jobs?

26. Write about any of the following topics on your campus: (1) date rape, (2) abortions, (3) skateboarding and skating, and (4) student loans and the difficulty of repaying the loans after graduation.

27. Interview the youngest or oldest student on your campus, or the youngest or oldest faculty member.

28. Localize a national phenomenon, such as hazing, grade inflation or students who take forever to graduate.

29. Describe your campus' vegetarians and their philosophy, health and problems.

30. Find and write about a campus club that involves an element of danger, such as scuba diving, skydiving, mountain climbing, hang gliding or spelunking.

31. What is your campus doing to recruit more women and minorities for its faculty—and how successful is it? Why? How do other faculty members feel about the issue?

32. About how many students flunk out of your college each year? Why? Is the problem more common in some majors than others? Interview several of the students.

EXERCISE 3

FEATURE STORIES

INFORMATION FOR FEATURES

Write feature stories based on the following sets of information. Correct all errors.

1. DEER FARMS

Kyle White is a farmer, age 41, in your county, married to his wife Rebecca, 42, and parents together of 4 children (3 girls and 1 boy). Their farm is located a distance of approximately 7 miles south of your city.

Their farm originally covered a total of 240 acres of land but eleven years ago they bought a second farm, a retiring cousins, which covered an additional 120 acres of land, so they now farm a total of 360 acres.

Little of the land is good for crops. Its too hilly and swampy, with lots of woods. A low area along the Mequin river often floods in the spring and then remains in a flooded condition for a period of time. Six years ago, Mr. White abandoned his diary herd and hay and vegetables, and pigs, chickens, and other crops and started a new crop: deer. Why? Big bucks.

Some sleek brown bucks weigh as much as 240 pounds or more. Leaner ones (visible in a pasture you visited) weigh only about 160 or so pds. They're kept on the farm by an 8-foot fence topped by barbed wire that now encircles the entire farm area. "The heaviest ones we sell," White said.

Who to? Fine restaurants throughout the entire state. They charge their diners a premium for tender venison which has much less fat than cow or pig. Some day White also hopes to sell his deer which he butchers himself directly to gourmet sections of supermarkets. Its a national trend, he said. Nearly 700 farmers nationwide now belong to the North American Deer Farmers Assn. established in 1978 by German immigrants who established the first United States venison ranch in the 1960s on a remote patch of rugged hills and woods in upstate New York. All venison ranchers now hope to capitalize on Americans current desire to be healthy—to eat well while staying fit. All tout venison as "the meat of the future"—red meat for health-conscious calorie counters. Nutritionists say among red meats only buffalo is healthier. Some animal rights activists raise a ruckus about the human consumption of deer and some consumers shudder at the thought of eating Bambi or any of the other beautiful, graceful members of the species, but deer farmers believe they can gain converts by rattling off the real statistics to further educate consumers. A 7-ounce serving of venison steak gets only 3.2% of its 316 calories from fat. Ground beef is nearly 10% fat and a 7-ounce portion weighs in at far more calories, a whopping total of 432. "Venison has less fat—and fewer calories—than even skinned chicken," White told you. At 6′2″ in height, White weighs only a thin 162 pounds and is red headed with a full red beard and red mustache. Others agree about the healthful nature of venison. The American Heart Assn. lists wild game as a good choice for your daily serving of meat, poultry, or fish. Weight Watchers also recommends venison as a lean, low-calorie alternative to fatty beef. Still, its a tough sell. Tests show farm-raised venison tastes tender and mild and the meat tends to be smooth without the grains that streak beef steak. Yet many Americans tend to associate venison with the tough, gamey, shoe-leather meat that many amateur hunters often drag back home after a kill while hunting in the fall and bagging a deer that isn't as well fed and cared for as Mr. Whites.

Plus there's what the farmers call the Bambi Syndrome. Graceful, brown-eyed, white-tailed deer seem to generate more sympathy than almost any other animal but dogs and cats which, by law, many states prohibit people in the U.S. from eating although both animals are eaten elsewhere in the world along with horse. "Most consumers don't see cows as cute and cuddly like they do a veal calf or lamb or deer," said a spokesman for the national Beef Industry Council. There are doom-and-gloom predictions about the future of beef with all the new competition from deer and other species, even ostrich, but cattle ranchers tend to brush off claims of venisons surging popularity. After all, Americans gobble up, on national average for every man, woman and child in this great country, a grand total of 63 pounds of beef each year despite relentless warnings from assorted medical authorities and nutritionists against fat and cholesterol. The average American persons diet also includes 47 lbs. of pork each and every year and almost as much chicken. By comparison, the average American now eats no venison, none whatsoever, which remains at this point in time largely a novelty, sold at a few fine restaurants—never at popular, fast-food restaurants where so many Americans eat so many of their meals, but those facts also show the markets untapped potential. White says: "Everyone has prejudices, and many involving deer are unfounded: emotional, not intellectual. People see deer on television or movies, then they don't want to eat them. Kids especially, but deer are good for kids, healthy for everyone. Its healthy, tasty, and inexpensive considering the fact its all meat, not fat."

2. SCHOLARSHIP SEARCHES

Are you thinking about going to college anytime soon? Are you already there? Are you a parent with a kid in college or about to go to college. If so, beware! Don't be swindled like the thousands of other poor innocent victims swindled every year. This story comes in part out of the U.S. capital of Washington, D.C. The Federal Trade Commission issued a warning today. The F.T.C. said there are some legitimate businesses in the field but there are also bogus scholarship search services that fast talk students and their families out of millions of dollars in cash each and every single year. Just last month the same Federal Trade Commission (FTC) in Washington filed charges against eleven companies that it claims stole a total of nearly about $10 million dollars from students located in all of the 50 states who plan to start college next year or who are already in college and from their families. The companies promised to look for money to help the swindled students and their families pay the outrageous cost of college tuition, fees, room and board, and other expenses incurred while attending a college. The numbers are astonishing, truly astonishing. The FTC estimates that each and every year as many as 300,000 students and their families fall for the swindle. They're defrauded. Fooled! Cheated! Swindled! Companies promise to find a scholarship or grant, which are free, never having to be repaid. Some promise to find a scholarship or grant for each and every one of the students using their service and to return peoples money if they don't, but then they don't find financial aid and don't return the money. The FTC said today in its new warning they may never look or they may send you a useless and totally worthless computer printout which lists dozens, even hundreds, of scholarships none of which you may be currently eligible for at all. The FTC warns, simply, that "If you have to pay money to get money it might be a scam. Be wary." Matt Adamopoulos, head of the Office of Financial Aid at your school, points out the fact that high school and college counselors provide free services. So do libraries. He recommends that people use free services exclusively.

None guarantee success. "That's impossible," Adamopoulos told you in an exclusive interview today. "We can almost always help really exceptional students, and sometimes the poor. Its those in the middle we have the toughest time with," he went on to add that. The FTC also warns people not to do stupid things like give these or other companies their credit card numbers or bank account numbers or even social security numbers, since other abuses are also committed, such as emptying a victims bank account or adding other charges to his/her credit cards. But people are desperate, overwhelmed and shocked and frightened by the high and escalating and ridiculous cost of college educations in the United States nowadays which threaten to nearly bankrupt some families, especially those with multiple kids. In desperation, and because they are unfamiliar with the process, they are in many cases easy victims for swindlers. The FTC normally seeks temporary restraining orders prohibiting companies from engaging in activities the FTC has challenged. Or, the FTC freezes the companies assets. But companies can close, move to another city or state and in a matter of a very few days open a new company with a new name that continues the same practices with the same people involved. 17-year-old Susan Carigg of your city is an example of victims of the fraud along with her parents, Susan and Craig Carigg. Young Susan is a senior at your citys Martin Luther King Jr. High School and wants to attend college next year but doesn't have a lot of money or extraordinarily high grades, just a solid 3.34 gpa. She, who wants to be a nurse and her parents paid $799 to the Scholarship Search Institute 3 days after receiving a flier in the mail from its headquarters located in the city of Phoenix. The flier promised that people are "guaranteed many times their investment back" in scholarships, grants, and other financial aid. But the Carigs haven't received anything since sending in their check. Now they can't even find the company anywhere. Postal authorities they called for help are also looking for the company, and say thousands of other gullible people who fell for the scam are doing likewise. An FTC official who asked that she not be identified admitted they almost never recover anyones money. Al Giangelli, another high school senior in your city, whose parents are divorced and who lives with his mother at 214 Lake Dr., sent $999 to a similar company, Financial Aid Finders, using money he saved working at a Burger King. "I want to go to a private school," Al told you in an exclusive interview today. "I figure that'd cost maybe $20,000 a year, probably more, and they promised to help, said they help everyone, that there's lots of money for everyone. Now I'm worse off than before. I worked hard for that money and they stole it. Its a ripoff, a damn ripoff. They're crooks is what they are."

3. MISSING PEOPLE

You won't believe the numbers involved. They're astonishingly high. Its typical of the situation in each and every one of the nations 50 states. Last year alone in just your one state alone a total number of 57,152 men, women, and children were reported at one time or another to be "missing." A total of 48,384 of the missing individuals sooner or later reappeared or were found or otherwise recovered. But nearly 9,000 remain missing, and that seems to be a typical number for a years total annual figures for your one state. Some of the missing people each year are kids—runaways. Others are very old people with Alzheimers who wander some distance away from their homes. There are deadbeat dads and deadbeat moms too. There are people trying to run away from their debts. There are always young men and women running away with lovers with whom they are deeply and idealistically and perhaps unrealistically in love. And there are each year a few, very few, bona fide crime victims: people apparently kidnapped or robbed or murdered, with their bodies hidden, perhaps burned or buried or tossed into some deep body of water somewhere and thus hidden.

Police estimate that the true crime victims total no more than 100 in number and perhaps as few as 40 or 50. A woman may disappear, and everyone—friends, co-workers, relatives, everyone—swears that she was a totally reliable person and happy and stable, so everyone believes shes a victim of foul play. 5 years later she may call her parents to say she's now happily married and has three kids, a new job, and a new name, and ran off 5 years ago because she was in love with someone her parents didn't like, or didn't like pressures at home or work or just wanted to try someplace new, or hated a boyfriend or her husband at the time who, unknown to all others, perhaps drank or beat her or abused her both physically and mentally.

"I've worked around missing persons for the past 10 years, and it's rare finding someone after more than a year," said Sgt. Manuel Cortez of your citys police dept. "We find a lot of people disappear because they've got troubles, want to leave them behind and start over again. A lot of people think about it, and some do more than think about it. Normally its more men than women, except among juveniles. Among juveniles, runaway girls outnumber boys 3 to 1. Kids, particularly those 11 to 17, flee in droves." Another authority, Psychology Prof. Alan Christopher, says, "Most adults will stick around and handle their problems, but a lot of kids think its easier to run away. Or they just don't think. They see some place on television, and it looks good, so they try to go there." Nationwide, 450,700 youngsters were reported to have fled their homes and juvenile facilities and all sorts of other places they were supposed to be living last year and another 127,100 were "thrown away," meaning their parents or guardians or whoever in the world was caring for them would not let them come back, according to statistics compiled by the U.S. Justice Dept.

Three-fourths of the missing persons in your state last year were runaway juveniles. Nearly 6,500 have not yet been found or located. Sabrina Diaz, a 14 yr. old, is an example, now residing at 1987 Holcrofte Ave. in your city. "My parents got divorced" she told you after you promised not to use her last name. "I hated my stepfather. He's a jerk. He got drunk and hit my Mom and expected us to wait on him like we were his slaves or something.

"So, uh, I met this guy who was moving to New York. He didn't want to take me, said I was too young, but I, uh, got him to change his mind. So, uh, like I was there two years, then got caught shoplifting and prostituting and the cops somehow they came up with my real name and my mom came and got me. She's dropped the jerk, so it's better now, just the two of us, and so we can, uh, talk and everything." Jason Abare is a 31 year old man currently residing in your county jail on charges of nonsupport. At the time of his divorce from his wife, Anne, of 9 years, he was ordered to pay alimony and child support for his four kids, a total of $840 a month. Ann currently resides at 855 Tichnor Way. "I wasn't going to give her a penny, not with the hell that woman put me through," he said. He left the state.

"It was easy, real easy," he told you during a jailhouse interview today.

"I'm in construction, a carpenter, and good, so I can pick up a job almost anywhere and kinda drifted around. If I liked where I was I'd stay a couple months, even a year. Other times I just stayed a week or two until I got my first payday then skipped town. I figured no one could ever find me that way. I got caught last month, charged with drunken driving and didn't have a drivers license anymore so they checked my prints and found out who I really was and returned me here. Bad luck, that's what it was, just bad luck."

CHAPTER 15

PUBLIC AFFAIRS REPORTING

Knowledge will forever govern ignorance, and a people who mean to be their own government must arm themselves with the power that knowledge brings.

(President James Madison)

Sometimes people refer to the news media as "the Fourth Estate." Some historians attribute that phrase to a British politician and political thinker, Edmund Burke, who supposedly once said the three traditional classes, or estates, of society—the nobility, the clergy and the commoners—were represented in Parliament but in the reporters' gallery sat a fourth estate more powerful than the other three. Whatever its origin, the term recognized the power of the British and American press around 1800 to inform and shape popular opinion on public affairs.

News organizations continue to devote substantial time and money to reporting on public affairs. The term "public affairs reporting" encompasses more than reporting on government, but that remains one of journalism's most important tasks. For reporters on the local newspaper's police beat as well as those covering the White House for the television networks, recording the actions and policies of government consumes much of the working day. This chapter introduces public affairs reporting at the local level, focusing on the coverage of crimes and accidents, local government officials and agencies, and criminal and civil court cases.

The public affairs reporter, to be successful at any level, must cultivate certain habits. Among them are the following:

- Diligence: Public affairs reporters, whether assigned to the county courthouse or the Pentagon, must follow a regular pattern of checking sources. Reporters have discovered important stories simply by regularly inspecting documents filed with the register of deeds or contracts awarded by government agencies.
- Knowledge of sources: The sources for public affairs stories may be the people who work in government or who are affected by its decisions. Or the sources may be the records governmental agencies keep. Public affairs reporters must know how to use both people and documents to find information quickly.
- Accuracy: Government agencies deal with complicated matters. The reporters who cover public affairs must report the details of these issues correctly, whether they

are the name and address of a person arrested for a crime or a contractor's winning bid on a street improvement project.

- Ability to write clear explanations: Reporters not only must understand what government agencies are doing but also must be able to explain issues and decisions clearly to readers, listeners or viewers. Unless reporters explain governmental actions clearly, citizens will not understand how their lives and interests may be affected.

Reporters who develop these traits may find public affairs reporting to be the most rewarding and satisfying aspect of their work, for nothing else a journalist does can affect so many people.

CRIME AND ACCIDENTS

The first assignment many newspaper reporters have is the police beat. Beginning television or radio reporters may have more varied assignments, but covering crimes and accidents will be a major part of their jobs.

Not all police reporters are beginners; some have covered that beat for many years. Nevertheless, the police beat is an excellent training ground, for several reasons:

- It forces young reporters to learn the community, both geographically and sociologically.

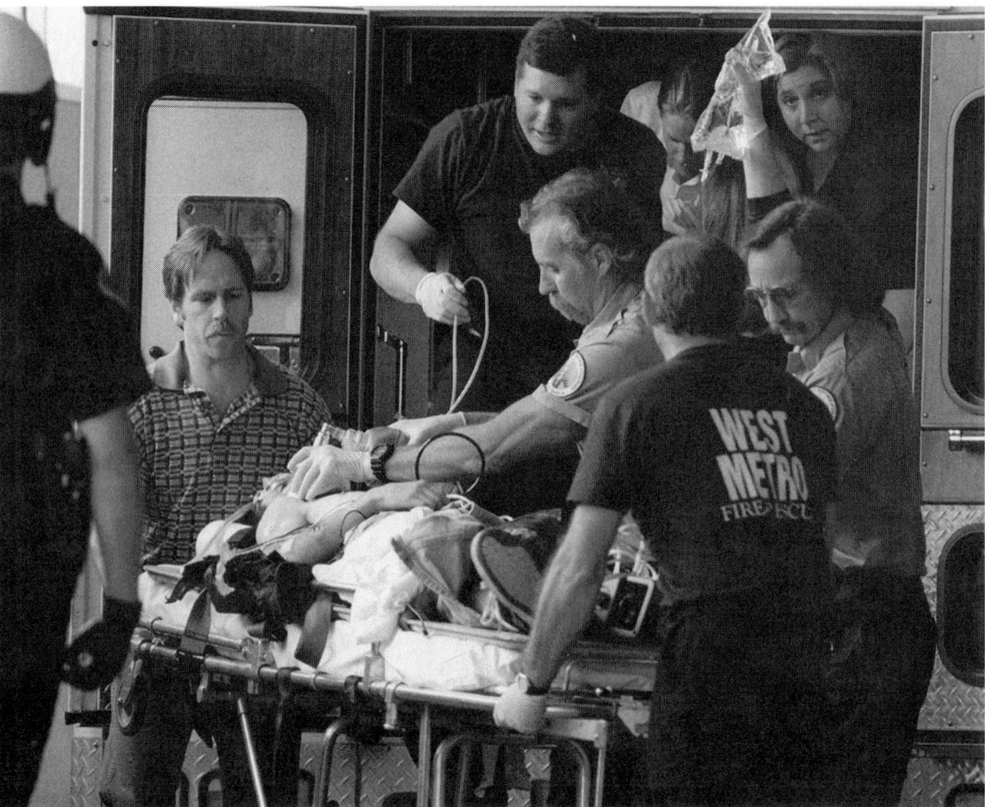

Reporters assigned to the police beat often cover life at its rawest and most violent. Here, medical workers load one of the victims of the shootings at Columbine High School in Littleton, Colo., into an ambulance.

COVERING THE SEARCH FOR A SERIAL KILLER

Charlotte Murray Pace had fought for her life as her attacker stabbed her repeatedly. Police later said her killer probably had been covered in blood when he left Pace's Baton Rouge, La., townhouse.

Such a crime would draw news coverage and public attention under any circumstances, but neither police nor reporters realized Pace's murder would put them on the trail of a serial killer.

Pace, a 22-year-old who had just earned a master's degree from Louisiana State University, was alone in the home she had moved into days earlier when her killer arrived on a late-May afternoon.

Eight months earlier, Gina Wilson Green, a 41-year-old nurse, was found strangled in her home on Stanford Avenue. At the time, Pace lived only three houses away from Green. Pace had not known Green, but the coincidence of their having been neighbors started some residents to wondering. So, too, did the disappearance of Christine Moore, 23, another LSU graduate student who had lived in the same neighborhood as Pace. Her skeletal remains were found only a couple of weeks after Pace's murder.

Melissa Moore, who had been covering police for the Baton Rouge Advocate for 10 years, doubted that the killings were connected. When some Advocate staffers suggested a story raising the possibility the murders were linked, Moore argued against it.

"We had talked about it," Moore recalled. "I said no. We have to be really careful about this."

That changed one month and nine days after Pace's killing. Police announced that DNA evidence proved Pace and Green had been killed by the same person. With that announcement, Moore said, the Advocate began planning a piece about the unsolved murders of Pace, Green, Christine Moore and a number of other Baton Rouge-area women.

The story Moore wrote—with contributions from Brett Barrouquere, Marlene Naanes, Ryan Goudelocke and James Minton—said the deaths of Pace, Green and Christine Moore were only three of 29 unsolved homicides in the Baton Rouge area over the past 10 years.

The Advocate staff prepared the list of unsolved homicides without help from the police. Moore and her colleagues had searched their clip files and their memories for unsolved murders, excluding those that involved multiple victims.

The story did not say the same person killed all 29 women, but it ran with a map that named each woman, included photos of some of them, and showed where each body had been found.

"I was comfortable with the story, but I was uncomfortable with the map, which connected cases that I did not think were connected," Melissa Moore said. The decision to run the map was her editor's, Moore said, and although it generated public interest in the story, it also left some misconceptions in the minds of readers. "I still get e-mails about the serial killer who's killed 30 women," Moore said several months later.

Baton Rouge police were also uncomfortable with the story. "They clearly were not happy," Moore said. "But it was accurate. They couldn't say it was unfair or inaccurate." Public reaction to the story, however, was strongly favorable. People started saying they had not realized how bad the problem was, Moore said.

The publication of the story about the many unsolved homicides of women coincided with the discovery of the body of another victim: Pam Kinamore, a 44-year-old

(*continued*)

businesswoman. She had been abducted from her home a few days earlier. Her throat had been slashed, and her body had been dumped near Interstate 10 outside Baton Rouge. A few weeks later, DNA evidence would show that the same person who had killed Green and Pace had also killed Kinamore.

For nearly 11 months, police sought the south Louisiana serial killer, and local and national news organizations followed the investigation. By the time a suspect, Derrick Todd Lee, 34, was arrested, the serial killer had murdered two more women: Trineisha Dené Colomb, 23, and Carrie Lynn Yoder, 26. Colomb died just a couple of months before she had planned to join the Marine Corps. Yoder was a doctoral student in biological sciences at LSU. Months after Lee's arrest, police had DNA evidence linking him to the murders of Randi C. Mebruer, 28, in 1998 and Geralyn DeSoto, 21, in 2002, and they were looking for evidence to connect him to still more killings.

Reporters covering the serial killer investigation had to cope with the unwillingness of the police to disclose information, a practice that not only frustrated journalists but also angered relatives of the victims. Melissa Moore said police were stingy with information about the homicides. Law enforcement officers said they did not want to release information that might help the killer, but that rationale did not explain all decisions to withhold information.

The police admitted they had DNA evidence linking all five murders; they also consistently referred to the suspect as "he." But they never admitted the obvious: that the victims had been raped. Moore said Baton Rouge police traditionally were reluctant to discuss rapes. "They're weird about sexual assault cases all the time, not just these (serial killer cases). They hate talking about it—hate it, hate it, hate it," she said.

The reluctance of the police to talk meant reporters had to look elsewhere for information. Moore ran a listserv for Criminal Justice Journalists, an organization for reporters who cover cops and courts. She used that listserv to find outside experts, people who had helped other reporters cover crime. Once she'd found sources, however, she still had to evaluate their expertise. Who else had quoted them? What had they written? What did other people in the field think of these experts? Did what these experts say correspond with what Moore had read and learned in her years of covering police? Asking these questions, Moore said, helped her eliminate one source who seemed to be an expert but who was considered a fraud by others in the field.

The hardest part of covering the serial murders was dealing with the families of the victims. "My heart just breaks for them," Moore said. When Pam Kinamore was abducted, her relatives were eager for news coverage as a way of helping get her back. "It was horrible to go back there after her body was found," Moore said. She persuaded the Kinamore family to talk to her by saying she wanted to write about Kinamore's life as a businesswoman, mother and wife and not about her death.

Although Moore left the Advocate to become the adviser to the LSU student newspaper before the serial killer suspect was arrested, she said the experience had reinforced some lessons about police reporting.

- Know what questions to ask by learning how police operate: "Read about it," Moore said. "Read 'Homicide' by David Simon. Read some Edna Buchanan. I tell people three-quarters of my job is knowing which questions to ask, and until you understand what happens in an investigation, you'll never know what questions to ask."
- Know how to use and manage a data base. "You never know what piece of information is going to be important later," she said. "So I've learned to manage little bits of information that don't make it into stories."
- Build good relationships with law enforcement agencies: "When I was a new reporter," Moore said, "if I could get a detective to let me hang out

Byron Kinamore (center), husband of Pam Kinamore, joins other family members in mourning his wife, who was one of the victims of a serial killer in the Baton Rouge, La., area. Melissa Moore, a reporter for The Advocate in Baton Rouge, covered the investigation of the killings. One of the most challenging parts of the job, she said, was dealing with the families of victims.

with him, we had breakfast, we had lunch, we had dinner, we had coffee. It helped me understand how they do what they do." Getting the story right, however, is the most important way to build trust, she said. Officers are more likely to trust reporters who have been getting the facts right for six months or a year than someone who is new or who has a reputation for making mistakes.

- Request public records early: Once a story develops into a big controversy, it becomes a madhouse for reporters and public officials, Moore said. Getting records then can be very difficult.
- Be willing to listen to people off the record: Although some reporters refuse to talk to someone who wants to go off the record, Moore said she was always willing to listen. "I'd always rather know than not know," she said, "even if the only reason for knowing is that it helps me know what context to put a story in."

- It trains reporters in news values and in the need for accuracy.
- It gives reporters an opportunity to develop sources who will serve them for many years.

The police beat imposes a great deal of stress on reporters. Police reporters mostly cover breaking news, so the deadline pressures are constant. Additionally, their jobs expose them to the harshest aspects of urban life: homicides, fatal accidents and suicides. And being on the streets places police reporters in more danger than most other reporters. Some reporters burn out because of the stress of police reporting, while others thrive on it. Many news organizations rotate police reporters to other beats after a few years, partly to prevent burnout but also to prevent reporters from becoming too friendly with the police officers they cover.

The work of police reporters varies with the size and type of community they are covering. In a small community, almost any crime, even a minor theft, may be newsworthy. In big cities, where two or three homicides a day are common, only the most bloody, most unusual crimes will receive detailed coverage. Police reporters also cover the activities of the department, including community service projects, promotions, retirements and internal investigations. They may cover traffic accidents, but usually only the most noteworthy ones.

A lot of the information for these stories is available at police headquarters or the precinct stations. Reporters may be able to write their stories without ever leaving headquarters or the newsroom. But experienced reporters know that they must go to the scenes of crimes and accidents to be able to report on them vividly. The reporter needs to be on the street, talking to the victims, witnesses, suspects and investigating officers.

Police Sources

Reporters and law enforcement officers are often leery of one another, and that suspicion sometimes prevents thorough reporting. Police forces are organized along military lines, and many members follow the military ideals of duty, discipline and deference to superior officers. Reporters tend to be more individualistic and less deferential to authority than police officers are. A more important obstacle is that police officers are wary of news coverage. They fear stories will sensationalize their work, portray them in a bad light or get them in trouble with their superiors. They usually see few, if any, benefits from news coverage, except under circumstances they can control. For their part, reporters tend to see police officers as tight-lipped and secretive, using claims of privacy or investigative necessity to keep interesting and important information from the public.

Reporters try to set aside their prejudices and work to overcome the suspicion and distrust of police officers, because they need information from police sources to write their stories. The first step toward gaining the confidence of police officers is to spend as many hours as possible at police headquarters and precinct stations. Reporters should chat with officers about their work and their professional concerns. They also should try to get permission to ride with officers in patrol cars. Those who do will see how officers spend their time and will learn what officers' lives are like. The best way reporters build trust with police officers is to prove their professionalism by reporting on police matters accurately and thoroughly and by treating sources fairly.

Different police departments handle relations with news organizations in different ways. In some communities, a police department public affairs officer might conduct daily briefings for all reporters on the beat. That officer might provide reporters with printouts or copies of police activity logs for the past 24 hours, describe some of the more significant events and then answer questions from reporters. Other cities might dispense with regular briefings and deal with reporters individually. Some departments might allow reporters to speak directly with the officers and investigators who are working on a particular crime or accident. Other departments permit only certain senior officers, perhaps a public information officer or shift captains, to talk to reporters. Police reporters prefer to speak directly to the officers who are handling a case.

Edna Buchanan, a former police reporter for The Miami Herald, says journalists, especially print reporters, need details to make their stories complete. A police department's public information officer, who may never visit a crime scene, cannot furnish those details. Only the officers who were present know what a reporter needs. Buchanan learned the importance of asking for details when she neglected to do so while covering a homicide. The case appeared to be routine: A man had been shot and his body dumped in the street. Only later did Buchanan learn that the victim had been wearing a black taffeta cocktail dress and red high-heeled shoes.

Reporters will find it easier to get the information they need for their stories if they develop good work habits. This means following a regular pattern for checking sources, such as police reports, jail records, the medical examiner's office and the department's public information officer. Other helpful sources reporters should cultivate are police union leaders, prosecutors, defense attorneys and bail bond agents. They also need to develop the skill of listening to the police scanner. Reporters should know the most frequently used channels for police and fire communications, including the special ones used by SWAT teams or other emergency units. The chatter on the scanner is preliminary information at best, however, and reporters must check it out thoroughly before publishing it.

Documentary Sources

Police keep records of most of their activities. The records help police plan their investigations, keep track of suspects, prepare to testify in court and justify their budget requests, among other things. Police officers do not prepare their records for the convenience of news reporters, but many police records are open to the public, and journalists should learn how to use them. What follows is a brief description of some of the records of crimes and accidents available from police departments and other agencies:

- **Police blotter.** This document goes by different names, but it usually records all calls for assistance received by the police. The log provides such basic facts as the location of an event, the time and a brief description. It may also tell who has been arrested, the charge and the time of the arrest. Blotter information is sketchy and best serves as a lead to other sources.

- **Incident reports.** The incident report gives a more complete description of a crime. It describes the nature of the crime, the location, the name of the victim, when the crime occurred, what property was stolen or damaged (if relevant) and the name of the investigating officer. Other information may or may not be available, depending on the law of the state. For example, Alaska law prohibits the disclosure of the addresses and phone numbers of all witnesses and victims; it also keeps confidential the names of victims of kidnappings, sex crimes and certain crimes involving minors. Some states make available sections of the incident reports that provide a narrative of the crime; other states consider that information part of the investigative record and close it to the public. Police generally treat as confidential any portion of the record that identifies suspects who have not been arrested.

- **Arrest warrants, search warrants and affidavits.** Police officers usually have to get a warrant from a magistrate before they can arrest a suspect or legally search private property. Police investigators get warrants by filing affidavits with a court identifying the suspect they want to arrest or the place they want to search and what they are searching for. The warrants also provide more details about the suspects and their alleged crimes than police might be willing to divulge directly to reporters. Nevertheless, the warrants and the affidavits usually become public records once the arrest or search is complete. The affidavits help reporters understand what police are doing and why. After a search has been conducted, police also must file a report of what items were actually taken during the search. Warrants, affidavits and related documents are usually found in district or circuit court files, not at the police station. Sometimes courts temporarily seal the warrants and the affidavits if the search or arrest is part of a larger investigation and police do not want to alert other possible suspects.

- **Jail booking records.** These records indicate when a person is taken into custody and when that person is released. The booking records will even show people who are in custody but have not been charged with a crime and who, therefore, may not show up on other records.

- **Autopsy reports.** In cases involving violent or unexplained deaths, coroners perform autopsies to determine the cause and manner of death. The cause of death is the medical reason the person died, such as gunshot wound to the heart or poisoning. The manner of death refers to the circumstances under which the person died: accident, suicide or homicide. Autopsy reports are not public records in all states. In Massachusetts, for example, they are considered medical records that are closed to the public. In Kansas, Maryland and Wyoming, however, autopsy reports are explicitly identified as public records.

- **Medical examiner's report.** This report may be separate from the autopsy, and it often includes information about the crime scene, witnesses and next of kin that may not be in the police incident report.

- **Arrest reports.** The arrest report describes a person who has been arrested and the offense, names the officers involved, lists the witnesses and, eventually, gives the outcome of the case.
- **Criminal history information.** Information that a suspect has prior arrests and convictions is likely to turn public opinion against that person and make it harder for him or her to receive a fair trial. To protect the suspect's right to a fair trial, law enforcement authorities hesitate to disclose such information. Some states severely limit access to it; others erase or expunge it after time and under certain other conditions. Most states, however, consider criminal history information public record.
- **Police misconduct investigation records.** Sometimes citizens complain that police officers have broken the law or violated department regulations. The complaints usually lead to an internal investigation. In some states, police use laws protecting personnel records or investigative records as a reason to withhold information about investigations of police misconduct. Elsewhere, complaints and the disposition of those complaints are public record.
- **Accident reports.** These records describe motor vehicle accidents and identify the time and place of the accident, drivers involved, passengers, injuries and property damages. The reports usually describe how the accident occurred as reconstructed by the investigating officer.

Although a number of records are available to reporters, most states allow police to withhold investigative records. Some states allow the withholding of almost any kind of investigative record, even if it is not part of a criminal investigation. Other states say police can withhold only the records of active criminal investigations; once the investigation is complete, the records become public. The names of confidential sources and undercover police officers, along with information about confidential investigative techniques, usually can be withheld indefinitely. Privacy laws may also allow police to keep some records confidential, such as the names of rape victims or the identities of juvenile suspects. These secrecy provisions mean the police reporter must combine human and documentary sources to prepare complete news reports.

In addition to knowing the records that track specific crimes and suspects, police reporters should be familiar with a variety of other documents pertaining to the police department. The department's rules and regulations along with training manuals will tell the reporter how the department is supposed to work. Some police departments are accredited by a national organization, and they must prepare a detailed report as part of that accreditation process. The accreditation report can show how well the department is meeting its goals and where it is falling short. The annual budget reveals how and where the department is spending its money. That can be compared with the community's crime statistics to give some indication of whether the department is addressing real problems. If, for example, the department is pouring resources into low-crime neighborhoods while shorting neighborhoods where the crime rate is rising, that fact may be a lead to an important story.

Libel, Sensationalism and Other Problems

A story saying that a person has been arrested in connection with an infamous crime is likely to harm that person's reputation. Therefore, reporters covering the police and courts must be careful to avoid libel suits. Reporters can say a person has been charged with a crime. However, reporters cannot say or imply the person is guilty until after that person has been convicted by a judge or jury. Criminal defendants in the United States are presumed innocent and have a right to be tried in a court of law, not by a mob on a street corner or by their local newspaper or television news broadcast.

The following story does not libel the defendant because it never reports or implies that the defendant committed the crime. Rather, the story seems to be describing two different people: (1) the defendant and (2) the criminal. The reporter carefully avoids saying the defendant actually committed the crime:

> A 27-year-old woman is suing a downtown hotel because she was raped in the hotel's parking garage on her wedding night.
>
> On Tuesday, the woman filed a suit in Circuit Court, charging that the Grand Hotel failed to adequately protect its guests.
>
> The hotel's general manager, Lillian DeLoy, responded that the hotel's security is adequate.
>
> According to the woman's attorney, James R. Lopez, the rape took place in front of an empty security office—a glassed-in booth with a view of the entire garage.
>
> The attack occurred when the bride returned to her parked car for a suitcase at about 11 p.m. Police arrested a suspect a short time later.
>
> The suspect, Myron Jaco, 18, of 141 Pine St., has been charged with sexual battery and is scheduled to stand trial next month.

Several recent criminal investigations have illustrated how thoughtless crime reporting can injure the reputations of innocent people or interfere with police work. Richard Jewell was a private security guard working at the Atlanta Olympics. After a bomb exploded in a park filled with Olympic spectators, killing one person and injuring several others, Jewell became a suspect. He was never charged with a crime, but law enforcement sources leaked their suspicions about him to local and national news organizations. To millions of news readers and viewers, Jewell appeared to be the prime suspect. Eventually, investigators focused on a different suspect, Eric Rudolph, who was arrested years later. Jewell sued several news organizations for libel; some settled out of court, but he has not won any judgments in court.

A similar media frenzy developed a few years later when a scientist at the nuclear weapons laboratories at Los Alamos, N.M., was suspected of having given China top-secret information about the most advanced thermonuclear warheads in the U.S. arsenal. Leaks, again from investigators, portrayed the scientist, Wen Ho Lee, as a spy who had compromised national security. The government held him in solitary confinement for nine months until its espionage case against him collapsed.

A third incident just two years after the Lee frenzy showed that news organizations had not learned the lesson. Federal investigators trying to find out who had mailed letters laced with anthrax to members of Congress and the news media told reporters that Steven J. Hatfill, a former bioweapons expert, was a "person of interest" in their investigation. The phrase "person of interest" has no legal significance, but it strongly implies the person is a suspect if not actually guilty. After the attacks of Sept. 11, Americans are worried—with good reason—about terrorists who might use biological or chemical weapons, but news stories that tarnish people who have been neither arrested nor charged with any crime only add to hysteria rather than calm it.

The hunt for the Washington, D.C., area sniper exposed other problems with news coverage of crime. Over nearly three weeks, 12 people in the District of Columbia area were shot and 10 killed. As the series of murders continued, news coverage increased in intensity, especially on the cable television news channels. Law enforcement officials complained the coverage was so intense it interfered with the investigation. After one of the shootings, a Washington television station revealed that the killer had left behind a tarot card with the words "Mr. Policeman, I am God" scrawled on it. The note on the card had also asked police not to reveal it to the press. Charles Moose, who was then the police chief in Montgomery County, Md., complained that the disclosure had severely impaired the investigation. Later Newhouse News Service reporter Dru Sefton showed that the sniper was responding to news reports. After a school official appeared on television to reassure parents their children were safe, the sniper shot a 13-year-old boy outside his school. And when a profiler noted that all of the killings had been on weekdays, the next shooting came on a Saturday. Eventually, John Allen Muhammad, 41, and Lee Boyd Malvo, 17, were arrested and charged with the killings. In separate trials, each was convicted of one of the killings. Muhammad was sentenced to death and Malvo to life in prison. They may be tried in connection with others in the series of killings.

Much of the criticism of media coverage of the sniper killings focused on the sources some news organizations used. One Fox News correspondent, Rita Cosby, turned to another serial murderer, David Berkowitz, the "Son of Sam" killer. In a letter to Cosby that she shared with viewers, Berkowitz opined that the D.C. sniper was driven by anger and rage against law enforcement. Critics wondered whether it was appropriate to ask one serial killer to analyze another. More commonly, however, reporters turned to unofficial experts who offered their opinions about who was committing the crimes. And often those opinions were wrong. Profilers, criminologists and psychologists quoted in newspaper stories and interviewed on television news shows led journalists and the public to believe that the sniper was likely to be a white man in his mid-30s. Muhammad and Malvo are both African-American and neither is in his 30s. Perhaps, the fault for the errors lies not in the reporters' star sources but in the reporters themselves and the questions they ask. Instead of asking the experts to make guesses and predictions, reporters should ask for facts and background, such as how profiling works and what information police look for to construct a profile.

Elements of Crime and Accident Stories

Most crime stories have summary leads that identify the central point immediately. Usually, that point is the aspect of the crime that makes it newsworthy—deaths, large amounts of money taken or some unusual or ironic twist to the story. When writing about unusual crimes, reporters sometimes use delayed leads, which place an anecdote or a description of a scene or person ahead of the nut paragraph containing the central point. Nevertheless, all crime stories contain basically the same information:

- Any deaths or injuries. When they occur, these are often the most important facts and should appear early in the story.
- The nature and value of any property stolen or damaged.
- As complete an identification of the suspect as possible: the suspect's full name, including middle initial, as well as his or her age, address and occupation. Complete identification of the suspect guards against the possibility that readers or viewers will confuse the suspect with someone else who has a similar name; that kind of confusion leads to libel suits.
- Identification of victims and witnesses. To protect them, some news organizations will not publish their addresses. News organizations also routinely withhold the names of victims of sex crimes.
- Whether weapons were used in the commission of the crime and, if so, what types.
- The exact charges filed against the suspect.
- A narrative of the crime.

News stories should describe the specific crimes involved, not just the legal charges. The legal charges often fail to reveal exactly what happened. Moreover, because they are expressed in general terms, the same legal charges could be repeated in thousands of stories:

VAGUE: Three people arrested in a church parking lot Sunday morning were charged with petty larceny.

REVISED: Three people arrested in a church parking lot Sunday morning were charged with siphoning gasoline from a car.

Never report a suspect's race or religion unless it is clearly relevant to the story. In the past (and sometimes even today) reporters mentioned the race only of suspects and criminals who were minorities. Race is relevant, however, in the description of a suspect who is at large:

> Witnesses described the thief as a white man, about 25 years old and 6 feet tall. The thief has a mustache and a scar on his left cheek and is missing several front teeth.

While describing a crime, do not mention the fact that it was committed by an "unidentified" man or woman. Criminals rarely announce their identities, and most crimes are never solved. Thus, most criminals are never "identified." Similarly, if police do not know a criminal's identity, the story cannot report that the police are looking for "a suspect." If the police do not know who committed a crime, they have no suspect.

Accident stories resemble crime stories in many of their elements. The central points usually emphasize deaths, property damage or unusual circumstances. Here are some of the major points to include in accident stories:

- Any deaths or injuries. Again, this is usually the most important information.
- Property damage.
- The identities of the people involved in the accident.
- The types of vehicles involved, such as cars, trucks or buses.
- Any citations given to any of the drivers.
- Any unusual conditions at the time of the accident, such as fog, rain or snow.
- A narrative of the accident.

Do not say that a person "received" injuries. People "receive" gifts, but they normally "suffer" injuries.

For both crime and accident stories, report only what occurred, not what has not occurred. Avoid statements like the following:

> No one was hurt.
> There are no suspects.
> Officers searched the neighborhood but were unable to find the vandals.

LOCAL GOVERNMENT

The phrase "public affairs reporting" calls to mind news about the federal government: the president, Congress and the federal bureaucracy. Certainly those institutions can affect millions of Americans with their actions. Yet, for the vast majority of Americans, contact with the federal government or federal officials is a rarity. Citizens are more likely to deal with local and state governments. Local governments provide police and fire protection, pave streets, provide water service and run schools and hospitals—services many people use frequently, even every day. Citizens want to know how the construction of a new freeway will affect property values and the environment. They want to know what will happen to local schools if the state limits property tax rates. And they want to know how tax incentives designed to attract businesses to a community affect the tax burdens on the rest of the people. Citizens turn to print and broadcast news reports for information about issues such as these, but too often they fail to find what they are looking for.

Obstacles to Thorough Coverage

Some numbers help explain why coverage of local government is incomplete even though journalists and citizens agree on its importance. There are 87,849 local units of government in the United States, including cities, counties, school districts and a variety of special districts that oversee such things as housing, water and power. By comparison, there are only 1,468 English-language daily newspapers and 1,686 television stations. True, there are also 13,012 radio stations and 6,476 weekly newspapers, but many stations broadcast little or no news, and weeklies often cover only the immediate community. Still, local government units outnumber media organizations by nearly four to one.

The picture appears more dismal when one compares numbers of employees. The total full- and part-time employment for all local governmental units is 13.1 million. Not all of the government employees make news, but the corps of journalists who cover government is much smaller. Federal labor statistics show only 280,000 employees identify themselves as editors or reporters. Many probably work for specialized media such as trade publications or magazines that focus on hobbies. And of the editors and reporters who work for television or radio news or daily newspapers, many cover business, sports or lifestyles. The proportion of journalists who cover public affairs is probably quite small.

Small numbers of reporters in newsrooms across the country have the difficult task of watching many governmental units and their departments and subdivisions. Even a small daily paper may have to cover a dozen city and county governments. In urban areas, a daily newspaper's coverage area may include hundreds of governmental units. Television journalists often must cover more governmental units than print reporters because their signals reach larger areas. Given these realities, it is no wonder many people complain about the superficiality of much local news coverage.

City and County Governments

City governments provide a wide range of services for their residents: police and fire protection, sewage treatment, water, street construction and maintenance, and parks and recreation services. Some cities also provide trash pickup and disposal, public transportation and electricity or natural gas. Others operate hospitals or have some control over the local school system. They also adopt ordinances regulating such things as local speed limits, zoning and the use of outdoor signs by businesses.

County governments usually have more limited powers. They collect taxes levied by all the agencies in the county. They may assess the value of all real and personal property, and they may hear appeals from citizens who believe those assessments are too high. County governments are repositories for records of births, deaths, marriages, real estate transactions and motor vehicle registrations. County governments also supervise elections and handle voter registration in many states.

Although it is difficult to generalize, city governments tend to have more professional managers than county governments, and cities tend to be less open than counties to the press and public. Usually, only the mayor and city council or city commission members are elected. In many cities, the mayor has little real power; much of the responsibility for administering the city rests with a city manager, who is hired by the council. Cities usually hire other top officials, such as the police chief, fire chief, finance director and public works director. The professionals hired to run most city departments may disdain news coverage, except for making routine announcements. They see themselves as accountable to the city manager or city council who hired them and not to the public generally.

The list of elected officials is longer in counties than in cities, sometimes including the county commissioners or supervisors, the clerk, register of deeds, assessor, sheriff and treasurer. These elected officials may feel more need to respond to the public, so they may be more accessible to reporters and citizens. Counties also may conduct their business in less formal ways than cities. The "good ol' boy" atmosphere of the 1940s and 1950s lingers in many county courthouses.

Local Budgets and Taxes

Reporters covering city or county government may write about a wide variety of issues, including the awarding of contracts for construction or major equipment purchases, creation of fire protection districts, zoning disputes and the regulation of adult movie theaters. The most important story, however, is the budget. The budget determines how much money a local government will have to collect from taxpayers and how it will spend that money for the coming year. It is the blueprint by which a local government works.

City budgets are set by the council or commission, county budgets by the commissioners. Usually department heads or officeholders submit their budget requests for the coming year. The council or the commission reviews the requests and makes the changes it considers prudent. Some states have statutory limits on the amounts by which local governments may increase their spending; others have been forcing local governments to roll back their taxes and spending. Tax and spending limits force the council or commission to make difficult budget choices.

Local governments get some money from federal and state governments, sales taxes, local income taxes, user fees and other miscellaneous sources, but property taxes provide the bulk of local revenue in most communities. Personal property includes such things as automobiles, boats, stocks and bonds. Real property is land and buildings. The assessor tries to determine the market value—how much it would sell for—for every piece of property in the county. That number is called the property's assessed valuation. Some states tax property on its full market value. Others apply the tax to only a portion of the market value. Still other states assess different classes of property differently, applying the tax to, say, 100 percent of the market value of residences but to only 80 percent of the market value of farmland.

A local government determines how much money it must raise from property taxes by deciding how much it needs to spend in the coming year and then subtracting all revenue from sales taxes, federal or state grants, user fees, income taxes and so forth. The remainder is divided by the total assessed valuation of all property in the community to produce the tax levy.

Here's an example: Say a city council has decided to set next year's budget at $19 million. The council expects to take in $8 million from sales taxes, state and federal grants and various fees. The remaining $11 million will have to come from property taxes. Assume the total assessed valuation of all property in this city is $875 million. Dividing $11 million by $875 million produces a tax rate of .01257. That means a person would pay 1.257 cents in taxes for every $1 in taxable property he or she owns. Sometimes property tax rates are expressed as mills. A mill equals one-tenth of a cent, so the tax rate in this example is 12.57 mills. Most readers and viewers will see the tax rate, whether expressed as cents or mills, as just another number. The news reporter must explain it in terms that will have meaning to them. One way is to say how much people will have to pay in taxes for every $100 in the assessed valuation of their property. Multiplying the tax rate of .01257 by $100 yields $1.26. That means people will pay about $1.26 in taxes for every $100 of taxable property they own.

Another way to explain property taxes to readers is to show what the tax bill would be for a typical home or car. Say the average price of a home in a community is $105,000 and personal homes are assessed at 100 percent of their market value. Multiply $105,000 by the tax rate, .01257. The result, $1,319.85, is the amount the owner of an $105,000 home would have to pay in real property taxes next year.

Residents of a community may pay taxes to several different governments: the city, county, school district, fire protection district, sewer district, natural resources district and others. The combination of taxes any individual pays will vary from city to city or even within cities.

The annual budget is a news story in itself, but it can also be the starting point for other important and interesting stories about local government. For instance, how much is the city or county spending on road repair? And is the spending concentrated in certain neighborhoods? Readers or viewers may want to know if the mayor's neighborhood is getting a disproportional amount of the road repair work. Another possible story would list the highest paid officials in the city or county and how much they are earning. Reporters might also look at something like the amount budgeted for snow removal or storm damage cleanup and whether it's in line with what has actually been spent over the last several years. Dramatic changes in revenue from fees, such as building fees, might be a story, too. If revenues from building permits has increased markedly, that may show a building boom in the community. A curious reporter who examines a local government budget closely can discover a wealth of story possibilities.

City and County Sources

Covering city hall or the county courthouse requires establishing a routine for visiting the various offices and departments and taking the time to get to know each officeholder or department chief. Reporters also should cultivate contacts among the assistants, staff members and secretaries who work in the various offices. Such workers can steer reporters to information for a story.

Some local officials fear press coverage or want to control information released to the press. Official policies that prohibit government employees from speaking to reporters or that punish those who do usually run afoul of the First Amendment. More successful are government efforts to channel the flow of information through public information officers, who present only the information top officials want revealed.

When they do talk, government officials often speak in jargon and technical terms: "ad valorem taxes," "capital outlays," "declaratory judgments," "percolation ponds," "promissory notes," "rapid infiltration basins," "secured and unsecured debts" and "tangible personal property." If a legal or technical term is essential to a story, the reporter should define it. Otherwise, those terms should be replaced with simpler and more familiar words. For example, while writing about plans to fix a sewer system, one reporter explained that the repairs were necessary "because of groundwater infiltration." Another reporter explained more clearly that the sewer pipes were so old and cracked that water was leaking into them.

City hall and county courthouse reporters also need to be familiar with public records. Not every document held by government is a public record; nevertheless, here are some local government records usually available to the public:

City or County

- **Purchase orders (paid and not paid).** These show what products or services were obtained from what vendors at what prices.
- **Payroll.** This record tells not only how much each employee was paid but also deductions, time records, sick leave, vacations and other absences. Although payroll information is usually obtainable, governments can and do withhold the Social Security numbers of employees. Other personnel information often is exempt from disclosure.
- **Expense records.** These may show which public officials are traveling, where they are going and how much they are spending. Telephone records, including cell phone records, for top officials may show who is trying to influence government decisions.
- **Bids and bid specifications.** When a governmental unit plans a major construction project or a major equipment purchase, it usually asks for bids. State laws usually require local governments to seek bids for all purchases above a certain amount. The bid specifications are the government agency's description of what it wants to buy or build and are sent to all contractors or vendors that might want to submit bids. The businesses submit sealed bids, which are opened at a public meeting. The specifications are public records as soon as the local government has distributed them. The bids become public records when they are opened.
- **Contracts.** When a government buys goods or services, it often signs a contract with the vendor or provider. Sometimes, it awards contracts without taking competitive bids. The contract shows who's getting paid, how much and for what. If certain companies seem to get the lion's share of government business, a reporter should ask why, particularly if the company's executives are major contributors to the campaigns of government officials.
- **Licenses.** Cities issue licenses for various kinds of businesses (liquor stores and food markets), occupations (private detectives and security guards), pets and a

variety of other things. In some communities, governments limit the number of liquor licenses they issue. Who gets a license may be determined by political connections and contributions.

- **Inspection reports.** Fire department officers inspect certain public buildings regularly for fire hazards. The reports they prepare usually are public records. So are reports prepared by building inspectors who make sure new buildings adhere to construction codes and by health inspectors who examine restaurants.
- **Zoning records.** Maps, reports, petitions and case files pertaining to planning and zoning actions are usually public.
- **Campaign contributions and financial statements.** Many states require public officials, both state and local, to disclose who contributed to their campaigns and how they are spending the money. Officials may also have to disclose the sources of their income and where they have their money invested. If an official makes a decision that benefits a business in which he has an investment, that may be a conflict of interest, and in some states, it may be illegal.
- **Resumes.** Resumes tell where public officials were educated, where they have worked in the past and what they've done. Although it may seem like a stupid thing to do, some people have falsified their resumes. When Notre Dame University fired its head football coach at the end of a season, it hired George O'Leary as the new coach. But within days, O'Leary had to resign when news reports disclosed he had lied about his achievements on his resume.

County

- **Tax assessment records.** These records reveal the owner, legal description and assessed value of the land and buildings for each piece of property in a community. The records usually are cross-indexed so they can be accessed in a number of ways.
- **Motor vehicle registration records.** These records show who owns what vehicles, their value and the taxes paid on them. In some states, counties keep tax records on motor vehicles; in others, the state keeps all motor vehicle and driver's license records. In 1994, Congress passed a law requiring states to make personal information on driving and motor vehicle records confidential. Some states challenged the law as interfering with their sovereign rights under the 10th Amendment, but the U.S. Supreme Court has ruled that the law is constitutional. The law does not prohibit public access to information about automobile accidents, driving violations and the status of drivers licenses. In the past, however, reporters have used computer databases of motor vehicle records to find such things as how many school bus drivers in a state have convictions for driving while intoxicated. The new federal law will make it much more difficult for reporters to do such stories in the future.
- **Deeds.** The register of deeds office keeps track of all transfers of real property in a county. The records reveal who owns what property, when it was purchased and from whom. In some states, the actual sales price of a piece of real estate is confidential.

For generations, local governments have kept these records and many others on paper. Now, computers are changing the way governments do business. The electronic transformation of public records has created both problems and opportunities for reporters. Most states consider records public whether they are in electronic or paper form. However, states differ on whether reporters and citizens should be able to get copies of records in electronic form. The difference is important because reporters can analyze data that are available in electronic form in ways that would be impossible with paper documents.

Erik Kriss and Jon Craig of the Syracuse (N.Y.) Herald-Journal matched data from two computer databases to show that the New York Legislature had padded its payroll with more than 800 political appointees, given jobs to many relatives of legislators, kept retired legislators on the payroll and operated three duplicate radio and television stations, among other things. Boston Globe reporters David Armstrong, Shelley Murphy and Stephen Kurkjian used a computer database with information on 30,000 elevators and escalators in Massachusetts to prepare a story documenting the decline in elevator safety. These stories were possible because reporters could use computers to examine quickly the electronic versions of thousands of public records. To sift through so many paper records would have taken more labor than most news organizations could afford to devote to a single project. Of course, the reporter must understand database and spreadsheet programs to be able to use electronic records effectively.

Geographic information systems—known by the acronym GIS—are an especially powerful tool for analyzing computer data. These sophisticated systems can combine information in government databases with maps showing terrain, roads, buildings and political boundaries. The Omaha (Neb.) World-Herald used GIS to identify high-crime areas of its metropolitan area and show how violent and nonviolent crime rates had changed over time. The Charlotte (N.C.) Observer also used GIS in its study of how a plan to send children to neighborhood schools instead of busing them would affect racial distributions. The Observer's five-part series helped persuade a federal judge to halt school busing.

School Districts

Public education absorbs more local tax money than any other area of government. That fact should encourage local news organizations to provide thorough and continuing coverage of schools. Most journalists, however, say education is poorly covered.

The responsibility for the poor news coverage of education rests partly with journalists and partly with educators themselves. Understanding what teachers and administrators are doing requires that reporters learn something about curriculum, educational methodology and child psychology, as well as budgets, taxes and school finance laws. These are difficult subjects to master, so many news organizations simply focus on what school boards decide or top administrators say. Yet such coverage reveals little of what happens to children in the classroom. Educators have compounded the problem with their fondness for opaque jargon, calling libraries "learning resource centers" and schools "attendance centers." Many of them also tend to fear news coverage, sometimes out of a desire to protect students and teachers, but other times to protect themselves from criticism.

Important stories about education will interest readers, but they require patience and time. When he was governor of Minnesota, Jesse Ventura noted that tuition at many private schools in the Minneapolis area was less than what the city's public schools spent annually per pupil. Ventura said that showed something was wrong with public schools. But Norman Draper of the Minneapolis Star Tribune took a closer look and found a more complicated picture. Private school tuition often did not cover the full cost of educating pupils. The difference was made up by contributions from parents and alumni and by state aid to pay for such things as bus service, school nurses, textbooks and equipment.

Some states have turned to charter schools as a way to improve education. Charter schools are privately operated schools that receive tax money but are not accountable to local school districts and often receive little state oversight. Timothy Egan of The New York Times found that in Texas, California and Arizona—states that had been in the forefront of promoting charter schools—charter schools were overcharging the state and underperforming public schools. In Texas, fewer than 50 percent of students in some charter schools were passing standardized state achievement tests that 82 percent of public school students were passing.

The Wichita, Kan., school board for several years had a contract with a private company, Edison Schools Inc., to operate four public schools. The district hoped Edison would improve student achievement, according to stories by education reporter Josh Funk for the Wichita Eagle, but problems developed instead, including cheating on achievement tests encouraged by administrators at one school, near loss of accreditation at the same school, unpaid utility bills, high teacher turnover amd low enrollment. A couple of Edison-operated schools did produce some improvement in student achievement, but the school board concluded it was not dramatically better than performance at district-operated schools while the Edison schools were much more costly to run. The Wichita school board terminated its contract with Edison, ending an eight-year experiment with privatization.

Many newspapers have been preparing report cards for school districts for several years. Reporters have discovered that they must do more than simply report scores on standardized tests and compare scores from different schools and different districts. Test scores can be dramatically affected by such things as the proportion of pupils who have one or more parents with a college degree, parents' income (often assessed by the proportion of pupils who qualify for free or reduced-price lunches), what percentage of pupils enter or leave school during the year and the percentage of pupils for whom English is their second language. Accumulating all of the data for a school report card and analyzing it correctly can take months, but the work can pay off in a story or series that many people will read or watch.

School Sources and Documents

Education reporters need to recognize the hierarchy of sources in school districts. The sources who are highest and most often quoted may have the least knowledge of what is happening in classrooms. Boards of education may concentrate on financial and administrative matters and pay less attention to curriculum issues. The superintendent of schools has day-to-day authority to direct the district and carry out policies set by the board. Superintendents generally deal willingly with reporters, but their knowledge of the classroom is limited. In larger districts, a number of assistant superintendents and program administrators may report to the superintendent. They may have information about specific areas, such as elementary education, art education, nutrition and foreign language instruction. Principals and teachers know the most about what is happening in classrooms, but they may be among the least accessible sources. Some of the best sources for school stories may be next door—or at the next desk. Neighbors, friends and colleagues may be parents with school-age children. They may have a wealth of story ideas or anecdotes for fleshing out stories.

Schools are semipublic places. Officials try to control access to school buildings to protect students and prevent disruptions of the educational atmosphere, but sometimes officials use the restrictions to harass reporters. When a lesbian group started handing out fliers at a school, the Springfield (Mass.) Union-News sent a reporter to cover the event. The reporter was questioning demonstrators and taking photographs when the superintendent arrived and asked the demonstrators and the reporter to leave. They did, but later the superintendent sent the newspaper a letter saying that the reporter was barred from all public schools in the district and if she entered any school it would be considered trespassing. The Union-News sued to prevent the district from enforcing that decree, but the suit was withdrawn after a settlement allowed the reporter to enter schools but only to attend public meetings. In another incident, a reporter for the Manassas (Va.) Journal Messenger was arrested for trespassing at a high school. The reporter, Kelly Campbell, was working on a story about a biology project in which students were assigned to care for baby ducks. She went to the school at the invitation of the receptionist. After Campbell arrived, the principal agreed to speak to her. But when Campbell asked for the name of the teacher whose class was conducting the project, the principal ended the interview and told Campbell to leave. The reporter was arrested before she left the building. Campbell eventually pleaded guilty to misdemeanor trespass charges and was sentenced to one year of probation and 50 hours of community service. Such confrontations are rare, but reporters who want to cover stories about classroom activities should arrange their visits in advance with the teacher and the building principal and possibly with the superintendent as well.

Some school records are closed to the public. Educational records on specific students are closed by state and federal laws. Directory information on specific students—name, age, address, major areas of study, and height and weight (for athletes)—is usually available unless a student objects to its release. Personnel records for district employees and supervisors usually are confidential, too.

Although student and personnel records are closed, state laws open other records that can assist reporters.

- **Laws and policies.** State education laws and school board policies should be a starting point for any story about or investigation of a school. Until reporters know how a school or a program is supposed to run, they cannot evaluate how well it is running.
- **Budget and financial records.** All records on school district revenues and expenditures are open to the public. The budgets show the district's priorities, and a comparison of budgets over several years can show how those priorities have shifted. Bills and warrants show how a district actually spent its money. Documents about federal grants are worth a look, too. Reporters can compare what administrators said the grant would be used for with the vouchers showing how the money was actually spent.
- **Salary information.** Some states make only salary ranges or salary scales available. Other states make public the salaries of employees in administrative positions. The employment contracts for school superintendents and principals are public record in many states. The contracts reveal what perks the administrator is getting in addition to a salary—travel expenses, automobile allowances and club memberships are some possibilities.
- **Accreditation reports, state audits and other assessment records.** Many public schools are accredited, a process that requires the school to prepare a self-study report. A visiting team uses the self-study to guide its on-site investigation of the school and then issue a final report. In addition, districts and individual schools usually prepare a variety of reports for state education officials. School districts may submit several reports describing curriculum, personnel, students and district finances. The reports, which may include recommendations for upgrading school facilities, curriculum or personnel, can give reporters criteria for evaluating school performance and progress over time.
- **Food service records.** Reporters probably can find records about the school lunch program, including analyses of menus and receipts and expenditures.
- **Transportation records.** If a district operates school buses, it probably keeps inspection and servicing records on those buses. Accidents, even minor ones, often must be reported, too.

COURTS

A handful of trials—the murder trial of O.J. Simpson, the prosecution of four white New York City police officers for the killing of an unarmed black man and the Microsoft antitrust trial—attract national media attention. From these sensational trials, Americans acquire misconceptions about legal procedures. People might think criminal prosecutions depend heavily on scientific evidence, such as DNA tests. In fact, police and prosecutors on tight budgets often skimp on laboratory tests and rely on confessions to build their cases. People also might think court trials are long, requiring weeks or even months. In fact, most trials last less than a week. And the sensational cases might make people think lawyers engage in courtroom theatrics and make inflammatory statements to reporters. In fact, attorneys generally behave courteously toward one another and are restrained in what they say to the media. Some have a policy of never talking to reporters.

Even if most trials lack the ballyhoo of O.J. Simpson's, they still may make interesting and important news stories. Crimes disrupt the community and challenge its moral order. People want to know that the moral order will be maintained. Citizens in Jasper, Texas, were shocked when James Byrd Jr. was chained to a pickup truck and dragged to his death for no reason other than he was black. People there and around the nation wanted to know that those responsible for the murder would be punished.

Citizens also want to know that law enforcement officers, prosecutors, defense attorneys and judges are doing their jobs. In most instances, the law enforcement system works well, but in a number of cases, innocent people have gone to prison. Reporters who cover the courts must remain vigilant and skeptical of what police, prosecutors and judges do. Here are just a few examples of the judicial system malfunctioning:

- In Tulia, Texas, 46 people—39 of them African-American—were arrested and charged with trafficking in drugs. Most were convicted solely on the strength of the testimony of Tom Coleman, a police officer, who claimed to have bought drugs from the suspects during an 18-month undercover investigation. But Coleman, who frequently referred to African-Americans with an insulting racial epithet, had no video or audio tapes of the drug buys, nor did he have any witnesses. Nevertheless, 38 people were convicted. The longest sentence handed out was for 90 years. Coleman was named Texas' Lawman of the Year. But some civil rights groups and some news organizations continued to question the convictions. Eventually a special hearing reviewed the cases, and the judge who presided concluded Coleman's testimony was not credible. The judge recommended the convictions be set aside. The governor pardoned all of the defendants, who also won a $5 million judgment for violation of their civil rights. Coleman, meanwhile, was facing charges of having perjured himself by lying about his background during a hearing related to the drug cases.
- In New York City, five young men were convicted in the rape and beating of a woman who had been jogging in Central Park. The most persuasive evidence against the five, whose ages ranged from 14 to 16, was their videotaped confessions. Years later, DNA evidence showed that none of the five had raped the woman. Instead, a sixth man confessed to having committed the crime alone, and his DNA matched that found on the victim. If the five young men were all innocent, why did they confess? Psychologists and other experts said the suspects had all been subjected to intense interrogation for 24 hours or more with little rest. In such situations, a simple statement like "If you cooperate, we can all go home" may lead a suspect to believe that a confession will end the whole ordeal. This case and some others where confessions later proved false have led to efforts to require police to videotape entire interrogations and not just confessions.
- In Burlington, N.C., Ronald Cotton was arrested as a suspect in two rapes and eventually convicted in one, largely on the strength of the eyewitness testimony of the victim, Jennifer Thompson. She described how during the ordeal she had tried to observe her assailant and remember his face. She unequivocally identified Cotton as the rapist. Cotton won a second trial two years later, but this time he was convicted of both rapes. Several years later, new attorneys for Cotton had DNA tests run on the evidence taken from the victims. The tests excluded Cotton as the assailant and showed that another man had committed the rapes. Experts say this case shows how error prone eyewitness testimony can be. Jennifer Thompson now lectures about her experiences and the danger of convicting suspects solely on the testimony of one or two eyewitnesses.

General Information About the Court System

Criminal cases begin when the state charges someone with violating a criminal statute. Courts also hear cases in which one individual sues another. These are called civil cases, and they involve such matters as divorce, contracts, personal injury and antitrust issues. Civil cases rarely attract as much press attention as criminal cases, but they may change more lives. The arrest, prosecution and conviction of actress Winona Ryder on charges of shoplifting $6,355.40 in designer merchandise from a Saks Fifth Avenue department store was a leading story in many newspapers and broadcasts, but the case affected no one other than Ryder. Less covered was the civil suit between Debra Moran of Illinois and Rush Prudential HMO Inc. Rush Prudential refused to cover the cost of surgery to treat numbness in Moran's shoulder. Moran asked an independent review board created under Illinois law to determine whether the procedure was medically necessary and should be covered by Rush Prudential. The board ruled in Moran's favor, but Rush Prudential still refused to pay, saying a federal law exempted it from state regulation. Eventually, the U.S. Supreme Court said Rush Prudential could be required to pay for Moran's surgery. Although the case involved only two parties—Moran and Rush Prudential—the result may influence the cost and availability of health care for millions of Americans.

Knowledge of the court system is important for all reporters, not just those who make the courts their beat. Courts are important sources for all kinds of information. Business reporters, education reporters, even sports reporters may follow paper trails to state and federal courts. A business reporter may want to find information about a corporation that plans to locate a new factory in the community. The corporation's public relations office may provide a lot of facts, but only what the corporation is willing to release. To go beyond that, the reporter needs other sources, and one possibility is court records. If the corporation has sued or been sued, it will have disclosed a lot of information to the other party as part of a pretrial process called "discovery." Some of that information may become part of the court record available to the public. The records may reveal the corporation's finances, structure and operating style.

Court systems vary from state to state, but the general outlines are similar. Both state and federal court systems have three tiers. At the lowest level are the trial courts, which have either limited or general jurisdiction. The courts with limited jurisdictions usually hear misdemeanor cases and civil cases involving claims below a dollar amount specified in state laws. They may also hear traffic violation cases. A person accused of a felony may be brought before the court of limited jurisdiction for an initial appearance and to enter a plea. But once that person pleads not guilty, the case is transferred to a court of general jurisdiction. The courts of limited jurisdiction have varied names. At the federal level, they are called magistrate courts. Some state courts of limited jurisdiction are also called magistrate courts, but elsewhere they may be called county courts or municipal courts.

The trial courts with general jurisdiction are the ones that receive the most attention from the public and from the news media. These courts at both the federal and state levels try felony cases, such as homicides and drug trafficking cases, and civil lawsuits involving claims above a statutory minimum. In California, the trial courts are called superior courts; in New York, supreme courts. Elsewhere they may be called district courts or circuit courts. States also may have specialized lower courts, such as juvenile courts, probate courts and others. In the federal system, the courts of general jurisdiction are called district courts. The federal system has specialized courts, too, such as bankruptcy, tax and claims courts, which hear cases only of a particular kind.

The second tier of the court system is the intermediate courts of appeals. In the federal system, it is the U.S. Court of Appeals, which has 13 circuits, most of which hear appeals from courts in specific regions of the country. The state intermediate courts may be known as courts of appeal or as appellate divisions.

The highest tier contains the final appellate courts. In the federal system, that is the U.S. Supreme Court, which hears an appeal only when the justices think a case involves an important legal issue, when lower courts have reached conflicting results or when a decision seems contrary to established law. Each state also has a final appellate court, but again the names vary. In New York, the Court of Appeals is the highest appellate court. In Massachusetts, it is called the Supreme Judicial Court. Most states call it the supreme court.

One popular misconception about appellate courts is that they review the evidence introduced at the trial in the lower court, in effect retrying the case. For the most part, appellate courts limit themselves to making sure the trial courts follow the correct procedures and apply the law correctly. They do not rehear the evidence. After appellate courts hear a case, they either affirm or reverse the verdict of the lower court. If they reverse it, they may send the case back to the lower court for a new trial or hearing.

The steps in a court case are similar for criminal and civil cases, but there are differences that may affect news coverage. Also, court procedures may differ from one state to another or between federal and state courts. Reporters who are going to cover courts regularly should spend some time with local judges, prosecutors and defense attorneys to learn the procedures in the state. Bar and press associations in many states have collaborated to produce handbooks for reporters. These handbooks can be valuable resources as reporters follow court cases, both criminal and civil. What follows is a summary of some of the major phases in criminal and civil cases and issues they present for news coverage.

Criminal Cases

Pretrial Stages

Court action in a criminal case usually begins when a complaint is filed against the defendant. This happens at the initial appearance, when the defendant is brought before a judge in a magistrate or county court and informed of the charges. Misdemeanors can be settled at this level. If the case is a felony, the judge sets bail and a date for a preliminary hearing in a court of general jurisdiction.

The purpose of the preliminary hearing is to persuade a judge that the state has probable cause to believe a crime has been committed and the defendant committed it. Preliminary hearings are open to the press and public, but judges and attorneys worry the press and public will hear facts that are prejudicial to the defendant but that will never be introduced at the trial. Judges may try to avoid this problem by sealing statements and evidence and by closing portions of the preliminary hearing. At the end of the preliminary hearing, the judge may either free the defendant or have the defendant bound over for trial.

Most states use preliminary hearings in place of grand jury action. Only about half the states use grand juries, and their use is often limited to investigating public corruption or some similar task. In the federal system, however, no person can be tried for a felony unless that person has been indicted by a grand jury. Grand jury proceedings are closed to the press and public, but reporters can sit outside grand jury rooms and watch who goes in to testify. Members of a grand jury and attorneys are sworn to secrecy. Anyone who violates that oath risks being charged with contempt of court. Reporters who publish stories based on grand jury leaks may be subpoenaed to testify about their sources; if they refuse to identify the sources, they may be held in contempt. Grand jury witnesses usually are free to talk to reporters and to describe their testimony after they have been examined. When a grand jury finds probable cause to believe the defendant committed a crime, it will vote a bill of indictment, or a "true bill." Grand juries also may issue presentments, which give the results of their investigations.

Once defendants have been charged either by a grand jury indictment or by an information filed by a prosecutor, they are arraigned in the trial court. The defendants enter their pleas, and trial dates are set. Because a defendant has a constitutional right to a speedy trial, the trial usually begins within two or three months of the arrest. Before the trial begins, each side must disclose to the other all witnesses and exhibits. Also, the defense and the prosecution at any time may reach a plea agreement, which usually requires the defendant to plead guilty to a lesser charge or to some of the charges if others are dropped.

Trial

The trial begins with the selection of the jurors (unless the judge alone hears the case in what is called a bench trial). Prospective jurors are asked whether they have a connection to the case or any of the people involved. If they do, they can be dismissed. Attorneys for each side also have a limited number of opportunities to dismiss prospective jurors without giving a reason. These are called peremptory challenges, and lawyers use them to exclude prospective jurors who they believe will view their clients unfavorably.

Jury selection, like the rest of the trial, is almost always open to the public and the press, although in highly publicized cases, the court may protect the jurors' identities. The prospective jurors may be referred to by number rather than by name. In this way overly eager reporters and people with opinions about the case cannot speak to a juror by telephone or in person.

Courts always hear testimony in public, unless some overriding interest justifies closing the courtroom. Such an interest might be the protection of a child from the emotional trauma of testifying in public about a sexual assault. Documents introduced as evidence become court records and also are open to the public. Here, too, the court may limit access in certain cases. For example, the court may prohibit public access to or copying of photographs, audiotapes or videotapes containing salacious or gory material.

The central point of a story about court proceedings should emphasize the most important testimony or ruling of the day. Mistakenly, beginners often emphasize a witness' identity or topic of the witness' testimony instead of summarizing what the witness specifically said. Leads usually do not have to reveal whether a witness testified for the state or defense; that can be reported later. The news—a summary of the witness' most telling remarks—is more important:

> VAGUE: The trial of William Allen Lee, who is accused of shooting his girlfriend, began Tuesday with the testimony of a prosecution witness who described what he saw on the day of the murder.
>
> REVISED: A neighbor testified Tuesday that he saw William Allen Lee shoot his girlfriend, then carry her body into a house the couple shared at 914 W. 22nd St.

The trial ends when the jury delivers its verdict. Jury deliberations are closed to the public, but reporters try to talk to jurors after the trial to find out what evidence and arguments were most persuasive and how the jurors evaluated the witnesses, the attorneys and the defendant. Occasionally judges try to protect jurors from news reporters even after the trial is over. After a notorious securities fraud case, the judge advised jurors not to speak to the press and prohibited journalists from repeatedly asking jurors for interviews. A federal appeals court ruled that this order violated the First Amendment rights of news organizations. The appeals court left intact that part of the trial court's order prohibiting journalists from asking jurors about comments by or opinions of other jurors. In another case, however, a different federal appeals court upheld a trial judge's order prohibiting post-trial interviews with jurors. The trial involved six defendants, including two former Louisiana state senators, who were accused of trying to influence legislation governing video poker. The appeals court said the extensive news coverage justified the restraint, although jurors who wanted to talk to the press were free to initiate contacts with reporters.

Post-Trial

If the trial ends in acquittal of the defendant, the reporter will want to interview the defendant, the defense attorney, the prosecutor, the jurors and the witnesses for a post-trial wrap-up. If the defendant is convicted, the next major step is sentencing. Congress and state legislatures in recent years have taken away some of the discretion judges traditionally have had in imposing sentences. Nevertheless, judges still can impose sentences within fairly broad ranges, depending on the crime.

Convicts usually undergo a series of examinations by psychologists and penologists to determine the appropriate sentence. These officials' recommendations are contained in presentence evaluations. The severity of the sentence depends partly on these evaluations and partly on such factors as mitigating or aggravating circumstances associated with the crime. Presentence evaluations are closed to the public, although some of the information in them may come out at the sentencing hearing, which is open to the public.

Prosecutors cannot appeal an acquittal, but defendants always have the right to appeal a conviction. To succeed on appeal, defendants must show that the trial court made some error of law that was so grave as to warrant reversing the conviction and ordering a new trial. Appeals courts are reluctant to do so. Nevertheless, the appeals process may go on for years, particularly in cases in which the death penalty has been imposed. The appeal process may take a case through several state and federal courts.

Civil Cases

Pretrial

A civil case begins when one party files a complaint in court against another party. The person filing the complaint is the plaintiff and the other party is the defendant. The complaint states the factual and legal basis for the lawsuit and tells the court what kind of remedy the plaintiff wants. In many cases, the plaintiff wants money to compensate for injuries, lost wages, lost property or misfortunes arising from the defendant's conduct. Other times, the plaintiff may seek a court order prohibiting the defendant from doing something or requiring the defendant to do something. This is called "equitable relief." Plaintiffs may ask for both kinds of remedies in some cases.

Reporters should be skeptical of the amounts of money demanded in lawsuits. Plaintiffs can demand any amount they want, even though it is obviously exorbitant. To attract news coverage, some lawyers encourage their clients to demand huge amounts, even millions of dollars, as compensation for minor injuries. The plaintiffs normally settle for much less, often a small fraction of what they demanded. Consequently, news story leads generally should not emphasize the amount demanded.

The complaint presents only the plaintiffs' charges; defendants are likely to deny those charges, and a judge or jury may decide (months or even years later) that the charges are unfounded. Thus, a news story should indicate clearly that the charges are the plaintiffs' allegations, not accepted facts. For example:

> INCORRECT: Because of the accident, Samuelson will require medical care for the rest of his life.
>
> REVISED: Samuelson's lawsuit says he will require medical care for the rest of his life.

Whenever possible, the story should include the defendant's response to the charges. If the case file does not include the defendant's response, reporters often can obtain it by calling the defendant or his or her attorney. The following example and revision illustrate the inclusion of a defendant's response. They also illustrate the need to condense, to simplify and to attribute the claims in a plaintiff's lawsuit:

> INCORRECT: He was caused to slip, trip and fall as a direct result of the negligence and carelessness of the store because of a liquid on the ground. This fall injured his neck, head, body, limbs and nervous system and caused him to be unable to lead a normal life and to lose his normal wages for a prolonged period of time.
>
> REVISED: The suit charges that he slipped and fell on a wet sidewalk outside the store, dislocating his shoulder and tearing several ligaments.
>
> The store's manager responded, "He was running to get out of the rain and slipped and fell on the wet pavement."

Defendants who cannot persuade the court to dismiss the complaint must file answers, which set forth their version of the facts and interpretation of the law. Both complaints and answers are public records.

As the case goes forward, both sides engage in the discovery process, during which they take sworn statements from witnesses and from the opposing parties. They seek documents and other evidence from each other. The discovery process happens outside of court, and the press and public have no right of access to it. Information exchanged between the lawyers for the two sides remains confidential unless it is filed with the court. Even then, the side producing the information may ask that the court seal information that is highly personal or that might disclose trade or business secrets.

In some jurisdictions, the practice of sealing the records in court cases has become almost routine. Reporters have even found cases with names like "Sealed vs. Sealed." Sealing court records offers something for everyone involved in the case: Defendants want records sealed to avoid bad publicity; plaintiffs sometimes can get larger payments from defendants in return for agreeing to seal records; and judges like anything that encourages pretrial settlements and reduces caseloads. But the practice deprives the public and even government agencies of information about problems and about how the courts function. The Boston Globe won a Pulitzer Prize for its stories about sexual abuse of parishioners in the Roman Catholic Archdiocese of Boston, but it was able to report on the problem only after persuading courts to unseal documents in scores of lawsuits. Tread separation in Firestone tires mounted on Ford Explorers led to many accidents and lawsuits, but agreements to keep documents and settlements secret hid the extent of the problem for years. Some states have tried to limit the sealing of court records, either through legislation or through changes in court rules.

Trial

The civil trial proceeds much as a criminal one, and it is usually open to the press and public. The trial may be heard by a judge, who decides the case alone, or by a jury. Some states use juries that have fewer than 12 members to hear civil cases.

A civil trial, like a criminal one, ends with the jury presenting its verdict. However, a civil trial is more likely to be halted by a settlement between the parties. At any time in a lawsuit, the two sides may reach an agreement to end it. Judges usually encourage such settlements, preferably before trial but even after the trial has started. The parties to the case usually keep secret the terms of any agreement. Sometimes, however, a settlement must have court approval and so may become public record.

Post-Trial

Losing parties in a civil case may ask the judge to set aside the jury's verdict and render a verdict in their favor; this is called a judgment as a matter of law. The loser also may ask for a new trial. Neither request is granted frequently. More commonly, the losing party appeals the verdict to a higher court. Again, the loser must argue that the trial court committed a legal error so serious as to warrant a reversal of the verdict or a new trial. Appeals are usually unsuccessful.

CHECKLISTS FOR PUBLIC AFFAIRS REPORTING

Crimes and Accidents

1. Spend time at the police station and talk to officers; try to learn their concerns.
2. Get as much information as possible from the investigating officers, witnesses, victims and suspects.
3. Learn what records are available at the police station and what information they contain and do not contain.
4. When writing crime stories, avoid implying that a suspect is guilty.
5. Avoid referring to a suspect's race or religion unless it is clearly relevant to the story.

Local Government

1. Learn how your local governments are organized, what their powers and limitations are and how the various governmental units interact.
2. Study the budgets of local government units, and learn how governments raise their money.
3. Develop a routine for visiting the local government offices on your beat, and become familiar with the people who work in those offices.
4. Learn what public records are kept in each office and how to use them.
5. Go beyond covering school board meetings; visit schools and talk to principals, teachers, parents and students.

Courts

1. Remember that the state files criminal charges against people suspected of violating criminal laws, whereas civil cases are usually between private parties.
2. Learn how state courts are organized, the names of the various courts and what kinds of cases they hear.

3. Learn how court records are kept and how to find the records on any particular case.
4. Do not imply that a defendant in a criminal case is guilty; only the jury, or the judge in a bench trial, can decide that.
5. Be skeptical of allegations and damage claims that appear in civil complaints; they present only one side of the story.
6. Be alert to the possibility that a plea bargain or a settlement will end a case before or during a trial.

A NOTE ABOUT THIS CHAPTER'S EXERCISES

Many of the documents available to a public affairs reporter—lawsuits and police reports, for example—provide all the information needed for minor stories. Examples of such documents are reprinted in the following exercises. Write a news story about each document. Unless the instructions say otherwise, assume that the police reports have been prepared by officers who investigated incidents in your community, and that all other legal documents have been filed in your city hall, county courthouse or federal building.

Most of the exercises use genuine copies of actual government documents. Even the most unusual police reports are based on actual cases.

THE WRITING COACH

THE "KNOWS" HAVE IT FOR POLICE AND COURT REPORTERS

By **Joe Hight**
Managing Editor of The Oklahoman

As a police and court reporter, you should know:

1. How to balance notebooks: writing short stories on breaking news while writing trend and issues stories, and so on.
2. People: secretaries, cops on streets, lawyers and judges. People in these areas may be able to provide useful news tips.
3. Your libel and open records laws in your state. Know how to request records and other materials.
4. How to attribute properly and treat both sides fairly.
5. How to face and interview victims:

    - Victims must be treated with dignity and respect.
    - Victims should be approached but allowed to say no. If the answer is no, the reporter should leave a card or number so victims can call back later. Oftentimes, the best stories come this way.
    - Each victim is an individual and must be treated that way, not just as part of an overall number.
    - Little things count. Call victims back to verify facts and quotes. Return photos.

6. How to use words properly. Don't throw "allegedly," "suspect" and other words such as this into your stories like you would throw mashed potatoes at a food fight.
7. That descriptions can proliferate stereotypes: three black men in a car; a Native American was last seen at the convenience store before the robbery, and so on. Don't use them unless absolutely necessary and the description is specific.
8. How to turn it off. Don't install a scanner at your home. You'll burn out.
9. To find a mentor: an editor or person who has done the beat who can coach you on such things as proper techniques and how to handle the beat.

SUGGESTED READINGS

American Society of Newspaper Editors, Readership Issues Committee. *The Local News Handbook.* Reston, Va.: ASNE, 1999.

Blau, Robert. *The Cop Shop: True Crime on the Streets of Chicago.* Reading, Mass.: Addison-Wesley, 1993.

Buchanan, Edna. *The Corpse Had a Familiar Face.* New York: Random House, 1987. (Reprinted in paperback by Charter Books.)

Campbell, Don. *Inside the Beltway: A Guide to Washington Reporting.* Ames, Iowa: Iowa State University Press, 1991.

Gelman, Mitch. *Crime Scene: On the Streets with a Rookie Police Reporter.* New York: Times Books, 1992.

Haltom, William. *Reporting the Courts: How the Mass Media Cover Judicial Actions.* Chicago: Newlson-Hall, 1998.

Houston, Brant, Len Bruzzese and Steve Weinberg. *The Investigative Reporter's Handbook: A Guide to Documents, Databases and Techniques,* 4th ed. Boston: Bedford/St. Martin's, 2002.

Killenberg, George M. *Public Affairs Reporting: Covering the News in the Information Age.* Boston: St. Martin's, 1992.

Lisheron, Mark. "Stalking a Sniper," *American Journalism Review,* December 2002, pp. 20–27.

McIntyre, Bryce T. *Advanced Newsgathering.* New York: Praeger, 1991.

Press, Charles, and Kenneth Verburg. *American Politicians and Journalists.* Glenview, Ill.: Scott, Foresman/Little, Brown, 1988.

Protess, David L., Fay Lomax Cook, Jack C. Doppelt, James S. Ettema, Margaret T. Gordon, Donna R. Leff and Peter Miller. *The Journalism of Outrage: Investigative Reporting and Agenda Building in America.* New York: Guilford Press, 1991.

Scheuren, Claire E., ed. *The Reporter's Source Book.* Corvallis, Ore.: Center for National Independence in Politics, 1993.

Smolkin, Rachel. "Into the Spotlight," *American Journalism Review,* November 2002, pp. 50–55.

———. "Off Target," *American Journalism Review,* December 2002, pp. 26–31.

Weaver, Paul H. *News and the Culture of Lying.* New York: Free Press, 1994.

Wilson, Theo. *Headline Justice: Inside the Courtroom—The Country's Most Controversial Trials.* New York: Thunder's Mouth Press, 1996.

USEFUL WEB SITES

SearchGov: http://searchgov.com (Links to Web pages of federal, state and local governments.)

University of Michigan Documents Center State Government and Politics: http://www.lib.umich.edu/govdocs/state.html

The White House: http://www.whitehouse.gov

U.S. Congress: http://thomas.loc.gov

U.S. General Accounting Office: http://www.gao.gov

Criminal Justice Journalists: http://www.reporters.net.cjj

Investigative Reporters and Editors: http://www.ire.org

The Poynter Institute: http://www.poynter.org

Freedom of Information Center: http://www.missouri.edu/~foiwww

EXERCISE 1

PUBLIC AFFAIRS REPORTING

911 EMERGENCY: A CHILD'S HEROISM

A 6-year-old girl placed the following call to a 911 dispatcher. Assume that the girl placed the call in your city today. She is Laura Burke, the daughter of Lynn and Randy Burke of 412 Wilson Avenue.

Police arrested a neighbor, Andrew Caspinwall of 416 Wilson Avenue, and charged him with raping Mrs. Burke. Bail has been set at $250,000, and Caspinwall, 24, is being held in the county jail.

DISPATCHER: "911 emergency. Hello?"
GIRL: "My mommy needs help."
DISPATCHER: "What's wrong?"
GIRL: "Somebody's hurting my mommy."
DISPATCHER: "Where do you live?"
GIRL: "At home with my mommy and daddy."
DISPATCHER: "No, uh, that's not what I mean. Can you tell me where your house is, your address?"
GIRL: "Wilson Avenue."
DISPATCHER: "Do you know the address, the number?"
GIRL: "Hurry. My mommy's crying."
DISPATCHER: "No, honey, do you know your address?"
GIRL, CRYING: "I gotta think. It's, uh, it's, uh, 4 something, I'm not sure. 412. 412."
DISPATCHER: "OK. I'll send help."
GIRL, CRYING: "Hurry."
DISPATCHER: "What's your name?"
GIRL: "Laura. Laura Anne Burke."
DISPATCHER: "Can you tell me what's wrong, who's hurting your mother?"
GIRL: "A man. He came in the back door and hit my mommy."
DISPATCHER: "Where are you now?"
GIRL: "Upstairs."
DISPATCHER: "Does the man know you're there?"
GIRL: "No. I'm hiding."
DISPATCHER: "Where are you hiding?"
GIRL: "In my mommy and daddy's room. Under the bed."
DISPATCHER: "Can you lock the door?"
GIRL: "I don't know. Maybe."
DISPATCHER: "Don't hang up. Just put the phone down and go lock the door. Then come back, talk to me some more."
GIRL: "My mommy. What'll happen to my mommy?"
DISPATCHER: "We've got three police cars coming. They'll be there in a minute. Now go lock the door, and don't let anyone in until I tell you. OK?"
GIRL: "I guess so."
DISPATCHER: "Hello? Hello? Laura, are you there?"
GIRL: "I locked the door."
DISPATCHER: "How old are you, Laura?"

GIRL: "Six."
DISPATCHER: "You're doing a good job, Laura. You have to be brave now to help your mommy. Tell me, is the man armed?"
GIRL: "What's that mean?"
DISPATCHER: "Does he have a gun?"
GIRL: "No. A knife."
DISPATCHER: "OK, a knife. Is the man still there, Laura?"
GIRL, SOBBING: "I don't know. I'm afraid. Will he hurt me, too?"
DISPATCHER: "No one will hurt you, Laura. Be brave. The police are outside now. They'll be coming into your house. You may hear some noise, but that's OK. Stay in the bedroom, and don't let anyone in, OK?"
GIRL: "OK."
DISPATCHER: "Your daddy's coming, too. We've found your daddy."
GIRL: "Soon?"
DISPATCHER: "The police say they're in your house. They're helping your mommy now. They've found your mommy, and they're going to take her to a doctor, a hospital."
GIRL: "The man?"
DISPATCHER: "He's been caught, arrested. It's OK. It's safe to go downstairs now. There are people there to help you. They want to talk to you, Laura. Can you unlock your door and go downstairs? Laura? Hello? Are you there? Laura? Hello? Laura?"

EXERCISE 2

PUBLIC AFFAIRS REPORTING

911 EMERGENCY: THE DAHMER TAPES

Police officers in Milwaukee, Wis., found 11 mutilated bodies in an apartment rented by Jeffrey L. Dahmer. Dahmer, 31, confessed to killing a total of 17 people and pleaded that he was insane. One of Dahmer's victims was a 14-year-old Laotian boy, Konerak Sinthasomphone, whom the police might have saved. When he was finally arrested, Dahmer told police that two officers had been at his apartment two months earlier to investigate a 911 call involving the 14-year-old. The officers left the boy at the apartment, and Dahmer then killed him.

The police later released this transcript of the 911 call. It reveals that a Milwaukee resident named Glenda Cleveland called the police at 2 a.m. the previous May 27. Mrs. Cleveland told a 911 dispatcher that her daughter and a niece had seen the boy naked on a street corner and that the boy needed help. In a follow-up call, Mrs. Cleveland, 37, asked the officers if they were certain that the boy was an adult.

A week before the tape's release, the two officers were suspended with pay but not identified. A lawyer representing the officers said they had seen no evidence at Dahmer's apartment to suggest that anything was wrong. Also, they believed that the naked male was a man living with Dahmer. The officers' lawyer added that they tried to interview the boy, but that he seemed to be seriously intoxicated.

Assume that the Milwaukee police (1) have already found the bodies and interviewed Dahmer, (2) suspended the officers one week ago and (3) released the transcript today. Write a news story that summarizes the transcript's content. Since this is a verbatim copy of the transcript, you can quote it directly. Include whatever background information seems necessary.

DISPATCHER: "Milwaukee emergency. Operator 71."

WOMAN: "OK. Hi. I am on 25th and State. And there's this young man. He's butt-naked and he has been beaten up. He is very bruised up. He can't stand. He is . . . butt-naked. He has no clothes on. He is really hurt. And I, you know, ain't got no coat on. But I just seen him. He needs some help."

DISPATCHER: "Where is he at?"

WOMAN: "25th and State. The corner of 25th and State."

DISPATCHER: "He's just on the corner of the street?"

WOMAN: "He's in the middle of the street. He (unintelligible). We tried to help him. Some people trying to help him."

DISPATCHER: "OK. And he's unconscious right now?"

WOMAN: "He is getting him up. 'Cause he is bruised up. Somebody must have jumped on him and stripped him or whatever."

DISPATCHER: "OK. Let me put the fire department on the line. They will send an ambulance. Just stay on the phone. OK?"

WOMAN: "OK."

[The dispatcher transferred the call to the fire department, and the woman asked for an ambulance, saying a "butt-naked young boy or man or whatever" needed help.]

WOMAN: "He's been beaten up real bad. . . . He can't stand up. . . . He has no clothes on. He is very hurt."

FIRE DEPARTMENT DISPATCHER: "Is he awake?"

WOMAN: "He ain't awake. They are trying to get him to walk, but he can't walk straight. He can't even see straight. Any time he stands up he just falls down."

DISPATCHER: "25th and State? All right. OK."

[The woman hung up. The next part of the tape is a police radio transmission of a dispatcher reporting the woman's call to a street officer.]

DISPATCHER: "36. I got a man down. Caller states there is a man badly beaten and is wearing no clothes, lying in the street, 2-5 and State. Anonymous female caller. Ambulance sent."

OFFICER: "10-4."

[A Milwaukee emergency operator received information from the sheriff's department, checking on another call that reported a male dragging a naked male who looked injured.]

EMERGENCY OPERATOR: "OK. We will get someone out."

[The next conversation involved an officer reporting back to the dispatcher over the police radio.]

OFFICER: "36. . . . Intoxicated Asian, naked male. (Laughter.) Was returned to his sober boyfriend. (More laughter.)"

[An officer advised (C-10) that the assignment was completed (C-18) and the squad was ready for new duties (10-8). There was a 40-second gap in the tape, then:]

OFFICER: "Squad 65."

DISPATCHER: "65."

OFFICER: "Ah, give myself and 64 C-10 and put us 10-8."

DISPATCHER: "10-4 64 and 65."

OFFICER: "10-4. It will be a minute. My partner is going to get deloused at the station. (Laughter.)"

DISPATCHER: "10-4."

[A woman later called Milwaukee Emergency and told the dispatcher that 10 minutes ago her daughter and niece "flagged down" a policeman after they "walked up on a young child being molested by a male guy." She said the officers took no information from the girls, and the boy was naked and bleeding. The woman said further information "must be needed." The dispatcher asked the location of the incident, and the woman repeated that her daughter's and niece's names were not taken.]

WOMAN: "The fact is a crime was being committed. I am sure you must need, you know, some kind of information based on that."

[The call was transferred, and the woman repeated the squad number and the address of the incident. The woman asked if squad car 68 "brought someone in, a child being molested by an adult that was witnessed by my daughter and niece."]

WOMAN: "Their names or nothing was taken down and I wonder if this situation was being handled. . . . What it indicated was that this was a male child being raped and molested by an adult."

[The police agent referred the call to another district after getting the address of the incident. The woman repeated her story again to another official. Eventually, she reached an officer who was at the scene.]

OFFICER: "Hello. This is . . . of the Milwaukee Police."

WOMAN: "Yes. There was a squad car number 68 that was flagged down earlier this evening. About 15 minutes ago."

OFFICER: "That was me."

WOMAN: "Ya, ah, what happened? I mean my daughter and my niece witnessed what was going on. Was anything done about the situation? Do you need their names or information or anything from them?"
OFFICER: "No, not at all."
WOMAN: "You don't?"
OFFICER: "Nope. It's an intoxicated boyfriend of another boyfriend."
WOMAN: "Well, how old was this child?"
OFFICER: "It wasn't a child, it was an adult."
WOMAN: "Are you sure?"
OFFICER: "Yup."
WOMAN: "Are you positive? Because this child doesn't even speak English. My daughter had, you know, dealt with him before, seeing him on the street."
OFFICER: "Hmmm. Yea. No. He's, he's, oh, it's all taken care of, ma'am."
WOMAN: "Are you sure?"
OFFICER: "Ma'am. I can't make it any more clear. It's all taken care of. That's, you know, he's with his boyfriend and, ah, his boyfriend's apartment, where he's got his belongings also. And that is where it is released."
WOMAN: "Isn't this, I mean, what if he's a child and not an adult. I mean are you positive this is an adult?"
OFFICER: "Ma'am. Ma'am. Like I explained to you. It is all taken care of. It's as positive as I can be. OK. I can't do anything about somebody's sexual preferences in life."
WOMAN: "Well, no, I am not saying anything about that, but it appeared to have been a child. This is my concern."
OFFICER: "No. No. He's not."
WOMAN: "He's not a child?"
OFFICER: "No, he's not. OK? And it's a boyfriend-boyfriend thing. And he's got belongings at the house where he came from."
WOMAN: "Hmmmm. Hmmm."
OFFICER: "He has got very . . . pictures of himself and his boyfriend and so forth. So. . . ."
WOMAN: "Oh, I see."
OFFICER: "OK."
WOMAN: "OK. I am just, you know, it appeared to have been a child. That was my concern."
OFFICER: "I understand. No, he is not. Nope."
WOMAN: "Oh. OK. Thank you. 'Bye."

EXERCISE 3

PUBLIC AFFAIRS REPORTING

Assume that the following complaint report and missing person report were released by the Sheriff's Department in your county this morning. Write separate stories based on the two reports. Your instructor may ask you to write a story about just one of the reports.

SHERIFF'S OFFICE

COMPLAINT REPORT

ZONE 1 UNIT 5, 3, 9, & 14 CASE NO. K51-1020C

GRID One PAGE One OF One OTHER AGCY CASE NO. None

MESSAGE NUMBER 31847P DATE Today (MONTH DAY YR)

TIME RECEIVED 01:22 TIME DISPATCHED 01:22 TIME ARRIVED 01:30 TIME IN-SERVICE 03:12 WEATHER NA

NATURE OF CASE Armed Robbery CHANGED TO F.S.S. FEL. MISD.

LOCATION OF OCCURRENCE (INCL. NAME OF BUSINESS/SCHOOL) Jiffy Foods, 4010 Holbrook Dr.

VICTIM Terry DaRoza (LAST) (FIRST) (MIDDLE) AGE 34 R/S DOB MO. DAY YR

HOME ADDRESS 410 University Boulevard #80 PHONE 823-4771

CITY Yes/Local STATE ZIP

BUSINESS ADDRESS 4010 Holbrook Dr. PHONE 823-0333

CITY Yes/local STATE ZIP

REPORTER ☐ WITNESS ☐ See below PHONE

CITY STATE ZIP

PROPERTY MISSING/STOLEN			EST. VALUES	
QUAN	ITEM	DESCRIPTION - SERIAL NO. - MFG NO. - ETC	STOLEN	RECOVERED
		Cash register contained approx $80 but nothing was actually stolen		

■ MISSING ■ SUSPECT ■ ARRESTED ■ WITNESS ■ OTHER

NAME Suspect #1: Keel, Timothy (LAST) (FIRST) (MIDDLE) AGE 19 R/S DOB MO. DAY YR

ADDRESS 1413 Griese Dr. PHONE 823-3411

CITY Yes/local STATE ZIP

BUSINESS OR SCHOOL ADDRESS Plaza Barber Shop 2140 West Av.

HEIGHT 5′ 4″ WEIGHT 120 HAIR Black EYES Black COMPLEXION Pocked OCCUPATION Barber

CLOTHING, ETC., Blue plaid shirt, tan pants, dark blue jacket, Braves baseball cap

VEHICLE INVOLVED

☒ USED ☐ STOLEN ☒ TOWED ☐ DAMAGED ☐ BURGLARIZED ☐ WRECKER ☐ OTHER

YEAR '94 MAKE Toyota MODEL Celica BODY STYLE 2-door COLOR Brown DECAL

LICENSE TAG NO. STATE YEAR EXPIRES I.D. OR VIN NO.

REMARKS

ENTERED FCIC/NCIC ☐ YES ☐ NO BOLO ☐ YES ☐ NO MESSAGE NO.

NARRATIVE The complainant is currently employed full-time as a clerk at Jiffy Foods, a convenience store open 24 hrs. DaRoza states 2 men entered said premises approx. 01:15 today. DaRoza was cleaning a popcorn machine when the 2 asked to use the toilet. DaRoza walked behind the counter to get the key and was followed by Keel who then pulled a knife. DaRoza was recently injured in a construction job, with one leg still in a cast, and uses a cane. DaRoza adds he swung the cane as hard as he could into the arrestee's face, hitting him repeatedly. Paramedics say Keel's nose and jaw and other facial bones are broken. Suspect #1 fell to the floor and suspect #2 then tried grabbing the cane from DaRoza, who proceeded to turn it on him. While suspect #2 fled, DaRoza got help from an entering customer, Stuart Adler, 1847 Oakland Boulevard, who helped tie suspect #1 with their belts until we arrived. Keel is charged with armed robbery and resisting a merchant. DaRoza said he was not injured. He is 6′ 4″ tall and weighs about 260 pds and works at the store while

DISPOSITION: recuperating from injuries received in a construction job accident.

FURTHER POLICE ACTION TAKEN ☐ YES ☒ NO REFERRED TO Robbery Division

S. Cullinan — REPORTING OFFICER'S NAME (PRINT)

I.D. NO. (INITIAL) D. Aneja

APPROVED BY

SHERIFF'S DEPT.

MISSING PERSON

2. CASE NO. 74-A14963

11. RADIO NO.	12. ZONE	5. DATE	6. DISP.	7. ARR.	8. IN SERV.	1. O.D.C.N
#482792	2	Yesterday	18:12	18:27		

87. ☒ MISSING PERSON ☐ RUNAWAY: Amber Hall — DOB: Age 6 — A / S / R — RES. PH. 823-4702 — BUS. PH.

ADDRESS: 34 Magee Ct. — CITY — STATE — ZIP

HEIGHT: 3'7" — WEIGHT: 42 — EYES: Blue — ☐ SHORT ☒ LONG — HAIR COLOR: Blond — OTHER

91. RELATIVES OR FRIENDS: See below — DOB — A / S / R — RES. PH. — BUS. PH.

ADDRESS — CITY — STATE — ZIP

15. REPORTED BY: Grandparents — DOB — RES. PH. 823-4682

RELATIVES OR FRIENDS (B): Samuel/Terese Pinckney — DOB — A / S / R — RES. PH. 823-4682 — BUS. PH. Retired

ADDRESS: 976 Grand Av. — A / S / R — BUS. PH. None

ADDRESS: 976 Grand Av. — CITY — STATE — ZIP

85. LAST PERSON SEEING SUBJECT: Grandparents — DOB — RES. PH.

92. DATE & TIME SUBJECT LAST SEEN: ☐ ADULT ☒ JUVENILE About 16:00 yesterday

94. LOCATION LAST SEEN: Grandparents yard

ADDRESS: 976 Grand Av. — A / S / R — BUS. PH.

97. BIRTH DATE: Age 6 — PLACE: Mercy Hospital

99. SCHOOL ATTENDING: Hawthorne Elementary — GRADE: 1 — PHONE

88. DATE & TIME SUBJECT LEFT HOME — 74. DATE

90. PARENT(S) OR GUARDIAN(S): (A) Marci Hall — DOB — AGE 38 — SEX F — RACE W — RELATIONSHIP: Mother — ADDRESS (GIVE NAME & ADDRESS OF BUSINESS IF RES IS SAME AS 87): 34 Magee Ct. — PHONE: 823-4702

(B) — PHONE

106. LOCATED MISSING BEFORE ☐ YES ☒ NO — PREVIOUS CASE NO ______

107. LOCATED PREVIOUSLY AT

101. PROBABLE DESTINATION: Unknown/Assumed probably lost in woods

100. FORMER ADDRESS OF SUBJECT: Las Vegas

63. OCCUPATION: 1st grade student

102. MENTAL CONDITION ☐ YES ☒ NO

104. RELIGION ☐ PROTESTANT ☐ CATHOLIC ☐ JEWISH ☒ OTHER

93. ALIAS AND/OR MAIDEN NAME

103. PERSONAL HABITS (UNUSUAL): Friendly, curious

105. JEWELRY, PAPERS, ETC. CARRIED: None

41. PERSON OR UNIT NOTIFIED: Missing Persons & Las Vegas police — TIME: 20:00

96. MARITAL STATUS ☐ MARRIED ☒ SINGLE ☐ DIVORCED ☐ OTHER

WAS PHOTOGRAPH OBTAINED ☒ YES ☐ NO

TYPE OF CLOTHING: See below

50. VEHICLE USED — MODEL — MAKE — YEAR — BODY STYLE: No known vehicle at this time.

53. COLOR — 52. LICENSE — STATE — YEAR — 55. IDENT. MARKS — 47. STORAGE RECEIPT

60. CONTACT INFORMATION

33. NARRATIVE
Amber was playing in her grandparents back yard at approx. 16:00 yesterday when they went in to start dinner and answer a phone call which Mr. Pinckney says lasted less than 5 minutes. When he returned to the outside back yard Amber was gone. We arrived at 18:27 and started a search of the area, calling for help at 20:00. Then a full search was instituted

20. REPORTING OFFICER'S SIGNATURE: (A) D. Aneja — ID NO. 482 — 13. DISTRICT — 10. APPROVED BY: C.L. — 21. PERSON REPORTING CRIME: Grandparents

(B) — ID NO. — 36. GRID: 11 — 22. FOREIGN AGCY — 23. LOCAL MSG NO.

28. REFERRED TO: Missing Persons & Las Vegas police — SIGNATURE — 27. RECORDED BY — 25. INDEXED BY — 24. STATISTICS

30. DISPOSITION ☐ CLEARED BY ARREST ☐ UNFOUNDED ☐ EXCEPTIONALLY CLEARED ☒ PENDING

18. MULTIPLE CLEAR UP RET. CASE NO.

ASSIGNED TO ______ DATE ______

SUPERVISOR ______ DATE ______

COMPLAINT NO. 74-A14963

Missing Hall child (continued)

by helicopter and about 20 officers on foot but failed to uncover the girl. The grandparents live in a rural area with their property backing up on a woods that, in turn, leads into the Twin Rivers State Park. Altogether the total wooded area is believed to cover about 1200 acres of land. The grandparents say the girl often played near the woods and sometimes went into it with them, especially chasing small animals, but was forbidden to enter it alone and was normally an obedient child. We have established a command post at Temple Israel 2 blocks from the scene and at sunrise today will start a full-scale search, starting in the backyard, with sheriffs deputies, friends, neighbors and volunteers (some on horseback) as well as the dept. helicopter and possibly some tracking dogs which we're trying to arrange.

The girls mother fears she may possibly have been snatched by her noncustodial father, Jack Allen Hall, currently of Las Vegas, where the entire family formerly lived, but efforts are nevertheless concentrating on the area search. An aunt in Las Vegas went to Hall's last known address last night but reports seeing no sign of him or any vehicle on the property and she does not know his current employer. The girls parents separated in Las Vegas 3 years ago and Amber lives solely with her mother who said their divorce was especially bitter as both parents fought for custody. Amber was last seen wearing pink pants, a pink and white striped long sleeved shirt and red slip-on shoes. She may have a white sweater but, still, would have been cold last night. A neighbor reported spotting a man on the edge of the woods in the vicinity yesterday morning. The neighbor questioned the man who said he was looking for his dog. Shown photos of Hall the neighbor said the man resembled Hall but he could not positively identify him as the man in the woods. Hall is described by his wife as a white male 6'3" in height, heavy set, weight approx. 220 pds., with dark brown hair, a mustache, and a small birthmark on the back of his neck. He is believed to drive a late model black chevy pickup truck.

ANY MEDIA: We are asking the publics cooperation, that anyone who may have seen this little girl immediately call us at 824-2424. Also anyone who wants to volunteer to aid in the search should report to Temple Israel.

Name ______________________ Class ______________________ Date ______

EXERCISE 4

PUBLIC AFFAIRS REPORTING

Assume that the Health Department for your city released these following two restaurant inspection reports this morning. Write one story that summarizes both. Your instructor may ask that you write about only one of the reports.

HEALTH DEPARTMENT
RESTAURANT DIVISION

Inspection Report

Time and date of inspection: 2 p.m. yesterday Previous inspection date: 4 months ago

Restaurant name: Deerfield Country Club

Address: 4720 Country Club Rd.

Name of owner: Alex Meserole Telephone: 672-4400

Nature of inspection: ______ Routine ______ Followup ______ Complaint __X__ Emergency ______ Problem list

Nature of visit: ______ Announced __X__ Unannounced

Inspector's commentary and report:

We conducted this inspection in response to numerous complaints of illness. In addition to this restaurant's regular dining room service it caters for special occasions such as anniversaries and weddings. Last Saturday evening beginning at approx. 5pm it catered a wedding reception for bride and groom Ms. Jena Cruz, 48 DeLaney, and Allen Farci, 818 Texas Av. By 6pm Sunday almost half of the approx. 120 guests at the wedding reception became ill with nausea, cramping, and diarrhea. Nine were treated in local emergency rooms over the weekend and 3 were admitted for further treatment to alleviate their symptoms. Doctors reported to the Health Dept. other cases of food poisoning coming to their offices Monday from the reception. The symptoms are consistent with a virus that is spread by sick workers who handle food without properly washing their hands.

During previous inspections we found workers contaminated food. The basic problem was workers who failed to follow basic rules of cleanliness. We found employees went from cleaning a counter to making a sandwich without using soap and water. Food was stored in a sink and employees were eating during previous visits while working with clean dishes. Those previous problems resulted in an $800 fine last year and the owner ordered to attend a Hospitality Education Program.

This new inspection yesterday led us to observe workers placing bare hands in bowls of shrimp, chicken, and sauces to place on salads. One worker was observed rinsing her hands off in a sink and wiping them on a soiled apron. Another problem is with food kept at room temperature when it should be cooled and food debris on steam tables. The food service license is expired. Some fruits and vegetables were stored in boxes kept on the floor and their contents appeared rotten and/or mouldy.

Standard areas of inspection and results:

__OK__ Cooking utensils __NA__ Food preparation __NA__ Food storage __NA__ Personnel hygiene

__NA__ Refrigeration __OK__ Restrooms __OK__ Serving areas __OK__ Serving dishes __OK__ Waste disposal

NA = Needs action

Inspector's name: Don Brame Signature: Don Brame

HEALTH DEPARTMENT
RESTAURANT DIVISION

Inspection Report

Time and date of inspection: 8 pm yesterday Previous inspection date: 3 months ago

Restaurant name: Deacosti's Restaurant

Address: 2048 Main Street

Name of owner: Peggy/Michael Deacosti Telephone: 420-9330

Nature of inspection: ____ Routine ____ Followup ____ Complaint ____ Emergency X Problem list

Nature of visit: ____ Announced X Unannounced

Inspector's commentary and report:

Due to findings of repeated violations, this restaurant has been on our Problem List for the past 2 years. This inspection was unannounced to determine whether or not all the problems found 3 months ago were corrected as directed. Four separate food poisoning incidents have been traced to the establishment since it was purchased by its present owners 2 years ago. Here are the results of yesterdays inspection:

FOOD HANDLING – Buffet items were kept at dangerously low temperature. Plus there were other temperature problems in the kitchen. There were no thermometers in the refrigerators, and some meats did not appear to be properly cooled.

EMPLOYEE HYGIENE – During this visit I noticed a cook coughed into his hand, picked up trash, and resumed handling food without washing. Other employees were observed eating, drinking, or smoking while handling food or near prepared food.

CLEANLINESS – There is a continued problem with cleanliness. Splash ledges on the fountain drink dispenser were dirty. The food slicer was dirty. We found dead roaches on the kitchen floor and rodent droppings. Food packages of macaroni, rice pilaf, dinner rolls, and croutons were gnawed through by rodents. The restrooms were another problem with a leaking urinal.

In summary, during the last inspection 90 days ago we itemized fifteen problems, 7 of which have not yet been corrected, and new problems have arisen. RECOMMENDATION: we recommend immediate closing of the restaurant, suspending its food service license.

Standard areas of inspection and results:

OK Cooking utensils NA Food preparation NA Food storage NA Personnel hygiene

NA Refrigeration NA Restrooms OK Serving areas OK Serving dishes OK Waste disposal

NA = Needs action

Inspector's name: Don Brame Signature: *Don Brame*

Name ______________________ Class ______________________ Date ________

EXERCISE 5

PUBLIC AFFAIRS REPORTING

Assume that the Police Department in your city released the following injury reports this morning. Write a story that summarizes both reports. Your instructor may ask that you write about only one of the reports.

Submitting Agency: Police Dept.

Description of Victim	Sex	Descent	Age	Height
	M	Hispanic	20	6'
Weight	**Hair**	**Eyes**	**Build**	**Complexion**
160	Brown	Brown	M	Clear

Identifying Marks and Characteristics: None visible at scene

Clothing & Jewelry Worn: Restaurant uniform of tan pants & shirt & cap

Victim's Name (last - first - middle)	Comp. No.
Alvarez, Thomas J.	87B-1241-GL

Location of Occurrence	Dist.	Type
Tom's Pizza	4	

Date & Time Occurred	Date & Time Reported to P.D.
11 PM yesterday night	11:07 PM yesterday night
Type of Premises (loc. of victim)	**Cause of Injury (instr. or means)**
Carry-out pizza restaurant	Pistol
Reason (Acc.-ill health, etc.)	**Extent of Injury (Minor or Serious)**
Robbery/shooting	Fatal
Remove To (address)	**Removed By**
County morgue	Coroners office

Investigative Division or Unit Notified & Person(s) Contacted: Homicide

INJURY REPORT — UCR

CODE R - Person Reporting D - Person Discovering W - Witness

Code	Victim's Occupation / Name	Resident Address City	Res. Phone	x	Bus. Phone	x
	College student/part-time worker	854 Maury Rd., Apt. 11B	823-8892		823-5455	
W/R	Anne Capiello	8210 University Blvd., #311	823-4117		None	
W	Andrew Caspenwall	416 Wilson Avenue	823-4417		823-5455	

(1) Reconstruct the circumstances surrounding the injury. (2) Describe physical evidence, location found, & give disposition.

The deceased, a pizza clerk, was shot fatally at about 11pm in a failed robbery attempt. A lone gunman entered the premises and faked that he wanted a pizza. When asked what he wanted on it suspect #1 said "I really want all your money". The clerk appeared to reach beneath the counter and suspect #1 then shot him although we found no alarm or weapon the clerk might have reached for, but our suspect claims that's what triggered the shooting. The suspect then ran behind the counter and tried to open the register, even throwing it to the floor but didn't know how to open it and then emptied his gun into it, 5 or 6 shots. He proceeded to run outside to a waiting vehicle described by 2 eyewitnesses as an old Ford mustang white in color. It was driven by another white male, and a deliveryman arriving at this time chased the perpetrators vehicle. In the area of Pauley Park the perps fired several shots at deliveryman Caspenwall who was not hit. Said getaway vehicle attempted to make a left turn onto Parkvue Av. but was speeding too fast and flipped on its side. Suspect #1 William McDowell, 1429 Highland Dr., was found dazed inside but otherwise unhurt and was identified as the shooter. We are continuing to look for suspect #2. Witness #1 (Capiello) identified herself as the victims girlfriend. She was present when the shooting occurred, and the gunman may not have seen her as she was studying in a back corner of the kitchen. McDowell said he has no job and admits to having a crack problem and that he went in to rob the place for money. He's charged with murder.

If additional space is required use reverse side.

Supervisor Approving	Emp. No.	Interviewing Officer(s)	Emp. No.	Person Reporting Injury (signature)
Sgt. A. Wei		Detective J. Noonan		Anne Capiello

602 - 07 - 23A INJURY REPORT

Submitting Agency	Police Dept.			
Description of Victim	Sex: M	Descent: AA	Age: 8	Height: 4′ 1″
Weight: 70	Hair: Black	Eyes: Black	Build: Medium	Complexion: Clear

Identifying Marks and Characteristics

Chipped front tooth.

Small scar on lower left leg.

Clothing & Jewelry Worn

T-shirt, bluejeans,

white sneakers.

Victim's Name (last - first - middle)		Comp. No.
Curtis, Derek Andrew		87B-1336K
Location of Occurrence: 663 Harding Av.		Dist.: 2 / Type:
Date & Time Occurred: About 4PM yesterday	Date & Time Reported to P.D.: 6:52 PM	
Type of Premises (loc. of victim): Family home	Cause of Injury (instr. or means): Fall into freezer	
Reason (Acc.-ill health, etc.): Accident	Extent of Injury (Minor or Serious): Fatal	
Remove To (address): Mercy hospital	Removed By: Paramedics	
Investigative Division or Unit Notified & Person(s) Contacted: None. No further action required		
INJURY REPORT		UCR

CODE R - Person Reporting D - Person Discovering W - Witness

Code	Victim's Occupation / Name	Residence Address	City	Res. Phone	x	Bus. Phone	x
	Child	663 Harding Av.	Yes	823-8019			
R	Sara Curtis	663 Harding Av.	Yes	823-8019		823-6400	
D	Danny Jones, grandfather	1152 Arlington	Yes	823-1097		823-4110	

(1) Reconstruct the circumstances surrounding the injury. (2) Describe physical evidence, location found, & give disposition.

The deceased was located in a box-type freezer in the garage area at his home. He apparently fell in while trying to reach some popsicles. There was a small tool chest and some other boxes piled in front of the freezer that he apparently used as steps. It now appears that the deceased crawled high enough to open the lid and tumbled in. The lid closed on him & latched. We were dispatched to the scene in answer to a call of a missing child. The victims mother Sara Curtis said the boy disappeared at about 4pm after returning from school. He'd asked for one of the popsicles and she said she told him to eat some fruit instead. Neighbors aided in the search and at 8:30pm we instituted a full scale search of the neighborhood using dogs, the dept. helicopter, and more than twenty officers. The boy was recovered during a 3rd search of the premises by a grandfather at 11:10pm. Paramedics already on the scene said the boy, who was age 8, had no heartbeat and a body temperature of only 70. Icicles had formed on his body and he apparently spent approximately around 7 hours trapped inside the freezer. Hospital personnel said they managed to get the boys heart beating and returned his body temperature to normal while on life support but he never regained consciousness and died shortly after 1am today. When we opened the lid and let it go it did fall back in place and latch itself each time. A box of popsicles was open and its contents scattered over the bottom of the freezer, which was only about 1/3 full of food.

If additional space is required use reverse side.

Supervisor Approving	Emp. No.	Interviewing Officer(s)	Emp. No.	Person Reporting Injury (signature)
Sgt. T. Dow		M. Hennigen		Sara Curtis

602 - 07 - 23A INJURY REPORT

Name ______________________ Class ______________________ Date ______

EXERCISE 6

PUBLIC AFFAIRS REPORTING

Assume that the Fire Department in your city released the two following reports this morning. Write a story that summarizes both reports. Your instructor may ask that you write about only one of the reports.

FIRE/INCIDENT REPORT

Date of incident: Today Time call received: 01:34 Time of arrival on scene: 01:38

Time of return to station: 08:12 Total time at scene: 6 hr., 34 min. Response time: 4 min.

Address of location: 2048 Main Street Type of premises: 218 seat restaurant

Name of owner: Mr./Mrs. Michael Deacosti Telephone: 823-0666

Nature of call: ______ 911 X Phone ______ Box ______ Police ______ Other ______ Alarms sounded: 1 (2) 3 4 5

Units dispatched: 4 Pumper 2 Ladder 1 Rescue ______ Chemical X District Chief ______ Other

Injuries: X Yes ______ No ______ Fatalities: ______ Yes X No

Commanding officer's narrative: First call came by phone from a passing motorist at 01:34 today regarding a fire at Deacosti's Restaurant. The structure was already fully involved when the 1st units arrived on the scene with flames having broken through the roof and shooting some twenty to thirty ft. up into the air. Heavy black smoke was pouring from the structure and flames flaring out the front door. We got 4 men inside via a west side window and a second alarm was immediately sounded. Upon arrival the District Chief ordered everyone outside for safety reasons.

The original building is old, having been opened somewhere around 1940 and was a wooden structure, remodeled and expanded several times. Fire was between and behind the current walls and difficult to reach and extinguish. Two tower trucks and 4 pumpers with deck guns doused all the flames by approx. 02:30. Two pumpers remained at the scene until approx. 08:00 when power company and other crews began coming to the scene in case any flames were re-ignited. Fire apparently started in the back NE corner of the restaurant, in either the kitchen or possibly an adjacent office area, possibly due to electrical problems, after the 11:00 closing hour. Private investigators from the insurance company are helping in the inquiry and an electrical engineer will inspect the damages later today. This may be a slow investigation because of extensive damage to the building which was totally and completely destroyed. There were no sprinklers. If it was constructed or remodeled today current codes would require the restaurant to have a sprinkler system. It would have been a whole different story if there were sprinklers. Sprinklers possibly could have saved the building.

2 firefighters were injured. FF John Charlton was taken to Mercy Hospital for treatment of smoke inhalation and released this a.m. FF Al Moravchek received 2nd and 3rd degree burns to his face, hands, and neck and is reported to be in satisfactory condition at the same hospital where he remains, having suffered said injuries during an explosion within the kitchen area at about 02:08 that sent a ball of flames up into his overhead ladder. No estimate of damage is likely to be available for several days. The premises were insured for $1.2 million.

Alarm system on premises: ______ Yes X No Alarm system activated: ______ Yes ______ No

Sprinkler system on premises: ______ Yes X No Sprinkler system activated: ______ Yes ______ No

Premises insured: X Yes ______ No Insurer notified: X Yes ______ No

Recommended followup:
______ None ______ Arson Squad X Fire Marshal ______ Inspection Division ______ Prevention Division

Commanding officer's name: Lieut. Ron Sheppard Signature Ron Sheppard

FIRE/INCIDENT REPORT

Date of incident: Yesterday Time call received: 16:48 Time of arrival on scene: 16:52

Time of return to station: 17:57 Total time at scene: 1 hr., 5 min. Response time: 4 min.

Address of location: West end of Liberty Av. Type of premises: Pond/undeveloped field

Name of owner: Wagnor Development Corporation Telephone: 823-3404

Nature of call: X 911 X Phone ___ Box ___ Police ___ Other Alarms sounded: (1) 2 3 4 5

Units dispatched: 1 Pumper 1 Ladder 2 Rescue ___ Chemical X District Chief ___ Other

Injuries: ___ Yes X No ___ Fatalities: X Yes ___ No

Commanding officer's narrative: The victim has been positively identified as a boy, age eleven, by the name of James Roger Lo, son of Joan and Roger Lo, home residence at 1993 Collins Av. The deceased was a student at Lincoln Elementary School. Witnesses at the scene said the deceased and 3 other neighborhood boys were digging a tunnel in the side of a hill overlooking a pond at the West end of Liberty Av. and it collapsed. One boy ran for help while the others began trying to dig him out. The one boy's mother dialed 911, then ran directly to the scene with neighbors. When we arrived about twenty adults from the neighborhood and passing motorists were at the scene, digging mostly with their hands and few shovels. We took over the work and got the boys head exposed about ten minutes into the rescue but before medics could begin resuscitation efforts another collapse occurred. Victim was freed at 17:24, taken to the Regional Medical Center, and pronounced dead there by doctors from an extensive lack of oxygen. The collapse occurred about 16:40.

Neighbors and witnesses at the scene were angry, expressing that they had told the property owner on numerous occasions and written him that the area was dangerous and that they needed a good fence around the entire pond area so none of the neighborhood children would drown in it, as it was apparently a popular play area for them. The survivors said they were building a fort and while the deceased was in it the walls caved in. When we arrived the boy had been buried about 12 minutes and completely covered. We found his body six feet from where the opening had been. It was basically a crawl-type cave, and getting the boy out was difficult because dirt (the sides and roof) kept collapsing back on us, and we had to be careful not to hit and further injure the victim without equipment. For that reason we were unable to use any heavy equipment. To expedite the rescue we tore sections from a fence at a residence at 8397 Liberty Av., using it as makeshift shoring in an effort to hold back the sand and dirt continuing to cave in on our men removing the interior dirt. The homeowner should be contacted as they may file a claim or have to be compensated for fence repairs.

Alarm system on premises: NA Yes ___ No Alarm system activated: ___ Yes ___ No

Sprinkler system on premises: NA Yes ___ No Sprinkler system activated: ___ Yes ___ No

Premises insured: ___ Yes ___ No Insurer notified: ___ Yes ___ No
Unknown

Recommended followup:
___ None ___ Arson Squad ___ Fire Marshal ___ Inspection Division ___ Prevention Division
Notify City Attorney of fence and Zoning Board of possible hazard for children.

Commanding officer's name: Lt. Steven Chenn Signature *Steven Chenn*

EXERCISE 7

PUBLIC AFFAIRS REPORTING

Write a news story based on this court document.

In the Circuit Court of
The 9th Judicial Circuit
in and for (your) County

Division: Civil

Case No.:1-78-1440

THADDEUS DOWDELL
and LAURA DOWDELL,
individually and as next friends
and parents of JAMES
DOWDELL, a minor, *Plaintiffs,*

vs.

MARVIN FERRELL,
GREG HUBBARD
and (YOUR CITY'S)
SCHOOL DISTRICT, *Defendants.*

COMPLAINT

COME NOW the Plaintiffs, THADDEUS DOWDELL and LAURA DOWDELL, individually and as next friends and parents of JAMES DOWDELL, a minor, by and through their undersigned counsel, and sue the Defendants, MARVIN FERRELL, GREG HUBBARD, AND (YOUR CITY'S) SCHOOL DISTRICT, jointly and severally, for damages and allege:

1. That this is an action for damages of $500,000, exclusive of interest, costs and further demands.
2. That at all times material to this cause, JAMES DOWDELL was and is the minor son of THADDEUS DOWDELL and LAURA DOWDELL, residing together with them in a family relationship as residents of this county.
3. That at all times material to this cause, the Defendant MARVIN FERRELL held and now holds the position of Principal of Kennedy High School, and that the Defendant GREG HUBBARD held and now holds the position of School Superintendent.
4. That the minor JAMES DOWDELL is and has been a student in Kennedy High School for the past three years and has been told that he will graduate from that school on or about the First Day of next June.
5. That the minor, JAMES DOWDELL, of this date, can barely read or do simple arithmetic and obviously has not learned enough to be graduated from high school or to function successfully in a society as complex as ours.

6. That the problem is not the fault of the minor JAMES DOWDELL, who, according to tests administered by guidance counselors at the high school, enjoys a normal IQ of 94.
7. That the failure of the minor JAMES DOWDELL to master the skills expected of high school students is the fault of the Defendants, MARVIN FERRELL, GREG HUBBARD, and (YOUR CITY'S) SCHOOL DISTRICT, that said defendants failed to employ competent teachers, to maintain discipline, to provide remedial help, and to provide an atmosphere in which learning might take place.

WHEREFORE, the Plaintiffs, THADDEUS DOWDELL and LAURA DOWDELL, individually and as next friends and parents of JAMES DOWDELL, a minor, sue the Defendants MARVIN FERRELL, GREG HUBBARD and (YOUR CITY'S) SCHOOL DISTRICT, jointly and severally, for compensatory damages in the amount of $500,000, exclusive of interest and costs.

FURTHER, the Plaintiffs demand that the minor JAMES DOWDELL be retained in Kennedy High School until he masters the skills expected of a high school graduate.

FURTHER, the Plaintiffs demand trial by jury of all issues triable as of right by a jury.

PILOTO and HERNDON, Attorneys
1048 Westmore Drive
Attorneys for Plaintiffs

BY: Kenneth T. Piloto
KENNETH T. PILOTO

EXERCISE 8

PUBLIC AFFAIRS REPORTING

Write a news story based on this court document.

In the Circuit Court of
The 9th Judicial Circuit
in and for (your) County

Division: Probate

Case No.:PR 67-1381

IN RE: GUARDIANSHIP
OF PATRICIA JEAN
WILLIAMS, an Incompetent
JOHN RUSSELL
WILLIAMS, as Guardian
of the Person of
PATRICIA JEAN
WILLIAMS, *Plaintiff,*

vs.

MERCY HOSPITAL;
ROSS R. GRAHAM,
M.D.; RICHARD M.
CESSARINI, M.D.;
RAMON HERNANDEZ,
DISTRICT ATTORNEY, *Defendants.*

FINAL DECLARATORY JUDGMENT

THIS CAUSE came for hearing upon the Complaint for Declaratory Relief because of the uncertainty of the law by JOHN RUSSELL WILLIAMS as Guardian of the Person of PATRICIA JEAN WILLIAMS, an Incompetent, against MERCY HOSPITAL; ROSS R. GRAHAM, M.D.; RICHARD M. CESSARINI, M.D.; and RAMON HERNANDEZ, DISTRICT ATTORNEY for the city, the Defendants, wherein Plaintiff seeks a Declaratory Judgment as to the following:

Authorization for JOHN RUSSELL WILLIAMS, as Guardian of the Person of PATRICIA JEAN WILLIAMS, an Incompetent, to direct MERCY HOSPITAL; ROSS R. GRAHAM, M.D.; RICHARD M. CESSARINI, M.D.; and all other attending physicians and health care providers to discontinue and to withhold all extraordinary measures such as mechanical ventilators, respirators, antibiotics, cardiovascular or similar type drugs; that these extraordinary measures should not be utilized, but be discontinued or withheld, in that the doctors agree there is no reasonable possibility of the Ward ever recovering from her present, persistent, "vegetative" (coma-like) state, which is irreversible;

That your Petitioner, JOHN RUSSELL WILLIAMS, surviving son; MERCY HOSPITAL; ROSS R. GRAHAM, M.D.; RICHARD M. CESSARINI, M.D.; and all other treating and consulting physicians and health care providers shall not be held civilly or criminally liable for taking the above action; and

That an appropriate restraining order be issued restraining the Defendant, RAMON HERNANDEZ, DISTRICT ATTORNEY, from prosecuting any of the above named individuals and organizations for withdrawing or withholding all extraordinary measures such as mechanical ventilators, respirators, antibiotics, cardiovascular or similar type drugs.

The Court makes the following findings of fact:

1. That this action is properly brought as a suit for declaratory judgment and relief, and that Plaintiff is the proper party to bring this action.
2. That at all times material hereto, the Plaintiff is a resident of the county in which this action is brought, and PATRICIA JEAN WILLIAMS, the Ward, has been maintained at MERCY HOSPITAL since she was involved in a serious motor vehicle accident 73 days prior to the issuance of this order.
3. That the following findings are based upon reasonable medical certainty and derived from the testimony of ROSS R. GRAHAM, M.D.; RICHARD M. CESSARINI, M.D.; and the records of MERCY HOSPITAL:
   (a) That four electroencephalograms, commonly referred to as EEGs, were performed on PATRICIA JEAN WILLIAMS, the Ward. None of the electroencephalograms indicated any cortical response. The only indication was a flat line.
   (b) That the Ward has suffered severe brain damage, which brain damage is totally irreversible and untreatable with no hope of recovery; and that the Ward is in a chronic and persistent "vegetative" (coma-like) state.
   (c) That the testimony of the doctors revealed that it was their respective medical opinion that all measures which are considered extraordinary lifesaving measures should not be utilized with respect to the Ward, but be discontinued or withheld; however, the decision to withdraw or withhold extraordinary lifesaving measures should be made by the Plaintiff and the family of the Ward.
   (d) That PATRICIA JEAN WILLIAMS, the Ward, requires constant care, and will so require IN THE FUTURE.

4. That PATRICIA JEAN WILLIAMS, the Ward, requires constant care, which care invades the Ward's body and violates the Ward's right to privacy as guaranteed by the Constitution of the United States of America and of this State; and that the State does not have an overriding interest it needs to protect, nor are there overriding medical interests that need to be protected.
5. That the son, JOHN RUSSELL WILLIAMS, has determined, subject to the approval of this Court, that all extraordinary lifesaving measures should not be utilized with respect to the Ward, but be discontinued or withheld from the Ward, PATRICIA JEAN WILLIAMS, and that MERCY HOSPITAL has no objection.

It is, therefore, ORDERED AND ADJUDGED:

1. That JOHN RUSSELL WILLIAMS, as the Guardian of the Person of PATRICIA JEAN WILLIAMS, an Incompetent, has full power to make decisions with regard to the identity of the Ward's treating physicians.
2. That MERCY HOSPITAL; ROSS R. GRAHAM, M.D.; AND RICHARD M. CESSARINI, M.D., are authorized to discontinue or to withdraw all extraordinary measures and life-support systems upon written direction of JOHN RUSSELL WILLIAMS, as Guardian of the Person of PATRICIA JEAN WILLIAMS, an Incompetent.

3. That no one shall be held civilly or criminally liable for taking action authorized by this Order.
4. That the Defendant, RAMON HERNANDEZ, as District Attorney for the city, shall be bound by this decision.

DONE AND ORDERED in Chambers.

BY: Randall Pfaff
Circuit Judge

EXERCISE 9

PUBLIC AFFAIRS REPORTING

HOUSE BILL 371

Write a news story about the bill reprinted here and about your state Senate's debate on the bill, which follows. You may quote the senators' remarks directly. Assume that the Senate debate and vote on the bill happened today. Assume also that your state's House of Representatives has already passed the bill by a vote of 101 to 23. In the text of the bill, the passages that have lines through them will be deleted from the current law, and passages that are underlined will be added to the law.

H.B. 371

An Act relating to crimes and offenses.

Section 1. Section 28-105, Revised Statutes, is amended to read:

28-105. (1) For purposes of the Criminal Code and any statute passed by the Legislature after the date of passage of the code, felonies are divided into eight classes which are distinguished from one another by the following penalties which are authorized upon conviction:

Class I felony	Death
Class IA felony	Life imprisonment
Class IB felony	Maximum—life imprisonment
	~~Minimum—ten years imprisonment~~
	<u>Minimum—twenty years imprisonment</u>
Class IC felony	Maximum—fifty years imprisonment
	Mandatory minimum—five years imprisonment
Class ID felony	Maximum—fifty years imprisonment
	Mandatory minimum—three years imprisonment
Class II felony	Maximum—fifty years imprisonment
	Minimum—one year imprisonment
Class III felony	Maximum—twenty years imprisonment
	Minimum—one year imprisonment
Class IV felony	Maximum—five years imprisonment
	Minimum—none

(2) <u>A person convicted of a felony for which a mandatory minimum sentence is prescribed shall not be eligible for probation.</u>

Section 2. Section 28-1205, Revised Statutes, is amended to read:

28-1205 (1) Any person who uses a firearm, a knife, brass or iron knuckles, or any other deadly weapon to commit any felony which may be prosecuted in a court of this state, or any person who unlawfully possesses a firearm, a knife, brass or iron knuckles, or any other deadly weapon during the commission of any felony which may be prosecuted in a court of this state commits the offense of using firearms <u>a deadly weapon</u> to commit a felony.

(2) (a) Use of firearms <u>a</u> ~~deadly~~ <u>weapon other than a firearm</u> to commit a felony is a Class III felony.

<u>(b) Use of a deadly weapon which is a firearm to commit a felony is a Class II felony.</u>

Section 3. Section 28-1206, Revised Statutes, is amended to read:

28-1206. (1) Any person who possesses any firearm ~~with a barrel less than eighteen inches in length~~ or brass or iron knuckles who has previously been convicted of a felony or who is a fugitive from justice commits the offense of possession of ~~firearms~~ a deadly weapon by a felon or a fugitive from justice.

(2) (a) Possession of ~~firearms~~ a deadly weapon other than a firearm by a felon or a fugitive from justice ~~or a felon~~ is a Class IV felony.

(b) Possession of a deadly weapon which is a firearm by a felon or a fugitive from justice is a Class III felony.

Section 4. Section 29-2221, Revised Statutes, is amended to read:

29-2221. (1) Whoever has been twice convicted of a crime, sentenced, and committed to prison, in this or any other state or by the United States or once in this state and once at least in any other state or by the United States, for terms of not less than one year each shall, upon conviction of a felony committed in this state, be deemed a habitual criminal and shall be punished by imprisonment in a Department of Correctional Services adult correctional facility for a ~~term of not less than ten nor~~ mandatory minimum term of ten years and a maximum term of not more than sixty years, except that:

(2) If the felony committed is manslaughter, armed robbery, rape, arson or kidnapping, as those terms are defined in the Criminal Code, or vehicular homicide while under the influence of alcohol, and at least one of the habitual criminal's prior felony convictions was for such a violation or a violation of a similar statute in another state or in the United States, the mandatory minimum term shall be twenty-five years and the maximum term not more than sixty years.

Section 5. Section 29-2262, Revised Statutes, is amended to read:

29-2262. (1) When a court sentences an offender to probation, it shall attach such reasonable conditions as it deems necessary or likely to insure that the offender will lead a law-abiding life. No offender shall be sentenced to probation if he or she is deemed to be a habitual criminal pursuant to section 29-2221.

Section 6. Section 29-2525, Revised Statutes, is amended to read:

29-2525. (1) In cases where the punishment is capital, no notice of appeal shall be required and within the time prescribed by section 25-1931 for the commencement of appeals, the clerk of the district court in which the conviction was had shall notify the court reporter who shall prepare a bill of exceptions as in other cases. The Clerk of the Supreme Court shall, upon receipt of the transcript, docket the case. The Supreme Court shall expedite the rendering of its opinion on any appeal, giving the matter priority over civil and noncapital matters.

Section 7. The following shall be added to the Criminal Code of the Revised Statutes:

(1) A person commits the offense of assault on an officer using a motor vehicle if he or she intentionally and knowingly causes bodily injury to a peace officer or employee of the Department of Correctional Services (a) by using a motor vehicle to run over or to strike such officer or employee or (b) by using a motor vehicle to collide with such officer's or employee's motor vehicle, while such officer or employee is engaged in the performance of his or her duties.

(2) Assault on an officer using a motor vehicle shall be a Class IV felony.

EXCERPTS OF FINAL DEBATE IN THE SENATE

Sen. Dan Twoshoes, D-Henderson: "If a farmer finds a weasel in his henhouse, he shoots it. I wish we could do the same with some of the two-legged weasels. But at least we can lock them up and keep them away from decent people. That's what this bill will do. It increases the prison sentence for criminals who use deadly weapons—especially guns—in the commission of crimes and it increases the penalties on felons and fugitives who possess deadly weapons. This bill will keep criminals off our streets by preventing judges from placing criminals on probation when this legislature has imposed a mandatory minimum sentence. And most importantly, this bill sets a mandatory minimum sentence for habitual criminals who commit serious crimes."

Sen. Sally Ong, R-Wakarusa: "I agree with Sen. Twoshoes that we need to keep habitual criminals off our streets, and if it were not for one provision, I could support this bill. I speak of the inclusion of vehicular homicide while under the influence of alcohol as one of those offenses requiring a 25-year mandatory minimum sentence. I understand the pain felt by those who lose a loved one in an accident caused by a drunken driver. That's how my brother died five years ago. But the people who drive while drunk need help, not a 25-year prison sentence."

Sen. John Percy, D-(Your city), and chairman of the Judiciary Committee: "I want to address Sen. Ong's concerns about the vehicular homicide provision. The Judiciary Committee debated this provision extensively, and we heard testimony from many people in law enforcement and social work. It was clear to us that a person who abuses alcohol and then drives an automobile is aware that she or he is behaving recklessly. If a habitual criminal engages in such reckless behavior and causes a fatal injury, then that should be treated as an extremely serious crime."

Sen. William Antonucci, R-(Your city): "We're fooling ourselves if we think that this bill will have any impact on crime in this state. Criminals don't think they'll be caught when they rob or kill, so increasing the penalties means nothing to them. What we'll be doing is wasting money warehousing criminals for years and years. The more people we jam into our prisons, the more we are going to have to pay to operate the prisons—even if we let the prisons become pigsties. We would do better to hire more police, prosecutors and judges. We will deter more crime by increasing the chances that crooks will be caught and prosecuted than by increasing the sentences for the few who now are prosecuted."

After debate, the Senate voted 40-12 in favor of the bill. The bill now goes to the governor, Laura Riley, who must sign it before it can become law. Her press secretary says the governor supports the bill and intends to sign it.

EXERCISE 10

PUBLIC AFFAIRS REPORTING

SCHOOL DISTRICT BUDGET

Write a news story summarizing the statement from the superintendent of schools and the proposed school district budget which follows. The statement appears verbatim and may be quoted directly. Accompanying the budget are figures showing enrollment by grade and the number of people the district employs. As you write your story, you may want to use a calculator (or a computer spreadsheet program) to find some numbers the budget does not provide, such as the percentage by which spending will increase or the average annual salary for teachers.

STATEMENT ON THE PROPOSED BUDGET

By Gary Hubbard
Superintendent of Schools

The development of this budget for the coming year was a challenging process. The district staff had only one overriding premise: What educational programs will provide every student with the opportunity to reach his or her fullest potential and provide the community with contributing citizens? This is an important goal because if this community is to continue to grow, prosper and maintain its quality of life, we must have educated citizens. This community historically has committed itself to maintaining the quality of the school system, and we are sure it will continue to do so.

This budget proposal shows what the district staff thinks is necessary to maintain the quality of schools and is based on certain assumptions which should be made public:

1. We expect growth in the district's assessed valuation of 28% next year. The county assessor will not certify the final assessed valuation for the district until after the deadline for adopting this budget.
2. The Legislature changed the formula by which state aid is distributed. The impact of that change is not clear, but we expect that state aid will increase only slightly for the next year, but more substantial increases of $700,000 to $1 million may be coming in the two or three years after next.
3. Student spending will remain at about $3,000 per pupil, and the district's enrollment will grow modestly.
4. The ratio of teachers to students will remain constant.
5. No new programs will be started.
6. No programs will be restarted.
7. Salaries and fringe benefits will not increase, but spending on nonsalary items will increase 2.5% in accordance with the consumer price index.

The General Fund Budget shows the staff's proposals for expenditures for most of the district's day-to-day operations, including all instructional programs. All expenses for operating the district's three high schools, nine middle schools and thirty-three elementary schools are in the general fund. It also includes all salaries for administrators, certified teachers and classified non-teaching employees.

The Building and Construction Budget shows spending on the construction of three new elementary schools and the work being done to renovate and remodel two middle schools. The district is nearing completion of the building program voters approved five years ago when they passed a $54-million bond issue. Some of the construction and renovation work that had been budgeted for this year was delayed because of bad weather. Therefore, money the district had expected to spend last year has been included in this year's budget.

The Interscholastic Athletics Fund Budget covers expenditures on interscholastic sports, such as football, girls' volleyball, girls' and boys' basketball, boys' baseball and girls' softball. Salaries for full-time coaches come from the General Fund. The salaries paid from the Interscholastic Athletics Fund go to referees, parking attendants, concessions workers and security personnel.

The Debt Service Fund shows district payments on the principal and interest for the various bond issues outstanding.

Definitions of Budget Categories:

- Salaries—Funds paid to employees under regular employment contracts with the district.
- Benefits—Funds for the district's share of Social Security, retirement, unemployment benefits, health insurance and death benefits.
- Contracted Services—Funds to pay for services provided by individuals or firms outside the district. Examples are attorneys' fees, consultant fees and maintenance agreements on equipment.
- Supplies—Funds for consumable materials used in providing district services, such as textbooks, pencils, chalk, paper, floor wax, gasoline, etc.
- Instructional Development—Funds allocated to improve instructional programs and for professional growth activities by employees.
- In-District Travel—Funds paid to reimburse district employees who are required by their job assignments to travel within the district.
- Repair Equipment—Funds allocated to repair equipment such as typewriters, film projectors, lighting fixtures and musical instruments.
- Replace/New Equipment—Funds for the purchase of equipment to provide new services or enhance current programs. Examples are microcomputers, copying machines, vehicles, tools and furniture.
- Fixed Charges—Funds allocated to purchase various kinds of insurance for the district.
- Transfer—Funds transferred from the General Fund to support athletics, debate, journalism and other student activities.
- Contingency—Funds budgeted for unexpected personnel and non-personnel items and which can be expended only with board approval.

SCHOOL DISTRICT BUDGET

Description	Last Year Actual	This Year Budget	Next Year Proposed
GENERAL FUND			
Beg. Balance 9/1	14,727,807.00	17,552,056.00	14,174,366.00
Receipts			
Property Taxes	91,798,484.00	91,485,010.00	102,793,572.00
State Aid	29,236,428.00	31,373,050.00	31,427,590.00
Other Local	5,785,741.00	5,847,000.00	5,971,000.00
County	857,522.00	1,000,000.00	841,000.00
State	18,744,139.00	21,566,000.00	21,451,000.00
Federal	2,950,850.00	3,457,000.00	3,625,000.00
Total Receipts	149,373,164.00	154,728,060.00	166,109,162.00
Total Revenue Available	164,101,335.00	172,298,116.00	180,283,528.00
Property Tax Rate	1.5571	1.6453	1.4126
Valuation	5,572,804,000.00	5,702,528,000.00	7,301,758,000.00

Description	Last Year Actual	This Year Budget	Next Year Proposed
Expenditures			
Personnel Expenses			
Salaries			
Administration	7,924,457.00	8,320,440.00	8,447,610.00
Certificated	76,144,423.00	80,556,450.00	87,034,960.00
Classified	19,413,780.00	21,297,550.00	21,982,000.00
Total Salaries	103,482,660.00	110,174,440.00	117,464,570.00
Benefits	26,117,570.00	29,405,560.00	30,723,020.00
Total Personnel Expenses	129,600,230.00	139,580,000.00	148,187,590.00
Non-Personnel Expenses			
Contract Services	1,716,125.00	2,588,010.00	2,570,590.00
Supplies	6,685,297.00	7,586,510.00	7,650,980.00
Utilities	3,081,556.00	3,036,980.00	3,566,700.00
Professional Development	386,739.00	384,430.00	391,930.00
In-District Travel	171,513.00	163,900.00	163,750.00
Repair Equipment	265,977.00	317,430.00	317,930.00
Replace/New Equipment	2,738,604.00	3,093,640.00	3,147,250.00
Fixed Charges	1,507,858.00	1,409,200.00	1,447,400.00
Transfers	395,380.00	363,650.00	348,150.00
Total Non-Personnel Expenses	16,949,049.00	18,943,750.00	19,604,680.00
Total Expenses	146,549,279.00	158,523,750.00	167,792,270.00
Contingency	0.00	100,000.00	0.00
Grand Total Expenses	146,549,279.00	158,623,750.00	167,792,270.00
Ending Fund Balance	17,552,056.00	13,674,366.00	12,491,258.00
BUILDING AND CONSTRUCTION FUND			
Beginning Balance 9/1	3,383,807.00	54,536,777.00	46,633,343.00
Receipts			
Property Taxes	8,206,489.00	7,895,636.00	6,419,926.00
In Lieu of Taxes	241,790.00	260,000.00	260,000.00
Interest on Investments	97,280.00	1,550,000.00	1,730,000.00
Land Leases	5,024.00	10,000.00	5,000.00
City Reimbursements	510,898.00	580,000.00	75,000.00
Miscellaneous	42,394.00	50,000.00	50,000.00
Roof Replacement Fund	0.00	1,000,000.00	900,000.00
Motor Vehicle Taxes	28,578.00	20,000.00	20,000.00
Bond Proceeds	53,705,054.00	0.00	0.00
Tax Anticipation	0.00	5,828,700.00	3,198,344.00
Total Receipts	62,837,507.00	17,194,336.00	12,658,270.00
Total Available	66,221,314.00	71,731,113.00	59,291,613.00
Expenditures			
Construction	8,535,662.00	29,923,852.00	55,390,460.00
Renovation	2,933,242.00	1,150,000.00	1,000,000.00
Connectivity	0.00	0.00	1,225,000.00
Roof Replacement	0.00	1,000,000.00	959,153.00
Purchase of Sites	7,883.00	0.00	0.00
Tax Collection Fee	75,892.00	80,000.00	82,000.00
Rating and Management Fees	131,858.00	0.00	0.00
Contingency	0.00	500,000.00	0.00

Description	Last Year Actual	This Year Budget	Next Year Proposed
Not Completed Projects	0.00	3,545,348.00	1,000,000.00
Principal/Interest Accrual	0.00	0.00	335,000.00
Total Expenditures	11,684,537.00	36,199,200.00	59,991,613.00
Ending Balance	54,536,777.00	35,531,913.00	0.00
DEBT SERVICES FUND BUDGET			
Beginning Balance 9/1	799,305.00	8,689,915.00	1,342,124.00
Receipts			
Property Tax	2,305,785.00	7,075,000.00	7,442,500.00
In Lieu of Tax	61,198.00	100,000.00	100,000.00
Motor Vehicle Taxes	7,578.00	10,000.00	10,000.00
Interest	159,196.00	218,660.00	100,000.00
Refunding	7,945,815.00	0.00	0.00
Total Receipts	10,479,572.00	7,403,660.00	7,652,500.00
Total Available	11,278,877.00	16,093,575.00	8,994,624.00
Expenditures			
Bond Principal			
4,280,000 Issued six years ago	325,000.00	3,225,000.00	0.00
5,000,000 Issued five years ago	345,000.00	4,005,000.00	0.00
3,500,000 Issued four years ago	240,000.00	380,000.00	415,000.00
4,220,000 Issued three years ago	110,000.00	180,000.00	190,000.00
8,020,000 Refunding two years ago	430,000.00	1,255,000.00	1,285,000.00
54,480,000 Issued last year	0.00	475,000.00	1,475,000.00
Total Principal	1,450,000.00	9,520,000.00	3,365,000.00
Bond Interest	1,091,477.00	6,096,168.00	5,529,489.00
Tax Collection Fee	21,455.00	70,000.00	70,000.00
Management Fees	26,030.00	33,241.00	30,135.00
Total Expenditures	2,588,962.00	15,719,409.00	8,994,624.00
Ending Balance	8,689,915.00	374,166.00	0.00
INTERSCHOLASTIC ATHLETICS FUND BUDGET			
Beginning Balance 9/1	71,272.00	72,303.00	72,229.00
Receipts			
Football	125,036.00	75,000.00	75,000.00
Basketball (Boys')	48,922.00	40,000.00	50,000.00
Basketball (Girls')	24,794.00	25,000.00	25,000.00
Other	104,148.00	100,000.00	100,160.00
Transferred from General Fund	294,120.00	238,390.00	228,230.00
Total Receipts	597,020.00	478,390.00	478,390.00
Total Available	668,292.00	550,693.00	550,619.00
Expenditures			
Salaries, supplies, equipment	595,989.00	505,964.00	505,964.00
Total Expenditures	595,989.00	505,964.00	505,964.00
Ending Balance	72,303.00	44,729.00	44,655.00

Description	Last Year Actual	This Year Budget	Next Year Proposed
SUMMARY OF ALL FUNDS			
Total Available Revenues	242,269,818.00	260,673,497.00	249,120,384.00
Total Expenditures	161,418,767.00	211,048,323.00	237,284,471.00
Ending Balance	80,851,051.00	49,625,174.00	11,835,913.00

DISTRICT ENROLLMENT

Grade	Last Year	This Year	Next Year
Kindergarten	2,348	2,193	2,349
1st	2,367	2,347	2,225
2nd	2,378	2,377	2,347
3rd	2,415	2,371	2,373
4th	2,421	2,406	2,386
5th	2,326	2,424	2,398
6th	2,322	2,319	2,435
7th	2,292	2,367	2,302
8th	2,071	2,289	2,335
9th	2,118	2,082	2,265
10th	2,078	2,141	2,112
11th	1,969	2,015	2,089
12th	2,070	2,057	2,006
Special Education	296	367	367
Head Start	267	265	265
Total	29,738	30,020	30,254

DISTRICT EMPLOYMENT (FULL-TIME EQUIVALENCY)

Category	Last Year	This Year	Next Year
Administration	127.95	131.30	132.30
Certificated	2,225.63	2,313.38	2,369.26
Technician	62.00	65.70	136.14
Office Personnel	270.60	274.55	263.05
Paraeducators	574.74	599.97	549.54
Tradespersons	435.13	467.50	467.55
Total	3,696.05	3,852.40	3,917.84

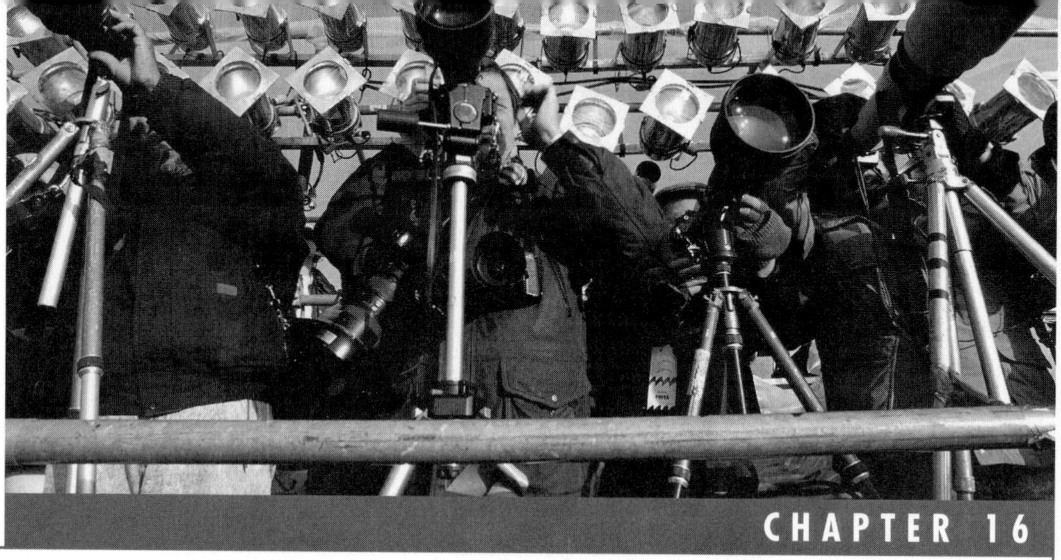

CHAPTER 16

UNDERSTANDING AND USING THE INTERNET

Just because it's digital doesn't mean it's true.

(Stephen Miller, journalist)

Editors in most news organizations require reporters to know how to use the Internet to gather information for stories. They expect reporters to use e-mail to interview potential sources and the Internet to find background information on issues, events, officials and experts. In a recent study of the nation's newspapers, the Pew Center found that most reporters gather 40 percent of the information for their stories from the field, 40 percent from the telephone and a growing 20 percent from the Internet.

The Internet can be described as a worldwide system of computers connected indirectly to one another, allowing the transfer of information in seconds. Most people think the Internet and the World Wide Web are the same thing, but the Web is a subset of the Internet. And, like such systems as e-mail, Usenet, FTP (file transfer protocol) and Telnet, the Web requires particular software for Internet users to access it.

A BRIEF HISTORY

The Internet was the brainchild of scientists who wanted to build computer networks so that researchers worldwide could share ideas. This project was named ARPANET, in honor of the agency that paid for it—the Advanced Research Projects Agency within the Department of Defense. In 1969, the network connected four computer sites (UCLA, the University of California at Santa Barbara, the Stanford Research Institute and the University of Utah). In 1971, it reached two dozen sites, and 10 years later, more than 200 were on the network. ARPANET grew initially because anyone who received ARPA funds for a project was required to be connected to the network.

Although the computers held a lot of information, users had difficulty obtaining the data because the network lacked standardized log-in procedures and directories of the connected computers and their stored information. To answer these problems, researchers at the University of Minnesota developed the original browser (the ancestor of Netscape Navigator and Microsoft's Internet Explorer) in 1991 and named it in honor of the university mascot—Gopher. This software grouped information into categories, automated different log-in procedures, found the requested information and brought it back to the user's computer. When the World Wide Web was developed in 1993, interest in the Internet exploded. The Web uses HTML (hypertext markup language), which enables a person to find information worldwide by simply clicking on a word that leads to another document in a different computer. By 2004, more than 204 million people in the United States had access to the Internet from their homes, and they spent an average of of eight hours a week online. More than 460 million people worldwide had Internet access from their homes.

JOURNALISTS AND THE INTERNET

Journalists use the Internet daily as a tool for reporting events and issues comprehensively to viewers and readers. The Internet helps every stage of the reporting process from thinking of a story idea to presenting the story. Reporters go to the Internet to find story topics, identify experts and monitor a subject. Editors use it to check names, addresses and other facts. The Internet helps journalists tackle broad themes, find background information on unfamiliar people or issue and keep up with developments.

The Internet saves journalists time and news organizations money. Only a few years ago, journalists found information by driving to libraries and other places in the community. Many towns lack large libraries with reference materials, so reporters had to travel to nearby cities or settle for incomplete information. Even with the telephone, journalists had to make many calls, leave messages and wait for return calls before finding the information they needed. With the Internet, reporters can find diverse voices and up-to-date information quickly, and at their fingertips. News organizations no longer have to pay journalists to spend as much time tracking down information. The Internet enables reporters to write more stories and better stories.

The Internet also has some disadvantages. Journalists may have a hard time sifting through the mountains of knowledge on the Internet. And, much of the information is questionable—up to 90 percent, according to some Internet experts. Furthermore, journalists should not depend on online sources alone because many important documents are not online.

In spite of the drawbacks, the Internet gives reporters new choices for finding information. They can use e-mail, go directly to a Web site, browse the Internet, explore a subject directory or a search engine, participate in a mailing list or read messages in a newsgroup or on 'blogs.

E-MAIL

The advent of telephone service in the 19th century revolutionized newsgathering. Electronic mail is doing the same thing at the dawn of the 21st century. Reporters use e-mail to contact hard-to-reach or reluctant sources. Even people who travel a lot make time to check their e-mail. Sometimes sources who dodge phone calls or hesitate to return phone messages will answer a reporter's e-mail. A reporter who is trying to contact several sources for similar information can use e-mail to send the same message to each of them. E-mail is also a way of keeping in contact with sources, exchanging ideas with colleagues or communicating with readers or viewers. Journalists keep their e-mail as a record of an interview in case a source disputes what was said.

Reporters are as polite in their e-mails as they are in person or on the telephone. They use a salutation (such as "Dear Mrs. Ramirez,") and identify themselves and the news organization they represent. They usually review the background of an event or issue before they ask their questions. Reporters also tell sources their deadline, and they thank the sources for their time and expertise. (After all, the sources are not getting paid to answer the reporter's questions, but are donating their time.) Reporters do not write in all capital letters because many e-mail users regard it as shouting. Journalists also avoid using acronyms, such as "BTW," because not everyone knows what they represent ("by the way").

E-mail interviews—or e-interviews—do not replace personal interviews. Reporters learn a lot about sources through their body language, facial expressions, pauses and voice tone. Such nonverbal information is available in personal or telephone interviews but not in written answers to e-mailed questions. E-mail interviews also give sources time to carefully prepare and check answers, whereas personal interviews consist of spontaneous responses. Sources can delete words from a computer screen, but they find it harder to take back the spoken word. Another advantage of personal and telephone interviews is that the spontaneous nature of such conversations allows reporters to gain additional insights and information by quickly following up on a source's offhand comment.

Journalists can learn a lot about a source from the person's e-mail address. An e-mail address usually consists of a person's user ID and the address of the computer that provides the person's e-mail service, sometimes called a domain. These parts are similar to a person's name and the postal address where the person receives mail. For example, one of the authors of this textbook had the following as her e-mail address: "davenpor@pilot.msu.edu." (This can be read aloud as "davenpor at pilot dot m-s-u dot e-d-u.") The "@" symbol separates the personal ID and the computer in which the mail resides. The dots separate sections of the computer's name.

Here are what the parts of the address mean for "davenpor@pilot.msu.edu":

The ".edu" at the end describes the type of setting in which the computer is located—"edu" indicates an educational institution. Other descriptions are:

.org—nonprofit organization
.com—commercial organization
.gov—government
.mil—military
.net—network provider or Internet service provider (ISP)
.int—international organization

A suffix is added at the end to denote addresses in countries outside of the United States. For example:

.ca—Canada
.fr—France
.jp—Japan

The "msu" is the registered Internet name of the organization (in this case, Michigan State University) that owns or leases the computer where messages are stored and serves as a gateway to the Internet. Every computer on the Internet has a unique identification number, but most organizations use an alias made up of letters. For example, Scientific Computing and Instrumentation magazine's unique ID number is 199.100.12.25, but its alias is "scamag.com." This is why numbers instead of letters sometimes appear in the locator space of the browser.

The word "pilot" identifies the specific computer on which the user's account resides. (MSU has many computers on campus.) Many addresses do not include this subdomain because the system automatically knows where to route the message.

The "davenpor" is the individual's personal identification or user name.

INTERNET ADDRESSES, WEB SITES OR URLS (UNIVERSAL RESOURCE LOCATORS)

The amount of information on the Internet is hard to imagine. Some experts say that Internet volume doubles every 90 days. Everyone has a reason to put information on the Internet: Businesses want consumers to buy products or services; nonprofit organizations want to influence people about an issue; government agencies want to show citizens that they are doing their jobs; and individuals use their Web sites to present electronic resumes or to publish online diaries called Web logs or 'blogs. Certainly, since the terrorist attacks on the World Trade Center and the Pentagon, thousands of new Web sites have popped up with opinions and "facts" about terrorism, Iraq, Afaghanistan, the United Nations, the policies of President George W. Bush and other world leaders and more. Because so many people use the Web for so many reasons, journalists must question the reliability of Web-delivered information. Reporters need to find out who put the information on the Web and why, and then verify any information they use.

Every screen of information on the Internet has an address, called its URL or universal resource locator. Once journalists become familiar with the parts of an Internet address, they can find many Web sites simply by using logic. For example, to look for job openings listed with the Investigative Reporters and Editors, a professional organization for journalists, one types in:

http://www.ire.org/jobs/look.html

The "http" is the protocol or computer scheme used to access information. The "www.ire.org" is the "home page," which refers to the introductory screen of related information. The "www.ire.org/jobs/look.html" identifies the electronic path to the specific screen ("look.html") holding the desired information. Here are what the parts of the address mean:

The "http:" means "hypertext transfer protocol." This protocol allows computers to move information (text, graphics, audio and video) around the Web. It allows a person to click on words to find another document residing in another computer.

The "www" is part of the host computer's name. Not every address on the World Wide Web has "www" as its prefix.

The Investigative Reporters and Editors organization uses its abbreviated name, "ire," as the designation of its Web site.

The IRE is a nonprofit organization, which is indicated by ".org" in the address.

The phrase "/jobs" is a filepath name, routing the researcher to the information about jobs.

And the phrase "/look.html" identifies the exact screen where one can look at job openings in different news organizations. (If one wanted to post an opening, the page name changes to "/post.html.") The software used to develop this screen supports hypertext markup language ("htm" or "html"—depending on the system), which contains text and graphics and links to words found in other computers on the Internet.

Web sites are reorganized often. If journalists can't go directly to the file they need, they omit the filename and filepath, and type in the Web site's home page (www.ire.org). Then they'll look for the desired information by using the home page's links.

Try to find the screen with job postings by starting at the Investigative Reporters and Editors home page (www.ire.org). Watch the URL locator (address) change with each click on a button or link.

Journalists' URLs

Journalists keep at their desks for easy access lists of important telephone numbers and addresses. They might keep source lists on paper taped to a wall or consult cards in a Rolodex file. Now, journalists also keep an electronic address book of sources' telephone numbers and e-mail addresses and they "bookmark" a source's or reference's Web page. ("Bookmarks" can be found on the menu bar of Netscape Navigator and "Favorites" on Internet Explorer, for example.) Other journalists maintain a list of online references on their own Web page. By using electronic bookmarks or listing URLs on a Web page, journalists can link to online information quickly. Here are a few sites that help reporters obtain information, verify news and find sources for their general and beat assignments. Some sites are helpful for journalists wanting to know more about the media industry.

Government

http://www.fedworld.gov
http://thomas.loc.gov
http://www.whitehouse.gov

http://www.access.gpo.gov
http://archives.gov
http://www.vote-smart.org
http://www.census.gov
http://campaignfinance.org
http://www.rcfp.org/foi.html
http://findlaw.com

Business and Industry News

http://prnewswire.com
http://www.businesswire.com

Finding People, Businesses and Organizations

http://www.switchboard.com
http://www.infospace.com
http://www.guidestar.org

Finding Experts

http://www3.profnet.com
http://www.experts.com

Mapping

http://www.mapquest.com
http://www.mapblast.com
http://www.worldatlas.com
http://www.nationalgeographic.com/maps

General Reference

http://refdesk.com
http://www.reference.com
http://www.ipl.org

Investigative Resources

http://www.virtualgumshoe.com
http://www.journalismnet.com
http://journaliststoolbox.com
http://powerreporting.com
http://www.cyberjournalist.net
http://www3.niu.edu/newsplace
http://reporter.umd.edu

Media Directories

http://newslink.org
http://cjr.org/mediafinder

Wire Services

http://www.ap.org
http://www.reuters.com
http://www.journalismnet.com/news/newsagencies.htm

Media Industry News and Professional Organizations

http://ajr.org
http://www.cjr.org
http://www.editorandpublisher.com
http://www.ap.org/pages/indnews
http://www.rtndf.org

Reporter Training and Help Sites

http://www.poynter.org
http://americanpressinstitute.org

SEARCH ENGINES AND SUBJECT DIRECTORIES

Sometimes reporters do not know where to look for information or whether the information they need is online. In these cases, journalists turn to a few of the Internet's 1,500 subject directories and search engines. Reporters who do not understand how search engines work simply type in keywords and receive hundreds of responses—many of them irrelevant. Frustrated at having to look through so much information, they abandon search engines. Yet, subject directories and search engines are a big help when used correctly.

Help Sections and Advanced Searching Areas

Learning about one or two search engines makes searching more efficient and productive. Reporters look at two areas in search engines to learn how to use them well. The first area is the "help" section. Help sections usually describe how search engines sort through the millions of Web sites on the Internet to find links to pages that seem to match the topic. This section often has lists of frequently asked questions and tips for doing searches. A second helpful area to review is "advanced searching." Using a search engine's advanced searching capabilities, reporters can refine their searches so that the computer responds with a handful of highly relevant Web sites.

How Search Engines Work

When journalists type the same keyword into different search engines, the results vary because each search engine operates in a different way. All search directories contain large databases. These databases are the search engine's copied version of the Internet. Sophisticated software—called a spider, bot or crawler—within each search engine goes out onto the Internet and compares each Web page it finds with the Web page in its database. If the software encounters updated pages, it replaces the old pages in its database. If the software encounters a new Web site, it adds the site to the database. The same Web site may appear more than once in response to a query because some search engines do an inadequate job of clearing out the old Web page from their database.

Search engines vary in the frequency of Web crawling—some search engine programs index the entire Internet in four weeks; some index it in six. Thus, some search engines respond to a query with more recent Web sites than others. Furthermore, search engine databases vary in volume, offering different numbers of responses to their searches.

Relevancy Ranking

Search engines are not thinking people. Unlike librarians, they cannot ask a journalist to tell them more about the topic or ascertain what way the journalist is using a keyword. The search engine identifies all Web sites containing that keyword, no matter the definition or context. It then lists the Web sites containing the keyword, according to how pertinent the Web site is to the journalist's keyword search. This is called relevancy ranking. Search engines' programming tells them how to compare the keyword with other words on a Web page for relevancy ranking.

The search engine programs use a location-and-frequency method to rank sites. Using the location variable, the search engine compares the keyword with the Web site's title, assuming that if the keyword appears in a URL address or a Web page title (which appears in the window's title bar), then the site must have something to do with that subject. It also compares the keyword to words appearing near the top of the Web page, such as in the headline or in the first few paragraphs. Using the frequency variable, the search engine analyzes how often the keyword appears in relation to other words in the page. The more frequently the keyword appears, the more relevant the engine judges the Web site to be. Some search engines include the number of links to a Web page in its relevancy ranking. The help section of a search engine describes its particular method of relevancy ranking.

Formulating Queries

Search engines use varied combinations of searching methods. To formulate a query, journalists must identify the concepts of their topic. They determine likely keywords and specify logical relationships between the words. Search engines support different methods to identify relationships and employ various search procedures. Some of those procedures are described below and may be explained more fully in a search engine's help section or used in an advanced searching area:

1. Boolean logic employs connectors—"OR," "AND" and "NOT"—to determine the relationship between words. "OR" means that the Web page can have either word. For example, to search for information about gas taxes, a reporter might specify "fee or tax" to appear because different writers may use different words to mean the same thing. "AND" signifies that both words, such as "tax and gas," must appear somewhere on the same Web page. "NOT" removes unnecessary Web pages that otherwise might be included as relevant pages. In this instance, a reporter would type, "gas NOT natural." Thus, the search string might look like: "fee OR tax AND gas NOT natural."

   Some search engines recognize implied Boolean logic, which uses symbols in place of "OR," "AND" and "NOT." A space between words implies the connector "OR," a plus sign replaces "AND," and a minus sign (a hyphen) signifies "NOT."

Boolean Logic	**Implied Boolean Logic**
fee OR tax	fee tax
tax AND gas	+tax +gas
gas NOT natural	+gas −natural

   Once journalists learn how different search engines use implied Boolean logic, they understand why a search using the keywords "sex discrimination" yields thousands of Web pages about sex as well as sex discrimination.
2. Truncation characters substitute for precise keyword spelling. For example, the exclamation mark replaces an undetermined number of letters at the end of a word. "Gas!" will produce pages with the word "gas" or "gasoline," but it might also yield pages with the word "gaseous." In many search engines, an asterisk substitutes for only one character. For instance, "wom*n" will result in Web pages containing "woman" or "women" or "womyn."
3. Proximity operators tell a search engine how close keywords need to be in relation to each other. For example, journalists may use "Elizabeth w/3 Ebony" to include Web pages that have "Elizabeth" and "Ebony" within three words of each other. Results would include "Elizabeth Ebony," "Elizabeth 'Beth' Ebony" or "Elizabeth W. Ebony." Other proximity operators may be "near" and "adjacent."
4. Field searching tells the search engine where to look for the keywords. "T: plutonium" means that the word "plutonium" must appear in the URL title of the document. Journalists can also search according to author, among other fields.
5. Phrase searching—with words inside parentheses or quote marks—helps journalists who need an exact phrase. For instance, typing in "radio-controlled airplanes" tells the search engine to find these exact words in this exact order.
6. Relevancy ranking tells reporters how relevant the Web pages probably are to their search.
7. Concept searching enables the reporter to choose synonyms to help with keyword meaning.

Most reporters experiment with a variety of subject directories and search engines. Then they choose a couple they like most and become familiar with their unique characteristics and search procedures.

Choosing a Search Engine or Subject Directory

The programs used to search the Internet fall into three groups: subject directories, search engines and metasearch engines. This section lists some of the most popular search programs. More information about each can be found at its Web site.

A subject directory is a database of Internet files selected by human site creators or evaluators (called "editors") and organized into subject categories. These vary considerably in selectivity. Reporters should consult a directory's policies when choosing a search program:

Yahoo!—http://www.yahoo.com
Infomine—http://infomine.ucr.edu
Internet Public Library—www.ipl.org
About—http://about.com
Google Directory—http://directory.google.com

A search engine is a database of Internet files collected by a computer program (called spiders, bots and crawlers). No selection criteria exist for the database:

Google—http://www.google.com
All the Web—http://www.alltheweb.com
AltaVista—http://www.altavista.com
Lycos—http://www.lycos.com
Ask Jeeves—http://www.ask.com

A metasearch engine searches multiple search engines and subject directories simultaneously. Many journalists prefer to use a metasearch engine because it will retrieve the most relevant (but not all) documents from each engine it searches:

Hotbot—http://www.hotbot.com
MetaCrawler—http://www.metacrawler.com
Profusion—http://www.profusion.com
Query Server—http://www.queryserver.com

Deep Web

Much of the information on the Web is invisible to search engine spiders and will not show up in query results. This invisible content is referred to as "deep Web" and is organized in databases stored in programs such as Access, FoxPro, Excel, Oracle, SQL Server and DB2. Search engine spiders also cannot see indexes and nontextual files, such as multimedia files, graphical files and portable document format (.pdf) files. However, search directories will link to database Web sites and search engines will find Web sites with searchable databases. Furthermore, many search engines offer their own searchable databases, such as phone books and maps.

MAILING LISTS AND NEWSGROUPS

Mailing lists and newsgroups are generally called discussion groups, and they exist for different reasons. Sometimes, an organization finds a discussion group is the most efficient way for its members to communicate quickly. Or an online group may form so people with similar interests can exchange ideas, no matter how far apart they live.

Reporters use mailing lists and newsgroups for a variety of reasons. They identify experts within discussion groups who can speak on a specialized subject. They also find people who have had interesting experiences that add human interest to news stories. Reporters obtain story ideas from discussion groups by reading what others are interested in. Also, reporters use discussion groups to keep up with their own profession. They find out what is happening in their field or ask professional questions to other reporters across the globe when they need help with a story.

Both mailing lists and newsgroups resemble ongoing discussions. However, mailing lists resemble magazine subscriptions because a member must ask to participate in the private discussion. Newsgroups resemble bulletin boards in coin-operated laundries because all who come by can read messages and post their own comments on the public conversation. Also, while mailing list messages come to subscribers in their mailboxes, newsgroup readers must go to the messages in newsgroups located somewhere on the Web.

Mailing Lists

Generally, information in mailing lists is more reliable than that in newsgroups. First, people generally think the information derived from the discussions in topical mailing lists is worth the effort of subscribing to the list. Second, their requests to subscribe along with their e-mail addresses, names and sometimes more are verified by individuals or computers. Third, individuals knowledgeable or interested in the topic usually make up the mailing list. And, fourth, many newsgroups are run by a moderator, who guides the discussion, curbs digressions in topics and keeps participants' tempers in check. Newsgroup readers, however, simply respond—sometimes on the spur of the moment—to anyone who posts a public message about anything that somes to mind.

When someone sends a message to a mailing list, the program automatically duplicates the message and sends it to the mailboxes of all subscribing members. Reporters use lists to ask general questions about sources, current events or help with researching their stories. They usually receive a variety of responses. Sometimes these public responses turn into a "thread" of conversation (many messages on the same topic) that all subscribers may read and contribute to. Other times, instead of continuing a public conversation, two list members may continue a private conversation through personal e-mails. For example, once a reporter asks a question to members of the mailing list and subsequently identifies an expert, the reporter may follow up with questions to the expert in private e-mail.

The process for joining mailing list discussions is fairly simple. Journalists must first find the e-mail address of the desired mailing list. Then, to subscribe to that mailing list, they send an e-mail request addressed to the mailing list management software (programs that run mailing lists) at the list's host computer address. Three types of mailing list management software are Listserv, Listproc and Majordomo, and each has a slightly different way of receiving a request.

TO: listserv@	BODY: subscribe [name of list]
TO: listproc@	BODY: subscribe [name of list] [your first and last name]
TO: majordomo@	BODY: subscribe [name of list] [your e-mail address]

An e-mail request to join the Society of Professional Journalists mailing list (SPJ-L) located in a host computer at The Pennsylvania State University would look like the following:

TO: listserv@lists.psu.edu
FROM: (leave blank because the address is automated)
SUBJECT: (leave blank)
BODY OF MESSAGE: Subscribe SPJ-L

The reporter will receive a message from the management program, asking for confirmation of the subscription request. Once the reporter confirms, the system will respond again with an automated message containing completed application information and frequently asked questions (FAQ) about the mailing list. (The most important information to keep is the command to unsubscribe, addressed again to the mailing list system.)

Now messages from the mailing list will appear automatically in the reporter's e-mail. The reporter can simply read the messages and do nothing. However, if reporters would like to participate in a discussion or ask list members a question, then they need to address their e-mail to the mailing list's name (and not the management software). A message to the SPJ-L members might resemble the following:

TO: SPJ-L@lists.psu.edu
FROM: (leave blank because the address is automated)
SUBJECT: Online Interviews
BODY OF MESSAGE:
Dear Journalists,
I am considering the ethical issues that might occur when interviewing someone online. Can you please tell me what problems I might enounter and advice on how to avoid them?
Thank you, [Your name]

The number of responses often varies with the number of members. Activity usually will be higher for lists with several hundred members, whereas fewer messages will appear from lists with only several members. Journalists may find many mailing lists are not conversations, but announcements or newsletters about a particular subject.

A directory of journalism-related mailing lists ranging from industry news to help on covering beats and stories can be found on Christopher Callahan's "A Journalist's Guide to the Internet": http://reporter.umd.edu/listserv.htm.

Reporters also like to keep up with news about their beats or attend discussions on a topic or story they are covering. They can find the names of thousands of mailing lists by going to mailing list directories on the Web. Some of the following directories use keywords to search for both topical lists and individual messages:

Catalist—http://www.lsoft.com/lists/listref.html
Tile.Net—http://www.tile.net/lists
Topica—http://lists.topica.com/dir

These Web sites also have sufficient help areas for new members. However, the following sites contain information on each of the three mailing list management programs:

Listserv instructions: http://www.lsoft.com/lists/listref.html
Listproc instructions: http://www.listproc.net
Majordomo instructions: http://www.menet.umn.edu/docs/software/majordomo

Newsgroups

Whereas messages in mailing lists are somewhat private and appear in a subscriber's e-mail, messages in newsgroups are public and open to anyone who stops to read them. Anybody using anyone's e-mail can post messages. Reporters need to verify all information from Internet sources, but that's especially true of newsgroups.

Newsgroups originated on Usenet, a system of discussion groups. Similar to the World Wide Web, Usenet is a component of the Internet. Reading and responding to messages in some newsgroups may require news reader software (Outlook Express, Netscape Messenger) usually provided by the Internet service provider (ISP), such as a college or university. Other news reader software is embedded in the browser, such as Netscape and Explorer.

Newsgroups are categorized by subject. The type of newsgroup is indicated with a prefix to its name. For example, biz.soccer might be a newsgroup with messages on the economics of managing a soccer team, rec.soccer might have the rules of soccer or the best type of playing field and alt.soccer members might discuss the private lives of players. The following are some general newsgroup categories:

alt.—topics on anything
biz.—business products, services, vendors
comp.—computer hardware, software and reviews
humanities.—fine art, literature, philosophy

misc.—other varied topics, such as health or employment
news.—Usenet information
rec.—hobbies and recreation
sci.—applied and social science
soc.—culture and social topics
talk.—current issues

Two online directories that list newsgroups are Google Groups (http://groups.google.com) and Tile.Net (http://tile.net/news). It is best to read their help sections when starting to use newsgroups. Journalists use keywords not only to search for particular newsgroups, but also to find messages on desired subjects.

Try typing in "journalism" as a keyword to find how many journalism-related newsgroups exist. Journalists also use these directories to find newsgroups that will give them tips about covering their beat or to better understand an issue or event.

Reporters use the following Web site if they have basic questions about a subject discussed in newsgroup: http://www.faqs.org/faqs. Reading each newsgroup's FAQs eliminates common questions, which can test members' patience.

ETHICAL CONSIDERATIONS

The Internet is a useful tool for reporters. However, it is only a tool, supplementing the traditional skills that make great journalists. Reporters still need to exercise good news judgment, write well, interview sources successfully, do research and acquire background information to give a story meaning and context.

The World Wide Web was developed in 1993. Much information compiled earlier is not yet on the Internet. Reporters who rely exclusively on Web sources for their news gathering might unwittingly write inadequate stories. Also, reporters have been duped by Internet sources who pretend to be someone they are not. The pranksters have led reporters to write inaccurate stories, embarrassing themselves and their news organizations. Thus, reporters must verify information, quotes and identities with telephone calls.

Finding experts and businesses in online directories for stories is relatively easy. Yet, many directories do not evaluate or verify "experts." These sources and companies sometimes pay a fee to be included in a directory. In addition to verifying the source's qualifications, journalists should ask themselves why a person would volunteer as an expert.

When journalists participate in mailing lists, newsgroups and chats, they behave online as they would in public and according to their newsroom's code of ethics. Indeed, the Web is a very public place, where the personal opinions of reporters can be traced and their biases publicized. Some news organizations ask their reporters to be circumspect about the opinions they express in personal e-mails and 'blogs. All journalists forego using their business IDs for personal use.

On the job, journalists do not join conversations under false pretenses. They identify themselves and request their information carefully. (In a public arena, such as the Web, other reporters might read inquiries for information and scoop their competition.) If reporters want to quote a participant in an online conversation—not from an interview—then reporters use e-mail to ask sources if they may be quoted, and they follow-up with a phone call to verify the source.

Journalists must confirm the accuracy of all information, but they must use special care with information from the Internet. Anyone can put information—reliable or otherwise—online. Journalists ask questions about accuracy, authority, objectivity and timeliness when evaluating a Web site and its information: Who wrote the content on the Web page and is contact information provided? Who publishes the Web page and what are their creditials? Where is the page published? Why are the page and this information published? Is the coverage comprehensive or does the Web site require specialized software or registration fees for the complete presentation of a subject? Also, when was the information posted and is it still accurate? Reporters use tools, such as Better—whois.com, which lists information about the company or person who has registered a Web site's name.

When journalists use information from the Internet, they attribute it to the author or the Web site or ask the site's administrators for permission to use the material. Web sites are electronic publications, and copying someone else's work and material is unethical and illegal; it is called plagiarism.

SUGGESTED READINGS

Reddick, Randy, and Elliot King. *The Online Journalist,* 3rd ed. Fort Worth, Texas: Harcourt College Publishers, 2001.

Reevy, Matthew M. *Introduction to C-A-R*. Mountain View, Calif: Mayfield Publishing, 2001.

Schlein, Alan M. *Find It Online,* 2nd ed. Tempe, Ariz: Facts on Demand Press, 1999.

USEFUL WEB SITES

For more information on understanding the Internet, see http://library.albany.edu/internet.

For more information on using the different subject directories and search engines, see http://library.albany.edu/choose.html.

EXERCISE 1

USING THE JOURNALISTS' URLS

Use the Journalists' URLs on pages 449–451 in this chapter to help you with this exercise. You will have to go past the home page and into the Web site for most of these exercises. Document where you found your answer and whether you found the Web site useful and efficient for finding information. Explain why or why not.

1. Choose one of the Web sites from each section of the journalists' URLs listed on pages 449–451 in this chapter. In what kind of stories do you think the site's information would be useful? Illustrate the site's usefulness to others in the class.

2. It is a slow news day and you are looking for a feature story. Try the Farmer's Almanac to find out what happened on this day in history.

3. You need more information about starfish for an environmental story. You might look in an online encyclopedia to find another name for starfish, the variety of their colors and the number of their legs.

4. Local gun control experts are not returning your calls or e-mails, and your deadline is looming. Go online to an experts database. Find sources willing to talk on the subject of gun control legislation. Examine their bios. Why are they good sources? What makes them "experts"? Have they published research or work professionally in this area? (Or, did they simply pay a fee to be included in the database?)

5. You are new in town and need to get to your city hall to cover a demonstration. Go online to get a map and directions.

6. You are working on a fire story. You wrote in your notes a phone number with no name attached. It has the local area code and the last four digits of 3479. You cannot remember if it belongs to the victim or the accused. Not wanting to make a faux pas, you use the reverse directory online. Find out whose phone number it is. Also get a map and directions to person's house. Use a criss-cross directory, which lets the user find a person by either name, address or phone number, to find neighbors to interview.

7. Yours is the last of four universities the president is visiting this week to discuss the economy and its effect on higher education. In preparation to report the story, you want to know how the president's visit went at the three other institutions. Where would you go online to find the other student newspapers and how they covered the visit?

8. You are writing a story to cover the anniversary of Sept. 11, 2001. You used a search engine to find a Web site with information about the tragedy. Now, you need to use a domain registration site to contact the owner of the Web site and verify its contents.

9. You want to pitch a few stories to the editor during your interview for a reporting position at your hometown daily. Find out about your audience using census information. In addition to examining government Web sites, check your hometown's community server for demographic information.

10. Just out of curiosity, you want to check the National Register of Sex Offenders. Do you have any offenders living nearby? You might compare the results to state and local registries.

EXERCISE 2

SUBJECT DIRECTORIES AND SEARCH ENGINES

Use the subject directories and search engines on page 453 in this chapter to help you with this exercise. Document the number of responses to your search query and state whether you found the subject directory or search engine useful and efficient for finding information. Explain why or why not. Share your reactions with your classmates.

1. Become familiar with the five subject directories by using their subject categories to search for the same topic. Which one did you like the most, and why?

2. Read the "help" sections of the five subject directories. Using the advanced search areas, carry out the same search on all the subject directories. Compare your results.

3. Become familiar with the five search engines. Using the same search query, repeat assignments No. 1 and No. 2 using search engines.

4. Become familiar with the four metasearch engines. Using the search query, repeat assignments No. 1 and No. 2 using metasearch engines.

5. Do several searches to compare and contrast your favorite subject directory, search engine and metasearch engine. Which one do you like most? Are subject directories better for some searches and search engines better for others?

EXERCISE 3

USING MAILING LISTS AND NEWSGROUPS

Use the mailing lists and newsgroups directories on page 455 in this chapter to help you with this exercise. For each of these assignments, document your procedure and participation in the discussion group. Did you find the mailing lists and newsgroups useful and efficient for gathering information? What are your reactions to the different discussion groups? Compare your experience with that of others in your class.

1. Join a mailing list. It may be about journalism generally, a reporting beat or information for a story. Initiate or participate in a discussion, and then write an analysis of how useful it was.

2. Join a newsgroup discussion. It may be about journalism generally, a reporting beat or information for a story. Again, initiate or participate in a discussion and write an analysis of the experience.

3. Compare your mailing list and newsgroup experiences. Do you like one more than the other? Are lists or groups better for newsgathering purposes?

4. Join a listserv or newsgroup on any topic of your liking, such as a hobby or special interest. How do these conversations differ from those about professional topics?

5. Choose a story appearing in the news. Search some discussion groups for ideas and sources for follow-up stories. List 10 story ideas and 10 experts who might be good sources for some or all of the stories.

EXERCISE 4

UNDERSTANDING AND USING THE INTERNET

Document your Web site journey for these assignments. You might want to share your experience with your class.

1. Find an interesting story in the local news. Using the Internet, investigate follow-up story ideas or sidebars to the main story. What ideas did you find and how? How would you develop these ideas?

2. Locate the Web site of a local news organization (print, broadcast or online) that has a public bulletin board where people can post e-mail messages. Do some of these messages give you story ideas or follow-up story ideas? If so, what are they?

3. Identify a story from the local broadcast news or newspaper. Imagine the story is online. Which words in the story would you use as links to more information, giving readers a more comprehensive understanding of the event or issue? Highlight those words. To which Web sites would you link them? Try this assignment with two other stories.

4. Use the Web to compare local coverage: Identify an event that affects more than one area. How does each online newspaper or broadcast Web site cover the event for its community? Can you explain any differences in the coverage?

5. Use the Web to compare international news coverage. Identify an issue or event that affects more than one country. How do the online newspapers or broadcast Web sites of the different countries report on it? Can you explain any differences in the coverage?

6. Observe how press releases are used: Find day-old press releases online. Then find the newspapers online that covered this news. How was the press release incorporated or used in the story? How much of the press release's information did the newspaper use?

7. Compare the online and print or broadcast products of some news organizations. Are the stories edited or written differently? What are the strengths and weaknesses of each medium?

Name ______________________ Class ______________________ Date ______

EXERCISE 5

UNDERSTANDING AND USING THE INTERNET FOR STORIES

Use some of the Web sites mentioned in this and other chapters to help you with this exercise. Document helpful Web sites and the information you would use in your story.

1. It is election year and your editor has asked you to write bios for the members of Congress from your state who are running for office again. Identify those officials. Then find information for their bios. Try the Senate and House of Representatives Web sites. Perhaps these officials have their own Web sites. What other Web sites might be helpful?

2. It is a week later, and your editor now wants a follow-up story on the legislators' voting records—how they voted on different issues and their voting attendance records. Your first thought is to use Project Vote Smart (vote-smart.org). Would you want to use any other sites?

3. While making your rounds to the schools for your education beat in Michigan, you learn that yet another student has been expelled for verbal assault. Go online to find the top 10 reasons students are expelled from schools in Michigan. A source told you that the Center for Educational Performance and Information, which is in the Office of the State Budgets, collects that information. Can you find the survey online? Where would you find someone to interview? Who are your experts and why? Try finding the same information for your state.

4. You are assigned to cover an important meeting in a township on the outskirts of your city. Your editor tells you the meeting is on a controversial zoning ordinance. Some residents want more development, while others want to keep the area a nature preserve. Your editor says to expect a huge attendance and a demonstration. You need to get some background on the township. (For purposes of this assignment, identify a similar township near you.) The U.S. Census is your best bet for demographic information. You can search geographically or by name or place. Can you compile a profile of township folks?

5. A truck carrying methyl bromide has overturned on a highway in your city. What can you find out quickly about this chemical? Do residents need to be evacuated? What subject directory, search engine or metasearch engine gave you the best results?

6. The oldest man in the United States has died. He was from your state. You want to know what is the longest anyone has lived. Can you find a book of records? The general reference Web sites might help.

7. A woman in your town is leading a strike against funeral homes because of what she says is the high cost of burials; her husband's cost about $5,000. Find out the range of funeral and burial expenses to put her costs and complaints into perspective. Would the fedworld.gov Web site have funeral statistics? Where else could you go

online for information or experts? Perhaps you should check mailing lists and newsgroups for other complaints.

8. Your governor strongly suggests that to attract industry, your state must remove local minimum-wage laws. She says local wage laws set wages higher than the national minimum and are inconsistent throughout the state. A colleague tells you that the Michigan Legislature had this debate in early 2003. You might go to various Michigan newspaper or broadcast Web sites to search their archives. Or, examine your library's online newspaper databases, such as ProQuest, to find the Michigan articles. These stories will give you ideas on how to cover the issue and questions to ask sources. In addition, you might check Michigan government Web sites. Do not forget to find out about the federal minimum wage. Where would you find information to help you with this story?

9. Children must take the state's standardized test to gauge their academic progress. This year's results have just been published. Go to education Web sites to find out more about the education assessment program, procedures and scores, and their importance to school officials and parents. Put your local schools' scores into perspective with state and national averages.

10. Members of the trucking industry are holding a Truck Exposition and Safety Forum conference in your city. Your editor tells you to make your stories more interesting by adding statistics about the trucking industry. What information would you include and where would you find it? Where would you find sources to interview?

EXERCISE 6

UNDERSTANDING AND USING THE INTERNET FOR STORIES

The assignments below need background, statistics and context. As you gather this information, document the following: beneficial search engines and keywords, and useful Web sites, information and experts.

1. The president influences federal legislation. His or her opinions and decisions have important effects on industries. Special-interest contributors give money to politicians in the hope of winning their support. You want to write a story on who contributed to the president's campaign and what effects campaign contributions might have had on any decision-making. Based on this information, what might people expect from the Oval Office? Using the Internet, find out who were the president's top contributors. Also interview some experts through the Internet and get their opinions on the issue.

2. A common concern among all news organizations is diversity on the staff. Some people think that an organization's staff should reflect the makeup of the community. Your editor wants you to write a column about diversity in the newsroom. You'll need the help of a U.S. Census Web site to find your community's demographics. What does the trend seem to be? Compare your community to surounding counties or the state. What does this mean about the ideal composition of your local newspaper's staff? (You'll also have to find out about the makeup of your local paper's news staff by asking the appropriate executive in the newsroom.) Check online what experts say.

3. GM has announced it will begin making Camaros again. You want to profile the older muscle car and compare it with the newer car in your story. How and where do you find out about the history of the car and sources to interview?

4. Junior high school authorities have expelled a student for three days for bringing a pocketknife to school. With Columbine still in mind, emotions run high about children carrying weapons and killing or injuring other children. Some educators say that the media have blown this issue out of proportion. Your editor wants you to write a story about this issue. You will need to find national statistics on juvenile offenders and juvenile victims. Can you find anything local? Identify experts online to interview.

EXERCISE 7

UNDERSTANDING AND USING THE INTERNET FOR CONTEXT

Good reporters do not merely report on local happenings; they also put local events and issues into a national context. Use the Internet to find all the pertinent information you can to give a national context to the local situations presented in this exercise. Do all the research up to the point of writing a story. For each exercise, answer the following: What search engines and keywords did you use? What Web sites did you find useful to the story and why? Would any mailing lists or newsgroups be helpful to your story? Where did you find experts to interview? What makes them authoritative?

1. People in your community are complaining about pollution from carbon dioxide emissions from several local plants. You want to check online whether there is any change of standards for carbon dioxide emissions and how the problem of pollution caused by carbon dioxide is tackled nationwide. You also want to interview some experts through the Internet and get their opinions. This information should give national context to the local situation.

2. Look at the Census online to find out if more people are moving into your community or leaving it. In a survey, people most often cited living costs and crime rates as reasons for leaving a community. Is this still the case? Using the Internet, find the main reasons U.S. citizens move. What do experts say? This information should help prepare you for a story comparing and contrasting the local situation to the national picture.

3. Drunken drivers have caused several car accidents recently in your community. You want to write a story on drunken driving with a national scope. You need to check online the nature and frequency of drunken driving accidents nationwide. See if any national regulations of drunken driving have been proposed or passed recently. If so, how would new federal legislation affect the local regulations? Also, whom would you interview?

4. "Vitamania" is the increased sale of vitamins and other supplements in your state, according to a recent report. Some scientists warn that people should be cautious when using vitamins and other nutrition supplements. Find what most people think when they use vitamins and other nutrition supplements, and check what experts say about vitamin use.

CHAPTER 17

ADVANCED REPORTING

Journalists seem to believe that democratic politics, which alone underwrites their craft, is a self-perpetuating machine that can withstand any amount of undermining. They are wrong.

(James Carey, journalism educator)

This chapter contains advanced reporting skills and exercises. To do well on the exercises, the student must apply the skills developed in the earlier chapters, as well as new ones explained in this chapter. Some of the exercises are longer and more complex than those in previous chapters. However, all the exercises involve the types of stories editors assign reporters during the first years of their careers. The exercises are divided into five categories:

- In-depth stories (Exercises 1-3). These three exercises are genuine; they involve actual letters, statements and other documents. Only a few names and dates have been changed. Unless the exercises mention another time and location, assume each story occurred in your community today.
- Statistical material (Exercises 4-6). These exercises range from the simple to the complex. The challenge is to interpret the numbers and make them interesting to the reader.
- Informal polls (Exercise 7). This group of exercises requires you to pose questions to gauge how people feel about issues and events. The central point of the stories should be about the issue and the results of the poll.
- Computer-assisted reporting (Exercises 8-10). These exercises involve sets of questions to get you thinking like a journalist about where to get information and how to use it to support a story.
- Converging media (Exercise 11). This exercise involves strategies in gathering and presenting news. It employs the newsgathering skills that were discussed in previous chapters along with presentation skills mentioned above.

USING STATISTICS

Much of the information reporters gather comes in the form of statistics. Statistics appear almost daily in news stories concerning budgets, taxes, census data, sports, politics, profits, dividends and annual reports. Other news stories based largely on statistics report rates of crime, productivity, energy consumption, unemployment and inflation. Reporters must learn to present statistics to the public in a form that is both interesting and understandable.

The reporter who writes a news story based on statistics begins best by translating as many numbers as possible into words, which readers can understand more easily. The reporter also tries to analyze the statistics, explaining their significance instead of simply reporting the numbers. Explaining the statistics requires that the reporter looks for and emphasize major trends, record highs and lows, the unusual and the unexpected.

Emphasizing the story's human interest is another technique for explaining statistical stories. Until it was revised, the example below gave numbers only in a routine and dull series. The revision includes a human element. The reporter found someone who received first aid from the fire department. Another version could have examined the false alarms in greater detail. Did they come from a certain area of the city? Was anyone caught and prosecuted for setting off those false alarms? Where were the bomb threats? Was anyone injured?

> The Fire Department's annual report states that last year it responded to the following numbers and types of calls: bomb threats, 60; electrical fires, 201; false alarms, 459; first aid, 1,783; mattress fires, 59; burned pots left on stove, 78; rescues, 18; washdowns, usually of leaking gasoline at the scene of automobile accidents, 227; and water salvage, 46.
>
> REVISED: When Sarah Kindstrom needed help, the fire department responded. Kindstrom's heart attack last week was one of 5,024 calls the department answered last year. First aid requests were the most common, according to the department's annual report, which was released today.
>
> The five leading types of calls included, in order of frequency: first aid, 1,783; false alarms, 459; washdowns, usually of leaking gasoline at the scene of automobile accidents, 227; electrical fires, 201; and burned pots left on stoves, 78.
>
> Other types of calls were bomb threats, 60; mattress fires, 59; water salvage, 46; and rescues, 18.

Stories that rely too heavily on numbers can be deadly for readers, who may perceive them as boring and hard to understand. The reporter's job is to make the numbers interesting so readers will stay with the story from beginning to end. The unusualness of statistical information and its impact on people are what make the story interesting.

Reporters describing election results tell readers more than who won and the number of votes that each candidate received. They search for additional highlights: Did incumbents win or lose? Was any bloc of voters (such as ethnic groups, women or conservatives) decisively for one candidate or another? Were there significant differences in precincts or voting districts from previous elections? Did any candidates win by unusually large or small margins? Answering those kinds of questions can make an election story more interesting than merely reporting who won what races.

Reporters who must include statistics in their stories try to present them as simply as possible. They avoid a series of paragraphs that contain nothing but statistics. Instead, they use transitions, explanations and narrative to break up long strings of numbers and make the information clearer. Reporters also avoid the temptation to editorialize about statistical information. Readers or viewers may not agree with a reporter's characterization of a budget increase as "big" or "huge." While one person may think a 2 percent increase in a $1 billion budget is small, another person may think that adding $20 million to the budget is a great deal.

Reporters who do not present statistical information carefully can mislead the reader. To write that the traffic accident death rate in a small town increased by 100 percent or doubled this year may be accurate. It also may be misleading, however, if one person was killed in a traffic accident last year and two people were killed this year. Placing the statistics in a context that makes their significance clear will prevent distortion.

CONDUCTING INFORMAL POLLS

Reporters often want to know what people think of issues in the news. Traditionally, reporters have gathered opinions by interviewing local experts or people they encounter on the street. Informal polls of this type are fast and cheap, but they cannot accurately describe public opinion because they do not use truly random samples that represent a cross-section of the general population. If reporters go where banks and law offices are concentrated to get public reaction to some issue, they are likely to hear comments different from those that factory workers might express. For this reason, reporters cannot generalize about the results of informal polls. They can report only the opinions of the people interviewed; they cannot suggest that the opinions reflect the sentiment of the community as a whole.

The unreliability of informal polls has encouraged some news organizations to employ more scientific techniques. To conduct a truly accurate poll, reporters must interview a random sample chosen from all the residents in their community. Because that is difficult, some news organizations hire professional pollsters to conduct their polls, especially during election campaigns. A few organizations employ reporters who have the expertise to conduct scientific polls using random samples—usually samples of several hundred people. Because of their more scientific procedures and carefully worded questions, the reporters can accurately determine public opinion about important issues.

Still, informal polls often are interesting and enable reporters to localize issues in the news. Reporters assigned to conduct informal surveys—to ask a dozen people whether they favor a new tax, for example—encourage people to respond with more than a simple yes or no. They ask people why they favor or oppose the tax. If respondents answer with vague generalities, reporters ask them to be more specific. If the responses to the questions are dull, vague or unclear, the story will be equally uninteresting.

The lead should describe as specifically as possible the major finding, which usually is the opinion expressed by a majority of the people interviewed. The lead must do more than report that a poll was conducted or that the respondents were "divided" about the issue. People are divided about every controversial issue, and conducting a poll is not newsworthy. Only the results are likely to interest readers. For these reasons, three of the following leads need to be revised. Only the fourth is well-written:

> NOT NEWS: One hundred college students were polled Tuesday about the war in the Middle East. (This fails to report the news—the results of that poll.)
>
> OBVIOUS: One hundred college students responded with varied answers Tuesday when they were asked, "Should the United States go to war in the Middle East?" (This states the obvious—the fact that people disagree about a controversial issue.)
>
> VAGUE: One hundred college students were interviewed Tuesday, and a majority said the United States should go to war in the Middle East, but only if attacked first. (This lead is too vague; it fails to reveal the size of the majority.)
>
> BETTER: Sixty-eight out of 100 college students interviewed Tuesday said the United States should go to war in the Middle East, but only if attacked first. (Note that this lead does not imply that 68 percent of all college students hold this opinion.)

The two or three paragraphs following the lead should summarize other highlights or trends. The fourth paragraph might quote the exact question asked of each respondent. If the story shifts directly from the lead to a quotation from one of the people interviewed, the transition may be too abrupt and the story will seem disorganized. Also, if the quotation placed in the second paragraph reflects the opinion of just one person, it is probably not important enough to merit that position in the story.

Reporters arrange quotations in a logical order, grouping similar responses and placing transitions between those groups. They look for trends—perhaps consistent differences between the responses of men and women, young and old, students and nonstudents. (When the story is based on an informal poll, reporters are careful not to imply that such trends are present in the entire population.)

After the lead and two to four paragraphs summarizing the results, poll stories usually begin by quoting respondents who expressed the majority viewpoint, then people who expressed opposing viewpoints. Some opinions may be divided into even smaller groups. For example, if the respondents who favor an issue gave four reasons for their beliefs, the story first might quote respondents who mentioned the most popular reason, then quote those who cited the second, third and fourth most popular reasons.

Transitions should be logical and informative, linking ideas from preceding paragraphs. Many summarize the viewpoint of the group of quotations that reporters are about to present. The following transitions appeared in a story about high school students' opinions of the Army. The paragraphs following each transition quoted students who expressed the viewpoint summarized in the transition:

> Fourteen students said they consider service in the Army a patriotic duty.
>
> Seven students said they plan to join the Army because they want to travel but cannot afford to go overseas by themselves.
>
> Four women said the Army offers higher salaries than civilian employers and is more willing to promote women.

Reporters do not quote simple yes or no responses when reporting the opinions of respondents. If the fourth paragraph in a story quotes the question that each respondent was asked, and the 10th paragraph reports that one person responded yes, readers may not realize the person was responding to the question presented six paragraphs earlier:

> Rebecca Pearson of 318 Ashton Drive responded, "Yes."
>
> REVISED: Rebecca Pearson of 318 Ashton Drive agreed that the cost of housing in the city is becoming too expensive for most home buyers.

Reporters also try to be specific and clear in characterizing responses, even if it means briefly restating an idea:

> Sandy Roach, a senior biology major, more or less agreed with Miss Hass.
>
> REVISED: Sandy Roach, a senior biology major, agreed that government workers are overpaid but said it is the fault of politicians, not of unions representing government workers.

Poll stories should identify fully every person quoted. Reporters identify most sources by name, age and address (or hometown for people from outside the community). Because of concerns about privacy, some news organizations no longer use addresses; instead, they identify sources by occupation, neighborhood or hometown. Experts or community leaders should be identified by name, title and organization. Identification for students should consist of major and year in school; for faculty, their rank and department; and for nonacademic employees, their departments and job titles.

Some people may refuse to identify themselves. Reporters have three choices for dealing with them: (1) Ask them why they do not want to be identified and try to overcome their objections; (2) offer to identify them by age or occupation instead of name; or (3) thank them and find others who are willing to be identified. Editors and news directors tell their reporters which of these options to follow. But it is important that opinions be attributed to their sources so readers don't think they are the reporter's views.

A poll story needs to quote only those respondents who say something colorful, important or unusual, not every person interviewed. Reporters paraphrase or discard responses that are awkward, wordy, unclear or repetitious. They select the most interesting statements, then devote several paragraphs to those remarks. A story that quotes 10 or 20 people and devotes one paragraph to each will seem choppy and superficial.

If two people make similar replies to poll questions, reporters combine their responses in a single sentence or paragraph. Note, however, that because two people are unlikely to use exactly the same words, the same direct quotation cannot be attributed to both of them. Instead, reporters paraphrase their responses or say several people expressed the same opinion, then quote one of them to illustrate that point of view. For example:

> Lionel Jackson and Eugene Bushnell, both seniors majoring in political science, said that the state's tax discriminates against the poor.
>
> Three students said they dropped out of college for a year or more. Marsha Dilte, a senior, explained: "I was running out of money, and I really wasn't certain what I wanted to do. After two years of working as a secretary, I had enough money to finish college, and I knew I wanted to be a nurse."

Reporters should never criticize or attach labels to respondents' answers. They do not refer to any answers as "interesting," "thoughtful" or "uninformed." They simply report whatever respondents said and let readers judge the remarks for themselves. (Readers' conclusions may be quite different from the reporter's.) Reporters also avoid making comments about the manner in which people responded to questions, and they are especially careful to avoid trite generalities. For example, they do not report that one person seemed "sincere" or that another seemed "apathetic." However, they may report specific details; for instance, a reporter might describe how one person paused for nearly a minute before answering a question, then addressed the issue for nearly 30 minutes.

Some people reporters attempt to interview may be undecided about or unfamiliar with the topic. People who are undecided or uninformed usually constitute a small minority and can be mentioned in the story's final paragraphs. The final paragraphs also might describe the methods reporters used to conduct the poll: the exact number of people interviewed and the way they were selected. The closing paragraphs, however, should never summarize the findings; a news story contains only one summary, and it belongs in the lead.

USING COMPUTERS TO GET ANSWERS

Newspapers have been using computers for many years. They make writing, editing and page layout and design (pagination) much faster and flexible. In addition, most papers use computers for handling photographs, eliminating the need for a darkroom. However, news organizations have found an even more powerful use for computers—as a means to gather and disseminate statistical information. Over the past decade, as much information went online or was stored in databases, journalists began viewing numbers in a different way. At many news organizations today, computers rather than pocket calculators help reporters analyze budgets, reports, surveys and polls.

Twenty years ago, only national or large regional newspapers were using computers to help spot trends and patterns in the information that crossed their desks. A recent compilation of 100 computer-assisted reporting stories showed that small news outlets have jumped on the technology bandwagon. Surveys of newspaper editors have found that more than 66 percent of their newspapers use computers as reporting tools in some manner.

Journalists apply the term "computer-assisted reporting" to a wide range of practices. Computers provide access to the Internet, where reporters use e-mail to communicate with sources and other reporters. Journalists also use the World Wide Web to gather information. Perhaps the most sophisticated use of computers in news reporting, however, is to analyze information in electronic databases that reporters have compiled on their own or have obtained from government agencies. These databases may contain vast amounts of information, and analyzing them without computers would consume months of time. With computers, however, reporters can analyze data quickly and thoroughly.

Databases are nothing new. A common example is a city directory—an alphabetical listing of people and businesses. But because the data are in a paper format, analysis would be difficult. For example, it would be difficult to calculate what percentage of the people listed in the city directory owned their homes instead of renting. Once the data are in electronic form, that calculation can be performed quickly using a database management program.

Computer-assisted reporting projects often compare two or more databases to see what they have in common. The Ann Arbor (Mich.) News followed up a tip that a local judge running for the state Supreme Court was strong-arming attorneys for campaign contributions. A reporter approached the story with three databases: a list of all the campaign donations for the judge, a list of attorneys practicing in the county and the results of cases those attorneys argued before that judge.

Other news organizations have used computer-assisted reporting to obtain stories about agriculture, business, child welfare, crime, discrimination, education, the environment, health care, highway safety and the justice system, to name some general areas. The opportunities are endless. And the stories often attract readers and viewers.

Computer-assisted reporting is an extensive topic, and this section offers only a glimpse of its uses. With continuing advances in computer technology, even small papers can employ computer-assisted reporting to give their readers more in-depth information on issues. News editors and station managers are requiring more computer-assisted reporting skills of the new reporters they hire. The student who graduates with some basic computer skills in using spreadsheet software (such as QuattroPro, Excel and Lotus 1-2-3) and relational databases (such as FoxPro, Paradox, dBase and Access) will move to the front of the line in the job market. It also will be important for students to prove they can apply that knowledge to real stories. Reporters must learn to see the possibilities, develop story ideas and write stories that use these skills.

Computer-assisted reporting does not replace good, old-fashioned reporting skills. Computers do not interview sources, and they are only as good as the information that goes into them. They are merely another tool used by reporters to provide information to the public.

CONVERGING MEDIA

Journalists in the future will have to be flexible. Because of technological advances as well as changes in the business of news and mass communication, news writers will need more skills to navigate the profession of journalism. Students will need not only to become good writers and editors but also to develop good oral communication skills to present news in real time. The growth of media conglomerates owning newspapers, radio stations and television stations or networks, cable news channels and Web sites means news and information may be processed and disseminated in a variety of ways by the same reporter. Print journalists working on a story for their newspaper may find themselves presenting the same story in a segment of the news organization's television station or posting the story to the newspaper's Web site. Photojournalists may go to a news event armed with a digital still camera and a digital video camera to capture photos for the newspaper and video for the Web site. The term being used for this phenomenon is "media convergence."

The Orlando (Fla.) Sentinel, starting in the mid-1990s, was one of the first news organizations to bring together a newspaper, television news station and a Web site in presenting news to a changing audience. In fact, television, newspaper and Web reporters share the same building. This allows the station manager and production people for the television station to stay in close contact with the news editors on the print side and the Web page editors on the Internet side. Ideas for stories are shared among the three entities and teams of reporters from each entity often work on stories together.

Media convergence is not only a phenomenon that affects future journalists who gather and disseminate information, but also a phenomenon that affects audiences who seek and assimilate information. In the past, people read a newspaper and talked to other people to find out what was going on in their communities and around the world. Today, people seek information from many sources. A news report emanating from a clock radio may start their day. As they eat breakfast or get ready for work they may watch one of the 24-hour cable news channels. As they drive to work they may listen to an all-news/talk station on their car radio. When they get to work, they turn on their computer and may connect to a newspaper Web site for the business news. When they get home at night, they may sit down with a newspaper or magazine. People get their information from many sources today, and the trend is expected to continue.

To prepare for the future, students will need to learn to adapt the information they gather for presentation on a number of platforms. Beginning journalists will need to learn how to write well because no matter what platform the information is presented on, the content needs to be well-written. Once they learn the mechanics of grammar and spelling, AP style and news story structure, students will need to learn to prepare the information for dissemination in print, on the Web and in video. In addition to learning how to write news stories, students also should learn to shoot and edit video, create digital radio spots and make Web animations. The key to learning about convergence is to be flexible.

CHECKLIST FOR USING STATISTICS

1. Verify the accuracy of statistical information.
2. Make the central point of your story reflect the most important or unusual aspects of the statistical information.
3. Present statistical information in a concise and understandable way.
4. Look for links between statistics that may make the story more interesting for the reader.
5. Do not editorialize about statistical information. Let the numbers speak for themselves and let readers make their own judgment.

CHECKLIST FOR CONDUCTING INFORMAL POLLS

1. Ask questions that encourage respondents to say more than yes or no. Try to get beyond vague generalities to more specific issues and details.
2. Make the lead as specific as possible in describing the results of the poll.
3. Don't shift abruptly from the lead to quotations from respondents. Use three or four paragraphs after the lead to describe the findings and report the exact wording of the question asked.
4. Look for trends or groups of similar responses.
5. Write strong transitions between sections of the story.
6. Do not criticize or editorialize about the responses; simply report them.
7. Never imply that the results of an informal poll can predict how the community in general thinks about an issue.

A Memo From the Editor

GOOD WRITING'S GREAT, BUT IT'S NOT ENOUGH

By **Tommy Miller**

Journalists put a lot of emphasis on writing—good writing. That's good, but an unbalanced focus on writing style overlooks a key element of good writing—reporting. Good reporting is the foundation for good writing.

And, occasionally I'm concerned that journalists concentrate so much on writing style, especially in feature stories, that the importance of strong enterprise news reporting is overlooked.

(*continued*)

The writing is important, but the primary emphasis of any good newspaper should be news. Here are some key points, or reminders, for digging up strong news stories:

- **Think news first.** The features will come naturally. Think about stories that have impact, stories that mean something to the lives of readers. Stories that make readers snap back and say "Wow! I didn't know about this!"
- **Read, read, read!** Obviously, you must read your own newspaper. And you should read other regional and national newspapers. You need to know what's in the papers, what stories are hot and what stories are not. Scan media and Web news sources as needed to learn of emerging stories. Good reporters should have a feel for what's going on.
- **Develop sources.** Beat reporters, of course, know that source development is essential to good reporting. But general assignment reporters too often have poorly developed sources. It's important for GA reporters to get out of the office, to meet people who can serve as reliable sources for story information. And remember that every source in one story is someone who may call later about another story.
- **Be aggressive.** At times, reporters and editors go into a reporting situation with the attitude that there is no story. Reverse the thinking. Go into each situation believing that a story is there. Then, either support it or knock it down with good reporting.
- **Localize, localize.** Look for ways to spin off local stories from stories in other newspapers.
- **Develop an area of expertise.** This is especially important for general assignment reporters. For example, a Houston Chronicle reporter once produced good stories for weeks about the zoo and zoo safety after a lion killed a local zookeeper. She extended topical immigration amnesty issues into a minibeat and produced a number of very good spot news stories. Another reporter did the same for the subject of care for the mentally ill in Texas.
- **Follow up, follow up, follow up!** Pursue loose ends and holes in previous stories. The reader expects a follow up on good stories. Especially Page One stories. If a story is good enough for Page One, it deserves a follow-up story the next day.
- **Keep up pursuit on a major story.** On a continuing story, keep pursuing fresh angles until the story is exhausted.
- **Aggressively pursue tips.** A tough part of reporting is filtering the good tips from the bad tips and deciding whether a potential story is "gettable." Initially, any reasonable tip must be checked out.

  For example, after joining the Philadelphia Inquirer in the 1980s, John Woestendiek was assigned to the prisons beat, which one editor described as a less than glamorous assignment. Woestendiek worked the beat hard and read every letter sent to him by inmates. One day he got a letter from an inmate who insisted he had information that would prove that another inmate wasn't guilty of murder. Woestendiek worked the story and finally convinced himself and then-Inquirer Editor Gene Roberts of the convicted killer's innocence. Eventually, the man was pardoned. Woestendiek won a Pulitzer Prize for his work in 1987.

- **Focus on detail in your reporting.** The more detail the better. The Anchorage Daily News won a Pulitzer Prize in 1989 with a series of stories that stemmed from a follow-up and ended with a powerful collection of details.

  The story began when the state's epidemiologist revealed massive underreporting of Alaska's suicide statistics, particularly in rural areas.

  Daily News reporters and editors followed up that study by re-examining routine obituaries of Alaskan Eskimos, Indians and Aleuts. After the reporters discovered that many had not died of natural causes, the newspaper got to work and later produced a series that ran for 10 days, showing how widespread despair among native men led to suicides, murders and sexual assaults.

- **Think about a news lead before a feature lead.** If you have a strong news story, consider a straight news lead over an alternative lead. Sometimes, the impact of a story is lost by backing into it with a nicely written feature lead. Sometimes the best lead is a straightforward approach, one that simply tells the story.

  Perhaps the late New York Times sports columnist Red Smith said it best. For a newspaper reporter, Smith said, "the essential thing is to report the facts; if there's time for good writing as well, that's frosting on the cake."

Adapted from "Good Writing's Great, But It's Not Enough," published in September 1988, in The Write Stuff, an in-house publication of the Houston Chronicle.

Tommy Miller holds the Roger Tatarian Endowed Chair of Professional Journalism at California State University, Fresno. He is a former managing editor of the Houston Chronicle.

SUGGESTED READINGS

Barnett, Tracy L., ed. *IRE 100 Selected Computer-Assisted Investigations*, Book II. Columbia, Mo.: Investigative Reporters and Editors and the National Institute for Computer-Assisted Reporting. Hillsdale, N.J.: Erlbaum, 1995.

Fink, Arlene, and Jacqueline Kosecoff. *How to Conduct Surveys: A Step-by-Step Guide*. Beverly Hills, Calif.: Sage, 1985.

Garrison, Bruce. *Computer-Assisted Reporting*. Hillsdale, N.J.: Lawrence Erlbaum Associates, 1995.

Gunter, Barrie. *News and the Net*. Mahwah, N.J.: Lawrence Erlbaum Associates, 2003.

Jaeger, Richard M. *Statistics: A Spectator Sport,* 2nd ed. Newbury Park, Calif.: Sage, 1990.

Houston, Brant. *Computer-Assisted Reporting: A Practical Guide*. New York: St. Martin's Press, 1996.

———, Len Bruzzese and Steve Weinberg. *The Investigative Reporter's Handbook: A Guide to Documents, Databases and Techniques,* 4th ed. New York: Bedford/St.Martin's, 2002.

Keenan, Thomas W., and Wendy Hui Kyong Chun, eds. *New Media, Old Media: Interrogating the Digital Revolution*. New York: Routledge, 2003.

McCombs, Maxwell, and Amy Reynolds. *The Poll with a Human Face: The National Issues Convention Experiment in Political Communication*. Mahwah, N.J.: Lawrence Erlbaum Associates, 1999.

Reddick, Randy, and Elliot King. *The Online Journalist*. Fort Worth, Texas: Harcourt College Publishers, 1995.

Virtual Reality: Newspapers and the Information Superhighway. Reston, Va.: American Press Institute, 1994.

EXERCISE 1

ADVANCED REPORTING IN-DEPTH STORY

JUDICIAL PAY RAISES

This is a statement by the American Bar Association from a report of the National Commission on Public Service regarding the disparity of salaries for federal judges compared to the executive and legislative branches of government. Write a story summarizing its content. At the end of the story, list the sources you would interview to write a more thorough story, along with questions you would ask each source.

Congress should grant an immediate and significant increase in judicial, executive and legislative salaries to ensure a reasonable relationship to other professional opportunities.

Judicial salaries are the most egregious example of the failure of federal compensation policies. Federal judicial salaries have lost 24 percent of their purchasing power since 1969, which is arguably inconsistent with the Constitutional provision that judicial salaries may not be reduced by Congress. The United States currently pays its judges substantially less than England or Canada. Supreme Court justices have pointed out in testimony before the National Commission on Public Service that, in 1969, the salaries of district court judges had just been raised to $40,000 while the salary of the dean of Harvard Law School was $33,000 and that of an average senior professor was $28,000.

That relationship has now been erased. A recent study by the Administrative Office of the U.S. Courts of salaries of professors and deans at the twenty-five law schools ranked highest in the annual U.S. News and World Report survey found that the average salary for deans of those law schools was $301,639. The average base salary for full professors at those law schools was $209,571, with summer research and teaching supplements typically ranging between $33,000 and $80,000. Federal district judges currently earn $150,000.

Also in testimony before the Commission, the Chief Justice of the Supreme Court noted that, according to the Administrative Office of the United States Courts, more than 70 Article III judges left the bench between 1999 and May 2002, either under the retirement statute, if eligible, or simply resigning if not, as did an additional number of bankruptcy and magistrate judges. During the 1960s on the other hand, only a handful of Article III judges retired or resigned.

The lag in judicial salaries has gone on too long, and the potential for diminished quality in American jurisprudence is now too large. Too many of America's best lawyers have declined judicial appointments. Too many senior judges have sought private sector employment—and compensation—rather than making the important contributions we have long received from judges in senior status.

Unless this is revised soon, the American people will pay a high price for the low salaries we impose on the men and women in whom we invest responsibility for the dispensation of justice. We are not suggesting that we should pay judges at levels comparable to those of the partners at our nation's most prestigious law firms. Most judges take special satisfaction in their work and in public service. The more reasonable comparisons are with the leading academic centers and not-for-profit institutions. But even those comparisons now indicate a significant shortfall in real judicial compensation that requires immediate correction.

Congress should break the statutory link between the salaries of members of Congress and those of judges and senior political appointees.

Congress has traditionally tied the salaries of senior executive branch employees and federal judges to its own. In 1989 the linkage was set in statute. Given the reluctance of members of Congress to risk the disapproval of their constituents, a phenomenon first seen in 1816, Congress has regularly permitted salaries to fall substantially behind cost-of-living increases and trends in private, educational and not-for-profit compensation.

We are aware that recent research suggests that pay disparities at the middle and lower levels of the federal workforce may be less significant than previously believed. However, the "pay gap" at the top of the salary structure is indisputable, as are its consequences in lost morale and uncertain accountability. Its consequences also are clear in the presidential appointments process, which must increasingly focus on the relatively affluent or those for whom an appointment process represents a dramatic increase in compensation, neither of which is appropriate in itself for public service.

We believe that members of Congress are entitled to reasonable and regular salary adjustments, but we fully understand the difficulty they face in justifying their own salary increases. Whatever political difficulties they face in setting their own salaries, however, members of Congress must make the quality of the public service their paramount concern when they consider salary adjustments for top officials of the other branches of government. We believe that executive and judicial salaries must be determined by procedures that tie them to the needs of the government, not the career-related political exigencies of Congress.

Although members of Congress have the power to adjust their own salaries, judges and senior executives do not have such power. Under current law, they are at the mercy of the Congress when it comes to salary adjustments. That mercy should not be strained by the inherent difficulty of congressional salary decisions. Salaries for leaders of the other branches should be based on the compelling need to recruit and retain the best people possible. Delinking congressional salaries from theirs is a first step in accomplishing that.

EXERCISE 2

ADVANCED REPORTING IN-DEPTH STORY

HEALTH CARE GRANTS

Write a news story that summarizes this report about health care grants awarded by the U.S. Department of Health and Human Services. At the end of your story, list the sources you would interview to write a more thorough story, along with the questions you would ask each source.

The U.S. Department of Health and Human Services announced Monday the awarding of grants to support health care services. A total of 19 new grants were awarded to help communities provide comprehensive health care services to an estimated 150,000 people, including many without health insurance.

Health centers deliver preventive and primary care to patients regardless of their ability to pay. Almost half of the patients treated at health centers have no insurance coverage, and others have inadequate coverage. Charges for health care services are set according to income, and fees are not collected from the poorest clients.

The grants continue the department's and the government's five-year initiative to expand health centers around the country. Launched in 2002, the initiative will add 1,200 new and expanded health center sites and increase the number of people served annually from about 10 million to 16 million by 2006.

"These grants will help to extend the health care safety net for Americans without health insurance," HHS Secretary Tommy G. Thompson said. "We are committed to expanding health centers in underserved rural and urban communities as part of our broader strategy to address the needs of Americans without health insurance."

HHS' Health Resources and Services Administration (HRSA) manages the Consolidated Health Centers Program, which funds a national network of community health centers, migrant health centers, health care for the homeless centers and public housing primary care centers.

Expanding health centers in underserved communities is a key component of the government's broad strategy for expanding access to health care for the more than 40 million Americans without health insurance. The government's fiscal year 2004 budget plan also would strengthen and modernize the Medicaid program, offer health tax credits to help individuals obtain insurance, and extend Medicaid and State Children's Health Insurance Program (SCHIP) coverage to more Americans who otherwise would go without coverage.

"Since the initiative started, we have created hundreds of new health center sites and expanded other sites," HRSA Administrator Elizabeth M. Duke said. "We are providing access to comprehensive health care to some 2 million additional Americans, including many uninsured Americans who otherwise might not get needed care and prevention services."

The list of grant recipients follows.

Fiscal Year 2003 Health Center New Access Point Grants

Organization	City	State	New Users	Proposed Area	Award
Mountain Park Health Center	Phoenix	Ariz.	7,000	Phoenix, Maricopa County	$858,633
Community Health Systems, Inc.	Bloomington	Calif.	4,850	Riverside, Riverside County	376,227
San Diego Family Care	San Diego	Calif.	28,026	San Diego, San Diego County	650,000
North East Medical Services	San Francisco	Calif.	4,600	San Francisco, San Francisco County	325,000
Brookside Community Health Center	San Pablo	Calif.	3,000	Richmond, Contra Costa County	450,000
Limon Doctors Committee dba Plains Medical Center	Limon	Colo.	12,207	Lincoln, Elbert, Kit Carson, Adams and Arapahoe Counties	650,000
McKinney Community Health Center, Inc.	Waycross	Ga.	4,494	St. George, Charlton County	550,000
Family Christian Harvey Health Center	Harvey	Ill.	9,443	Harvey, Cook County	649,707
Detroit Health Care for the Homeless, Inc.	Detroit	Mich.	7,675	Brightmoor, Cody/Rouge and Redford communities of Detroit, Wayne County	866,667
Peoples' Health Center of Lincoln	Lincoln	Neb.	8,900	Lincoln, Lancaster County	650,000
Community Healthcare Network	New York	N.Y.	5,040	Washington Heights, Manhattan	650,000
Betances Health Center	New York	N.Y.	10,624	Lower East Side of Manhattan	650,000
Goshen Medical Center, Inc.	Faison	N.C.	8,411	Beulaville, Duplin County	325,000
Central City Concern	Portland	Ore.	8,770	Portland, Multnomah County	650,000
Umpqua Community Health Center, Inc.	Roseburg	Ore.	1,500	Glide, Douglas County	365,950

Organization	City	State	New Users	Proposed Area	Award
Christ Community Health Services, Inc.	Memphis	Tenn.	18,715	Memphis, Shelby County	650,000
Bear Lake Community Health Centers, Inc.	Garden City	Utah	1,480	Rich County, Utah; Lake County, Idaho	384,658
Valley Health Systems, Inc.	Huntington	W.Va.	5,900	Westmoreland, Wayne County	603,394
Community Health Center of Central Wyoming, Inc.	Casper	Wyo.	2,500	Dubois, Fremont County	445,313
Total					**$10,750,549**

EXERCISE 3

ADVANCED REPORTING IN-DEPTH STORY

JUVENILE SHOPLIFTING

Write a news story that summarizes this report about juvenile shoplifters. At the end of your story, list the sources you would interview to write a more thorough story, along with the questions you would ask each source.

THE JUVENILE SHOPLIFTER

Shoplifting is the largest monetary crime in the nation. Annual retail losses have been recently estimated at $16 billion nationally and as high as 7.5% of dollar sales. Shoplifting-related costs have been cited as a prime cause in one-third of all bankruptcies in small businesses. Shoplifting losses are on the rise with a 300 percent increase in the incidence of this crime during the 1990s alone.

Juveniles make up the largest percentage of shoplifters. Several studies have revealed that juvenile shoplifters account for approximately fifty percent of all shoplifting.

To gain further insight into the shoplifting problem, George P. Moschis, Professor of Marketing at Georgia State University, and Professor Judith Powell of the University of Richmond surveyed 7,379 students ages 7 to 19 in urban, suburban and rural areas using methods that insured anonymity of responses.

Some key findings:

- Approximately one out of three juveniles said they had shoplifted.
- Among teen-agers ages 15 to 19, about 43% had shoplifted.
- Male youths shoplift more than females; approximately 41% of the males and 26% of the females reported having shoplifted at some time.
- A large amount of shoplifting is done by relatively few juveniles. Approximately 14 percent of those who admitted to shoplifting indicated repeat shoplifting behavior.
- In comparison with non-shoplifters, youths who shoplift are more likely to believe that shoplifting is not a crime.
- Motives for shoplifting are primarily social rather than economic, especially among girls.
- A great deal of shoplifting is done because of peer pressure, especially among girls.
- About half of the time shoplifting takes place in the presence of peers.
- Shoplifting with peers is more common among girls than boys (61% vs. 47%).
- Females show greater tendency to shoplift with others than males.
- Females tend to shoplift more frequently in the presence of others with age.
- Boys tend to shoplift more frequently alone (less frequently with others) with age.
- Shoplifting done by juveniles is primarily impulsive; four times out of five it is done on impulse.
- Female juveniles who shoplift are more likely to shoplift on impulse. Approximately 87% of females and 76% of males who admitted they had shoplifted decided to shoplift after they entered the store.

- Older teen-age girls are more likely to shoplift on impulse than older teen-age boys.
- Older boys tend to plan out shoplifting more than girls.
- There is a decline in impulse shoplifting with age and an increase in planned shoplifting among boys. No decline in impulsive shoplifting behavior is shown for girls.
- Impulsive (unplanned) shoplifting in the presence of others is not only more common among girls, but it also becomes more frequent with age. Impulsive shoplifting among boys in the presence of others does not increase with age.

The findings regarding differences in shoplifting behavior due to age and sex characteristics are expected to apply to other parts of the country, and they are consistent with the results of previous studies.

The authors recommend two broad strategies for reducing shoplifting losses: shoplifting prevention and shoplifting detection. Among shoplifting prevention methods, the authors suggest promotional campaigns that would increase awareness of the seriousness of the crime, and methods that would increase the difficulty of shoplifting. Proposed shoplifting detection strategies focus on educating security-detection personnel to be alert to the shoplifter's early warning signals, including knowledge of characteristics of youths most likely to shoplift.

EXERCISE 4

STATISTICAL MATERIAL

Write a news story about the services provided over the past year by your state's Department of Human Services for victims of domestic and sexual violence. Develop a list of sources you would interview to write a more complete story, along with questions that you would ask each of them.

SUMMARY OF SERVICES PROVIDED BY DOMESTIC AND SEXUAL VIOLENCE SERVICE PROGRAMS

JANUARY THROUGH DECEMBER

Your state's Department of Human Services administers funding for both domestic violence shelter and related services contracts and for sexual assault crisis lines and crisis center contracts.

Last year, DHS contracted with 23 agencies throughout the state that provided crisis lines, emergency shelters and related services to survivors of domestic violence and their children. DHS also contracted with 27 agencies last year that provided crisis line and crisis center services to survivors of sexual assault. Twenty-five of those agencies also had contracts for domestic violence services. One agency subcontracted with two additional agencies for specialized services to survivors of sexual assault.

DHS began administering the sexual assault support program in July 2000 with the first contracts being awarded in May 2001. Programs now report whether the primary issue for the survivor was:

- domestic violence (DV),
- sexual assault (SA) or,
- both domestic violence and sexual assault (DV/SA).

During the past year, 30 contracted programs operated shelter facilities. The remaining four used safe homes and/or motels.

There are approximately 570 shelter beds for both adults and children in these shelters. This is supplemented by safe homes and motels, but still cannot meet the need. The domestic violence programs kept track of the number of times victims requested shelter, but were not sheltered due to lack of space.

The following table shows the number of adult victims who received emergency shelter through all programs, the number of adult shelter nights, the number of children, the number of child nights, and the number of requests for shelter from adults that could not be met due to lack of space. That number may include duplication as women may have contacted more than one shelter.

# of adult women	2771
# of adult nights	44,189
# of children under 6	1464
# of children 6 & older	1259
# of child nights	42,310
# of unfilled adult requests	11,760

The number of adults sheltered decreased slightly from the previous year, but the number of adult nights increased.

The following table shows the pattern of stays for adult victims.

# of Nights	# of Adults	Percent
1 to 3	924	33.35%
4 to 7	426	15.37%
8 to 15	465	16.78%
16 to 31	544	19.63%
over 31	412	14.87%

The following three tables show demographics characteristics by numbers of those adult victims sheltered, either in shelter facilities, safe homes or motels. For this year's report, we combined ages over 55 into one category.

Age	# of Adults	Percent
under 21	247	8.91%
21-30	908	32.77%
31-45	1214	43.81%
46-55	293	10.57%
over 55	91	3.28%
unknown/blank	18	0.65%

Ethnic Background	# Adults	Percent
Asian/SE Asian	37	1.34%
African-American	200	7.22%
European Descent/Caucasian	1918	69.22%
Native American or Alaskan Native	150	5.41%
Native Hawaiian or other Pacific Islander	11	0.40%
Hispanic/Latina	343	12.38%
Middle Eastern/Arabic	2	0.07%
Multi-cultural/racial	65	2.35%
unknown/blank	45	1.62%

Beginning this year, DHS added the categories "former co-habitant" and "dating partner" to the relationship of the abuser.

Relationship of Abuser	# Adults	Percent
spouse	926	33.42%
ex-spouse	140	5.05%
child	18	0.65%
co-habitant	1131	40.82%
parent	68	2.45%
dating partner	103	3.72%
other	276	9.96%
unknown/blank	109	3.93%

NON-SHELTER SERVICES

Programs also operate crisis lines and offer non-shelter services to victims of sexual assault and/or domestic violence. During 2002, there were over 189,800 calls to domestic violence and/or sexual assault programs. Calls included both crisis and non-crisis service calls. The calls were coded as being primarily:

domestic violence	88,520
sexual assault	8278
domestic violence & sexual assault	14,427
other issue (suicide, homelessness, etc.)	78,601

Programs also provide services to victims who are not in emergency shelter. The table below shows the number of adults who received those in-person services. Victims are counted only once per month, even though they may receive more than one service during that month. The monthly average is a way to reduce some of the duplication in the count.

The services provided include:

PEER SUPPORT: group or individual sessions designed to validate the experience of the victim, explore with her options and advocate for her safety, build on her strengths, and respect her right to self-determination.

ADVOCACY: assistance in obtaining needed services when victims were unable to adequately represent themselves.

INFORMATION AND REFERRAL: brief assessment of needs and provision of appropriate referrals to meet those needs.

Programs report whether the primary issue for the survivor was:

- domestic violence (DV),
- sexual assault (SA) or,
- both domestic violence and sexual assault (DV/SA).

An average of 2946 adults per month received in-person services from the domestic violence and sexual assault service providers.

	DV	DV/SA	SA
transportation for adults	10,726	1099	388
accompaniment of adults to hospital	627	155	263
court advocacy for adults	10,464	1555	446
speaking engagements	2156	1228	614

Volunteers play key roles in providing services. They answer the crisis lines, staff shelters, advocate in court, serve on boards of directors, do fund-raising and educate their community. During the fiscal year, there were a total of over 282,000 volunteer hours donated to the programs.

EXERCISE 5

STATISTICAL MATERIAL

The Uniform Crime Report for your state has just been released. Write a news story about the rates of crime in your state, which are listed below.

The state police conduct its Uniform Crime Reporting Study each year. It collects the statistics from local police departments. The results, released today, cover Crime Index Offenses, which are considered to be the most serious and most likely to be reported crimes.

Also, develop a list of sources you would interview to improve the story, along with questions that you would ask each of them.

UNIFORM CRIME REPORT

There were 987,037 actual crimes of all types reported to the Uniform Crime Report Program by law enforcement agencies throughout the state last year. This total represents a rate of 8,195.2 crimes per 100,000 estimated population, an increase of 4.1 percent over last year's total of 948,320 actual crimes.

Crime Index Offenses are considered to be both the most serious and most likely to be reported and are used nationally as the standard base for comparisons. They are crimes identified by law enforcement that readily come to the attention of police and occur with a frequency great enough to be reported as a separate category. They include: murder and non-negligent manslaughter, forcible rape, robbery, aggravated assault, burglary, larceny/theft, motor vehicle theft and arson.

There were 408,546 Crime Index offenses reported to the state police by local law enforcement agencies. That represents an average of 1,119.3 offenses reported each day or one every minute and 17 seconds. This is an increase of 0.9 percent over the 404,738 offenses reported last year. The Crime Index rate was 3,392.1 crimes per 100,000 estimated population.

The following table lists a time scale breakdown of Crime Index offenses:

- One Index Crime every 1 minute 17 seconds.
  - One violent crime every 10 minutes 18 seconds
    - One murder every 10 hours 55 minutes
    - One rape every 2 hours 48 minutes
    - One robbery every 25 minutes 22 seconds
    - One aggravated assault every 19 minutes 56 seconds
  - One property crime every 1 minute 28 seconds
    - One burglary every 6 minutes 18 seconds
    - One larceny/theft every 2 minutes 30 seconds
    - One motor vehicle theft every 8 minutes 47 seconds
    - One arson every 2 hours 19 minutes

The following table lists the number and percentage distribution of Crime Index Offenses and the clearance rate (percentage of cases solved and arrests made). The CIO is divided into Violent Crime and Property Crime.

Violent Crime	# Reported	% of Total	% Cleared
Murder	802	0.2%	80.7%
Aggravated Assault	26,358	6.5%	62.7%
Forcible Rape	3,130	0.8%	64.1%
Robbery	20,718	5.1%	32.0%
Property Crime			
Burglary	83,341	20.4%	16.6%
Arson	3,775	0.9%	22.9%
Motor Vehicle Theft	59,818	14.6%	17.6%
Larceny/Theft	210,604	51.5%	24.6%

To assist the state in distributing funding support for local law enforcement agencies, the state is divided into six "common human service regions," or CHSRs. These regions are used for planning and reporting purposes. The following table summarizes the distribution of the Crime Index Offenses among the six regions.

CHSRs	Crime Index Offenses	Percent Distribution	Crime Index Rate	Percent Change from Last Year	Cleared Offenses	Percent Cleared
State Total	408,546	100.0	3,392.1	0.9	102,782	25.2
Southeast	179,837	44.0	4,715.9	−0.8	44,298	24.6
Northeast	53,139	13.0	2,687.9	7.8	12,208	23.0
Southcentral	46,896	11.5	3,043.6	4.5	13,959	29.8
Central	23,643	5.8	2,192.9	1.0	7,158	30.3
Southwest	80,296	19.7	3,023.9	−1.4	17,886	22.3
Northwest	24,735	6.1	2,526.1	1.0	7,273	29.4

EXERCISE 6

STATISTICAL MATERIAL

UNITED STATES DEPARTMENT OF EDUCATION
WASHINGTON, D.C. 20202

UPDATE ON ADULT ILLITERACY

THE SOURCE

The English Language Proficiency Survey was commissioned by the U.S. Department of Education and conducted by the Bureau of Census during the last summer. At that time, simple written tests of English comprehension were administered in the home to a national sample of 3,400 adults, ages 20 and older.

MAJOR FINDINGS

Between 17 million and 21 million U.S. adults are illiterate, for an overall rate of nearly 13 percent. In contrast to traditional estimates of illiteracy based on completion of fewer than six years of school, this new study shows that illiterate adults are now much more likely to be located in our major cities, and most are under the age of 50. Immigration and reliance on non-English language are also major factors; nearly half of all adults using non-English language at home failed the test of English proficiency. More specifically,

- **OF ALL ADULTS CLASSIFIED AS ILLITERATE:**

—41 percent live in central cities of metropolitan areas, compared to just 8 percent in rural areas;
—56 percent are under the age of 50; and
—37 percent speak a non-English language at home.

- **AMONG NATIVE ENGLISH-SPEAKERS CLASSIFIED AS ILLITERATE:**

—70 percent did not finish high school;
—42 percent had no earnings in the previous year; and
—35 percent are in their twenties and thirties.

- **AMONG ILLITERATE ADULTS WHO USE A NON-ENGLISH LANGUAGE:**

—82 percent were born outside the United States;
—42 percent live in neighborhoods where exclusive reliance on English is the exception rather than the rule;
—21 percent had entered the U.S. within the previous six years; and
—About 14 percent are probably literate in their non-English language (judging from their reported education).

THE TEST AND THE DEFINITION OF ILLITERACY

The test employed is called the Measure of Adult English Proficiency (MAEP). The written portion of MAEP consists of 26 questions which test the individual's ability to identify key words and phrases and match these with one of four fixed-choice alternatives. Based on an analysis of the number of questions answered correctly out of 26, a literacy cutoff of 20 was selected as providing the best discrimination between high and low risk groups. Specifically, among native English speakers, less than 1 percent of those completing some college scored below 20, in contrast to a failure rate of more than 50 percent for those with fewer than 6 years of school.

ACCURACY OF THESE ESTIMATES

The standard error of our point estimate (18.7 million) is about 1 million. Thus, we can be quite confident (95 chances out of 100) that the true figure is in the range of 17 to 21 million.

IDENTIFICATION OF HIGH-RISK GROUPS

Six factors were found to be strongly correlated with performance on the written test: age, nativity, recency of immigration for non-natives, race, poverty status, and amount of schooling and reported English speaking ability (of persons who use non-English language at home).

ILLITERACY RATE ESTIMATES*

	Rate	Inverse Rank		Rate	Inverse Rank
UNITED STATES	13				
			MASSACHUSETTS	11	17
ALABAMA	13	31	MICHIGAN	11	17
ALASKA	7	2	MINNESOTA	9	9
ARIZONA	12	25	MISSISSIPPI	16	47
ARKANSAS	15	40	MISSOURI	12	25
CALIFORNIA	14	33	MONTANA	8	4
COLORADO	8	4	NEBRASKA	9	9
CONNECTICUT	12	25	NEVADA	9	9
DELAWARE	11	17	NEW HAMPSHIRE	9	9
D.C.	16	47	NEW JERSEY	14	33
FLORIDA	15	40	NEW MEXICO	14	33
GEORGIA	14	33	NEW YORK	16	47
HAWAII	15	40	NORTH CAROLINA	14	33
IDAHO	8	4	NORTH DAKOTA	12	25
ILLINOIS	14	33	OHIO	11	17
INDIANA	11	17	OKLAHOMA	11	17
IOWA	10	14	OREGON	8	4
KANSAS	9	9	PENNSYLVANIA	12	25
KENTUCKY	15	40	RHODE ISLAND	15	40
LOUISIANA	16	47	SOUTH CAROLINA	15	40
MAINE	11	17	SOUTH DAKOTA	11	17
MARYLAND	12	25	TENNESSEE	15	40

	Rate	Inverse Rank		Rate	Inverse Rank
TEXAS	16	47	WASHINGTON	8	4
UTAH	6	1	WEST VIRGINIA	14	33
VERMONT	10	14	WISCONSIN	10	14
VIRGINIA	13	31	WYOMING	7	2

*Rates apply to the adult population age 20 and over. All rates have been rounded to the nearest whole percent.

EXERCISE 7

INFORMAL POLLS

CONDUCTING AN INFORMAL POLL

Interview a minimum of 10 people, about half men and half women. Ask for their views concerning a controversial issue, then write a news story about their opinions. The respondents may be students, professors, nonacademic employees, visitors or anyone else you encounter on campus. Conduct your interviews separately, not simultaneously with other members of your class—if only because it is disconcerting for a respondent to be approached by two or three people, all asking the same controversial question. Identify yourself, explain why you are conducting the poll, then ask the question selected by your instructor or class. You may want to use one of the following questions:

1. Do you believe that newspapers and radio and television stations in the United States report the news fairly and accurately?
2. Should faculty members be allowed to date their students, or should your college or university adopt some rules prohibiting the practice?
3. Should your college or university adopt rules prohibiting faculty and students from saying things that are racist or sexist?
4. Would you want your state legislature to adopt a law making it legal—or illegal—for women to serve as surrogate mothers for childless couples?
5. If you saw another student cheating on a test, would you try to stop the student or report the student to your teacher?
6. If the administrators at your school learned that several students had AIDS, would you want them to allow the students to continue to attend classes with you?
7. Should state prison officials allow journalists to photograph or videotape executions?
8. Should the government prohibit the sale of pornographic magazines or the showing of pornographic movies?
9. Should churches and other religious organizations be required to pay taxes for the municipal services, such as police and fire protection, that they receive?
10. Should the federal government allow media companies to own a newspaper and a television station or two or more TV stations in the same town?
11. Do you think the number of terms any one person may serve in Congress should be limited by law?
12. Do you think an unwed mother should be required to identify the father of her child before she can receive welfare benefits so the father can be ordered to help support the child?

After you have conducted your poll, write a story about the results. You will have to do additional research to get background information about your poll issue to write a complete story. You may want to do follow-up interviews with experts on the issue to get their interpretation of the poll results.

EXERCISE 8

COMPUTER-ASSISTED REPORTING

1. If you don't have one already, get an e-mail address for yourself through the proper agency on your campus and subscribe to a journalism discussion list (a number of Web sites have such discussion groups). Prepare a weekly report about the mail on the list summarizing what journalists talk about. Discuss the mail in class. What does it tell you about journalists and the journalism profession?

2. Read this chapter's Exercise 3 about juvenile shoplifting. What databases could be checked or developed that would help you find out whether the recommendations for dealing with shoplifting might be effective? Discuss your ideas with the other members of your class and your instructor.

3. Develop a computer-assisted reporting project from the information given below. What databases could be generated? What information would be important for your story? What comparisons need to be made? Who needs to be interviewed? What questions need to be asked?

   County commissioners for the past 10 years issued licenses for duck hunting on three small, unoccupied islands in Ford Lake. Each year there are nearly 100 applications for the five licenses the commissioners award. Over the past several years, developers have built a number of homes along the waterfront around the lake. Visitors and residents use the lake for recreational activities—boating, swimming, fishing and picnicking. This year, homeowners want duck hunting to stop. They claim development around the lake has made hunting dangerous. They say pellets from the hunters' guns could hit houses and people along the shoreline. Hunters say the pellets never reach shore.

4. How could computer-assisted reporting help you with a story based on the information given below? What other databases would be helpful? Can the health report listed below be divided into sub-databases? What information would be important for your story? What comparisons need to be made? Who needs to be interviewed for the story? What questions need to be asked?

   Every year, the county health department releases a report that lists the leading causes of death. This report provides the address, age, gender and race of each decedent, as well as the cause of death and the date of death. There were 3,245 deaths in the county last year, including 1,201 from all types of cancer. Other leading causes of death were: automobile accidents (525), heart attacks/strokes (432) and gunshot wounds (57).

5. Your editor hands you a CD-ROM with a database containing information about the 4,000 parking tickets your local police department wrote over the past year. For each ticket, the database contains this information: license plate number, state where license was issued, year license was issued, the ticket number, where the ticket was issued (including street and block), time of day the ticket was issued, day of the week the ticket was issued, date the ticket was issued, type of parking violation (expired

meter, no parking zone, double parked, etc.), make of the vehicle, amount of the fine, date the fine was paid and name of the officer issuing the ticket.

Before your editor will allow you to use the computer to manipulate the data, she wants you to develop three ideas for stories that could result from this single database. She also wants you to list the sources you will need to talk to about each story once the data have been analyzed. Prepare a report for your editor addressing these requirements.

EXERCISE 9

COMPUTER-ASSISTED REPORTING

MARKET BASKET STUDY

This assignment will give you experience in gathering information from a basic source and compiling a database of statistical information. In addition, it will give you experience in turning the statistics into a meaningful story that interprets the information for your audience. In teams of two to four students, visit two or more grocery stores in your community and create a computer database comparing prices of 100 food and household items. Design your database so that items are categorized by product type and brand for comparison between stores and the results can be easily turned into charts or graphs for the story you will do. Then conduct interviews with shoppers and other sources, including secondary sources, to give a perspective to the information gathered for the database. Write a consumer-oriented story about your findings.

1. Before you start, ask yourself some questions that consumers, who are your readers, would want to know. Is it cheaper to shop at one store or another? Where do you get the best food bargains? Overall, where will your dollar go further? What are the best buys? These are questions that will help you focus your story.

2. Gather background information on such things as consumer spending patterns, percent of income spent on food and household goods or differences in food-buying habits of single people and families. These and other topics can be used in your story.

3. As you select the 100 items for your study, be aware that not all stores carry the same brand of products. You may want to gather information only on national brands that each store carries. Or you may have to compare similar products of different company brands. In that case, make certain that you compare similar-size containers.

4. After gathering the prices of the products, create a database for the statistical material either in a spreadsheet program, such as Lotus 1-2-3 or Excel, or a relational database program, such as FoxPro or Access.

5. Divide your database of costs into categories for food items—subdivided into grocery items (such as canned goods), meats, dairy products and produce—and nonfood items, such as household cleaning products and detergents for each store.

6. Make cost comparisons based on individual products, groups of products and the entire selection of products.

EXERCISE 10

COMPUTER-ASSISTED REPORTING

CRIME STORY

Your editor has assigned you a story about "Crime in America." The story is to deal with trends in violent crime in the United States—crimes such as murder, assault, rape and domestic violence. You are to research the topic and gather information from the variety of electronic sources available on the Internet or the government documents available at your institution's library. Create a database of the crime data for several years so you can make comparisons and develop trends in the data. With the information in your database, conduct a statistical analysis of the data and then write a story. Your story should focus on interpreting the statistics for your readers, noting trends that may be apparent in your data. Follow the trail of information you gather wherever it leads to a good, interesting story about crime in America.

1. Some of the questions you may want to ask yourself for this assignment include: Are violent crimes on the increase or decrease in the country? Who are the victims—urban, suburban or rural citizens? What are the levels of violent crime by age group? Are younger people committing more crimes than older people? How many violent criminals are there in prison today? These are just some possible directions the story could take.

2. The first step will be to create a search strategy for locating information on the Internet or in library databases by determining which Web sites and databases will serve your needs. Before you begin searching, decide on the central point of your story. Put your objectives in writing, then begin searching for databases and Web sites. Make a list of keywords to use in your search.

3. When you begin to search online, make a list of the various government or criminal justice Web sites that provide information for your story. You should document where you are getting your information, both for your story and future reference. You will need to attribute where you are getting the information in your story.

4. The CD-ROM databases in your library can provide a wealth of information for your story. Many government documents are now available on CD-ROM and require much the same search strategy that you used for your online search of the Internet. You may use the same list of keywords for the CD-ROM databases, or you may add to the list to find the information you need.

5. The list of databases and sources that you use may change as your search progresses—you may find additional information as you conduct your searches, and some databases will provide interesting information that will be irrelevant to the central point of your story. Not all sources will be electronic. Some computer searches may refer you to printed material that you can use in your story.

EXERCISE 11

CONVERGING MEDIA

WORKING IN PRINT AND ELECTRONIC MEDIA

The following exercise requires you to use material discussed in several chapters in your text.

1. Develop an idea for a story. It could be a hard news story about your local government or your college or university. It could be a feature story from your community or your college or university, such as a personality profile of an individual.

2. As you are thinking about the story, consider the visual possibilities, such as video or still digital images that could be used to illustrate the story. List the types of shots that you would like to use with the story.

3. Check with your department, university library or campus media services department to see about borrowing a digital still camera and a digital video camera. If you do not have access to a digital still camera, use a traditional film camera and get the film developed. You will have to scan the prints or negatives depending on what scanner technology you have available. Take both the still camera and the video camera with you when you cover the story and conduct interviews.

4. Collect images (both still and video) during your interview, being sure to identify the people and scenes you are photographing. Make sure your interview is thorough. Make sure you obtain the full name and title of those you interview for the story.

5. Write the story and download the still and video images onto a computer. Edit the story and select the still photographs and about a minute of digital video to use in a film clip. You will have more visual images than you will need, so edit the images carefully to find the most dramatic and meaningful ones for the story.

6. Now, turn the camera on yourself. If you don't have a tripod or a steady flat surface on which to set the video camera, ask a classmate to operate the camera for you. Do a 15-second stand-up promotion about the story. You will want to put together a script in order to have notes to follow for the promo. Tell potential viewers and readers about the story, highlighting important details and telling them what to expect in the story.

7. If you have access to a Web page, you may want to upload the images and the story to the Internet for viewing electronically.

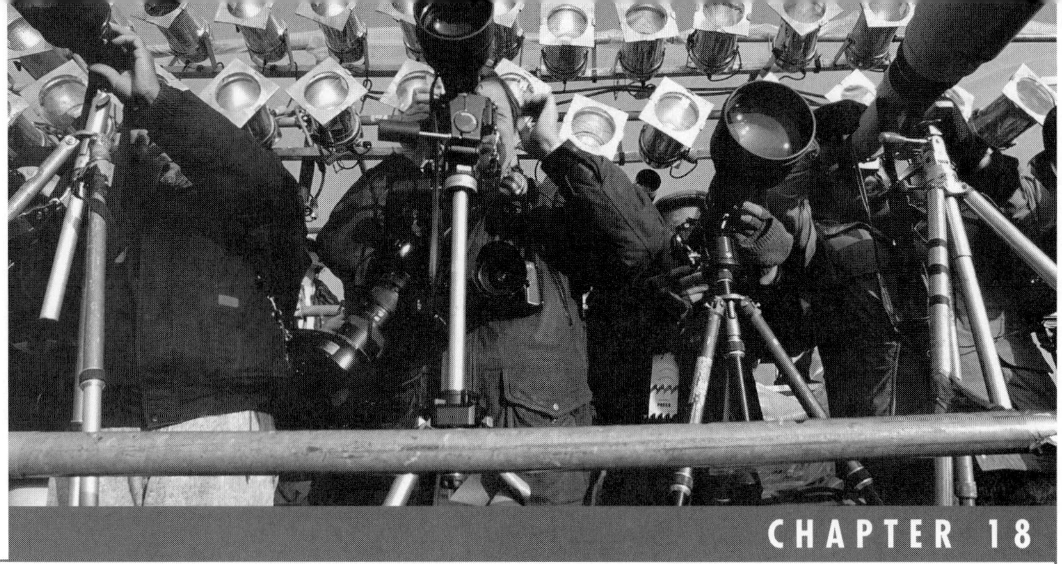

CHAPTER 18

WRITING FOR BROADCAST

Our job is to tell people the things they don't know. Our job is to tell people the things they can't ask for in a survey.
(Carol Marin, television news correspondent)

Print and broadcast media both inform their audiences, but they do so in different ways. Print news is written for readers scanning a page with their eyes. Broadcast news is written for listeners and viewers tuning in with their ears and sometimes eyes. Another difference is that words in print can be reread. Broadcast words, once spoken, are gone forever; listeners cannot hear them again if their attention wanders or if they need to clarify a fact or issue. Furthermore, most people like the newspaper for its detailed information but enjoy broadcast news for quick, up-to-date information. Thus, the story organization and writing style for broadcast news differ from those for print because of the nature of the media and how people use them.

Although the writing styles for print and broadcast are different, the types of stories chosen are not. The best stories in broadcast are also the best stories in print. They involve the audience. Compelling themes draw audience members into a story or involve them in the story in some way.

In addition to emphasizing similar news elements, print and broadcast journalists must do the same type of reporting work. Both reporters must identify a central point. They must research their topic to find the best angle, conduct background research on their sources to ask the best questions and employ good interviewing skills to obtain interesting quotes. Furthermore, they must be good writers and spellers so their copy flows easily for both the announcer reading the story and the listener hearing it.

This chapter presents the basics of broadcast news writing, which begins with radio, and compares it to print news writing. Progression into radio news writing would discuss writing the text of stories around natural sound and interviews. Advanced instruction would indicate the finer differences between radio and TV news writing styles and copy, and how to package information into different presentation formats for TV.

WRITING FOR YOUR LISTENER

Broadcast journalists adhere to a combination of Associated Press general rules and a broadcast presentation style. Many networks and stations have their own style guides. The broadcast guidelines presented in this chapter point out the major differences between print and broadcast writing styles.

A broadcast journalist must think in terms of listening and viewing time, whereas a print reporter thinks in terms of newspaper space. Broadcast news writers appeal to the ear in order to attract and hold the attention of listeners who may be doing other things while the news broadcast airs. The following guidelines help journalists meet the challenge of keeping the audience interested:

- **Adopt a conversational, informal and relaxed style.** Broadcast news is written in the way one friend talks to another. Often, news coaches emphasize, "Tell the story the way you'd tell it to your mother." Sometimes this style includes using contractions, incomplete sentences and first and second person pronouns ("I," "me," "us," "we," "you") to establish a rapport with listeners. Yet, one should keep the conversation more formal than casual.

- **Write short, declarative sentences that are to the point and limited to one idea.** People cannot listen to a long sentence and always associate the end with the beginning. The sentences often have fewer than 15 words, and none should have more than 25 words. They should be simple sentences in the active voice, keeping the subject, verb and object together—and in that order. And writers should put parenthetical information in a separate sentence:

  WRONG: The apartment building, says the landlord of several rental properties, Shellye Wyath, who once was a volunteer firefighter in Shermanville, near the reservation, has been the scene of two other fires—two arsons—in the past three months.

  RIGHT: A third fire in as many months has occurred in the same apartment complex on the north side of town.

  The landlord of Sundown Apartments says she believes the fire is connected to two prior arsons.

  Shellye Wyath met this morning with police officials to . . .

- **Present information in an up-to-date format.** Broadcast news airs several times a day because news is happening NOW. Avoid saying "today" because listeners assume the story describes a recent event or a current issue. Instead, give the most up-to-the minute news account possible by stressing "this morning" or "this afternoon." Use "yesterday" and "tomorrow" instead of days of the week except in the first sentence.

- **Use present-tense verbs.** This emphasizes recency. Use "Says," not "said"; "is searching," not "searched." If the present tense does not work, then try the present perfect tense:

  A wildlife biologist has traced two eaglets to a large nest on Jamison Island.

  If past tense is used, try to include the time element to reflect recency and place it immediately after the verb:

  Comptroller Mia Macabee [MEE-uh MAC-uh-bee] announced this morning a new free online payment service for state taxes.

- **Round numbers.** It is difficult for someone to remember the exact figure of 3,984. It is easier to remember "almost four-thousand."

- **Give numbers meaning.** What does it mean to the listener that the governor's proposed budget will cut more than 100-thousand-dollars from the school district? Sound overwhelming? Saying the cut is "about 55-dollars per student" gives listeners a personal context and clearer understanding.

- **Shorten long titles.** Titles sometimes fail to describe a person's job. Also, long titles make people forget what else the story has to say. For example, Andrea Maye supervises the Pharmacy Program of the Health Regulation Division in the Office of Health Services of the Bureau of Occupational and Professional Regulation in the Michigan Department of Commerce. This long title would use most of the time allotted to the story. Shorten the title to a word or two, such as "a supervisor," or to a brief description of the person's job, such as "a state health official."

- **Never put an unfamiliar name first in a story.** Listeners might miss it. Also, sometimes the indivual's name is less important than the position he or she occupies. Delay the name until the story has captured the audience's attention:

  The state Parks and Recreation Director says the state will set aside ten-thousand acres of swampland to preserve wildlife habitats.

- **Omit a person's middle initial.** Use an initial only if it is commonly recognized as part of that person's name. Remember that broadcast writing uses a conversational style, and speakers rarely refer to others by their initials in conversation.

- **Place the description, age or identification before a person's name.** The newspaper style of placing a description after the name is not conversational. Instead, describe the person beforehand to keep the subject, verb and object together:

  WRONG: Jorges Morales, 13, a Riversmeet Middle School student, has won the national championship spelling bee.

  REVISED: A Riversmeet boy is being celebrated this afternoon in Washington, D.C.

  Thirteen-year-old Jorges Morales [HOR-hay mor-AL-es] spelled remblai [ron-BLE] to win the national championship spelling bee. . . .

- **Leave out ages and addresses if they are not important to the story.** Time is short in broadcast, and usually ages and addresses are not central to the news angle. However, writers use information that differentiates individuals with the same name, especially in stories reporting arrests or allegations of criminal conduct.

- **Place the attribution before what is said.** The broadcast formula "Who Said What" is the opposite of newspaper style ("What, Said Who."). In broadcast news, reporters need to prepare listeners for the quote or paraphrase coming next, to allow them to concentrate on what is being said:

  The president said in his televised address this evening that the people of the United States are lucky to have such brave men and women serving our country.

- **Avoid direct quotes.** Listeners cannot see a quotation mark, so a journalist needs to paraphrase what someone said. If a direct quote is necessary, use special language make it clear:

  And quoting directly here, " . . .

  As she put it, " . . .

  In her own words, " . . .

- **Avoid homonyms.** Words that sound alike but have different meanings and spellings can confuse listeners. ("He was a real bore/boor in polite company.")

Audience members may miss the rest of the story if they spend time wrestling with a confusing sentence.

- **Try to avoid pronouns.** With several women in a story, for instance, it is often difficult for a listener to figure out to whom the announcer is referring: "Keesha and Sooyoung found her dog in her car."
- **Use descriptive language, but sparingly.** Some descriptive words help a listener better visualize an event (e.g., "hurled" instead of "threw"). However, too much description can take away from the rest of the story by confusing the listener or using precious seconds needed elsewhere.

WRITING FOR YOUR ANNOUNCER

Broadcast copy must be "announcer-friendly." At some stations, the writer is the announcer, but often, writers and announcers are different people. Writers may finish their copy minutes before a newscast airs, allowing announcers only a quick practice read before going on-air. Therefore, broadcast journalists must write stories so they can be delivered aloud by someone else.

Here are common writing tips broadcast writers use to make announcing easier:

- **Add phonetic spelling.** To mispronounce a name on the air is a sin. However, not everyone knows how to pronounce everything correctly. Announcers often need the name of a place or person spelled out phonetically, which the writer places in square brackets either directly after or in the space above the word. The Voice of America has a pronunciation guide online for names, places and other words that are in the national and international news.

  Juanita Diaz [Wha-NEE-ta DEE-ahz] has placed first in the Rifle Club's annual sharpshooters' contest.

  Sometimes, the same spelling is pronounced differently in different regions of the United States. Thus, "Charlotte" can be [SHAR-lot] in North Carolina or [shar-LOT] in Michigan. Or, the same word can have different spellings: al Qaeda or al Qaida [al-K-EYE-(eh)-duh].

- **Hyphenate words that go together in a group.** Announcers will then avoid taking a breath between these words, saying them as a group:

  The 75-year-old woman finished the race.

  The 19-25 dictionary sold for 45-dollars.

- **Spell out numbers up to and including eleven.** Spell out eleven because it may look like ll (two letter l's) instead of 11 (two numeral ones). For example, an announcer may pause when reading "11 llamas" instead of "eleven llamas."
- **Use numerals for 12 to 999,** unless they begin a sentence or indicate an age, address or date.
- **Use a combination of numerals and words for large numbers** (e.g., "40-thousand"). Announcers may pause at the numeral "$10,110,011," but can glide along more easily when reading (and rounding) "about ten-million-110-thousand-dollars." The numeral "6,500" should be written as "six-thousand-500" or as "65-hundred."

- **Use words instead of abbreviations:** Spell out rather than abbreviate titles, states, months of the year, measurements and other words so announcers can easily recognize and pronounce them without guessing their meaning.

  Saint or Street—not St.

  Association—not Assn.

  miles-per-hour—not m.p.h.

- **Spell out figures, signs and symbols.** And, never use a period for a decimal. Try to round numbers or use fractions instead of decimals.

  50-percent—not 50%

  200-dollars—not $200

  seven-and-a-half-million—not 7.5 million or seven-point-five-million

- **Hyphenate some numbers and some abbreviations on second reference.** Hyphens let an announcer know that the letters are to be read not as a word, but individually:

  A-B-C News

  N-double-A-C-P

  Acronyms, such as NATO and NASA, are written without hyphens because they are pronounced the way they are spelled.

- **Use hyphens for numbers to be read individually.** Numerals in phone numbers and addresses are usually read individually or as two-digit numbers.

  That telephone number is 6-7-6-3-4-2-2.

  Her address is 14-21 Grecian Drive.

- **Avoid alliterations or tongue twisters that might trip an announcer.** The late Laurie MacMillan, a BBC radio announcer, refused to read on air a story with the phrase, "dismissed this as a myth," fearing she might stumble over the words. Also avoid words in a series that have several snaking "S" sounds or popping "P's." They don't translate well into a microphone.

LEADS FOR BROADCAST STORIES

The summary lead used for print news often is too long for broadcast news and too difficult to follow when read aloud. Too much information (who, what, where, when, why and how) frustrates listeners. They cannot digest it all at once. The audience will understand the story better if the information is delivered in separate sentences.

Broadcast news stories follow a "pyramid" formula: The most important element of a story comes first, followed by the rest of the information. The lead rarely tells the whole story, however. And, because newscasts are timed before they air, journalists can write a complete story without fearing that the ending sentence or paragraph will be edited out at the last moment.

A broadcast lead must capture the attention of listeners immediately or they will be lost to the story forever. The lead should tell listeners one or two important facts and ease them into the rest of the story.

The best leads capture attention by involving listeners in some way. Many people are going to care about a story regarding a new corn hybrid. Even if they are not farmers, they will be affected by the impact the hybrid corn has on the supermarket price of corn and meat from animals fed on corn. In a college town, most students will be interested in new bicycle laws that will affect the way in which they get to their classes. For others, the story will explain the new paths they see crisscrossing campus.

Yet the lead must not give away too much important information. Listeners usually don't hear the first two or three words of a lead, but they "tune in" when they hear something that interests them.

Broadcast journalists rewrite leads throughout the day for ongoing stories. Whereas newspapers are published once a day and give yesterday's news, broadcast news can air any time of the day, as often as necessary. With hourly updates, broadcast stories can tell today's news as it happens. Thus, writers freshen the lead with each broadcast to update or localize the story.

Four common types of leads are the hard lead, the soft lead, the throwaway lead and the umbrella lead. Each is written to intrigue and interest the listener and provide a transition to the rest of the story.

The Hard Lead

Hard leads give important information immediately. Some broadcasters believe that, as a result, listeners may misunderstand a story because they weren't paying attention to important facts reported at the beginning. Yet, some listeners want to hear the most meaningful information first.

> LEAD: A Grand County man charged this morning with two counts of sexual assault also may be responsible for similar attacks in neighboring counties.
>
> REST OF THE STORY: Thirty-seven-year-old Marcus Sodderby [SODer-bee] would look for the glow of computer screens and TV sets in windows late at night when hunting for his victims. . . .

Here is another example of a hard lead:

> LEAD: The county has started giving 9-1-1 domestic violence the same priority as homicide, assault and rape calls.
>
> REST OF THE STORY: Police Chief Hugh Joplin says that the policy changes were incorporated after a woman was killed while on the phone to a 9-1-1 dispatcher. The call terminated abruptly and police arrived about an hour-and-a-half later to find the woman and her husband dead. . . .

The Soft Lead

The soft lead tells a broadcast audience that something important is coming up and invites them to continue listening to hear the story. Soft leads, similar to soft-news stories, "featurize" information before getting to the hard news. A soft lead usually tells listeners why the information is important or how it affects them:

> LEAD: After last month's deadly porch collapse, a state lawmaker wants to put warning signs on porches.
>
> REST OF THE STORY: State Representative Josie Williams of Cleveland wants the signs to state the exact number of people who can be on a porch at the same time. . . .

Here is another example of a soft lead:

> LEAD: State officials say they spent a record amount this year to maintain our roads and bridges.
>
> REST OF THE STORY: Transportation Department Director Jason Taylor says the state spent about one-billion-dollars on 513 road projects this year, making this year the costliest in state history. Some of that money was spent on overtime for workers, enabling about 80-percent of the year's road construction projects to end on time.

The Throwaway Lead

The throwaway lead intrigues listeners. After they have "tuned in" to the story, the next sentence begins the real lead. A story would make sense without the throwaway lead—but without it, the story might not have attracted listeners:

> LEAD: What was anticipated to be a zoo of a sale turned out to be just that.
> REST OF THE STORY: Hundreds of brides-to-be mashed into Bobbi's Bridal Boutique in the Galleria to save on gowns, all of which were on sale for 225-dollars. Some of the dresses were originally priced at 10-thousand-dollars. . . .

Here is another example of a throwaway lead:

> LEAD: Finally, it's beginning to feel a lot like Christmas.
> REST OF THE STORY: After more than a week of unseasonably warm weather across our state, cold temperatures are back. Light snow is possible today in the Upper Peninsula and in other parts of the state. Today's highs are expected to reach about 42-degrees.

The Umbrella Lead

The umbrella lead summarizes or ties together two or more related news stories before delving into each separately. The lead tells listeners the relationship between the stories:

> LEAD: Fires at two area churches last night have police asking whether they're both arson cases.
> REST OF THE STORY: Flames destroyed the education building of the Faith, Hope and Love Church on Clinton Avenue at about one o-clock this morning.
> About three hours later, firefighters were called to the scene of a fire at Divinity Chapel on Cooper Street that caused about 50-thousand dollars in damages.

THE BODY OF A BROADCAST NEWS STORY

The inverted-pyramid print news story presents its facts in descending order of importance. After each sentence or paragraph, the reader can leave the story, having gleaned an increasingly detailed sense of what happened. Also, print editors can cut the story almost anywhere, knowing that the most important information has already been presented.

In broadcast news, every sentence of a story is important because when listeners leave the story, they are usually leaving the newscast. In addition, listeners generally cannot digest a lot of information all at once, so broadcast stories are short. Every sentence needs to be heard. Stories need to be tight, with no extraneous information or loose ends. Although the most important information is given first, what follows is important, too. Sometimes facts are presented in descending order of importance, sometimes in chronological order with a narrative format. Overall, sentences are shorter and contain fewer facts than those used in print stories.

Descending Order of Importance

The broadcast journalist must first figure out the most significant piece of information to tell listeners. It usually goes in a story's lead. Then the journalist must anticipate what else listeners want to know. This information makes up the body of the story.

Although a story may contain several pieces of information, their order is usually dictated by the facts given in the lead. If the lead says a minister was killed late last night, listeners will want to know the victim's name. They will also want to know where, how or why the victim was killed. And they will want to know what police are doing about the case. This fact pattern is similar to using "blind leads" in print writing, as described in Chapter 6:

> Police are looking for a man who posed this afternoon as an evangelist and used a hammer to attack a Roseville couple.
>
> Janna and Dylan Banner are in stable condition at Community Hospital after Marten Keller repeatedly hit the couple and forced his way into their home.
>
> By the time police responded to a neighbor's 9-1-1 call, Keller had already fled in his car, a 1997 white Taurus.
>
> Janna Banner had a restraining order on Keller, who is her ex-husband.
>
> Keller has brown hair and eyes and is six-feet-tall and was last seen wearing a light blue suit.

Chronological Order

In the chronological type of broadcast news story, the climax—the most significant part—makes up the lead. Then, as in chronological print stories, the details are related to listeners in the order of their occurrence. Journalists relate the story in the order events happened, not the order in which they learned each fact:

> A Roseville couple was hospitalized this afternoon after being repeatedly attacked with a hammer by the woman's ex-husband.
>
> Authorities say Marten Keller knocked on the Banner's door at noon, posing as an evangelist. When Dylan Banner tried to shut his door, Keller became violent, repeatedly hitting Banner with a hammer while forcing his way into the house. Keller then attacked Janna Banner when she came to the aid of her husband.
>
> Keller had already disappeared in a 1997 white Taurus by the time neighbors called police, who arrived about 15 minutes later.
>
> An ambulance took the Banners to Community Hospital, where they are in stable condition.
>
> Police are looking for Keller, who has brown hair and eyes, is six-feet-tall and was wearing a light blue suit at the time of the attack.

UPDATING BROADCAST NEWS STORIES

Many radio stations have newscasts throughout the day. Although new stories may replace old ones, stations must keep listeners up to date on important, ongoing events. Thus, the same story may be repeated throughout the day, but freshened with new angles, additional interviews or more recent information. The lead sentence and body of the story should never stay exactly the same in successive newscasts. Here are three updated leads:

> A Roseville man accused of a hammer attack on his ex-wife and her new husband has been arrested in Houston. (Or, Police have arrested a Roseville man. . . .)

> Police say the man who attacked his ex-wife and her new husband was trying to regain custody of his son.

> A woman and her husband are out of the hospital this afternoon after her ex-husband attacked them with a hammer Thursday.

GUIDELINES FOR COPY PREPARATION

The format and aesthetics of broadcast news copy are important because too many extraneous marks can distract an announcer and, consequently, detract from the news story. If an announcer gets confused, then listeners surely will be, and they may turn the dial.

Most of the information in this chapter applies to both radio and television broadcasts. However, these copy guidelines and some of the following sections are written mostly with the radio journalist in mind, because many students learn about radio before advancing to television. Copy preparation differs from station to station, but the basics are outlined below:

- Use standard $8\frac{1}{2}$- by 11-inch paper so that all stories fit neatly together and smaller ones don't slip out.
- Type on only one side of the paper so an announcer knows immediately where the next story is. This also prevents on-air paper shuffling.
- Set margins for 65 characters a line as a universal line measurement for announcer timing. (Fifteen lines of 65 characters each make up about one minute of air time; the exact timing depends on the individual announcer's pace.)
- Double or triple space to visually separate lines for announcing and to give more room for editing.
- Standardize copy with either all uppercase or upper and lowercase letters.
- Place only one story on each page. If more stories are written than can be used during a newscast, the announcer may become confused about which of two stories on a page should be omitted.
- Put a slug in the top left corner of the page. The slug contains the story identification in one or two words, the reporter's name, the date and the time of the newscast. If the story runs longer than one page, the slug on subsequent pages should include the page number, repeated several times for clarity (e.g., "2-2-2"). Rarely is a story longer than one page.
- Begin each story about six lines below the slug. The space between the slug and the story can be used for editing or adding transitions between stories.
- Omit datelines because most broadcasts reach only local listeners. (National wires use datelines because they are syndicated across the country.)
- Indent the first line of each paragraph of a story five spaces to indicate a new paragraph.
- Never split words or related phrases between lines of copy. End lines at natural breaks between words or phrases to avoid leaving an announcer unprepared and listeners wondering. For example:

  She has been in the news
room.
- Never split a sentence or paragraph between pages of copy. The announcer needs to read smoothly and should not have to look for extended endings on other pages. Furthermore, the story will sound less confusing if a thought (paragraph) is completed even though the rest of the story happens to be on another page that is missing.
- Use an end mark at the end of the story to indicate there is no more. Some journalists prefer a traditional end mark ("###" or "30"), while others use their initials.
- Add "more" or a long arrow pointing to the bottom of the page to indicate that the story continues onto the next page.

BROADCAST COPY EXAMPLE

Escaped Convict
Davenport
1/12/00
6 p.m.

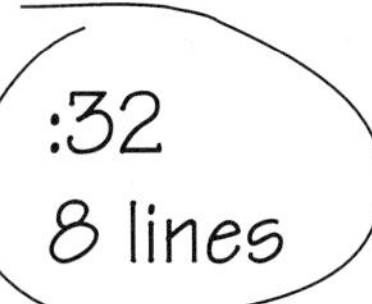

Police are looking for a Lansing woman who fled the Jackson County Courthouse moments after being convicted today.

Assistant prosecutor Reggie Maxim says the trial had just ended when Lucretia Morris hit a guard and ran to freedom, at about three o'clock.

The 28-year-old Morris had just been convicted of assault and robbery charges from last May.

Sheriff Bobbi McNeil says the woman was wearing jeans, and a white short-sleeved shirt and tennis shoes.

Police say Morris is dangerous.

EDITING COPY

- Never use newspaper copy-editing symbols. They are too difficult for an announcer to interpret while reading on-air.

WRONG: Police are ~~are~~ looking for a Kalamazoo woman who feld the Jackson County court house momments after being convicted today.

- To edit a word, black it out completely and rewrite it in the space above it:

> looking fled
> RIGHT: Police are ~~are~~ for a Kalamazoo woman who ~~feld~~ the Jackson County
> Courthouse moments
> ~~court house~~ ~~momments~~ after being convicted today.

- Limit the number of handwritten words inserted into copy.
- If the copy requires a lot of editing, type a clean copy. The fewer editing marks, the fewer times an announcer hesitates or stumbles while reading.
- Write the timing of the story (for example, ":20") and number of lines in the top right-hand corner of the copy page. Remember that for most announcers, 15 lines of copy equal one minute of reading time. Some journalists prefer to denote only the number of lines. (Count two half lines as one complete line.)
- Circle all information that is not to be read on-air, such as the slug, end mark and timing.

PUTTING TOGETHER A NEWSCAST

Tight, efficient—but thorough—story writing is imperative in broadcast news. Local and national television newscasts usually are 30 minutes long. Some public radio newscasts span an hour or more, but many commercial radio newscasts are only five minutes long, made up of mostly 15- to 30-second news stories.

Time for news stories becomes even shorter once the opening and closing for the newscast, commercial breaks, teasers and promos (to keep people tuned in after the commercial), transitions between stories, weather and sports are deducted from the original time.

Reviewing Copy

A journalist or announcer should read aloud all copy to become familiar with what has been prepared for the newscast. While reading each story, the announcer should confirm that his or her reading time matches the average number of lines per minute. The announcer should also mark—or personalize—the copy for word emphases or difficult pronunciations.

Timing the Newscast

Let's say that five minutes are allotted every hour on the hour for a radio newscast. To figure out how much copy is needed, begin by subtracting one minute for a commercial break and 15 seconds each for opening and closing to the newscast. That leaves three and a half minutes, which equals about 52 lines of copy. Weather and sports updates consume 20 seconds each, taking a total of 10 lines (five lines each). That leaves 42 lines for news copy. With this number in mind, review each story, find the important ones, and add the total lines of copy (by adding the number of lines in all the stories, which should be noted in the top right-hand corner of each copy page). Remember to add a few seconds for transitions between stories. In addition, always keep an extra story available in case it is needed to fill time.

A newscast's length is its "running time." Some announcers combine running time with "back timing" the last two or three stories. For example, the announcer does a practice reading of the last few stories, in this case sports and weather, and notes the exact time it takes. Then the announcer subtracts that time from the end of five minutes—what the clock should say at this exact point. Thus, the announcer will know where in the newscast he or she should be at this exact time while on-air. When the announcer reaches these stories on air, he or she compares the time with the run-through. If the announcer is under the allotted time, then the last stories should be read more slowly or another short story should be added. If the announcer is past the allotted time, he or she should speed up the last few stories to end exactly on time.

Organizing Stories

The order in which stories appear in a newscast often depends on station policy. Some stations begin with local news, progress to state news and end with national or international news. Others use just the opposite order. Within each news category, start with the best stories to gain the listener's attention at the beginning. If the first story—whether local, national or international—is an attention-grabber, then a listener is unlikely to change stations. Some broadcast journalists look for a "kicker" to run at the end of the newscast: a lighthearted or good-news story that listeners will enjoy. Some kickers are humorous; others emphasize human interest.

Adding Transitions

Transitions make newscasts more conversational. As you review each story before a newscast, think about the transitions needed to move from story to story, and pencil them on the copy. Transitions smooth out the potentially abrupt movement from one subject to another by tying different subjects together. In addition, transitions signal the end of one story and the beginning of another. Transitions may be phrases such as "meanwhile" or "closer to home."

To make a transition from one story to another, seek a commonality in both. Commonalities might include geographic proximity, time sequence or action:

> You might think it's hot today, but forecasters are predicting even hotter temperatures tomorrow. . . .

Or, transitions can point out differences:

> While southern Texas is experiencing heat waves, fierce thunderstorms are ravaging the northern part of the state. . . .

SOURCES FOR BROADCAST NEWS

Broadcast journalists get news from the same sources print journalists use. However, instead of writing down what a source has said, broadcast reporters tape their sources' comments to be played on the air. This change in voice—the use of sound bites—gives variety to newscasts and lends authority to the news. In addition, broadcasters sometimes use the telephone rather than personal interviews. Because newscasts are so frequent, little time is available to work on stories. Common sources for broadcast news include news services and wire feeds, people, newspapers and news releases or video news releases from public relations agencies.

News Services

In days gone by, wire machines would continuously print out all news, weather and sports stories that correspondents wrote from different parts of the country and beyond. Typically, a subscribing station's morning reporter would open the office door to find on the floor yards of paper filled with stories from a wire machine, which typed throughout the night. This Teletype machine would continue to print news and information throughout the day, occasionally ringing a bell for a particularly important story, and stopping only for someone to change its ribbon or paper.

The old term "rip and read" came from reporters ripping stories off the Teletype and immediately reading them over the air. Often nothing was changed because wire copy coming into broadcast stations was already written in the accepted broadcast style.

Today, the wire services are termed "news services," and Teletype machines have been replaced by computers. The steady clacking of Teletype keys and ringing of the bell are gone. News service stories continue to stream into stations, but they are no longer printed. Instead, the stories are recorded in a computer system. Reporters look at national or regional headings and read every story on a computer screen. They then print only the stories they want to use.

News feeds are another news source. These also come from news services, but instead of being written, they are audio or video stories that journalists can tape and integrate into their newscasts. At designated times of the day, forthcoming story topics and lengths are listed on a computer, and the news feeds are transmitted to subscribing stations. Journalists can tape any stories they want. Once the story is taped, journalists simply add the opening and closing to the story.

Newspapers

Newspapers are an important source of information. Frequently, commercial broadcast stations have only one or two news reporters, not enough people to cover all stories in person. Thus, they learn about many important events from a local newspaper. Broadcast journalists rewrite the story in broadcast style for newscasts, giving credit to the newspaper.

Public Relations News Releases

The government and businesses hire public relations practitioners to promote their image or product. News organizations receive a flood of print and video news releases announcing events or happenings, such as the promotion of an executive officer or the introduction of a new product line. Rarely are news releases objective; never are they negative.

However, news releases can be quite helpful on slow news days. Journalists can look to them for additional information about changes within the community or updates on local companies. Ideally, the release should be regarded as a news tip, to be followed up with background research and interviews with competing organizations or people with opposite viewpoints. Unfortunately, too many journalists simply take a news release, shorten it for broadcast and read it on the air.

People

Many good news tips come from people who call stations to give information about an event that has just happened or is about to happen. Some stations encourage these tips by advertising a telephone number people can call with news or by publicizing their e-mail addresses or Web site. Following up the tips with in-depth questions and research can uncover more sources and interesting stories. In addition, interviewing people about one subject can lead to tips and ideas on additional subjects.

THE NEWSROOM ENVIRONMENT

Commercial television and public radio stations typically schedule longer and more frequent news and information programs than do commercial radio stations. Thus, they need more journalists, more space for newsrooms and a larger news budget. Commercial radio stations often regard news as a brief update for their listeners. They have small news budgets and sometimes only one journalist. That one journalist, who has the title "news director," is the entire news staff.

This journalist is responsible for obtaining the news from news releases or local newspapers, calling sources to verify information or to ask for interviews, writing the news and reading it over the air. This person lacks time to research stories in depth, and covering events in person is out of the question.

Journalists who prefer talking to a lot of people and covering stories in depth would probably like working at a television station or public radio station better than at most commercial radio stations. Those who can become proficient at conveying the heart of a story in a few words should do well in broadcast news.

CHECKLIST FOR BROADCAST NEWS WRITING

Writing Style

1. Write in a conversational style for the listener.
2. Make your copy announcer-friendly for quick, easy reading.
3. Use sentences of about 15 words or fewer.
4. Write in the present tense.
5. Write simple sentences in subject-verb-object order and eliminate parenthetical phrases.
6. Find the one important news element and highlight it in the lead. The rest of the information should follow in small doses.
7. Do not start a story with a person's name or important information; save it for later when the listener has "tuned in."
8. Use few numbers, round them and give them meaning.
9. Write out titles, numbers and symbols.
10. Use descriptive language, but sparingly.

Copy Format

1. Use only one side of the paper.
2. Triple space.
3. Set margins for 65-character lines.
4. Do not split phrases or words between lines. Do not split a sentence or paragraph between pages.
5. Put the slug in the top left-hand corner, then skip about six lines to begin the story.
6. Write the number of lines and reading time for the story in the top right corner.
7. Black out words to be edited. Write in the corrected word above the line.
8. Circle all parts of the text that are not to be read by the announcer.

SUGGESTED READINGS

Kalbfeld, Brad. *The Associated Press Broadcast News Handbook*. Burr Ridge, Ill.: McGraw-Hill, 2000.

Lindner, Ken. *Broadcast Realities: Real Life Issues and Insights for Broadcast Journalists, Aspriring Journalists and Broadcasters*. Chicago: Bonus Books, 1999.

Papper, Robert A. *Broadcast News Writing Stylebook*. Boston: Allyn & Bacon, 2001.

Tuggle, C.A., Suzanne Huffman and Forrest Carr. *Broadcast News Handbook*. Burr Ridge, Ill.: McGraw-Hill, 2003.

USEFUL WEB SITES

Abe Rosenburg's broadcast newswriting tips: http://www.newswriting.com
National Association of Broadcasters' information on the industry: http://www.nab.org
Broadcast Education Association's information on the industry: http://www.beaweb.org
Television Newswriting Workshop with Mervin Block: http://www.mervinblock.com
Voice of America pronunciation guide: http://www.voa.gov

Name ______________________ Class ______________________ Date ______

EXERCISE 1

WRITING FOR BROADCAST

IDENTIFYING BROADCAST STYLE

The following are correctly written broadcast leads. Explain how they differ stylistically from leads written for newspapers. Think about time, verb tense, titles, personal identification, amount of information and a conversational mode.

1. Observing the 15th anniversary of Americans with Disabilities Act, President Bush said this morning that the civil rights law had improved people's lives.
2. A five-year-old girl is credited with saving a man's life near Tulsa, Oklahoma.
3. Council member Jebb Locket wants motorized scooters to be a thing of the past.
4. Four cars were stolen last night in different incidents in the downtown area.
5. The U-S has begun extradition procedures against the political leader of an Islamic militant group.
6. Prosecutors want more time to build a case against a city official accused of illegal trading.
7. We are in for some really warm weather tomorrow.
8. A city police officer is clinging to her life after a shooting that killed a fellow officer.
9. Purple wreaths are disappearing from cemeteries across the county.
10. Several break-ins on campus this weekend are causing dormitory residents to lock their doors more often.

Name ______________________ Class ______________________ Date ________

EXERCISE 2

WRITING FOR BROADCAST

IDENTIFYING DIFFERENT BROADCAST LEADS

The following broadcast leads and the second paragraphs are written correctly. Identify the style of each lead: hard news, soft news, throwaway or umbrella.

1. LEAD: The man who raped three St. Louis men, killing one of them, was sent to prison for life today.

   REST OF THE STORY: Ervine McMitchelle drew a life term for the first-degree murder of Henry LaForge last year. County Circuit Judge Ashley Monahan also gave McMitchelle 50-to-75-years for each of three counts of rape. The rapes occurred over the last three years.

2. LEAD: If you think your pampered pooch or cuddly kitty deserves the national spotlight, here's your chance.

   REST OF THE STORY: The International Pet Cemeteries Foundation in Austin, Texas, plans to build a National Pet Hall of Fame within two years. The president of the foundation, Heidi Hills, says members hope to provide education about pets and also memorialize famous and not-so-famous pets.

3. LEAD: A Friendswood teenager is the center of attention today at the governor's mansion.

   REST OF THE STORY: Sixteen-year-old Gordon Elliott has received the state's Good Citizenship Award for saving two children from drowning in Grand River last fall.

4. LEAD: Smoke still fills the air over western Colorado.

   REST OF THE STORY: A wild fire that injured 30 firefighters and threatened homes has already burned 12-thousand acres. High temperatures and strong winds make the job harder for the 15-hundred firefighters who continue working around the clock.

5. LEAD: A Presbyterian minister has been found dead in her church office.

   REST OF THE STORY: First Presbyterian Church secretary Robert Abrahm found the door unlocked and the Reverend Sarah Chen dead when he came to work this morning.

6. LEAD: Police are looking into the possibility of a connection among 20 recent dognappings in the area.

   REST OF THE STORY: Parson's Animal Shelter Director John Ertos says he has received 12 inquiries about lost dogs since yesterday. Most of these dogs were in fenced-in back yards or on leashes.

   In nearby Colleyville, police Officer Annie Bearclaw says the station has logged eight calls reporting missing dogs within two days.

7. LEAD: Police are looking for a South Bend man who fled the Johnson County Courthouse moments after being convicted today.

   REST OF THE STORY: Assistant Prosecutor Lonnie Howard says the trial had just ended when Lee Chang hit a guard and ran to freedom, at about three o'clock.

8. LEAD: The chair of the House Ways and Means Committee says she wants to abolish our current tax structure.

   REST OF THE STORY: Texas Republican Rachael Morgan set that as her goal today as she opened hearings on our tax system.

9. LEAD: You can be 25-thousand-dollars richer if you tip police with information that helps solve a homicide case.

   REST OF THE STORY: Metropolitan Police Chief Stone Willows says that people who provide information that leads to a conviction stand to receive ten-thousand-dollars more than they did last year.

10. LEAD: More than 165 passengers are safe, after a seven-47 jetliner made an emergency landing at the Minneapolis Metro Airport today.

    REST OF THE STORY: Airport director Jean Richards says shortly after takeoff, a door blew open in the luggage compartment. The plane then dumped its fuel and returned to the airport.

Name ______________________ Class ______________________ Date ______

EXERCISE 3

WRITING FOR BROADCAST

IDENTIFYING DIFFERENT BROADCAST LEADS

The following broadcast leads and the second paragraphs are written correctly. Identify the style of each lead: hard news, soft news, throwaway or umbrella.

1. LEAD: Thanksgiving holiday traffic accidents in our state have claimed at least five lives.

   REST OF THE STORY: The victims include three Jonesville residents killed in a rollover accident in Ingham County. They're identified as 22-year-old Marie Wildflower and her passengers, 28-year-old Jesse Wildflower and his sister Margaret Quinn, who was 25-years-old. Officials in Greene County say 44-year-old Jimmie Lincoln and 62-year-old Zackory Timbs died in a two-car accident. Both men are Centerville residents.

2. LEAD: There is confirmation that inflation is not a problem.

   REST OF THE STORY: A representative of the Labor Department says that the June Producer Price index dropped one-tenth of one percent. Not counting food and energy, the index was ahead a modest two-tenths of one percent. The index shows a big decline in energy costs and the largest drop in fruit prices in nearly 20 years.

3. LEAD: A New York man who tried to exterminate his girlfriend's family will spend the rest of his life in prison.

   REST OF THE STORY: A federal judge in Rochester, New York, today gave Hiram Evans five consecutive life terms and four additional life sentences to be served concurrently.

4. LEAD: Suburban Detroit automotive supplier Lear is cutting 28-hundred jobs.

   REST OF THE STORY: The cuts amount to about four-percent of Lear's employees. About eleven-hundred of the employees will be cut in North America, the rest in Europe. Company representative Jill Li says that Lear hopes the reorganization saves more than 40-million-dollars yearly.

5. lEAD: Shakespeare's ghost may live again.

   REST OF THE STORY: After about 400 years, actors are again on the stage of the Globe Theatre in London. It's a copy of the old building where the playwright's productions were first performed.

6. LEAD: About a dozen people were killed this morning when a charter flight out of Chicago hit thunderstorms.

   REST OF THE STORY: The Sunshine Company plane was rising above lightning and torrential rain on its way to Reno when its engines apparently failed.

7. LEAD: Several U-S industries are experiencing the effects of NAFTA.
   REST OF THE STORY: Asparagus growers are finding that more fresh asparagus is being imported from Mexico because of cheaper prices.

8. LEAD: Even the North is no escape for hot weather this week.
   REST OF THE STORY: According to the National Weather Service, temperatures in northern Arizona will remain in the scorching three digits.

9. LEAD: Three area people were killed in two separate highway accidents this Labor Day.
   REST OF THE STORY: A DeWitt construction worker was killed when a truck driver fell asleep and his semi slid into Jackson Perlini's [per-LEE-nee's] southbound lane on Highway 127 in Fullbright. The driver of the truck, Joey McCabe, was uninjured.
   Two Holt sisters were pronounced dead on arrival at Community Hospital after a drunken driver crossed the median on Interstate 69, just south of Eagle River. . . .

10. LEAD: A police officer in New York has quit his job in deference to his principles.
    REST OF THE STORY: At a press conference in Manlius today, Jesse Morales called the judicial process a revolving-door penal system.

EXERCISE 4

WRITING FOR BROADCAST

WRITING BROADCAST STORIES

Write broadcast stories about the following events. Write at least one soft news, one hard news and one throwaway lead. Check for wordiness. Your stories should not run more than 30 seconds. Correct any errors in spelling and grammar.

1. Previously, anyone who parked in a spot reserved for the handicapped in your city would be fined $20. However, your city council met last night and heard complaints that other motorists often use the spaces, making it harder for handicapped people to shop or eat out or go to movies. As a result, the council voted 5-2 to raise the fine to $250—the highest in the state—to discourage able-bodied drivers from using the parking spots reserved for the handicapped. Those spaces normally are close to store entrances. Two members of the Paralyzed Veterans Association were at the meeting to lobby for the stiffer fine, saying it might be the only way to stop offenders. The new law will go into effect in 30 days. State law allows half of the money collected through such fines to go toward enforcing and administering the parking regulations. The rest may be used to build wheelchair ramps and other improvements to enhance access to public buildings.

2. J. T. Pinero is a developer in your community. He is planning to build 350 houses in a 120-acre subdivision which he has named "Deer Run." This morning he was cited by the city. The city also stopped all work on the development. The land had been wooded, and Pinera was charged with clearing the first 30 acres without obtaining city permits. Mayor Serena Datolli said it was the most flagrant violation of the citys tree protection code since her election five years ago. Pinero was cited for cutting down more than 500 pines, oaks, maple, birch and other trees. Under city codes, unauthorized destruction of of each tree is punishable by a fine of up to $500. Datoli added that she and other city officials are negotiating with Pinero and his attorney for landscaping and replacement of all the trees. Pinero must also post a $100,000 bond or letter of credit to ensure restoration. If the work is done, Datoli said, Pinero might not be fined for this, his first offense. Pinaro said he did not know of the land-clearing and tree-removal permits required by the city.

3. Liz Holton operates a doughnut shop at 2240 Broadway Avenue. Today she was ordered to appear in court at 10 a.m. tomorrow morning. One of her employees is Mildred McCartey. Ms. McCartey was called for jury duty on Monday of last week and served the entire week. When she returned to work at 7 a.m. Monday of this week she found that she had been replaced, fired because of her absence last week. State law prohibits an employer from firing or threatening to fire an employee called for jury duty, and Judge George C. LeClair has ordered Liz to appear in his courtroom to determine whether she should be held in contempt of court. Interviewed today, Liz said she did not know of the law and never knew of it. She said she works 12 to 16 hours a day in the doughnut shop, which she owns. McCartney is her only full-time employee, and she said she cannot afford to have her away for several days at a time—she is unable to run the business by herself with only her part-time help. If

held in contempt, she could be fined up to $10,000 and sentenced to six months in jail.

4. Wesley Barlow is an inmate in a Nebraska state prison. He has been charged with swindling dozens of widows out of thousands of dollars. Barlew, 32, is serving an 8-year sentence for burglary. Today he pleaded guilty to new charges against him and was sentenced to an additional 10 years on top of the old sentence. Barlow had mailed letters to men who recently died not long ago. The letters were then received by the mens widows. The letters sought payment—usually less than $100—"for maintenance and repairs." Some women paid because they assumed their dead husbands had some work done before their deaths, a detective thought. Barlow said he got their names from the obituaries in an Omaha newspaper. The scam was discovered when the mother of an Omaha detective received one of the letters.

5. Researchers at your college issued a report today. After three years of study, they confirmed the widely assumed link between drinking and birth defects. They warned that pregnant women who drink risk injury to their children. Because the scientists don't know how much alcohol may be safely consumed by pregnant women, they recommend absolute and total abstention from all alcoholic beverages during a womans 9-month term of pregnancy. What the doctors found during their three years of study is that children born to pregnant women who drink have higher rates of mental and physical abnormalities. The most common problems among such infants are mental retardation and delays in their physical development. Pregnant women who drink also experience more miscarriages and premature births. The reason for the problems is that alcohol from a mothers system passes directly into the bloodstream of her developing child, and that the alcohol remains in the fetal system longer because it is not metabolized and excreted as fast as it is by an adult. Scientists call the problem the fetal alcohol syndrome.

EXERCISE 5

WRITING FOR BROADCAST

WRITING SHORTER BROADCAST STORIES

Write broadcast stories about the following events. Write at least one soft news, one hard news and one throwaway lead. Check for wordiness. Although you may find it difficult at first, limit your stories to 20 seconds or less. Correct any errors in spelling and grammar.

1. Although three straight national girls' marbles champions have come from your city, it gives them no place to play or practice. Their coach, whos Cheryl Nichols, is looking for donations to build marble shooting rings. "If we had rings, then we could recruit more kids and turn out more champions," said Cheryl. "And, it would be great for tourism." Cheryl is a an avid supporter of the sport. She won the 1980 national championship and has coached the last 7 out of 10 winners, including Tim Onn and Wendy Jaco, of your city, who won this years championship. To practice, the kids must use portable rings or go to LaSage, which is forty minutes away. Some kids have parents who cannot travel the distance on a regular basis. Cheryl said that it takes several years and about 4,000 hours of practice to make a champion. Cheryl thinks it would cost about $700 to build a ring—a 14 × 14 foot smooth, concrete pad—and that at least 4 are necessary. Donated materials and labor would lower the cost.

2. The state has initiated a new drug program and is happy with the response. The new drug program is to help low-income Medicare folks buy prescription drugs at reduced prices. "We are happy with the early response," said Edwin diMarco, your states health secretary. The State Pharmacy Discount Program was approved by the state legislature about 3 years ago, and was finally inacted at the beginning of this month. People who can take advantage of the program are Medicare recipients with incomes up to 175% of the federal poverty level—$15,715 for an individual or $21,210 for a family of two. Members already get a 15% discounted price that the state negotiates with pharmaceutical manufacturers for the Medicaid program. The new program enables them to get a 35% discount off of that. Edwin says that this is a substantial savings. The problem, he says, is that a majority of people who are eligible havent enrolled yet. The challenge is to get the word out. About 4 thousand elderly citizens have enrolled, although the state estimates 50,000 citizens are eligible for the program. He is using Dr.'s offices and senior citizen centers to spread the word. Prescription drugs is a very high concern for seniors. To inquire about the program, request an application or just talk to someone about it, you can call toll free 1-800-555-5555.

3. From 11 at night to 4 in the morning, people more easily can pick up or drop off airline passengers at the airport. Community Capital Airport is now offering free parking for drivers and their passengers. "You must park in the hourly garage and only between those times," said Sherman Kirpatrick, the director of the airport. They will not be having police officers there to check your vehicle. If you mess up where you park, then you have to pay that area's full fees. If you park earlier or later than

the designated times, then you must pay the full price of $8 an hour. The airport and the airlines are trying to encourage people to travel at all times of the day and night. And, they are trying to make it a nicer experience for night travelers and their drivers.

4. The police have not identified a suspect or motive, but the physician—Richardo Cessarini—who was shot Tuesday evening about 7 p.m. in his driveway—on Cypress Blvd.—has now died—at Community Hospital, where he has been in critical condition since the shooting. Before he died it was not a homicide case, but now authorities say it is. Cessarini was shot, in the head, as he got out of his 2002 Mercedes. His wallet and other items on him were not taken. The police have been questioning neighbors, looking for clues. They are following up on a tip that a light colored Navigator was seen leaving the scene. Cessarini was described by family and friends as a kind, loving father and a giving doctor who had time for everyone.

5. The city hopes to save about $3 million this year in its first stage of a new program that it hopes could eventually save 10 times that amount in the future. The mayor said she hopes to do this through bulk buying and consolidation of contracts. "We should manage our spending—buy in bulk—just like families do and operate our budget—including consolidating our contracts—just like a Fortune 500 company does." Mayor Datoli noted, for example, that the city had 30 different contracts for buying computers and software and 40 different contracts for janitorial supplies. "That's changed," she says. Also, with bulk buying, things cost less: a whole puncher used to cost $11.57, and now costs $5.03; a 100 watt light bulb that had cost $0.42 now costs $0.21. However, citizens should not expect to see this savings reflected in lower city taxes. "This savings will be applied to reducing the budget's deficit," said Tony Ferguson, the City Treasurer.

EXERCISE 6

WRITING FOR BROADCAST

WRITING BROADCAST STORIES FROM MORE FACTS

Write broadcast stories about the following topics. Write at least one soft news, one hard news and one throwaway lead. Check for wordiness. Your stories should not run more than 30 seconds. Correct any errors in spelling and grammar.

1. The citys Board of Education met at 8 p.m. yesterday in the board headquarters. The board considered four proposals. First it awarded Certificates of Appreciation to 17 retiring teachers. Second it approved the appointment of Reba Caravel, now vice principal at Central High School, to principal of Martin Luther King Jr. High School. Third it approved a proposal to let individual high school PTAs decide whether or not to require school uniforms. And fourth it approved a 3.6% raise for all teachers and administrators. "We'll be trading designer jeans and stylish shirts and $200 sneakers for blue-and-white uniforms," said Priscilla Eisen, president of the Kennedy High School PTA. "Everyone favors this. Jumpers or skirts and blouses for girls and trousers, shirts and ties for every boy." Thus, the city will join a small but growing number of public schools nationwide hanging up fashion trends. Supt. Gerrie Hubbard said uniforms may not be suitable for every public school, but it will benefit students, since uniforms are an equalizer, a way to make poor kids indistinguishable from more affluent kids, and a way to end a clothes competition that seems to dominate some schools. "We're not interested in the best-dressed child here," said Hubard. "We're interested in emphasizing achievement and raising self-esteem. We want to stop concentration on clothes and start concentration on basic skills." School officials hope the idea may also be a unifier, creating more of a sense of togetherness and also instill a greater pride in school. "We decided we needed something to bring everyone together. It also imposes discipline and reduces thefts, especially of clothing. And it alleviates a lot of financial problems for parents. Kids can be cruel," Hubard said. "They'll make fun of someone who's wearing $9.99 Kmart specials instead of $95 Gloria Vanderbilts. Uniforms take a lot of pressure off the kids and parents." The uniforms will cost about $30 each, and provisions will be made for students who can't afford to buy three of them.

2. Its a tragedy being investigated in your city. Your city has many homes for the elderly, including Elder Haven at 1040 Broughton Drive. In the last 3 months alone 4 residents of the home passed away. Today, the citys social service agencies announced they are launching an investigation into the deaths. A team of doctors and nurses will look into why 4 residents of the state-licensed manor died and whether the deaths could have been prevented. Two died while suffering from severe bed sores and urinary infections. A watchdog group, your states Department of Health and Rehabilitative Services, inspects nursing homes, normally once a year, and gave the home a rating last year of "marginally acceptable," citing numerous problems to clear up. People wonder whether social workers for the department could have prevented the deaths. Critics say the department failed to act in time. The first incident being investigated occurred 3 months ago when a 85 year old resident was admitted to a local hospital. He was dehydrated, his body temperature dangerously low, and his

body covered by bruises and bed sores. He died a week later. Six weeks ago city inspectors found two other patents who needed "immediate medical attention." One was a 69-year-old woman, the other a 76-year-old man, and both eventually died. Yet another woman died just last week.

3. Sara Howard of 812 Bell Av. is a hero. She has the bad burns to prove it. "It wasn't that big a deal," she said to you. Police officer Howard, 28, was on routine patrol, starting her shift at 7 a.m. today. Her first call concerned a car-truck collision on Heritage Road. Gas was spewing from the cars punctured fuel tank, and Howard could see that three women were inside. "I just waited for an opening in the flames and then went for the door," Howard said. Three times the officer charged the car and three times was driven back by the raging, hot, fiery flames. Howard then proceeded to empty an extinguisher in her car on the flames and two of the women were able to get out largely under their own power but in the backseat was 78-year-old Suzanne Kopp. Howard, feeling the searing heat along her left side, finally succeeded in grabbing the woman and tugged her to safety. They looked back and "the whole car was just a total fireball," a witness at the scene said. Other witnesses at the scene were awestruck. "How many people would go into a car completely engulfed?" asked Charles Kalani, another witness. "Not very many, I think." None of the women in the car was badly hurt but Howard ended up in Regional Medical Center with serious 2nd and 3rd burns on her left side from her ankle to her arm and face. She remains hospitalized and will miss at least a week of work, maybe a month. "I just hope that somebody would do the same thing if it were my parents or grandmother in her car," Howard said. Her boss, Police Chief Bary Kopperud said the women in the burning car were lucky Howard drove by. "She's really brave," Kopperuud said. "It didn't surprise me a bit what she did, and I've recommended her for our Medal of Valor—its the highest award we give—for risking her life to save others."

4. In the past citys have offered cash for guns and the response has been good. Police in those cities have collected hundreds, sometimes thousands, of guns, mostly pistols which they want to get off the streets, but also rifles and shotguns. Now your city is planning a new program called "Toys for Guns." Anyone who turns in a gun will be given a gift certificate worth $100 at Toys R Us. Local businessmen are providing the money. They hope people will give up their guns to get toys for their kids, especially at Christmas. So far the program has received a significant amount in donations and expects much, much more. "Its a simple solution to a serious problem" says local businessman Minny Cosby, who thought of the idea. "You have to put something in a persons hands once you take something out of their hands." There are an estimated 200 million firearms in the U.S. In other cities people have been given football tickets, a choice of sporting events, rock concerts or fancy restaurant meals. Critics say most guns collected are from law-abiding citizens, not criminals. "If you get even one gun off the street you may prevent a tragedy," Cosby responds however. "Besides, if honest people turn in their guns, they can't be stolen. That's where a lot of criminals get their guns." The police promise to ask no questions and to destroy the guns. Cosby proposed the idea at a recent regular monthly meeting of the citys Chamber of Commerce and other people in attendance at the meeting immediately pledged additional contributions which has thus far reached a grand total of $43,500 and is still growing.

5. Lynn Aneja is a 14-year-old teen-ager. She is the daughter of Mr. and Mrs. David Aneja, 489 Tulip. Her father is a deputy sheriff with the county sheriffs department. Her mother is a homemaker known for volunteering much of her time—20 or more hours a week—to help the homeless in your city by running a soup kitchen for the

hungry and homeless at Calvary Assembly of God Church. Lynn, an only child, told police that her dad came to her bedroom last night where she was studying at about 10 p.m. and said goodnight and that he loved her very much and hugged her. Earlier, she said, she'd heard her parents arguing. Minutes after her dad left her room Lynn heard a series of shots, one after the other. She ran to her parents bedroom. Both were dead. She promptly dialed 911. Police responding to her call found two bodies in the bedroom: her mother and her father. Sheriff Gus DeCessari said in a press conference this morning: "Its hard, these tragedies, hard on everyone: the family, neighbors, co-workers, everyone. David was a 17-year veteran and was recently promoted from corporal to sergeant." A preliminary investigation suggests that David shot his wife three times, then turned the gun on himself. Both were dead when police arrived on the scene. The investigation is continuing, and autopsies are scheduled for today. The daughter, Lynn, is staying with neighbors. Sheriff DeCessari said David had an exemplary record, and no one knows any reason for the murder/suicide apparently committed with Davids service revolver.

CHAPTER 19

THE NEWS MEDIA AND PR PRACTITIONERS

The inherent worth of . . . speech in terms of its capacity for informing the public does not depend upon the identity of the source, whether corporation, association, union, or individual.

(Justice Lewis Powell, U.S. Supreme Court)

News reporting and public relations are two different professions, but they share the goals of communicating with and informing an audience. They often share the same audience. Also, reporters and PR practitioners work in a symbiotic relationship. PR practitioners want to reach journalists' large audience of daily viewers and readers. Journalists turn to PR practitioners to get sources and information for stories. For that relationship to work, each must understand how the other thinks and operates.

Public relations practitioners provide a valuable service for both their clients and the public. To succeed, they must understand how the media operate and provide information that is clear, concise, accurate and objective.

Public relations practitioners need good writing skills; the ability to translate complicated information into clear, readable stories; and an understanding of journalists' definitions of news. They need to be available and respond quickly to questions from reporters. The best practitioners know their client or organization well, locate information quickly and arrange interviews with experts and top executives when needed. PR practitioners use these skills to build trust and a working relationship with reporters.

WHAT IS PUBLIC RELATIONS?

Public relations is planned and continuous communication designed to project a positive image about an organization, an issue or a product to the public. Unlike advertising, which is paid promotion, public relations uses the news media as a means to promote an organization or a product.

Public relations practitioners and reporters cross paths almost daily. Most PR practitioners want to get their client's name in the news without having to pay for the publicity, so the practitioner's allegiance is to the client. The reporter's objective, on the other hand, is to inform readers or viewers, so the reporter judges a news release on its value to the public. In addition, space in a newspaper or time on radio and television is limited.

It is important, then, that PR practitioners think and write like reporters. Those who do will write news releases that are both newsworthy and conform to news style. News releases should sound and look as though they were written by reporters.

Public Relations Agencies

Some practitioners work in a public relations agency, representing companies or other organizations either throughout the year or for special events, such as a festival or sporting event, the launch of a new product or service, a fund-raising campaign or a political election campaign. Public relations practitioners in agencies handle several "accounts" simultaneously. Agencies may be as small as a one-person consultant contracted to write and edit a company's communications, develop brochures or shoot videotapes for training employees. Or an agency can be a large, international network of offices. International conglomerates usually hire worldwide agencies to handle their public relations needs in different countries and cultures.

Corporate and Nonprofit Public Relations

Many public relations practitioners work within a company or nonprofit organization, such as General Motors or the American Heart Association. Practitioners in corporate and nonprofit settings have two audiences they must communicate with—an internal audience of officers and employees and an external audience of consumers, investors and the general public. Practitioners may handle either internal or external communications, or both, depending on the size of the organization.

Internal Communications

Practitioners handling internal communications keep company employees informed about the organization. They ensure that all employees, whether in the same building or in a branch office several states away, think of themselves as part of the company.

For example, employees in a General Motors plant in Texas may believe administrators in the Detroit headquarters do not care much about them or understand production problems that affect their work. The public relations practitioner creates lines of communication between administrators and employees to make the employees aware of their roles in and contributions to the company's operations. Through the company newsletter or annual report, the practitioner informs employees of activities at the headquarters as well as other plants or offices. The practitioner helps employees understand changes in policies or business practices, such as the closing of a plant, that will affect them.

Some practitioners send birthday cards to all employees to show the company cares about them. Others publish photographs and brief biographies of new employees in a newsletter or news video. Still others hold companywide competitions or host award banquets for all personnel. Usually the public relations practitioner stays in the background, allowing company executives to benefit from the increased goodwill. A department head signs the birthday cards the practitioner sends. The CEO shakes the hands of the winners of the companywide contests, and a president reads the practitioner's prepared speech at the awards banquet. In many ways, the practitioner resembles the theater director who never appears onstage but coordinates the performances of others.

External Communications

Public relations professionals in the world of corporations or nonprofit organizations also have to deal with the public—the people outside the organization who are its investors, customers, clients or contributors. PR practitioners promote a positive image of the organization by identifying the different publics that affect the organization and researching the best ways to reach them. To influence or project a positive image, most practitioners write news releases and features and send them to the media. Other PR tools and skills include developing press kits that contain information about the company; setting up speakers' bureaus; staging events; filming news clips; writing public service announcements; holding meetings; and designing posters, brochures and pamphlets. All these activities help disseminate information about the company or its products to the public. Many companies have public relations departments that manage all external communications, while other companies hire public relations agencies to handle special needs.

Whether corporations or organizations have an internal public relations department or hire a public relations agency to represent them, they may sometimes face a crisis that requires working with the news media to keep the public informed. Hiding information from the media and the public can create a crisis in public confidence toward the corporation or organization. The accounting scandals at Enron, WorldCom and other large corporations shook public confidence in the financial markets and the corporate world. PR practitioners must deal with such crisis situations and get truthful information out to the external publics the organization serves in order to protect the organization's reputation.

BECOMING A PUBLIC RELATIONS PRACTITIONER

Numerous U.S. universities and colleges offer majors in public relations. Usually, schools require PR majors to enroll in a newswriting and reporting class. The class teaches students such things as the media's definitions of news, newswriting style and the importance of deadlines. Public relations professionals agree on the class's importance. A survey of 200 members of the Public Relations Society of America found that professionals consider a news reporting course more important for PR majors than any course in public relations.

Many journalists who decide to leave the traditional news business accept jobs in public relations. Companies hire reporters and editors as public relations practitioners because they have writing skills that are essential to the job.

WORKING WITH NEWS MEDIA

Public relations practitioners use the media to get information about their client to the public. Therefore, practitioners must determine which media outlets—newspapers, trade publications, radio or television—will best serve their purposes. In addition, practitioners know the writing styles, deadlines and other procedures of each target medium. News releases sent to newspapers are written in Associated Press style. Releases sent to radio stations are written in broadcast style and format so radio announcers do not have to rewrite them; they can read them verbatim over the air.

To make their promotional efforts effective, PR practitioners must also learn whom to contact. They should identify the proper news departments and the people in charge of the departments before sending out a release. "Shotgunning" a release, or sending to multiple departments and department heads in a news organization, wastes time and money. For example, most editors will discard a news release about a company employee's promotion, but a business editor might report the promotion in a weekly column or section devoted to local promotions. Similarly, most editors would discard a news release about a Christmas program at a church, but a religion editor might mention it in a roundup about Christmas activities. By sending their news releases to the right editor, practitioners increase the likelihood that the releases will be used and decrease the chance of harming their reputations by wasting an editor's time.

Many news stories have public relations origins. PR practitioners bring information about a company or organization to journalists' attention, often through a news release. If the release is well-written and a journalist believes it contains something newsworthy, it has a better chance of being used by the media. If the news release is poorly written or contains nothing newsworthy, it usually receives only a quick glance before landing in a trash basket.

Reporters also might follow up an idea presented in a news release, but interview their own sources, write their own stories and present their own angles. Thus, while it appears PR practitioners are using journalists to achieve their goals, news releases help journalists stay informed about their community. Journalists choose whether or not to use the releases.

ELEMENTS OF A NEWS RELEASE

Journalists reject news releases for many reasons:

- They are too long.
- They are not newsworthy.
- They are poorly written.
- They fail to include important information.
- They have not been localized.
- They arrive too late.
- They are mailed to the wrong person.
- They are written more for clients than for the public.

The following suggestions describe how to write a successful news release for print media, but they also apply to writing releases for broadcast news.

List a Contact Person and a Follow-Up

Reporters may want to follow up a news release to verify information or answer a question. They need to know whom they can call to get more information. Thus, an effective news release lists the name and phone number of a contact person, someone familiar with the subject of the release who can answer questions.

Reporters often complain that no one is available to answer questions about a release. If a contact person is not available, then another person in the organization should be briefed about the release and given authority to respond to questions.

Some news releases, such as those for a new organization or product, may include a cover letter to the editor telling more about the sponsoring company. Some practitioners use cover letters to suggest ideas for using the attached release. Such suggestions may help the editor decide whether to use the release, or may help in developing story ideas involving the organization or product.

Send the Release on Time

Timely information is as important to PR practitioners as it is to news reporters. Timeliness is one of the several characteristics of news and is used by reporters to judge the importance of a story. A news release received too close to deadline is unlikely to be published or broadcast because editors have little or no time to verify information or get answers to questions.

News releases can be sent to news organizations by conventional mail, fax or e-mail. If releases are sent by conventional mail, PR practitioners must allow adequate time for mail to be handled and delivered. If they send releases by fax or e-mail, PR practitioners must know the correct telephone fax number or e-mail address so the information gets to the proper department or person. Whether releases are sent through conventional mail or faxed, practitioners need to know news organization procedures and deadlines and deliver the release in time for processing for publication.

Use Journalism's Five W's

The opening paragraph, or lead, of a news release should provide the who, what, when, where and why of the subject of the release. Journalists respect public relations practitioners who understand their definitions of news. Journalists want to be informed about major stories. They do not want to be bothered with stories that are obviously not newsworthy. Unfortunately, most news releases either lack any news or are written so poorly the news is buried near the end of the release.

The best news releases are so good that it is difficult to distinguish them from the stories written by a news organization's own staff. Here are three examples:

> The Ashton Community Senior Center, 115 N. Locust St., will hold a flea market and bake sale from 8 a.m. to 2 p.m. Friday to benefit the senior center's emergency food pantry.
>
> John Jacobs, editorial cartoonist for the Newtown Daily News, will speak about the role of editorial cartooning in a democratic society at the Newtown Public Library at 7 p.m. Wednesday.
>
> St. Joseph Medical Center's Women's and Children's Services will present "Confident Parenting I," a program about children's physical and social development, from 6:30 to 9 p.m. Monday in the hospital's Reed Memorial Annex, 805 S. Virginia Ave.

Analyze those leads. Notice that, like good news story leads, all three emphasize the news—and are clear, concise and factual. They also follow Associated Press style in regard to addresses, time elements and sentence structure.

Write Well

Editors complain that many news releases are poorly written or written for the wrong audience. Newspapers have a diverse audience whose reading abilities range from elementary to college level. For a news release to be used in a newspaper, it must be written so all readers can understand it. News organizations usually write for an 11th-grade reading level. Journalists will throw away difficult-to-understand releases. News organizations would reject this news release:

> Systems Status, Inc. (SSI), developers of fully integrated PCI/release shipping control applications for the food service industry, announces that the National Food Service Industry Council (NFSIC) has approved AutoShip Version 7 for SRO (Stock Replacement Optimization) PCIFACS processing and that on-site testing of the shipping processing software for PCIFACS (Personal Computer Interface for Acquiring Continuous Supplies) will begin in January at 250 fast-food restaurants throughout the United States.

Editors would reject it because it is written more for the client than the public and contains jargon that few people would understand. When writing a news release, practitioners should write as journalists. Words should be simple. Sentences should average about 20 words. Paragraphs should be short and get to the point immediately. Practitioners should write in the active voice, using the passive voice only when necessary.

Proofreading is essential. Editors reject news releases with grammar and spelling errors or missing, buried or erroneous information. Practitioners must care about the quality of the work they produce in order to see it used in newspapers and news broadcasts.

Practitioners should think of their news releases as a community service providing information the public needs. Their writing should be lively and to the point, not boring and literary.

Localize Information

News releases often present generalized information and fail to tell how that information affects people in a community. Too often practitioners confuse "localization" and "proximity." In fact, localizing can mean reflecting a psychological as well as geographical closeness. A university's health science center submitted the following news releases, which illustrate that principle:

> While many Americans may be eating less red meat to lower cholesterol and fat levels, researchers at the University of Florida are investigating the possibility that older Americans should, in fact, be eating more.

> Doctors have some unseasonable advice for pregnant women heading outdoors to enjoy this summer's warm weather: Bundle up.
>
> Although the risk is small, they could get bitten by ticks carrying Lyme disease, a rare but disabling illness that University of Florida physicians say can be transmitted by infected mothers-to-be to the unborn babies.

The first news release discusses a topic that concerns many adults—their cholesterol level—but it also points out an unusual or unexpected twist: that older Americans may need more red meat. The second news release concerns another unusual topic: the fact that pregnant women need to bundle up, even in summer, to protect their unborn babies from Lyme disease (a disease often in the news). Identifying the source, in this case the University of Florida, localizes the releases geographically. But because the releases discuss topics that affect the everyday lives of hundreds of thousands of readers and viewers, they are also psychologically close to the audience.

Provide Visuals

Visuals, such as photographs, graphs or charts, catch the eye of readers, draw them into the story and illustrate major points. Many newspapers use visual elements on their pages so their audience can get information easily and quickly.

Public relations practitioners should think about what visuals might be relevant to a release. Can a photograph help illustrate the information in the release? Can an infographic, chart or other visual help the audience grasp the information? Thinking visually can help practitioners get their releases accepted by editors. But don't overwhelm editors with visuals. Keep them simple and to the point. Usually, one or two will do.

Provide a Link to a Web Site

The Internet has become a major source of information, and research can be conducted quickly and efficiently from a newsroom when reporters have a link or URL address to get to a Web site.

Most organizations or corporations have Web sites, which can provide additional information on the topic addressed in the release. Statistical information to support the release or links providing additional information can be included with the release to help reporters answer questions they may have. In addition, many corporations or organizations belong to trade or professional associations that can supply expert sources for a story if reporters want to follow up on information. Links to those associations also can be provided in the release. It is important that the release provide not only adequate information, but also the means for reporters to get additional information.

Format the News Release Properly

News releases should follow a standard format so an editor can quickly determine who sent it and what it is about.

Include the complete address of the organization sending the release in the upper left corner of the page. Along with the address, provide the name and telephone number of a contact person the editor or reporter can call in case of questions. It is a good idea to include both daytime and nighttime telephone numbers since many reporters and editors work at night.

A release date should appear just below the address block on the right side of the page. The release date tells the editor when the information may be published. The release date may say, "For Immediate Release" or "For Release at Will" (whenever the newspaper has space available), or it may specify a date and time after which it may be published. News organizations have no legal obligation to adhere to release dates, but they usually do so as a matter of professional courtesy. Failing to honor a release date can cost a news organization its credibility with sources and, perhaps, deprive it of information in the future. Another problem with not honoring a release date is that the information could turn out to be inaccurate. The information in a release may change between the time it was written and the release date. The source of the release may have been prepared to update it in light of changing circumstances. If a news organization, however, has already published the release, both the source and the news organization look foolish.

The body of the news release should begin one-third of the way down the page to allow space for the editor to make comments to the rewrite person who will prepare it for publication. A headline or title for the release should appear above the text of the release. The headline should be placed on the left side of the page and typed in capital letters. It typically should not extend beyond the address block. If the headline requires two lines, it should be single-spaced. The body of the news release should be double-spaced.

If the release runs more than one page, the word "more" should be placed within brackets or dashes (—more—) at the bottom center of the page. The following pages of the release are identified by a slug line (a word or short phrase indicating the topic of the release) followed by dashes and the page number at the top of the page, either on the left or the right side of the page.

At the end of the release, type the word "end" or the number "30" within quotes or dashes to indicate to the editor that there is no more text. Some editors use three number signs (###) to indicate the end of the text.

Here's a sample format for a news release:

> American Conference of Homebuilders
> 129 South Construction Way
> Rockville, MD 12345-7890
>
> CONTACT: Amanda James
> Office phone (301) 555-1212
> Cell phone (301) 999-4444
>
> E-mail ajames@ach.org
>
> Release Date and Time
>
> (Body text of the release begins one-third down the page.)
> <u>THE TITLE GOES HERE IN UPPER CASE AND UNDERLINE.</u>
>
> Body of the release begins under the title and is double-spaced, making it easier for editors to edit the copy.
>
> At the end of the release, type an end mark to indicate the text is finished.

TYPES OF NEWS RELEASES

News releases serve a variety of objectives, such as publicizing a new company, announcing a new product or pointing out the effects a company has on a community. The most common types of news releases are advance stories, event stories, features and discoveries.

Advance Stories

Practitioners write announcements whenever their company or client will sponsor an activity such as a speech or seminar. Advance stories often use an "agenda" lead like the following to provide information on the activity or event to the public:

> The Bloomington Teen Athletic Challenge will be held beginning at 9 a.m. Saturday, June 28, on the athletic fields of the Bloomington High School, 1479 W. Maple Ave.
>
> The all-day event is open to boys in grades eight to 12 and girls in grades six to 12. The cost is $45 for students of Bloomington Area School District and $55 for those participants from outside the district.
>
> For registration and more information about the all-day competition, call 555-2121 or 1-800-000-0000.

Event Stories

When practitioners write a story prior to an event, they write it as though the event already has happened and the news organization is reporting on it. A release written in this manner serves two main purposes: First, it lets reporters know what will occur at the event, in case they want to cover it; second, it frees reporters from writing the story.

Reporters rarely publish such a release verbatim, however. They may attend the event, perhaps simply to verify the release's accuracy. Reporters often rewrite releases so identical accounts do not appear in other publications.

Practitioners also give reporters copies of speeches before they are delivered. This practice enables reporters to quote the speakers accurately. However, reporters usually attend the speeches because speakers may change some of their comments at the last moment.

The following release was written about a forthcoming presentation at a chemical society's convention. The headline, "Leaves Found to Be Rich Source of Protein for Humans," indicates that the story concerns a topic—health trends—that interests many readers. However, this advance could be improved:

> Tobacco and soybean leaves are a better source of protein for human consumption than egg whites, cheese and milk, scientists said today. Tobacco protein, particularly, has a more complete complement of essential amino acids, they said.
>
> The researchers have been experimenting with tobacco protein for several years, and have demonstrated that it can be whipped into meringue toppings or added to any foods that are whipped or jellied.
>
> Now they say edible proteins can be extracted as well from the leaves of alfalfa, soybean and sugar beets. Unlike traditional protein sources like meats, eggs and milk, the plant leaves contain no fat or cholesterol, said Austin Black of the University of Iowa today. He spoke here at the 99th national meeting of the Midwestern Chemical Society.
>
> With world population increasing and a shortage of protein for human nutrition imminent, Dr. Black said leaf protein, being the most abundant protein on earth, can alleviate the supply-and-demand problem. He also said that after extracting the protein and removing undesirable leaf constituents, the fiber and juice from the leaf could be processed into smoking materials that are less harmful than those on the market now.
>
> "This is especially important for developing countries where the smoking population is increasing and human malnutrition is overwhelming," Dr. Black said.
>
> He described two forms of leaf protein, fraction-1-protein (F-1-p) and fraction-2-protein (F-2-p). F-1-p accumulates inside chloroplasts—where the green pigment chlorophyll occurs—and is the enzyme responsible for fixation of carbon dioxide in photosynthesis. F-2-p represents the remaining protein that surrounds the nuclei of the leaf cells.
>
> The tobacco F-1-p has a protein content of 99.5%; F-1-p's from soybean, sugar beet and alfalfa range between 97.3%-98.4% in protein. All F-1-p's are odorless and tasteless, as are all F-2-p's, but they are beige to yellow in color.
>
> In food applications, plant leaf protein can be added to any food that will be whipped or jellied. Dr. Black said these proteins could serve the same function as egg white and the protein casein in the new commercial fat substitutes. The result would be an even lower fat content and nearly equal or better protein level, he said.
>
> Dr. Black noted that tobacco F-1-p may have pharmaceutical uses, particularly for renal and post-surgical patients. For patients undergoing dialysis, tobacco F-1-p provides a near ideal combination of protein and amino acids and it would be nutritious for post-surgical patients also, he said.

This release has several problems. One is that it deviates from Associated Press news style—for example, the use of "%" rather than spelling out "percent." Another problem is that the release contains too many words and phrases that experts might understand but that the general audience would not. And although the first paragraph notes "scientists," only one is named and quoted throughout the news release. Dr. Black or the event—the chemical society's meeting—

should be mentioned sooner in the story. In addition, the release should be simplified by eliminating much of the information in the last four paragraphs.

Features

Practitioners often write feature stories as press releases. Many features can interest a national audience. They may provide interesting and important information and deal with subjects ranging from health, medicine and science to home and auto care. A well-written feature should appear to be an information piece rather than a blatant publicity piece for a client or organization. Sometimes features mention the client or organization as the sponsor of an event; at other times, they quote the client or organization as an authority or source for the article.

The following feature describes homebuilders using the Internet for information. The feature includes quotes from the manufacturer, for whom it was prepared, and mentions a specific distributor:

> Nearly 80 percent of homeowners now consider themselves buy-it-yourselfers. Yet, only one in five say they rely on the advice of professionals to assist in their product-buying decisions, according to a survey by Better Homes and Gardens Special Interest Publications.
>
> Instead, that advice could be coming from one of the fastest-growing sources of information for homeowners—the Internet's World Wide Web—say building product manufacturers. The Web grew by 360 percent in just the last quarter, according to Open Markets Inc.
>
> "Buy-it-yourselfers demand information about home products where they can reach it, when they want it," said Daniel Hobbs of Stevens Construction Inc., the local distributor of Jackson Windows and Doors. He said area homeowners are seeking product information once requested only by builders and contractors. "They demand competitive comparisons, details of product features and examples of what the product will look like installed."
>
> Right now, more homeowners are looking for this kind of information on the Internet. "If it's not there, that product may not be considered when it's time to buy," said Marvin Espinoza, vice president of marketing for Jackson Windows, which recently established a site on the Web to provide on-demand information about windows and doors.
>
> With a home computer, modem and browser software, homeowners have everything from product photographs to technical information at their fingertips. And, while only 2 percent of building materials manufacturers have World Wide Web sites now, according to WebTrack's InterAd Database, Espinoza expects that number to rise quickly.
>
> Like Jackson Windows, Frigidaire, Electrolux, Master Lock and Grohe Faucets have anticipated this demand and established sites on the Web.
>
> Upon accessing Jackson's home page (http://www.jack.com) through an online service, users may choose informational paths including "Windowscaping," which provides photography and descriptions of design ideas; "Crash Course," including a glossary of window and door terms and energy efficiency ratings terminology; "Jamb Session," which highlights product line options and benefits; and "Windows of Opportunity," where users can request free information about making window decisions by entering their name and mailing address.
>
> "We expect the Web to support our sales personnel," said Hobbs. "Buy-it-yourselfers now have the window and door information they demand—at their fingertips—when and where they demand it."
>
> For free literature about making window decisions, call 1-800-000-0000, or visit Jackson Windows on the World Wide Web at http://www.jack.com.

Most news organizations would eliminate the feature's last sentence and both mentions of the company's online home page to keep it from sounding too much like an advertisement. They might also rewrite parts of the release, condensing and simplifying it.

Discoveries and Results

Universities, hospitals, corporations and research institutions want the public to know about their discoveries and the results of their work. Announcements of discoveries highlight and enhance an organization's reputation, as well as keeping the public aware of new advances in science and technology.

A news release from Tulane University typifies press releases that announce discoveries. The beginning of the release provides the central point of the news. The rest of the release explains the significance of the discovery:

> NEW ORLEANS—Smoking cigarettes may increase the levels of three novel risk factors for cardiovascular disease, say Tulane University researchers in this month's Annals of Internal Medicine. Smoking has long been known to increase a person's risk of heart disease, but the relationships between cigarette smoking and several recently identified risk factors have not been studied thoroughly.
>
> Heart disease and strokes (cardiovascular disease) are leading causes of death and disability in most Western countries. Smoking, high-fat diets, high cholesterol, high blood pressure, diabetes and kidney disease increase a person's risk for cardiovascular disease. Recently, researchers identified several novel risk factors that indicate additional risk for cardiovascular disease. These newer risk factors include proteins that are involved in blood clotting and are released in response to inflammation (fibrinogen and C-reactive protein). They also include an amino acid (homocysteine) that may be elevated when intake of vitamins, such as folic acid, is low.
>
> Researchers looked at data that was collected from 1988 to 1994 from 17,353 adults nationally. Participants in the survey answered questions about cigarette smoking and their medical history. They also had their blood pressure and weight measured, and gave blood samples that were used to measure newer risk factors. The researchers then looked at whether people who smoked were more likely to have elevated levels of the newer risk factors, even after controlling for other traditional risk factors, such as diabetes and high blood pressure.
>
> Cigarette smoking was associated with elevated levels of fibrinogen, C-reactive protein and homocysteine. Current smokers had higher levels of these risk factors than former smokers. Also, smoking more cigarettes daily was associated with higher levels of the risk factors.
>
> "These data indicate that cigarette smoking may promote cardiovascular disease by increasing the levels of blood fibrinogen, C-reactive protein and homocysteine," said Dr. Jiang He, the senior author.
>
> The full report is titled "Relationship Between Cigarette Smoking and Novel Risk Factors for Cardiovascular Disease in the United States." It is in the June issue of Annals of Internal Medicine. The authors are Tulane epidemiologists Lydia Bazzano, Jiang He, Paul Muntner, Summa Vupputuri and Paul K. Whelton.

THE JOURNALIST'S PERSPECTIVE: WORKING WITH PRESS RELEASES

Newspapers are besieged by individuals and organizations seeking publicity. Large newspapers receive thousands of news releases and other requests for publicity each week. Even small-town newspapers receive hundreds of releases in a week.

For most news organizations, news releases are an important and convenient source of information and story ideas. No news organization can afford to employ enough reporters to cover every story occurring in a community. Instead, news media depend on readers and viewers to notify them about church and school activities; charitable events and fund-raisers; business and medical news; art, music and theater events and schedules; speakers; and festivals.

Reporters handle news releases as they would any other type of story. Their first task is to identify a central point. If the release lacks a central point, the reporter discards it. If a central point is there, then the reporter identifies the relevant information and discards the rest. Reporters also use the central point to identify what information is missing.

Reporters then critically examine whatever information the news release provides and summarize that information as clearly, concisely and objectively as possible. The task often is difficult because some news releases fail to emphasize any news. Others contain clichés, jargon and puffery. Moreover, most fail to use the proper style for capitalization, punctuation and abbreviations.

Typically, editors discard 100 news releases for every three or four they accept. Even those they accept usually must be rewritten. Some editors do not even open all the news releases they receive in the mail. Rather, they glance at the return address to see who sent the release, then immediately throw it away if they recognize that it came from a source that regularly submits trivial information. For example, journalists are unlikely to use a news release from a company that has no presence in a community or surrounding area, such as manufacturing plants or franchise outlets. Yet some companies send out announcements about the promotion of executives at corporate headquarters hundreds of miles away. Few news organizations use such releases because they hold no interest for people in their community.

The worst news releases, usually those submitted by local groups unfamiliar with the media, lack information that reporters need to write complete stories. They also omit the names and telephone numbers of people whom the reporters might call to obtain more information, or explanations of unclear facts. Some news releases provide telephone numbers that journalists can call only during the day, not during the evening, when the reporters employed by morning dailies and the broadcast media often work.

Editors usually do not use news releases as submitted. Instead, they have reporters rewrite them, confirming the information and adding to it with quotes and additional facts. These editors may explain that they want their stories to be distinctive. Also, they may distrust the accuracy and truthfulness of the information submitted by publicists.

Other editors use news releases primarily as a source of ideas. If editors like an idea provided by a news release, they will assign reporters to gather more information and write a story. Sometimes the published story is much different from the picture presented in the news release.

THE NO. 1 PROBLEM: LACK OF NEWSWORTHINESS

Journalists obviously prefer news releases about topics that satisfy their definitions of news. They look for topics that are new, local, interesting, unusual, relevant and important to their audience. Journalists also look for information likely to affect hundreds or even thousands of people. Action is more newsworthy than opinions, and a genuine or spontaneous event is more newsworthy than a contrived one. Unless they serve very small communities, news organizations increasingly refuse to publish news releases about ribbon-cutting and groundbreaking ceremonies. Newspapers also generally refuse to publish photographs showing people passing a check or gavel.

Limited Interest

News organizations may not use releases like the following because their topics would not interest many people—except, of course, members of the organizations they mention. Those organizations can use other means, such as newsletters, to communicate with their members. That is not the job of a news organization:

> The Central States Podiatrist Association held its annual membership drive during its winter meeting this week in Springfield.

> Janice Harbaugh, owner and operator of Harbaugh's Gift Emporium, has been selected to attend the third annual Small Business Owners Conference to be held in Kansas City, Mo., beginning March 30.

Contrived Events

Reporters are likely to discard the following news releases because they announce contrived events:

> The president has joined with the blood bank community in proclaiming January as National Volunteer Blood Donor Month and is urging everyone who is healthy to donate blood to help others.
>
> Gov. Donald Austin has proclaimed April 20-26 as American Literacy Week in the state, to coincide with the president's declaration of National Literacy Week during the same period.

Every week and every month of the year is dedicated to some cause, and often to dozens of causes. For example, May is Arthritis Month, National High Blood Pressure Month, National Foot Health Month, Better Speech and Hearing Month, National Tavern Month and American Bike Month. Furthermore, the two news releases state the obvious. Most responsible adults would urge "everyone who is healthy to donate blood to help others." In the second release, since a National Literacy Week already exists, a state declaration is an unnecessary duplication. Stories about such proclamations are often trite, dull, repetitive and devoid of news value.

Rewriting for Newsworthiness

Many of the people writing news releases seem to be more interested in pleasing their bosses than in satisfying the media and informing the public. To please their bosses, they begin news releases with their bosses' names. Or, they may begin with the organization's name and information about the organization before focusing on the news aspect of the release.

> Rep. Wayne Smith, R-Mo., is leading the fight to push the Federal Trade Commission to combat predatory and exorbitant interest rates charged by the nation's banks and credit card companies.
>
> Smith is sponsoring legislation in Congress to cap interest rates that can reach as high as 24 percent on some credit cards. In addition Smith says banks and credit card companies continue to send out credit card solicitation offers to people who already are weighed down by a mountain of debt.
>
> "These solicitations go out to everyone, but young people, seniors and minorities are among the most affected by these practices because they can get into debt quickly and never get the balances paid off," Smith said. "The payments are so low on many of these cards that the only thing that gets paid if there is a balance due each month is the interest.
>
> Smith said many people carry huge amounts of credit card debt because the high interest rates add so much to the balance each month.
>
> REVISED: Congress is considering legislation to lower the interest rates that banks and credit card companies charge consumers.
>
> The legislation, sponsored by Rep. Wayne Smith, R-Mo., will seek to have the Federal Trade Commission investigate lending institutions accused of charging consumers exorbitant interest rates on their credit cards or practicing predatory soliciting to get consumers' business.

Other news releases are editorials that philosophize or praise rather than report information beneficial to the public. A news release submitted by a state's beef producers declared:

> Red meat makes a contribution to America's health and vitality and should be saluted.
>
> We often overlook the fact that American meat products are known throughout the world for their quality, wholesomeness and delicious flavor. This week is National Meat Week, and it is an excellent opportunity to recognize the important contribution red meat makes to the diets of more than 250 million Americans who have made meat

> one of the country's favorite foods. Meat is more than a satisfying meal—it's part of a healthy, well-balanced diet.

Newspapers and newscasts should not praise or editorialize in a news story. That is not their job, nor is it ethical for them to do so.

News organizations might use the following releases because they describe topics likely to interest some readers. However, both news releases require some rewriting to emphasize the news and conform to the style—especially the type of lead—suitable to newspapers.

> The president of a national organization representing psychiatrists all over the United States marked National Mental Health Week by calling for better care for America's seriously mentally ill citizens. The National Psychiatric Association, which represents medical doctors who diagnose and treat severe mental illness, is focusing considerable time and effort on the issue during National Mental Health Week to galvanize support and awareness in its selfless struggle to shed light on these terrible human conditions.
>
> During his opening address at the National Psychiatric Association annual conference, National Psychiatric Association President Dr. Paul Steinmetz demanded that state and federal legislation be implemented that would require the health insurance industry to stop discriminating against the mentally ill and provide sufficient care under health care plans provided by public and private employers.

> REVISED: The president of the National Psychiatric Association today called for state and federal legislation that would require insurance companies to provide health benefits for the mentally ill.

> Programs making war violence exciting and fun entertainment are said to lead the new Fall programs, according to the National Coalition on Television Violence (NCTV). NCTV has just released its most recent monitoring results of prime-time network programs. Violence is portrayed at the rate of about seven violent acts per hour, with new programs taking three of the top four violent spots. ABC continued to be the most violent network for the fourth quarter in a row.

> REVISED: Prime-time network programs contain about seven acts of violence every hour, and this fall's new programs are among the most violent, according to the National Coalition on Television Violence.

THE NO. 2 PROBLEM: LACK OF OBJECTIVITY

Too many news releases promote rather than report. They contain laudatory adverbs and adjectives, not facts.

Advertisements

The worst news releases are blatant advertisements, obviously written to help sell commercial products. Most journalists would reject the following news releases for that reason.

> Dogs may be considered man's best friend, but for many walkers, joggers, and cyclists, dogs can be their worst enemy. According to the American Veterinary Association (AVA) more than a million people are treated each year for dog attacks and on average, 12 people a year die as the result of dog attacks.
>
> Some of these victims are walkers, joggers and cyclists who are attacked by dogs while enjoying the sport they love. Meeting the needs of today's sports-minded and exercise-dedicated active Americans, Pace Consumer Products (PCP) is introducing DOG GONE! Canine Repellant Spray. Based on proven technology developed for law enforcement agencies, DOG GONE! is a nonlife-threatening, momentarily debilitating chemical spray that causes temporary irritation of an animal's nose and eyes, rendering it incapable of attack.

> Fashion designer Beth Engalls and Ribbon Inc. will launch the first line of Beth Engalls Fashion Glasses next spring, according to a licensing agreement signed on Friday. The new line will be available to the trade in March and will appear on retail shelves by late spring.
>
> Ribbon will distribute the line through department stores, sunglass specialty shops, retail chains and optical stores nationwide, as well as Engalls' U.S. boutiques. The line will debut in Engalls' runway presentation for spring at Abby Park in the Mayes Pavilion.
>
> The collection, consisting of eight ophthalmic and eight sunglass styles, exudes all the charm, whimsical creativity and wit that characterizes the work of Beth Engalls. The styles are designed to enhance one's look with sophisticated coloration and subtle detailing, and will feature Engalls' trademark crown logo on the temple. They will be manufactured to Ribbon's renowned high-performance eyewear standards.

While most newspapers would not use such releases, they might be valuable to the trade press or news media in affected communities as leads for stories in the business section of the newspaper.

Laudatory Adjectives and Puffery

Journalists eliminate laudatory adjectives in rewriting news releases. Terms such as "world famous," the "best" or the "greatest" are subjective at best and difficult to verify. Every speaker does not have to be called a "guest speaker," and none should be labeled "famous," "prominent," "well-known" or "distinguished." If a speaker truly is famous, the public already will know the person and will not have to be told of his or her fame.

No news story—or news release—should call a program "wonderful," "successful," "timely" or "informative." Similarly, nothing should be called "interesting" or "important." Reporters also avoid phrases such as "bigger and better," "the best ever" and "back by popular demand."

Puffery often appears in leads of news releases:

> Dr. Paul W. Rust, an internationally known and recognized expert on adolescent learning disorders, will be the guest speaker at a symposium on learning disorders Friday, Nov. 10, at the Convention Center. An extraordinarily gifted and knowledgeable speaker who has written three critically acclaimed and highly interesting books on learning disorders, Dr. Rust will speak about the role of parents and other family members in helping a child with a learning disorder adapt to the challenges the child will face in society.
>
> REVISED: Dr. Paul W. Rust, who studies adolescent learning disorders, will speak about the role of parents and family members in helping a child with a learning disorder adapt to society at a symposium on learning disorders Nov. 10 at the Convention Center.

Reprinted by permission: Tribune Media Service.

The Creative Art Gallery, devoted exclusively to fine art photography, proudly announces an event of international significance in the photographic community: an exhibition of the works of Jerry N. Uelsmann and Diane Farris.

REVISED: The Creative Art Gallery, 324 N. Park Ave., will exhibit the photographs of Jerry N. Uelsmann and Diane Farris from Jan. 4 to Jan. 29.

Telling the Public What to Do

Instead of reporting news, some releases urge readers and viewers to donate their time and money, to buy new products, to attend events or to join organizations. For example:

You have to see this display to believe it!

Every dollar you give—whether $10, $100 or $1,000—stays in your community. So give—you'll be glad you did.

Tickets are available for $60 per person, or reserve a table of eight for $400. That's a savings of $80. Seating is limited so get your tickets right away!

Journalists delete such editorial comments or rewrite them in a more factual manner. Reporters may summarize a story and then, in the final paragraph, tell readers how they can respond, but not say that they should respond:

Tickets for the program are available to the public at the Performing Arts Center and by calling 422-4896, for $5 each. Seating will not be reserved, so the public is urged to arrive early to hear this most important message on the subject of health care.

REVISED: Tickets cost $5 and can be obtained at the Performing Arts Center or by calling 422-4896.

OTHER PROBLEMS WITH NEWS RELEASES

Stating the Obvious

Public relations writers who lack journalism training and do not know what makes a successful news story often write releases that state the obvious:

The state fire marshal's office today emphasized the importance of having working smoke detectors in homes and businesses as a way to save lives.

Parents are worried more than ever about the amount of violence in our society.

A fire marshal is expected to encourage the use of smoke detectors to save lives. That is a routine part of the official's job, and not news. Similarly, violence has always been a problem; generations of parents have worried about it.

In many releases, the real news is buried in the second—or even 22nd—paragraph.

Helping people is a rewarding experience, especially for those who volunteer their time or donate money for their local communities. The reward is seeing friends and neighbors, as well as strangers, benefit from the time and money donated for community projects. Dr. Ronald Bishop, a social psychologist specializing in the subject of private giving, claims that the act of giving is part of the social fabric of a community and helps people become more connected to their community.

Bishop is one of several experts who will present a program on volunteerism and how to get involved with your community that will be presented at 7 p.m. Tuesday, March 5, in the Town Hall auditorium. This interesting and challenging program is designed to raise awareness of volunteering as a way for communities to help themselves develop and achieve common goals.

REVISED: Ronald Bishop, a specialist in private giving, will be one of several people presenting a program on volunteerism and community involvement at 7 p.m. March 5 in the Town Hall auditorium.

Absence of Solid Facts

Some news releases contain sentences stating generalities, platitudes, self-praise and gush, but not facts. While rewriting releases, journalists eliminate every one of those sentences. Here are three examples:

> It will be an exciting theatrical presentation that will heartily reward audiences.
>
> An impressive array of speakers will share their wonderful experiences.
>
> The library has a reputation as a friendly, pleasant place to visit.

Such gush often appears in direct quotations, but that never justifies its use. If a quotation lacks substance, reporters will discard it, too:

> City Council Member Jaitt stated, "The fair is the best ever, with a dazzling lineup of new entertainment."
>
> "We're very excited about the opening of the new store," said Mark Hughey, president. "The store represents a new direction for us and extends our commitment to provide customers with the highest quality products at the lowest possible prices."

The platitudes and generalities sound familiar because they are used so often. For example, the following platitudes are similar but appeared in news releases that two different companies used to describe new employees:

> We are fortunate to have a woman with Russell's reputation and background as a member of the team. Her knowledge and experience will be invaluable as we broaden our sales and marketing base.
>
> We were impressed with Belmonte's accomplishments and his professionalism. We're extremely pleased with our good fortune in having him join us.

One-Sided Stories

People and organizations submit news releases to the media because they hope to benefit from the stories' publication. Almost all news releases are one-sided. They present only the sources' opinions and often present those opinions as fact. The news releases that do mention opposing views usually try to show that the other side is wrong.

Reporters may be tempted to accept the information provided by a news release because doing so is fast and easy. Reporters who fail to check the facts, however, are likely to make serious errors. For example, a college newspaper missed a major story because it received and immediately published a news release announcing that eight faculty members had received tenure and promotions. The news release failed to reveal the real story: the fact that the college had denied tenure to a dozen other faculty members, including some of the college's most popular teachers, because they were not considered good researchers. Moreover, the faculty members who did not get tenure were, in essence, fired. A single telephone call to a faculty representative would have uncovered the real story.

Using the Media

Other news releases encourage controversy. Here, too, media that publish such news releases allow themselves to be used. For example, Paul N. Strassels, a former tax law specialist for the Internal Revenue Service, has charged that the IRS uses the media to scare taxpayers. Each year, stories about tax evaders who have been sentenced to prison begin to appear in the media shortly before the April deadline for filing income tax returns. Strassels explains: "It's the policy of the IRS public affairs office to issue such stories at the time when you are figuring your taxes. The service knows that prison stories make good copy. It's simply manipulation." A member of Congress accused the IRS of waging "a campaign of terror among the American people." He explained the IRS uses tactics "carefully designed to threaten the American taxpayer"—to keep people in a constant state of fear so that fewer will cheat on their taxes.

In dealing with these and all the other problems that they encounter while handling news releases, reporters regularly condense four- and five-page handouts into three- and four-paragraph stories.

SOME FINAL GUIDELINES

Whenever possible, reporters localize the news releases they handle. A release distributed by the American Journalism Foundation began:

> ARLINGTON, Va.—Sixty-seven students, representing the best of the country's future journalists, will receive more than $186,000 as winners of American Journalism Foundation Scholarships.
>
> The American Journalism Foundation Scholarship Program provides scholarships of $2,500 a year to undergraduates and $4,000 a year to graduate students pursuing full-time journalism or mass communication degrees at four-year U.S. colleges and universities.

The news release ended with a list of the winning students and their universities. Perceptive reporters would localize their stories' leads, focusing on the winning students from their area.

Second, avoid unnecessary background information, especially statements about a group's philosophy, goals or organization. The information rarely is necessary. Moreover, it would become too repetitious and waste too much space if reporters included it in every story about a group:

> MDCA is a private, nonprofit arts organization dedicated to the presentation and advancement of the fine arts in our area.

> Throughout the year volunteers give unselfishly of their time as Big Brothers and Big Sisters. "The lives of boys and girls in this community are enriched by their caring," said Joe Midura, Executive Director, in announcing the Volunteer Appreciation Week event.

CHECKLIST FOR PR PRACTITIONERS

When writing a news release, ask yourself the following questions:

Does the News Release Provide the Proper Information?

1. Does it list a contact person and a telephone number?
2. Does it list the address of the public relations agency or department?
3. Does it clearly identify the client?
4. Does the news release have a release date, indicating an appropriate publication date? Normally, news releases are written in advance of an event.
5. Does the release include a cover letter to the editor indicating more about the sponsoring company or ideas for using the attached news release?

Is the News Release Written in Journalistic Style?

1. Does the opening paragraph, or lead, of the release focus on the who, what, when, where and why of the story?
2. Is there a short headline summarizing the contents of the release?
3. Does the text begin one-third of the way down the page and use "more" or "#" or "end" on the appropriate pages?
4. Does the text conform to Associated Press style, especially in the handling of addresses, employee titles, dates and time elements?
5. Are creative visuals, such as graphs or charts, or photographs, included with the story? Visuals catch the eye of readers, drawing them into the story, and help illustrate a point.

CHECKLIST FOR HANDLING NEWS RELEASES

When evaluating a news release, ask yourself the following questions:

Does the News Release Have News Value?

1. What is the central point of the release?
2. Is it newsworthy?
3. Does it involve an issue likely to interest or affect many members of your community—or only a few, such as the members of the organization distributing the news release?
4. Does it involve a genuine rather than a contrived event, such as a proclamation, groundbreaking or ribbon cutting?

Does the News Release Need Rewriting?

1. Does the lead emphasize the news, or is it buried in a later paragraph?
2. Does the lead begin by stating the obvious?
3. Does the lead begin with an unnecessary name?
4. Does the lead need to be localized?
5. Is the story clear and concise?
6. Does the story contain only information necessary to fully develop the central point of the news release?
7. Does the story omit any information necessary to develop the central point?
8. Does the story contain clichés, jargon or generalities? Even if they appear in direct quotations, eliminate them.
9. Whom does the news release benefit, the public or its source?
10. Is the story objective?
    —Does it contain any puffery: words such as "best," "exciting," "famous," "interesting," "important," "successful" or "thrilling"?
    —Does it promote a private company or commercial product?
    —Does it make unsubstantiated claims about a product or service being the "cheapest," "biggest" or "best"?
    —Does it urge the public to act?
11. Does the news release present every side of a controversial issue? If it does, are its presentations adequate—that is, fair and thorough?

Guest Column

TRANSPARENCY IS PARAMOUNT

By **Robert S. Saline, APR,* as edited by Nance McGown**

Are writers born, or just trained? The answer to this age-old question is "both." Some writers possess natural talent, while others acquire skills through education. For both, hard work and dedication are key to mastering the writing process and product.

Yet writing skill is not enough. In order to be truly great writers, print and broadcast journalists as well as public relations practitioners must go beyond mechanics, beyond carefully chosen words, beyond well-crafted sentences—they must also meet the highest standards of ethical excellence.

*Accreditation in Public Relations.

(continued)

In a democratic society, these often-dueling professions carry immense responsibility. For both, achieving ethical standards—and even their livelihoods—depends on maintaining credibility between the writers themselves, the communications vehicle and the intended readers.

What constitutes ethical standards in journalistic and public relations writing? Professional organizations in both fields offer codes of ethics by which members are expected to carry out their duties. For example, the code of ethics (updated 1996) of the Society of Professional Journalists establishes four core values for journalists to follow:

- seek truth and report it with honesty, fairness and courage;
- minimize harm by treating sources, subjects and colleagues as human beings deserving of respect;
- act independently to serve the public's right to know;
- be accountable to readers, listeners, viewers and each other.

Likewise, the Public Relations Society of America (PRSA) Member Code of Ethics 2000 asks members to sign a pledge to six professional values and six code principles:

- advocacy in responsible service to the public with a voice in the marketplace;
- honesty in adhering to the truth for both clients and publics;
- improving expertise through lifelong learning and efforts to build mutual understanding;
- independently providing objective counsel and accountability for actions;
- loyalty to those represented while honoring an obligation to serve the public interest;
- fairness while dealing with stakeholders and respecting their right to free expression.

As a public relations counselor for more than 35 years, I frequently turn to the PRSA Code of Ethics 2000 to help me in decision-making. And I share with my journalist counterparts a commitment to protect the free flow of accurate and truthful information, to promote healthy and fair competition, to foster open communication to facilitate informed decision-making and to build the trust of the public.

Both journalism and public relations curricula generally include ethics components. Developing story angles, finding and verifying facts with multiple sources and writing to capture the reader's interest are standard journalism study fare. And fostering two-way communication between publics and organizations, dealing openly and fairly with media professionals and telling the truth at all times are key ideas in public relations studies. Yet these basic ethical principles are often put to the test once journalism and public relations graduates have a diploma in hand and enter the highly competitive marketplace.

It is the journalists' repeated decisions during each step of the story thought process—the research, the writing, and the editing—that reminds them to follow their conscience and recall their ethical training. It will force them to verify and reverify sources; it will encourage them to avoid mixing biases with facts, and it will help them push the limits of their personal and career safety envelopes.

PR professionals face their own ethical dilemmas. From writing a persuasive brochure, reporting to executives on research of public opinion about their organization's image, or handling media inquiries during a highly visible crisis situation, public relations practitioners must also turn to their inner moral compass and learned ethical standards. Whether working for a not-for-profit, a corporation or a service organization, PR professionals must first be committed to their broader role in meeting society's need for truth. That commitment will require them to embrace their role as a conduit of free-flowing communication to and from society, to and from their leadership.

As our global society becomes more and more capable of instantaneous international communication, striving for and maintaining organizational transparency is paramount. Corporate malfeasance, leadership isolation, and elitism and injustice to our fellow world citizens find no place in truly successful organizations. And now, more than ever, knowledge is power—power derived from truthful communication.

Journalists and public relations practitioners daring to commit to the highest ethical standards of their respective professions will help carve the next block of organizational leadership. It will take constant vigilance and increased dedication to ensure a bright future for the truth.

SUGGESTED READINGS

Bivins, Thomas. *Handbook for Public Relations Writing*, 4th ed. Lincolnwood, Ill.: NTC Business Books, 1999.

Fisher, Lionel L. *The Craft of Corporate Journalism: Writing and Editing*. Chicago: Nelson-Hall, 1992.

Guth, David W., and Charles Marsh. *Public Relations: A Values-Driven Approach*, 2nd ed. Boston: Allyn & Bacon, 2003.

Mogel, Leonard. *Making It In Public Relations: An Insider's Guide to Career Opportunities*. Mahwah, N.J.: Lawrence Erlbaum Associates, 2002.

Newsom, Doug, Judy VanSlyke Turk and Dean Kruckeberg. *This Is PR: The Realities of Public Relations*. Belmont, Calif.: Wadsworth, 1996.

Ryan, Michael, and David L. Martinson. "Journalists and Public Relations Practitioners: Why the Antagonism?" *Journalism Quarterly*, Spring 1988, pp. 131-140.

Seib, Philip, and Kathy Fitzpatrick, *Public Relations Ethics*. Fort Worth, Texas: Harcourt College Publishers, 1995.

Smith, Ronald D. *Becoming a Public Relations Writer: A Writing Process Workbook for the Profession*, 2nd ed. Mahwah, N.J.: Lawrence Erlbaum Associates, 2003.

Wilcox, Dennis L., and Lawrence W. Nolte. *Public Relations Writing and Media Techniques*. New York: Harper & Row, 1990.

Wilcox, Dennis L., Phillip H. Ault, and Warren K. Agee. *Public Relations Strategies and Tactics*. New York: Longman, 1998.

Name ______________________ Class ______________________ Date ______

EXERCISE 1

PUBLIC RELATIONS: THE NEWS MEDIA AND PR PRACTITIONERS

EDITING A NEWS RELEASE

Public relations practitioners and reporters must learn to include only essential information in a news release. Many news releases include information that merely pads the length of the release and is not essential. The following news release is too long and could be reduced by half. Edit the release for publication by eliminating unnecessary information and correcting any errors in AP style and possessives.

NEWS RELEASE

Sonya Clayborn, soloist and president of the Immaculata Inspirational Gospel Choir, will be one of the featured soloists when the Immaculata Inspirational Gospel Choir presents its fall concert at 7 p.m. in the evening on Saturday, October 17 in Ryan Concert Hall, located in the Immaculata University Theater Arts Building, 401 Park Street.

Clayborn has been a featured soloist with the Gospel Choir since her freshman year and has performed in more than 40 concerts at Immaculata and around the United States. In addition, she was the featured soloist when the Gospel Choir traveled last year on an extensive tour of Europe, performing in concert halls in London, Paris, Munich, and Salzburg, Austria. Clayborn won rave reviews during the European tour, with audiences praising her "strong and vibrant soprano voice" that "showed a magnificent range of maturity and emotion."

Clayborn began her singing career as a member of the Sacred Heart Church Children's Choir when she was six years old. She became a soloist for the choir when she was eight and performed in a number of children's holiday and Christmas concerts broadcast on television and radio. She continued to sing as a soloist with the Sacred Heart Adult Choir before enrolling at Immaculata

University as a sociology major and joining the Immaculata Inspirational Gospel Choir when she was a freshman.

Clayborn says the fall concert program will include contemporary gospel songs and anthems, as well as some older familiar standards that audiences will truly enjoy. Among the contemporary pieces to be presented are "Perfect Security," by James Hall; "Balm in Gilead," by Karen Clark-Sheard; and Hezekiah Walker's "Sweeter as the Day Goes By" and "A Second Chance." Clayborn added that several other of the choir's 53 members will also be featured as soloists during the concert.

The Immaculata Inspirational Gospel Choir is directed by Mary Ann McCarty, assistant director of financial aid at Immaculata, who serves as advisor to the choir. Organ and piano accompanist for the choir is Jaclyn Saunders, a first year student from Chicago, Illinois.

The concert will begin promptly at 7:00 p.m.. Tickets are $10.00 for adults and $5.00 for children under 12 years of age and are available at the Theater Arts Building box office, 401 Park Street. Tickets are also available by telephone by calling 581-3030, Ext. 2100, between the hours of 9 a.m. and 5 p.m. weekdays.

EXERCISE 2

PUBLIC RELATIONS: THE NEWS MEDIA AND PR PRACTITIONERS

WRITING NEWS RELEASES

The following information is from actual news releases. Write a news release from each set of details. Remember to use Associated Press style. Use as much information as you think is necessary to create an effective release. Add phrases and transitions to make the news releases acceptable to editors. List yourself as the contact person for each sponsor, decide on the release date and write a headline.

1. The following program is being sponsored by your state's department of health.
   - West Nile Surveillance Program
   - A joint effort by local, state, federal and private agencies.
   - Free testing for human arboviral infections and expanded mosquito trapping in every county of the state.
   - Last year there were 27 human cases of mosquito-transmitted West Nile virus infection reported to the department of health.
   - In addition, West Nile infections were identified in 759 horses and 185 birds.
   - The testing is being funded through the Centers for Disease Control and Prevention in Atlanta, Georgia.
   - The surveillance program includes reporting and testing sick horses and dead birds, trapping and testing mosquitoes, and monitoring symptoms and illnesses in humans.
   - Mosquitoes in your state may carry viruses that cause western equine encephalitis, St. Louis encephalitis and most recently West Nile encephalitis.
   - Most people infected with diseases transmitted by mosquitoes—including West Nile virus—experience no symptoms or have only mild symptoms such as fever or headaches. More severe infection can include high fever, severe headache, stiff neck, altered mental state and death.
   - Information on the program is available through the state department of health at 1-800-555-1212.
   - Since the best means to detect the virus is to test wild birds, state health officials are asking citizens to report observations of any sick or dying birds, especially crows and blue jays.
   - A person cannot catch the virus by touching a dead bird, but health officials recommend wearing protective gloves as a precaution.
   - The surveillance program will remain in effect until November.
2. The following program is being offered by the Student Government Association at your university.
   - Adopt-A-Street program
   - More than 600 students from eighteen on-campus organizations are involved in the program.
   - Students will be working with members of the community to help clean up and beautify the community and the campus.

- Members of the program meet at 8 p.m. Tuesdays in Room 210 of the universitys student union building to plan projects and coordinate cleanup schedules.
- The program is the latest volunteer service project by members of the university community, including students, staff and faculty.
- Students annually contribute more than 10,000 hours of volunteer service to the community, while staff and faculty contribute several thousand more hours with various community groups.
- Community members or students interested in participating in the Adopt-A-Street program can call the Student Government Association through the universitys student affairs office at 555-1111.
- The first cleanup project is planned for sometime in the fall semester and will involve basic cleanup and leaf raking in selected areas.
- Cleanup projects also will be assigned to groups for the spring semester to remove trash and debris left from the winter months.
- Participating groups include the Greek Affairs Council (representing 12 fraternities and sororities), the Resident Halls Association, Student Senate, Criminal Justice Club, ROTC, the Public Relations Student Society of America and the Womens Caucus.
- The university still is looking for volunteers from the community, as well as the university.
- Streets selected for cleanup this fall include Richard Avenue, High Street, Fort Street, Britton Road, Queen Street, Burd Street, Earl Street, Prince Street, King Street, Martin Avenue, Middle Spring Avenue, Orange Street, Fayette Street Morris Street and Washington Street.

3. The results of a study on property loss and violent weather were released today by the National Institute of Insurance Underwriters and Claims Adjusters (NIIUCA).
   - James Addison, President of the National Institute of Insurance Underwriters and Claims Adjusters, addressed more than 3,500 insurance agents and claims adjusters at the institute's convention in San Diego, California, yesterday.
   - The insurance industry paid more than $2.5 billion dollars in the past year to repair or replace property damaged in hurricanes, tornadoes, and floods. The amount is nearly 25 percent more than the industry paid the previous year.
   - Addison noted that severe flooding in Texas, California and the Southeastern United States was a major cause of property damage and accounted for much of the 25 percent increase. Most homeowners who have flood insurance are insured through the federally funded National Flood Insurance Program (NFIP).
   - Hurricanes that struck Mississippi, Alabama, Louisiana and Florida caused an estimated $512,000,000 in damage to homes, businesses and personal property.
   - "These projections are very preliminary. The total number of claims and their costs could vary depending on the amount of federal aid that was provided, but it still was a costly year for the insurance industry," Addison said.
   - Some insurance experts attending the conference are questioning whether global weather patterns are changing and could be responsible for the increase in severe weather.
   - For further information, contact NIIUCA at its headquarters at One Insurance Plaza, 2305 Connecticut Avenue Northwest, Washington, D.C., 20071. Or telephone 1-800-555-0000.

EXERCISE 3

PUBLIC RELATIONS: THE NEWS MEDIA AND PR PRACTITIONERS

WRITING NEWS RELEASES

The following information is from actual news releases. Write a news release from each set of details. Remember to use Associated Press style. Use as much information as you think is necessary to create an effective release. Add phrases and transitions to make the news releases acceptable to editors. List yourself as the contact person for each sponsor, decide on the release date and write a headline.

1. The following program is sponsored by Sacred Heart Hospital's Women's Health Center and the local county chapter of Women In Need.
   - Last year, 277 women in the county were victims of domestic violence and another 182 women were the victims of sexual assault.
   - A new program to help victims of domestic violence and sexual assault is being supported by grants from the state Department of Human Services and the federal Department of Health and Human Services.
   - The Domestic Violence and Sexual Assault Support Center offers a 24-hour crisis hotline for victims of domestic violence and sexual assault.
   - The support center is free of charge.
   - The center offers a 30-day shelter equipped to handle the victim and her children in a secure and supportive environment.
   - The shelter provides 170 beds for adults and children in three protected-environment locations. Security is provided by the county sheriffs department.
   - Individual and group counseling is provided by Sacred Heart Hospital's Mental Health and Counseling Department.
   - Those needing the services of the center can call 555-7732 or 1-800-555-1431.
   - Center counselors and support personnel also will aid victims in getting protection from abuse orders, accompany victims for court appearances and aid in obtaining crime victim compensation.
   - Center personnel also participate in community education outreach programs to raise the awareness of domestic violence and sexual assault.

2. The following program is sponsored by your state's Art and Cultural Affairs Council.
   - Your county is one of 8 counties in the state receiving eleven grants to support arts and cultural affairs education in the state.
   - A total of $495,500 has been awarded to 11 recipients out of 21 grant applicants.
   - The grant program, "Lessons in Art and Culture," is funded through the National Endowment for the Arts' Challenge America Program, which is designed to teach students about art and culture.
   - "Our state's tremendous cultural resources add beauty and richness to the lives or our citizens," said Wallace Chandler, director of the state Department of History, Arts and Libraries, which is administering the NEA-funded program. "This program

will help to build connections between schools, students, arts and cultural institutions, and artists."

- Projects funded by the program are intended to aid development of student interest in the arts, support partnerships between schools and cultural institutions, improve arts education curriculum in schools, and introduce students and teachers to the rich variety of art and culture in the state.
- "Lessons in Art and Culture" also will target teacher education in the arts, striving to improve the quality and depth of arts education.
- Information on the "Lessons in Art and Culture" program is available at (111) 555-4444.

3. The following program is co-sponsored by your local chapter of the American Lung Association.
    - The local chapter of the American Lung Association is co-sponsoring a quit-smoking campaign.
    - The six-week Freedom from Smoking Clinics are scheduled to begin next month at convenient locations throughout the area.
    - Smokers can register for the Freedom From Smoking Clinics or receive the free manuals by calling the nearest American Lung Assn. office.
    - The Health Care Coalition United is co-sponsoring the Freedom From Smoking Clinics and free Freedom From Smoking Self-Help Manuals through its "Break Away From the Pack" campaign.
    - Smokers who quit for twelve weeks are eligible to win a 7-day cruise for two in the Caribbean. Their names will be entered in the Coalition's Grand Sweepstakes Drawing, with the name of one lucky winner drawn in each State.
    - More people die each year from smoking than from any other cause.
    - The clinics cost $50.00, with a $25 rebate for all those who quit. The Self-Help Manuals are free.
    - More than 20 smoking clinics will be offered at a variety of convenient locations in the area, including schools, churches and hospitals.
    - For local smokers, there has never been a better time to quit.

Name ______________________ Class ______________________ Date ______

EXERCISE 4

PUBLIC RELATIONS: THE NEWS MEDIA AND PR PRACTITIONERS

EVALUATING NEWS RELEASES

Critically evaluate the newsworthiness of the following leads. Each lead appeared in a news release mailed to news organizations. Determine whether each release is usable as written, and why. Then discuss your decision with your classmates.

1. Pregnant women throughout the state are finding it more difficult to locate an obstetrician willing to deliver their baby because of the number of obstetricians—80 last year alone—who are discontinuing the practice because of the high cost of malpractice insurance, according to a survey by the State Obstetric and Gynecologic Society.

   EVALUATION: ______________________

2. During October, millions of high school seniors and their families will attend college fairs and tour campuses nationwide as they select a college for next fall. Planning experts at Morris College say that families should not automatically eliminate a college because of its sticker price.

   EVALUATION: ______________________

3. High interest rates, coupled with low prices for most agricultural commodities, are causing serious "cash flow" problems for farmers, pushing some toward bankruptcy, according to a study by the Institute of Food and Agricultural Sciences (IFAS) at your state university.

   EVALUATION: ______________________

4. Nail polish remover is still being dropped into the eyes of conscious rabbits to meet insurance regulations, infant primates are punished by electric shocks in pain endurance tests and dogs are reduced to a condition called "learned helplessness" to earn someone a Ph.D.

   With the theme "Alternatives Now," People for the Ethical Treatment of Animals (PETA) is sponsoring a community rally on Friday—World Day for Laboratory Animals—at 1 p.m.

   EVALUATION: ______________________

5. Until recently, a missing lockbox key could be a major security problem for homeowners selling a house. But today, a missing electronic key can be turned off, protecting clients and their homes. More and more homesellers are using an electronic lockbox, the Superior KeyBox from Williams, on their properties to provide added safety, security and convenience for their homes.

   EVALUATION: ______________________

6. Natural Gardening, the world's largest-circulation gardening magazine, has announced that it has retained Balenti Associates to represent its advertising sales in the Midwest and Western United States. The 27-year-old company is one of the largest advertising sales firms in the United States, with sales offices in the top five U.S. markets as well as major European cities.

   EVALUATION: ______________________________

7. "The Changing Face of Men's Fashion" will be illustrated in a fashion presentation in Robinson's Mens Shop at 5:30 on Thursday. A special feature of the event will be commentary on the distinctive directions in men's designs by fashion designer Anna Zella.

   EVALUATION: ______________________________

8. In cooperation with the U.S. Consumer Product Safety Commission (CPSC), the Moro division of the Petrillo Group of Italy is announcing the recall of 31,000 London branch LP gas Monitor Gauges. Some of these gauges may leak highly flammable propane gas that could ignite or explode. CPSC is aware of 5 incidents of gas leaks catching fire. Two of these fires resulted in burn injuries.

   EVALUATION: ______________________________

9. Dr. Zena Treemont, who recently retired after 35 years with the U.S. Department of Agriculture, has assumed her new duties as Chief of the Bureau of Brucellosis and Tuberculosis with the State Department of Agriculture and Consumer Services, Commissioner Doyle Conner announced today.

   EVALUATION: ______________________________

10. Women have made much progress against discrimination through social and legal reforms, but they are still the victims of a very disabling form of discrimination that largely goes unnoticed: arthritis.

    Of the more than 31 million Americans who suffer from arthritis, two-thirds are women, according to the Arthritis Foundation.

    EVALUATION: ______________________________

EXERCISE 5

PUBLIC RELATIONS: THE NEWS MEDIA AND PR PRACTITIONERS

ELIMINATING PUFFERY

Rewrite the following sentences and paragraphs to make them more objective. Many contain puffery. Also, correct any errors of style, spelling and grammar.

1. Patricia James is a stellar talent whose powerful mezzo-soprano voice rings clear as a bell in the night. James' wonderful vocal presence will grace the stage of Memorial Auditorium for five nights, May 20-24, so place your order for tickets now.

2. As executive director of the Georgia Building Trades Association, Barton brings a tremendous amount of expertise to the job. He has promised to lead the association and its members in an effort to improve salaries, benefits and working conditions for all of Georgia's dedicated and hardworking construction workers.

3. In a move that shows how decisive she can be, the chancellor of the state system of higher education today appointed a highly qualified search committee comprised of 14 distinguished members of the academic community to find a replacement for retiring board of trustees president Harold Walters. The chancellor charged the committee with the task of finding a replacement who could match Walters magnificent dedication toward education in the state.

4. Oak Ridge Homes is proud to announce the opening of its newest and most spectacular subdivision—Oak Crest. These unparalleled luxury four- and five-bedroom homes with spectacular views of Paradise Valley offer some of the latest in-home conveniences new-home buyers will surely want in their new homes. Built on $\frac{1}{4}$-acre lots and beginning at $350,000, the quality of these new luxury homes has to be seen to be believed. Open houses are being scheduled by six of the areas finest and most prestigious real estate firms that have been selected to list homes in the Oak Crest subdivision.

5. If you're looking for something out of the ordinary for an evenings entertainment, the Downtown Performing Arts Center is the place for you this weekend. The center, known for its support of fresh and innovative theater productions by some of today's most distinguished young producers and directors, is presenting Director Lyle Peters exciting and laugh-filled new romantic comedy "Love in the Pits." The play, certain to please the whole family, will be performed at 7 p.m. Friday and Saturday nights and at 2 p.m. Sunday afternoon. Tickets are only $12.50 per person, which is an incredibly low price for such a sure-fire hit as this.

6. Emerson is dedicated and committed to his work as president of the board of directors and while serving in that capacity has distinguished himself admirably as a proven leader. Other executives can't hold a candle to his unmatched drive to make Emerson Industries an unrivaled leader in precision manufacturing processes. During Emersons

visionary leadership, production and sales of the companys products have increased a spectacular 37 percent for the year so far.

7. The outrageously funny British farce, RUN FOR YOUR WIFE!, will romp across the Lake Street Players stage may 25-27 and May 31-June 2. It will be a fun-filled evening for the entire family, with each hilarious performance starting promptly at 8 p.m. in the evening.

8. As a proponent of innovative hiring practices, the companys president has worked diligently to hire older workers, disabled workers and the homeless.

EXERCISE 6

PUBLIC RELATIONS: THE NEWS MEDIA AND PR PRACTITIONERS

REWRITING NEWS RELEASES

These are actual news releases mailed to daily or weekly newspapers. Only the locations and the names of some individuals have been changed. Your instructor may ask you to write only the lead for each news release or to write the entire story.

1. IAMSICK.COM

With an estimated 76 million foodborne illnesses and as many as 5,000 deaths every year in the United States, the Centers for Disease Control and Prevention in Atlanta, Georgia, and the National Intstitutes of Health in Washington, D.C., are providing states with funding to develop awareness campaigns about food poisoning.

Whether it is macaroni salad left sitting in the sun, insufficiently cooked hamburgers or chicken that has been chopped on the same cutting board as the salad greens, summer holidays and vacations can create gastrointestinal problems if people are not careful.

If the state's citizens find themselves suffering from what they think is a foodborne illness, they can now get help at a new state Website, IAmSick.com. The new website will also help state health officials to track outbreaks and determine whether additional intervention by health officials is needed.

"This new Web site will allow food poisoning victims and state officials to compare notes to determine if the illness is just an isolated case or something more serious," said Melinda Borden, director of the food safety education program for the state Department of Health.

The website is being funded through a $600,000 grant from the NIH and the CDC.

Symptoms of foodborne illness can include nausea, diarrhea and abdominal cramps. Stomach and abdominal pain, cramps, and spasms are the No. 1 reason people go to a hospital emergency room or clinic.

Last year there were 203 outbreaks of foodborne illnesses, affecting more than 2,100 people in the state. More than one-third of those outbreaks required hospitalization.

"Before the website was developed, no one—not victims or state health officials—knew if the illness was an isolated case brought on by merely a poorly cooked hamburger at a restaurant or potato salad that was left sitting on a picnic table too long, said Dr. Peter Collins, a medical specialist in nutrition and food safety with the state Department of Health. "Many people who get sick automatically blame something they ate at their last meal, but foodborne illnesses sometimes can take several days to develop in the human body. By tracking what and where people ate, health officials can get a handle on any serious food-related outbreaks."

People who are experiencing sudden vomiting and diarrhea—strong symptoms of food poisoning—can visit the Website to see if anyone else has reported eating similar foods or has reported similar symptoms. Visitors to the site fill out a form online, listing the foods they ate and where they ate them over the past several days. The information is then processed and analyzed by health officials at the Department of Health. The web site is secure, and all information submitted by victims is kept confidential.

For more information on the IAmSick.com website, call the Department of Health at (200) 555-8998 or 1-800-000-0000.

2. DEPARTMENT OF DEFENSE HOMETOWN NEWS

September 28—Navy Petty Officer 3rd Class Anthony J. Blake, son of Carl P. and Amanda C. Blake of (your city and state), recently completed Exercise Rim of the Pacific (RIMPAC) while aboard the aircraft carrier USS Chester A. Nimitz, home ported in San Diego, Calif.

Blake was one of more than 25,000 Sailors, Marines, Airmen, Soldiers and Coast Guardsmen from across the Pacific to participate in the month-long exercise conducted near Hawaii. More than 50 ships and 200 aircraft were involved in RIMPAC including naval forces from Australia, Canada, Japan, the Republic of Korea and the United States.

During the final evolution of the exercise, Blakes ship led 10 ships across the Pacific Ocean in front of Waikiki Beach, Hawaii, for a pass and review.

RIMPAC was a large-scale, multi-faceted exercise conducted to improve the interoperability of combined and joint forces in tactics, command and control, logistics and communications. RIMPAC was the latest exercise in a series which began in 1971 as an annual exercise and became a biennial exercise in 1974.

Aircraft carriers, like the USS Chester A. Nimitz, are forward deployed around the world to maintain a U.S. presence and provide rapid response in time of crisis. They serve as a highly visible deterrent to would-be aggressors and, if deterrence fails, offer the most versatile and powerful weapons available, including Tomahawk cruise missiles, tactical aircraft and combat-ready Marines.

He is a graduate of Middle Valley High School.

3. BIRTH RATE

The U.S. birth rate fell to the lowest level since national data have been available, reports the latest Centers for Disease Control and Prevention birth statistics released today by the Department of Health and Human Services in Washington, D.C.

HHS officials also noted that the rate of teen births fell to a new record low, continuing a decline that began in 1991.

The birth rate was 13.9 per 1,000 persons last year, a decline of 1 percent from the rate of 14.1 per 1,000 the year before last and down 17 percent from the recent peak in 1990 (16.7 per 1,000), according to the CDC report. The current low birth rate primarily reflects the smaller proportion of women of childbearing age in the U.S. population, as baby boomers age and Americans are living longer.

There has also been a recent downturn in the birth rate for women in the peak childbearing ages. Birth rates for women in their 20s and early 30s were generally down while births to older mothers (35-44) were still on the rise. Rates were stable for women over 45.

Birth rates among teenagers were down last year, continuing a decline that began in 1991. The birth rate fell to 43 births per 1,000 females 15-19 years of age last year, a 5-percent decline from the previous year and a 28-percent decline from 1990. The decline in the birth rate for younger teens, 15-17 years of age, is even more substantial, dropping 38 percent from 1990 to last year compared to a drop of 18 percent for teens 18-19.

"The reduction in teen pregnancy has clearly been one of the most important public health success stories of the past decade," said HHS spokesperson John Smith. "The fact that this decline in teen births is continuing represents a significant accomplishment."

More than one fourth of all children born last year were delivered by cesarean section; the total cesarean delivery rate of 26.1 percent was the highest level ever reported in the united States. The number of cesarean births to women with no previous cesarean birth jumped 7 percent, and the rate of traditional births after previous cesarean delivery dropped 23 percent. The cesarean delivery rate declined during the late 1980s through the mid 1990s but has been on the rise since 1996.

Among other significant findings:

- Last year, there were 4,019,280 births in the United States, down slightly from the previous year (4,025,933).
- The percent of low birthweight babies (infants born weighing less than 2,500 grams) increased to 7.8 percent, up from 7.7 percent the previous year and the highest level in more than 30 years. in addition, the percent of preterm births (infants born at less than 37 weeks of gestation) increased slightly over the year before last, form 11.9 percent to 12 percent.
- More than one-third of all births were to unmarried women. The birth rate for unmarried women was down slightly last year to 43.6 per 1,000 unmarried women, reflecting the growing number of unmarried women in the population.
- Access to prenatal care continued a slow and steady increase. Last year, 83.8 percent of women began receiving prenatal care in the first trimester of pregnancy, up from 83.4 percent the year before that and 75.8 percent in 1990.

Data on births are based on information reported on birth certificates filed in state vital statistics offices and reported to CDC through the National Vital Statistics System.

4. ANTI-IRS DRIVE

State Rep. Constance Wei today joined with your states largest small-business advocacy organization—the National Federation of Independent Business—in support of the NFIB's petition drive to abolish the IRS Tax Code. Wei is among the legislative sponsors of a resolution urging Congress to sunset the entire IRS code as unfair and innately burdensome.

Wei called the IRS Code "an injustice to the hard working small business owners of this state." She added that "Congress has tried to amend and simplify the Tax Code for years and it just hasn't worked. The time has come to scrap the Tax Code and start from scratch." As a substitute, Wei suggests a flat tax or national sales tax. At a rally at the state capitol, Wei was joined by Andrew Santana, President of the National Federation of Independent Business (NFIB), members of the states congressional delegation, other state lawmakers, and small business owners.

Last month NFIB launched a national petition drive to sunset the IRS Code and replace it with a simpler, fairer code that rewards work and savings. NFIBs goal is to present one million signatures to Congress by June 17th—opening day of the Congressional Small Business Summit sponsored by NFIB.

"Small business owners are overwhelmed by a Tax Code that is complex, confusing, and disproportionately biased against people who run small businesses," said Santana, president of NFIB. "How can anyone understand a code that contains 7 million words and forces people to spend millions of hours trying to comply."

Alan Wilke, State Director for NFIB, commended Wei for her support of NFIBs campaign. "The fight to dump the Tax Code isn't restricted to the halls of Congress," Wilke said. We'll only win this fight because of the dedication of small business owners and the hard work and leadership of Wei and other pro-business members of our state legislatures."

5. ENVIRONMENTAL PLAN

Gubernatorial candidate Hector R. Salvatore today unveiled a comprehensive and innovative plan that will protect and preserve the states environment. The backbone of Salvatore's plan, called Preservation Forever, will provide over $3 billion over 10 years to protect environmentally sensitive lands.

"Our state is known around the world for its magnificent natural environment," Salvatore said during the unveiling of his Preservation Forever plan. "Over the course of the next decade our efforts to save hundreds of thousands of environmentally sensitive acres will take resolve and creativity, but as our legacy to future generations we can offer no greater gift."

Salvatore said Preservation Forever will carry forward two themes that will be central to his administration if he is elected in November: an emphasis on community-based governance and the use of private stewardship incentives and not exclusively regulation to protect our environment.

The Preservation Forever plan will include these features:

- $3 Billion to Buy Lands: Over the next ten years the state will provide $300 million each year in bond proceeds to purchase, protect, and improve environmentally sensitive lands and urban greenspaces.
- Doubling Local Land Buys: The state will double the amount of money currently given to local governments for the purchase of environmentally sensitive land and urban greenspaces. This initiative will provide at least $600 million to local governments over ten years, encouraging greater citizen involvement in land purchases at the local level, and providing immediate access to natural areas.
- Providing the Public Better Access and Amenities: The program will permit the use of bond proceeds to provide capital improvements on acquired lands and, in fact, will promote greater public access and the use of amenities that are consistent with the purposes of the acquisition.
- Protecting State Lands through Management and Maintenance: Preservation Forever will dedicate greater resources to managing and maintaining the properties that the state purchases, including lands previously purchased.
- Using Innovative Land Acquisition Techniques to Lower Costs: The program calls for providing incentives to purchase development rights and conversion easements to protect lands at a lower cost than an outright acquisition. In addition the proposal calls for a change in the state's land-buying practices so that land sellers can offer the state a discount to save taxpayers money.

With its pristine rivers and incredible biological diversity, the state's natural environment is one of the most varied and valuable in the world. With this complexity comes fragility, and increasingly the state's wilds are affected by encroaching development. Salvatore proposes that the state should fashion his Preservation Forever program in a way that reflects the state's changing needs and makes improvements based on the practical knowledge gained from earlier efforts.

6. MEMORIAL SERVICE

A memorial service to commemorate the anniversary of the September 11, 2001, attack on America is planned for Wednesday on your campus. Other events throughout the week have also been scheduled to remember the victims of 9-11.

Beginning with "A Day of Deliberation" on Monday, a panel discussion titled "Loving Your Enemy?: A Theological Response to 9-11" will be held in the Student Union Building auditorium. The panel discussion program is a regular forum held each week on campus in which students, faculty, staff and the public can come together to discuss topics. The 9-11 panel discussion will begin at 7 p.m. The public is welcome to attend this discussion and as always, the program is free.

Tuesday will be dedicated as "A Day of Honor" to remember the attack. Members of the Student Activities Board will distribute red, white and blue ribbons to students, faculty and staff to honor the memory of the victims of the attack and support those who are survivors.

Wednesday has been set aside as "A Day of Remembrance" and will include a memorial service on campus to be led by university and community officials, student government leaders and campus ministry. The service will begin at 7:30 a.m. and continue until 9:30 a.m. During the service the names of all the victims who died during the terrorist attack will be read.

Thursday's activities will feature "A Day of Renewal" on campus. Campus ministry and the departments of sociology and history will hold services and programs to mark the tragedy of 9-11 and its impact on the United States and the world. Campus ministry will hold a special service at 11 a.m. featuring speakers from several faiths who will address the need for spiritual healing among all peoples and nations. From 1-4 p.m. the history and sociology departments will feature a roundtable of speakers and quests who will address the ramifications the terror attacks have had on America as a nation and the world as a whole.

All the events planned for the week of remembrance are free and open to the public. For information on the events, contact John Andersen, director of Campus Ministry, at 555-5566, or Mary Stevens, Dean of Student Affairs, at 555-8888.

Name ______________________ Class ______________________ Date ______

EXERCISE 7

PUBLIC RELATIONS: THE NEWS MEDIA AND PR PRACTITIONERS

REWRITING NEWS RELEASES

This is an actual news release mailed to a news organization. Only the locations and the names of some individuals have been changed. Use the name of your university as the source of the release. Your instructor may ask you to write only the lead or to write the entire story. The exercise contains numerous errors in style, spelling and punctuation. Correct all errors.

UNIVERSITY STUDENT VOLUNTEERS HELP MEET COMMUNITY NEEDS

Press Release

The universitys Volunteer Services Office serves as a center for five service-oriented groups on campus and provides opportunities for students and others who want to volunteer there time to help others. The V.S.O. also acts as a clearinghouse for community agencies seeking university student volunteers. This service is completely free of charge to the community.

Almost 400 students, including many repeat volunteers, worked on projects as diverse as cleaning up Duncan State Forest, helping the elderly in local retirement homes, and assisting the Red Cross with a blood drive.

Tara Osborn started volunteering as a freshman to meet the requirements of her social work classes at the university but, like a lot of other students, she discovered she enjoyed volunteering and continued her service without further classroom credit.

"I really liked it," said Osborn, a junior who heads T.O.U.C.H., a campus group that promotes volunteerism. "I like making a difference and helping people."

Osborn and other students volunteered 1,714 hours during the fall semester, donating time and energy to about thirty projects on campus and the surrounding communities.

They volunteered through TOUCH (Today's Organization Utilizing Concerned Humans) and other student-run organizations including Alpha Phi Omega, Big Brothers/Big Sisters, Circle K, Student Environmental Action Coalition and Women's Rights Council. Circle K members, for example, volunteered 564 hours, including forty-seven at Valley View Retirement Community, where they helped push residents in wheelchairs to and from therapy sessions.

"That is a high-energy job," said Linda Ellerman, director of volunteer services at Valley View. "That is definitely a great help for us. A lot of our other volunteers are retirement-age people and they are not able to take on that kind of responsibility."

The residents benefit from interacting with young people, she said. "Just seeing the young faces in the building and having the compassion of a young adult is a very positive thing."

The students, in turn, gain an understanding of the aging process and an appreciation for the work at a retirement home. "They could choose that as a career," Ellerman said. "We've seen that a couple of times."

Other T.O.U.C.H. projects included volunteering at a local homeless shelter, visiting the elderly at Manor Rest Nursing home and working with Head Start children at the university's daycare center. The Student Environmental Action Coalition helped with recycling drives in Gibson City and clean-ups in Duncan State Forest. Alpha Phi Omega members visited the old folks at Episcopal Village Retirement Center. Circle Ks other projects included helping with the Red Cross blood drive, cleaning a local highway and rails-to-trails path, and volunteering at the King's Kettle Food Pantry. Big Brothers/Big Sisters members spent a total of 464 hours with area children, including activities such as bowling and camping.

For the number of groups that we have, I think they've done an excellent job," said Ann Hoffman, director of volunteer services at the university. "It gives students some life experiences as far as feeling they have accomplished something for themselves. They certainly grow and learn from their experiences."

Student volunteers are planning a number of projects to be held over the next few months including the eighteenth annual Childrens Fair to be held in the universities athletic center. It will feature games, prizes, food, a petting zoo, educational displays and entertainment.

TOUCH members and other students spent 52 hours at the County Youth Development Center, tutoring and providing recreational activities for adjudicated delinquents aged twelve to eighteen.

It's very important, because all the kids need remedial work," Said Larry Davis, director of the center. "They're all behind their schoolwork by several grades. It's a good service. There's no doubt about it."

Mary Hastings, a junior who tutored the boys in reading and math, said she enjoys going to the center. "I don't know what I'll do when I graduate", said Hastings, whose majoring in social work. "That might be an option, getting into juvenile justice."

Anyone interested in recruiting students for service projects can call the universitys Volunteer Services Office at 555-4444, ext.101. The service is absolutely free of charge to the community.

CHAPTER 20

COMMUNICATIONS LAW

Congress shall make no law respecting an establishment of religion, or prohibiting the free exercise thereof; or abridging the freedom of speech, or of the press; or the right of the people peaceably to assemble, and to petition the Government for a redress of grievances.

(The First Amendment to the U.S. Constitution)

The First Amendment's guarantee of "freedom of the press" has never afforded complete freedom to publish anything at any time. From the very beginning of the republic, courts have held that states may punish obscene or libelous expression. In the 20th century, the courts, particularly the U.S. Supreme Court, elaborated on the meaning of the First Amendment. They found that it does not apply to advertising, movies and broadcasting in the same way that it applies to newspapers and books. They also found the right to gather information less broad than the right to publish it. And they said that the First Amendment does not insulate media businesses from the taxes and regulations to which all other businesses are subject.

Communications law is a broad area involving many aspects of the mass media and a variety of legal principles. Journalism students usually investigate this subject in detail in specialized media law courses. This chapter introduces three areas of communications law that news reporting and writing students need to know as professionals-in-training. Libel and privacy are covered extensively because the danger of a lawsuit is high and the cost of defending or losing one can be great. Newsgathering is also covered, though in less detail.

LIBEL

"Libel" is defamation by written words or by communication in some other tangible form, whereas "slander" is defamation by spoken words or gestures. Traditionally, the law has treated libel more harshly because the written word is more permanent and may reach more people than the spoken word. Courts said the greater power of written words to injure reputation justified harsher penalties and legal rules more favorable to libel plaintiffs than to slander plaintiffs. One might think that broadcast defamation should be treated as slander since it is spoken, and some states do so, either by statute or by judicial interpretation. More commonly, however, courts treat broadcast defamation as libel, because it can reach millions of listeners and be as durable as written defamation.

Libel is a major concern for the mass media. People who feel injured by something in a broadcast, a newspaper story or an advertisement may be quick to sue. The costs of a lawsuit can be great. Juries may award millions of dollars to a successful libel plaintiff. The Media Law Resource Center reports that in recent years, libel plaintiffs have recovered an average of $2.9 million in damages. Damage awards of $30 million, $40 million and $50 million are not uncommon. The largest jury award ever was $223 million—$200 million in punitive damages—against Dow Jones for a story published in The Wall Street Journal. That award was reduced by the judge and later set aside entirely because of misconduct by the plaintiffs.

Even when media organizations win libel suits, they still may spend millions on court costs and attorneys' fees. William Westmoreland, a retired general who had commanded U.S. forces in Vietnam, sued CBS for libel in the 1980s. The trial ended in an agreement that involved no monetary settlement, but the two sides spent an estimated $8 million on legal fees; more than half of that expense was borne by CBS.

Libel suits place at risk not only the news organization's pocketbook but also its reputation. News organizations build their reputations on fairness and accuracy. A libel judgment blemishes that reputation, sometimes irreparably. Individual reporters, producers and editors also depend on their reputations for accuracy, thoroughness and responsibility. If they lose a libel suit, they may lose that reputation. They may even lose their jobs. For these reasons and others, journalists must know what constitutes libel and what defenses can protect them in a libel suit.

The Elements of a Libel Suit

A plaintiff in a libel suit involving a statement published in the mass media usually must prove six things: (1) defamation, (2) identification, (3) publication, (4) falsity, (5) injury and (6) fault.

Defamation

The essence of a libel suit is vindication of one's reputation. The plaintiff, therefore, must prove defamation, meaning injury to reputation. A statement is defamatory if it injures a person's reputation, lowering that person in the estimation of the community or deterring third persons from associating or doing business with that person. Judging whether a statement is defamatory involves two steps. The first step requires a judge to determine that the statement is capable of a defamatory meaning; in the second step, the jury decides whether a substantial and respectable segment of the public actually understood the statement as defaming the plaintiff.

Some statements obviously are capable of defaming a person or business. A report that a bank was founded with drug money and that the president of the bank was a drug trafficker and money launderer implied the bank and its managers engaged in illegal activities (Banco Nacional de Mexico S.A. vs. Rodriguez, 30 Media L. Rptr. 1129 [N.Y. Sup. Ct. 2001]). Few people would want to do business with such a bank. However, just because a statement angers a person does not make it defamatory, even if the statement is false. In one recent case, a former member of a corporation's board of directors sued the corporation because it told shareholders and the U.S. Securities and Exchange Commission that the director had retired from the board. In fact, she had not been renominated. A federal district court dismissed the director's lawsuit, however, saying the corporation's statements had not held her up to ridicule or contempt (Farmer vs. Lowe's Companies Inc., 188 F. Supp. 2d 612 [W.D.N.C. 2001]). The Utah Supreme Court ruled that a newspaper column saying a town's mayor had engaged in "repeated, and not too subtle, attempts to manipulate the press" was not capable of a defamatory meaning. The court said the statement amounted to an accusation the mayor had used his office to influence the dissemination of information to the public. The statement did not suggest the mayor had engaged in any illegal or unethical acts (West vs. Thomson Newspapers, 872 P. 2d 999 [Utah 1994]).

For a statement to be defamatory, it must be phrased in such a way that the ordinary reader would understand it as stating facts about the plaintiff. If the statement is so wildly improbable that no one would understand it as factual, it cannot be the basis for a libel suit. Former Beatle George Harrison and the Honolulu Advertiser were sued by two of Harrison's neighbors. The newspaper had reported on Harrison's objections to a court order allowing his neighbors to cross parts of his property. "Have you ever been raped?" Harrison told the Advertiser. "I'm being raped by all these people. . . . My privacy is being violated. The whole issue is my privacy." The neighbors claimed Harrison's remarks accused them of the crime of rape, but the Hawaii Supreme Court concluded that "rape" was being used in a metaphorical rather than a literal sense and that reasonable readers would understand it as such (Gold vs. Harrison, No. 20468, Hawaii, July 8, 1998). The Virginia Supreme Court reached a similar conclusion in a libel suit brought by Sharon Yeagle, an administrator at the Virginia Polytechnic Institute and State University, against the student newspaper. The newspaper had quoted Yeagle in a story, and part of the quotation was repeated in a large-type drop quote. The drop quote identified the speaker as "Sharon Yeagle, Director of Butt Licking." The identification was apparently dummy copy that an editor had forgotten to change. Yeagle contended that the identification accused her of committing a criminal sex act, but the Virginia Supreme Court said readers would not interpret the statement as factual (Yeagle vs. Collegiate Times, 497 S.E.2d 136 [Va. 1998]).

Some statements obviously have the power to injure reputations—for example, statements that a person has committed a crime, has a loathsome disease, is incompetent in her or his business or has engaged in serious sexual misconduct. In other cases, a statement conveys no obviously defamatory meaning. Rather, a reader or listener must put a statement together with previously known facts to come up with a defamatory conclusion. In one case, the owner of a kosher market sued the meatpacking firm of Armour & Co. for libel because it had published an advertisement listing his store as one that sold Armour bacon. Saying that a person sells bacon is not defamatory by itself, but it becomes defamatory when it is combined with the extrinsic fact that the store is kosher (Braun vs. Armour & Co., 173 N.E. 845 [N.Y. 1939]). In cases like this one, the plaintiff must prove that readers or viewers knew the additional facts and that he or she actually lost money as a result as a result of the defamatory statements.

Libel plaintiffs usually sue over statements made in the body of a news story, but they may sue over pictures, cartoons, headlines or some combination of words and pictures that create a defamatory meaning. Brian "Kato" Kaelin sued the supermarket tabloid National Examiner over a headline that ran on the issue it published one week after O.J. Simpson was acquitted of murdering Nicole Brown Simpson and Ronald Goldman. The headline said, "COPS THINK KATO DID IT!" The story said the police suspected Kaelin had perjured himself when testifying at Simpson's trial, but Kaelin argued the headline implied he was suspected of having committed the murders. A federal appeals court agreed with Kaelin (Kaelin vs. Globe Communications, 162 F.3d 1036 [9th Cir. 1998]). An ABC News documentary about prostitution included a visual of a woman walking along an urban street. The woman, Ruby Clark, was not a prostitute, but a federal appeals court found that the juxtaposition of her photograph with the narrative, which discussed prostitution, created the implication that she was a prostitute (Clark vs. American Broadcasting Companies Inc., 684 F.2d 1208 [6th Cir. 1982]).

Identification

The libel plaintiff must also prove he or she was identified with the defamatory statement. This requires proving that reasonable readers, listeners or viewers would have understood that the statement was about the plaintiff. Whether the publisher of the statement intended to refer to the plaintiff does not matter.

Usually, libel plaintiffs have no trouble establishing identification in cases involving the news media. News stories usually identify sources or subjects clearly by name. In fact, detailed identification protects reporters against libel suits. Many suits arise from situations in which similar names create confusion. If a Sam Johnson is arrested for selling cocaine, the commonness of the name creates the possibility of confusion. By identifying the person arrested as Samuel H. Johnson Jr. of 3517 N. Forest St., Apt. 303, the reporter has eliminated the possibility of inadvertently defaming any other Sam Johnsons in town.

The publication of a name is not necessary for identification. A California jury awarded damages to a psychologist, Paul Bindrim, who said he had been libeled by a novel. Bindrim conducted nude encounter-group workshops, one of which was attended by Gwen Mitchell, a novelist. Mitchell later wrote a novel about a psychiatrist who conducted similar nude workshops. The fictional psychiatrist had a different name and different physical characteristics from Bindrim, but the real-life psychologist persuaded the jury there were enough similarities that readers could infer that the novel was about him (Bindrim vs. Mitchell, 155 Cal. Rptr. 29 [Cal. Ct. App. 1979]).

Publication

Obviously, when a statement has appeared in a newspaper or on a television broadcast, it has been published. But a statement does not have to be so widely disseminated for a person to sue for libel. All the law requires is that the defendant made the defamatory statement to someone other than the person defamed. In one case a man dictated a letter to his secretary, accusing the addressee of larceny. The secretary then typed the letter. The New York Court of Appeals held that publication took place when the secretary read and transcribed the stenographic notes (Ostrowe vs. Lee, 175 N.E. 505 [N.Y. 1931]). If the man had written his own letter and sent it to the addressee in a sealed envelope, it would not have been published.

Once a libel is published, the plaintiff must sue within the time specified by the state's statute of limitations. In most states, the statute of limitations is one or two years. A few allow as many as three years. In all states, the statute of limitations runs from the most recent publication, so republishing a defamatory statement extends the time during which the plaintiff may sue.

The Internet has complicated some of these publication issues. With a daily newspaper or a news broadcast, the statute of limitations starts running the day of publication. But what if the defamatory story is on a Web site? Someone may easily access that site and the defamatory story weeks, months or even years later. And what if the Web master updates the site regularly but does not change the defamatory story? Does each update of the site constitute a new publication of the defamatory story? The New York Court of Appeals recently answered these questions in a manner favorable to the media. The court said the statute of limitations would start running from the day of the initial publication, and updates to the Web site would not constitute republication (Firth v. State of New York, 2002 N.Y. Lexis 1901).

Falsity

For generations, courts presumed defamatory statements were false. A series of U.S. Supreme Court decisions beginning in 1964 changed that. Now many libel plaintiffs must prove falsity when the allegedly defamatory statements involve matters of public concern. In many libel cases, the Supreme Court has said, the parties argue over whether a defamatory statement is true. In those cases, the party that must prove truth or falsity is more likely to lose. Making plaintiffs prove falsity means some defamed persons may not be able to recover damages, but making defendants prove truth means some truthful publications will be punished. When the mass media publish statements about matters of public concern, the Supreme Court said, the First Amendment requires tipping the balance in favor of freedom of the press (Philadelphia Newspapers vs. Hepps, 475 U.S. 767 [1986]).

Although the plaintiffs must prove falsity only when the defamatory statement involves a matter of public concern, the requirement will apply in most cases involving the mass media. Courts usually conclude that if a statement appears in a newspaper or a news broadcast, it involves a matter of public concern.

Injury

Under traditional libel law, courts presumed that obviously defamatory statements had injured the plaintiff. The plaintiff did not have to produce any evidence showing that she or he had suffered injury to reputation, monetary loss or emotional suffering. The U.S. Supreme Court said in 1974 the presumption of injury was incompatible with the First Amendment. Since then libel plaintiffs have had to prove "actual injury" in order to recover damages from publishers who negligently made defamatory statements. Actual injury includes more than provable monetary loss. Evidence of damage to reputation, humiliation and mental anguish also count.

A candidate for sheriff in a Tennessee county published campaign advertisements that said the incumbent sheriff's deputy was guilty of abusing a woman he had been living with. The deputy sued, but the trial court granted summary judgment to the defendant. On appeal, an issue was the sufficiency of the deputy's evidence of injury. He said some people had asked him about the advertisements and he had found the questions embarrassing. He also said he had not been invited to a few parties because of the campaign ads; however, he offered no evidence to support this claim. The Tennessee Court of Appeals said the deputy's evidence failed to prove he had been injured. Whatever embarrassment or discomfort he had suffered had not been a daily problem nor had it interfered with his ability to perform his duties, the court said. (Murray vs. Lineberry, 69 S.W.3d 560 [Tenn. App. 2002]).

Although the plaintiff must show some injury, the injury need not be great. The Arkansas Democrat-Gazette was reporting on the prosecution of Little Rock lawyer Eugene Fitzhugh in connection with the Whitewater scandal and erroneously substituted J. Michael Fitzhugh's photograph for that of Eugene Fitzhugh. J. Michael Fitzhugh, a lawyer in Fort Smith, Ark., sued and won a $50,000 jury verdict. Fitzhugh was unable to show that anybody had shunned him as a result of the publication or that anybody actually believed he was being prosecuted in the Whitewater affair, but he did present testimony that at least some people thought he might be involved in the scandal. That was enough, the Arkansas Supreme Court said, to establish injury (Little Rock Newspapers vs. Fitzhugh, 954 S.W.2d 650 [Ark. 1997]).

Sometimes the plaintiff does not have to prove injury. If the defendant published the defamatory statement with actual malice (which will be explained in the next section), then the courts can presume injury. Publications that do not involve a matter of public concern are another exception.

Fault

The most crucial issue in modern libel cases is fault. "Fault," in libel law, refers to the state of mind of the person responsible for the allegedly defamatory statement: Was the statement made intentionally, recklessly or negligently? Before 1964, many states said publishers of defamatory statements would have to pay damages even if they had taken every reasonable step to ensure the accuracy of the story. Starting in 1964, the U.S. Supreme Court changed that in the case of New York Times vs. Sullivan (376 U.S. 254) and changed it further in its 1974 Gertz vs. Robert Welch Inc. (418 U.S. 323) decision. Now plaintiffs must prove some level of fault. The level of fault a plaintiff needs to prove depends on whether the plaintiff is (1) a public official or public figure or (2) a private individual.

Public officials and public figures must prove that the statement was published with the knowledge that it was false or with reckless disregard for whether it was false. This is called "actual malice," a term that causes confusion since many people think it means ill will, but whether the defendant disliked or wanted to harm the plaintiff is not an issue. All that matters is whether the defendant knew the statement was false or had a high degree of awareness of the statement's probable falsity when it was published. Proving this can be difficult, since the plaintiff must produce evidence about the defendant's state of mind.

Private individuals have less difficulty winning libel suits. In most states, they have to prove only that the defendant acted with negligence in order to recover actual damages. Negligence essentially means acting unreasonably under the circumstances. Usually, the jury decides whether a defendant's actions were unreasonable. In a libel case, an error such as failing to check public records, misspelling or confusing names or accidentally transposing dates or figures might be considered negligence.

The difference between actual malice and negligence is sometimes confusing, but two cases may clarify the distinction:

Chris Gatto, a reporter for the Belleville Post in New Jersey, rewrote a story from a larger paper about an investigation of problems with the New Jersey School Board Association's insurance group. Lawrence Schwartz, a local attorney, represented the school board association in the investigation. Unfortunately, Gatto's understanding of the case was weak and his story was confused. When the story reached Post editor Joseph Cammelieri, Gatto was out of town on another assignment. Cammelieri had to figure out the story on his own and incorrectly concluded that the focus of the investigation was Schwartz—specifically, whether the $353,851

Schwartz had received from the association in legal fees was excessive. Cammelieri later said: "I was confused. So in my confusion, I saw a local person; and I assumed that oh, this local person must be the primary focus of the story and I was trying to simplify it." Schwartz sued for libel. The New Jersey courts said he was a public figure and had to prove actual malice. But the most he could prove was that Gatto and Cammelieri had been negligent. Gatto should have checked his facts more carefully, and Cammelieri should not have assumed Schwartz was the focus of the story. But there was no evidence that either had the high degree of awareness of probable falsity required to prove actual malice (Schwartz vs. Worrall Publications Inc., 20 Media L. Rptr. 1661 [N.J. Super. Ct. App. Div. 1992]).

A Virginia physician proved actual malice in a libel case against WJLA-TV in Washington, D.C. The issue was the technique the physician, Stephen M. Levin, used to treat piriformis syndrome in female patients. The piriformis muscle, in the buttock, sometimes irritates or pinches the sciatic nerve, causing pain in the lower back, buttock and leg. Levin treated female patients with this condition by intervaginally manipulating their piriformis muscle. Some of Levin's patients considered the treatment abusive and humiliating. They complained first to the Virgina Board of Medicine, which investigated and cleared Levin of any wrongdoing. One of the patients then took her complaint to WJLA-TV, which investigated and prepared a story. After the story aired, Levin sued. A jury eventually awarded him more than $2 million in damages. WJLA appealed the verdict to the Virginia Supreme Court, arguing among other things that Levin had failed to prove actual malice. The court, however, agreed with Levin. For one thing, WJLA had interviewed a specialist who at first said he had never heard of vaginal manipulation as a treatment for piriformis syndrome. The specialist later disavowed the remarks, but knowing that, WJLA aired the interview anyway. Another piece of evidence contributing to a finding of actual malice, the court said, was the promotional advertisements WJLA aired for its report on Levin. Those spots said or strongly implied Levin had sexually abused his patients, but WJLA news staff knew the Board of Medicine had cleared Levin of any wrongdoing (WJLA-TV et al. vs. Levin, 564 S.E.2d 383 [Va. 2002]).

Actual malice is difficult to prove. Simple mistakes in handling a story are not enough. Nor is evidence that the defendant disliked the plaintiff. But the U.S. Supreme Court has said actual malice can be found when the defendant:

- Knew facts that would call the story into question;
- Refused to examine evidence that would prove or disprove a charge;
- Relied on an inherently unbelievable source;
- Published an improbable story without investigation; or
- Simply fabricated the story.

Public Officials, Public Figures and Private Individuals

The most important decision in many libel cases is whether the plaintiff is a public official or public figure. That decision determines whether the plaintiff will have to prove actual malice and what damages he or she can recover. A public official or public figure must prove actual malice to win any damages, actual or punitive. A private individual need prove only negligence to recover actual damages but would have to prove actual malice to win punitive damages. The U.S. Supreme Court has provided only hazy guidelines for distinguishing public officials and public figures from private individuals. The guidelines have left a good deal of room for states to expand or contract those categories.

The more clearly defined category is that of public official. The Supreme Court has said public officials must hold some government position. The category of public officials includes not only elected officials, such as U.S. senators, state legislators and city council members, but also appointed officials and government employees. Even unpaid government officials may be public officials for purposes of libel law. Just being on the government payroll does not make a person a public official, however. The person also must have or appear to have substantial

Reprinted by permission: Tribune Media Service.

authority over governmental affairs. A low-ranking worker in the city sanitation department or a secretary in the city attorney's office probably would not be a public official. Also, to be considered a public official, the employee must hold a position important enough that the public would have an interest in his or her qualifications even in the absence of a specific news event or controversy (Rosenblatt vs. Baer, 383 U.S. 75 [1966]).

A gray area exists between government leaders, like mayors, who are clearly public officials, and minor employees, like city file clerks, who are not. Whether people in the gray area are public officials may depend on how a state's courts have interpreted the law. Some states have found public school principals and teachers to be public officials, while others have said they are not. Most courts have found law enforcement officers and others who make decisions that affect the rights, liberty, health and safety of the public to be public officials.

Identifying public figures is even more difficult than identifying public officials. A judge in one libel case complained, "Defining public figures is much like trying to nail a jellyfish to the wall." Part of the problem is the vagueness with which the U.S. Supreme Court has defined the term "public figure" and part is the court's reluctance to impose any uniformity on the states.

After it decided that public officials would have to prove actual malice, the Supreme Court recognized that certain people who did not hold official government positions nevertheless exercised great influence over public affairs and public opinion. The court decided that these public figures also should have to prove actual malice, but the justices tried to define "public figure" in a way that would keep the category small. The Supreme Court in the Gertz decision identified three types of public figures: (1) involuntary, (2) general-purpose and (3) limited-purpose. The court said the essence of public-figure status is that a person has voluntarily assumed some special prominence or role in society; therefore, the category of involuntary public figure must necessarily be very small, almost to the point of being nonexistent. The other two categories are somewhat larger.

The general-purpose public figure, the Supreme Court said, has such persuasive power and influence as to be a public figure for all occasions. Celebrities from the entertainment and sports industries, such as David Letterman, Jennifer Lopez, Denzel Washington, Meryl Streep, Tiger Woods and Bret Favre, would probably fit this definition. So would people from other walks of life who have become unusually prominent—people like Ann Coulter, the Rev. Jerry Falwell, Martha Stewart and Bill Gates. The Supreme Court said this category, too, must be small because few people attain such widespread notoriety.

The largest category of public figures consists of those who hold that status for the limited purpose of commenting on some particular topic or issue. These public figures have thrust themselves to the forefront of a controversy in order to affect its resolution. People who organize an abortion-rights march or who lead an effort to persuade a school board to change the curriculum in history classes or who argue publicly for laws allowing people to carry concealed weapons would be examples of limited-purpose public figures.

Richard Jewell, the private security guard who became a suspect in the Olympic Park bombing in Atlanta, became a limited-purpose public figure, a Georgia appeals court ruled. Jewell had discovered the bomb and had helped get people out of the park before it exploded. At first, he was considered a hero, but FBI investigators soon were telling local reporters on background that Jewell was a suspect. Eventually, Jewell was cleared, but his reputation had been tarnished and he sued for libel. The Georgia Court of Appeals, however, ruled he had to prove actual malice. His willingness to speak to reporters after the bomb incident and help persuade visitors they would be safe at the Olympics had made him a public figure (Atlanta Journal-Constitution vs. Jewell, 555 S.E.2d 175 [Ga. Ct. App. 2001]).

The Supreme Court has left the definitions of "public figure" so vague lower courts have had trouble applying them. Some court decisions seem to contradict one another. For example, one court said a life insurance company had become a public figure through its advertising and public relations efforts dealing with the health-care funding controversy (National Life Insurance Co. vs. Phillips Publishing Inc., 20 Media L. Rptr. 1393 [D. Md. 1992]). Another court said neither of two corporations engaged in competitive and comparative advertising focusing on the cost and quality of their health insurance programs was a public figure (U.S. Healthcare vs. Blue Cross of Greater Philadelphia, 17 Media L. Rptr. 1681 [3rd Cir. 1990]).

Journalists need to remember that just being involved in a newsworthy event does not make a person a public figure. The U.S. Supreme Court has said that people involved in civil court cases, criminal suspects and defendants, individuals and businesses who receive money from the government, and lawyers representing people in court are not automatically public figures. The court has said that such people have not necessarily stepped forward to influence the resolution of a public controversy.

Major Defenses to Libel Suits

The difficulty plaintiffs have in proving actual malice has become the major defense for media organizations in libel cases. Other defenses are available, and they can be important in some cases. Of these defenses, the main ones are (1) truth, (2) fair-report privilege and (3) fair comment and criticism.

Truth

The use of truth as a defense arose when courts presumed defamatory statements were false. Now, plaintiffs must prove falsity; but proving a statement true can still defeat a libel claim.

Proving truth does not mean proving a news report accurate in every detail. Most courts require only proof that the sting or the gist of the charge is true. A former president of the Kansas Farm Bureau sued the bureau over a statement its attorney had made to the board of directors. The attorney had said the former president needed to reimburse the bureau for $10,467 in travel expenses, when he actually owed only $5,888. The Kansas Supreme Court said that even though the attorney had misstated the amount owed, the statement was substantially true. The former president's reputation suffered no more from the inaccurate statement than it would have if the statement had been accurate (Hall vs. Kansas Farm Bureau, 50 P.3d 495 [Kan. 2002]).

The Nevada Supreme Court used similar reasoning to uphold the dismissal of a libel suit brought by James Mortensen, who had been arrested for removing artifacts from an archaeological site in Nevada. He later pleaded guilty to selling archaeological resources illegally. Newspaper stories, based on press releases from the U.S. Attorney's office, described Mortensen as having looted and robbed graves. Mortensen contended he had not looted or robbed and that the site from which the artifacts had come was not a grave. The Nevada Supreme Court said the terms "looter" or "robber" accurately described Mortensen's conduct, even though they were not the actual charges brought against him. Also, the site from which the artifacts were taken was described in the U.S. Attorney's press release as a burial ground, and the news organizations were justified in relying on that description (Mortensen vs. Gannett, No. 27724 [Nev. S.Ct., Oct. 1, 1997]).

If a news story misuses a technical term to create a substantially false and defamatory impression, then courts will not consider the story true. A Minnesota appeals court upheld a $676,000 damage award to a Duluth street maintenance supervisor over a series of stories and editorials in a local newspaper. The stories and editorials said the supervisor had arranged to have the clay road in front of his home paved. In fact, the street was not paved but repaired with asphalt shavings. The difference is that paving an unpaved road is a major improvement, for which the adjacent property owners would have to pay. Repairing a road with asphalt shavings is routine maintenance, and homeowners do not pay any of the costs. The difference, the Minnesota appeals court said, is substantial enough to create the false and defamatory impression that the supervisor had misused his office (LeDoux vs. Northwest Publishing Inc., 521 N.W.2d 59 [Minn. Ct. App. 1994]).

Crucial omissions can defeat the defense of truth even if every fact in a news report is accurate. A Memphis newspaper reported that Ruth Nichols had been shot in the arm by another woman. The story said, "Officers said the incident took place Thursday night after the suspect arrived at the Nichols home and found her husband there with Mrs. Nichols." That was true, but the story failed to mention that Ruth Nichols' husband and two other people also were present. Nichols successfully sued for libel, saying that the omission created the false and defamatory impression that she was having an affair with the other woman's husband (Memphis Publishing Co. vs. Nichols, 4 Media L. Rptr. 1573 [Tenn. 1978]).

The defense of truth does not protect the accurate republication of defamatory charges made by other people. A news organization that reports a defamatory statement a bank president makes about a competitor cannot escape liability by proving that it accurately quoted the bank president. The news organization is responsible for proving that the underlying statement was true, not merely that it had quoted the source accurately. There are some exceptions to this rule, the main one being the fair-report privilege that news organizations have to report on official proceedings and documents.

Fair-Report Privilege

The law recognizes certain occasions when people need absolute protection from libel suits. People called to testify in court, for example, cannot be sued for defamation because of what they say on the witness stand. And members of legislative bodies, such as Congress and state legislatures, cannot be sued over remarks they make in the course of their official duties. News organizations enjoy a similar, although qualified, privilege to report on what happens in courtrooms and legislative chambers and what is said in official documents. So a news reporter covering a trial cannot be sued for reporting false and defamatory statements made by a witness so long as the reporter's story is full, fair and accurate.

A reporter for the Lamar (Mo.) Democrat covered a meeting of the City Council of Golden City, Mo., at which the members discussed the fitness of the town's chief of police and its only patrolman. The council also heard comments from citizens, including one person who said his 16-year-old daughter had been "knocked up" by the patrolman. That comment appeared later on the front page of the Democrat, and the patrolman sued for libel. The Missouri Court of Appeals said newspapers have a privilege to report on public meetings about matters of public concern so long as the reports are fair and accurate, and this one was (Shafer vs. Lamar Publishing Co., 7 Media L. Rptr. 2049 [Mo. Ct. App. 1981]).

Under the qualified privilege defense, the Lamar Democrat was not responsible for proving that the deputy in fact had gotten a 16-year-old girl pregnant; it was responsible only for showing that it had accurately reported what was said at the council meeting. If the report inaccurately summarizes an official meeting or an official document, the privilege may be lost. So when a broadcast news report said an attorney had been found guilty of conspiring to help a client evade the federal income tax, when in fact the attorney had been acquitted, the station could not claim that it had made a fair and accurate report of an official proceeding (Western Broadcasting vs. Wright, 14 Media L. Rptr. 1286 [Ga. Ct. App. 1987]).

Journalists have this fair-report privilege when describing such governmental proceedings as court hearings, administrative agency meetings and legislative sessions at all levels of government from town council to Congress. In most states, the privilege extends to official documents, such as police reports, health inspection reports, depositions, official government correspondence and grand jury transcripts. In some states, the privilege also applies to reports of nongovernmental meetings open to the public for discussion of matters of public concern.

Including in a news report information gathered from sources other than official meetings or records can defeat the fair-report privilege. A citizen complained during a meeting of the Crookston, Minn., City Council that a police officer, Gerardo Moreno, had been selling drugs out of his police car. Mike Christopherson, the city editor of the Crookston Times, attended the council meeting and heard the charge. He did not report it until several days later, after he had heard that an officer was about to be arrested. Christopherson asked the police chief about the rumors. The chief denied Moreno was about to be arrested, but he also said the department would investigate the drug-selling accusation. Christopherson's story included information from the council meeting and from his later investigations. Moreno sued the Times for libel. The newspaper argued it was protected by the fair-report privilege. The case eventually reached the Minnesota Supreme Court, which said the privilege did apply to information gathered in official city council meetings—about three paragraphs of the story. But the Supreme Court said the trial court needed to determine whether Moreno had been defamed by any of the information Christopherson had gathered outside the council meeting (Moreno vs. Crookston Times Publishing Co., 610 N.W.2d 321 [Minn. 2000]).

Fair Comment and Criticism

Everyone has the right to an opinion, even an opinion that might injure another person. The fair comment and criticism defense evolved in the late 19th and early 20th centuries to protect from libel suits expressions of opinion about matters of legitimate public interest. The defense applied only if the opinions were based on true facts, were the sincere opinions of the speakers and were not motivated solely by ill will.

The U.S. Supreme Court seemed to expand the opinion defense in 1974. The court, in deciding the Gertz vs. Robert Welch Inc. libel case, made the passing remark that there is "no such thing as a false idea." Many lawyers and judges took that as creating a nearly complete defense for any statement that could reasonably be classified as an opinion. So lower courts developed elaborate tests for distinguishing statements of fact from statements of opinion.

The Supreme Court threw this area of libel law into disarray in 1990 when it declared in Milkovich vs. Lorain Journal (497 U.S. 1 [1990]) that a sports writer's opinion column could be the basis for a libel suit. The court said opinions enjoy no special protection from libel suits. Chief Justice William Rehnquist, who wrote the majority opinion in Milkovich, said existing principles of libel law provide sufficient protection for expressions of opinion. He said an editorial, column, letter to the editor or other expression of opinion can be libelous if it says something about a person that can be proved false and defamatory.

Many legal scholars worried that the Milkovich decision would expose all manner of opinions to libel litigation. To some extent, that has happened, but it appears courts are analyzing such cases in a manner like that used before the Milkovich case. Now, however, instead of talking about whether a statement is fact or opinion, courts talk about whether a statement can be proved false. The result, in many instances, is the same, but a crucial question remains: How much emphasis should be given to the context in which a defamatory statement appeared?

A case involving a book review published in The New York Times provides a good look at how the opinion defense works in the wake of the Milkovich decision. Dan Moldea, an investigative reporter, wrote "Interference," a book that describes organized crime's influence on professional football. Gerald Eskenazi reviewed the book for The New York Times and concluded that the book contained "too much sloppy journalism." Moldea thought the remark libeled him and sued. A federal district court granted The Times' motion to dismiss the case. Moldea appealed to the U.S. Court of Appeals for the District of Columbia Circuit. The appeals court issued two opinions in the case, the second dramatically reversing the first.

The first time the court of appeals considered Moldea's case, it ruled that the statement about "sloppy journalism" was sufficiently factual that a jury could decide whether it was true. Furthermore, the court said the Milkovich decision prevented it from attaching much weight to the fact that the statement appeared in a book review.

A short time later, the appeals court reconsidered its ruling and concluded that the Supreme Court had not intended to prevent courts from considering context in libel cases. Context had been irrelevant in the Milkovich case, the appeals court said, but when it is relevant, context helps indicate whether readers will understand a statement as factual. The court said in the context of a book review the accusation of sloppy journalism was exactly the kind of thing a reader would interpret as opinion and not as something that could be proved true or false (Moldea vs. New York Times, 22 Media L. Rptr. 1673 [D.C. Cir. 1994]).

The fair-comment-and-criticism defense does not protect all editorials, columns and reviews. Any opinion based on or implying false facts can be the basis of a libel suit. However, the fair comment defense may apply outside the opinion pages. News stories often report the opinions of others. If those opinions are based on true facts or cannot be proved false, they enjoy protection.

Legislative Trends

The principles of libel law are shaped largely by court decisions. In a few areas, however, state legislation has an impact. Two areas of recent activity are retraction statutes and agricultural product-disparagement laws.

Most states have retraction statutes that limit damages or prevent libel suits in cases where a full, prompt and prominent retraction has been published. The statutes vary greatly in their terms. Some states prohibit a plaintiff from recovering punitive damages when a retraction has been published; others say a plaintiff cannot seek punitive damages unless she or he has first requested a retraction. And a few statutes require a person to seek a retraction before filing a libel suit. Some retraction statutes have been rendered obsolete by U.S. Supreme Court decisions over the last 40 years.

In 1993 the National Conference of Commissioners on Uniform State Laws proposed a uniform correction or clarification act that would harmonize the state laws and provide an alternative to costly and confusing libel suits. The proposed statute would limit the damages a libel plaintiff can recover to provable economic loss when the defendant publishes a retraction. The defendant would benefit from having a cap placed on damage awards, and the plaintiff would benefit from prompt vindication of her or his reputation and reimbursement for economic loss. Only one state—North Dakota—has adopted the Uniform Correction or Clarification of Defamation Act and only a handful of other states have considered it. The proposal has the support of several journalism organizations—the National Newspaper Association, the American Society of Newspaper Editors, the Associated Press Managing Editors and the Media Law Resource Center, among others—but it also has its critics. Some contend the proposal puts libel plaintiffs at a disadvantage. Others contend that the corrections statute may encourage news organizations to sacrifice their credibility in order to avoid costly libel suits.

Agricultural product-disparagement laws—sometimes called veggie libel laws—are a new trend. After "60 Minutes" reported that many apple growers used a pesticide linked to cancer, the market for apples collapsed and apple producers lost millions of dollars. Some producers sued, unsuccessfully. As a result, some state legislatures have passed laws creating a right on the part of producers of agricultural products to sue when those products are disparaged. In some states, the rules for these lawsuits are more favorable to plaintiffs than the rules governing personal libel suits, leading some legal authorities to say most of the laws are unconstitutional.

The Texas agricultural product-disparagement act, which applies to perishable food products, was tested in a widely publicized, but inconclusive, lawsuit. "The Oprah Winfrey Show" had broadcast a segment on mad-cow disease which included derogatory statements by Winfrey and her guest about beef. Some Texas beef producers sued in federal court under the agricultural product-disparagement law and the common law of product disparagement. The judge dismissed the charges brought under the Texas statute on two grounds: Cattle are not a perishable food product, and Winfrey and the other defendants had not knowingly made any false statements. The jury found in favor of Winfrey on the remaining charges. The U.S. Court of Appeals for the 5th Circuit affirmed the decision in Winfrey's favor (Texas Beef Group vs. Winfrey, No. 98-10391 [5th Cir., Feb. 9, 2000]). Thirteen states have enacted veggie libel laws: Alabama, Arizona, Colorado, Florida, Georgia, Idaho, Louisiana, Mississippi, North Dakota, Ohio, Oklahoma, South Dakota and Texas. Several other states have considered such laws.

12 STEPS FOR AVOIDING LIBEL SUITS

No checklist or set of steps can guarantee that a news organization will never be sued for libel. Some news organizations have checked stories and found evidence for every potentially defamatory statement but still have been sued. Usually, the conscientious news organization will win, but the cost of defending against the libel suit can be daunting. Nevertheless, here are some things journalists can do to protect themselves and their employers:

1. Make sure everything in the story, especially any potentially defamatory statement, is newsworthy. Nothing is gained by risking a lawsuit over a statement that has no news value.
2. Identify everyone mentioned in the story as fully as possible.
3. Ask persons who are attacked or criticized in news stories to respond and include the response in the story, even if it is just a flat denial. If the person refuses to respond, say so in the story.
4. If a person who has been attacked or criticized presents credible evidence to support his or her denials, check out that evidence.
5. Interview every relevant source and read every relevant document; do not ignore sources or information that may contradict the central point of a story.
6. Find out what basis a source has for making a defamatory charge and what the source's motives might be.
7. If a source for a story has credibility problems, explain in the story what those problems are.
8. Avoid confidential or anonymous sources. Reporters may be asked to reveal their sources at a libel trial. If the reporters refuse to do so, judges may tell jurors to assume the reporters made up the information.
9. Never use confidential or anonymous sources for making attacks on a subject. Use them only for factual information that can be verified by other sources or documents.
10. If a story uses documentary sources, make sure the documents are understood and quoted accurately. Double-check the information in any documents; even official records may have errors.
11. If a story is not breaking news, take additional time to make sure the investigation is thorough and the story is accurate.
12. Adhere to organizational policies regarding keeping notes, tapes and other materials. If the policy is to keep all such materials, be sure everything is kept. If the policy is to destroy materials, make sure all are destroyed. Do not destroy some and keep others.

PRIVACY

The right to sue for invasion of privacy is little more than 100 years old. Already, lawsuits over various forms of invasion of privacy have become a major concern to media organizations because people are worrying more about their privacy.

The law recognizes four kinds of invasion of privacy: (1) intruding on a person's seclusion or solitude, (2) giving publicity to private facts, (3) placing a person in a false light, and (4) appropriating a person's name or likeness for one's own benefit. The last of these is primarily a concern for advertisers, although news and advertising messages could be the basis for a lawsuit over any of the four forms of privacy. The status of these four forms of invasion of privacy varies from state to state. Some states have recognized them in statutes; in others, court decisions have recognized privacy rights even in the absence of specific statutes. Some states do not recognize all four forms. Nebraska, for example, does not recognize a right to sue for giving publicity to private facts, and Texas does not recognize false-light actions.

Intrusion

A lawsuit for intrusion requires that one person intentionally intrude on the solitude or seclusion of another in a manner that would be highly offensive to a reasonable person. Courts do not consider ordinary newsgathering techniques intrusive. Gathering information about a person by examining public records and interviewing friends, relatives, enemies and associates is perfectly legal, even if the subject of an investigation objects. Nor are reporters intruding on a person's solitude or seclusion by requesting interviews. To commit intrusion, they would have to invade some area in which the person had a reasonable expectation of privacy.

Intrusion cases deal with a number of newsgathering techniques and issues. Some deal with newsgathering in private or semiprivate places, and others deal with newsgathering in public places.

News reporters must have permission to enter private property. Entering a person's home without consent would be a clear case of intrusion. It also would be grounds for a trespass action. It is possible to invade another person's privacy without physically entering that person's property, for example by using electronic eavesdropping devices, tapping a telephone line, looking into a bedroom window with binoculars or using a powerful telephoto lens to take pictures of people inside their homes. Even if some newsworthy event is happening on private property, a journalist may not enter without the owner's or legal occupant's permission.

A similar limitation applies to privately owned places that invite the public to enter, such as restaurants, shops, malls and other places of business. Because the right of privacy belongs only to people, a business or a corporation cannot sue for intrusion if a news reporter enters its premises without permission. It can sue for trespass or press criminal trespass charges, however. Also, individual patrons may sue for intrusion in some instances. An Iowa woman sued a television station that filmed her while she was dining in a restaurant. Although the Iowa Supreme Court did not say whether the woman's privacy had been violated, it did say that restaurant patrons may be able to sue depending on where they were seated in the restaurant and what they were doing at the time (Stessman vs. American Black Hawk Broadcasting Co., 416 N.W.2d 685 [Iowa 1987]).

What if reporters enter private property at the invitation or in the company of police officers or firefighters? Television "reality programs" that show actual drug busts or other police actions have generated cases raising that question. In some instances, the targets of the police raids have sued both the police and the media. They have claimed that the police and the media violated their Fourth Amendment rights to be free from unlawful searches and seizures, and they also have said the media intruded on their privacy. The U.S. Supreme Court has agreed with them.

The Supreme Court ruled that law enforcement officials who allow news reporters and photographers to accompany them on searches are violating the Fourth Amendment, which protects people against illegal search and seizure. The court said the presence of reporters and photographers when officers execute search warrants and arrest warrants serves no law enforcement purpose. Reporters ride along with police for their own purposes, not to help police execute search or arrest warrants. Whatever interests might be served by the journalist's presence—informing the public about police activities, guarding against police abuses and protecting officers from violence by suspects—were outweighed by the Fourth Amendment interests of the people who were arrested or whose property was searched (Wilson vs. Layne, 119 S.Ct. 1692 [1999]). The effect of the Supreme Court's decision is that not only may news organizations whose reporters accompany officers on raids be sued for invasion of privacy, but also that the law enforcement agencies may be sued for violating the target's Fourth Amendment rights. The news organizations may also be sued on Fourth Amendment grounds, too, if they collaborated with law enforcement in arranging the raid.

Under what circumstances a person might have a reasonable expectation of privacy is a matter of judgment. Obviously, a person's home is a private place, but one also may reasonably expect privacy in other places. Ruth Shulman and her son, Wayne, sued when a television crew taped efforts to aid the Shulmans after they had been involved in a traffic accident. The cameraman not only recorded what happened at the accident site, but also some of what happened in the helicopter ambulance that carried the Shulmans to the hospital. A nurse who provided medical assistance to the Shulmans at the scene was wearing a microphone, and her conversations with the Shulmans were recorded. A divided California Supreme Court said the mere presence of the camera crew at the accident scene did not invade the Shulmans' privacy, but the presence of the camera crew in the helicopter ambulance did. Patients have the same expectation of privacy in an ambulance as they would in a hospital room. Also, the recording of the Shulmans' conversations with rescue workers may have intruded on their privacy if the evidence showed it was unlikely passers-by could have heard what the Shulmans had said (Shulman vs. Group W Productions Inc., 955 P.2d 469 [Cal. 1998]).

The California Supreme Court has also found that the reasonable expectation of privacy extends to at least some workplace situations. An ABC reporter, Stacy Lescht, worked undercover for a company that offered psychic readings by telephone. While on the job, Lescht wore a hidden microphone and camera. She recorded conversations she had with some of her coworkers, among them Mark Sanders. After ABC aired a story about the telepsychic business on its "PrimeTime Live" show, Sanders sued for invasion of privacy. A jury awarded him compensatory damages, punitive damages and attorney's fees, adding up to $1.2 million. A California appeals court reversed the award, but the state Supreme Court later reinstated it. The main issue on appeal was whether Sanders had a reasonable expectation of privacy. Sanders, Lescht and the other telepsychics worked in cubicles that were not fully enclosed. Workers could sometimes overhear conversations in other cubicles. However, the Supreme Court said because the office was not open to the general public Sanders had a reasonable expectation that his conversations with his colleagues would not be recorded or photographed surreptitiously (Sanders vs. American Broadcasting Cos. Inc., 978 P. 2nd 67 [Calif. 1999]).

Generally, the right of privacy does not extend to things that happen in public places or on private property but that can be seen or heard from a public street or sidewalk. The reporters are free to stake out the home or business of someone in the news as long as they stay on public streets and sidewalks. They are free to report anything they see or hear without such things as telephoto lenses or powerful microphones.

Nevertheless, there are limits to what reporters can do even in public places. A free-lance photographer who specialized in photographing Jacqueline Kennedy Onassis—to the point that he put her life and safety in danger—was found to have invaded her privacy (Galella vs. Onassis, 353 F.Supp. 196 [S.D.N.Y. 1972]). And two independent photographers who surrounded and stopped an automobile carrying Arnold Schwarzenegger, his wife, Maria Shriver, and their son were convicted of false imprisonment (California vs. O'Brien, No. 75M02318 [Santa Monica Mun. Ct., Feb. 23, 1998]).

Outrage over the conduct of the aggressive photographers known as paparazzi who were following Princess Diana at the time of her fatal traffic accident prompted a number of federal and state lawmakers to propose restrictions on newsgathering. Many of the proposals were never enacted, but the California Legislature passed a law that allows a person to recover damages for "constructive" trespass, defined as using an auditory or visual enhancing device to obtain images or recordings that could not have been obtained otherwise except by physical trespass.

In both public and private places, the use of hidden microphones and hidden cameras is a difficult legal and ethical issue. It is legal in most states to record a conversation so long as one party to that conversation has consented. That means reporters may legally record their conversations with sources without informing them. Twelve states—California, Connecticut, Florida, Illinois, Maryland, Massachusetts, Michigan, Montana, Nevada, New Hampshire, Pennsylvania and Washington—require the consent of all parties to the recording of conversations.

In all states, the ethical practice is always to ask your sources for permission to record conversations. And almost all states prohibit recording or publishing a conversation where none of the parties has given consent.

In an unusual case, however, the U.S. Supreme Court ruled that news media could not be liable for publishing a recording of a conversation that had been made by someone else. During a heated labor dispute between a teachers union and the Wilkes-Barre, Pa., school district, someone recorded a cell phone conversation between the union's chief negotiator and its president. The president, complaining about the unyielding bargaining position of district officials, said, "If they're not gonna move . . . , we're gonna have to . . . blow off their front porches." Neither the negotiator nor the president was aware the conversation was being recorded. A copy of the tape was mailed to a local radio talk show host, who aired it. Both union officials sued, saying the airing of the tape violated federal and state wiretapping laws. The U.S. Supreme Court, however, said news organizations may not be held liable in such circumstances. The radio talk show host had not recorded the conversation, nor did he know who did. And while publishing an illegally recorded conversation might be illegal in most instances, the strong public interest in knowing about the labor negotiations outweighed the interest in deterring wiretapping, the court said (Bartnicki vs. Vopper, 121 S.Ct. 1753 [2001]).

Surreptitiously photographing people also presents legal problems. At least 24 states outlaw using hidden cameras in private places. The laws vary widely. Some apply only to unattended cameras; others prohibit only attempts to use hidden cameras to photograph people in the nude.

Reporters have defended the use of hidden microphones and cameras as the best and, occasionally, the only way to get some stories. Nevertheless, this practice is distasteful to many readers and viewers.

A federal jury in North Carolina gave tangible expression to that disgust when it awarded the Food Lion supermarket chain more than $5.5 million in damages against ABC News. The network had broadcast a "PrimeTime Live" report on how Food Lion handled meat and other products it sold. Two producers for the show falsified job applications and references to obtain jobs in Food Lion stores in North and South Carolina. While working at Food Lion, they wore hidden microphones and cameras, recording such things as washing spoiled hams in bleach and using barbecue sauce to disguise rancid meat. Although the supermarket chain disputed many of ABC's charges, the truthfulness of the story was not at issue in the trial. The jury considered only the newsgathering practices ABC and its producers had used and concluded they had committed fraud, breach of duty of loyalty, trespass and unfair competition. A federal appeals court, saying Food Lion had failed to prove fraud on ABC's part, reduced the damage award to $2 (Food Lion Inc. vs. Capital Cities/ABC, 194 F. 3rd 505 [4th Cir. 1999]).

Giving Publicity to Private Facts

Everybody has secrets, and most people would be upset if their secrets were made public. Giving publicity to private facts presents the greatest potential for conflict with the First Amendment because an unfavorable judgment may punish truthful publications. A person who sues for this form of invasion of privacy must prove that:

- Publicity has been given to a private matter;
- The matter publicized would be highly offensive to a reasonable person; and
- There is no legitimate public interest in the information.

The information must be truly private. Publicizing facts that appear in public records but that are not generally known cannot be the basis for a lawsuit. Property tax information is a matter of public record in most states. If a news organization publishes a list of the most valuable homes in the community, who owns them and how much the owners pay in property taxes, the people on that list cannot sue for invasion of privacy. Even if the information is not on a public record but is merely known to a large number of people, publicizing it does not invade that person's privacy. A San Francisco man named Oliver Sipple saved the life of President Gerald Ford by disrupting an assassination attempt. A newspaper column later revealed that Sipple was gay, and he sued for invasion of privacy. The courts ruled that Sipple's homosexuality was already so widely known in the San Francisco gay community that he could not sue (Sipple vs. Chronicle Publishing Co., 10 Media L. Rptr. 1690 [Cal. Ct. App. 1984]).

The information that is publicized must also be highly offensive to a reasonable person. Disclosure of information that is merely embarrassing rather than highly offensive cannot be the basis for a lawsuit. The "reasonable person" standard is imprecise, but it asks juries to decide not by what would be offensive to the most sensitive or insensitive individual but by what the reasonable person would find highly offensive. Not surprisingly, many of the cases involve sex or nudity. For example, a Florida woman was abducted by her estranged husband and forced to strip while he held her hostage in an apartment. The crisis ended when the husband shot himself. Police rushed in, grabbed the woman and rushed her out of the apartment, leaving her time only to grab a tea towel. The local newspaper published a photograph of her being escorted to a police car and clutching the towel to her front. The woman sued, saying the photograph invaded her privacy, but a Florida appeals court ruled that the picture was not offensive enough to support a lawsuit. The photo, the court said, showed little more than could have been seen had the woman been wearing a bikini on a public beach (Cape Publications Inc. vs. Bridges, 423 So.2d 426 [Fla. Dist. Ct. App. 1982]).

Even if the matter publicized is highly offensive to a reasonable person, the plaintiff still must prove that there is no legitimate public interest in the information. A South Carolina man who was charged with trying to murder his wife by dousing her with gasoline and setting fire to her mobile home was homosexually raped while in jail awaiting trial. The local newspaper learned about the rape and reported the incident, along with the victim's name. He sued the newspaper saying it had given publicity to private facts, but the South Carolina Supreme Court said the public had a legitimate public interest in learning about violent crimes jail inmates commit against one another (Doe vs. Berkeley Publishers, 496 S.E.2d. 636 [S.C. 1998]).

The public interest in information is broad, and courts generally have interpreted this requirement in a way favorable to the news media. The public interest is broader in people who are public figures—movie stars, sports heroes and important political figures—but it may also include private individuals who have been caught up in newsworthy events. Moreover, the public interest extends beyond the event or situation that brought the person to public notice and includes other aspects of the subject's life and information about her or his relatives. But there is a line. Courts have said that the public interest does not extend to a morbid and sensational prying into private affairs with which the reasonable person would say he or she had no concern.

False Light

A false-light invasion of privacy lawsuit is similar in many respects to a libel suit. In fact, a person often may sue for either or both on the same set of facts. The major difference between them is that a libel suit redresses injury to a person's reputation, whereas a false-light suit protects a person's interest in being let alone. A false-light suit requires that publicity place a person in a false light and that the false light be highly offensive to a reasonable person. A federal appeals court said "Baywatch" actor José Solano Jr. could sue the magazine Playgirl for false light. The magazine's senior vice president had ordered the editors to "sex up" the January 1999 issue. The cover of that issue carried a photo of Solano, used without his permission, and close to his photo were headlines saying, "12 Sizzling Centerfolds Ready to Score With You," "TV Guys: Prime Time's Sexy Young Stars Exposed," and "'Baywatch's' Best Body: José Solano." The appeals court said the juxtaposition of the photo and the headlines could convey the false and highly offensive impression that Solano had posed nude for Playgirl (Solano vs. Playgirl Inc., 292 F.3d 1078 [9th Cir. 2002]).

Because false light is so similar to libel, the U.S. Supreme Court has ruled that false-light plaintiffs, like libel plaintiffs, must prove actual malice. The court imposed that requirement in a 1960s false-light case, Time Inc. vs. Hill (385 U.S. 374 [1967]). The court left unresolved the question of who must prove actual malice in false-light cases. Must all false-light plaintiffs prove actual malice or only public figures, as in libel cases? Some states have adopted a negligence stan-

The woman in this photograph sued a magazine that used it for false light, a form of invasion of privacy. The magazine used the photo to illustrate an article about Alzheimer's disease. Originally, the photograph accompanied a news story reporting that when parents reach an old age, they sometimes experience a sharp role reversal with their children who must take care of them.

dard for private individuals, but until the Supreme Court speaks no one can be sure what standard the First Amendment requires. In Solano's case, the federal appeals court said the actor had evidence that might allow a jury to conclude Playgirl had published its cover with actual malice.

Appropriation

Anyone who uses the name or likeness of another for his or her own use or benefit may be sued for invasion of privacy by appropriation. This was the first form of invasion of privacy to be recognized by the law. The most common form of appropriation is the use of a person's name or likeness for commercial purposes, as in an advertisement or television commercial.

A promotional calendar for the profit-making Choices Women's Medical Center in New York City used photographs of people prominent in the women's movement and in women's medicine to illustrate each month. One photograph showed a physician whose consent the company had not obtained. She sued for appropriation and won. The court concluded the calendar's purpose was to stimulate client referrals to the clinic and the use of the physician's name and photograph was directly connected to that purpose (Beverley vs. Choices Women's Medical Center, 19 Media L. Rptr. 1724 [N.Y. 1991]).

The use of a person's name or likeness in a news story is not considered appropriation, even though it may benefit the newspaper, magazine or broadcast by attracting readers, viewers and advertisers. The use of the name or likeness must have some reasonably direct connection to a news event, but courts have been lenient in deciding both what is a reasonable connection and what constitutes a newsworthy matter. A case involving actress Ann-Margret illustrates how broadly courts have construed newsworthiness. A magazine called High Society, which specializes in photographs of naked women, obtained a photo of Ann-Margret performing a nude scene for one of her movies. The magazine ran the photo in a section called "Celebrity Skin," and Ann-Margret sued for appropriation. A federal court ruled in favor of the magazine, saying information about entertainment, such as Ann-Margret's decision to perform a nude scene, is newsworthy (Ann-Margret vs. High Society, 6 Media L. Rptr. 1774 [S.D.N.Y. 1980]).

The exemption from appropriation lawsuits for news publications and broadcasts extends to advertisements promoting them. A news interview program can use the name and likeness of a person who will be profiled in a future broadcast in advertisements promoting that broadcast. However, the advertisement must not suggest that the person is endorsing that program or station. Nor can a broadcast or publication infringe on a performer's right to make money from his or her act. The U.S. Supreme Court upheld a judgment against an Ohio television station that broadcast a human cannonball's act in its entirety. The court said the television station had infringed on the performer's right of publicity (Zacchini vs. Scripps-Howard, 433 U.S. 562 [1977]). The idea of a right of publicity is very similar to that of appropriation. To the extent that the two can be distinguished, the right of publicity protects more than just a person's name or likeness; it extends to other distinctive attributes of a person's identity, such as voice, appearance, personality or act.

NEWSGATHERING

The First Amendment expressly protects the right to speak and to publish, but it says nothing about the right to gather information. The Supreme Court has recognized that freedom of the press means very little if there is no right to gather information, but what rights news reporters have to information are largely defined by a hodgepodge of state and federal statutes and court opinions. This section covers three newsgathering issues: access to nonjudicial proceedings and records, access to judicial proceedings and confidentiality for sources and information.

Reporters should always remember that the First Amendment does not protect them from prosecution if they engage in illegal conduct in order to gather news. Posing as a police officer, buying drugs or stealing documents are all illegal activities, and reporters who are prosecuted for engaging in illegal activities will not be allowed to plead that they were doing so to gather information for a news story.

Access to Nonjudicial Proceedings and Records

News Scenes

News happens in all kinds of places; some of them are not generally accessible by the public. News reporters have no greater right of gather at news scenes than do ordinary citizens, but officials may extend access privileges to reporters as they see fit.

Journalists frequently cover accidents, fires, crimes and natural disasters, and in all cases, the photographers and reporters want to get as close to the action as possible. At the same time, police, rescue workers, firefighters and other authorities need to control such scenes to protect lives and property. The normal desire of the authorities to manage crisis scenes has intensified since the terrorist attacks of Sept. 11. Reporters and photographers across the country have encountered greater resistance to their efforts to gather news.

A photographer for the Brattleboro, Vt., Reformer was arrested after taking photographs of the Vermont Yankee nuclear power plant. The photos were for a story the newspaper was preparing on the power plant, and the photographer was not on power plant property when he was taking the photos. Nevertheless, the prosecuting attorney said Vermont law prohibited the taking of photographs at nuclear power plants during a time of war. Ironically, Vermont Yankee's own Web site carries a photograph of the power plant's control room. The photographer was never charged with any crime.

Some state and local governments have used the terrorist attacks as a rationale for imposing greater restrictions on access to government buildings by reporters. In Pennsylvania, the Department of General Services started issuing credentials to members of the Capitol press corps. And reporters seeking permanent access cards now have to undergo criminal background checks.

The Chicago Police Department started fingerprinting reporters seeking press credentials and checking their criminal background. The Omaha, Neb., Police Department imposed a similar requirement, but it decided to allow news organizations to conduct their own background checks of reporters and tell police who was eligible for credentials.

Reporters and photographers covering the protests accompanying meetings of the World Bank and International Monetary Fund and the beginning of the Second Gulf War have sometimes been arrested along with the demonstrators. Nick Varanelli, a photographer for the Sacramento, Calif., City College Express was arrested and charged with rioting and blocking traffic. He had been trying to photograph anti-war demonstrations in San Francisco. Varanelli tried to show police officers his press credentials, but they told him the only valid credentials were those issued by the San Francisco police. Even reporters with San Francisco credentials were detained, however. San Francisco Chronicle reporter Michael Cabanatuan was covering the same demonstration and was wearing a press pass issued by the San Francisco police. He was detained for more than an hour and a half after he was trapped by police along with 200 other people.

Journalists covering protests, demonstrations and riots face many risks, but they can do some things to minimize the chances of being harassed by police. The Reporters Committee for Freedom of the Press recommends reporters and photographers covering protests do the following:

- Always carry press credentials.
- Don't trespass on private property or cross clearly marked police lines.
- Don't take anything from a crime scene.
- Obey all orders from police officers, even if doing so interferes with getting the story or the photo. (The alternative may be going to jail.)
- Don't argue with arresting officers.
- Have $50 to $100 on hand to purchase bail bond.
- Have a government-issued photo ID.

Even when life and property are not at stake, reporters and photographers often must cope with formal and informal official efforts to restrict their access to news scenes. When the late King Hussein of Jordan arrived in Rochester, Minn., to receive cancer treatments, police at the airport shined headlights and flashlights directly at the photographers who were covering the event, interfering with their ability to take pictures of the king. A police official said the lights were used as a security precaution. Formal Senate rules prevented still photographers from attending and taking pictures of President Clinton's impeachment trial. The Senate also closed its doors to all members of the public and the media for discussion of some procedural issues and for final deliberations on the impeachment issue. Reporters were able to conduct only prearranged interviews with senators or spontaneous interviews in a controlled "pen" outside the Senate chambers.

Privacy concerns have motivated many decisions to narrow the scope of access to news scenes in recent years. A federal task force on assisting the families of aviation disaster victims recommended limiting media access to the names and families of victims. The task force said airlines should release names only after a reasonable time to allow notification of families and the National Transportation Safety Board should keep the media away from families. Similar privacy concerns persuaded a federal court in New York to rule that "perp walks" are unconstitutional. The "perp walk" is the police practice of walking a suspect past reporters and photographers solely so that they can see and photograph him.

Records and Meetings

The federal government and all state governments have laws that help citizens and reporters access government records. The main federal law is the Freedom of Information Act. (Some people pronounce the acronym FOIA as FOY-ya.) This law, enacted in 1966, opens to public inspection all records held by agencies of the federal executive branch. The law exempts from disclosure nine categories of records:

1. Classified information.
2. Information related solely to internal personnel rules and practices.
3. Information exempted by other statutes.
4. Trade secrets and confidential commercial information.
5. Interagency and intra-agency memoranda that would reveal decision-making processes.
6. Information that would be a clearly unwarranted invasion of personal privacy.
7. Law enforcement investigative files, the disclosure of which would or could cause certain harms.
8. Information about financial institutions.
9. Geological and geophysical information such as maps showing the locations of oil and mineral deposits.

Since passing the FOIA, Congress has amended it several times to expand or contract the amount of information that may be disclosed. It has excluded from the purview of the act information about foreign intelligence, counterintelligence and terrorism. It has also made it easier for law enforcement agencies to withhold information about their investigative procedures and techniques. Recently, when Congress created the Department of Homeland Security, it exempted from disclosure information the department receives from private businesses about weaknesses in the country's critical infrastructure.

Executive branch policies can affect the usefulness of the FOIA, too. Attorney General John Ashcroft issued a memorandum to all federal agencies saying the Justice Department would defend any agency that withheld information requested under the FOIA unless the decision lacked any sound legal basis or could lead to a court decision that would harm the ability of the government to protect information. The Ashcroft memo was widely criticized as an invitation to federal agencies to withhold information.

The FOIA says federal agencies should release nonexempt information in response to any written request that reasonably identifies the records. Furthermore, the agency is supposed to respond within 20 working days. If a request raises or involves unusual circumstances, the agency may have an additional 10 days to answer. Actually getting the information, however, may take much longer. Most agencies have backlogs of requests for information. Congress has encouraged agencies to reduce their backlog by making more information available over the World Wide Web. The change has dramatically reduced backlogs at some agencies, such as the National Aeronautics and Space Administration, but its impact at others, such as the Department of Justice, has been minimal.

Two other federal statutes, the Government in the Sunshine Act and the Federal Advisory Committee Act, promote access to meetings. The Sunshine Act opens to the public the meetings of federal agencies that are led by boards or commissions having two or more members. The law exempts several categories of meetings, and many federal agencies do not formally meet to do their business. Instead, members do much of their work by circulating documents among themselves. The Federal Advisory Committee Act applies to the plethora of advisory committees appointed by the president and Congress to study various issues. Again, exemptions allow many deliberations to occur in secret.

All states and the District of Columbia have laws opening government records and meetings to the public and the press. The terms of these statutes, and their effectiveness, vary considerably. Some laws are very broad and have few exemptions. Others exempt dozens of kinds of records or meetings or have other qualifications that limit access.

Some public officials dislike having their records opened to public inspection, so they flout or ignore the law. News organizations in about 30 states have conducted statewide surveys of official compliance with public records laws. In most, journalists found many instances in which records that were clearly supposed to be open to the public were withheld. New Jersey reporters, for instance, found that while they had no trouble getting local budgets, only 22 percent of their requests for police logs and 31 percent of requests for school superintendents' contracts were granted. In spite of instances of noncompliance, reporters rely almost daily on state open records laws because they apply to local governments, like cities, counties and school boards, as well as to state agencies.

Privacy concerns have driven some legislatures to close records that traditionally have been open to public inspection. An example is what happened in Florida after the death of NASCAR driver Dale Earnhardt in a crash during a race. Shortly before Earnhardt died, the Orlando Sentinel had published stories about the deaths of other drivers and how a device called a Head and Neck Support system, known as HANS, might have saved their lives. The Sentinel asked for access to the photos of Earnhardt's autopsy, records that were public under Florida law. The Sentinel's editors did not want to publish the photos; they wanted to have an independent expert examine them and determine whether the HANS system might have saved Earnhardt's life. Teresa Earnhardt, the racer's wife, sued to prevent the Sentinel from having access to the photos. Teresa Earnhardt and the Sentinel eventually reached an agreement allowing an expert to examine the photos, but the Sentinel never received any copies. The expert's report concluded Earnhardt's injuries were the type that the HANS system might have prevented. Meanwhile, the Florida Legislature, with the encouragement of Teresa Earnhardt and Gov. Jeb Bush, amended the state's Sunshine Law to exempt autopsy photos from disclosure.

Most people might think access to autopsy photos serves no legitimate public interest, but in a number of instances, media and other organizations have used autopsy photos to challenge official stories about how people have died. The photos have been particularly useful in cases in which people have died in police custody:

- Frank Valdes died on death row in Florida. Prison officials said he died of self-inflicted injuries when he flung himself off his bunk and thrashed about his cell. Autopsy photos showed a clear imprint of a boot in his skin, evidence that he had been beaten. Guards eventually confessed that Valdes had been beaten to death.
- Moises DeLao was arrested for public intoxication in Pasadena, Texas. Before he could be bailed out of jail, guards found him hanging by an electric cord. The police and the medical examiner declared the death a suicide, but autopsy photos showed DeLao had been badly beaten.
- In Buffalo, N.Y., Donald Fleming was arrested for robbery and died in police custody. Police said the cause of death was a heart attack, but witnesses said Fleming had been beaten, a claim supported by autopsy photos.

Access to Judicial Proceedings

Freedom of the press is only one of many rights the Constitution guarantees to people in the United States. The right of a person accused of a crime to have a trial by an impartial jury is another constitutional right. These two rights appear to conflict when news organizations publish information that may sway potential jurors. Some authorities have labeled this problem "free press vs. fair trial," suggesting that one right must be sacrificed to the other. Fortunately, most judges, including those on the U.S. Supreme Court, have not phrased the problem so starkly. Rather, they have said the judge presiding over a trial must protect both the right of a defendant to a fair trial and the freedom of the press.

In 1966, the Supreme Court said trial judges must protect judicial proceedings when there is a reasonable likelihood that news coverage may prejudice the trial. The court did not say what a judge may do to media organizations. Rather, it focused on steps a judge could take that would protect the trial without interfering with the news media. Among other things, the Supreme Court said, trial judges can sequester jurors, move trials to new locations if publicity becomes too intense, delay a trial and limit the kinds of statements prosecutors and defense attorneys may make to the press about a pending trial.

Although the Supreme Court said nothing about restraining what journalists say about court proceedings, soon judges started issuing "gag" orders prohibiting reporters from publishing certain information even when they learned it in open court. The Supreme Court declared this kind of limitation on the press a prior restraint (Nebraska Press Association vs. Stuart, 427 U.S. 539 [1976]). It is unconstitutional unless:

- A defendant's trial may be prejudiced by news coverage;
- No alternative to a prior restraint would protect the trial; and
- A prior restraint would be effective in preventing prejudice.

Some trial judges have dealt with prejudicial news coverage by denying journalists access to information. The easiest way to do this is by closing the courtroom door. The Supreme Court seemed to endorse that approach, at least in some situations, in a 1979 decision. Just a year later, the court revisited the issue and declared that the press and the public have a First Amendment right to attend trials. The Supreme Court has elaborated on this right of access through several decisions. As it now stands, the press and the public have a qualified First Amendment right to attend judicial proceedings to which there is a history of public access and at which the presence of the public benefits the process. Trials have a long history of public access, for example, and having the public present helps the trial process by encouraging witnesses to be truthful and by serving as a check on the conduct of the police, the prosecutor and the judge. Similar concerns argue for public access to pretrial hearings, preliminary hearings and jury selection.

Courts may abridge the right of the press and the public to attend judicial proceedings when:

- There is a substantial likelihood of prejudice to the case;
- Closure of the courtroom would prevent the prejudice; and
- There are no alternatives to closure.

This is a very difficult standard to meet, because it requires the court to find facts establishing all these conditions (Press-Enterprise vs. Superior Court, 478 U.S. 1 [1986]). Occasionally, courts are able to satisfy the test. A federal district judge in New Orleans prohibited reporters from talking to jurors after they had convicted four defendants charged with trying to influence legislation governing the video poker industry. The judge said the order was necessary to protect jury deliberations, which historically have been closed to the public. A federal appeals court agreed that the order was necessary to deal with the substantial threat to the judicial process created by publicity to the case (U.S. vs. Cleveland, 128 F.3d 267 [5th Cir. 1997]).

The right of the press and the public to attend juvenile court hearings, family courts, divorce courts and some other judicial proceedings often is more restricted. The Supreme Court has not specifically ruled on access to these, but many states allow public attendance only at the discretion of the judge or where the judge finds that it serves a substantial or compelling interest.

The problems with gag orders and court closures became so severe in the 1970s that some state press and bar groups collaborated to write guidelines for dealing with each other during trials. The guidelines were supposed to be voluntary, but they were also supposed to protect the interests of news organizations and of criminal defendants. The bar-press guidelines vary from state to state, but common provisions are outlined in a sidebar on page 583.

Protecting Confidential Sources and Information

For almost as long as reporters have written news, they have used confidential sources. And reporters routinely promise to protect the identities of those sources. Reporters depend on confidential sources for some of their best stories, and the sources will provide information only if they know their identities are safe.

BAR-PRESS GUIDELINES

Guidelines worked out by state bar and press representatives for reporting criminal matters generally say the media should be free to report the following:

- Basic information about a suspect, such as name, age, address and marital status.
- The charges against the suspect.
- The circumstances under which the suspect was arrested, including whether any weapons were used.
- The names of those who have filed complaints against the suspect.
- If the crime involved a death, who died and how.
- The identities of the investigating agencies and officers.

The following information should not be published under most bar-press guidelines:

- The existence and nature of any statement or confession the suspect made to authorities.
- The results of any tests.
- Opinions on the credibility of the suspect or any witnesses or any evidence.
- Opinions about the outcome of the trial.
- Any other statements made outside the presence of the jury that might be highly prejudicial.

The guidelines usually include special warnings about the publication of the past criminal record of an accused person. Such information is considered highly prejudicial, but it is also a matter of open record in many states. Besides, much of the information may already be in a newspaper's clip file. So it would be impossible to prevent its disclosure. Nevertheless, the guidelines strongly discourage reporting a suspect's record.

Sometimes law enforcement officials, grand juries, courts, legislative bodies or administrative agencies demand the names of a reporter's confidential sources or other information the reporter wants to protect. The lawyers and judges want this information because they think it is relevant to some criminal or civil court case. In such cases, reporters may receive subpoenas ordering them to appear and testify before some official body. The subpoena may also direct them to bring notes, photographs, tapes and other materials they may have collected in the process of gathering news. A person who fails to comply with a subpoena can be cited for contempt of court and sent to jail or fined or both.

Vanessa Leggett, a writer working on a book about a Houston murder case, spent 168 days in jail in 2001 and 2002 for refusing to turn over to a federal grand jury all tapes and transcripts of her interviews with her sources. Although Leggett was not the first U.S. journalist to go to jail to protect sources or information, her term was the longest served by any journalist on a contempt charge. Leggett was investigating the murder of Doris Angleton, the wife of a wealthy Houston bookie, Robert Angleton. Soon police focused on Robert and his brother, Roger, as suspects. Both were arrested and charged with the crime. While Roger was in jail, he met with Leggett many times for interviews. During the interviews, Roger confessed that he had killed Doris and that Robert had paid him to do it. Roger died in jail before the trial started, however.

The state's case against Robert collapsed, and he was acquitted. Federal prosecutors then started building a case against Robert Angleton, and among the evidence they wanted was all the information Leggett had accumulated. Leggett argued the First Amendment allowed her to protect confidential sources and information, but federal courts refused to recognize the claim. Leggett was released from jail only after the term of the grand jury had expired. A second grand jury indicted Robert Angleton on federal charges of conspiracy to commit murder and firearms violations. Because she may be called to testify at the trial, Leggett may again face the dilemma of turning over the tapes and transcripts or going to jail.

Subpoenas are a common problem for news reporters. The Reporters Committee for Freedom of the Press has been surveying news organizations for several years to determine the extent of the problem. Seventy-nine percent of the television stations and 32 percent of newspapers responding to a recent survey by the Reporters Committee for Freedom of the Press had received at least one subpoena during the previous year. Most of the subpoenas to radio and television stations asked for video or audio tapes that had not been broadcast (outtakes) as well as tapes that had aired. Newspapers were more likely to receive subpoenas demanding that reporters reveal confidential information or sources.

Reporters have had mixed success resisting subpoenas in the effort to protect their sources and to prevent interference with their newsgathering. The U.S. Supreme Court in the Branzburg vs. Hayes (408 U.S. 665 [1972]) case rejected the idea that the First Amendment gives journalists any special protection from being subpoenaed to testify before grand juries. The court said although newsgathering enjoys some constitutional protection, every citizen has a duty to provide relevant information to a grand jury. Some justices disagreed with the Branzburg decision. The dissents and the ambiguity of the majority opinion opened the door for most federal and state courts to recognize a qualified privilege for reporters to protect confidential sources or information or both. Since the Branzburg decision, nine of the 12 U.S. Circuit Courts of Appeals have recognized a qualified privilege based on the First Amendment or on common law. Two circuits have not spoken on the issue, and one has rejected the idea of a reporter's privilege. Appellate courts in many states have also said reporters have some degree of protection for their confidential sources and information.

The extent of the privilege these state and federal courts have recognized varies greatly, but usually it allows reporters to protect confidential sources except when the information is essential to a case, can be obtained in no other way and would serve a compelling governmental interest. Courts generally have held that this privilege does not apply to nonconfidential information and sources or to actions a reporter or photographer may have witnessed firsthand.

Another 31 states and the District of Columbia have shield laws that specifically guarantee a journalist's right to protect confidential sources or information. Again, the laws vary in the level of protection they offer. What is protected in one state may not be in another. Some state laws let journalists protect confidential sources and unpublished information. Others limit the protection to confidential sources. Also, some states grant reporters a nearly absolute privilege to refuse to testify, while others qualify the privilege. However, even in states that recognize an absolute privilege, journalists are required to provide information vital for securing a criminal defendant's constitutional right to a fair trial.

CHECKLISTS

Elements of a Libel Suit

1. **Defamation:** A communication is defamatory if it lowers the plaintiff in the estimation of the community and deters others from associating or doing business with him or her.
2. **Identification:** A reasonable reader or viewer would conclude that the defamatory statement was "of and concerning" the plaintiff.
3. **Publication:** At least one person other than the publisher and the plaintiff saw or heard the defamatory statement.

4. **Injury:** The defamatory statement injured the plaintiff financially or through loss of reputation, mental anguish or humiliation. (Not required if the plaintiff proves the statement was made with actual malice.)
5. **Falsity:** If the defamatory statement is about a matter of public concern, the plaintiff must prove it false.
6. **Fault:** If the plaintiff is a public official or public figure, he or she must prove actual malice, meaning the defendant knew the defamatory statement was false or had a high degree of awareness of its probable falsity. If the plaintiff is a private individual, he or she must prove that the defendant negligently published a false statement.

Public Officials and Public Figures

1. A **public official** is someone who has or appears to the public to have substantial control over the conduct of public affairs and who holds a position important enough that the public has an independent interest in his or her qualifications.
2. A **general-purpose public figure** is someone who has such persuasive power and influence as to be a public figure for all occasions.
3. A **limited-purpose public figure** is someone who has thrust himself or herself to the forefront of a public controversy in order to affect its resolution.

Libel Defenses

1. **Truth:** A defendant can win a libel suit by proving that the sting or gist of the defamatory statement is true.
2. **Fair-report privilege:** Journalists may report defamatory statements made in official proceedings or documents so long as their reports are full, fair and accurate.
3. **Fair comment and criticism:** Statements about matters of public interest that cannot be proved false or do not appear to state facts about the plaintiff are protected.

Privacy

1. A lawsuit for **intrusion** is possible when one party intentionally intrudes on another's seclusion or solitude in a manner that would be highly offensive to a reasonable person. This would include eavesdropping, electronic surveillance or photographing someone using a high-power telephoto lens.
2. A lawsuit for **publicity to private facts** requires proof that the facts were private, that their disclosure would be highly offensive to a reasonable person and that the information was of no legitimate public concern.
3. A plaintiff in a **false-light** lawsuit must show that the publication would portray the plaintiff in a false light that would be highly offensive to a reasonable person and was published with knowledge that the story was false or with reckless disregard for whether it was false.
4. Using another person's name or likeness for one's benefit without that person's permission may be an unlawful **appropriation** of that person's identity. Use of a person's name or likeness in connection with a matter of public interest is exempt.

Newsgathering

1. The U.S. Supreme Court has said the First Amendment affords some protection to newsgathering, but generally, reporters have the same right of access to places and information as ordinary citizens.
2. Some federal laws, mainly the Freedom of Information Act, require the federal executive branch to disclose information, with some exceptions.
3. State laws regarding open meetings and open records provide access to information about government at the state and local levels.
4. Judges presiding at trials must protect both freedom of the press and the right of the parties to a fair trial.

5. Judges can impose prior restraints on news reporters only if evidence shows there is a substantial probability of prejudice to the trial, no alternative to a prior restraint would protect the trial, and the prior restraint would prevent prejudice.
6. The press and the public have a First Amendment right to attend court proceedings when there is a history of public access to that type of proceeding and when public observation benefits the proceeding.
7. When the press and public have a First Amendment right to attend a court proceeding, judges can close the courtroom only if the evidence shows there is a substantial probability of prejudice to the trial, closure would prevent the prejudice, and alternatives to closure would not be effective.
8. The Supreme Court recognizes no First Amendment right for reporters to refuse to testify about confidential sources and information.
9. Many state and federal courts recognize a qualified privilege for reporters to withhold confidential information and sources.
10. Thirty-one states and the District of Columbia have shield laws that provide some degree of protection for confidential sources or information. The laws differ greatly as to who and what is protected and under what circumstances.

SUGGESTED READINGS

Bezanson, Randall P., Gilbert Cranberg and John Soloski. *Libel Law and the Press: Myth and Reality.* New York: The Free Press, 1987.

Gillmor, Donald M. *Power, Publicity, and the Abuse of Libel Law.* New York: Oxford University Press, 1992.

Goodale, James C., ed. *Communications Law 2000.* New York: Practising Law Institute, 2002.

Hammitt, Harry A., David L. Sobel and Mark S. Zaid, eds. *Litigation Under the Federal Open Government Laws 2002.* Washington: Electronic Privacy Information Center, 2002.

Hixon, Richard F. *Privacy in a Public Society: Human Rights in Conflict.* New York: Oxford University Press, 1987.

Hopkins, W. Wat. *Actual Malice: Twenty-Five Years After Times v. Sullivan.* New York: Praeger, 1989.

Lewis, Anthony. *Make No Law: The Sullivan Case and the First Amendment.* New York: Random House, 1991.

Powe, Lucas A., Jr. *The Fourth Estate and the Constitution: Freedom of the Press in America.* Berkeley, Calif.: University of California Press, 1991.

Sanford, Bruce W. *Don't Shoot the Messenger: How Our Growing Hatred of the Media Threatens Free Speech for All of Us.* New York: The Free Press, 1999.

———. *Libel and Privacy,* 2nd ed. Englewood Cliffs, N.J.: Prentice-Hall Law & Business, 1985, 1993.

Smolla, Rodney A. *Law of Defamation.* Deerfield, Ill.: Clark Boardman Callaghan, 1986, 1994.

———. *Suing the Press: Libel, the Media and Power.* New York: Oxford University Press, 1986.

Spence, Gerry. *Trial by Fire: The True Story of a Woman's Ordeal at the Hands of the Law.* New York: Morrow, 1986.

Zuckman, Harvey L., Robert L. Corn-Revere, Robert M Frieden, and Charles Kennedy. *Modern Communication Law.* St. Paul, MN: West Group, 1999.

USEFUL WEB SITES

American Civil Liberties Union: http://www.aclu.org
FindLaw: http://www.findlaw.com
Freedom Forum First Amendment Center: http://www.firstamendmentcenter.org
Freedom of Information Center: http://www.missouri.edu/~foiwww
Legal Information Institute: http://fatty.law.cornell.edu
Reporters Committee for Freedom of the Press: http://www.rcfp.org
Student Press Law Center: http://www.splc.org
The Thomas Jefferson Center for the Protection of Free Expression: http://www.tjcenter.org
U.S. Supreme Court: http://www.supremecourtus.gov

Name ______________________________ Class ______________________ Date ______

EXERCISE 1

LIBEL

Decide which of the following sentences and paragraphs are potentially libelous. Place a "D" in the space preceding each statement that is dangerous for the media, and an "S" in the space preceding each statement that is safe.

1. ________ The police officers said they shot and wounded Ira Andrews, a 41-year-old auto mechanic, because he was rushing toward them with a knife.
2. ________ Testifying during the second day of his trial, Mrs. Andrea Cross said her husband, Lee, never intended to embezzle the $70,000, but that a secretary, Allison O'Hara, persuaded him that their actions were legal. Her husband thought they were borrowing the money, she said, and that they would double it by investing in real estate.
3. ________ A 72-year-old woman, Kelli Kasandra of 9847 Eastbrook Lane, has been charged with attempting to pass a counterfeit $20 bill. A convenience store clerk called the police shortly after 8 a.m. today and said that she had received "a suspicious-looking bill." The clerk added that she had written down the license number of a car leaving the store. The police confirmed the fact that the $20 bill was counterfeit and arrested Mrs. Kasandra at her home about an hour later.
4. ________ Margaret Dwyer said a thief, a boy about 14, grabbed her purse as she was walking to her car in a parking lot behind Memorial Hospital. The boy punched her in the face, apparently because she began to scream and refused to let go of her purse. She said he was blond, wore glasses, weighed about 120 pounds and was about 5 feet 6 inches tall.
5. ________ Police said the victim, Catherine White of 4218 Bell Ave., was too intoxicated to be able to describe her assailant.
6. ________ "I've never lived in a city where the officials are so corrupt," Joyce Andrews, a Cleveland developer, complained. "If you don't contribute to their campaigns, they won't do anything for you or even talk to you. You have to buy their support."
7. ________ The political scientist said that Americans seem unable to elect a competent president. "Look at who they've elected," she said. "I'm convinced that Lyndon Johnson was a liar, Nixon was a crook, Carter was incompetent, and Reagan was the worst of all: too lazy and senile to be even a mediocre president."
8. ________ The newspaper's restaurant reviewer complained: "I've had poor service before, but nothing this incompetent. The service at The Heritage Inn wasn't just slow; it was awful. When she finally did get to us, the waitress didn't seem to know what was on the menu. Then she brought us the wrong drinks. When we finally got our food, it was cold and tasteless. I wouldn't even feed it to my dog. In fact, my dog wouldn't eat it. The stuff didn't even smell good."

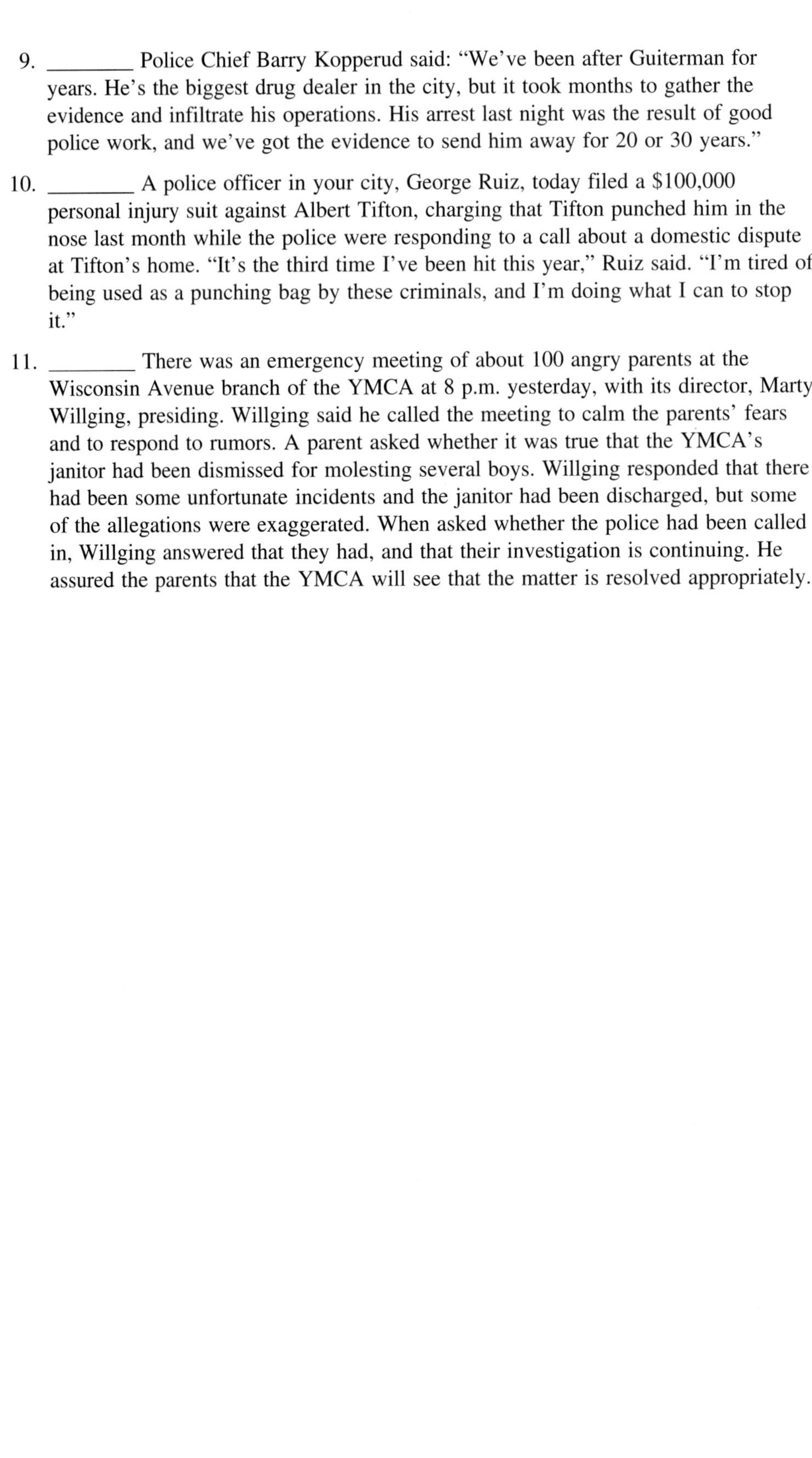

9. ________ Police Chief Barry Kopperud said: "We've been after Guiterman for years. He's the biggest drug dealer in the city, but it took months to gather the evidence and infiltrate his operations. His arrest last night was the result of good police work, and we've got the evidence to send him away for 20 or 30 years."

10. ________ A police officer in your city, George Ruiz, today filed a $100,000 personal injury suit against Albert Tifton, charging that Tifton punched him in the nose last month while the police were responding to a call about a domestic dispute at Tifton's home. "It's the third time I've been hit this year," Ruiz said. "I'm tired of being used as a punching bag by these criminals, and I'm doing what I can to stop it."

11. ________ There was an emergency meeting of about 100 angry parents at the Wisconsin Avenue branch of the YMCA at 8 p.m. yesterday, with its director, Marty Willging, presiding. Willging said he called the meeting to calm the parents' fears and to respond to rumors. A parent asked whether it was true that the YMCA's janitor had been dismissed for molesting several boys. Willging responded that there had been some unfortunate incidents and the janitor had been discharged, but some of the allegations were exaggerated. When asked whether the police had been called in, Willging answered that they had, and that their investigation is continuing. He assured the parents that the YMCA will see that the matter is resolved appropriately.

EXERCISE 2

COMMUNICATIONS LAW

LIBEL

Write an essay analyzing whether the news organization in the following situation can be sued successfully for libel. Consider all the elements of a libel case and how likely the plaintiff would be to prove each. Consider also whether the plaintiff is a public official, public figure or private individual. Finally, consider what defenses the news organization might use.

When Local 1313 of the Municipal Employees Union and the Beacon City Council negotiated a new labor contract for the city's employees last year, the union was represented by Sam Fong, its chief negotiator. The Beacon negotiations were stressful and stormy, with accusations of bad-faith bargaining made by both sides. At one point, the union threatened to strike if its demands were not met.

As the strike deadline approached, Hilda Jackson, reporter for the Beacon Daily Light, prepared a story that profiled Fong and described the union's negotiating strategy. Jackson talked to a number of people familiar with Fong and the way he conducted labor negotiations.

Jackson's story included the comments of Paula Williams, a city councilwoman, who said during a council meeting: "Fong is a first-rate bastard. That S.O.B. is trying to extort a fortune from the city. If we give him what he wants, we'll be broke, and if we don't, he'll shut down the city with a strike."

Another of Jackson's sources is Ben Davis, a union member with a grudge against Fong and a history of alcoholism. Davis said Fong had promised to keep union members informed about negotiations and to get their advice and guidance, but instead he had kept the members in the dark. Davis also said he suspected that union money had been used to hire prostitutes for union officials. He said a union bookkeeper had information that could confirm his story, but Jackson did not talk to him. Nevertheless, she included Davis' allegations in her story.

Jackson also reported that Fong had been convicted of automobile theft when he was 19 and had spent five years in a state penitentiary. Because Jackson failed to read the entire record of the case, her report was incorrect. Fong had served only 18 months of his five-year sentence and was placed on parole because of his good behavior.

Immediately after Jackson's story was published, Fong's wife sued him for divorce, alleging adultery and citing the allegation that union officials had engaged prostitutes as an instance of adultery. National union leaders also commenced an investigation of how Fong was spending his expense account money. The national union concluded that the charges of misuse of union money were groundless, but it dismissed Fong anyway for having failed to disclose his conviction for auto theft when he applied for his job.

Fong sued the Beacon Daily Light for libel.

EXERCISE 3

COMMUNICATIONS LAW

LIBEL

Write an essay analyzing whether the news organization in this situation can be sued successfully for libel. Consider all the elements of a libel case and how likely the plaintiffs would be to prove each. Consider also whether each plaintiff is a public official, public figure or private individual. Finally, consider what defenses the news organization might use.

U.S. policy toward the Central American country of Costa Grande, where there is a civil war, has been the subject of extensive debate in Congress, a key issue in some congressional elections and a major news story for some months. As part of its coverage of the topic, the Continental Broadcasting Co.'s Nightly News program has investigated and broadcast a story alleging that three people, including a prominent federal official, were involved in sending arms and supplies to rebels in Costa Grande in violation of U.S. law.

One was Russell Starr, a retired Army general, who is considered an expert on Central American insurgency movements. He is president of an organization that has promoted the cause of the Costa Grande rebels. He has written newspaper and magazine pieces about the justness of the rebels' cause and has defended them on television talk shows. The second figure is Ronda Vernon, who recently became the third wealthiest person in the country when she inherited the fortune her father earned in the computer software business. Vernon rarely appears in public and never comments on political matters, but through various trust funds that she and her family control, she has donated millions of dollars to controversial groups, including the Costa Grande rebels. The last key figure in the Nightly News piece is Sean Grady, assistant secretary of state for Central American affairs, the member of the administration with primary responsibility for formulating and carrying out U.S. policy in that region.

The Nightly News story said that Starr had used dummy corporations and numbered Swiss bank accounts to channel money from his organization to the purchase of arms and supplies for the rebels. Several men involved in the illegal arms trade, all convicted felons, told reporters about Starr's financial arrangements. The information from the arms dealers was corroborated for the most part with information from several reliable staff members of congressional committees. The congressional staffers were familiar with classified information on Starr's dealings. Starr denied any wrongdoing and steered reporters to sources who would back him up. But the Nightly News reporters ignored Starr's sources because none had any inside knowledge.

The Nightly News said that Vernon had contributed $3 million to Starr's organization in full knowledge that some of the money was being sent illegally to the Costa Grande rebels. This part of the story was based on interviews with various people who had helped manage some of the Vernon family trust funds and on financial statements. Because of a reporter's arithmetic error, however, the Nightly News exaggerated the size of Vernon's contributions to the Costa Grande rebels by $700,000.

As for Grady, the news broadcast said he had used his official position in order to persuade the FBI to ignore the trio's illegal activities. Nightly News' only source for this was another State Department official, who is known to covet Grady's job. The official said he learned about Grady's efforts to obstruct any federal investigation of Starr and Vernon when a glitch in the telephone system enabled him to overhear a conversation between Grady and an FBI agent. The network's reporters failed to check with the bureau to find out whether any of its agents had even tried to investigate the flow of arms and cash to the Costa Grande rebels.

Starr, Vernon and Grady all sued the network for libel.

EXERCISE 4

COMMUNICATIONS LAW

PRIVACY

Write an essay analyzing whether the news organization in this situation can be sued successfully for invasion of privacy. Consider all four forms of invasion of privacy and decide whether the plaintiff would be able to prove any of them.

Jasmine Lynd is a model-turned-actress who has appeared on the covers of many fashion magazines and in several major motion pictures. She attended a reception at the governor's mansion and stayed late for a private cocktail with the governor. The next day, Lynd reported to the police that the governor had raped her. The incident drew intense coverage from the press, including the Weekly Intelligencer, a tabloid newspaper sold mainly in supermarkets. In the past, Lynd had angered Intelligencer editors by refusing requests for interviews and threatening libel suits. One editor told the reporters covering the case, "This is our chance to pay her back."

Lynd would not talk to Intelligencer reporters, so they spoke to a number of her friends and acquaintances. One friend described Lynd's high school career, saying that she had been a "party girl" who had barely passed her courses and had frequently been in trouble with school authorities. Another source mentioned that Lynd had overcome, with great effort, a severe stuttering problem as a teen-ager.

Other Intelligencer reporters examined court records and learned that Lynd had three arrests for speeding and one for drunken driving. Other records showed that her husband had divorced her because she had been unfaithful. Her ex-husband said in an interview with reporters that he had discovered Lynd's infidelity when she gave him a venereal disease she had picked up from her lover, a professional wrestler. The wrestler told reporters that Lynd had an irrational fear of food preservatives, chewed her fingernails compulsively and always slept in the nude. Lynd has denied none of these statements.

The divorce records on file in district court also provided reporters with information about Lynd's finances, including the fact that she had purchased a controlling interest in a television production business and several pieces of commercial real estate, all of which more than tripled in value in only two years. One of Lynd's former friends, a woman who had known her in high school but had not seen her for 15 years, said that Lynd never made a business investment without consulting the famous astrologer Wesley Wilson. Wilson denied that Lynd was one of his clients, but the Intelligencer published the assertion anyway.

The Intelligencer's editors dispatched two teams of photographers to get photos for the story. One team followed Lynd wherever she went—work, shopping, social events—constantly snapping photos. On one occasion, trying to get a photo of her driving on the freeway, they maneuvered their car so close to hers that she swerved to avoid them and grazed a safety railing. Another team of photographers stationed themselves at the side of a highway on a hill overlooking Lynd's expensive home. From that location, the photographers used powerful telephoto lenses to get pictures of Lynd sunbathing and swimming in her back yard (which is surrounded by a high privacy fence).

Even though Lynd had not talked to reporters since she charged the governor with rape, the Intelligencer promoted its story about her with an advertisement in several newspapers saying, "Meet Jasmine Lynd. Find out what Lynd told the Intelligencer that she would tell no one else. You can depend on the Intelligencer—just as Lynd does—to deliver the truth!"

Lynd has filed a lawsuit alleging that the Weekly Intelligencer has invaded her privacy by placing her in a false light, giving publicity to private facts, intruding upon her solitude and seclusion and appropriating her name and likeness.

CHAPTER 21

ETHICS

Readers don't expect us to be guided by situational ethics, to speak high-mindedly then to pursue every hiccup as if it were The Truth.

(Sandra Mims Rowe, newspaper editor)

Every decision a journalist makes when gathering, organizing and presenting the news requires value judgments:

- Which story is more important to report?
- Whom to interview?
- What questions to ask?
- What angle to take?
- Whom to quote?
- Which side to present first?
- How long to make the story?
- Should photos or graphics go with the story?
- Should the photo be cropped?
- Should the subject for the video be a close-up or a medium or long shot?
- Where to place the story in a newspaper or broadcast?

Different decisions bring different results. All decisions have consequences that are direct and indirect, intended and unintended, short-term and long-term. And, journalists' decisions affect others.

Journalists examine their actions on the basis of professional and personal standards. They think about organization, industry and society norms. They want to make their news programs or newspapers as lively and interesing as possible, but they try to stay within the bounds of good taste and common decency. They also must balance competing interests, such as the need for the public to know about current events and the privacy interests of people involved in those events. Most journalists try to work ethically, which means acting and thinking morally. To be moral means to distinguish between right and wrong.

MEDIA CREDIBILITY

No matter what journalists decide, some audience members will criticize their decisions. Audiences have a wide range of complaints: Journalists do not respect other people; the media have become too big, powerful, arrogant and insensitive; the news reports are ideologically slanted; media report too much bad news; journalists seek only the sensational news. Some of these criticisms are justified. Others are stereotypes from the portrayals of journalists and news organizations in movies and on television. Also, the media are quick to report on journalists who act unethically, whereas the thousands of moral journalists who make good decisions do not make the news.

The media must maintain credibility for two main reasons. First, people depend on the media for their information. Research shows people use local and national television news programs to find out about breaking events, and they monitor radio news for updates. People who want more detail about issues or events turn to newspapers, the Internet and magazines.

Second, media must be credible to succeed as businesses. The media need readers, viewers and listeners to attract advertisers, who provide financial support. If audiences doubt the credibility of a particular news organization, they will change the channel or stop buying that newspaper. When audiences turn away, advertising revenues decline. Then the media organization's budget shrinks, which often means even poorer news coverage. The downward spiral usually continues until that news organization goes out of business.

ETHICAL DECISION-MAKING

When a story is wrong or unethical, people usually berate the organization that published it. The organization may then reprimand or dismiss the reporter or editor responsible for it. This alone gives journalists a powerful reason to think through ethical issues.

Guiding Questions

A journalist can ask several questions when facing an ethical decision. Two of the most important are:

- Who will be hurt, and how many?
- Who will be helped, and how many?

Many news stories hurt people. Weighing the hurt against the benefits, and justifying that hurt, can help journalists make the right choice. If the story hurts several people but helps several hundred, then publishing the story is most likely justified. Perhaps a physician has been accused of misdiagnosing patients' symptoms, which has led to incorrect surgeries. The story might embarrass the physician and his family, but it would help many patients and potential patients.

Sometimes, journalists get too involved with the details of writing and publishing a story and forget to ask the all-encompassing questions of "What is the objective of my story? And, will my decision contribute to the reason for writing the story?"

A retired journalist and professor, H. Eugene Goodwin, used to tell his reporters and students to ask themselves six questions while making an ethical decision:

1. What do we usually do in cases like this? (What is the news organization's policy on this type of situation, and is it a good policy?)
2. Is there a better alternative? (Harmful results often can be avoided or eased by trying something different.)
3. Can I look myself in the mirror tomorrow? (You must think about how you feel, and whether you can live with your decision.)

A furniture store owner in St. Louis, Ron Olshanger, received a Pulitzer Prize for spot news photography for his photo showing a firefighter giving mouth-to-mouth resuscitation to a child pulled from a burning building.

4. Can I justify this to family, friends and the public? (If we know we have to explain our decisions to the public—in an editor's column, for example—then we might be more careful about our decisions.)
5. What principles or values can I apply? (Some overarching principles, such as truth, justice or fairness, will take priority over others.)
6. Does this decision fit the kind of journalism I believe in and the way people should treat one another? (Our judgments should correspond with the way we believe the media ought to be and the way people in a civilized society ought to behave.)

Macro and Micro Issues

Journalists wrestling with ethical decisions should identify a story's macro and micro issues. The macro issue is the main reason for publishing the story. Micro issues—such as the wording of a story or its headline, what art to use with it and what facts to include or omit—tend to be less consequential, but still important. Too often journalists get caught up in micro issues and forget a story's macro issue. For example, state police received complaints from motorists that a rest stop was becoming a hangout for homosexual men, who were sexually accosting travelers in the men's toilet. The police videotaped the troublemakers in action and arrested some suspects. A local newspaper wanted to publish the story. Editors discussed printing the names of the accused. Many had wives, children and colleagues who knew nothing of their homosexuality or of their criminal actions. Editors realized that publicity could ruin reputations, marriages and careers. One man was a scout leader and another was in a seminary.

The editors' discussion focused on several micro issues: (1) placement—a story placed on an inside page is less damaging to the accused than a story on the front page; (2) space—a short story is not as noticeable as a longer one; and (3) graphics and visuals—the type and number of illustrations, if any, can set a tone.

The editors revisited the macro issue (the reason for the story): making the rest stop safe for community members and travelers. Once focused on the macro issue, they were able to resolve the micro issues more easily. The newspaper printed the story on Page 1 with a list of the names of the accused.

ETHICS ISSUES

The public questions the techniques some journalists use to obtain the news. Rude, aggressive reporters seem willing to do anything to get a story: invade people's privacy, invent details and interview the victims of crimes and accidents while they are still in shock. In the past, reporters slanted some stories and invented others. Some reporters stole pictures from the homes of people involved in the news. Other reporters impersonated police officers or accepted expensive gifts from people they wrote about.

Despite public perceptions, today's journalists act more ethically and professionally than their predecessors. They are better educated and better paid. They are also doing more to raise their ethical standards.

On some issues, American journalists have reached almost universal agreement. They agree, for instance, that it is unethical to fabricate information or to accept valuable gifts from a source. On other issues, ethical journalists may differ because competing values are involved. A journalist may want to report an important story but fear that it would intrude on an individual's privacy. Or a journalist may want to publish an important document but hesitate because a source stole the document or because a federal official insists that it is a "state secret." Furthermore, reporters must be concerned with audience perception of their behavior, even if they are acting ethically.

Each ethical situation is unique, and journalists must consider each individually, trying to balance the competing values or to decide which value is most important. While covering one story, journalists may decide to protect an individual's privacy. While covering another story, journalists may decide that the community's need to know is more important than protecting an individual's privacy. Regardless of what they decide, it is impossible for journalists to convince every person that they made the right decision. Thus, some criticisms are inevitable. The rest of this section discusses some of the major areas of ethical concern for journalists: maintaining objectivity, exploiting grief, using visuals, invading privacy, naming names, having conflicts of interest, witnessing crime and disasters, being deceitful, recording interviews, stealing and fabricating information, reporting rumors and speculation, publicizing terrorism, and accepting some types of advertising.

Maintaining Objectivity

Objectivity has two components: absence of bias and accuracy. Everyone has biases and opinions. Journalists' biases can greatly affect a story. Biases may subtly influence selection of story topics, sources, questions asked, story angle, organization and presentation. For instance, journalists who are pro-choice might have difficulty writing an objective story about a new federal bill limiting abortions. They may unintentionally interview only sources who share their opinions. Reporters should interview people who have other ideas or come from different cultures.

Sometimes, journalists aware of their prejudices may overcompensate in the opposite direction in their efforts to present an objective story. To alleviate the problem of bias, reporters avoid topics about which they have strong opinions and let their editors know when they cannot cover a subject objectively. The editor will then assign the story to another reporter.

Objectivity also means being accurate. However, objective facts without context can create inaccurate impressions. Journalists who report that a married female mayor often ate lunch and worked late with a male staffer may lead audiences to assume mischief is afoot. Even if accurate, the story needs the background information that will help readers correctly interpret the facts. In reality, the mayor may be working overtime with a staffer assigned to research an important budget issue the city council will vote on the following week.

The Cincinnati Enquirer ran an 18-page special section accusing Chiquita Banana International of improper business practices. Several weeks later, the newspaper paid $10 million to Chiquita to avoid a lawsuit, ran a front-page apology to the company for three consecutive days and fired its reporter, Mike Gallagher, for stealing Chiquita executives' voice mail messages. The apology was for the reporter's methods, but also for the conclusions about the company his stories reached. Taken out of context, the stolen voice mail made the company executives look like crooks. (Gallagher pleaded guilty to two felony charges and identified a confidential source—something many journalists say was unforgivable.)

Reporting or Exploiting Grief

A national public opinion survey found that 47 percent of the country's adults believe the media do not care about the people they report on. An even greater number—73 percent—believe the media have no regard for people's privacy. The public is especially critical of the way media cover death and tragedy by photographing and interviewing victims and grieving relatives.

Interviewing Victims

Few journalists are psychologists. They may not realize that many disaster victims and their family members experience shock for several days or months after an event. The shock can last for a few days or a long time and can affect people in different ways.

Reporters often harm a news organization's reputation when they scramble to get an early interview. Sometimes victims in shock inadvertently twist facts. Or, they may want to please the reporter by answering questions, even if they are not certain of the accuracy of the details they supply. Victims often complain later that they were in shock at the time of the interview and cannot recall even talking to a reporter. They sometimes recant their stories or accuse reporters of making up the interview.

Many journalists have found they obtain more accurate and complete stories if they wait several days to interview victims. Hard news stories can be written immediately after an event, with accurate, informative follow-up stories later.

Victims or their family members sometimes choose to speak to one reporter during their time of grief. Usually families select reporters who are respectful and considerate. These reporters ask to talk to the family's representative, who may be another family member or close friend. In addition, reporters give their names and telephone numbers to the victim or the victim's representative, not asking for an immediate interview, but asking the victim to call them if and when the victim feels ready to talk. Compassionate journalists, who do not pressure victims and their families, receive more in-depth information about the victim and the event.

Hurting Victims Again: The News Story as a Second Wound

A news story may inflict a second injury on victims and family members who lived through a disaster and experience it again when seeing it described on television or in a newspaper. For example, a young man was beaten and raped and his nude body was found along a deserted road. Had reporters described the tragedy in detail and used sensational photographs the story could have been painful for the victim's family. Instead, editors reviewed the objective of the story, omitted sensational details and published only what the public needed to know.

A 5-year-old boy drowned while swimming in Bakersfield, Calif. This photograph shows a rescue worker trying to console the victim's mother and siblings. The victim's father is on his knees. Robert Bentley, managing editor of The Bakersfield Californian, said: "I ran the picture because it was a powerful photograph, and it was news, and I'm a newsman." The picture also appeared in other newspapers, from Salt Lake City to Boston and Tampa.

The Californian received more than 400 telephone calls and 500 letters. A bomb threat forced employees to evacuate their office, and 80 readers canceled their subscriptions. People complained that the photograph showed a callous disrespect for the victim, and that it invaded the family's privacy at a moment of grief and shock. Bentley apologized, admitting that he had made a mistake. Photographer John Harte disagreed. "The picture should have run," Harte said. "It was a very good picture. This was an area where there have been a lot of drownings, and the photograph will have long-term benefits in making people aware of water safety and swimming safety."

Compassionate photojournalists, reporters and editors often ask themselves how they would want the press to treat them or their own family members if they were in the victim's situation. Journalists discuss the purpose of the story, what the public needs to know and alternate ways to portray the emotion. They also weigh the crucial questions: Who will be hurt, and how many? Who will be helped, and how many?

Using Visuals: Newsworthy or Sensational?

The visual coverage of Sept. 11, 2001, challenged many editors. For many, it was a fine line to fully represent the events without giving readers and viewers more than they wanted to see. Pictures of death and dying often anger audience members, which distracts them from the purpose of the story. Furthermore, too much repetition of the same images—the jetliners' flying into the World Trade Center Towers, for example—can numb viewers' reaction to the horrific events.

Editors and producers run photographs or videotapes because they help tell a story. People upset by the pictures accuse the media of sensationalizing stories to attract audiences rather than helping people in distress. Critics denounce a news organization's decision if a photo or video is used for shock effect only. Critics are concerned about a visual's effects: about whether the footage is too unpleasant, tasteless and upsetting.

Editors and producers often feel cornered. Should they shield the public from unpleasantness or educate them? Some newspapers and television news programs used shots of a dead American soldier being dragged by ropes through the streets of Mogadishu in Somalia. Viewers and readers were shocked. The soldier's body and the laughing faces of Somalians told a

Associated Press photographer Alan Diaz won a Pulitzer Prize for this photo of federal marshals taking Elian Gonzales into custody. The raid ended a weeks-long dispute over whether the U.S. government should return Elian to his father in Cuba or let relatives in South Florida have custody of him. The photograph also aroused anger against the U.S. government for using force. Sen. Bob Smith, R-N.H., said the photograph seemed to show the federal marshal was pointing his assault rifle right at Elian, and therefore proved the government had endangered the boy.

horrifying story. Because the soldier was not identified, hundreds of parents and wives were worried that the soldier was their relative, or that their son or husband might be next. Many editors wrote columns explaining they published the photo to help describe what was happening to the U.S. peacekeeping effort in Somalia. They said words alone did not convey the situation

Sometimes a photograph can have more impact than words. This image reflected the reality of a natural disaster's effect on humanity. About 74 percent of the San Jose (Calif.) Mercury News journalists said they would run this photo of a woman pulled from earthquake rubble, while 52 percent of their readers agreed.

Some editors who ran this photograph thought the image taught a lesson in a way words could not: This is what can happen when a youth tries to climb a six-foot fence with spikes on top. Twenty-six percent of the San Jose (Calif.) Mercury News journalists said they would publish the photo, and 23 percent of their readers agreed. (The boy survived the piercing.)

as well as this photograph did. Others, though, argued the situation in Somalia could have been portrayed in other ways.

Within one day, more than 100 people called the Milwaukee Journal Sentinel complaining about an accident story with a photo of two police officers shooting a fatally injured horse. The 4-column by 8-inch photo showed the horse down on the street with its head up looking at the officers. The story noted that after each gunshot, the horse "writhed in pain and appeared as if it was trying to stand. After the fourth shot, it was still." The editors said they were reporting the news. Many readers said the same news could have been presented differently. Nonetheless, many readers were confused as to the objective of the story.

News organizations must keep in touch with the public's attitudes. Journalists who see a lot of violence and unhappiness may not accurately judge what the public will find acceptable.

Invading Privacy

The media sometimes intrude on the privacy of individuals. Although they are often within their legal rights, do they have the moral or ethical right?

Respecting Private Individuals

Some events are more obviously newsworthy than others. People who become involved in major lawsuits, crimes and accidents may expect to be mentioned in news stories about them. Other citizens may be surprised to find themselves standing in the media spotlight.

Sometimes journalists must make difficult decisions about whom to subject to public scrutiny. News organizations usually do not identify juvenile delinquents. But if several teenagers are arrested and charged with committing rapes and burglaries that terrorized a neighborhood, editors may feel a need to identify the teenagers and perhaps their parents as well. Editors may decide their obligation to calm people's fears by informing the neighborhood about the arrests outweighs their normal obligation to protect the teenagers and their families.

Reporting on Public Figures

Journalists are often criticized for their treatment of government officials and other public figures. Journalists argue the public's right to know outweighs a government official's or public figure's right to privacy. Most Americans seem to agree journalists should expose government officials who abuse their power or who have personal problems, such as alcoholism, that affect their work.

But does the public have a right to know about a public official's private affairs, such as adultery? Some people say adultery does not affect a politician's public decision-making. Other critics argue that if a politician breaks a solemn promise, such as a wedding vow, then promises to his or her constituency may also be meaningless. These critics say the public has a right to know about the character of the person who represents them.

Larry Sabato, a political scientist who teaches at the University of Virginia, has argued that the press should have been more aggressive in reporting on John F. Kennedy's love affairs. Reporters who covered Kennedy during his presidential campaign and while he was in office were well aware of his many paramours, including Judith Campbell Exner. At the same time Exner was having an affair with Kennedy, she was also the girlfriend of Sam Giancana, a Chicago mob boss. Kennedy and Giancana were both aware of the other's involvement with Exner, which could have left Kennedy open to extortion by the mob. Sabato said Kennedy's womanizing interfered with his presidential duties. Occasionally, Kennedy would try to have more privacy with his lovers and evade his guards and the military officer who carried the codes that control U.S. nuclear weapons. None of these details became public knowledge until long after Kennedy's death. But when Bill Clinton's involvement with Monica Lewinsky surfaced, the press covered it in explicit detail—and many Americans found the coverage excessive.

Journalists also become involved in controversies after overhearing—and reporting—remarks that were not meant for publication. Speakers are outraged and accuse journalists of invading their privacy and acting unfairly and unethically. Journalists respond that the remarks are newsworthy and reveal the speakers' true feelings, character and behavior. When President Ronald Reagan joked about bombing the Soviet Union, journalists reported the story. Reagan told the joke just before a radio broadcast, and it was accidentally transmitted to a pressroom. During one of Jesse Jackson's campaigns for the presidency, journalists also heard—and reported—derogatory remarks the candidate made about Jews. Politicians charge that the press has gone too far. They wonder if the public really benefits from its scrutiny of public officials. Journalists respond that, unlike private citizens, politicians voluntarily place themselves in the public spotlight. They seek attention. In addition, most public figures should be role models for the citizenry they govern.

A Newsweek poll showed most people (76 percent) thought the news media had gone too far in the direction of entertainment and away from traditional reporting. Much of the entertainment includes delving into actors' and other public figures' private lives. Are all stories newsworthy? How important was it to follow and photograph Princess Diana and Dodi Fayed the night they died in an automobile crash in Paris? (French officials placed nine photographers and a press motorcyclist under formal investigation for manslaughter and failing to aid people in danger. The investigation eventually concluded the photographers and press motorcyclist had violated no laws.) Many charge that the press had pushed too hard to get photographs and information about Princess Diana.

Deciding When to Name Names

Normally, journalists want to identify fully everyone mentioned in their stories. Most news organizations have adopted policies requiring their reporters and editors to do so. But the participants in some stories may make forceful claims for anonymity: for example, juveniles accused of crime, rape victims, homosexuals, and prostitutes and their clients. Because each situation is different, reporters and editors examine them individually.

Juveniles Accused of Crimes

Journalists usually do not name children who are connected in any way to a crime. Children are not capable of dealing with the infamy associated with a news account that might affect them for the rest of their lives. Traditionally, the criminal justice system also has shielded children under 18 who are accused or convicted of a crime. This protection has been explained on the grounds juveniles understand neither what they did nor the consequences of their actions. In most cases, journalists cooperate by not publicizing juveniles' names. The main exception occurs when juveniles are being tried in adult court because the crimes of which they are accused are more serious than the ones juveniles usually commit or the suspects have already been punished for earlier serious offenses.

Victims of Sexual Assault

A national study showed most news organizations withhold the names of rape victims. Editors explain that the nature of the crime traumatizes and stigmatizes victims in unique ways. They also realize rape is an underreported crime, and news coverage discourages some rape victims from going to police. A recent study on rape victims found most victims were angry about being identified, and a few said they would not have reported the crime if they had known a TV station or newspaper would name them. As a result of being named, most victims reported emotional trauma as well as embarrassment, shame and difficulties in their relationships with others. One victim, who subsequently left college, realized reporters had discovered her school schedule when she found them waiting for her at the door of her classrooms and interviewing classmates.

Some critics say the practice of not naming rape victims constitutes a dual standard: Media identify people charged with rape but not their accusers. Another study, this time with readers and viewers, showed most people definitely opposed identifying rape victims. The respondents were divided about naming the rape suspect, but most indicated the accused's name should be included. Rape suspects, like those in all other crimes, are always identified so that the public will have full knowledge about how the law enforcement and judicial systems are performing their duties.

The same study concluded identifying victims had little effect on how people viewed either a rape story or the crime, but it had potentially negative effects on the victim. The study indicated naming the victim helps no one and hurts the victim again.

Other Cases

Journalists in doubt about publishing names ask their standard questions: Who will be hurt, and who will be helped? For example, an editor may decide that identifying prostitutes and their clients may hurt the offenders and their families but benefit an entire neighborhood by deterring prostitution. In some cities, coalitions of merchants, homeowners and government officials have organized to combat the problem. They encourage the police to make more arrests, and they ask newspapers to publish the names of both prostitutes and their "johns," or customers.

The macro issue is ridding the community of an unsavory business associated with drugs, violence and disease. The macro issue is also a matter of fairness, since news organizations were practicing a form of discrimination when they identified prostitutes (mostly women) and shielded customers (mostly men). Both, after all, were breaking the law.

Other kinds of lawbreakers may find their names in newspapers. Some papers in Iowa print the names of delinquent taxpayers as public notices. Newspapers in various states identify delinquent child-support payers in their news sections, which has helped the states collect hundreds of thousands of dollars in overdue child support each year. The Anderson (Ky.) News regularly publishes the jailhouse mugshots of people convicted of driving while intoxicated. Most community members support the policy. The objective, said the publisher, was to bring public attention to drunken driving in the county. The publisher decided against publishing the photos of convicted rapists, spouse abusers and child abusers because it would identify the victims as well.

Practicing Deceit: Is It Justified?

Journalists want everyone to believe and trust them. Most reporters believe deceit is a form of lying and lying is unethical. However, some journalists think deceit is the only way to get some stories. A story may be important and help thousands of people. It may, for example, expose crime or a government official's abuse of power. However, some journalists say the press should not criticize deceitfulness by public officials or businesses if reporters are lying while pursuing a story. And in most cases, an investigative story with many in-depth interviews and extensive background research provides a better story than one in which journalists misrepresent themselves.

Posing and Misrepresentation

Few reporters misrepresent themselves to sources. On some occasions, however, reporters may simply fail to reveal their identities. Restaurant reviewers would be ineffective if everyone knew their identities. Restaurant owners, eager to obtain favorable publicity, would cater to the reviewers, offering them special meals and special service. Reviewers would be unable to describe the meals served to the average customer.

Other journalists may want to shop anonymously at a store whose employees have been accused of misleading customers. Or reporters may want to visit a fortune teller or attend a protest rally. If protesters realized several reporters were present, they might either act more cautiously or perform for the reporters, behaving more angrily or violently to ensure that they got into the news. Protesters might also harass or attack reporters who identified themselves.

Usually, such instances of passive posing, in which the reporter may appear to the business owner or government official as simply another member of the public, present few ethical problems. The reporter is gathering only that information available to any person. More serious ethical—and legal—problems arise when reporters actively misrepresent themselves and gain access to places and information closed to the general public.

Journalists may lie about their identities by posing as patients to gather information about a mental hospital. Or they may pretend to be laborers while writing about migrant workers' exposure to the chemicals sprayed on farm crops. Although journalists may expose a social ill, they discover the public disapproves of their conduct. They may even face legal penalties because of their dubious methods in gathering information. The Food Lion case described in Chapter 20 is a good example of the ethical and legal problems that arise from undercover reporting.

Reporters must talk to their editors before they use any form of deceit. Typically, editors allow their reporters to pose only when a story is important and no other safe way exists to obtain it. In addition, reporters should admit their use of deception in the stories they publish and explain why it was necessary. Reporters also should call all people criticized in their stories and give them an opportunity to respond.

Recording Interviews: Tape Recorders and Video Cameras

Journalists are reluctant to secretly record their interviews with sources, because the tactic may seem devious and unfair. Journalists also fear that if sources learn that reporters secretly record some conversations they may hesitate to speak candidly or refuse to speak at all.

Reporters let sources know they would like to record the interview. They use tape recorders to protect themselves in case they are accused of lying. Reporters fear sources may claim the reporters had misquoted them or even fabricated the entire interview. Some sources honestly forget what they said. Others are shocked by how awful their statements appear in print. To defend themselves, the sources may claim the statements attributed to them are inaccurate. If reporters record their interviews, however, they can prove their stories are accurate. They can also protect themselves more easily in libel suits. When reporters record a conversation, most do so openly, with their sources' permission.

Sometimes reporters use concealed cameras, particularly video cameras, for gathering information. The use of hidden cameras raises some issues audio recordings don't raise. Audio tapes record only a person's voice, and reporters use them to make sure they have complete,

A photographer practiced for a month before secretly taking this picture of Ruth Snyder as she was electrocuted for murdering her husband. This photo appeared in the Daily News of New York. A mask had been placed over Snyder's head after she was strapped into the electric chair at Sing Sing prison on the night of Jan. 12, 1928. To avoid detection, the photographer–who posed as a reporter–tied a miniature camera to one ankle. He lifted his pants cuff to snap one photo as the first jolt of electricity surged through Snyder's body, and to snap another photo at the second jolt.

accurate information. Reporters rarely publish the tape itself or even a transcript of it. Video cameras, however, also record people's faces, clothing and actions. These tapes often end up on television. Many people would consider hidden cameras a greater violation of privacy than hidden tape recorders.

Lawsuits and public disapproval—time, money, bad publicity and the appearance of irresponsible behavior—should discourage journalists from using hidden cameras or tape recorders unless the story is extraordinarily important and they have exhausted all other means of getting the information they need.

Stealing and Fabricating Information: Never Acceptable

It is illegal for a journalist to use another's work; it also is unethical and says something about the journalist's moral character. Journalists who are caught plagiarizing or making up information are fired.

Twenty-seven-year-old Jayson Blair, a reporter for The New York Times, was reprimanded and then fired after editors found lies in about half of his national stories, which were written over seven months. His duplicity included making up sources, creating false quotes from real people, not personally covering events about which he had written and lifting major portions of his information from other news reports. A follow-up story in The New York Times stated that Blair "repeatedly violated the cardinal tenet of journalism which is simply truth." One bad reporter's decisions rarely affect just himself. Two top editors of the Times resigned because they had sent Blair to cover sensitive national stories after the paper's metro editors had raised questions about Blair's competence. After Blair was fired, a team of Times reporters reviewed all his work and found falsehoods and plagiarisms in hundreds of stories he had written over four years.

The New Republic fired Ruth Shalit, an associate editor who was caught in two acts of plagiarism. It also fired reporter Stephen Glass, who made up quotations, people, corporations, towns, legislation and other things. He backed his stories with forged notes and interview transcripts and other bogus documents. When a reporter for an online magazine wanted verification on a story, 25-year-old Glass created a phony corporation Web site and bogus voice mail.

Columnists as well as reporters are held to high standards of journalistic integrity. The Boston Globe warned two of its popular metro columnists about plagiarism and fabrication. Two years later, both were asked to resign for repeating these offenses. Patricia Smith, whose writing had been considered for American Society of Newspaper Editors and Pulitzer Prize awards, made up quotes and people in several of her columns. Mike Barnicle, who had worked for the Boston Globe for 25 years, made up information and lifted jokes from a book by comedian George Carlin. Barnicle said he was unaware of the book, but videotapes verified that Barnicle had promoted the book with Carlin on a television show Barnicle hosted.

Journalists who plagiarize often complain that deadlines and competition forced them to act unethically. Legions of other journalists, however, work under the same deadlines and uphold high principles. They understand that no matter the explanation, if they plagiarize or make up information, they are lying to the public. The Boston Globe argued in an editorial that journalists who make up stories or plagiarize are stealing something more valuable than money. They are stealing the public's trust and the newspaper's credibility.

Reporting Rumors and Speculation: Spreading Gossip or News?

Journalists are supposed to publish facts but are often tempted to publish rumors. If everyone in a community seems to be talking about a rumor, journalists may want to report it. Yet some rumors are impossible to verify and, by discussing a rumor, journalists may give it credibility it doesn't deserve. News stories may explain that the rumor is "unconfirmed," but audience members may fail to notice or remember the disclaimer. Some rumors concern topics that might affect an entire community. A news organization might report a credible rumor that a local bank has financial problems. The rumor might be false, but the publication could damage the bank, causing its owners and—if the bank is not insured—its depositors to lose their money. Journalists will investigate the rumors and generally report only those they find are true.

Sometimes, reports of unsubstantiated information can have a national impact. CNN and Time magazine recanted a heavily promoted TV report after it was aired. The report said the United States had used nerve gas in Laos during the Vietnam War. CNN and Time fired employees responsible for the story, and the organizations apologized after they found in separate investigations that the story was not properly substantiated. The Dallas Morning News retracted a story posted on its Web site inaccurately reporting that a Secret Service agent had seen President Clinton and Monica Lewinsky in a compromising position. Meanwhile, dozens of other news organizations repeated the allegations from the Web site in broadcasts and print publications. The story was only one of many media missteps during the Clinton-Lewinsky saga.

When an event occurs, some of the news elements, such as the "who," "what," "where" and "when," are readily available. It may take several days, weeks or months to find out the "why." Yet, journalists sometimes try to provide their readers and viewers with the "why" immediately, through speculation and interpretation, which may mislead readers and viewers. Theories and conjectures are not news and waste readers' time.

On two occasions, cars went off the side of the Mackinac Bridge in Michigan. After the second accident, in which the driver died, early follow-up stories seemed to accuse state officials of negligence for not placing higher side rails on the bridge. Additional stories delved into the driver's past and incorrectly insinuated he had been a reckless driver and, perhaps, intoxicated when he went off the bridge. Later, authorities determined that the accident was a suicide. Was it fair for reporters to publicize the man's driving record and to give their own conclusions?

In the absence of solid evidence to explain why TWA Flight 800 exploded shortly after takeoff, reporters repeated a variety of rumors and conspiracy theories involving the FBI and Navy, missiles and bombs. Some conjecture originated as messages on the Internet. Eventually, federal investigators concluded the most likely explanation for the crash was an explosion in the jetliner's center fuel tank caused by a short in the wiring.

Witnessing Crimes and Disasters

Reporters and photographers might witness terrible tragedies, such as people drowning, falling to their deaths or fleeing from fire. Journalists will help another person who is in danger, particularly if they are the only ones on the scene. Journalists say they would react the same way as they would if they saw a member of their family in physical danger. Furthermore, they hope other journalists would help—not simply record—human beings in trouble. But when a victim is already receiving help from rescue workers, police officers, firefighters or medical technicians, journalists will stay out of the rescuers' way and concentrate on reporting the event.

Reporters occasionally learn about a crime before it is committed or while it is in progress. They might either go to the police or watch the crime and interview the criminal. The St. Petersburg (Fla.) Times and WFLA radio in Tampa, Fla., were soundly criticized when they telephoned a killer holding a hostage. The man had killed a 4-year-old boy and three police officers and was holding a hostage in a gas station. WFLA called the gas station and aired live the conversation with the gunman. The Times also interviewed him. Ethics experts said the potential risk to the hostage outweighed the value of the information gleaned. The hostage situation was in progress. Listeners and readers would have been as well served if the news organizations had learned the information later from police as opposed to learning it at that moment from the killer. Furthermore, the news organizations interrupted police officers trying to do their jobs, which could have resulted in an obviously unstable person's killing another victim. Journalists are not hostage negotiators or psychologists.

Conflicts of Interest

A conflict of interest exists when journalists, their friends or relatives, or news organizations are in a position to benefit directly from the stories they cover. These conflicts can take various forms, but many news organizations have adopted policies to cover the most common ones.

Accepting Gifts—"Freebies"

Most journalists refuse to accept money or anything else of value from the people they write about. Gifts could bias a reporter's story. An editor at The Washington Post has said: "On some newspapers (this one included), the acceptance of a bribe—for that is what it is—is a firing offense."

Businesses usually do not give gifts without expecting something in return. Although journalists may believe their stories are not biased by gift-giving, they cannot control the public's perception of their reporting once it is known the journalist accepted a gift.

Most news organizations sharply limit the gifts reporters and editors may accept. Some news organizations allow their journalists to accept items worth only a few dollars: a cup of coffee or a souvenir T-shirt, for example. Other newsroom guidelines require journalists to politely return the gift, share the gift with everyone else in the newsroom or send the gift to a charity.

Accepting Trips—"Junkets"

Free trips, called "junkets," once were common. Fashion writers traveled to New York, and television critics to Hollywood, with all their expenses paid. Sportswriters might accompany their local teams to games in distant cities, with the teams paying all the writers' expenses.

Many travel writers insist they could not afford to travel if hotels, airlines or other sponsors did not pay for them. Their stories are often compromised and unrealistic, however, because people on holiday do not get all-paid-for trips with first-class traveling and managers' red-carpet treatment. Thus, the reporter's experience is neither similar nor helpful to the average traveler's.

Some journalists say junkets help them obtain stories that would otherwise be inaccessible. Walt Disney World invited thousands of journalists to fly to Orlando to celebrate its 15th anniversary, which coincided with the 200th anniversary of the U.S. Constitution. Each journalist was allowed to bring one guest. More than 5,000 people accepted Disney's invitation. They flew to Orlando from all 50 states and were joined by several hundred Canadians, about 200 Europeans and 20 Japanese.

The celebration cost about $7.5 million, but Disney contributed only $1.5 million. Seventeen airlines offered air travel free or at reduced rates. Hotels donated 5,000 rooms and free breakfasts. The state of Florida and several local groups, all established to promote tourism, contributed an additional $350,000 apiece. The sponsoring organizations spent $600,000 on a single party in downtown Orlando. The visiting journalists were also treated to a concert and a fireworks display and had Disney's Magic Kingdom to themselves for an entire evening. The Disney organization insisted journalists were under no obligation to give the theme park favorable publicity.

A writer for The Orlando Sentinel said the food, drink and lodging amounted to a bribe to get favorable coverage and the journalists who accepted it were a disgrace. A second critic complained that Disney's offer proved many U.S. news organizations were willing to sell favorable coverage to anyone who paid the price. Even the critics overlooked a more fundamental issue: Was the party newsworthy? Was Disney's 15th anniversary important enough to justify coverage by 5,000 media employees? Or did the recipients use Disney's anniversary as an excuse to accept a free vacation in Florida?

Disney obviously wanted publicity—and got it. A Disney representative called it "the biggest marketing project we have ever undertaken." Within three months, Disney estimated that it had received $9 million of free publicity. Disney publicists collected a two-foot stack of press clippings. Television stations broadcast 186 live reports during the extravaganza, and radio stations provided 1,000 hours of live coverage. Even major networks covered the story. Both ABC's "Good Morning America" and NBC's "Today" broadcast live from Disney World.

Participating in the News

Reporters have lives outside the newsroom, and sometimes those outside activities turn reporters into newsmakers. When that happens, editors worry that their reporters' involvement in events might undermine public confidence in the news organization's objectivity. Editors insist reporters' first obligation should be to their primary employer, and they say reporters continue to represent their employers even after they leave work for the day.

Editors generally agree reporters should not hold public office, either elected or appointed. Most editors also agree reporters should not serve as party officials or help with anyone's election campaign. Editors want to avoid even the appearance of a conflict. A business writer's running for city council might not pose a direct conflict; a business writer might never cover the city council. But the public might suspect that other writers would slant the news in favor of their colleague's campaign.

Journalists' activities can create the appearance of a bias. For example, a reporter for Florida's Vero Beach Press-Journal was fired after she sent letters and small copper coat hangers to all 160 members of the state Legislature. The legislators were meeting in a special session to consider the adoption of tougher abortion laws. The reporter, Vicky Hendley, said her job as a reporter should not require her to give up her involvement in a cause she believed in. Also, she had been covering education for two years and said the abortion issue never came up on that beat. Darryl Hicks, the newspaper's general manager, said Hendley was fired not because of her beliefs about abortion, but because she had violated company policy. In addition to writing the letters, Hendley had given interviews to other papers. "In all those she was clearly identified as a reporter for the Press-Journal," Hicks said. "We were drawn into it right away—clearly a conflict."

Freelancing

Journalists at most news organizations are free to accept outside jobs, provided they do not conflict with their regular work. Typically, reporters and photographers can work as freelancers, but they cannot sell their work to their employers' competitors, such as other media in the same market.

Similarly, newspapers may allow their journalists to teach at a community college, but not to serve as scorekeepers at the games they cover. As scorekeepers, the writers would become part of the stories they were covering. Their decisions might be controversial or influence who wins a batting title or other awards. Thus, the writers would have to report on their own actions. Newspapers also might tell a sports editor to stop serving as the host of a local radio program or to avoid appearing on local television programs, especially for pay. The newspapers want sports editors to give important news stories to their readers, not to television viewers.

Dealing with Pillow Talk and Cronyism

Increasingly, journalists face a newer conflict: their spouses' employment or position. To avoid a conflict, or the appearance of conflict, editors rarely allow reporters to cover any story in which their spouse is involved.

"Dateline" reporter Maria Shriver was on leave from NBC while she campaigned with her husband, Arnold Schwarzenegger, as he ran for governor of California. NBC News president Neal Shapiro said Shriver was welcome to return to "Dateline," but with the agreement that she not cover anything about California politics or issues relating to her husband. Shriver eventually quit her NBC job to be a full-time first lady for California. NBC News correspondent Andrea Mitchell, whose husband, Alan Greenspan, runs the Federal Reserve, covers foreign affairs for the network but avoids economics stories.

Another ethics problem, called "hobnobbery journalism," arises when journalists become good friends with their sources. After becoming friends, journalists cannot easily report objectively about their sources. Friends in politics presents the greatest problem; journalists are supposed to be the watchdogs, not friends, of politicians.

Reporting on Terrorism

Terrorists usually want publicity and have learned to create news so compelling that news organizations are unable to ignore it. The terrorists provide genuine drama: hijackings, demands, deadlines and the threat of mass murder—such as the attacks on the World Trade Center in New York and the Pentagon in Washington, D.C. Terrorists can add to the drama by moving from one place to another and by releasing or killing hostages.

To attract even more publicity, terrorists conduct press conferences. Some allow journalists to photograph and interview their captives. Others make videotapes of their captives, sometimes showing the hostages pleading for their lives, reading the terrorists' demands and warning that they will be killed if the demands are not met. The terrorists who kidnapped and killed Wall Street Journal reporter Daniel Pearl not only released photos of Pearl with a gun pointed at his head, but they also made a videotape of his murder, which some found on the World Wide Web.

Some critics insist the media coverage encourages terrorists. They believe that if the media ignored terrorists, they would become discouraged and abandon their acts of violence. Former British Prime Minister Margaret Thatcher urged journalists to stop covering terrorists, to starve them of "the oxygen of publicity." Other critics insist Americans have a right to know what is happening in the world and a news blackout might result in rumors that were more frightening than the truth about terrorists' activities. They also fear terrorists will escalate their violence if they are ignored by reporters. Eventually, the media would have to cover them.

Censoring Advertisements and Advertiser Pressure

Americans oppose censorship, and journalists are especially vigilant in their efforts to combat it. Yet news organizations regularly refuse to publish some advertisements submitted to them. They clearly have the legal right to do so. Courts have consistently ruled that the First Amendment gives editors the right to reject any advertisement they dislike, regardless of the reason.

For almost 200 years, newspapers published virtually every advertisement submitted to them. Editors rarely felt responsible for the content of advertisements. Rather, the editors' phi-

The body burning in the truck is that of one of 15 victims of a suicide bomber at the Red Cross headquarters in Baghdad, Iraq. Terrorists sometimes stage attacks specifically to generate publicity for their cause. This causes news executives and journalism critics to debate how much coverage acts of terrorism should receive.

losophy was one of "let the buyer beware." Before 1860, newspapers in both the North and the South published advertisements for slaves, prostitutes and quack medicines. Some medicines contained enough alcohol to inebriate the people using them. Others contained so much heroin, opium and morphine that the people using them became addicts. Even the "soothing syrups" sold for babies were spiked with drugs.

During the late 1800s, a few periodicals began to protect their readers from fraudulent advertising. When Cyrus H.K. Curtis took over the Saturday Evening Post in 1897, he began to reject advertisements for liquor and patent medicines. During the early 20th century, the St. Louis Post-Dispatch led the campaign to clean up newspaper advertising columns. The Post-Dispatch lost thousands of dollars in revenue, but its publisher never objected.

Now, news organization managers often reject advertisements that seem tasteless or promote illegal, immoral or harmful products. The managers want to act ethically. Some explain that they have always felt responsible for the content of their news columns, routinely deleting anything that seemed tasteless, inaccurate, unfair, libelous or obscene. Now, the managers say, they are accepting a similar responsibility for the content of their advertising columns.

Many daily newspapers reject advertisements for tobacco products and alcoholic beverages, especially hard liquor. Other dailies reject advertisements for movies rated X or NC-17, sexual aids, mail order goods, hair restorers and fortune tellers. Most dailies reject advertisements for abortion services and handguns. Many also reject advertisements for massage parlors and escort services. Some newspapers, concerned about their readers' health and safety, no longer accept restaurant and bar advertisements for "happy hours," during which drinks are cheap or free. News organization managers fear that the advertisements will contribute to drunken driving. Many readers agree with the managers' decisions. Others accuse them of censorship.

A growing concern among journalists is advertisers who want to dictate news content and placement of their ads. Kimberly Clark, the maker of Huggies diapers, insisted that its ads be placed adjacent to "happy baby" content. "60 Minutes" pulled a story about a tobacco company when the company threatened to sue the network. ("60 Minutes" eventually aired the segment.) Chrysler wanted to review in advance "any editorial content that encompasses sexual, political, social issues or any editorial that might be construed as provocative or offensive" in any magazine carrying its advertisements. The car maker demanded the right to see articles in advance and "a written summary outlining major themes/articles appearing in upcoming issues." As America's fifth largest advertiser, Chrysler wanted veto power over stories. (Chrysler later dropped its demand when the Magazine Publishers of America and the American Society of Magazine Editors issued a joint statement recommending their members not grant prior review to advertisers.)

CODES OF ETHICS

Major professional organizations in journalism have adopted codes of ethics. The codes encourage organization members to adhere voluntarily to the guidelines. They also serve as models that individual media companies follow when setting their own policies. Broadcast stations and newspapers adapt the ethics codes to reflect local standards. What is acceptable in a metropolitan area may not be permissible for news media in a rural community.

The American Society of Newspaper Editors adopted one of the industry's first codes, the Canons of Journalism, in 1923. Among other things, the ASNE declared that newspapers should act responsibly by being truthful, sincere, impartial, decent and fair. News organizations adopt codes of ethics to discourage the most obvious abuses, especially freebies, junkets and conflicts of interest. Although codes serve as guidelines for journalists' actions, exceptional cases arise. The codes cannot solve every problem in a free society. Thus, decisions will always vary from one news organization to another—and that may be one of the system's great strengths. After considering their news organization's code of ethics, journalists decide which course of action is right or wrong, ethical or unethical. Inevitably, some journalists will be mistaken. But any effort to change the system—to force every journalist to conform to a single standard—would limit the media's diversity and freedom. It would also limit Americans' access to information.

The professional standards in journalism are improving. Journalists are becoming better educated, more responsible and more ethical. However, journalists and their audiences often disagree about which stories the media should report and how the stories should be presented to the public. Whereas journalists are reluctant to suppress any stories, ethicists worry about the effects stories have on the people involved and on other readers and viewers.

CHECKLIST FOR IMPROVING MEDIA CREDIBILITY

The American Society of Newspaper Editors (ASNE) interviewed 3,000 Americans and ran 16 focus groups to find ways to improve public trust in journalism. The ASNE's study came up with six areas in which journalists should concentrate to improve news media credibility:

1. **Inaccuracies:** Factual, grammatical and spelling errors undermine a story and its reporter's credibility.
2. **Sensationalism:** Sensational stories are often chased and overcovered because they are exciting, but they may be less important than other stories.
3. **Objectivity:** Journalists should avoid the appearance of bias in their reporting—what stories are covered and how they are covered. Bias is defined as not being open-minded and neutral about the facts, having an agenda and shaping the news to advance that agenda, or showing favoritism to a particular social or political group.
4. **Freedom from manipulation of the press:** The public believes the press can be manipulated by powerful people, organizations and advertisers who want to shape news stories. A big criticism is that newspapers are trying to make a profit instead of serving in the public interest.

5. **Name sources:** Using anonymous sources lowers the credibility of a news story. Many people would not run the story at all if a source declined to go "on the record." Journalists should tell the public why an anonymous source is used.
6. **Corrections:** Admitting errors and running corrections help credibility, not hurt it.

A Memo From the Editor

SOME THOUGHTS ON PLAGIARISM

By **Tommy Miller**

Plagiarism is like speeding on the highways. It likely will never go away, but that doesn't mean a promising career can't crash and burn after one stupid lapse in judgment.

In the last 20 years, for example, plagiarism embarrassed the journalism profession a number of times. The most infamous, of course, came in 2003 when New York Times reporter Jayson Blair stole quotes and description from other stories and lied to readers by filing stories with false datelines.

Blair was fired, and the controversy over the Times' management style, or lack thereof, led to the resignation of Times Editor Howell Raines.

About 13 years earlier, plagiarism incidents occurred at several newspapers, including the Washington Post and the Fort Worth Star-Telegram, where editors wrestled with problems three times in a matter of a few months. The problems involved lifting part of a Washington Post story and using quotes from other newspapers without proper attribution.

All of this means that plagiarism needs constant vigilance and discussion.

Making up entire stories leaves the most damaging wounds on the reputations of newspapers and other news media, but typical plagiarism incidents focus on these questions:

- How should information be handled when it is obtained from other newspapers, wire services or the electronic media?
- What information can be used from other stories and what can't?
- What is background information and how should it be handled?
- When should quotes be attributed to other media?
- When are quotes in the public domain?
- When is a fact a generally known fact?

QUOTATIONS ARE SACRED

There is no room here for embellishing, fudging, or guessing.

Readership trust hinges on the belief that words inside quotation marks are true and that the person or entity the quote is attributed to can be held accountable.

BACKGROUND FACTS

Here's one rule you can count on: Generally known facts can't be plagiarized.

For example, for the second, third and fourth paragraphs of this story, I gathered information from several stories in other newspapers and trade publications. The information is background for this story, and the facts are that The New York Times editor resigned over a plagiarism controversy and about 13 years earlier several newspapers

(*continued*)

had problems with plagiarism. Some of the information for this story was written in much the same way that it was written in several other accounts. Because the information now falls into the category of generally known facts, there is no need for me to tell readers specifically where I got that information.

ATTRIBUTION

But consider this situation:

Let's say that a Washington Post moves a story on its news service reporting that former Houston Police Chief Elizabeth Watson will become the new police chief in Washington, D.C.

Of course, Houston Chronicle reporters would immediately try to confirm that report, and, if they did, no attribution to the Washington Post would be needed. But, if the Chronicle were unable to confirm the Post report, the Chronicle story would need attribution, such as: Former Houston Police Chief Elizabeth Watson will become the new police chief in Washington, D.C., The Washington Post reported.

The previous example seems elementary. But the debate about attributing information usually centers on information of much less impact, primarily because many newspapers lift what is often described as routine information from wire service stories without telling the reader where it was obtained.

For example, I once asked a Chicago newspaper reporter about one of her bylined clips about violence in Chicago theaters where the movie "Boyz N the Hood" was showing. The story carried no dateline and most of it focused on the Chicago incidents.

About midway through the story, the reporter had written: "In other incidents, reported across the nation Friday night:" This sentence was followed by a list with specific information about incidents in Sacramento; Milwaukee; Hollywood; Tuscaloosa, Ala., and other cities.

I asked the reporter where she had gotten the information for the list. "Oh," she said. "That came from the AP." In a spot news story such as this, a reporter should tell readers where the information came. For example, the sentence setting up the list should have said: "The Associated Press reported these other incidents across the nation." Or, at the very least, an Associated Press contributor line should have been at the bottom of the story.

PUBLIC DOMAIN

Background is substantiated information that has stood the test of time, putting it in the public domain.

Let's say that the first sentence in a newspaper editorial about a bank scandal is: "Asked why he robbed banks, Willy Sutton said, 'Because that's where the money is.'" The editorial doesn't say when Sutton said it, or where he said it, or who first reported that he said it. And the editorial assumes that readers know that Sutton was an infamous bank robber. Why? Because the quote has been used so much throughout the years that it's considered in the public domain and doesn't need attribution.

How do you decide what's in the public domain? Time is one element, such as how long has the quote been around. General usage is another. If the quote has been used often in a variety of media, it has moved into the public domain. The exclusive, initial report of a quote is usually the guideline for deciding when a quote is not in the public domain.

But plagiarism problems usually don't come from pragmatic bank robber quotes. It's the routine quotes that cause problems. Too often, reporters read stories from other papers, or from other media sources, and use quotes without attribution. There's no problem with using good quotes that are relevant and important to a story. They simply must be attributed to the proper source.

DESCRIPTION

Description can be another problem area.

For example, let's say you visit San Francisco and write a piece in which you say that San Francisco is a beautiful, haunting city. No problem there. In fact, your problem isn't plagiarism. Your problem is lifeless, bland description.

But let's say you write it this way: "It's the enchanting symphony of metropolitan noise—the stray foghorn in the night, the panting automobile in second gear, the golden clang of the cable car bell, the dreamy ageless silence of Golden Gate Park, the staccato snap of the traffic signal and the wail of the Ferry Building's noon siren, telling the world defiantly that the old landmark still has its job to do and is doing it."

Now you've got a problem, because that's San Francisco Chronicle columnist Herb Caen's description in a column on July 2, 1940.

But let's say you write it this way:

"It's the enchanting music of metropolitan sounds—the stray foghorn in the darkness, the struggling car in second gear, the golden ring of the cable car bell. . . ."

You've still got a problem. You've done nothing more than steal Caen's structure and cadence while filling in the blanks with other words.

What about press releases? Generally, press releases need more reporting and, therefore, should be rewritten. Additionally, length, style and the proper emphasis on the lead paragraph are frequently reasons for rewriting press releases.

As for quotes in news releases, tell readers that the quotes were in a news release or printed statement. This shows that the source provided the quotation in a printed statement or release and was not available for further questioning.

With some straightforward, routine public service news releases, rewriting simply doesn't make sense. For example, "The University library will display a rare collection of first edition William Faulkner books in its foyer from Aug. 1 to Aug. 20. Call 555-5555 for further information."

The bottom line on plagiarism is to do your own reporting, write your own description and attribute quotes and information whenever it is needed. Common sense usually indicates when material should be attributed. When in doubt, attribute! Or get a second opinion.

Adapted from "Some thoughts on plagiarism," published in August 1992 in The Write Stuff, an in-house publication of the Houston Chronicle.

Tommy Miller is the Roger Tatarian Endowed Chair of Professional Journalism at California State University, Fresno. He is a former managing editor of the Houston Chronicle.

SUGGESTED READINGS

Christians, Clifford, Mark Fackler, Kim B. Rotzoll and Kathy McKee, eds. *Media Ethics: Cases and Moral Reasoning,* 6th ed. Boston: Allyn & Bacon, 2000.

Cote, William, and Roger Simpson. *Covering Violence.* New York: Columbia University Press, 2000.

Gross, Larry, John Stuart Katz and Jay Ruby, eds. *Image Ethics in the Digital Age.* Minneapolis, Minn.: University of Minnesota, 2003.

Smith, Ron E. *Groping for Ethics in Journalism,* 5th ed. Ames, Iowa: Iowa State University Press, 2003.

Willis, Jim. *The Human Journalist: Reporters, Perspectives, and Emotions.* Westport, Conn.: Praeger Publishers, 2003.

USEFUL WEB SITES

Victims and the Media Program, School of Journalism at Michigan State University: Helping Journalists Cover Catastrophes and Victims of Crime: http://victims.jrn.msu.edu

The Poynter Ethics Journal of the Poynter Institute is devoted to mass media ethics: http://www.poynter.org/subject.asp?id=32

Suggestions on balance and fairness when it comes to statements or characterizations that cast a person or group of persons in a bad light: http://www.copydesk.org/balance.htm

National Center for Victims of Crime http://www.ncvc.org/ncvc

Society of Professional Journalists Code of Ethics: http://www.spj.org/ethics_code.asp

American Society of Newspaper Editors Statement of Principles: http://www.asne.org/kiosk/archive/principl.htm

Associated Press Managing Editors Code of Ethics: http://www.apme.com/about/code_ethics.shtml

Name ______________________ Class ______________________ Date ______

EXERCISE 1

ETHICS

DISCUSSION QUESTIONS

Read the following situations, marking those actions you would take. Discuss your decisions with the class.

1. Students are sometimes not sure about what constitutes plagiarism. Put a check in front of those actions that you consider a form of plagiarism. (Consider "newspaper" or "magazine" to mean print or online.)

   A. _____ To turn in a paper purchased online.

   B. _____ To use, without attribution, a 20-word sentence from a magazine.

   C. _____ To use, without attribution, a 60-word paragraph from a magazine.

   D. _____ While writing about a celebrity, to reuse several quotations you found in several other newspapers.

   E. _____ To use your own words, but another writer's ideas.

   F. _____ To use, but totally rewrite without attribution, a story from another newspaper.

   G. _____ To use, but totally rewrite with attribution, a story from another newspaper.

   H. _____ To use a press release without changing a word.

   I. _____ For background while working under deadline pressure at a newspaper, to reprint verbatim several paragraphs from an old story written by another reporter at your newspaper.

   J. _____ While working for a radio or television station, to read your city's daily newspaper to determine what's happening in your community and what stories you should cover.

   K. _____ While working for a radio or television station, broadcasting news stories published by your local paper without rewriting or attribution.

   L. _____ While working for a radio or television station, rewriting stories from your local newspaper and attributing them to the newspaper.

2. If you edited your student newspaper and received an anonymous letter that accused a faculty member of repeatedly making sexist remarks, would you publish the letter?

   _____ Yes _____ No

   If your answer is "No," mark the point below at which you would change your mind. (You can mark more than one response to this and other questions.)

   A. _____ The student who wrote the letter identifies herself but, because she fears retaliation, insists that you keep her name a secret.

   B. _____ Two more women come in and corroborate the letter's content but also insist that you keep their names a secret.

   C. _____ All three students agree to let you quote them and publish their names.

D. _____ The three students play a tape they secretly recorded in class, a tape that clearly documents their complaints.

E. _____ The students complain that the faculty member also touched them.

3. As editor of your student newspaper, mark any of the following gifts you would allow members of your staff to accept.

A. _____ Free tickets to local plays, movies and concerts for your entertainment editor.

B. _____ Free meals at local restaurants for your food critic.

C. _____ Free trips to out-of-town games with your college team for your sports editor.

D. _____ Free loan of a sophisticated computer that a computer manufacturer offers to your technology editor for the school year so she can test new games and software.

E. _____ Free one-week trip to Daytona Beach, Fla., for your entertainment writer and a friend to write about the popular destination for students on spring break.

4. As editor of your local daily, mark all the products and services for which you would be willing to publish advertisements.

A. _____ Pistols

B. _____ Cigarettes

C. _____ Fortune tellers

D. _____ Juice bars that feature live nude dancers

E. _____ Couples who want to adopt white newborns

F. _____ Abortion clinics

G. _____ Escort services and massage parlors

H. _____ An essay claiming the Holocaust is a hoax

5. As editor of your local daily, mark all the cases of deception that you would permit.

A. _____ Allow a young reporter to pose as a high school dropout and join a teen gang.

B. _____ Allow a reporter using a fake identity to join the Ku Klux Klan, which often marches and holds rallies in the region.

C. _____ After hearing that some people may be cheating local charities, collecting food and money from several simultaneously, allow a reporter to pose as a destitute mother who visits several local charities to see how much food and money she can collect in one day. The reporter promises to return everything after her story's publication.

D. _____ Allow two reporters to pose as a gay couple and try to rent an apartment. Friends have told members of your staff about instances of discrimination.

E. _____ A reporter informs you that his brother is opening a bar, and that city inspectors seem to be asking for bribes to approve the bar's plumbing, electrical and health inspections, for example. The reporter suggests that you notify the district attorney, install hidden cameras in the bar and begin to pay the bribes.

6. As editor of your local daily, mark the practices you would permit.

   A. _____ Allow the sports editor to host a daily program on a local radio station.

   B. _____ Allow the sports editor to appear in television advertisements for a chain of sports stores in the city.

   C. _____ Allow the business editor to own stock in local companies.

   D. _____ Allow the education writer to marry a high school principal.

   E. _____ Allow a popular columnist, a local celebrity, to charge $1,000 for each one-hour speech she gives.

7. Without your knowledge, a talented young reporter on your staff breaks into the computer system at a second daily in your city, a bitter rival. The reporter gives you a list of all the stories the rival's staff is working on. Would you:

   A. _____ Compliment the reporter on her initiative and quickly assign your own staff to cover the stories so you are not scooped?

   B. _____ Destroy the list and tell the reporter to never again enter the rival's computer system?

   C. _____ Reprimand the reporter, suspending her for a week?

   D. _____ Notify your rival and apologize for the reporter's actions?

   E. _____ Notify the police that the reporter may have unknowingly violated a state law?

8. One of your reporters is writing about a local country club that, she learns, excludes Jews, blacks and Hispanics. The reporter also learns that your publisher and other influential members of your community are members of the club. Would you:

   A. _____ Abandon the story?

   B. _____ Inform your publisher about the story and suggest that she resign?

   C. _____ Tell your reporter to interview the publisher and give her an opportunity to explain her membership in the club?

   D. _____ Publish the story but never identify any of the club's members?

   E. _____ Publish the story, listing your publisher and other prominent citizens who belong to the club?

   F. _____ List all 1,200 of the club's members?

9. Each year, a professional organization in your state sponsors an awards competition. Minutes ago, you learned that a reporter on your staff won second place in feature writing and that your chief photographer won third place in another category. However, another newspaper in the city—a bitter rival—won five awards, and a local television station won four. How would you handle the story?

   A. _____ Ignore the story.

   B. _____ Report all the awards, beginning with the first-place awards.

   C. _____ Report only the two awards won by your staff.

   D. _____ Start by reporting the two awards won by your staff, then briefly mention the awards won by all the other media in your city.

10. You edit your local daily, and a sports reporter mistakenly credited the wrong football player with scoring two game-winning touchdowns. Would you:
    A. _____ Publish a routine correction?
    B. _____ Publish a correction and identify the reporter responsible for the error?
    C. _____ Publish a correction and punish the reporter, placing him on probation?
    D. _____ Publish a correction that identifies the reporter and reports his punishment?
    E. _____ Order the reporter to write a letter to the school, apologizing for his error?
    F. _____ Privately punish the reporter, placing him on probation, but publish nothing, treating the incident as a private personnel matter?

11. Journalists must make difficult and controversial decisions. Decide how you would respond in each of the following situations.
    A. As news director of a local television station, you think an emphasis on crime and violence is bad journalism, but you don't know if it affects your newscasts' ratings. Would you continue to emphasize crime and violence? _____ Yes _____ No
    B. A reporter on your newspaper's staff with terrible eyesight undergoes a new laser procedure to correct her nearsightedness and wants to write a series about the operation and the doctor who successfully performed it. The story is likely to interest thousands of readers, but you learn that the reporter's operation was performed for free. Would you let her write the series? _____ Yes _____ No
    C. After serving three terms, your city's mayor—a popular and successful Republican—decides to step down. She then applies for a job as a political columnist for your editorial page and is obviously a good writer. Would you hire her? _____ Yes _____ No
    D. Thousands of people live in your city's slums, and most are poor and have little education. Advertisers prefer reaching people who are wealthy and well-educated. To improve your newspaper's demographics (the reader characteristics that attract advertisers) would you, as publisher, instruct your circulation staff to ignore your city's slums and their residents? _____ Yes _____ No
    E. A member of your state legislature proposes applying your state sales tax to advertisements, a policy that would cost the newspaper of which you are publisher millions of dollars a year. When asked, would you contribute $50,000 to a campaign your State Press Association is waging against the tax? _____ Yes _____ No

       Would you report in your newspaper your decision and the size of any contribution? _____ Yes _____ No
    F. Because of a decline in advertising revenue, you decide to lay off 42 employees, primarily employees in your newspaper's production department. Would you publish a story reporting the layoffs? _____ Yes _____ No Would you report your newspaper's annual profits? _____ Yes _____ No
    G. An extortionist says he has poisoned groceries in your town's largest chain of supermarkets. Customers continue to shop in the supermarkets. Police say that the threat is almost certainly a hoax and that it will be easier for them to catch the extortionist in a day or two if you delay publishing the story. Would you immediately publish the story? _____ Yes _____ No

Name ______________________ Class ______________________ Date ______

EXERCISE 2

ETHICS

STORIES THAT RAISE ETHICAL CONCERNS

Each of the following stories involves several ethical dilemmas. Write a news story based on each set of facts, thoughtfully deciding which facts to use and which to discard. Correct any errors you may find.

1. NURSING HOME EMPLOYEES

It's a shocking tale and an exclusive for your newspaper, revealed by a diligent and exhaustive month-long investigation by a team of 5 reporters and one editor on your staff. While visiting a nursing home where her mother is currently being cared for due to her deteriorating physical health, your police reporter recognized three faces, all ex-cons. She investigated, helped by other reporters, and here's all the information they gathered on the situation at hand. Felons can and do have daily contact with the most frail and defenseless of your citys elderly residents. No one can say how many nursing home orderlies, maids, cooks, janitors, and other employees have been convicted of theft, prostitution, domestic violence, or other crimes of all types and descriptions. That's because people in those jobs don't have to undergo a criminal background check. Unlike employees of daycare centers for children, school bus drivers, etc., there is no requirement for nursing homes to check the background of every person who works in their employment. Your paper compiled a list of the names of 412 nursing home employees in your city using city directories and a multitude of other sources to learn the names of as many such employees as at all possible and found that 1 in 5 had an arrest or conviction for a felony crime. Esther Onn, president of the state Coalition to Protect Elders, told you that she wants and is fighting for all nursing home employees to be screened and explains: "Our parents deserve the best care society can give them. They shouldn't have to worry about being robbed or beaten. In some nursing homes in the city we've found evidence of real brutality, of residents being terrorized by these thugs. These people work in nursing homes because they can get jobs there. The operators of the places know if they hire ex-cons, they don't have to pay them much. Giving them jobs at low wages increases the owners profits, and they're already exorbitant." But on the other hand Beatrice Rosolowski, spokesman for the State Federation of Nursing Homes, says checking on everyone goes too far and they themselves are pushing other reforms to the system they agree is flawed. "The cracks are there and they are big enough for people to be slipping through," Rosolowski admits. Theft is the most common crime against nursing home patients, and they are vulnerable you found because many residents are incapable of even reporting crimes against them, whether theft or brutality or intimidation or neglect. At least some of those crimes are committed by nursing home staffers, which is why people residing in nursing homes everywhere are told to keep their valuables hidden and drawers and doors locked. Even if background investigations of nursing home employees are conducted you learn they could be far from adequate since people convicted in other states would likely not be detected and background checks often are not run on people until after they have begun to work. And employees arrested or convicted after their initial check may not be detected until they apply for a job at another nursing home. Blanket screening would be expensive and not likely to make homes much safer. Another of your sources, Atty. Harold Murray, represents 150 clients currently suing nursing homes in and around the state. Some have been abused, he said, while others have had their possessions stolen by nursing home workers. "You've got housekeepers, custodians, dieticians, and a host of employees who go into these rooms every day and who have contact with residents. Who are these people?" Murray asks. While pursuing the lawsuits Murray obtained records of nursing home workers and did his own background check. Of 378 employee names he submitted, 76 had been arrested for or convicted of felonies. The convictions included prostitution, assault and spousal abuse. Two former prostitutes work at Elder Haven, 3110 East River Parkway, and so does a bank robber released after 14 years in prison. A convicted child molester, Grady Smith, was found by Murray working at Sunnyview Nursing Home, 1012 Peters Dr. In 1981, he was convicted and was in prison from '81 to '93, when he got his current job as a janitor at Sunnyview and, according to police, has been in no trouble since then. You have also heard—but have been unable to document—allegations that some nursing home employees strap some residents difficult to handle to their chairs or beds, leaving them in such condition for prolonged periods of time on a daily basis. You have also heard from unhappy residents families, but have been unable to document, allegations that some residents are kept heavily sedated even when there is no clear medical or physical reason to do so simply because it makes residents easier to handle.

2. TEEN GANG

Beginning at the start of last year the police in your city noticed an abrupt increase in crime, especially car thefts and residential burglaries, in the Oakwood Subdivision. As dawn broke early today police went to the homes of 4 teenagers, all students currently at Oakwood high school. The teens were arrested by police and police now say they were part of a ring suspected of involvement in a total of approximately 100 to 150 in number or more car and home burglaries. Police are looking for two other teens but did not identify them. All are white. All are male. Two of the 6 are on the schools honor roll, which requires a 3.5 gpa or higher. All are between the ages of 16 to 18 yrs of age. In a press conference today your citys police chief said the students apparently took orders from fellow students. His officers recovered property valued at $15,000, including radar detectors, televisions, stereos, cassette players, guns, cameras, stamp and coin collections, games, compact disc players and a trash bag full of cassette tapes. "Some of these kids were making a lot of bucks," the chief said. The youngest students, one age 16 and one age 17, were immediately taken to the county juvenile detention center for incarceration and were subsequently released to their parents. The other two, both 18, were charged with multiple counts of burglary, possession of stolen goods, and contributing to the delinquency of a minor, and are being held in the county jail with their bail set at $50,000. Because of the seriousness of their crimes, police charged all 4 as adults and identified them as:

- Claude Nunziata, 16, son of Carmen Nunziata
- Burt Dolmovich, 17, son of Sandra M. Dolomovich
- Michael Gandolf, 18, son of Sandra Gandolf
- Giles Grauman, 18, son of Alyce and Samuel Graumann

The police chief, who personally released the youths names to the press today, said, "The information our investigation is uncovering is that they've done a lot more than what we know. One of these punks told my men he'd been involved in at least 80 burglaries himself. What's worse, what's really depressing here, is that we think dozens of students at the school knew what they were doing and, because it was cheap, were buying things from them, things they knew were stolen." Police chief Barry Kopperud added that the parents of three of the boys voluntarily cooperated by allowing police to search their homes for stolen property taken in the crimes. Carmen Nunziata, the mother of Claude, refused to let the police into her home and refused to talk to the press when you called her today. Police subsequently obtained a search warrant, then proceeded to search the premises. She is divorced and on welfare, with a total of four children to support and is not currently working, having been on welfare for 11 years according to public records maintained by the city that you were able to see. The whereabouts of Nunziatas father is unknown at this point in time. "Some parents were aware their sons were wheeling and dealing with property, but they figured they were just swapping with one another," Kopperudd said. "I don't know, maybe some knew their kids were crooks." Some of the recovered property has been returned to its owners. For people who may be wondering whether or not some of the property could be theirs, Kopperud expressed that most of that which was recovered was stolen in the past 30 days and a lot of the rest was sold to other students and at flea markets, so its mostly now all gone.

3. BOY'S MURDER

Yesterday George Claunch, a 15-year-old high school student in your city, was stabbed to death. A student at Kennedy High School, his body was found inside a vacant house at 482 Fern Creek Dr. His body was found by police answering an anonymous call to them and was found tied to a chair with his hands tied behind his back and stabbed multiple times in the chest. There was evidence of torture preceding death: of cigarette burns and bruises as he had apparently been beaten. Police continue to search for answers in the case. The victims older brother, Tony, 19, today complained, "The cops aren't doing enough about his case. 'Cause of who he was they don't care." Tony acknowledges that his brother, the youngest of 5 siblings, had his fair share of run-ins with the law, that he was in and out of juvenile detention centers, cut classes, used marijuana, and may have belonged to a gang, although that is not known for sure at this point in time. For stealing a car he was on probation. The family is now dealing with its grief and searching for answers. A local police officer investigating the case, Detective Allison Biaggi, said the victim was apparently, they suspect, dealing drugs when he was killed, but police have not determined an exact motive, although there were drugs found at the scene. Those who might have information on the victims death, friends, acquaintances, even relatives, refuse to cooperate with detectives, Biaggi said. Another brother, Raymond, said, "I haven't accepted it yet. I fault myself a little for what happened. I think he wanted love and didn't get it. Our father died four years ago, and that confused him in a way. My mother really loved him, but he wanted to do his own thing even when she told him not to. He never listened. He'd do his own thing, and that's what always got him into trouble, plus the guys he ran with weren't good people. It was them that got him in trouble." George Claunch was the son of Amy Claunch of 2481 Seasons Court, Apt. B.

CHAPTER 22

CAREERS

I talk with people and notice things, and then I turn those things into a column for the most wonderful gift a storyteller can be given—an audience on the other end.

(Bob Greene, columnist)

Journalists are passionate about their work. They find their jobs varied, creative, important and challenging. Perhaps more than anyone else, journalists witness the kaleidoscope of the life within their communities: the good and the bad, the joyous and the tragic, the significant and the mundane.

John Mollwitz has been in the news business for more than 50 years. His passion for journalism led him to newspaper work that began with being a delivery boy and went on to being a reporter, copy editor, online editor and member of the board of directors, all for the Milwaukee Journal Sentinel. "Journalists are admitted everywhere and meet everyone," Mollwitz said. "One of the neatest perks of the job is being able to go up to public and corporate officials, as well complete strangers, and ask questions. In learning so many interesting things about people and issues, you learn things you never knew about yourself. You learn, too, that the people you interview and bring into your stories are also your readers, viewers or listeners. They trust you to get it right. Get it right and you sleep well. Fulfilling the public's trust—the public's right to know. What a way to live!"

Wherever they go, journalists share some of the power and prestige of the institutions they represent. Yet, they also represent the public when they cover a story. And journalists ask questions as a member of society. By providing citizens with the information they need to be well-informed, journalists perform a vital function within a democratic society.

In addition to obtaining information that makes events and issues understandable for the public, journalists get to do something else inspiring and fun: They get to write. And writing a good story—selecting the important facts, the correct words, the proper organization—is a highly creative process. It is also challenging. Within a few minutes, journalists may have to summarize a complex topic in a clear, accurate story that will interest the public. Within hours, even minutes, the story may be read, heard or seen by thousands of people.

Todd Beamon, business producer for the Baltimore Sun's baltimoresun.com and a 20-year veteran of metropolitan journalism, said: "Journalism still remains the highest form of public service. If you have a sense of serving the public, the best way you can do that—and still bring forth change—is through journalism. Journalism is the vehicle by which a variety of interests can, and should, be presented. Society, in America and across the world, continues to grow more diverse every day. This profession needs people who are broad-visioned, savvy and willing to take chances such that they can get out and talk to the various cultures of the community, city, state, nation or world—to understand their views, interests and concerns and to present it intelligently to readers."

Students who major in journalism learn how to write well, communicate clearly, do research and understand the importance of objectivity. These strengths are important in any area of communication. Knowing how to write well has one great payoff: Many journalists can switch their careers and still remain within the communication arena. Print reporters often become public relations practitioners; broadcast journalists move into print reporting, and magazine writers produce stories online. Many hard-news reporters who no longer want the stress of quick deadlines become wonderful feature writers. Furthermore, with more news conglomerates "converging" their different media companies under one roof, journalists might write a story for the newspaper, revise it for online and comment on it for live television.

Being able to think concisely and write well are advantages in almost any industry, not just journalism. One journalism graduate who enjoyed art landed a job in a metropolitan museum. Her ability to capture an artist's work in a few words was of great benefit when writing captions for creative works on display.

A JOURNALIST'S ATTRIBUTES

News executives want job applicants who are intelligent and well-informed and who have a sense of the news—what is happening in the community and what people want to know. They want talented writers: good grammarians who can spell and write clearly and accurately. They also want applicants who are prepared to report, write or edit.

The news industry seeks applicants who are honest, curious, aggressive, self-starting and dedicated. The best applicants are also clearly committed to careers in journalism, willing to sacrifice and likely to stay in their jobs for several years. Editors and news directors look for applicants who show a long-term interest in journalism. They want applicants who have demonstrated a desire to be journalists, perhaps by working for student media, freelancing or working at an internship.

When Benjamin Bradlee was the executive editor of The Washington Post, he said he looked first for energy, for commitment to the news business and for a willingness to take work home. After that, he looked for knowledge, ability and judgment.

Retired editor and publisher Pat Murphy said applicants should have imagination, energy, a flair for risks, a passion for long hours and demanding deadlines, and that indefinable "nose for news." Furthermore, applicants should be familiar with city and county governments; be able to cope with deadline pressures; and possess an adequate general background in economics, history, literature, philosophy and science.

About 75 percent of all newcomers to the field come directly from college journalism programs. News organizations rarely hire people without a college degree, and applicants who studied journalism in college are more likely to be hired.

Many news organizations are hiring more specialists, so editors are impressed by new graduates who have developed an interest or expertise in some area of specialization, such as medicine, science, the arts or the environment. Partly for that reason, many of the students who major in journalism also minor in another field.

Smaller newspapers, broadcasting stations and public relations firms often hire applicants who can write well and operate a video or digital camera, design a Web site and conduct research using the Internet. Knowing how to do more than one job is always an advantage. In the last few years, the newspaper industry has been short of copy editors, so it may be easier and more lucrative for journalism graduates to obtain jobs as copy editors than reporters.

BE THE APPLICANT WHO GETS HIRED

William Ruehlmann, author of "Stalking the Feature Story," tells of one of his first attempts at finding a newspaper job. He arrived in town a couple of days ahead of his scheduled interview, wrote three feature stories and submitted them to the paper as freelance pieces. The day he went in for the interview, the paper had already published one of his stories. He got the job.

Internships

Successful journalism students obtain some experience while still in school. Many students start by working for campus publications. Later, they may freelance or work part time for a local public relations firm or news organization. Internships enable students to acquire more job experience and become better acquainted with the editors who hire regular staff members. Internships provide a variety of benefits: They demonstrate a student's commitment to journalism, improve professional skills and provide the "clips" or "tapes" students need to obtain jobs when they graduate. Nearly three-fourths of the journalism graduates who find media-related jobs have worked previously as interns.

Newspaper editors value internships because a college degree alone is not enough preparation for a journalism career. Job applicants who show up with piles of clips and months of experience working for school newspapers or local dailies will need less on-the-job training. Also, the fact a job seeker had the initiative to find an internship proves he or she has enthusiasm for a career in journalism.

The media employ thousands of interns every summer. Many news organizations have internship programs in which recruiters visit colleges or universities to see all applicants who want an interview. Large organizations often set early application deadlines, such as November or December, for the following summer's internships. Unfortunately, many students do not interview with national or metropolitan news organizations because they assume they are not good enough to be chosen. This is not always the case. Some students who sign up with recruiters to practice their interviewing skills are offered a job because they are at ease in the meeting.

Many students work as interns for smaller news organizations or their hometown newspaper, radio station or TV station. Motivated students simply visit the business and ask for an internship. Managers may provide internships because they feel an obligation to support journalism education or because they want to help students get ahead in the field. Editors also use internships to observe talented young journalists whom they might want to employ after graduation.

Some news organizations expect interns to work for nothing. A few exploit interns, using them as free labor, often to replace vacationing employees. Better internships include formal training programs: orientation sessions, seminars with news executives, and regular reporting and editing duties. They also pay students the same salaries that beginning staff reporters receive.

Many colleges and universities include in their Web site a listing of internships and interviewing dates and professional jobs available to students and graduates. Applicants can use the Internet to find information about a company before interviewing.

Where to Look for a Job

Metropolitan news organizations look for people with several years of solid professional experience. However, students who have had an internship at the news organization have a good chance of being hired.

In addition, new graduates should consider applying to smaller news organizations and to those in smaller markets. These media receive fewer applications and are more likely to accept applicants with less experience. Also, jobs at smaller news operations often provide better experience because they offer journalists a variety of assignments and greater responsibilities. The experience young journalists gain working in a smaller market enables them to find jobs at metropolitan news organizations later. Another avenue for gaining valuable and marketable experience and skills is to work for a newsletter or other specialized publication that focuses on a specific topic such as criminal justice, oil spills or aerospace.

Graduates seeking journalism jobs should consult professional magazines covering specialized areas of the industry. For example, announcements of newspaper jobs would be in the help-wanted advertisements in Quill or Editor & Publisher, whereas broadcast positions are more likely to be advertised in Broadcasting & Cable. Students also should check for job listings or consider posting their resume on the Web sites of professional organizations. Some that carry job listings and resumes are the Society of Professional Journalists (http://www.spj.org), Investigative Reporters and Editors Inc. (http://www.ire.org), the Public Relations Society of America (http://www.prsa.org) and the Newsletter Publishers Association (http://www.newsletters.org). Students who attend conventions of these professional groups also can make valuable contacts for jobs. Furthermore, students should consider the following ethnic professional organizations online for job listings or resume postings:

Asian American Journalist Association: http://www.aaja.org
National Association for Black Journalists: http://www.nabj.org
Native American Journalists Association: http://www.naja.com
National Association of Hispanic Journalists: http://www.nahj.org

The Cover Letter, Resume and Work Examples

A resume is an opportunity for an applicant to highlight and summarize his or her work experience and skills to a prospective employer. If candidates apply for a position through traditional or electronic mail, they send their resume with a cover letter and work samples. If candidates apply for the position in person, they submit the resume and work samples when they fill out and turn in the company's job application form.

Resume formats vary. However, the layout and content of the resume should be designed to give a prospective employer a good understanding of the applicant within 30 seconds. Readability is a key ingredient. A cluttered resume is too hard to read quickly, and one with too much space wastes time. Too many underscores and bold characters lose their purpose of making a few, important points stand out. Many applicants reserve such typographical effects for section headings and the first words in a list. For example, the job position, company and dates of the employment might appear in bold followed by the job description in regular type.

A resume begins with the applicant's formal name and contact information, such as address, phone numbers and e-mail addresses. Some applicants state their career objectives next. The rest of the resume has sections describing the applicant's education, experience related to the prospective job, other work experience, skills related to the position, honors and awards, and perhaps hobbies or interests. Most resume styles call for the most up-to-date information to be listed first within each section because editors want to see what the applicant has done recently. The last section on a resume lists about three references—preferably previous employers, professors or other individuals who are knowledgeable about the applicant's accomplishments and work ethic.

The cover letter should be addressed to the specific individual at a news organization who is responsible for hiring and focus on the particular position for which the candidate is applying. A cover letter may include supplemental information to the applicant's resume, or it may highlight important points about the applicant for the editor to note. Successful applicants stress their particular strengths that can help the company. A good cover letters ends with the applicant displaying initiative by promising to call the editor in a few days to schedule an appointment. Wording for the cover letter should be specific, concise and direct. After all, applicants who cannot present a well-written cover letter may lack journalistic skills as well.

Work samples should be duplicated legibly and pertain to the job position. They represent the strongest examples of an applicant's work. Applicants should type notes at the top or the bottom of the example or attach sticky notes indicating what they did on the story. For example, the applicant might write that the story was written within a 30-minute deadline or describe the lengths the writer went to in finding a crucial fact.

The Job Interview

When an applicant's cover letter, resume and clips impress an editor, the applicant may be invited for an interview, a critical step in obtaining a job. When applicants appear for an interview, they bring evidence of commitment and experience, such as additional clips or other samples of their work.

An applicant's appearance in an interview is important. In a study done in 2002 by the National Association of Colleges and Employers, 92 percent of the employers of new college graduates said that a candidate's overall appearance influenced their opinion about the candidate. About 65 to 83 percent of the employers said that nontraditional attire—body piercing, obvious tattoos, unusual hair color and unusual hairstyles—negatively influenced them. Every applicant should appear clean, neat and in appropriate business attire. An applicant's appearance should not detract from what an applicant has to say.

During a typical interview, an applicant is likely to meet managers and editors and other members of a news organization's staff. Successful applicants are enthusiastic, honest, confident, consistent and positive. They use the person's name and speak in a relaxed yet assertive voice.

The editors will want to learn more about the applicant: strengths, personality, interests and intelligence. They will want to know about an applicant's expectations and understanding of journalism. Is the applicant realistic about the salary range and aware that work might include evenings, weekends and holidays? If the applicant wants to be a columnist, editorial writer or Washington correspondent, it may take several years to achieve that goal. And, if the applicant wants to be a foreign correspondent, the ability to speak foreign languages is an advantage.

Editors are likely to ask the following questions during an interview: What can you tell me about yourself? What books and magazines have you read during the last month or two? Why do you want to be a journalist? Why should I hire you? What are your short- and long-range goals? What is your ideal job? What are your principal strengths and weaknesses? Why do you want to work here? What is it that you like about this particular company? What would you like to know about us (the news organization and company that owns it)? Why do you want to leave your present job? Employers look for answers that provide evidence of an applicant's commitment, intelligence and initiative.

Applicants should ask questions, too. Questions that are thoughtful and informed impress interviewers. Applicants may want to ask about assignments or opportunities for advancement. Good questions include: Exactly what would I do here? Who would edit or produce my stories, and how much feedback would I receive about them? Who would evaluate my work, and how? Can I meet the editor or producer I would work for? Can I talk with other reporters (or other copy editors, if applying for a copy-editing position)?

Applicants should be prepared to talk intelligently about the media organization. Successful candidates will have studied the company and the area before the interview. They also will have examined recent editions of the newspaper (printed or online), newsletter or newscast.

After the interview, applicants write a letter thanking the editors and expressing a continued interest in the job. If they are not hired immediately, they continue to write to the editors every few months, submitting fresh clips or other samples of work.

When offered a job, it is important to understand the offer. Is it a full-time position? Does it begin with a probation period? If so, how long is that probation, and will the salary increase when probation is over? What do company benefits include, such as insurance coverage? Also, will the company provide a car for reporters and photographers? If not, will the company pay mileage and other expenses?

Job Testing

Increasingly, news organizations test job applicants. Some also test current employees who want a promotion. The tests range from simple typing exams to more elaborate tests of an applicant's personality, mental ability, management skills and knowledge of current events. News organizations everywhere are also testing applicants for drugs. Almost all news organizations that give entry-level tests want to learn more about an applicant's ability to spell and knowledge of grammar and punctuation. Most also test writing ability, and others check reporting and copy-editing skills. Applicants may have to write a story summarizing information from rough notes as a test of writing skills.

A growing number of large news organizations ask applicants to complete tryouts: spending one to several days working in the newsroom so editors can see how they handle everyday assignments. Editors may try out three or four applicants before deciding which one will get the job.

Starting Salaries

Generally, people with better education and more experience earn higher salaries.

Earnings for entry-level journalists depend on the type of job and on the size, location and type of news organization. For example, graduates with journalism and mass communication degrees frequently earned higher salaries in the West and Northeast.

In some markets, journalists have formed unions to represent them in salary negotiations. The Newspaper Guild represents reporters, copy editors, artists and photojournalists at some newspapers. The American Federation of Radio and Television Artists represents broadcast news personnel at some stations. Salaries at those news organizations are controlled by contracts negotiated with the unions.

The salaries and numbers of jobs in journalism and mass communication generally follow the nation's economy and job market trend. Professors at the University of Georgia have conducted annual surveys of jobs and salaries for journalism and mass communication graduates for more than 35 years. Information about the job market for recent graduates can be found at http://www.grady.uga.edu/annualsurveys.

News organizations often hire their new reporters on a probationary basis, then raise their salaries when they complete the probationary period satisfactorily. Also, many young journalists receive rapid promotions as their more experienced colleagues find jobs at larger publications. Many new reporters double their salaries in five years, especially if they move to larger markets. However, many journalists decide to stay where they are because they like their particular job, news organization or community.

Newsroom Organization and Procedure

Most journalism graduates who work for print or broadcast news organizations begin as reporters. As new reporters, they may spend the first several weeks in their offices, completing minor assignments that enable them to become better acquainted with their employers' policies, while allowing supervisors to evaluate their work more closely. Or, to become better acquainted with a city, newcomers may follow experienced reporters on their beats. Each beat involves a topic that is especially newsworthy or a location where news is likely to happen.

More experienced reporters have beats covering a specific building such as the city hall, county courthouse or federal building. Other beats involve broader topics rather than a geographical location. The most common of those beats are business, education, religion and features. Larger news organizations establish dozens of more specialized beats, covering such topics as agriculture, environment, art, medicine, science or consumer affairs. This system promotes efficiency, because reporters become experts on the topics they cover and cultivate important sources of information. Reporters often remain on the same beats for several years, become well acquainted with their sources and obtain information from them more easily than they could from strangers.

On a typical day, the reporter assigned to cover, say, the city hall for a medium-sized morning daily or TV station will arrive at the office about 9 a.m. The reporter may write minor stories left from the previous day, scan newspapers published in the area, rewrite minor news releases or study issues in the news. He or she is likely to confer with an editor about major stories expected to arise that day, then go to the city hall about 10 a.m. During the next hour or two, the reporter will stop in all the major offices in the city hall, especially those of the mayor,

Many reporters use laptop computers to write their stories and telephone lines to transmit those stories to their offices, whether across town or across the country.

council members, city clerk, city treasurer and city attorney. He or she will return to the newsroom and quickly write all the day's stories. Other reporters, meanwhile, will be gathering information from their respective beats. A few reporters may not even begin work until 3 or 4 p.m. The time that journalists report to work depends on the newscast or newspaper's deadline. TV stations usually have several newscasts: early morning, noon, evening and night. Newspapers have morning editions, afternoon editions or multiple editions. Some newspapers with morning editions have their copy to the printers by midnight. New technologies and digital transmission are making deadlines easier to meet. Copy editors at morning newspapers typically come to work in the afternoon and work until the final edition is published, which may be after midnight. At an afternoon daily, copy editors might start their shift at 6 a.m. and finish about 3 p.m.

THE INDUSTRY NEEDS MORE WOMEN AND MINORITIES

Traditionally, white men have made up the workforce in media organizations. As organizational experts have found in businesses around the world, managers hire and promote people most like themselves. This situation has made it difficult for women and minorities to win jobs and promotions. A goal for some news organizations is to have the same percentage of women, racial and ethnic minorities as found in the community or the U.S. population.

Leaders in the news business recognize that a news staff consisting entirely of white males, no matter how well meaning they may be, cannot accurately reflect the views and experiences of the community it serves. The news organizations that succeed will be those that have done the best job of building diverse staffs, most editors and reporters say.

FREELANCE WRITING

College students often dream of becoming freelance writers. As freelancers, the students imagine, they will be able to set their own hours, write only about topics that interest them, pursue those topics in greater depth, sell their stories to prestigious national magazines and live comfortably on their earnings.

Getting a start as a freelancer is often difficult. It takes time to understand what editors want. However, once editors accept a freelancer's work the first time, they will accept other articles because they have become familiar with the freelancer's writing. Once a relationship has begun, editors may ask freelancers they already know to write special articles.

Freelance writing can be an enjoyable hobby or part-time pursuit. It provides another outlet for people who like to write and enables them to supplement their incomes from other jobs. Beginners are most likely to sell their articles to smaller publications, such as special interest or city magazines. Those publications may not pay as much as The New Yorker, but they receive fewer manuscripts and are much less demanding. A freelancer's indispensable tool is a book titled Writer's Market. This guide, updated annually, lists thousands of markets for freelance writers and describes the types of articles each publication wants to buy and the fees it pays.

CHECKLIST FOR FINDING THE RIGHT JOURNALISM JOB

1. **Have a talk with yourself.** In what type of atmosphere can you work best—an online news organization, where new technology skills are used every day; a magazine, which has longer deadlines; a television station, where talent for oral presentation is valued; a small newspaper, which uses its entry-level reporters to do just about everything? Decide also where you want to live and work.
2. **Internship.** Working in a professional newsroom increases your experience, your work samples, your references and your ability to ask good questions during an interview. Also, internships might help you decide where you do not want to work, instead of finding out too late at your first professional job.
3. **Cover letter.** This should be one page, creative (not cutesy) and error-free. Use the name of the recruiter. The cover letter is the first part of your first impression.
4. **Resume.** This is the opportunity to tell someone about yourself—work experience, awards, travel and special skills such as computer-assisted reporting and foreign languages.
5. **Work samples.** Some recruiters skip the resume and go straight to the work samples. Send a variety that will let an employer know what you can do. Add a short explanation to every sample explaining what you did.
6. **References.** Include the names, titles and telephone numbers of three or four people who know your work. Former employers are best; professors are fine. Make sure your references can speak to your abilities as a journalist.
7. **Research.** Learn what you can about the news organization where you'll interview. Go to its Web site; read several issues of the newspaper or watch several broadcasts; and look it up in a directory, such as the Editor & Publisher Year Book for newspapers.

8. **Interview.** Dress in business attire. Bring several sets of the same or additional work samples. Ask recruiters questions that make them think, such as questions about competitive pressures or the news organization's goals. Show enthusiasm for being a journalist. Before leaving, obtain the recruiter's e-mail address or telephone number.
9. **Thank you.** Send a thank-you note within five days of the interview. Briefly review your skills and touch upon something the recruiter said in the interview. Call or e-mail the recruiter if you haven't heard anything by the deadline given you. Remember to respect publication deadline cycles when making calls.
10. **Learn from experience.** If you don't get the job, still thank the recruiter and ask what you can do to better your chances. You might consider reapplying to the same organization later.

SUGGESTED READINGS

Students should read professional journals such as *Quill, Editor & Publisher, Columbia Journalism Review* and *American Journalism Review.*

Beasley, Maurine H., and Sheila Jean Gibbons. *Taking Their Place: A Documentary History of Women and Journalism,* 2nd ed. State College, Pa.: Strata Publishing Inc., 2002.

Cronkite, Walter. *A Reporter's Life.* New York: Alfred A. Knopf Inc., 1996.

Schieffer, Bob. *This Just In: What I Couldn't Tell You on TV.* New York: Putnam Publishing Group, 2003.

Simpson, John. *Simpson's World: Tales From a Veteran War Correspondent.* Miramax, 2003.

Streitmatter, Rodger. *Raising Her Voice: African-American Women Journalists Who Changed History.* Lexington, Ky.: University Press of Kentucky, 1994.

Zinsser, William. *Speaking of Journalism: 12 Writers and Editors Talk About Their Work.* New York: HarperCollins, 1994.

USEFUL WEB SITES

The Job Board for Media Professionals: http://www.journalismjobs.com
The National Diversity Newspaper Job Bank: http://www.newsjobs.com
American Press Institute: http://www.journaliststoolbox.com/newswriting/jobs1.html
Poynter Institute: http://www.poynter.org
Rebecca Smith's eResumes and Resources: http://www.eresumes.com
Women in Communication Inc.: http://www.womcom.org
National Gay & Lesbian Journalists Association: http://www.nlgja.org

APPENDIX A

CITY DIRECTORY

Like other city directories, this directory lists only the names of adults (people 18 and older) who live in your community. The directory does not list children under the age of 18 or adults who live in other cities. Also, city directories (like telephone books) are published only once a year. Thus, they may not list people who moved to your community within the past year.

When it conflicts with information presented in the exercises, always assume that the information in this directory is correct and that the exercises are mistaken. You will be expected to correct the exercises' errors. If a name in an exercise is not listed in the directory, assume that the name is used correctly.

As you check the names of people involved in news stories, also check their addresses and occupations, since they may also be erroneous. Sources often make errors while supplying that information to police and other authorities. Also, a person's identity may add to a story's newsworthiness. You will find, for example, that some of the people involved in stories are prominent government officials.

Finally, assume that the people listed as university professors teach at your school.

SECTION I: DIRECTORY OF CITY OFFICIALS

Belmonte, William. Member, City Council
Brennan, Rosemary. Director, City Library
Cycler, Alice. Member, City Council
Datolli, Sabrina. Mayor
DeBecker, David. Member, School Board
Drolshagen, Todd. Director, Code Enforcement Board
Farci, Allen. City Attorney
Ferguson, Tony. City Treasurer
Gandolf, Sandra. Member, City Council
Graham, Cathleen, M.D. Director, City Health Department
Hernandez, Ramon. District Attorney
Hubbard, Gary. Superintendent of Schools
Kopperud, Barry. Police Chief
Lieber, Mimi. Member, School Board
Lo, Roger. Member, City Council
Lu, Judie. Member, School Board

Maceda, Diana. Member, School Board
Nemechek, Anna. Member, School Board
Nyad, Carole. Member, City Council
Nyez, Jose. Member, School Board
Onn, Tom. Director, City Housing Authority
Plambeck, Emil. Superintendent, City Park Commission
Ramirez, Luis. Member, City Council
Stoudnaur, Marlene, M.D. Medical Examiner
Sullivan, Tony. Fire Chief
Tribitt, Jane. Member, School Board
Tuschak, Joseph. Member, City Council
Vacante, Umberto. Member, School Board

SECTION II: DIRECTORY OF COUNTY OFFICIALS

Alvarez, Harold. County Administrator
Chenn, Anne. Member, County Commission
Dawkins, Kerwin. Director, Public Works
Dawkins, Valerie. Member, County Commission
DiCesari, Gus. Sheriff
Ellis, Faith. Member, County Commission
Gardez, Jose. Member, County Commission
Grauman, Roland. Member, County Commission
Hedricks, Donald. Assistant County Attorney
Laybourne, Raymond. Member, County Commission
McNally, Ronald. County Attorney
Morsberger, Diedre. Supervisor of Elections
Shenuski, Anita. Member, County Commission
Sindelair, Vernon. County Treasurer
Smith, Ronald. County Clerk
Wehr, Helen. Assistant County Attorney

SECTION III: JUDGES

Municipal Court

Hall, Marci
Kocembra, Edward

Circuit Court

Johnson, Edwin
Kaeppler, JoAnn
Levine, Bryce R.
McGregor, Samuel
Ostreicher, Marlene
Pfaff, Randall
Picott, Marilyn
Stricklan, Julian

SECTION IV: ABBREVIATIONS

acct	accountant
admn	administration
adv	advertising
agcy	agency
agt	agent
appr	apprentice
apt	apartment
archt	architect

asmbl	assembler
assn	association
asst	assistant
athom	at home
attnd	attendant
atty	attorney
aud	auditor
av	avenue
bkpr	bookkeeper
bldr	builder
blvd	boulevard
brklyr	bricklayer
bros	brothers
capt	captain
carp	carpenter
cash	cashier
cc	community college
ch	church
chem	chemist
chiro	chiropractor
cir	circle/circuit
clk	clerk
clns	cleaners
co	company
colm	council member
com	commissioner
const	construction
cpl	corporal
crs	cruise consultant
ct	court
ctr	center
cty	county
custd	custodian
dent	dental/dentist
dep	deputy
dept	department
det	detective
dir	director
dispr	dispatcher
dist	district
dr	drive/driver
drgc	drug abuse counselor
econ	economist
ele	elementary
electn	electrician
emp	employee
eng	engineer
est	estate
exec	executive
facty	factory
fed	federal
ff	firefighter
formn	foreman
gdnr	gardener
govt	government
h	homeowner
hairdrsr	hairdresser
hosp	hospital
hwy	highway
inc	incorporated
ins	insurance
insp	inspector
jr	junior
jtr	janitor
jwlr	jeweler
la	lane
lab	laborer
librn	librarian
lt	lieutenant
lwyr	lawyer
mach	machinist
mech	mechanic
med	medical
mfg	manufacturing
mgr	manager
min	minister
mkt	market
mstr	master
mtce	maintenance
muncp	municipal
mus	musician
nat	national
ofc	office
ofer	officer
opr	operator
optn	optician
pcpl	principal
pers	personnel
pharm	pharmacist
photog	photographer
phys	physician
pl	place
plmb	plumber
pntr	painter
po	post office
polof	police officer
pres	president
prof	professor
pst	postal
pub	public
r	resident/roomer
rd	road
recpt	receptionist
rel	relations
rep	representative
repr	repairer
rept	reporter
restr	restaurant

retd	retired
Rev	reverend
sav	savings
sch	school
sec	secretary
secy	security
sen	senator
serv	service
sgt	sergeant
slsp	salesperson
slsr	sales representative
soc	social
sq	square
sr	senior
st	street
stat	station
studt	student
supm	supermarket
supt	superintendent
supvr	supervisor
tech	technician
techr	teacher
tel	telephone
ter	terrace
treas	treasurer
univ	university
USA	U.S. Army
USAF	U.S. Air Force
USM	U.S. Marines
USN	U.S. Navy
vet	veterinarian
vp	vice president
watr	waiter
watrs	waitress
wdr	welder
wid	widow
widr	widower
wkr	worker

SECTION V: SAMPLE ENTRIES

Hurley Carl J & Mary; printer Weisz Printing Co & ofc sec Roosevelt Ele Sch
1 2 3 4 5 6
h 140 Kings Point Dr
7 8
Hurley Ralph studt r 140 Kings Point Dr
9 10 11 12

1 = Family name
2 = Names of spouses in alphabetical order
3 = First listed spouse's occupation
4 = First spouse's employer
5 = Second listed spouse's occupation
6 = Second spouse's employer
7 = Homeowner
8 = Home address
9 = Name of roomer or renter 18 years of age or older
10 = Roomer/renter's occupation
11 = Resident or roomer
12 = Address

SECTION VI: ENTRIES

Aaron Betsy retd r 410 Hillcrest St Apt 302
Abare Ann recpt Chavez Bros Chevrolet h 855 Tichnor Way
Abbondanzio Anthony & Deborah brklyr Wagnor Bros & athom h 473 Geele Av
Abbondanzio Denise pub rel rep Haile Associates r 3218 Holbrook Av Apt 832
Acevede Esther & Louis both retd h 8484 Highland Dr
Acevede Miguel atty h 812 Bell Av
Adams Jenna & Donald mgr Wendy's Old Fashion Hamburgers & pst wkr h 1943 Hope Ter

Adcock George & Lydia mgr Blackhawk Hotel & soc wkr Catholic Social Services h 141 N Cortez Av
Adler Sandra & Stuard athom & min Ch of Christ r 1847 Oakland Blvd
Adles Dora & John athom & rep Bach & Co h 1218 S 23rd St
Ahl Thomas C facty wkr Vallrath Plastics r 2634 6th St Apt 382
Ahrons Tommy managing editor The Daily Courier h 1097 Leeway Dr
Ahsonn Jeffrey R & Teresa both retd h 49 Groveland Av
Albertson Wanda pers dir Vallrath Plastics h 529 Adirondack Av
Alicea Carlos city emp h 2930 Leisure Dr
Allen Christopher univ prof Pierce CC h 1810 Collins Av
Allen James D & Margie mach opr Collins Industries & atty h 28 Rio Grande Rd
Allen Michael mech Allison Ford r 410 Hillcrest St Apt 82
Allersen Alice & Thomas athom & acct Mercy Hosp h 418 Meridan Av
Allyn Christopher & Julie dir Center for Arts & univ prof h 1504 Lincoln Dr
Alvarez Harold & Tina cty administrator & techr Washington Ele Sch r 854 Maury Rd Apt 11B
Alvarez Jose cpl state hwy patrol h 1982 Elmwood Dr
Alvarez Thomas studt r 854 Maury Rd Apt 11B
Amanpor Effie & Elton athom & technical writer Wirtz Electronics h 823 E Pierce Av
Ames Robert & Emily asst mgr University Bookstore & sec Cypress Av Med clinic h 2380 Wendover Av
Anchall Mildred dir Sunnyview Retirement Home r 2202 8th Av Apt 382
Andrews Ira auto mech Allison Ford h 561 Tichnor Way
Andrews Paula wid aud Blackhawk Hotel h 4030 New Orleans Av
Aneesa Ahmad univ prof h 1184 3rd Av
Aneja David & Tracy sgt sheriff's dept & carp h 488 Tulip Dr
Ansell Herman clk Blackhawk Hotel r 2814 Ambassador Dr Apt 61
Antonucci William plmb Rittman Engineering Co r 107 Hillside Dr Apt B
Arico James K pntr Kalina Painting & Decorating r 9950 Turf Way Apt 703C
Austin Anna & Terrance C chef & athom h 481 Cottage Hill Rd
Baille Maggy wdr Halstini Mfg h 810 N Ontario Av
Baliet Karen & Thomas adv exec Bailet & Associates & pres Republican Bldrs h 1440 Walters Av
Ball James studt r 1012 Cortez Av Apt 870
Barber Herbert & Irene vp Denny's Restr Group & athom h 2440 College Dr
Barlow Janet & Raymond hairdrsr Lynn's Styling & dir United Way h 2868 Moor St
Barlow Janie & Wesley r 977 4th St Apt 2
Barlow Kevin polof r 3363 Andover Dr
Barlow Robert A mech Allison Ford r 112 Hope Cir
Barsch Margaret & Michael athom & sgt police dept h 2489 Hazel La
Barton Eileen owner/mgr Barton Sch of Dance h 1012 Treasure Dr
Basa Shannon optn r 6718 Fox Creek Dr Apt 1010
Baugh Marcia state consumer advocate h 350 Meridan Av
Bealle Denise univ prof h 1018 Cortez Av
Beasley Ralph pntr Kalina Painting & Decorating r 810 Howard St
Beaumont Edward & Hazel pst wkr & athom h 7240 N Ontario Av
Beaumont Roger studt r 7240 N Ontario Av
Becker Maurine & Ricky athom & publisher The Daily Courier h 1521 Cole Rd
Belcuor Christine & Paul watrs Holiday House Restr & librn h 497 Fern Creek Dr
Belmonte Lucy & William mus & city colm & archt Belmonte & Associates h 177 Andover Dr
Berg Mildred univ prof h 984 Elmwood Dr
Best Bryan para Sacred Heart Hosp r 4320 Michigan Av
Biagi Allison polof r 2634 6th St Apt 906B

Biegel Franklin custd Filko Furniture r 782 12th Av
Blackfoot Jason & Veronica Dawn archt & atty h 2045 Wendover Av
Blake Amanda C & Carl P nurse & electn r 3314 Santana Blvd
Blanchfield Elaine owner/mgr Elaine's Jewelry r 780 Cole Rd Apt 282
Bledsoe Edward & Rosalie photog The Daily Courier & athom h 833 Meridan Av
Blohm Kevin cook North Point Inn r 5604 Woodland St
Bolanker Timothy studt r 854 Murray Rd Apt 107B
Boudinot Marilyn sec Westinghouse Corp r 4340 Virginia Av
Boyette Willis A jtr Barton Sch of Dance r 2121 Biarritz Dr
Boyssie Betty & Lee bkpr Allstate Ins & polof h 1407 3rd Av
Brame Don city emp h 3402 Virginia Av
Brayton Wayne studt r 410 University Av Apt 279
Brennan Rosemary dir City Library h 1775 Nair Dr
Brooks Oliver & Sunni univ prof & technical writer Halstini Mfg h 5402 Andover Dr
Brown Howard slsp Prudential Ins Co h 2745 Collins Av
Bulnes Karen atty sch board h 43 Princeton Pl
Burke Lynn & Randy athom & capt USA h 412 Wilson Av
Burmeister Abraham & Esther pres First Nat Bank & athom h 4439 Harding Av
Burmester Herman A & Sally const wkr Rittman Eng Co & athom h 1412 S 23rd St
Burnes James J min St. Mark African Methodist Episcopal Church r 3155 Marcel Av
Burnes Todd polof r 1502 Matador Dr Apt 203
Burnes Tyrone min United Methodist Ch r 8430 Wilson Av
Butler Irene & Max athom & courier First Nat Bank r 444 Jamestown Dr
Cain Fred & Irma mus & athom r 427 Hidden La
Cantrell Michael pres/mgr Mr. Muscles r 410 South St
Capiello Ann studt r 8210 University Blvd Apt 311
Capiello Otto A & Sandra J photog & wdr Rittman Industries h 47 Rio Grande Rd
Carey John priest St. John Vianney Catholic Ch r 2020 Oak Ridge Rd
Carey Myron univ prof h 641 N Highland Dr
Carigg Craig & Susan min Allen Chapel AME Ch & athom h 453 Twisting Pine Cir
Carigg James R studt r 453 Twisting Pine Cir
Carson Frank & Janice serv formn Allison Ford & athom h 2197 Marcel Av
Carter Deborah counselor Lovell Psychiatric Assn r 550 Oak Parkway Apt 821
Caruna Alyce min Howell Presbyterian Ch h 423 Charrow La
Carvel Reba techr Colonial Ele Sch r 1883 Hope Ter
Casio David & Gretta atty & athom r 711 N 31st St Apt 220
Caspinwall Andrew r 416 Wilson Av
Caspinwall Nadine phys h 416 Wilson Av
Cessarini Maxine & Richard M univ prof & phys r 4184 Cypress Av
Charton John city ff r 3158 Virginia Av
Cheesbro Marylin asst pub defender r 1010 Eastview Rd Apt 3
Cheng Beverly exec dir State Restr Assn h 643 Wymore Rd
Chenn Anne & Steven city com & lt fire dept r 91 Melrose Av
Chevez Larry det police dept h 4747 Collins Rd
Chmielewski Albert nurse Mercy Hosp r 2814 Ambassador Dr Apt 82
Christopher Alan univ prof h 4850 Elm Dr
Chuey Karen & William J slsp Allison Ford & clk police dept r 5710 Michigan Av
Cisneroes Andrew & Lillian min Redeemer Lutheran Ch & athom r 818 Bell Av
Claire Richard & Wanda dir state Dept of Corrections & athom h 12142 Decatur Rd
Clauch Amy clk Annie's Auto Parts r 2418 Seasons Crt Apt B
Clayton Amy univ pres r 820 Twisting Pine Cir
Cohen Abraham & Estelle asst dir computer serv city sch system & pub rel rep Evans Pub Rel Group r 1903 Conway Rd

Collin Ronald const wkr Wagnor Development Corp r 2814 Ambassador Dr Apt 47D
Colson Jonathan studt r 7240 N Ontario Av
Conaho Henry & Jeanne supvr sales ERA Realty & pres Lake CC h 820 Hope Ter
Correia Bobby & Dawn supvr Delta Airlines & athom h 9542 Holbrook Dr
Cortez Manuel & Nina polof & bkpr North Point Inn r 1242 Alton Rd
Cosby Minnie agt Watson Realty r 487 Jamestown Dr
Coto Jorge Alberto studt r 8210 University Blvd Apt 311
Courhesne Adolph & Gloria mech Fridley Volkswagen & athom h 1186 N Highland Av
Cowles Stephen jtr VFW Post 40 h 8217 Cypress Av
Cross Andrea & Lee chiro & city acct h 2 Virginia Av
Cross Dina & Raymond athom & pst wkr r 101 Charow La
Cruz Jena atty r 48 DeLaney Av
Cullinan Charles A & Susan both sheriff's dep r 848 Rio Grande Rd
Curtis Sarah sr vp SunBank r 663 Harding Av
Cycler Alice & Richard city colm & atty r 7842 Toucan Dr
Daigel Annette hairdrsr Anne's Beauty Salon r 431 E Central Blvd
DaRoza Sue & Terry studt & clk Jiffy Food Store r 410 University Av Apt 80
Datolli Roger & Sabrina retd & mayor r 845 Conway Rd
Dawkins Agnes & Kerwin athom & dir cty Dept of PubWorks r 2203 Coble Dr
Dawkins Ronald & Valerie bklyr & cty com r 1005 Stratmore Dr
Dawson Shirley wid techr Colonial Ele Sch h 492 Melrose Av
Deacosti Amy studt r 3254 Virginia Av
Deacosti Michael & Peggy pres Deacosti's Restr & hostess h 3254 Virginia Av
Deboare Ann & Jack R dir emp rel Rittmann Industries & mgr Lucky's Supm r 1415 Idaho Av
DeCastro Wilma teacher Kennedy High Sch h 3277 Pine Av
Dees Karen studt r 410 University Av Apt 52
DeLoy Joseph R phys r 280 Lancaster Rd Apt 110
Desaur Roland studt r 700 Classics St
DeVitini Brenda & Ronald asst min Redeemer Lutheran Ch & mach Rittman Industries r 313 Coble Dr
DeWitt Tony studt r 2230 Cortez Av Apt 828
Deyo Ashley & Ralph graphic designer & dent r 2814 Ambassador Dr Apt 7
DeZinno Marc & Nancy asmbl Vallrath Industries & athom h 205 Rockingham Ct
Diaz Diane & Richard author & nurse St. Nicholas Hosp h 1978 Holcroft Av
Diaz Enrique & Lisa atty & pst wkr r 3224 Mt Semonar Av
Diaz Juanita watrs Pancake House r 408 Kasper Av Apt 322
DiCesari Gus & Henrietta cty sheriff & athom h 980 Atlantic Av
Dillan Martha atty Westinghouse Corp h 702 S Kirkmann Av
DiLorrento Anthony univ prof h 666 Texas Av
Dolmovich Sandra M clk Dayton-Hudson h 714 N 23rd St
Dow Tammy sgt police dept r 2208 17th Av
Dowdell Laura & Thaddeus clk & jwlr Dowdell Jewelry h 620 Lexon Av
Doyle Cynthia & Wayne techr Colonial Ele Sch & pres National Homebuilders Assn h 428 Wilson Av
Drolshagen Illse & Todd athom & dir City Code Enforcement Board h 2406 Alabama Av
Dwyer Margaret studt r 2047 Princeton Av Apt 405
Dysart Tony & Wendy athom & attnd Sunnyview Retirement Home r 724 Aloma Av Apt 24F
Edwards Traci psychiatrist h 3303 Lake Dr
Einhorn Doris & Robert athom & univ phys h 8320 Meadowdale Rd
Eisen Priscilla phys r 1118 Bumby Av Apt 204

Ellam Dorothy R & Roger A techr Madison Ele Sch & landscape contractor r 2481 SantanaBlvd
Ellerbe Robert widr pres Ellerbe's Boats h 3213 Hidalgo Dr
Emory Jonathan & Lori eng & athom h 849 Groveland Av
Eulon Harley & Martha jtr St. Nicholas Hosp & athom h 410 E 3rd St
Evans Mark & Trish W cty soc wkr & owner/mgr Evans Pub Rel Group h 4232 Stewart Av
Evans Nikki & Timothy loan ofer First Fed Sav & Loan & mgr Allstate Ins r 806 Apple La
Fairbairn Sean owner Advance Investments h 5235 Robinhood Dr
Farci Allen widr atty h 818 Texas Av
Favata Celia J wid h 9930 Bumby Av
Ferguson Marcia & Tony vet & city treas h 96 West Av
Ferrell Fannie & Melvin atty & pcpl Kennedy High Sch h 2384 West Av
Firmett Rene J serv stat attnd Bert's Shell Stat r 4474 Colyer Rd
Flavel Vernon J dir Becker Express h 827 Pigeon Rd
Forlenza Henry custd Kmart r 4620 Alabama Av Apt 22
Forsythe Scott cpl sheriff's dept h 1414 S 14th Av
Foucault Carmen wid techr Aloma Ele Sch h 1452 Penham Av
Foucault James studt r 1452 Penham Av
Fowler Barbara K & Fritz polof & owner Fowler Allstate h 88 Eastbrook Av
Fowler Joel studt r 2006 Hillcrest St
Franklin Allen sgt USA r 840 Apollo Dr Apt 322
Friedmann Leo asst dist atty r 2814 Ambassador Dr Apt C2
Fusner Charles tech h Peachtree Dr
Gable Frances & Jay athom & truck dr Becker Express h 1701 Woodcrest Dr
Gandolf Sandra wid city colm h 8 Hillcrest Av
Gant Diana univ prof h 810 Village La
Gardepe Ellen serv mgr Derek Chevrolet h 210 Lake Dr
Garland Charlotte & Chester athom & city health insp h 2008 N 21st St
Garner Cheryl & David athom & emp City Recreation Dept r 2814 Ambassador Dr Apt 88
Gianangeli David gdnr r 48 Stempel Apt 53D
Giangelli Marlene P pres Pestfree Inc h 214 Lake Dr
Gill Todd watr Fred's Steakhouse r 410 University Av Apt 279
Goetz Beryl dent & writer h 1010 McLeod Rd
Golay Evelyn & Thomas cash & ownr/mgr Tom's Liquors h 1203 Texas Av
Goree Linda exec dir city Girl Scout Council r 2202 8th Av Apt 302
Gould Darlene & Savilla athom & slsp Anchor Realty Co h 4178 N 11th Av
Graham Cathleen & Ross R dir City Health Dept & phys h 710 Harding Av
Grauman Alice & Samuel athom & min First Covenant Ch r 610 Eisen Av
Grauman Roland & Tina cty com & asst supt for pub education r 3417 Charnow La
Green Joey atty h 604 Michigan Av
Greenhouse Irwin & Trina administrator Mercy Hosp & athom h 9575 Holbrook Dr
Griffin Marlene det police dept h 3130 Joyce Dr
Guarino Anne chiro r 4100 Conway Rd Apt 611
Guarino Belva retd r 84 Lakeland Av
Guarino Gerhard chiro h 1813 Texas Av
Guarino Tony A techr Colonial High Sch h 6139 Eastland Dr
Guerin Anita & Ronald E athom & city ff r 1045 Eastvue Rd
Guitterman Daniel bartender Jim's Lounge r 550 Oak Park Way Apt 7
Gulas Gail & William J studt & phys h 3405 Virginia Av
Guyer Joseph & Rita artist & athom h 4043 S 28th St
Guzmann Trina mgr Sports Unlimited r 2032 Turf Way Apt 230

Haile Jeffrey polof r 2634 6th St Apt 847
Hall Marci muncp ct judge h 34 Magee Ct
Halso Beverly & Jeff pres Haslo Pub Rel & vet r 879 Tichnor Way
Hamill Kimberly mgr Albertson's supm h 811 N Cortez Av
Hamill Margaret studt r 811 N Cortez Av
Hammar Margaret J secy ofer Macy's Dept Store h 1181 6th St
Hana Edward & Jena min Unity Ch of Christianity & athom h 134 Eisen Av
Hana Kyle cust Unity Ch of Christianity r 134 Eisen Av
Hanson Lydia atty r 880 6th St
Hanson Myron widr retd h 880 6th St
Harmon Rhonda watrs Red Lobster r 816 Westwinds Dr Apt 8
Harnish Cheryl & David supvr sales Cargell Corp & state sen h 288 Hillcrest St
Harris Jerry R & Jewel asst mger House of Pancakes & athom h 2245 Broadway Av
Haselfe Jennifer & Richard athom & pres Haselfe Development Corp h 554 Beloit Av
Haserott Mildred wid ticket agt Greyhound Lines r 411 Wisconsin Av
Haskell Thomas widr lt fire dept h 2482 Elmwood Dr
Hattaway Willie widr retd r 411 Wisconsin Av
Hedricks Donald asst city atty r 4320 Elsie Dr Apt 884
Hermann Andrew J & Jennifer acct & teller First Nat Bank h 1888 Hope Ter
Hernandez Ramon dist atty h 84 Lake Cir
Herndon Joyce atty h 310 Mill Av
Herrin Raymond W univ prof h 410 Park Av
Herwarthe Gregory L & Ruth pres Knight Realty & asst mgr Harrington & Co Investments h 4410 Baltimore Av
Heslinn Allison & Burt clk Kmart & slsr Prudential Bache h 8197 Locke Av
Heslinn Dorothy L mgr Mr. Grocer r 8197 Locke Av
Higginbotham Gladdies Anne mgr Secy Fed Bank h 1886 Hope Ter
Hilten Randall J & Virginia lt fire dept & athom h 915 Baxter Dr
Hoequist Thomas owner/pres The Jewelry Shoppe h 2418 Collins Av
Hoffmann Vivian wid clk Quik Shoppe h 711 Meadow Creek Dr
Hoffsinger Nora wid retd r 411 Wisconsin Av
Holland George & Tanaka dr Greyhound Lines & athom h 4368 Normandy Dr
Holland Keith studt r 410 University Av Apt 11
Holland Maryanne adv exec Wilson Associates h 947 Greenbrier Dr
Holman Evelyn & Leonard athom & phys h 4366 Normandy Dr
Holten Liz owner Holten Doughnuts h 9512 Forest Grove
Holtzclaw Norma J wid slsp ERA Realty h 739 West Av
Horan Roger sheriff's dep r 118 Hillside Dr Apt C3
Howard Sarah polof h 812 Bell Av
Howe Lynn studt r 410 University Av Apt 318
Howland Ruth & Terry owner Blackhawk Hotel & secy ofer Memorial Hospital h 1808 Gladsen Blvd
Hubbard Gary & Peggy supt of city schs & athom h 384 Hilcrest St
Hyde Marie & Roger asst supt of city schs & slsp Ross Chevrolet h 1381 Lakeview Dr
Iacobi Neil atty r 6214 Maldren Av
Innis Alvin & Sarah lt police dept & athom h 1305 Atlantic Blvd
Jabil Stephen dr Becker Express r 800 Crestbrook Loop Apt 314
Jacbos Martha mgr Mom's Donuts r 1889 32nd St
Jaco Milan & Robyn dir Blood Bank & athom h 2202 S 8th St
Jacobs Bill & Carol sgt police dept & dispr Yellow Cab h 2481 Lakeside La
James Edwin cour Pinkerton Security Ser r 1010 Eastview Rd Apt 12
Jamison Peter J & Stephanie R phys & phys/surg Sacred Heart Hosp h 6004 Beech St
Janviere Jeanne techr Colonial Ele Sch r 1883 Hope Ter

Jeffreys Michael dir Humane Society h 2781 Collins Av
Jimenez Edwin C mgr Quik Shoppe r 3611 31st St
Joanakatt Cathy asst dir We Care h 2442 Collins Av
Johnson Edwin & Susan cir ct judge & athom h 148 West Av
Johnson Karen asst supt of city schs h 2344 S 11th St
Johnson Marc const wkr r 2643 Pioneer Rd
Johnson Mary bkpr Vallrath Plastics h 6181 Collins Rd
Jones Danny & Margaret min Metro Life Ch & athom h 1152 Darlington Av
Jones James dr City Cab Co r 977 4th St. Apt 10
Jones Lucinda & Samuel athom & lt USM h 4851 Edmee Cir
Jones Robyn & Sean med tech Mercy Hosp & capt USN h 4216 Winford Cir
Kaeppler JoAnn cir ct judge h 2192 West Av
Kaeppler Lori & Ronald athom & sgt USM h 9540 Holbrook Dr
Kalani Andrew mgr Kalani Bros Bakery h 2481 Kaley Way
Kalani Charles pres Kalani Bros Bakery h 2481 Kaley Way
Kasandra Kelli retd r 9847 Eastbrook La
Kasparov Linda univ dietitian r 9103 Lake St
Keegan Patrick Jr fed atty h 505 Walnut Dr
Keel Sally & Timothy asmbl Cargell Corp & barber Plaza Barber Shop h 1413 Griesi Dr
Kehole Marvin mtce wkr Cargell Corp r 182 W Broadway Av
Kernan Russell mach Vallrath Industries r 168 Lake St
Kindstrom Sarah watrs Steak & Ale h 4828 N Vine St
Kirkmann James dr Yellow Cab r 816 Westwinds Dr Apt 202
Knapp Erik A cook Frisch's Restr r 2314 N 11th St
Knoechel Alvin & Sara plmb & slsr The Daily Courier h 1112 E Lisa La
Kocembra Edward & Heather muncp ct judge & athom h 388 31st St
Koche Ellen Jane atty Neighborhood Law Ofc h 4214 Azalea Ct
Kopez Frank & Lisa city mech & athom h 1067 Eastland Av
Kopp Suzanne wid retd r 4200 S 11th St Quality Trailer Ct
Kopperud Barry widr chief of police h 458 Kaley Way
Kostyn Elizabeth & Ralph E athom & asst supt for ele education city schs h 284 Erie Av
Krueger Melody & William athom & pres Aladdin Paints h 48 Michigan Av
Kubic Marilyn & Ralph both techrs North High Sch h 1452 N 3rd St
Kunze Lauren & Robert athom & mach Vallrath Industries r 94 Jamestown Dr Apt 318
LaCette Cecil serv stat attnd r 2814 Ambassador Dr Apt 61
Lasiter Harriet & James athom & techr Roosevelt Ele Sch h 374 Walnut Dr
Layous Michael E studt r 212 N Wisconsin Av
LeClair George cir ct judge h 501 Mont Clair Blvd
Lee Fred owner/cook Kona Village h 1181 24th St
Leforge Ted dent h 537 Peterson Pl
Leidigh Floyd & Rose const wkr Rittman Engineering Co. & athom h 1812 Dickins Av
Levine Bryce & Trina cir ct judge & athom h 8521 Shady Glen Dr
Levine Ida mgr Mr. Waterbeds r 8521 Shady Glen Dr
Lewis Jacquelin & Jonnie watrs Holiday House & insptr Vallrath Industries h 1840 Maldren Av
Linn Eddy & Marie sgt police dept & athom h 6287 Airport Blvd
Linn Ronald studt r 6287 Airport Blvd
Lo Joan & Roger athom & city colm h 1993 Collins Av
Logass Jeffrey econ Larco Corp h 81 Venetian Way
Lowdes Enrico & Sandra dir Regional Medical Ctr & athom h 77 Maldren Av

Lowrie Catrina phys Regional Medical Ctr r 118 Hillside Dr Apt 74
Lowrie Cynthia studt r 118 Hillside Dr Apt 74
Lozando Marie clinical dir Mercy Hosp r 234 E Markham Dr Apt 4
Lucas Frank cpl hwy patrol h 2417 Country Club Dr
Lydin Charles R mgr LaCorte Printing Co h 888 Melrose Av
Macbos Martha dir of nursing Mercy Hosp h 1889 32nd St
Macco Alan mus r 503 29th St
Madea Ramon exec dir Bon Voyage Travel Agcy r 118 Hillside Dr Apt 606
Mahew Arthur mgr Fische's Bowling Alley h 1918 Pacific Rd
Majorce Albert & Monica archt & athom h 2882 Ambassador Dr
Marcheese Harvey O & Joyce min & organist Faith Baptist Ch h 1481 Cole Rd
Mariston Saundra watrs Freddy's Inn h 822 Kentucky Av
Matros Margo univ prof r 410 University Av Apt 818
McCartney Mildred wrk Holten Doughnuts h 1212 Alexandrea St
McCauley Melvin & Veronica truck dr Becker Express & athom h 540 Osceola Blvd
McDonald Herbert J & Rosalie owner/mgr Tastee Popcorn & athom h 1842 Hazel La
McDowell William pntr r 1429 Highland Dr
McEwen Lonnie & Victoria techr Washington Jr High Sch & athom h 1024 Nancy Cir
McFarland Charlotte nursing supvr Sand Lake Hosp h 1090 Timberline Trail
McFerren Patrick J widr U.S. postmaster h 1227 Baldwin Dr
McFerren Patti const wkr Rittmann Engineering Co r 816 Westwinds Dr Apt 3
McGorwann Karen cc prof r 4320 Elsie Dr Apt 6
McGowen Bill & Rosalind const wkr Rittmann Engineering Co & maid Hyatt Hotel h 4842 S Conway Rd
McGowin William sheriff's dep h 4224 N 21st St
McGrath Sunni jtr Washington Ele Sch h 109 19th St
McGregor Carol & Samuel mgr trainee Albertson's Supm & cir ct judge h 1501 Southwest Ct
McIntry Eugene & Irene pres McIntry Realty & athom h 2552 Post Road
Meir Sharon pers dir Vallrath Industries r 810 Kalani St Apt 2
Mejian Colette pcpl Risser Ele Sch h 415 Ivanhoe Blvd
Merrit Jacob & June eng WTMC-TV & athom h 301 Wymore Rd
Meserole Alexander & Teresa owner Deerfield Country Club Restaurant & adv slsr The Daily Courier h 5293 Mandar Dr
Meyer Robert & Sonia sgt USAF & credit mgr Sears h 811 Moor St
Miehee Margaret & Richard athom & asst U.S. postmaster h 1190 Euclid Av
Millan Timothy cook Grande Hotel r 1112 Huron Av
Miller Sharon optn LensCrafters h 2827 Norwell Av
Minh Stephen retd r 410 Hillcrest St Apt 842
Moravchek Albert & Dorothy city ff & clk police dept h 4187 N 14th St
Moronesi Donna slsr Adler Real Estate h 623 N 5th St
Morrell Cathy & Wayne athom & mgr Bon Voyage Travel Agency h 382 Arlington Cir
Morsberger Diedre city supvr elections h 898 Hemlock Dr
Muldaur Eddy studt r 660 S Conway Rd
Murhana Thomas lab Cargell Corp r 40 W Hillier Av
Murphy Joseph & Kathleen dir research Collins Industries & athom h 114 Conway Rd
Murray Blair & Patricia mgr Beneficial Finance & athom h 1748 N 3rd St
Murray Harold & Marty atty & curriculum resource techr h 1801 Hillcrest St
Neely Myron A det police dept h 1048 Jennings Rd
Nego Alan polof r 1840 Wymore Rd Apt 10
Nemnich Harland & Helen electr & retd h 1331 Mt Vernon Blvd
Nicholls Cheryl fed emp h 1287 Belgard Av
Nieves Erik & Krystal univ athletic dir & hairdrsr h 2894 Ambassador Dr

Noffsinger Nora wid retd r 411 Wisconsin Av
Noonan Jack widr det police dept h 5928 Jody Way
Nouse Sharon pilot Aerial Promotions Inc r 4740 Valley View La
Novogreski Harry R & Melba mach Keller Plastics & athom h 2891 Morris Av
Nunez Carolynn & Roger athom & eng Kelle-Baldwin Corp h 2820 Norwell Av
Nunziata Carmen h 1410 1st Av
Nyad Carol city colm h 850 Sutter Loop
Nyer Diana studt r 550 Oak Park Way Apt 264
Nyer JoAnne sec Washington Ele Sch r 550 Oak Park Way Apt 264
O'Hara Allison city sec r 4729 Texas Av
Oldaker George polof r 2117 Wisconsin Av Apt 488
Oldaker Thomas polof r 2117 Wisconsin Av Apt 488
Oliver Franklin R & Jeanette exec Gill Assoc Inc Pub Rel & athom h 1121 Elm Blvd
Onn Esther & Tom C athom & dir City Housing Authority h 3869 Jefferson Av
Ortiz Lynn & Randy athom & brklyr HomeRite Builders r 816 Westwinds Dr Apt 78
Ortson Martha & Thomas J athom & vp Secy First Bank h 810 N 14th St
Ostreicher Marlene wid cir ct judge h 449 Ferncreek Cir
Paddock Cynthia & Thomas C credit mgr Belks Dept Store & mach Cargell Corp h 1736 Hinkley Rd
Palomino Molly & Ralph R athom & vp Genesco Inc h 374 Douglas Rd
Parkinson Marie studt r 857 Murray Rd Apt 204A
Patterson Michelle electn r 1012 Cortez Av Apt 915
Patzell Bruce & MaryAnne carp & athom h 915 Bishop Dr
Patzell Larry studt r 915 Bishop Dr
Paynick Nina & Stanley techr Washington Ele Sch & owner Paynick's Carpets h 901 2nd St
Peerson Marc univ prof h 4851 Edmee Cir
Perakiss Ethel & Michael athom & atty h 876 Collins Av
Percy John atty h 1037 2nd St
Perez Jason const wkr Wagoner Development Corp r 2414 Skan Ct
Perez Joseph & Vicki city emp & lt police dept h 2414 Skan Ct
Petchski Pearl asst cash Morrison's Cafeteria r 411 Wisconsin Av
Peters Frederick & Rene C pharm Kmart & pres Humane Society h 484 Sugar Ridge Ct
Peterson Sara wid h 1671 Drexel Av
Pfaff Randall cir ct judge h 2134 Oak Ridge Rd
Phillips Teresa M clk The Jewelry Shoppe r 800 Crestbrook Loop Apt 228
Picardo Marie nurse r 510 Concord St Apt 48
Picott James & Katherine slsp Allison Ford & dent asst h 640 Lake Dr
Picott Marilyn cir ct judge h 901 2nd St
Piloto Claire & Kenneth T interior decorator & atty Piloto & Herndon h 1472 Bayview Rd
Pinccus Jennifer atty Piloto & Herndon r 2021 Dyan Way Unit 2
Pinckney Samuel & Terest retd & athom h 976 Grand Av
Pinero Jim Timmons dvlpr Pinero Developers h 2411 Windsong Dr
Ping Dorothy & Louis athom & plumb Lou's Plumbing h 348 Conroy Rd
Plambeck Dolly & Emil athom & supt City Park Com h 6391 Norris Av
Porej Irvin vp for loans First Fed Sav & Loan h 112 Anzio St
Povacz Julius city paramedic r 210 E King Av Apt 4
Proppes Richard E asst mgr Safeway Supm h 1012 2nd St
Pryor Lynne R const wkr Rittmann Engineering Co r 2634 6th St Apt 45
Rafelsin Louis lt police dept h 934 Old Tree Rd
Ramirez Harriet & Luis dent asst & city colm h 982 Euclid Av
Randolph James const wkr Rittmann Engineering Co r 654 Harrison St

Ray Elizabeth & William David both retd r 550 Oak Park Way Apt 157
Reeves Charlton E & Polly state health ofer & athom h 658 Lennox Av
Reimer Maurice & Mildred acct & athom h 2529 Barbados Av
Richards Patricia r 42 Tusca Trail
Richardson Inez & Thomas E athom & polof h 5421 Jennings Rd
Richbourg Bud & Kathleen owner/mgr Buddy's Lounge & athom h 1014 Turkey Hollow
Richter Robyn Anne retd h 42 Tusca Trail
Riggs Gladies Ann wid retd r 1080 Harvard Rd Apt 4
Rivera Hector phys Medi-First Clinic r 800 Crestbrook Loop Apt 38
Rivera Maxwell tech h 11 Calico Crt
Robbitzsch John W psychiatrist h 1014 Bear Creek Cir
Roehl Cecil & Esther polof & athom h 1228 Euclid Av
Romaine Gerri & Nickolas H athom & wdr h 2876 Post Av
Romansaik Michael const wkr Wagnor Development Corp r 118 Hillside Dr Apt 8
Rudnike Harold & Martha athom & sales mgr Vallrath Industries h 4825 N Vine St
Rue Alexander studt r 8420 University Blvd Apt 218
Rueben James & Elizabeth state sen & atty h 12494 Hillcrest Rd
Ruffenbach Laura univ prof h 6741 Waxwing La
Ruiz George & Lila polof & athom h 263 9th St
Ruiz Guillermo & Harriet asst city med examiner & dir pub affairs Regional Med Ctr h 4718 Bell Av
Rybinski Kim owner Kim's Pets r 2634 6th St Apt 710
Salcido Martha & Tony athom & city ff h 10 Exeter Ct
Saleeby Claire & John athom & lt colonel USA h 626 N 3rd St
Saleeby Henry widr retd r 84 Sunnyvale Rd
Saleeby Olivida & Wesley both retd h 1916 Elizabeth La
Salvatore Hector R & Juanita M atty & athom h 1716 Forest Ridge Rd
Sanchez Gumersinda hairdrsr Lillian's Beauty Salon h 173 Burgasse Rd
Satava Kenneth widr techr Kennedy High Sch h 2204 Marcel Av
Saterwaitte Benjamin widr retd h 307 E King Blvd
Sawyer Betty & Harley athom & techr Kennedy High Sch r 2032 Turf Way Apt 512
Sawyer Claire min Christian Redeemer Ch h 7400 Southland Blvd
Schifini Destiny vp SunBank h 3620 Timber Ter
Schipper Michele studt r 4100 Conway Rd Apt 814
Schweitzer Ralph city building insp r 816 Westwinds Dr Apt 160
Scott Kerry & Nancy slsp Kohlerware & athom h 4189 Hazel St
Scott Milan & Nancy techr Kennedy High Sch & techr Wilson Ele Sch h 20 Magee Ct
Sessions Jeffrey D & Michelle A emer rm phys/dir emer sers Sacred Heart Hosp & athom h 9303 Vale Dr
Shadgott Carol & Frank D athom & phys h 8472 Chestnut Dr
Sharp Lynita L clk Jiffy Foods r 5836 Bolling Dr
Shattuck Christina & Dennis A mgr Perkins Restr & emp city garage h 532 3rd St
Shearer Ethel cocktail watrs Melody Lounge r 408 Kasper Av Apt 718
Shenuski Anita & Frederic cty com & dis mger IRS h 1230 Embree Cir
Shepard Frank & Helen techr & rept The Daily Courier h 107 Eastbrook Av
Shepard Linn Marie studt r 854 Murray Rd Apt 107B
Sheppard Ronald lt fire dept r 2024 Vincent Rd Apt 1020
Shisenauntt Arthur & Lillian secy consultant & pharm Walgreen h 1243 Washington Av
Shoemaker JoAnn techr Colonial High Sch r 6139 Eastland Dr
Silverbach Daniel G & Jill polof & athom h 3166 Wayne Av
Simmons Karen dist dir Greenpeace r 708 E Lisa La

Simmons Rachel & Wayne athom & slsp Prudential Ins h 708 E Lisa La
Sindelair Elaine & Vernon athom & cty treas h 4164 Mandar Dr
Skinner Dorothy & Roger clk typist Lawson Bros & polof h 2080 Washington Av
Skurow Melvin widr carp h 4138 Hennessy Ct
Slater Carolyn & David athom & chiro h 8443 Turkey Hollow
Smith Grady r 8213 Peach St
Smith Linda M & Ronald studt & city clk h 1814 N 3rd St
Smitkins Marlene & Myron athom & mach Kohlarware h 417 Huron Av
Smythe Asa A & Carol city emp & athom h 4280 Timber Trail
Smythe Terry bartender Bayside Bar & Grill r 4280 Timber Trail
Snow Dale & Terri athom & nurse Mercy Hosp h 4381 Hazel St
Snowdin Elizabeth clk state employment ofc h 952 Kasper Av
Snyder Christina dir pub rel Mercy Hosp h 711 Broadway Av
Sodergreen Karl & Lillian phys & athom h 788 Timber Trail
Sota Mimi dir Drug Abuse Unit Mercy Hosp h 655 Brickell Dr
Stevens Julie Ann mus h 624 N 3rd St
Stockdale George & Lillian capt USM & athom h 472 Bolling Dr
Stoudnaur John & Marlene mgr Rexall Drugs & city med examiner h 1350 41st St
Stovall Iris wid mgr Quikke Clns h 7204 Southland Blvd
Straitten Karen & Walter athom & city building insptr r 4450 Richmond Rd
Stricklan Julian cir ct judge h 4268 Wayne Av
Sulenti Allen D studt r 800 Crestbrook Loop Apt 1010
Sullivan Tony widr fire chief h 863 Benchwood Ct
Svec Wallace A mech Allison Ford r 4320 Elsie Dr Apt 1
Svendson Lillian & Wayne athom & city paramedic h 814 Washington Av
Swaugger Charlotte & Samuel cc prof & rept The Daily Courier h 4987 Huron Dr
Sweers Daniel & Karen fed emp & det police dept h 108 Eastbrook Av
Tai Wendy housekeeper Hilton Hotel r 84 Chestnut Dr
Talbertsen Sarah A artist h 3214 Riverview Dr
Taylor Frederic C r 4828 N Vine St
Taylor Marsha L mgr McDonald's h 2012 Lincoln Av
Temple Roger polof r 2032 Turf Way Apt 818
Thistell Dirk & Mildred R eng Rittmann Industries & counselor Roosevel High Sch h 528 Kennedy Blvd
Thomas Joseph techr Kennedy High Sch r 2848 Santa Av Apt 2
Thompsen Yvonne studt r 1012 University Av Apt 812
Tifton Albert & Marsha capt fire dept & athom r 2814 Ambassador Dr Apt 417
Tijoriwalli Cathy owner Cathy's Sandwiches r 1320 Embree Cir
Tiller Ida & Julius athom & polof h 539 Sheridan Blvd
Tilman Marion & Randall C athom & city health insptr h 818 N 41st St
Tontenote Eldred L & Lisa mech Ace AutoBody & athom r 2634 6th St Apt 17
Totmann Gloria & Marvin dent asst & secy guard Brinks h 1818 4th St
Tribitt Jane mgr Colonial Apts r 1040 Colonial Way Apt 101
Tuschak Arlene & Joseph master electn & city colm h 2094 Byron Av
Ungarient James R & Margaret both attys The Law Office h 7314 Byron Av
Uosis Bobbie & Michael both retd h 4772 E Harrison Av
Vacante Mary & Umberto athom & technical writer Lockheed Martin h 3202 Joyce St
Vacanti Carlos & Carol polof & athom h 4910 Magee Ct
Valderama Lynn dir secy JC Penney h 1020 Lincoln Av
Valesquez George & Paula archt/owner Valesquez Design Group & atty univ bd of trustees h 5405 Conway Rd
Van Atti Joseph & Trina city ff & athom h 960 Stratmore Dr
Van Den Shuck Margaret pub serv rep Allstate Ins h 7663 Robinhood Dr

VanPelt Audrey W & James min First United Methodist Ch & serv mgr Lane Toyota h 420 N Wilkes Rd
Vasquez Guillermo & Miranda dir State Dept of Corrections & athom h 2801 Norwell Av
Veit Helel Lynn min First Covenant Ch h 184 Nelson Av
Verdugo Maureen pcpl Kennedy High Sch r 816 Westwinds Dr Apt 482
Verkler LeeAnn univ prof r 800 Crestbrook Loop Apt 10A
Vernell Cathy S dr Yellow Cab r 1010 Vermont Av
Vorholt Andrew A owner/mgr Hallmark Cards h 10 E Lake Rd
Wagnor Kristine & Timothy Sr athom & owner/mgr Tim's Coffee Shop h 418 N Wilkes Rd
Ward Frances & Jon H athom & sgt/recruiter USA r 3113 DeLaney Av
Ward Lonnie D mtce wkr Colonial Apts r 2814 Ambassador Dr Apt 22
Warniky Clara & Wayne mgr Hertz Rent A Car & polof h 428 N Wilkes Rd
Washington Bruce R atty David Casio & Associates r 1104 Esplada Av Apt 19
Waundry James R & Lisa mgr 2-Hour Clns & athom h 5310 Stratmore Dr
Weber Nancy techr Washington Ele Sch h 44 E Princeton St
Wehr Helen asst cty atty h 1298 Vermont Av
Wei Albert sgt police dept h 964 Jody Way
Wei Constance P & Donald S state rep & atty h 206 N Wabash Av
Weinstein Jeanette techr Colonial High Sch h 6139 Eastland Dr
Weiskoph Herman asst min John Calvin Presbyterian Ch h 4817 Twin Lakes Blvd
Wentilla Lorrie & Reid R athom & pres Keele-Baldwin Corp h 640 Clayton Av
West Billy L asst min John Calvin Presbyterian Ch h 452 Central Blvd
Whidden Bonnie sec cty fair h 2913 Oak La
White Katherine mgr Blackhawk Hotel h 4218 Bell Av
Whitlock Randall vp Wagnor Development Corp h 504 Sutter Loop
Wiess Robert A wkr Belks Moving & Storage r 2032 Turf Way Apt 338
Wilke Alan & Tracie state dir National Federation of Independent Business & techr North Mid Sch h 818 Woodland Dr
Wilke James & Laura sgt police dept & sheriff's dep h 2420 Highland Av
Willging Judy & Jurgen athom & owner/mgr Choice Video Rentals h 2204 S 8th St
Willging Marty & Tessie dir YMCA & athom h 1808 Gadsden Blvd
Williams Jon R tech K107 Radio r 814 Harding Av
Williams Patricia J retd h 1338 Biarritz Dr
Williams Phyllis nurse Lovell Psychiatric Assn r 1220 Jasper Av Apt 56
Williams Thomas & Mary Lee emp Parson's Funeral Home & athom h 2338 Vermont Av
Wong Phyllis & Steven I mgr Sears & athom h 441 S 28th St
Woods Amy dir State Federation of Independent Businesses h 640 Sherwood Dr
Wymann Barbara & Paul athom & mech Layne Toyota h 2020 Lorry La
Yamer Frank studt r 118 Hillside Dr Apt 1020
Yapenco Nancy & Thomas athom & writer h 4941 Pine St
Younge Rachel techr Kennedy High Sch r 3361 Bolling Dr
Zarrinfair Lois retd r 411 Wisconsin Av
Zerwinn Sarah h 2021 Dyan Way
Zito Allen & Linda archt Zito Associates & marketing dir Blood Bank h 818 Jamestown Dr
Zito Nancy & Robert athom & pharm Kmart h 328 Winford Cir
Zozulla Wesley polof h 5219 Ranch Rd
Zumbaddo Carlos mgr cty fair h 1902 White Av

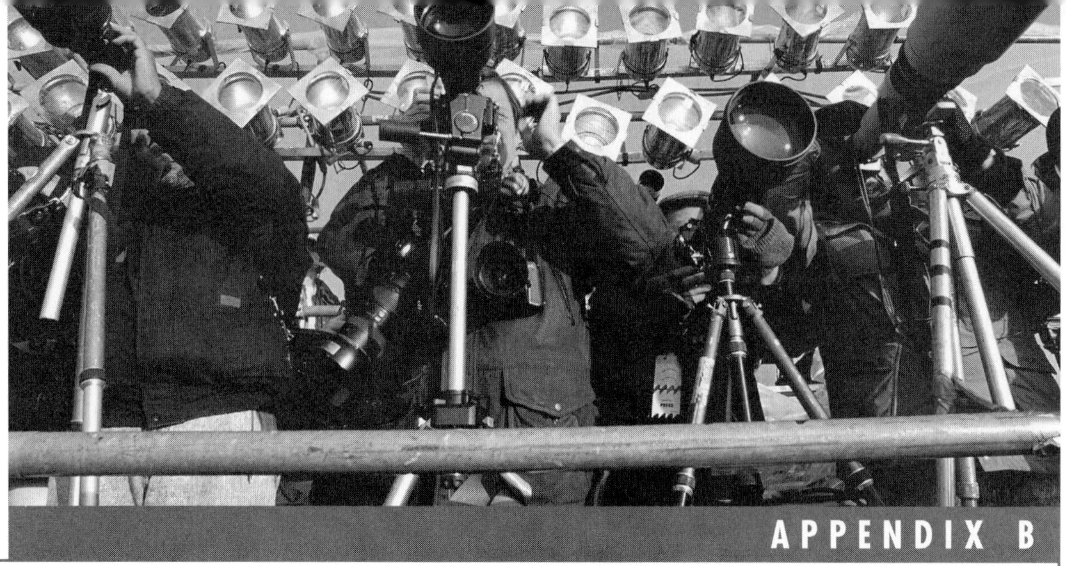

APPENDIX B

THE ASSOCIATED PRESS STYLEBOOK

The following pages summarize the most commonly used rules in The Associated Press Stylebook and Briefing on Media Law. Section and subsection numbers have been added. These selected rules have been reprinted with the permission of The Associated Press. Most newspapers in the United States—both dailies and weeklies—follow the rules it recommends.

Complete copies of The Associated Press Stylebook and Briefing on Media Law can be ordered from most bookstores.

SECTION 1: ABBREVIATIONS

1.1 COMPANY. Abbreviate and capitalize *company, corporation, incorporated, limited* and *brothers* (*Co., Corp., Inc., Ltd.* or *Bros.*) when used after the name of a corporate entity. *Gateway Inc. builds computers.* Do not capitalize or abbreviate when used by themselves: *She works for the company.*

1.2 DEGREES. Generally avoid abbreviations for academic degrees. Use instead a phrase such as: *Edward Huston, who has a doctorate in history, gave the lecture.* Use an apostrophe in *bachelor's degree, a master's, doctor's degree.* Use abbreviations such as *B.A., M.A., LL.D.* and *Ph.D.* only when identifying many individuals by degree on first reference would make the preferred form cumbersome.

1.3 DO NOT ABBREVIATE. *assistant, association, attorney, building, district, government, president, professor, superintendent* or the days of the week, or use the ampersand (&) in place of *and* in news stories.

1.4 INITIALS. A few organizations and government agencies are so widely known that they may be identified by their initials on first reference: *CIA, FBI, NASA, YMCA* (no periods). For other organizations, use their full names on first reference. On second reference, use abbreviations or acronyms only if they would be clear or familiar to most readers.

1.5 JUNIOR/SENIOR. Abbreviate and capitalize *junior* and *senior* after an individual's name: *John Jones Jr.* (no comma).

1.6 MPH/MPG. The abbreviation *mph* (no periods) is acceptable in all references for miles per hour. The abbreviation *mpg* (miles per gallon) is acceptable only on second reference.

1.7 STATES. Do not use postal abbreviations for states. Eight state names are never abbreviated: *Alaska, Hawaii, Idaho, Iowa, Maine, Ohio, Texas* and *Utah.* Abbreviations for other states are: *Ala., Ariz., Ark., Calif., Colo., Conn., Del., Fla., Ga., Ill., Ind., Kan., Ky., La., Md., Mass., Mich., Minn., Miss., Mo., Mont., Neb., Nev., N.H., N.J., N.M., N.Y., N.C., N.D., Okla., Ore., Pa., R.I., S.C., S.D., Tenn., Vt., Va., Wash., W.Va., Wis.* and *Wyo.*

1.8 TITLES. Abbreviate the following titles when used before a full name outside direct quotations: *Dr., Gov., Lt. Gov., Rep., the Rev., Sen.* and certain military titles such as *Pfc., Cpl., Sgt., 1st Lt., Capt., Maj., Lt. Col., Col., Gen., Cmdr.* and *Adm.* Spell out all except *Dr.* when used before a name in direct quotations.

1.9 U.N./U.S. Spell out *United Nations* and *United States* when used as nouns. Use *U.N.* and *U.S.* (no space between initials) only as adjectives.

SECTION 2: ADDRESSES

2.1 ADDRESSES. Always use figures for an address number: *9 Morningside Circle.*

2.2 DIRECTIONS. Abbreviate compass points used to indicate directional ends of a street or quadrants of a city in a numbered address: *562 W. 43rd St., 600 K St. N.W.* Do not abbreviate if the address number is omitted: *East 42nd Street.*

2.3 STREETS. Spell out and capitalize *First* through *Ninth* when used as street names; use figures with two letters for *10th* and above: *7 Fifth Ave., 100 21st St.* Use the abbreviations *Ave., Blvd.* and *St.* only with a numbered address: *1600 Pennsylvania Ave.* Spell out and capitalize *Avenue, Boulevard* and *Street* when part of a formal street name without a number: *Pennsylvania Avenue.* All similar words (*alley, drive, road, terrace,* etc.) are always spelled out.

SECTION 3: CAPITALIZATION

In general, avoid unnecessary capitals. Use a capital letter only if it is required by one of the principles listed here.

3.1 ACADEMIC DEPARTMENTS. When mentioning an academic department, use lowercase except for words that are proper nouns or adjectives: *the department of history, the history department, the department of English, the English department.*

3.2 AWARDS/EVENTS/HOLIDAYS/WARS. Capitalize awards (*Medal of Honor, Nobel Prize*), historic events (*Camp David Peace Treaty*), periods (*the Great Depression, Prohibition*), holidays (*Christmas Eve, Mother's Day*) and wars (*the Civil War, Persian Gulf War*).

3.3 BIBLE/GOD. Capitalize *Bible* (no quotation marks) to refer to the Old and New Testaments and *God* to refer to any monotheistic deity. Lowercase pronouns referring to the deity (*he, his, thee*). The preferred spelling for the Muslim holy book is *Quran.*

3.4 BRAND NAMES. Capitalize brand names: *Buick, Ford, Mustang.* Lowercase generic terms: *a car.* Use brand names only if they are essential to a story.

3.5 BUILDINGS/ROOMS. Capitalize the proper names of buildings, including the word *building* if it is an integral part of the proper name: *the Empire State Building.* Also capitalize the names of specially designated rooms: *Blue Room, Oval Office.* Use figures (for room numbers) and capitalize *room* when used with a figure: *Room 2, Room 211.*

3.6 CAPITOL. Capitalize *U.S. Capitol* and *the Capitol* when referring to the building in Washington, D.C., or to state capitols.

3.7 CONGRESS. Capitalize *U.S. Congress* and *Congress* when referring to the U.S. Senate and House of Representatives. Lowercase when used as a synonym for *convention.* Lowercase *congressional* unless it is part of a proper name: *congressional salaries, the Congressional Record.*

3.8 CONSTITUTION. Capitalize references to the *U.S. Constitution,* with or without the *U.S.* modifier. Lowercase *constitutional* in all uses. Also capitalize *Bill of Rights, First Amendment* (and all other amendments to the Constitution).

3.9 DIRECTIONS/REGIONS. In general, lowercase *north, south, northeast,* etc., when they indicate a compass direction; capitalize when they designate geographical regions, including widely known sections of states or cities: *the Atlantic Coast states, Deep South, Sun Belt, Midwest. He drove west. The cold front is moving east. The North was victorious. She has a Southern accent. He grew up on the East Side of New York City. She moved to Southern California.*

3.10 DO NOT CAPITALIZE *administration, first lady, first family, government, presidential, presidency, priest,* seasons of the year (*summer, fall, winter, spring*), and years in school (*freshman, sophomore, junior, senior*).

Also lowercase the common-noun elements of all names in plural uses: *the Democratic and Republican parties, Main and State streets, lakes Erie and Ontario.*

3.11 EARTH. Generally lowercase *earth;* capitalize when used as the proper name of the planet.

3.12 GOVERNMENT. Capitalize *city, county, state* and *federal* when part of a formal name: *Dade County, the Federal Trade Commission.*

Also capitalize *city council, county commission, city hall, police department, legislature, assembly* and all other names for governmental agencies when part of a proper name: *the Boston City Council, the Los Angeles Police Department.* Retain capitalization if the reference is to a specific city council, legislature, police department, etc., but the context does not require the specific name: *The City Council met last night.* Generally, lowercase elsewhere: *The council approved the ordinance.*

3.13 HIGHWAYS. Use these forms, as appropriate in the context, for highways identified by number: *U.S. Highway 1, U.S. Route 1, U.S. 1, Illinois 34, Illinois Route 34, state Route 34, Route 34, Interstate Highway 495, Interstate 495.* On second reference only for Interstate: *I-495.* When a letter is appended to a number, capitalize it but do not use a hyphen: *Route 1A.*

3.14 MILITARY. Capitalize names of the U.S. armed forces: *the U.S. Army, the Navy, Marine regulations.* Use lowercase for the forces of other nations: *the French army.*

3.15 NATIONALITIES/RACE. Capitalize the proper names of nationalities, races, tribes, etc.: *Arab, Caucasian, Eskimo.* However, lowercase *black, white, mulatto.* Do not use the word *colored.* In the United States, the word is considered derogatory.

3.16 PLURALS. To form the plural of a number, add *s* (no apostrophe): *1920s.* To form the plural of a single letter, add *'s.* To form the plural of multiple letters, add only *s*: *Mind your p's and q's. She knows her ABCs.*

3.17 POLITICAL PARTIES. Capitalize both the name of a political party and the word *party: the Democratic Party.* Also capitalize *Communist, Conservative, Republican, Socialist,* etc., when they refer to a specific party or to individuals who are members of it. Lowercase when they refer to a political philosophy. After a name, use this short form, set off by commas: *D-Minn., R-Ore., Sen. Hubert Humphrey, D-Minn., said. . . .*

3.18 PROPER NOUNS. Capitalize proper nouns that constitute the unique identification for a specific person, place or thing: *Mary, Boston, the Columbia River.* Lowercase common nouns when they stand alone in subsequent references: *the party, the river, the city.*

3.19 SATAN. Capitalize *Satan* but lowercase *devil* and *satanic.*

3.20 TITLES. Capitalize formal titles when used immediately before a name: *Mayor, Chairman, former President Bill Clinton.*

Lowercase formal titles used after a name, alone or in constructions that set them off from a name by commas. Use lowercase at all times for terms that are job descriptions rather than formal titles: *astronaut John Glenn, movie star Tom Hanks, peanut farmer Jimmy Carter.* Do not capitalize or abbreviate *professor* when used before a name.

SECTION 4: NUMERALS

For general purposes, spell out whole numbers below 10, use figures for 10 and above.

Exceptions: Figures are used for all ages, betting odds, dates, dimensions, percentages, speeds, times and weights. Also, spell out a number at the beginning of a sentence, except for a calendar year. Avoid beginning a sentence with a large number or a calendar year.

4.1 AGES. Use figures for all ages. Hyphenate ages expressed as adjectives before a noun or as substitutes for a noun: *a 5-year-old boy, the 5-year-old,* but *the boy is 5 years old. The boy, 7, has a sister, 10. The woman is in her 30s* (no apostrophe).

4.2 CENTS. Spell out the word *cents* and lowercase, using numerals for amounts less than a dollar: *5 cents, 12 cents.* Use the *$* sign and decimal system for larger amounts: *$1.01.*

4.3 DECADES/CENTURY. Use Arabic figures to indicate decades of history. Use an apostrophe to indicate numbers that are left out; show the plural by adding the letter *s*: *the 1890s, the '90s, the Gay '90s, the mid-1930s.* Lowercase *century* and spell out numbers less than 10: *the first century, the 21st century.*

4.4 DOLLARS. Lowercase *dollars.* Use figures and the *$* sign in all except casual references or amounts without a figure: *The book cost $4. Dollars are flowing overseas.* For amounts of more than $1 million, use the *$* sign and numerals up to two decimal places: *He is worth $4.35 million. He proposed a $300 million budget.*

4.5 ELECTION RETURNS/VOTE TABULATIONS. For election returns, use the word *to* (not a hyphen) in separating different totals listed together: *Al Gore won the popular vote from George Bush 50,996,116 to 50,456,169.* For results that involve fewer than 1,000 votes on each side, use a hyphen: *Bush defeated Gore in the electoral vote 271-266; The House voted 230-205 to pass the bill.* Spell out numbers below 10 in other phrases related to voting: *the five-vote majority.*

4.6 FRACTIONS. Spell out amounts less than one, using hyphens between the words: *two-thirds, four-fifths, seven-sixteenths.* For precise amounts larger than one, convert to decimals whenever practical: *1.25, 3.5.*

4.7 MEASUREMENTS/DIMENSIONS. Use figures and spell out *inches, feet, yards,* etc. Hyphenate adjectival forms before nouns: *He is 5 feet 6 inches tall* or *the 5-foot-6-inch man. The rug is 9 feet by 12 feet* or *the 9-by-12-foot rug.*

4.8 MILLION/BILLION. Do not go beyond two decimals: *7.51 million people, $2.56 billion.* Decimals are preferred where practical: *1.5 million,* not *1 1/2 million.* Do not drop the word *million* or *billion* in the first figure of a range: *He is worth from $2 million to $4 million,* not *$2 to $4 million,* unless you really mean $2.

4.9 NUMBER. Use *No.* as the abbreviation for *number* in conjunction with a figure to indicate position or rank: *No. 1 woman, No. 3 choice.*

4.10 ODDS. Use figures and a hyphen for betting odds: *The odds were 5-4. He won despite 3-2 odds against him.*

4.11 PERCENTAGES. Use figures: *1 percent, 2.56 percent.* For amounts less than 1 percent, precede the decimal point with a zero: *The cost of living rose 0.6 percent.* The word *percent* should be spelled out; never use the % symbol.

4.12 RATIOS. Use figures and a hyphen for ratios: *The ratio was 2-to-1, a ratio of 2-to-1, 2-1 ratio.*

4.13 SCORES. Use figures for all scores, placing a hyphen between the totals of the winning and losing teams: *The Reds defeated the Red Sox 4-1. The Giants scored a 12-6 victory over the Cardinals. The golfer had a 5 on the last hole but finished with a 2-under-par score.*

4.14 TEMPERATURES. Use figures for all temperatures except *zero* and spell out *degrees: The high Wednesday was 5 degrees.* Use a word, not a minus sign, to indicate temperatures below zero: *minus 10 degrees.*

4.15 WEIGHTS. Use figures for all weights. *The police seized 2 pounds of marijuana and 13 ounces of cocaine.*

SECTION 5: PUNCTUATION

5.1 COMMA

5.1.1 AGE. An individual's age is set off by commas: *Phil Taylor, 11, is here.*

5.1.2 CITY-STATE. Place a comma between the city and the state name, and another comma after the state name, unless the state name ends a sentence: *He was traveling from Nashville, Tenn., to Albuquerque, N.M.*

5.1.3 HOMETOWN. Use a comma to set off an individual's hometown when it is placed in apposition to a name: *Mary Richards, Minneapolis, and Maude Findlay, Tuckahoe, N.Y., were there.* However, the use of the word *of* without a comma between the individual's name and the city name is generally preferable: *Mary Richards of Minneapolis and Maude Findlay of Tuckahoe, N.Y., were there.*

5.1.4 QUOTATION. Use a comma to introduce a complete, one-sentence quotation within a paragraph: *Wallace said, "She spent six months in Argentina."* Do not use a comma at the start of an indirect or partial quotation: *The water was "cold as ice" before the sun came out, the lifeguard said.* When the attribution follows the quotation, change the period at the end of the quotation to a comma: *"I will veto the bill," the governor said.* Always place commas and periods inside quotation marks. *"The journey must end," she said. "We cannot go on."*

5.1.5 SERIES. Use commas to separate elements in a series, but do not put a comma before the conjunction in a simple series: *The flag is red, white and blue. He would nominate Tom, Dick or Harry.*

5.2 COLON.

5.2.1 LISTS. The most frequent use of a colon is at the end of a sentence to introduce lists, tabulations, texts, etc: *There were three considerations: expense, time and feasibility.*

5.2.2 QUOTATIONS. Use a colon to introduce direct quotations longer than one sentence within a paragraph and to end all paragraphs that introduce a paragraph of quoted material.

5.3 POSSESSIVES. Appendix C contains the rules for forming possessives.

5.4 SEMICOLON. Use semicolons (instead of commas) to separate elements of a series when individual segments contain material that also must be set off by commas: *He leaves three daughters, Jane Smith of Wichita, Kan., Mary Smith of Denver and Susan Kingsbury of Boston; a son, John Smith of Chicago; and a sister, Martha Warren of Omaha, Neb.* Note that the semicolon is used before the final *and* in such a series.

SECTION 6: PREFERRED SPELLINGS

Adviser
Afterward (not afterwards)
All right (never alright)
Ax (not axe)
Baby-sit, baby-sitting, baby sitter
Backward (not backwards)
Damage (for destruction); damages (for a court award)
Employee (not employe)
Forward (not forwards)
Goodbye
Gray (not grey)
Kidnapping
Likable (not likeable)
Percent (one word, spelled out)
Teen, teenager (n.), teenage (adj.) (Do not use teenaged.)
Vice president (no hyphen)
Whiskey

SECTION 7: TIME

7.1 **HOURS AND MINUTES.** Use figures except for *noon* and *midnight.* Do not put a *12* in front of them. Use a colon to separate hours from minutes: *11:15 a.m., 1:45 p.m., 3:30 p.m.* Avoid such redundancies as *10 a.m. this morning* or *10 p.m. Monday night.* Use *10 a.m. today* or *10 p.m. Monday.* The hour is placed before the day; *a.m.* and *p.m.* are lowercase, with periods.

7.2 **DAYS.** Use the words *today, this morning, tonight,* etc., in direct quotes, in stories intended for publication in afternoon newspapers on the day in question, and in phrases that do not refer to a specific day: *Customs today are different from those of a century ago.* Use the day of the week in stories intended for publication in morning newspapers and in stories filed for use in either publishing cycle. Use *yesterday* and *tomorrow* only in direct quotations and in phrases that do not refer to a specific day.

7.3 **DAYS/DATES.** Use *Monday, Tuesday,* etc., for days of the week within seven days before or after the current date. Use the month and a figure for dates beyond this range. Avoid such redundancies as *last Tuesday* or *next Tuesday.*

7.4 **MONTHS.** Capitalize the names of the months in all uses. When a month is used with a specific date, use these abbreviations: *Jan., Feb., Aug., Sept., Oct., Nov.* and *Dec. Jan. 2 was the coldest day of the month.* Do not abbreviate *March, April, May, June* or *July. His birthday is June 26.* Spell out the names of all months when using alone or with a year alone.

When a phrase lists only a month and a year, do not separate the year with commas. *January 1978 was a cold month.* When a phrase refers to a month, day and year, set off the year with commas: *Feb. 14, 1976, was the target date.* Do not use *st, nd, rd* or *th* after the Arabic number in a date.

SECTION 8: TITLES

Formal titles that appear directly before a name are capitalized and abbreviated, when appropriate: *Gov. Arnold Schwarzenegger.* If the title comes after a name or is alone, then it should be lowercase and spelled out: *The president issued a statement. Pope John Paul II gave his blessing.* Do not repeat a title the second time you use a person's name: *Sheriff Sam Smith arrested the driver. Smith did not give details of the arrest.* Some titles, such as *mayor, sheriff* and *president,* have no abbreviations.

8.1 **BOY/GIRL.** The terms *boy* and *girl* are applicable until the age of 18. Use *man, woman, young man* or *young woman* for people 18 or older.

8.2 **COMPOSITIONS.** Capitalize the principal words in titles of books, movies, operas, plays, poems, songs, television programs, lectures, speeches and works of art. Put quotation marks around the names of all such works: *Tom Clancy wrote "The Hunt for Red October."* Do not underline or italicize the titles of any of these works.

8.3 **CONGRESSMAN.** Use *congressman* and *congresswoman* only in references to specific members of the U.S. House of Representatives. Use *representative* if the gender is unknown or when referring to more than one member of the House, and abbreviate it when it used before a name: *Rep. John Dingle; Reps. Tom DeLay and Henry Hyde.*

8.4 **COURTESY TITLES.** In general, do not use the courtesy titles *Miss, Mr., Mrs.* or *Ms.* on any reference. Instead, use the first and last names and middle initial on first reference to a person. A woman's or man's marital status should not be mentioned unless it is clearly pertinent to the story.

For a married woman, the preferred form on first reference is to identify her by her own first name and the last name she uses, which could be her spouse's or her birth name: *Susan Smith.* Use *Mrs.* on the first reference only if a woman requests that her husband's first name be used or if her own first name cannot be determined: *Mrs. John Smith.*

On the second reference, use only the last name of a man or woman, unless the courtesy title is needed to distinguish between two people with the same name in the same story. On first reference to couples, use both first names: *John and Mary Smith.*

8.5 INITIALS. In general, use middle initials to help identify specific individuals. Middle initials are most helpful in such things as casualty lists and stories naming a person accused of a crime.

Use periods and no space when an individual uses initials instead of a first name: *O.J. Simpson.* Do not give a name with a single initial (*O. Simpson*) unless it is the individual's preference or the first name cannot be learned.

8.6 MAGAZINES. Capitalize magazine titles but do not place them in quotes or italics. Lowercase *magazine* if it is not part of the publication's formal title: *Newsweek magazine.*

8.7 NEWSPAPERS. Capitalize *the* in a newspaper's name if that is the way the publication prefers to be known: *The New York Times.* If the state in which the newspaper is published is needed but is not part of the official name, use parentheses: *The Huntsville (Ala.) Times.* Do not underline or add quote marks.

8.8 REFERENCE WORKS. Capitalize, but do not use quotation marks around, the proper names of books that are primarily catalogs of reference material: *The Reader's Guide.* These rules also apply to almanacs (*the Farmers' Almanac*), directories (*the Columbus City Directory*), dictionaries (*Webster's New World Dictionary*), handbooks (*the News & Record Employee Handbook*) and encyclopedias (*the Encyclopedia Britannica*).

8.9 REVEREND. When using the title *Rev.* before a name, precede it with the word *the*: *the Rev. Jerry Falwell.*

SECTION 9: WORDS

9.1 INJURIES. Injuries are suffered, not sustained or received.

9.2 INNOCENT/NOT GUILTY. Use *innocent* rather than *not guilty* in describing a jury's verdict to guard against the word *not* being dropped inadvertently.

9.3 MASS. It is celebrated, not said. Always capitalize when referring to the ceremony, but lowercase any preceding adjectives: *high Mass, low Mass, requiem Mass.*

9.4 NOUNS/VERBS. Nouns that denote a unit take singular verbs and pronouns: *class, committee, family, group, herd, jury, team. The committee is meeting to set its agenda. The jury reached its verdict.* When used in the sense of two people, the word *couple* takes plural verbs and pronouns: *The couple were married Saturday.*

9.5 PERSON/PEOPLE. Use *person* when speaking of an individual. The word *people* (not *persons*) is preferred in all plural uses. *Some rich people pay little in taxes. There were 17 people in the room.*

9.6 RAISED/REARED. Only humans may be *reared.* Any living thing, including humans, may be *raised.*

9.7 REALTOR. The term *real estate agent* is preferred. Use *Realtor* only if the individual is a member of the National Association of Realtors.

9.8 WORDS TO AVOID. Do not use the following words in news stories: *kids, irregardless, ladies* (as a synonym for *women*), *cop* (except in quoted matter) or *entitled* (when you mean *titled*).

APPENDIX C

RULES FOR FORMING POSSESSIVES

1. For common or proper nouns, whether singular or plural, that do not already end in the letter *s,* add an apostrophe and *s* to form the possessive. For example:

SINGULAR	man	child	Johnson	Microsoft
SINGULAR POSSESSIVE	man's	child's	Johnson's	Microsoft's
PLURAL	men	children	alumni	
PLURAL POSSESSIVE	men's	children's	alumni's	

2. If the word is a singular common noun that already ends in the letter *s,* add an apostrophe and *s* to form the possessive, unless the next word also begins with an *s*.

the hostess's request	the hostess' seat
the witness's answer	the witness' story

3. If the word is a singular common or proper noun that ends in a letter other than *s* but has an *s* sound (such as *ce*, *z* and *x*), add an apostrophe and an *s*.

   the fox's den
   Butz's policies
   Marx's theories
   the prince's life

4. Singular proper nouns that end in *s* add only an apostrophe:

   Descartes' philosophy
   Hercules' labors
   Socrates' execution
   Tennessee Williams' plays

5. Plural common and proper nouns ending in s add only an apostrophe:

   the churches' association
   the girls' toys
   the horses' food
   the Smiths' car
   the Williamses' children
   the Carolinas' coastline

6. If a term is hyphenated, make only the last word possessive:

SINGULAR	mother-in-law	She is my mother-in-law.
SINGULAR POSSESSIVE	mother-in-law's	It is my mother-in-law's car.
PLURAL	mothers-in-law	The program featured mothers-in-law.
PLURAL POSSESSIVE	mothers-in-law's	The mothers-in-law's cars were damaged by vandals.

7. If an object is jointly possessed by two or more people or entities, make only the last noun possessive:

   Mary and Fred's entry won a prize.
   Acme Co. and Smith Corp.'s joint business is profitable.
   My mother and father's home was destroyed by fire.

8. If the objects are not jointly owned—if they are separate objects owned or possessed by different people—make both nouns possessive:

   Mary's and Fred's entries won prizes.
   The Smiths' and the Browns' luggage was lost.

9. Indefinite pronouns such as *everyone* follow the same rules. However, personal pronouns have special forms that never use an apostrophe. Personal pronouns include such words as: *his, mine, ours, theirs, whose* and *yours.*

10. Generally, avoid making inanimate objects possessives. Instead, try to rewrite the passage, either dropping the possessive or converting the passage to an *of* phrase:

    AWKWARD: the table's leg
    BETTER: the table leg OR the leg of the table

    AWKWARD: the book's chapter
    BETTER: the book chapter OR the chapter of the book

11. When mentioning the name of an organization, group or geographical location, always use the common or preferred and official spelling. Some names use the possessive case, such as *Actors' Equity Association*, but others, such as *Pikes Peak,* do not.

12. The word *it's,* spelled with an apostrophe, is a contraction of *it is.* The possessive form, *its,* does not contain an apostrophe:

    WRONG: Its higher than I thought.
    RIGHT: It's higher than I thought OR It is higher than I thought.

    WRONG: It's height scares me.
    RIGHT: Its height scares me.

APPENDIX D

ANSWER KEYS

CHAPTER 1: THE BASICS: FORMAT AND AP STYLE

EXERCISE 4

AP STYLE

1. The priest celebrated Mass during their marriage ceremony.
2. Morgan's new book is titled "Rachael's New Glasses."
3. His dad celebrates his birthday in August.
4. The jury found him innocent.
5. The miniature ponies were raised in Elliott County.
6. The mayor lives at 49 Morning Glory St.
7. Seven of the people in the room were reading newspapers.
8. Jean and Diane's room was in a mess.
9. Neither Jason nor his friends were going to the party.
10. The wine was bottled in October 2002.
11. Most news organizations want a reporter with a bachelor's degree in journalism.
12. The police clocked the mayor going 30 mph over the speed limit.
13. The address is 21 Merryweather Road.
14. The attorney and her assistant went into the government building to meet with their clients.
15. She will remember Sept. 11, 2001, always.
16. Manuel Middlebrooks Jr. works for the FBI.
17. President Bush has a ranch in Midland, Texas.
18. The capital of Idaho is Boise.
19. The journalism class had its last meeting Wednesday.
20. Hers was the No. 1 book on the best sellers list.

CHAPTER 2: GRAMMAR AND SPELLING

EXERCISE 1

SECTION I: AGREEMENT

1. The committee submits its data this weekend and expects it to help the church.
2. She said the company failed to earn enough to repay its loans, and she does not expect it to reopen.
3. The jury reached its verdict at 1 a.m., concluding that the media were guilty of libeling the restaurant and its 22 employees.
4. The decision allowed the City Council to postpone its vote for a week, and it suggested that the site's developer design a plan to save more trees.
5. A representative for the organization said it helps people who are on welfare obtain some job training and raise their self-esteem.

SECTION II: POSSESSIVES

1. The women's car was parked nearby, and sheriff's deputies asked to see the owner's driver's license.
2. The woman said she opposes assisted suicide "because a doctor's job is to save peoples' lives, not end them."
3. Last year's outstanding teacher insisted that people's complaints about the school's problems are mistaken.
4. Katrina Jones' parents said their younger children's teacher earned her bachelor's degree in philosophy and her master's degree in education.
5. Everyone's money was stolen, and the neighborhood association's president warned that the police are no longer able to guarantee people's safety in the city's poorest neighborhoods.

SECTION III: PLACEMENT

1. The Board of Trustees voted 8-1 during an emergency meeting Thursday morning to fire the college president for his sexual misconduct.
2. When the guests arrived, the hotel manager took their bags to their rooms.
3. At the Unitarian church Sunday, the union representative urged Americans to support better working conditions for the nation's migrant workers.
4. A thorn bush ripped a hole in her shirt as Jill jogged around campus.
5. A suspect in the burglary case involving two lawn mowers stolen from a hardware store was arrested after a high-speed chase.

SECTION IV: PERSONIFICATION

1. Slamming on the brakes, the driver turned the car to the left, narrowly missing the dog.
2. The city officials said they cannot help the three businesses whose owners asked for better lighting.
3. After detecting the outbreak, the hospital administrators admitted that seven babies born this month were infected, including one who died.
4. Firefighters treated the child for smoke inhalation, then transported her to Mercy Hospital, where her broken legs were treated.

5. The corporation officers, who denied any responsibility for the deaths, will appear in court next month.

SECTION V: PARALLEL FORM

1. He was charged with driving drunk and having an expired license.
2. Karen Kim was a full-time student and Air Force reservist and part-time worker for a veterinarian.
3. To join the club, one must be a sophomore, junior or senior; study journalism; be in good academic standing; and have demonstrated professional journalistic ability.
4. The mayor warned that the neighborhood's high crime rate causes residents to flee, contributes to more unemployment for workers, deprives the city of tax revenue and lowers everyone's property values.
5. She said the other advantages of owning her own business include being independent, not having a boss, having flexible hours and enduring less stress.

SECTION VI: MULTIPLE ERRORS

1. A sheriff's deputy arrested the driver after he saw the teen-ager pull the Chevrolet out of the alley and drive recklessly without headlights.
2. City officials also said that they cannot silence Sooyoung Li, the woman who fears pollution is likely to affect the neighborhood's 300 residents.
3. Seeking more money, publicity and help for the poor, the church's members said they want the city to help them by providing food and housing for the homeless.
4. A spokesman said the Public Works Department could pave the development's road itself for less than $1.2 million. The Roess Company submitted a bid of $2.74 million.
5. A jury awarded almost $10.5 million to the operators of an abortion clinic who charged that picketers tormented them and their clients. The clinic's operators praised the jury's verdict, saying the jurors' courage and understanding set a needed precedent.

CHAPTER 3: NEWSWRITING STYLE

QUIZ

1. She was in a ~~quick~~ hurry and warned that, ~~in the future~~, she will seek ~~out~~ textbooks that are sexist and demand ~~that~~ they be ~~totally~~ banned.
2. ~~As it now stands~~, three ~~separate~~ members of the committee said they will try to prevent the city from closing ~~down~~ the park during the winter ~~months~~.
3. His convertible was ~~totally~~ destroyed, and ~~in order~~ to obtain the money necessary to buy a new car, he ~~now~~ plans to ask a ~~personal~~ friend for a loan ~~to help him along~~.
4. After police found the ~~lifeless~~ body, the ~~medical~~ doctor conducted an autopsy ~~to determine the cause of death~~ and concluded the youth had been strangled ~~to death~~.
5. ~~In the past~~, he often met ~~up with~~ the students at the computer lab and, because of their future potential, invited them to ~~attend~~ the convention.
6. Based upon her ~~previous~~ experience as an architect, she warned the committee members that constructing the ~~new~~ hospital ~~facility~~ will be ~~pretty~~ expensive and suggested ~~that~~ they ~~step in and~~ seek ~~out~~ more donors.
7. The two men were hunting in a ~~wooded~~ forest ~~a total of~~ 12 miles ~~away~~ from the nearest hospital ~~in the region~~ when both suffered severe ~~bodily~~ injuries.

8. Based upon several studies ~~conducted in the past~~, he ~~firmly~~ believes that, when ~~first~~ started next year, the two programs should be ~~very~~ selective, similar ~~in nature~~ and conducted only in the morning ~~hours~~.

EXERCISE 5

SECTION I: REMAINING OBJECTIVE

1. The speaker will discuss the relationship of economics and poverty at tonight's presentation.
2. Police have identified the man who attacked the 65-year-old woman.
3. The man was presented with an award for his efforts on behalf of the agency.
4. Tickets for the community theater production of "Cats" cost $20.
5. The board ended its water service contract with the company.

SECTION II: AVOIDING REDUNDANT PHRASES

1. conclusion
2. experience
3. tracked
4. tangled
5. solution
6. cause
7. hoist
8. identical
9. debt
10. green

SECTION III: AVOIDING WORDY PHRASES

1. face
2. escaped
3. summoned
4. never
5. married
6. much
7. know
8. investigated
9. postpone
10. favored

SECTION 1V: AVOIDING UNNECESSARY WORDS

1. Firefighters responding to ~~the scene of~~ the blaze found the warehouse ~~fully~~ engulfed in flames.
2. ~~There is a possibility~~ the board may postpone ~~until later~~ a decision on rezoning the city park.
3. The city council commented ~~to the effect~~ that no ~~qualified~~ experts were consulted in the report.
4. The woman set an ~~all-time~~ record in the marathon despite ~~the fact~~ that she was having muscle cramps the last two miles ~~of the race~~.
5. The accident occurred when the driver of the pickup ~~truck~~ failed to yield ~~the right of way~~.

SECTION V: TESTING ALL YOUR SKILLS

1. She broke her leg and lost her sight in the accident.
2. The attorney's evidence helped the jury reach a decision.
3. Councilperson (or councilwoman) Janet Rose and others said the budget increase should be eliminated. (NOTE: You may want to discuss the use of councilman, councilwoman and councilperson with your instructor.)

4. Police released the suspect because he had not been identified as the gunman.
5. Candidate Donna Moronesi has raised more than $1 million before the campaign has begun. (NOTE: Are the woman's attractiveness and hair color relevant to the story? Would you mention such things if you were writing about a male candidate? You may want to discuss this problem with your instructor and classmates.)
6. The information was presented now because all members of the board were present and could vote on increasing contributions to the employees' retirement accounts. (NOTE: The word "employees' " is a plural possessive.)
7. The article examines problems of migrant workers.
8. The mayor said she considered the attorney's proposal to settle the suit filed by the man over the death of his dog in the city pound, but decided the settlement was not in the best interests of the city and its residents. (NOTE: Attribution is important in this sentence to avoid the possibility that it will sound like the writer's opinion.)
9. Michael and Peggy Deacosti and their two children, Mark and Amy, were invited to meet the president. (Caution: See the City Directory, Deacosti's name was misspelled.)
10. Before children can begin school, they must be able to read and write their name. (NOTE: The word "child" is singular and the pronoun "they" is plural. Nouns and pronouns must agree. It is easier to make "child" plural ["children"] than making "they" singular [he or she]. Avoid using the masculine "he" when you are referring to any or every child, both male and female.)
11. The state representative recommended purchasing 150 acres of land near the capital and combining it with the 300 existing acres of the park to provide more recreation space.
12. The sheriff said overcrowded conditions in the county jail was the reason he is seeking a federal grant.

CHAPTER 4: THE LANGUAGE OF NEWS

EXERCISE 6

1. The employees ignored the company president's plea to support the restructuring plan.
2. People became violent when the club doors were closed, leaving them outside.
3. The governor said the election results favored his party.
4. The students believed the program would fail because few supported it.
5. Soldiers fought a group of guerrilla fighters.

SECTION II: IMPROVING VERBS AND SENTENCE STRUCTURE

1. Officials postponed a decision on the project's final plans until later this year.
2. The mayor said planning for her fall re-election campaign will begin soon.
3. Their lawsuit says the bottle contained an insect.
4. The computer expert said the file server lacked the space for the web site.
5. Witnesses told police the gunman approached the woman and demanded the keys to her car.

SECTION III: KEEPING RELATED WORDS AND IDEAS TOGETHER

1. She sent her husband, who is with the U.S. Army in Iraq, a letter about the birth of their baby boy.
2. The senator addressed her colleagues in a speech on the Senate floor Monday afternoon asking them to provide funding to get the bill passed.

3. The police department waited until it had sufficient evidence to arrest the suspect and put him in handcuffs before he could flee the country.
4. She said students face a high risk of dropping out of high school if they fail two or more subjects, are frequently absent, have discipline problems and show signs of low self-esteem, loneliness or stress.
5. The accident victim was found trapped under the motorcycle with cuts on his arms and legs.

SECTION IV: TESTING ALL YOUR SKILLS

1. The envelope containing their test scores was delivered at 8 a.m.
2. The mayor said residents must all work to improve the city's streets and neighborhoods.
3. The police officer and the firefighter both said they would vote for the ban on smoking at their stations.
4. Workshop participants agreed that the nurses should get a 15- to 20-percent pay raise.
5. The woman said it was unlikely she would shop at the supermarket again after finding a cockroach in her box of cereal.
6. The author said anyone could learn the sport of bowling.
7. The city council voted 6–1 to increase funding for the program to help expectant mothers regardless whether the city would be able to pay for the program.
8. Many people say they will support her nomination to the board of directors despite protests about her $35,000 annual salary.

SECTION V: AVOIDING JOURNALESE

1. She incurred $30,000 in medical expenses. OR Her medical expenses reached $30,000.
2. He approved spending $26,000 for the car.
3. The program will help high school students.
4. The new building will cost about $6 million.
5. Three council members opposed the proposal.

SECTION VI: AVOIDING JARGON

1. Police said the burglary suspects would be arraigned later in the week.
2. Teresa Phillips, who also uses the name Marie Phillips, testified that she helped the defendant steal jewelry from the store around the 9th of last month. (Caution: See the City Directory. Teresa Phillips name was misspelled.)
3. The company said it would use every department to overcome the budget crisis.
4. The mayor said he would order other city workers to drive the trash trucks if sanitation workers went on strike.
5. Brown's lawsuit says that he suffered physical and mental injuries, and aggravated a previous condition, as well as lost his ability to earn a living, because of the accident.

EXERCISE 7

1. She said she was an alumna of the university.
2. The stockholders received a 15 percent dividend.
3. Police placed the envelope with the ransom money in the mailbox.

4. Legislators passed the statute that will add 3,000 acres to the national park.
5. The principal said he plans to block parents from developing their own sports program.
6. She said the job was too hard for the average person to complete in one hour.
7. The portrait of the president hung in the rotunda of the Capitol building.
8. The concept was too elusive to ensure success.
9. She said she plans to lie on the beach all day.
10. At one time, Poland was a member of the Soviet bloc.
11. Police said it was only a minor accident, but the man suffered several injuries.
12. Joanne is not averse to the trip, but thinks people should pay their own meals and hotel room.
13. He has blond hair, but some people say it is dyed.
14. She described the purse-snatching suspect as someone who preys on lone women.
15. The nurse gave the soldier a snake bite antidote at the site of the bite.
16. Bob's youngest sister is the only one whose advice he will take.
17. Do you know who will be at the meeting?
18. The committee is composed of four women and three men.
19. Ellen should fare well in this year's bike race.
20. The man was sentenced to prison because he incited a riot that caused three deaths.
21. If she decides to go along, then the rest of their journey will take longer.
22. She alluded in her testimony that the company president had taken the funds.
23. The attorney said it was a bizarre incident that led his client to sue the company.
24. The president's confidant said the president was willing to work with Congress on the legislation.
25. The mayor said the media are unfair and implied that they have no right to offer dissent of her programs.

CHAPTER 9: QUOTATIONS AND ATTRIBUTION

EXERCISE 2

1. "Our goal is peace," the president said. (Use a comma, not a period, before the attribution and place the punctuation mark inside the quotation mark. Transpose the attribution's wording so the subject appears before the verb. Avoid using "claimed" as a word of attribution.)
2. Benjamin Franklin said, "Death takes no bribes." (Use a comma, not a colon, before the one-sentence quotation. Because it is a complete sentence, capitalize the first word of the quotation. Place the final period inside the quotation mark.)
3. She said her son calls her literary endeavors "mom's writing thing." (Condense the attribution and place the period inside the quotation mark. Normally, you do not need a comma before a partial quote.)
4. He is a scuba diver and pilot. He also enjoys skydiving and explains, "I like challenge, something exciting." (Clearly attribute the direct quotation.)
5. The Mideast crisis is likely to last indefinitely, the president said. (The quotation can be paraphrased more clearly and simply. Place the paraphrase before the attribution.)
6. "Freedom of the press is not merely freedom to publish the news," columnist Jack Anderson said during a speech last night. "It is also freedom to gather the news. We cannot publish what we cannot gather." (Place the attribution near the beginning, not the end, of a long quotation. The attribution should be preceded by a comma, not a period. Quotation marks do not have to be placed around every sentence in a continuing quotation. Use the normal word order in the attribution.)

7. "I think that America has become too athletic," Jesse Owens said. "From Little League to the pro leagues, sports are no longer recreation. They are big business, and they're drudgery." (The attribution "expressed the opinion that" is wordy. Do not place quotation marks around every sentence in a continuing quotation. If it remains at the beginning of the quotation, the attribution should be followed by a colon. Attribute a continuing direct quotation only once.)
8. The man smiled and said: "It's a great deal for me. I expect to double my money." (Because the quotation contains more than one sentence, "said" should be followed by a colon, not a comma. Do not use "smiled" as a word of attribution. Place quotation marks at the beginning and end of the direct quotation, not at the beginning and end of every sentence. Attribute a continuing direct quotation only once.)
9. The woman said she likes her job as a newspaper reporter and explained: "I'm not paid much, but the work is important. And it's varied and exciting. Also, I like seeing my byline in the paper." (Reporters should stress their source's answer to a question, not the question. Attribute a continuing quote only once. Avoid "grinned" as a word of attribution. The attribution "responded by saying" is wordy.)
10. The librarian said the new building will cost about $4.6 million. (The attribution can be condensed, and, by paraphrasing, you can simplify the quotation. Also, virtually all the news published in newspapers is given to reporters. You do not have to mention that routine detail in every story.)
11. "Thousands of the poor in the United States die every year of diseases we can easily cure," the professor said. "It's a crime, but no one ever is punished for their deaths." (Use the normal word order: "the professor said." Place the attribution at the beginning or end of a sentence or at a natural break in a sentence. Attribute a direct quotation only once, and place quotation marks at the beginning and end of the quotation, not at the beginning and end of every sentence.)
12. Thomas said students should never be spanked. "A young boy or girl who gets spanked in front of peers becomes embarrassed and the object of ridicule," he said. (Clearly attribute the direct quotation. The City Directory reveals that Thomas is a male. Thus, in this case, use of the masculine "he" is correct. Do not, however, assume that every public figure or other source is a male.)
13. The lawyer said: "He ripped the life-sustaining respirator tubes from his throat three times in an effort to die. He is simply a man who rejects medical treatment regardless of the consequences. He wants to die and has a constitutional right to do so." (Because the quotation includes more than one sentence, use a colon, not a comma, after "said." Attribute a direct quotation only once.)
14. Bobby Knight, the basketball coach at Indiana University, said: "Everyone has the will to win. Few have the will to prepare. It is the preparation that counts." (Use a colon, not a comma, after "said," because the quotation includes more than one sentence. Attribute a continuing quotation only once. Place quotation marks at the beginning and end of a direct quotation, not at the beginning and end of every sentence.)
15. She said the federal government must do more to help cities support and retrain the chronically unemployed. (Condense the attribution and avoid orphan quotes—quotation marks placed around one or two words.)

APPENDIX E

COMMON WRITING ERRORS

The Writing and Editing Committee of the Associated Press Managing Editors Association prepared this list of common newswriting errors, arranged alphabetically. The list has been edited and condensed for this book.

1. **Affect, effect.** Generally, *affect* is the verb; *effect* is the noun. "The letter did not affect the outcome." "The letter had significant effect." But *effect* is also a verb meaning to bring about. Thus: "It is almost impossible to effect change."
2. **Afterward, afterwards.** Use *afterward.* The same rule applies to *toward* and *towards, backward* and *backwards,* and *forward* and *forwards.* Use *toward, backward* and *forward.*
3. **All right.** That's the way to spell it. *Alright* is not acceptable in standard usage.
4. **Allude, elude.** You *allude* to (or mention) a book. You *elude* (or escape) a pursuer.
5. **Annual.** Do not use "first" with it. If it's the first time, it cannot be annual.
6. **Averse, adverse.** If you do not like something, you are *averse* (or opposed) to it. *Adverse* is an adjective and means unfavorable: *adverse* (bad) weather, *adverse* conditions.
7. **Block, bloc.** A *bloc* is a coalition of people or a group with the same purpose or goal. Do not call it a *block,* which has some 40 dictionary definitions.
8. **Compose, comprise.** Remember that the parts *compose* the whole, while *comprise* means to include or embrace. *Comprise* in the sense of compose or constitute is regarded as poor usage. Water is *composed* (not *comprised*) of hydrogen and oxygen.
9. **Demolish, destroy.** They both mean to do away with completely. You cannot partially demolish or destroy something, and *totally destroyed* is a redundancy.
10. **Different from.** Things and people are different *from* each other. Do not write that they are different *than* each other.
11. **Drown.** Do not say someone *was drowned* unless an assailant held the victim's head under water. Just say the victim *drowned.*
12. **Due to, owing to, because of.** We prefer the last.
    WRONG: The referees canceled the game *due to* rain.
    STILTED: *Owing to* rain, the referees canceled the game.
    RIGHT: The referees canceled the game *because of* rain.
13. **Either.** It means one or the other, not both.
    WRONG: There are goal posts at *either* end of a football field.
    RIGHT: There are goal posts at *each* end of a football field.

14. **Funeral service.** A redundant expression. A funeral is a service.
15. **Head up.** People do not *head up* committees. They *head* them.
16. **Imply, infer.** The speaker *implies*; the hearer *infers.*
17. **In advance of, prior to.** Use *before*; it sounds more natural.
18. **It's, its.** *Its* is the possessive; *it's* is the contraction of *it is.*
    WRONG: What is *it's* name?
    RIGHT: What is *its* name? *Its* name is Fido.
    RIGHT: *It's* the first time she scored tonight.
    RIGHT: *It's* my coat.
19. **Lay, lie.** *Lay* is the action word; *lie* is the state of being.
    WRONG: The body will *lay* in state until Wednesday.
    RIGHT: The body will *lie* in state until Wednesday.
    RIGHT: The prosecutor tried to *lay* the blame on him.
    However, the past tense of *lie* is *lay.*
    WRONG: The body *laid* in state from Tuesday until Wednesday.
    RIGHT: The body *lay* in state from Tuesday until Wednesday.
    The past participle and the plain past tense of *lay* is *laid.*
    RIGHT: She *laid* the pencil on the pad.
    RIGHT: She had *laid* the pencil on the pad.
    RIGHT: The hen *laid* the egg.
20. **Less, fewer.** If you can separate items in the quantities being compared, use *fewer.* If not, use *less.*
    WRONG: The Rams are inferior to the Vikings because they have *less* good linemen.
    RIGHT: The Rams are inferior to the Vikings because they have *fewer* good linemen.
    RIGHT: The Rams are inferior to the Vikings because they have *less* experience.
21. **Like, as.** Do not use *like* for *as* or *as if.* In general, use *like* to compare with nouns or pronouns; use *as* when comparing with phrases or clauses that contain a verb.
    WRONG: Jim blocks the linebacker *like* he should.
    RIGHT: Jim blocks the linebacker *as* he should.
    RIGHT: Jim blocks *like* a pro.
22. **Marshall, marshal.** Generally, the first form is correct only when the word is a proper noun: Susan Marshall. The second form is the verb form: She will *marshal* her forces. The second form is also the one to use for a title: *fire marshal* Cynthia Anderson, *Field Marshal* Erwin Rommel.
23. **Mean, average, median.** Use *mean* as synonymous with *average.* Both words refer to the sum of all components divided by the number of components. The *median* is the number that has as many components above it as below it.
24. **Nouns.** There is a trend toward using nouns as verbs. Resist it. *Host, headquarters* and *author,* for instance, are nouns, even though a dictionary may say they can be used as verbs. If you do so, you will come up with a monstrosity like: *"Headquartered at her country home, Allison Doe hosted a party to celebrate the books she authored."*
25. **Over, more than.** They are not interchangeable. *Over* refers to spatial relationships: The plane flew *over* the city. *More than* is used with figures: *More than* 1,000 fans were in the crowd.
26. **Parallel construction.** Thoughts in series in the same sentence require parallel construction, meaning each thought takes the same grammatical form, such as noun phrase, verb phrase or prepositional phrase:
    WRONG: The union demanded *an increase* of 10 percent in wages and *to cut* the work week to 35 hours.
    RIGHT: The union demanded *an increase* of 10 percent in wages and *a reduction* in the work week to 35 hours.

27. **Peddle, pedal.** When selling something, you *peddle* it. When riding a bicycle or similar form of locomotion, you *pedal* it.
28. **Principle, principal.** A guiding rule or basic truth is a *principle.* The first, dominant or leading thing is *principal. Principle* is a noun; *principal* may be a noun or an adjective.
    RIGHT: It's the *principle* of the thing.
    RIGHT: Liberty and justice are two *principles* on which our nation is founded.
    RIGHT: Hitting and fielding are the *principal* activities in baseball.
    RIGHT: Jessica Jamieson is the school *principal.*
29. **Redundancies.** Avoid the following redundant expressions:
    Easter Sunday. Make it *Easter.*
    Incumbent representative. Use *representative.*
    Owns her own home. Make it *owns her home.*
    The company will close down. Use *The company will close.*
    Jones, Smith, Johnson and Reid were all convicted. Use *Jones, Smith, Johnson and Reid were convicted.*
    Jewish rabbi. Just *rabbi.*
    8 p.m. tonight. All you need is *8 tonight* or *8 p.m. today.*
    Both Reid and Jones were denied pardons. Use *Reid and Jones were denied pardons.*
    I am currently tired. Just *I am tired.*
    Autopsy to determine the cause of death. Just *autopsy.*
30. **Refute.** The word connotes success in argument and almost always implies editorial judgment.
    WRONG: The Rev. Bury *refuted* the arguments of the pro-abortion faction.
    RIGHT: The Rev. Bury *responded* to the arguments of the pro-abortion faction.
31. **Reluctant, reticent.** If someone does not want to act, that person is *reluctant.* If someone does not want to speak, that person is *reticent.*
32. **Say, said.** The most serviceable words in the journalist's language are the forms of the verb *to say.* Let a person *say* something, rather than *declare* or *admit* or *point out.* Never let a person *grin, smile, frown* or *giggle* a quote.
33. **Slang.** Do not try to use "with-it" slang. Usually a term is on the way out by the time we get it in print.
34. **Temperatures.** They may get higher or lower, but they do not get warmer or colder.
    WRONG: Temperatures are expected to warm up Friday.
    RIGHT: Temperatures are expected to rise Friday.
35. **That, which.** *That* tends to restrict the reader's thought and direct it the way you want it to go; *which* is nonrestrictive, introducing a bit of subsidiary information. For instance:
    RESTRICTIVE: The lawnmower *that* is in the garage needs sharpening. (Meaning: We have more than one lawnmower. The one in the garage needs sharpening.)
    NONRESTRICTIVE: The lawnmower, *which* is in the garage, needs sharpening. (Meaning: Our lawnmower needs sharpening. It's in the garage.)
    RESTRICTIVE: The statue *that* graces our entry hall is on loan from the museum. (Meaning: Out of all the statues around here, the one in the entry hall is on loan.)
    NONRESTRICTIVE: The statue, *which* graces our entry hall, is on loan. (Meaning: Our statue is on loan. It happens to be in the entry hall.)
    Note that *which* clauses take commas, signaling they are not essential to the meaning of the sentence.
36. **Under way, not underway.** But do not say something *got under way.* Say it *started* or *began.*
37. **Unique.** Something that is unique is the only one of its kind. It cannot be *very unique* or *quite unique* or *somewhat unique* or *rather unique.* Do not use it unless you really mean unique.

38. **Up.** Do not use *up* as a verb.
    WRONG: The manager said he would *up* the price next week.
    RIGHT: The manager said he would *raise* the price next week.
39. **Who, whom.** A tough one, but generally you are safe to use *whom* to refer to someone who has been the object of an action. *Who* is the word when somebody has been the actor.
    RIGHT: A 19-year-old woman, to *whom* the room was rented, left the window open.
    RIGHT: A 19-year-old woman, *who* rented the room, left the window open.

CREDIT LINES

TEXT

ALBANY (N.Y.) TIMES UNION. For various excerpts. Reprinted with permission.
THE ANN ARBOR (MICH.) NEWS. For various excerpts. Copyright © The Ann Arbor News, all rights reserved. Reprinted with permission.
THE ASSOCIATED PRESS. For various selections. Reprinted with permission of The Associated Press.
ATLANTA JOURNAL CONSTITUTION. For excerpt of story by Rachel Sauer. Copyright © Cox Newspapers, 2001.
THE BOSTON GLOBE. For excerpt dated July 6, 2002. Reprinted Courtesy of The Boston Globe.
BOSTON HERALD. For various excerpts. Reprinted with permission of the Boston Herald.
THE CHICAGO TRIBUNE. For various excerpts. Copyright © Sept. 12, 2001, Oct. 12, 2001, and June 23, 2002, Chicago Tribune Co. All rights reserved. Used with permission.
THE DALLAS MORNING NEWS. For selection dated June 15, 1997. Reprinted with permission of The Dallas Morning News.
THE DENVER POST. For an excerpt by John Aloysius Farrell. Copyright © May 26, 2003, The Denver Post. All rights reserved. Reprinted by permission.
THE DETROIT NEWS. For three excerpts. Reprinted by permission.
GREAT FALLS (MONT.) TRIBUNE. For selection dated March 12, 2002.
JOE I. HIGHT, Managing Editor, The Oklahoman. For 12 columns. Reprinted with permission.
MATTHEW HANSEN, reporter for the Lincoln Journal Star. For "It's Dick Cavett." Reprinted with permission.
HOUSTON CHRONICLE. For excerpt. Copyright © 1994 Houston Chronicle Publishing Co. Reprinted with permission. All rights reserved.
LANSING (MICH.) STATE JOURNAL. For excerpt dated April 23, 2003. Reprinted with permission.
THE LOS ANGELES TIMES. For excerpts dated Jan. 23, 2001, and March 23, 2003. Copyright © 2001 and 2003 The Los Angeles Times. All rights reserved. Reprinted by permission.
TOMMY MILLER, Roger Tatarian Chair of Professional Journalism at California State University, Fresno, and former managing editor of the Houston Chronicle. For four columns. Reprinted with permission.
MIAMI HERALD. For excerpt Copyright © 2003 Miami Herald. Reprinted with permission.
NEW YORK POST. For except dated Aug. 9, 2002. Copyright © New York Post. Reprinted with permission.
THE NEW YORK TIMES. For various excerpts. Copyright © 1994, 1995, 2000, 2001, 2002, 2003 by The New York Times Co. Reprinted with permission.
THE ORLANDO (FLA.) SENTINEL. For various excerpts published 1992, 1998, 2001 and 2002. Reprinted with permission.
PHILADELPHIA INQUIRER. For excerpt dated 2001. Reprinted with permission.
PITTSBURGH POST-GAZETTE. For various excerpts. Reprinted with permission.
SAN FRANCISCO CHRONICLE. For an excerpt. Copyright © The San Francisco Chronicle. Reprinted with permission.
ERIN SCHULTE. For a column. Reprinted by permission.
SIOUX FALLS (S.D.) ARGUS LEADER. For an excerpt. Reprinted with permission.
ST. LOUIS POST-DISPATCH. For an excerpt. Copyright © St. Louis Post-Dispatch. Reprinted with permission.
TIME MAGAZINE. For an excerpt. Copyright © 2002 TIME Inc. Reprinted by permission.
USA TODAY. For two excerpts. Copyright © 2002 USA Today. Reprinted with permission.
U.S. NEWS & WORLD REPORT. For an excerpt. Copyright © U.S. News & World Report. Reprinted with permission.
THE WASHINGTON POST. For various excerpts and a story. Copyright © 1992, 1995, 1997, 2001, 2003, The Washington Post. Reprinted with permission.
WESTCHESTER (N.Y.) JOURNAL NEWS. For an excerpt. Copyright © 2001 The Journal News. Reprinted with permission.
JEFF ZELENY. For a column. Reprinted by permission.

**All other text credits are listed within the text.

PHOTO AND CARTOON

p. 8 Calvin & Hobbes © 1992 Watterson. Reprinted with permission of Universal Press Syndicate. All rights reserved.

p. 92 The Far Side® by Gary Larson © FarWorks, Inc. All Rights Reserved. Used with permission.

p. 98 © 2000 Benson. Reprinted with permission of United Features Syndicate. All rights reserved.

p. 124 Reprinted with permission of the Biloxi Sun Herald. Photo: AP/Wide World Photos. Photo: David Purdy/The Sun Herald.

p. 125 From the San Francisco Examiner, Sept. 12, 2001. Photo: Kristen Brochmann/The New York Times.

p. 134 Chris O Mera/The Ledger.

p. 139 © 2001 The Record (Bergen County, NJ), Thomas E. Franklin, Staff Photographer.

p. 151 Michael Kamber/The New York Times.

p. 188 PA News/David Cheskin.

p. 345 Reprinted by permission: Lincoln (Neb.) Journal Star.

p. 378 AP/Wide World Photos.

p. 394 McConnell/Denver RMN/Corbis Sygma.

p. 397 Reprinted with permission of the Baton Rouge Advocate. Photo: Arthur Lauck.

p. 537 Reprinted by permission: Tribune Media Service.

p. 567 Reprinted by permission: Tribune Media Service.

p. 577 © Oliver Rebbot 1980/Woodfin Camp & Associates.

p. 595 Photo courtesy of Ronald Olshwanger.

p. 598 John Harte/The Bakersfield Californian.

p. 599 AP/Wide World Photos.

p. 599 © Dan Coyro.

p. 600 AP/Wide World Photos.

p. 604 New York Daily News Photos.

p. 609 Joao Silva/The New York Times.

p. 628 Getty Images/Kim Steele.

INDEX

Abbreviations, 502, 646–647
Access
  to judicial proceedings, 581–582
  to meetings and records, 579–581
  to news scenes, 578–579
  to schools, 409
Accident reports, 400
Accidents, 394, 397–403, 416, 574
Accreditation reports, 410
Accuracy, 138–141, 393–394, 597
Accuracy checking, 9–11
Active voice, 38, 151–152
Addition, as transition, 216
Addresses, 647
Adjective pronouns, 32
Adjectives, 30–31, 94–95, 537–538
Advance stories, 312–313, 322, 530
Adventure features, 375–376
Adverbs, 32, 36, 94–95
adverse, averse, 665
Advertisements
  censorship of, 608–610
  of job listings, 625
  news releases as, 536–537
  privacy, 578
affect, effect, 665
Affidavits, 399
afterward, afterwards, 665
Ageism, 70
Agendas, 155, 313–314
Agreement, 38–40, 49, 52
Agricultural product-disparagement laws, 571
all right, 665
allude, elude, 665
Alsop, Joseph, 135
American Society of Newspaper Editors code of ethics, 610
Anecdotes, 319
Animal stories, 344, 352
Ann-Margret *vs.* High Society, 577–578
Anniversaries, 375
annual, 665
Anonymous sources, 252–253
Antecedents, 34–35, 39, 40
Appeals, 414, 416
Appearance, personal, 626
Appellate courts, 412–413
Appropriation of likeness, 577–578
Armstrong, David, 408
Arrest, danger of, 579
Arrest reports, 400
Arrest warrants, 399
Articles (part of speech), 31–32
as, like, 666
Associated Press Stylebook and Briefing on Media Law, 8, 646–654
Atlanta Journal-Constitution *vs.* Jewell, 567–568
Attribution
  in broadcast copy, 500
  checklist, 256
  exercises, 260–264
  in leads, 154
  levels of, 251
  and plagiarism, 612
  in speeches and meetings, 319
  style of, 246–253
  word choice, 250–251
Audience, 157, 498–501. *See also* Readers
Audit reports, 410
Autopsy photos and reports, 399, 581
average, median, mean, 666
averse, adverse, 665

Back timing, 508–509
Background, 204, 251, 611–612
Banco Nacional de Mexico S.A. *vs.* Rodriguez, 562
Barnicle, Mike, 605
Barlett, Donald, 61–62
Batten, James K., 135
Beamon, Todd, 622–623
because, due to, 44, 665
beg the question, 92
Behind-the-scene features, 378–379
Bentley, Robert, 598
Bergstrom, Bill, 381
Bernstein, Carl, 139

Beverley *vs.* Choices Women's Medical Center, 577
Bias, appearance of, 607. *See* Objectivity
Bids and specifications, 406
Bindrim vs. Mitchell, 563–564
Biographical obituaries, 293–295
Blair, Jayson, 140, 604–605, 611
Blind leads, 148
bloc, block, 665
Blotters, police, 399
Bobbitt, Lorena, 99
Body, of a news story
  checklist, 222
  focus style, 208–210
  hourglass style, 206–208
  inverted pyramid, 200–206
  narrative style, 211–215
  in obituaries, 294–295
  rewriting exercises, 226–233
Book reviews, 570–571
Booking records, 399
Boolean logic, 452
Bradlee, Benjamin, 253, 623
Branzburg *vs.* Hayes, 584
Braun *vs.* Armour & Co., 563
Brights, 343–344, 348, 352–354
Brinkley, David, 123, 131
Broadcast news
  body, 504–505
  checklist, 511
  copy preparation, 505–507
  exercises, 512–523
  leads, 502–504
  updating, 505
  writing style, 498–502
Buchanan, Edna, 63, 157, 398
Budgets, 404–405, 410, 441–445
Buried leads, 183–184
Bush, George W., 334–336
Business features, 380
Bylines, 8

Cabanatuan, Michael, 579
California *vs.* O'Brien, 574
Callahan, Christopher, 455
Cammelieri, Joseph, 565–566
Campaign contributions, 407
Cape Publications Inc. *vs.* Bridges, 576
Capitalization, 255, 647–649
Carville, James, 242
Cases, of pronouns, 33–34
Causation, 216
Cause of death, 296
Cavett, Dick, 370–375
Celebrities, 298–301, 567
Censorship, 608–610
Central point
  accident stories, 403
  crime stories, 402
  feature stories, 369
  identification, 59–62
  obituaries, 294–295
  speeches and meetings, 314–316
Character, 382
Charter schools, 408
Chartrand, Sabra, 183
Chronology, 154–155. *See also* Time
Circuit courts, 412
City government, 404–408
Civic journalism, 133–135
Civil cases, 411–412, 415–416
Clarity, 47, xii
Clark, Roy Peter, 72, 206
Clark *vs.* American Broadcasting Companies Inc., 563
Clauses, 37–38
Clichés, avoiding like the plague, 95–97, 115, z117
Clinton, Bill, 337–338
Coble, Henry, 129
Collective nouns, 39
Commas, 36, 254
Comparison, 30–31, 32, 216
Compassion, 597–598
Complex stories, 204–205
Complex subjects, 272
compose, comprise, 665
Confidentiality, 582–584
Conflict, 130, 382
Conflict of interest, 606–608
Conjunctions, 35–36, 37
Consent, 277
Contacts, 526, 527
Context, 570–571, 597
Continuations, 3
Contracts, 406
Contrast, 216
Contrived events, 535
Controversy
  attribution, 247
  characteristics, 130
  in news releases, 539
  in obituaries, 299–300
  source selection, 272
Copy editing
  broadcast copy, 507–508
  exercises, 12–18, 23–28
  for print, 4–7, inside front cover
Copy production, 2, 11
Corrections, 141
Correlative conjunctions, 36
Cosby, Rita, 402
County government, 404–408
Court documents, 433–437
Courts
  access to, 581
  checklist, 416–417
  fair-report privilege, 569
  overview, 411–413
  reporting on, 410–416
Cover letters, 625
Craig, Jon, 408
Credentials, 578–579
Credibility, 594, 610–611
Crime. *See also* Trials
  checklist, 416
  details, 137–138
  exercises, 419–426, 429
  reporting on, 394–403
  witnessing, 606

Criminal cases, 413–414
Criminal history, 400
Criticism, 570–571
Croteau, Maureen A., 73
Curiosity, value of, xi–xii
Curtis, Cyrus H.K., 609

Dahmer, Jeffrey L., 421–423
Databases, 451
Datelines, 4
Deadlines, 11
Death notices, 293
Deceit, 603
Deeds, 407
deep background, 251
Deep Web, 453
Defamation, 562–563
Defendants, 400–401
Delayed leads, 183–184, 381
demolish, destroy, 665
Demonstrative pronouns, 33
Denham, Bryan, 383
Dependent clauses, 37–38
Descriptions
  in body copy, 219–221
  in broadcast copy, 501
  in leads, 186–187
  plagiarism, 613
  qualities of, 256–258
  of speeches and meetings, 321–322
destroy, demolish, 665
Details
  broadcast copy, 504–505
  descriptive writing, 220, 258
  inverted pyramid style, 201–202
Dialogue, 382
Diaz, Alan, 599
different from, 665
Diligence, need for, 393
Dillow, Gordon, 67
Direct objects, 36
Direct quotations, 239–241, 248–249
Disasters, 606
Discoveries, 533
Discovery process, 412, 415
Discussion groups (electronic), 453–456
District courts, 412
Documents, as sources, 398–400, 409–410
Doe *vs.* Berkeley Publishers, 576
Draper, Norman, 408
drown, 665
Drudge, Matt, 137
Drug overdoses, 296
due to, because, 44, 665

E-mail, 273–274, 447–448
Eavesdropping, 573
Echoes, 101
Editing, 189–191, 222. *See also* Copy editing; Rewriting
Editorialization. *See* Objectivity
Education, 408–410
effect, affect, 665
Egan, Timothy, 408
either, 665
Electronic sources, 407–408, 471–472, 493–496. *See also* Internet
Elizabeth, Queen Mother, 299
Ellipses, 246
elude, allude, 665
Empathy, xii
Employment, 624–625, 629–630
End marks, 3–4, 506
Endings, 223
Engagement, xi–xii
Enthusiasm, 46, 101
epicenter, 92
Ethics
  codes of, 610
  decision-making, 594–596
  exercises, 615–621
  issues in, 596–610
  of recording devices, 574
  transparency, 541–543
Euphemisms, 98–99
Event stories, 531
Exaggeration, 101, 156
Examples, use of, 219
Exclamation points, 36
Expense records, 406
Experts, finding, 271, 449–451
Explanations
  in attribution, 250
  in body copy, 217–219
  of jargon, 406
  need for, 394
  of quotations, 243–244
Explanatory features. *See* Sidebars
External communications, 525–526

Fabrications, 140, 604–605
Fact checking, 10–11, 139–140, 320–321
Facts
  generally known, 611–612
  lack of, in news releases, 539
Fair comment, 570–571
Fair-report privilege, 569–570
Fairness, 221–222, 234–238
Fallows, James, 131, 133
False light, 576–577
Falsity, 564
Farmer *vs.* Lowe's Companies Inc., 562
Farrell, John Aloysius, 240
Fault, 565–566
Feature obituaries, 298–300
Feature stories
  body, 381–382
  endings, 382
  exercises, 385–392
  leads, 380–381
  news releases, 532
  skills for, 383
  topic selection, 368–369
  types, 370–380
Federal Advisory Committee Act, 580
fewer, less, 666

Financial records, 410
Financial statements, 407
Fires, 431
First-person reference, 100
Firth v. State of New York, 564
Focus style, 208–210
Follow stories, 314–320, 322
Follow-up stories, 345–347, 348, 355–360
Food Lion Inc. *vs.* Capital Cities/ABC, 575
Food service records, 410
Freebies, 606
Freedom of Information Act, 579–580
Freelancing, 607–608, 629
Fritz, Sarah, 74
Fry, Don, 211
Funeral notices, 293
funeral service, 666
Funk, Josh, 408
Fuson, Ken, 135

Gag orders, 582
Galella *vs.* Onassis, 574
Gatto, Chris, 565–566
Gellman, Barton, 220
Geographic information systems, 408
Gertz *vs.* Robert Welch Inc., 570
Gifts, 606
Gilliland, Pat, 223
Glass, Stephen, 605
Goddard, Mary, 73, 278
Gold *vs.* Harrison, 563
Goodwin, H. Eugene, 594–595
Gossip, 605–606
Government in the Sunshine Act, 580
Government officials, 271, 566–567
Grady, Sandy, 299
Graham, Katharine Meyer, 299–300
Grammar checklist, 45
Grammatical errors, in quotations, 244–246
Grand jury proceedings, 413
Grief, 597–598
Gross, Terry, 277
Guilt, 400–401
Gush, 101, 539

Hall *vs.* Kansas Farm Bureau, 568
Hansen, Matthew, 370–375
Hard leads, 503
Harrington, Walt, 378
Hart, Jack, 104, 123, 159, 189, 240
Harte, John, 598
Hartman, Steve, 368
Hatfill, Steven J., 401
head up, 666
Headlines, 8
Hendley, Vicky, 607
Hesman, Tina, 348
Hicks, Darryl, 607
Hidden cameras and microphones, 574–575, 604
Hight, Joe. *See* Writing Coach
Historical features, 375
Hoaxes, 300–301
Hobby features, 377
Hohler, Bob, 298–299
Homonyms, 500–501
Hourglass style, 206–208
How-to-do-it features, 376–377
Hull, Anne, 63
Humor, 221
Hyphenation, 3, 501, 502

Identification, of subjects, 470, 563–564
Imagery, 258
Impact, 123
imply, infer, 666
Imus, Don, 137
in advance of, prior to, 666
In-depth stories, 476–482
Incident reports, 399
Indefinite pronouns, 33
Independent clauses, 37–38
Indirect objects, 37
Indirect quotations, 241–243, 249–250
infer, imply, 666
Injury, 564–565
Inspection reports, 407
Interjections, 36
Internal communications, 525
Internet
  addresses, 448–451
  ethics, 456–457
  exercises, 458–466
  history, 446–447
  mailing lists and newsgroups, 453–456
  search engines, 451–453
  use by journalists, 447
Internships, 624
Interrogative pronouns, 33
Interviews
  e-mail and, 448
  exercises, 280–291
  for jobs, 626
  location, 273–274
  purposes, 269–270
  recording ethics, 603–604
  source selection, 270–272
  timing, 272–273
Intrusion, 573–575
Inverted pyramid style, 200–206
Investigative stories, 270
Irony, 187
its, it's, 41, 666

Jail records, 399
Jargon
  avoiding, 97–98
  in education, 408
  exercises, 119
  explaining, 406
Jewell, Richard, 401, 567–568
Journalists
  attributes, 623, xi–xii
  value of, 622–623

Journalists' URLs, 449–451, 458–459
Judgment, 258
Junkets, 606–607
Juries, 413–414
Juveniles, reporting on, 138, 600–601, 602

Kaczynski, Theodore J., 136
Kaelin *vs.* Globe Communications, 563
Kay, Jane, 218
Keywords, 451–452
Kickers, 208–209, 210
Kolata, Gina, 348
Kovaleski, Tony, 271
Kriss, Eric, 408
Krugman, Paul, 219
Kurkjian, Stephen, 408

Labels, 155–156
Landers, Ann, 298
LaRocque, Paula, 63, 72, 149, 191
Law enforcement officers, 398, 573–574
lay, lie, 666
Le Doux *vs.* Northwest Publishing Inc., 568–569
Leads
  advance stories, 313
  alternative forms, 181–189
  alternatives, exercises, 192–199
  broadcast news, 502–504
  broadcast news, exercises, 513–516
  characteristics, 158
  common errors, 154–157
  criticism of, 182–183
  exercises, 161–180
  exercises, from speeches and meetings, 324–325
  feature stories, 380–381
  focus style stories, 208, 210
  follow stories, 315–317
  guidelines, 149–154
  length of, 184
  news releases, 528
  obituaries, 294
  other media, 157–158
  roundups, 347
  sentence structure, 148–149
  summary nature, 146–148
  unusual methods, 184–189
Leapfrogging, 203
Lee, Wen Ho, 401
Leggett, Vanessa, 583–584
Legislation, 438–440
less, fewer, 666
Lewinsky, Monica, 99
Libel
  avoiding suits, 572
  checklist, 584–585
  in crime reports, 400–401
  defense of, 568–571
  elements, 562–566
  exercises, 587–590
  legislative trends, 571
  overview, 561–562
  and quotations, 245
Licenses, 406–407
lie, lay, 666
like, as, 666
Lindley, Ernest K., 251
Line breaks, 3
Lists
  in body copy, 205–206
  explaining, 219
  in leads, 156
  from speeches and meetings, 315–316
Little Rock Newspapers *vs.* Fitzhugh, 565
Local angle
  historical features, 375
  lead exercises, 171–174
  leads, 152–153
  news releases, 528–529, 540
  research on, 349–351
  sidebars, 348
Local government, 403–410, 416, 427–428
Luvison, Kelly, 99

MacMiller, Laurie, 502
Macro and micro issues, 595–596
Magistrate courts, 412
Magnitude, 152
Mailing lists (electronic), 453–455, 461
Malcom, Janet, 245
Malice, 565–566, 576
Margaret, Princess, 300
Margins, 3
Marshall, marshal, 666
McCabe, Carol, 245
McGown, Nance, 541–543
McHam, David, 256
McNulty, Henry, 68
McPhee, John, 278
McQuain, Jeffrey, 103, 279
mean, average, median, 666
Mears, Walter R., 183
Media convergence, 1, 472–473, 497
median, mean, average, 666
Medical examiner's reports, 399
Medical features, 379
Meetings
  advance stories, 312–313
  checklist, 322
  exercises, 339–342
  follow stories, 314–320
  news releases, 531
  reports, and libel, 569–570
  tips for covering, 313–314
Memos from the Editor
  "Descriptive Writing: Turning a Good Story into a Great Story," 256–258
  "Good Writing's Great, But It's Not Enough," 473–475
  "History, Traditions and Culture: Old Glory and Noodle," 349–351
  "Some Thoughts on Plagiarism," 611–613
Memphis Publishing Co. vs. Nichols, 569
Metaphors, 258, 278–279
Metasearch engines, 453
Milkovich *vs.* Lorain Journal, 570

Miller, Tommy. *See* Memos from the Editor
Mills, 405
Minorities, 628–629
Misrepresentation, 603
Modifiers, 42–43, 43, 101
Moen, Daryl, 278
Moldea vs. New York Times, 570–571
Mollwitz, John, 622
Moore, Melissa, 395–397
more than, over, 666
Moreno *vs.* Crookston Times Publishing Co., 569
Mortensen *vs.* Gannett, 568
Motor vehicle registrations, 407
Murphy, Pat, 623
Murphy, Shelley, 408
Murray, Donald, 74
Murray *vs.* Lineberry, 565
Myers, DeeDee, 131

Names
  accuracy checking, 9–10, 140
  brands, 138
  in broadcast copy, 500
  dullness of, 204
  ethical issues, 601–602
  in leads, 147
Narrative style, 211–215
National Life Insurance Co. *vs.* Phillips Publishing Inc., 568
Nebraska Press Association *vs.* Stuart, 582
Negative construction, 100–101
Negatives, 156
Newman, Bruce, 258
News
  buried in news releases, 538
  characteristics, 123–125, 129–131
  lack of, in news releases, 534–536
  selection, 135
  selection exercises, 143–145
  types of, 131, 133
News organizations, 130–131, 292–293
News releases
  and broadcast news, 510
  characteristics, 527–530
  checklists, 540–541
  editing exercise, 544–545
  evaluation exercises, 550–551
journalist's perspective, 533–540
  problems, 534–540
  rewriting exercise, 554–560
  types, 530–533
  writing exercise, 546–549
News services, 509
News stories, 2–4, 277–278
Newscasts, 508–509
Newsgathering, 573–574, 578–584, 585–586
Newsgroups (electronic), 455, 461
Newspapers, 9, 510
Newsrooms, 510, 627–628
Nicholson, Jim, 297
Nobel, Alfred, 300
Notes, 276–277
Nouns, 29–30, 39–40, 666

Numbers
  AP style, 649–650
  in broadcast copy, 499, 501
  explaining, 218
  statistics, 468–469, 473
Nut graph
  after soft leads, 181, 183
  feature stories, 381
  focus style stories, 208, 210

Obituaries
  considerations, 301–302
  exercises, 303–311
  policies on, 292–293
  types, 293–300
Objectivity
  ethical concerns, 596–597
  exercises, 76, 86, 87
  lack of, in news releases, 536–538, 539
  in leads, 153–154
  need for, 66–70
  in news selection, 135
  and quotations, 246
  sources' friendship, 608
  using quotations, 246
Observation, 257
Obvious, stating the, 156
Occupational features, 377
Occupations, 500
off the record, 251
Offensive details, 136
Ogden, Karen, 211
Olshanger, Ron, 595
Omissions, 569
on the record, 251
Opinions, 247, 469–471, 570–571. *See also* Objectivity
Organization, of stories, 60–62
Orphan quotes, 243
Ostrow vs. Lee, 564
Outlines, 60–61
over, more than, 666
Overholser, Geneva, 98
Overwriting. *See* Simplicity
owing to, because, due to, 665

Page breaks, 3
Pagination, 9
Paparazzi, 574
Paragraphs, 3, 64, 506
Parallelism, 44, 51, 53, 666
Paraphrasing, 241–243, 249–250, 613
Parenthetical phrases, 243–244
Partial quotations, 249
Participatory features, 379
Parts of speech, 29–36
Passive voice, 38, 151–152
Payroll information, 406, 410
pedal, peddle, 667
Perp walks, 579
Personal experience features, 377–378
Personal pronouns, 33–34
Personality profiles, 270, 370–375

Personification, 43–44, 50, 53
Philadelphia Newspapers vs. Hepps, 564
Photographers, 578–579
Phrases, 38
Plagiarism, 604–605, 611–613
Plaintiffs, 562
Platemaking, 9
Platitudes, 99–100, 539
Plots, 382
Plurals, 40–41, 49–50, 52
Poetry, in language, 278–279
Police. *See* Law enforcement officers
Police beat, 394, 397–398
Police misconduct investigations, 400
Polls, 469–471, 473, 494–492
Posing, 603
Possessives
  exercises, 49–50, 52
  formation, 40–41
  rules, 655–656
Post-trial stages, 414, 416
Praise, 537–538
Precision, 91–93, 115
Preliminary hearings, 413
Prepositions, 34–35
Press-Enterprise *vs.* Superior Court, 582
Press releases. *See* News releases
Pretrial stages, 413, 415
Prewriting process, 59–62
Price, Debbie, 139
principle, principal, 667
Prior restraint, 582
prior to, in advance of, 666
Privacy
  checklists, 585
  ethical issues, 600–601
  exercises, 591–592
  invasion of, 572–578
  news access, 579
Private facts, 575–576
Private individuals, 567–568, 600–601
Private property, 573
Product-disparagement laws, 571
Profanity, in quotations, 246
Prominence, 123, 125
Pronouns
  ambiguity, 40
  in broadcast copy, 501
  gender-neutrality, 69–70
  shift, with quotations, 249
  use, 32–34
Property taxes, 405
Prostitution, 602
Protests, 579
Provost, Gary, 103, 223
Proximity, 129
Public affairs reporting, 133–135, 393–394
Public domain, 612
Public figures, 567–568, 585, 601
Public interest, 576
Public officials, 566–567, 585
Public records
  access, 579–581
  private facts, 575
  as source material, 271
Public relations
  and broadcast news, 510
  checklist, 540
  ethics, 541–543
  and news media, 526–527
  overview, 524–526
  practitioners, 526
Public Relations Society of America (PRSA) code of ethics, 542
Publication, and libel, 564
Publicity, 608
Puffery, 537–538, 552–553
Punctuation, 102, 253–254, 650–651
Purchase orders, 406

Queries, 452
Questions
  5 W's, 133–134, 146–147, 528
  ethical decision-making, 594
  in interviews, 242, 274–275
  in leads, 185–186
  before quotations, 244
  as transitions, 217
Quotation marks, 243, 253–254
Quotations
  attribution, 248–250
  in broadcast copy, 500
  changing, 244–246
  checklist, 255
  clarity, 73
  editing, 190
  effective use, 47, 278
  exercises, 265–268
  in leads, 184–185
  and libel, 569
  mechanics of, 253–255
  from meetings, 321
  in narrative copy, 243–246
  in obituaries, 295
  poll stories, 469–470
  sanctity of, 611
  use of, 239

Race, 402–403
Racism, 68
Raines, Howell, 611
Rape, reporting on, 137–138, 602
Reactions, 318–319
Readability, 63, 201
Readers. *See also* Audience
  addressing in leads, 187
  characteristics, 132
  and speeches and meetings, 320–321
Real estate, 407
Reality programming, 573
"Reasonable person" standard, 576
Recording. *see* Tape recording
Redundancy, 64–66, 101, 667
Reflexive pronouns, 34
refute, 667
Relative pronouns, 34

Relevancy, 451–452
reluctant, reticent, 667
Reporting, key points, 473–475
Reputation, 562–563
Research, 272–273
Results, 533
Resumes, 407, 625
reticent, reluctant, 667
Retraction statutes, 571
Rewriting, 46–47, 73–74, 535–536
Ride-alongs, 573–574
Rogers, Fred, 298
Rosen, Jay, 133
Rosenblatt vs. Baer, 567
Roundups, 347, 348, 361–363
Ruehlmann, William, 624
Rumors, 137, 605–606
Running time, 508–509

'S (apostrophe s), 40–41
Sabato, Larry, 601
said, say, 250, 667
Salaries, of journalists, 627
Saline, Robert S., 541–543
Sanders *vs.* American Broadcasting Cos. Inc., 574
say, said, 250, 667
School districts, 408–410
Schulte, Erin, 126–127
Schwartz *vs.* Worrall Publications Inc., 565–566
Search engines, 451–453, 460
Search warrants, 399
Seasonal features, 376
Second paragraphs, 203, 224
Secrets, 575–576
Sefton, Dru, 401
Semicolons, 36
Sensationalism, 136–137, 401–402, 598–600
Sentences
  in broadcast copy, 499, 506
  in leads, 148–149
  simplification, 62–64, 79–80
  structure, 36–38, 117
  as transition, 217
Sept. 11, 2001, 122–123, 124–129
Sexism, 68–70, 81
Sexual assault, 137–138, 602
Shafer vs. Lamar Publishing Co., 569
Shalit, Ruth, 605
Shield laws, 584
Shulman *vs.* Group W Productions, 574
Sidebars
  checklist, 348
  described, 347–348, 376
  exercises, 364–367
Similes, 278–279
Simplicity
  in leads, 154
  sentence exercises, 79–80, 84–85
  tips, 72–73
  withdrawal, 87–88
  word exercises, 77–78, 83–84
Singularity, 129–130
Sipple *vs.* Chronicle Publishing Co., 576
Slander. *see* Libel
Slang, 97, 117, 667
Sluglines, 2–3
Smith, Patricia, 605
Smith, Red, 474
Society of Professional Journalists code of ethics, 542
Soft leads, 503
Solano *vs.* Playgirl, 576–577
Sources
  for broadcast news, 509–510
  documents, 398–400
  evaluation, 272
  friendship with, 608
  identification, 251–253
  Internet, 449–451, 456–457
  local government, 406–408
  need for, 393
  protecting confidentiality, 582–584
  school-related, 409–410
  selection for interviews, 270–272
Spangler, Todd, 298
Specificity, 150–151, 257, 568–569
Speculation, 605–606
Speeches
  advance stories, 312–313
  checklist, 322
  exercises, 326–338
  follow stories, 314–320
  news releases, 531
  tips for covering, 313–314
Spell-checkers, 45
Spelling
  AP style, 651
  in broadcast copy, 501
  exercises, 55–58, 120–121
  importance, 44–45
Statistics, 468–469, 473, 483–490
Statute of limitations, 564
Steele, James B., 61–62
Stereotyping, 67–70, 81–82
Stessman *vs.* American Black Hawk Broadcasting Co., 573
Stith, Pat, 272
Style, 8, 19–28
Subject directories, 453, 460
Subjects, 36–37, 39
Subpoenas, 583–584
Suicides, 296
Superior courts, 412
Surprise, 343–344
Survivors, 296–297
Suspense, 186

Tape recording, 276–277, 574–575, 603–604
Tax assessment records, 407
Taxes, 404–405
Technical language, 97–98
Telephones, 273
Temperature, 667
Tenses, 30, 102
Terrorism, 608
Texas Beef Group *vs.* Winfrey, 571

that, which, 41, 667
Thien, Dick, 381
Thompkins, Al, 369
Throwaway leads, 504
Time
  AP style, 652
  in broadcast copy, 504–505
  in feature stories, 382
  in leads, 154–155, 159–160
  references, 102
  transitional words, 216
Time Inc. *vs.* Hill, 576
Timeliness, 123
Timing, 508–509
Tips, 474
Titles, 652–653. *See also* Headlines; Sluglines
Tomalin, Nicolas, 123
Trade names, 138
Transitions
  about speeches and meetings, 320
  in broadcast news, 509
  exercises, 225
  in news stories, 215–217
  poll stories, 469–470
  with quotations, 248
Transportation records, 410
Trespassing, 409, 573, 574
Trials
  access to, 581–582
  civil cases, 416
  criminal cases, 413–414
  reporting on, 410–416
Trips, 606–607
Truth, 157, 564, 568–569
Turn paragraphs, 206
Twain, Mark, 300–301
Twists, 187
Tyler, Patrick E., 251
Typing, 3

Umbrella leads, 504
Unabomber, 136
under way, 667
Undercover work, 603
Uniform Correction or Clarification of Defamation Act, 571
unique, 667
Universal needs, 369
Unusual, emphasizing the, 177–180
up, 668
Updates, 152–153
URLs (uniform resource locators), 449
U.S. Healthcare *vs.* Blue Cross of Greater Philadelphia, 568
U.S. *vs.* Cleveland, 582

Varanelli, Nick, 579
Verbs
  in broadcast copy, 499
  exercises, 112–113, 117
  in leads, 151–152
  in prepositional phrases, 35
  sentence use, 36–37
  strong choices, 93–94, 103–104
  subject agreement, 39
  use, 30
Victims, reporting on, 417, 597–598, 602
Visuals, 529, 598–600
Vocabulary
  AP preferences, 653–654
  exercises, 105–111, 120–121
  in leads, 188
Voice, 38, 151–152

Web sites, 529, 564
West *vs.* Thomson Newspapers, 562
Western Broadcasting *vs.* Wright, 569
which, that, 41, 667
who, whom, 42, 668
Wilber, Rick, 190–191
Williams, Ted, 298–299
WJLA-TV et al. *vs.* Levin, 566
Woestendiek, John, 474
Women, in the workforce, 628–629
Woodward, Bob, 139
Worcester, Wayne A., 73
Word division, 3
Work examples, 625
Workplace, 574
World Wide Web, 446, 448–451
Writing Coach
  "Acronyms Lift Your Writing," 45–47
  "Become a Power Lifter When Picking Verbs," 103–104
  "Figure It: Poetry Can Be in Newspaper Stories," 278–279
  "Find the Clear Path to Writing Glory," 72–74
  "Go Beyond the Stick," 323
  "How to Find the Endings to Stories," 223
  "Lucky 13 Ways to Become a Good Writer," 10
  "Oh Where, Oh Where Does the Time Element Go?", 159–160
  "The 'Knows' Have It for Police and Court Reporters," 417
  "Too Many Words Can Muddle Writing," 189–191
Writing style
  bad examples, 70–71
  checklist, 71–72
  great, but not enough, 473–475
  prewriting, 59–62

Yeagle *vs.* Collegiate Times, 563

Zaccini *vs.* Scripps-Howard, 578
Zeleny, Jeff, 127–129
Zinsser, William, 74, 103
Zoning records, 407